THE AMERICAN SOUTH

THE
AMERICAN
SOUTH
A Brief History

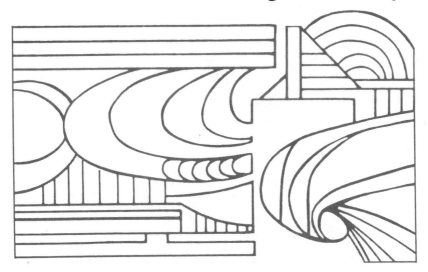

Monroe Lee Billington
NEW MEXICO STATE UNIVERSITY

Charles Scribner's Sons
New York

Printed in the United States of America
SBN 684–12324–X College
SBN 684–10025–8 Trade
Library of Congress Catalog Card Number 73-132573

*To Marion, Martha, and Melinda—without whose
assistance this book would have been written sooner*

Preface

The American South has been the subject of hundreds of books published in recent years. Northern travelers and journalists have reported upon their brief tenures in the region, southerners have opened their hearts and minds by printing their memoirs and personal observations, and scholars in both North and South have written on specific topics or limited periods of time. The Old South continues to fascinate writers, and Civil War themes apparently will never run dry. Politics, economics, society, and race relations in the changing modern South have all received due attention. With so much having been written, why then another book on the South? Despite the proliferation of monographs on important but specific aspects of the nation's most distinct region, no new survey of the South's entire history has been published for more than a decade. Works which appeared before the traumatic events following World War II are now badly outdated, and most histories written during the postwar era have unfortunately neglected the major events in the South's most recent past. The need for a general, up-to-date, interpretive history of the American South is transparent. This volume, briefly surveying the South's history but with emphasis upon modern times, is designed to fill that void.

Many writers who have concerned themselves with the South have used the term non-South in reference to the remainder of the nation, but this word seems to be negative and inappropriate. Throughout this work, for lack of a more satisfactory word, the traditional term North is applied to the remainder of the nation, even though that word may not in all instances be entirely accurate. Upon occasion, I speak of the West, when the subject under discussion demands that that region be specifically identified, but at other times I depend upon the context to inform the reader of the area to which I am referring when I write of the North.

In this age of racial crises, the most sensitive terms I use are Negro and black. I employ these words interchangeably, although I am aware that the former, which was for years a term of respect, is now held in low esteem by many younger members of the nation's largest racial minority. My usage is not intended to alienate those who dislike that designation. As a matter of fact, the word Negro is the term most preferred by this minority population. A recent Gallup poll published in *Newsweek* (June 30, 1969, p. 20) revealed these responses:

	Like most	Like least
Negro	38%	11%
Colored People	20	31
Blacks	19	25
Afro-Americans	10	11
Don't Care	6	6
Not Sure	7	16

The strong opposition to the term colored compels me not to use it, even though it is preferred by a sizable number.

While this volume is designed to stand alone, I have deliberately made it brief. Its restricted length has prohibited me from writing about some subjects which might otherwise be considered in order to deal reasonably adequately with the material which is included. However, readers may be stimulated to delve more deeply into a particular subject, and to assist in that end, brief bibliographical essays follow each chapter and a lengthy paperback listing appears at the end of the volume. Also intended to be of specific aid to the reader are the full-color maps in the middle of the volume.

I could not have written this book without consulting the works of dozens of writers who preceded me. While I have engaged in a certain amount of original research on those sections dealing with the near-present, in the remainder of the pages I have relied heavily upon the work of my colleagues in the profession, and I hope they will not be offended if I have closely followed their ideas. I was first introduced to the South as a field of study when I enrolled in a course taught by John S. Ezell at the University of Oklahoma. I pursued further graduate work in southern history at the University of Kentucky, where I had the good fortune to study under Thomas D. Clark, Clement Eaton, and Albert D. Kirwan. I am immeasurably indebted to these four friends who over the years have shaped my thoughts about southern history in lectures, conversations, monographs, and scholarly essays. I hope they will consider it a compliment if on occasion their works or ideas are reflected in the succeeding pages. To be sure, factual errors and faulty interpretations are my responsibility alone. I must express my thanks to Mrs. Rita Granger who with patience and good humor typed too many drafts of too many chapters of the manuscript; to Mrs. Nancy Julian who did much of the spade work on the sections where secondary volumes were not yet available; and to Mrs. Elsie Kearns of Charles Scribner's Sons who offered invaluable editorial suggestions and assistance. My deepest appreciation goes to my wife, Mary Elizabeth, who served as typist, grammarian, critic, sounding board, and sentry at the study door.

Table of Contents

List of Maps

THE AMERICAN SOUTH

INTRODUCTION

No other region of the United States has attracted so much attention as the South. And rightly so. Throughout the nation's history and in its own distinct way, the South has greatly affected the remainder of the nation. It is difficult to imagine what American history would have been like from 1800 to 1860 without the South; and the Civil War and its long aftermath continue to have their effect upon everyone. The racial tension of recent years, while now national in scope, has its roots in the relationship of the races when southern white men enslaved their black-skinned brothers. To consider the United States without the South is a virtual impossibility. Certainly the nation's history would have been far different had the South never existed, and while this rapid survey focuses upon the South itself, its readers should relate the region's history to the national experience.

The South has many images. When Americans—either southern or non-southern—think of the South of the past they may call to mind contented slaves harvesting white cotton fields, or prosperous plantation owners leisurely quaffing mint juleps on the verandas of white-columned Georgian homes, or beautiful and beautifully dressed southern belles strolling in shady gardens of an Old South era forever "gone with the wind." Or they may visualize poor rural whites eking out a living in worn-out fields beside a Caldwellian tobacco road, or poor urban whites riding to the end of the line on a "streetcar named Desire," or degenerates in Yoknapatawpha County intent on rape, incest, and murder. On the other hand, some mind's eyes may see the more recent industrialization of the South: blast furnaces in Birmingham, oil and gas refineries near Houston, coal mines in West Virginia and Kentucky, cotton textile mills in North Carolina. Others may recall with pleasure Miami Beach and Key West, while some may soberly contemplate Cape Kennedy and the American space race with the Russians. The Negro may come first to the American's mind: Uncle Tom speaking kindly to a little white girl; Booker T. Washington addressing a mixed audience in Atlanta, Georgia; Martin Luther King, Jr., in jail dramatizing the Negro's second-class citizenship; James Meredith appearing on a racially tense Ole Miss campus; persons unknown bombing Negro churches; whites harassing Negro first-graders as they enter a formerly all-white school. H. L. Mencken summarized his picture of the "Sahara of the Bozart" when he quipped: "Fundamentalism, Ku Kluxry, revivals, lynchings, hog wallow politics—these are the things that always occur to a northerner when he thinks of the south." But such mental pictures reflect an incomplete, stereotyped, and sometimes distorted and inaccurate picture of that region. The South is surely something more than that seen by novelists, playwrights, tourists, and daily newspapers.

Definitions of the South vary greatly. No one will deny that five states often called the Deep South, are indisputably southern—Louisiana, Mississippi, Alabama, Georgia, and South Carolina would surely make every list—but authoritative sources disagree on which other states constitute the South. A glance at a physical map of the United States reveals why this disagreement exists. Not separated from the remainder of the United States by a mountain range, the South is physiographically related to non-southern areas. Instead of being a distinct geographical entity, the South itself is divided into a number of separate regions. Along the Atlantic seaboard and the Gulf of Mexico lies the Tidewater region, a flat, sandy, coastal plain stretching west and north to the fall line and the low-lying red hills of the Piedmont. Beyond these foothills rise highlands collectively called the Appalachian Mountains, including the Blue Ridge, Great Smoky, and Clinch mountains, as well as the Alleghenies, the Shenandoahs, and the Cumberlands. The mountain ranges are separated by many valleys such as the Shenandoah and the Tennessee. Adjacent to the mountains on the west are the Cumberland Plateau in Tennessee and the Bluegrass country of central Kentucky. Farther west appear alluvial lowlands filled with bluffs, flood plains, bayous, and delta lands drained by the Mississippi River. And beyond the Mighty Mississippi, the Boston, Ozark, and Ouachita mountains, isolated hills rising out of the fertile black soil of Arkansas, Missouri, and Oklahoma. The western edge of the South ends with vast, semiarid stretches of land characterized by the high plains of the Edwards Plateau of southwestern Texas, and interrupted only temporarily by the stark, rocky Wichita Mountains of western Oklahoma. The South is not a region, but a congeries of regions, a conglomeration of physiographical elements, a collection of diverse districts. If the

South exists it is not because of physiography, terrain, topography, or soil similarity. The South exists despite these geographical conditions.

Acknowledging that geography does not define the South, the historian is to some extent bound by place as well as time and events. For this volume's purposes, the colonial South was composed of Maryland, Virginia, North and South Carolina, and Georgia. In the antebellum period the South was made up of the eleven states which formed the Confederate States of America (Alabama, Arkansas, Florida, Georgia, Louisiana, Mississippi, North Carolina, South Carolina, Tennessee, Texas, and Virginia), as well as the slaveholding states of Missouri and Kentucky which the Confederates claimed. After the Civil War, the South consisted of the seventeen states and the District of Columbia which had compulsory school segregation prior to May 1954. Besides the eleven Confederate states, this included Oklahoma, Missouri, Kentucky, West Virginia, Maryland, and Delaware. Because various authorities have delimited the South for their own purposes, the outer boundaries of the South in any particular discussion in this volume are sometimes narrower than this and are not always precisely defined.

If not geography then perhaps climate is the South's most distinguishing characteristic. Ulrich B. Phillips opened his classic *Life and Labor in the Old South* (1929) with: "Let us begin by discussing the weather, for that has been the chief agency in making the South distinctive." On its surface this statement appears to have some validity because the South has long been noted for mild winters, long growing seasons, hot summers, and heavy rainfall. Actually, three belts of climate exist: the upper South, where the growing season is six months; the middle South, eight months; and the lower South, nine months. Killing frosts come regularly in Missouri and Kentucky, but only occasionally in Florida and south Texas. Also, a wide variation of rainfall occurs in the Southland. While the upper South averages about forty inches of annual precipitation, the lower South often has more than sixty. Along the Gulf coast the rainfall is so abundant that over seventy inches of rain are not unusual, while the western areas of Texas and Oklahoma may have less than twenty-five. Such variety of weather and precipitation can hardly make for a single distinctive South.

Because the South has been one of the most rural sections of the United States, possibly it can best be defined in terms of its agricultural traits. One writer has suggested that a chart of the nation's mule population would reveal the boundaries of the South. The region's devotion to the one-crop tradition, the use of Negro labor on plantations and farms, and the large number of rural dwellers seem to attest to the dominance of agriculture in the South. In 1930 when twelve southerners saw the South gradually bartering away its tranquil agricultural tradition and culture for dubious material gain, they took their stand against the trend of industrialization. Painting an image of an agricultural South with stable folkways, leisurely living, and an aristocratic society, they sought to defend this "southern way of life" against the "American way," and they agreed that the phrase "Agrarian *versus* Industrial" best represented that distinction. Since agrarianism and its values were the essence of the southern tradition, they requested antiindustrial measures to stop or revoke the advances of industrialism. The authors of *I'll Take My Stand* were dedicated to the proposition that the southern way would stand or fall with agrarianism, but they were championing a lost cause. Yet, despite the increased urbanization and industrialization of the southern states, the South as such remains. The definition of the South must be found elsewhere than in agrarianism.

C. Vann Woodward argues persuasively that the South can best be defined in terms of its history. By this he does not mean the worship of ancestors, nor written history and its interpretation; rather, he refers to the "collective experience of the Southern people." Woodward points out that Americans generally have known abundance, but southerners have lived in poverty; that the United States has experienced success, but the South has been familiar with frustration, failure, and defeat (including not only military defeat in the Civil War, but also the frustration of Reconstruction and long decades of failure in economic, social, and political life); that other Americans have claimed innocence, but the southerner has felt guilt; that most Americans were "born free," but many southerners were not. In short, Woodward says the South has had a tragic and unique history which has helped unify the section and which has contributed to its definition. The distinctions Woodward first noted in 1958 seemed less relevant in 1970 as all Americans became conscious of urban poverty, as they experienced the frustrations of a military stalemate in Southeast Asia, and as they struggled with other problems of society called to their attention by college students who felt at odds with the "Establishment."

Various additional criteria have been advanced to define the South. As the region has become urbanized, some have suggested that the South's identity lies in the survival of rural ways in the cities. Others have stressed the fundamental piety of the people, and still others have found importance in the southerner's emphasis on home life. Even diet has been advanced to explain the South, cornbread, yams, turnip greens, sorghum molasses, ham hock, and buttermilk being praised by a recording personality a few years ago in a popular ditty called, "That's What I Like About the South." But all of these have been characteristics of the South; they do not define the region.

In 1928 Ulrich B. Phillips advanced the thesis that the white people of the South have indomitably maintained a common resolve that the South remain a white man's country—and that this overriding conviction makes the South distinct. Does this mean that the South will disappear when white supremacy ends? Living at a time when the demise of white supremacy seemed almost completely outside the range of possibility, Phillips answered this question affirmatively when he stated that the South would be only another geographical region of the United States if white supremacy were somehow overcome. But living through those turbulent years following World War II, years which Phillips surely could not have foreseen, modern scholars tend to reject his conclusion. Even though the racial issue has been an important key to the South in the past, most historians of the South agree that in the light of recent events the color difference and its attendant ramifications cannot continue to be regarded as an immutable feature of southern life.

James G. Randall has suggested that southernism is like a poem, a song, or an emotion—a reality too elusive to be explained completely in terms of concrete definitions, origins, or cultural conditions. "Poets have done better in expressing this oneness of the South," remarked Randall, "than historians in explaining it." Said he, "Just as the name 'Dixie' loses something of its haunting melody when subjected to etymological analysis, so the quality called 'Southern,' and recognizable on the instant, seems to dissolve into thin air when wiseheads fall to explaining it. . . ." Vague though it is, perhaps Wilbur J. Cash's classic contention that the South is a state of mind is the most satisfactory way to describe the South.

Even the term southerner is difficult to define. There are, of course, the stereotyped descriptions. A southerner is the descendant of a family that early settled in the South, lived on a plantation, owned many slaves, and dominated the southern social and political scene before the Civil War. A southerner is one who seeks to defend the "southern way of life." A southerner favors segregation of the races and is willing to take extreme measures to insure that separation. A southerner is a man or woman who speaks with a southern accent. A southerner is one who believes in states' rights. A southerner is a man who sympathizes with the revived Ku Klux Klans and the objectives of the White Citizens Council. A southerner is a college student waving a Confederate flag at an intersectional football game who jumps to his feet and cheers when the band strikes up, "Oh, I wish I was in the land of cotton, old times there are not forgotten."

But these labels ignore a large segment of the population of the South. Are not those men who live in the South and who are trying to ease racial tension also southerners? Was not Ralph McGill, the Atlanta *Constitution*'s forward looking critic of many of the South's social customs, a southerner? What about the mid-twentieth-century southerners who know little and care less about their ancestors as they strive to improve their economic status in industry and agriculture? Are southern-born and edu-cated college professors who have made the deliberate choice to remain in the South not southerners because they are striving to bring under-standing to the region's new generations in an era of change? What about

the millions of Negroes who have lived in the South throughout that region's long history? Must they be denied the appellation southern? Is the
term southerner synonymous with white southerner? Is it not equally
appropriate to speak and write of black southerners? The term southerner,
like the South, is difficult to assess with any degree of finality. Perhaps
no more can be said than that a southerner is one who considers himself
a southerner, even though upon occasion he may feel the necessity to
preface the term with "white," "black," "liberal," "died-in-the-wool,"
"staunch," or "real."

The South, southerner, and southernism remain enigmatic terms,
and the region's diversity in geography and economy, in society and politics, in psychology and ideology resists any single, all-encompassing definition or explanation. Instead, many themes permeate the South's past. For
an understanding of the South as a distinct section, this volume will
study various aspects of that mercurial region: society, agriculture, education, literature, religion, slavery and the Negro, politics, industrialization,
urbanization, change, and resistance to change.

After a brief survey of the colonial and early national periods of
the South, attention will be directed to those factors in the Old South
which help explain its growth as a distinct section in the early nineteenth
century. Then came the Confederacy and the Civil War, the latter being
a major watershed in both the South's and the nation's history. The war
destroyed the Old South, and the region's history after 1865 became largely
a story of the development of a New South to replace the older society.
An important part of that story has been the resistance of some southerners to the changing times. Indeed, one of the South's major problems
since the Civil War has been to adjust southern ways of thinking and acting to those of other Americans. This adjustment to national norms has
brought much anguish and soul-searching to the southern people, but
many happy experiences have also resulted. If racial strife in the South
has brought mental turmoil to many southerners, economic progress has
produced a higher standard of living. If southerners recall with sorrow
the passing of a mythical Old South, few would actually be willing to substitute their region's present status for the "good old days." Many pages
hereafter will attest to the truth of these statements. Historians who write
books entitled *The Lasting South* and *The Everlasting South* contending
that there will always be a South are in direct disagreement with those
who argue that the South is rapidly disappearing or, indeed, has already
vanished. It may be fairly assumed that although the South as a distinct
society may not last forever, neither is it evaporating as quickly as some
contend. Assessing which parts of southernism have disappeared or are
fast disappearing, and which remain or are vanishing slowly, is an objective worth pursuing.

Suggestions for Further Reading

Monroe Billington (ed.), *The South: A Central Theme* * (New York: Holt, Rinehart & Winston, 1969) contains excerpts from a number of volumes which are concerned with the essential nature of the South. In addition to these, the following works deal directly or indirectly with that fascinating subject: Wilbur J. Cash, *The Mind of the South* * (New York: Knopf, 1941); C. Vann Woodward, *The Burden of Southern History* * (Baton Rouge: Louisiana State Univ., 1960); Francis B. Simkins, *The Everlasting South* (Baton Rouge: Louisiana State Univ., 1963); James McBride Dabbs, *Who Speaks for the South?* (New York: Funk & Wagnalls, 1964); Louis D. Rubin and James J. Kilpatrick (eds.), *The Lasting South* (Chicago: H. Regnery, 1957); Howard Zinn, *The Southern Mystique* (New York: Knopf, 1964); David Bertelson, *The Lazy South* (New York: Oxford, 1967); Earl E. Thorpe, *Eros and Freedom in Southern Life and Thought* (Durham: The Author, 1967).

Old but useful articles which attempt to delineate the South as a distinct section are: Phillips, "The Central Theme of Southern History," *American Historical Review,* vol. 34 (1928–29); Ransom, "The South Defends Its Heritage," *Harper's Monthly Magazine,* vol. 159 (1929); Keyserling, "The South—America's Hope," *Atlantic Monthly,* vol. 144 (1929); Zelinsky, "Where the South Begins," *Social Forces,* vol. 30 (1951–52). Other articles which may be profitably read are: Dykeman, "The Face of the South," *Current History,* vol. 35 (1958); Cappon, "The Provincial South," *Journal of Southern History,* vol. 16 (1950); Hesseltine, "Sectionalism and Regionalism in American History," *ibid.,* vol. 26 (1960); Shyrock, "Cultural Factors in the History of the South," *ibid.,* vol. 5 (1939).

* Available in paperback.

CHAPTER I

THE "PRE-SOUTH" SOUTH

"To write of the South when there was no South is a task not without difficulties," Wesley F. Craven penned in the preface to his volume on the southern colonies in the seventeenth century. The men and women who inhabited the South in the colonial period of American history did not consider themselves southerners, nor Americans for that matter. They were mostly transplanted Englishmen with a scattering of continental Europeans, and all of them thought in terms of their Old World antecedents. In the words of Stephen Vincent Benét:

> And those who came were resolved to be Englishmen,
> Gone to World's End, but English every one.*

Only as the American Revolution approached did some of the English colonials begin to be conscious of themselves as Americans, and awareness of sectionalism did not appear in an overpowering form until after the Revolution had ended. But if no southern consciousness existed in the colonial period, a number of events occurred then which were important to the development of the South as a distinct region.

* Benét, *Western Star* (New York, 1943), p. 116.

Colonial Antecedents of the South

English traditions modified by the New World environment were the bases for the colonial South. Although both the Spanish and the French explored and colonized in the area now called the South, the English were eventually supreme in the race for colonies in the southern regions. After several unsatisfactory attempts by Elizabethan Englishmen, including Sir Walter Raleigh's and Richard Hakluyt's failures to establish trading posts on or near Roanoke Island in the 1500s, a venture was begun in 1606 which proved to be the guiding force behind the first permanent English colony to be founded in the Western Hemisphere. In that year the London Company (subsequently called the Virginia Company) was organized, a joint-stock venture which had more resources, men, and desire than did the earlier colonizers. Hoping to convert the Indians, to discover gold, to locate the Northwest Passage to India, and to provide raw materials for England, the company sent three ships to establish a trading post on the shores of Virginia, claimed by England following the voyages of earlier English explorers and named after the Virgin Queen, Elizabeth I. Landing in the Chesapeake Bay region in April 1607, more than one hundred men and boys on this maiden venture founded a settlement they called Jamestown in honor of King James I. Overwhelmed by the natural beauty of the region, the leaders ignored the London Company's sound advice that the settlement be beside a navigable river, in a location not densely wooded, and on high ground away from marshes and swamps. Instead, they located on a peninsula thirty miles up the James River, in a heavily wooded area near a mosquito-breeding swamp. Malaria ultimately forced the abandonment of the original Jamestown site.

The colony's leaders made other grave mistakes. They set up a completely unworkable form of government headed by a president and a council, and in 1609 they experimented with a single governor who had dictatorial powers. The colony was torn by dissension, "gentlemen" did not want to soil their hands with manual labor, disease decimated their numbers, and the neighboring Indians were hostile. That the colony was saved from extinction was due in no small measure to Captain John Smith, a twenty-seven-year-old soldier of fortune. A confident and resourceful natural leader, Smith neutralized the Indians and traded with them for much needed corn. He also forced the "gentlemen" to plant more corn instead of searching for gold. The historian's main source for Smith's role in the salvation of the colony is Smith's own account, and older historians doubted the Captain's story which made the author the hero. Smith himself wrote, "I shall be taxed for writing so much of my selfe: but I care not much." Recent scholars have been inclined to accept his accounts as the "fabulous truth," and apparently he, more than any other person in Virginia, could grasp and cope with the almost overwhelming problems.

Additional shiploads of men arrived in Virginia from time to time, but the colony did not prosper. Lack of food supplies, disease, Indian raids, and inability to adjust to the new environment reduced the numbers of men in the colony almost as fast as the dead could be replaced. While some 6,000 colonists had migrated to Virginia from 1607 to 1624, in the latter year only 1,275 survived. The frightful toll of disease, starvation, and Indian massacres continued to be felt for years to come. But the colonists did not give up. The arrival of a shipload of women in 1619 signaled that the colony was not to remain only a distant English trading post struggling to survive, but that it intended to become the permanent home of migrating Englishmen who left the mother country for a better way of life in the New World. But the colony was not yet firmly established. Factionalism caused misrule of the colony, and more importantly the colony after eighteen years had not made a profit for the London Company. A huge investment of over £200,000 had resulted only in red ink upon the company's ledger. A hearing in 1624 in the King's court brought into the open the mismanagement of the colony by the company's council in England, and the court withdrew the charter from the company. Virginia's status became that of a royal colony, managed directly by the British government in the name of the King. Some of the company's stockholders who hoped to recoup their losses were unhappy over this turn of events, but subsequent years were to prove that for the Virginians themselves the government's action was beneficial. Although good times did not come immediately, eventually Virginia became firmly established under the King's rule and Virginians today can accurately recall that it was within their boundaries that the foundations for both American and southern civilizations were laid.

Contrasted with Virginia's difficult early experiences, Maryland, the Carolinas, and Georgia were settled without undue hardship. An investor in the Virginia Company, Sir George Calvert, developed plans for an economic enterprise on the upper Chesapeake, and after his death his son Cecilius inherited the elder Calvert's ambitions as well as his English title (Lord Baltimore). In 1632 King Charles I granted to the younger Calvert a slice of northern Virginia which contained nearly ten million acres and was named Maryland in honor of the King's wife. Two years later, under Lord Baltimore's authority over two hundred immigrants crowded into two small vessels to sail to the New World. Arriving at the mouth of the Chesapeake Bay in March 1634, the group sailed up the St. George River and established St. Mary's, about seventy miles north of Jamestown. The experience and propinquity of the Jamestown colony benefited the Marylanders. They located their first town on a high bank overlooking a good anchorage, they made peace with the Indians in the vicinity and purchased the land from them, and they planted crops immediately upon their arrival. Coming to America to found a colony rather than a trading post, these settlers lost no valuable time in futile searches for a passage to India or for nonexistent gold. Maryland avoided a "starving time" which had almost wiped out the earlier Virginia colony; indeed, enterprising settlers exported a shipload of Indian corn after their first harvest.

As sole proprietor of the colony, Lord Baltimore was granted the power to make ordinances, to appoint officials, and to administer justice, including meting out the death penalty. The charter under which Baltimore operated stated that the proprietor could make laws only with the assent and advice of the freemen and that the laws were to be reasonable and in accord with English law. The liberties of British subjects were extended to the colonists, and the King had no power to veto the colony's laws or to collect taxes. Like his father, the second Baltimore was motivated by the desire for economic gain when he established his colony as a haven for persecuted members of his faith. He did not prohibit settlers who were not Catholic; in fact, he promised religious toleration for all Protestants who settled in his domain. Taking Baltimore at his word, Protestants migrated to the colony and from the beginning constituted a numerical majority. To attract and protect both Catholics and Protestants, the Maryland Toleration Act of 1649 was passed, shielding the "conscience in matters of religion" for all who accepted the divinity of Jesus Christ. Continuing a policy Baltimore had unilaterally laid down when he first publicized his undertaking, this act resulted in increased migrations to the colony. Although it said nothing about the relationship of Church and State, it was nonetheless an important step in American and southern traditions well formulated in later years.

After the English Civil War and Oliver Cromwell's Protectorate, in 1660 Charles II was restored to the throne of England, an event which affected the settling of the area south of Maryland and Virginia. Wishing to reward his old friends and supporters who had helped him regain the English throne, Charles gave a huge area of land to eight important favorites, all of whom were interested in colonial affairs, including the Earl of Clarendon, Sir Anthony Ashley Cooper, and Sir William Berkeley, a former governor of Virginia. To honor the King the region was called Carolina. Carolina's charter, like Maryland's, allowed the proprietors wide authority in the colony. With the assistance of John Locke, the English political philosopher, the proprietors drafted a model government which they called Fundamental Constitutions. This curious document demonstrated Locke's and the proprietors' ignorance of actual conditions in America. They dreamed of a feudal system with the land divided into counties, seigniories, baronies, and precincts and the establishment of a hierarchy headed by the proprietors and lesser "landgraves" and "caciques." The proprietors and the nobility were to retain two-fifths of the land, the remainder to be granted to the common people. The manpower to support this feudal society was to come from peasants who were designated "leetmen." Grants of land were made to some landgraves and caciques, but they could not find leetmen willing to work on their great domains. Land was too readily available for migrants to remain landless peasants in Carolina, and the ambitious plans of the proprietors were never effected.

Encouraged by the proprietors, settlers arrived in 1670, most of them small English farmers from the sugar plantations of Barbados, who were unable to compete with the developing slave system in the West Indian Islands. Charles Town (Charleston), founded in 1680 on an excellent bay where the Ashley and Cooper rivers flowed into the Atlantic, became the center of economic and social activity in the southern part of Carolina. A northern region of the colony, the Albemarle district just south of Virginia, also became a population center, settled largely by squatters from Virginia who were permitted to govern themselves. Two strikingly different societies developed over the years. Because the proprietors gave more personal attention to the southern than to the northern portion of their grant, failing to provide even the rudiments of an adequate government for the distant settlements, the people of northern Carolina soon became unhappy. After 1691 the northern part of the colony was called North Carolina, and for a time both North and South Carolina were governed as one unit. In 1712 the proprietors designated a separate governor for the northern region. But the proprietors were unable to provide a satisfactory government for either part of their colony. After attacks from the Yamasee and Tuscarora Indians, the Carolinians petitioned the King to take over the colonies from the proprietors. Subsequently, South Carolina (1721) and North Carolina (1729) became royal colonies.

Georgia, the southernmost English colony on the North American mainland, was the only one of the original thirteen colonies not settled in the seventeenth century. Seventy years after the Carolina charter was issued, the King of England granted the land between South Carolina and Spanish Florida to a group of "trustees" who were to establish and manage a colony there without profit to themselves for a period of twenty years. Since the colony was viewed as a buffer against the neighboring Spanish, the Parliament promised an annual appropriation of £8,000 for its maintenance. The primary reason for the creation of Georgia stemmed from humanitarian motives. General James Oglethorpe, leader of the trustees, looked upon Georgia as a haven for the inmates of England's debtors' prisons. His plans called for the former prisoners to render military service, to abstain from drinking rum, and to work fifty-acre tracts of land without the benefit of slaves. Oglethorpe founded Savannah in 1733, but the records show that only a few of the settlers of Georgia were in fact former imprisoned debtors. Fearful of the Spanish and the Indians, most of the settlers of Georgia faithfully fulfilled their military obligations in order to protect their colony, but they refused to live the Spartan existence planned by the trustees. When settlers began to migrate from Georgia to colonies with fewer restrictions and greater economic opportunities, the trustees winked at violations and gradually relaxed their tight control over the lives of the settlers. Rum began to flow, slaves were imported, and landholding increased. When Georgia began to mirror the neighboring colony on the north, the disillusioned trustees abandoned their responsibilities and in 1752 Georgia became a royal colony.

"That Filthy Weed"

Whatever the primary motivation may have been for the settlement of the five southern colonies, each of them had to become self-sufficient in order to survive. The colonists therefore gave attention to crops which would provide food and bring cash to the colonies. Corn, the basic ingredient for bread, was the principal grain crop during the colonial era. A relatively small amount of wheat was grown in the southern colonies in the seventeenth and early eighteenth centuries. Wheat production in Virginia and Maryland increased somewhat after about 1730, and a greater increase in wheat production occurred after mid-century as the backcountry began to fill up. Small quantities of oats, rye, and barley were also grown. Corn and other grains were in such short supply in the early colonial years that laws were passed to prohibit their exportation.

Colonial company officials, proprietors, and the British government all encouraged the colonists to produce a variety of specialized crops. The cultivation of figs, olives, citrus fruits, almonds, ginger, and cotton was suggested and sometimes attempted. Virginia's first cotton crop was planted in 1607, but cotton did not become an important part of the colonial economy. On the eve of the American Revolution, the mainland colonies were exporting annually less than 45,000 pounds of cotton. The Virginia Company sent vine dressers from France to aid with the development of a grape and wine industry. The vineyardists succeeded in improving the Virginia grape and producing a desirable wine, but wine-making did not become commercially profitable. Silkworms were imported to feed on the native mulberry trees, and efforts were made to force colonists to care for the trees and worms, but only a small amount of silk was produced in the mainland colonies. Georgia's 1,084 pounds of silk exported in 1766–67 represented the apex of the colonial silk production, and the industry declined and disappeared shortly after that time. Colonial legislatures encouraged the production of flax and hemp in the early colonial period by paying bounties and premiums to those farmers who grew them. The crops were not generally successful until the 1750s, however, when hemp and flax were both being raised in abundance in interior regions. Neither became an important export crop.

By far the most important of the commercial crops of the colonial South was tobacco. Virginia's first desperate and lean years were overcome with the introduction of tobacco. In 1612 John Rolfe first carried to Virginia a West Indian variety of the "filthy weed" which was free from the strong bite of the tobacco native to the region. Despite sharp criticism of tobacco-using (King James I condemned the "black stinking fume"), Englishmen and continental Europeans had become addicted to the use of the plant, and a captive market awaited each hogshead. After 1616 when a successful curing process was developed in Virginia, many shiploads of tobacco were sent to Europe. So profitable was tobacco at one time that Virginians were growing it in the streets of Jamestown. With so much attention being directed toward that crop, Governor Thomas Dale feared for the food supply of the colony and tried to force each family head to plant at least two acres of corn.

Because tobacco could be grown profitably in the Chesapeake Bay country and the Albemarle Sound region, Maryland and North Carolina also turned to the growing of this money crop. To illustrate the attention tobacco received: before 1620 Virginia was already exporting over 60,000 pounds of the golden leaf annually. At five shillings a pound tobacco became a source of revenue more valuable for the English than was the gold of Peru and Mexico for the Spanish. By 1627 the colonists were exporting 500,000 pounds annually, and within a dozen more years the total production was 1,500,000 pounds. By the end of the century the crop was 40,000,000 pounds annually, and on the eve of the American Revolution the yearly crop amounted to over 100,000,000 pounds. The great importance of tobacco in the economy of Virginia and Maryland is pointed up by these figures: in 1766 those two colonies exported £880,000 worth of farm products, £768,000 of this being tobacco.

Throughout the colonial period, tobacco prices fluctuated wildly depending upon supply and demand. When prices were low colonists considered diversifying their production, but this was seldom done. The usual pattern was that during a depression the tobacco farmer put his efforts into producing food; then when reduced tobacco production resulted in higher prices, the farmer returned to growing more of the staple crop. Soil exhaustion and low prices were responsible for tobacco production shifting from the Tidewater area around 1750, but settlers moving westward planted tobacco, and production continued to expand. As early as 1629 the Virginia legislature attempted to control tobacco production by limiting each farmer to the cultivation of no more than three thousand plants. Another law made it illegal to harvest more than ten leaves from a single tobacco plant, while another ordered all inferior tobacco and half of the good tobacco to be destroyed. In 1665 the tobacco-producing colonies sought an agreement to have no tobacco planted for one full year following February 1666. When Lord Baltimore refused to approve this moratorium on tobacco-growing, the scheme to raise prices by planned scarcity did not become effective. In 1682 large surpluses resulted in such disastrously low prices that plant-cutting riots occurred in three counties of Virginia when small farmers sought to curtail the production of their larger competitors. In 1731 the Maryland legislature passed an act to provide for the payment of paper money to farmers who destroyed part of their tobacco crop. For every 150 pounds of tobacco burned or otherwise destroyed, the farmer was to receive fifteen shillings. The law did not go into effect, but it and other attempts in the colonial period to solve the problems of overproduction, surpluses, and resultant lower prices for farm products are historical reminders that most of the federal government's efforts in the twentieth century to raise prices by restricting farm production are not new.

While Virginia, Maryland, and upper North Carolina were exploiting—and being exploited by—tobacco, lower North Carolina, South Carolina, and Georgia were developing a commercial trade from naval stores, rice, and indigo. North Carolina's great coastal forests of longleaf pine were the source of turpentine, tar, pitch, and ships' masts, vital products to the British navy and shipping industry. The "Tar Heel" colony (and later, state) remained the principal source of naval stores in America until well after the American Civil War. In the late seventeenth century an important rice culture was begun in the inland swamps of South Carolina. Tradition has it that this cultivation began in 1694 when rice seed from Madagascar was brought to the colony. Whether true or not, by 1700 a considerable amount of rice was being exported from South Carolina. By the middle of the eighteenth century the center of South Carolina's rice production had shifted to swamplands lying beside the tidal rivers and inlets. A system of dikes and ingenious floodgates allowed fresh water into the fields as the tide rose; when the tide receded, the gates closed automatically to keep the water in. When the land needed to be drained, the process was reversed, the water running off fields as the tide fell. The rice culture spread to Georgia and the sea islands in the Atlantic, and by 1770 rice exports from the American colonies totaled 150,000 barrels annually. Indigo, the basis for certain widely used dyes, was another cash crop important in the Carolinas. Obtained from the leaves of a plant similar to asparagus, indigo was successfully produced in the colonies beginning in the 1740s. The need for indigo was so great that both England and South Carolina paid bounties to producers. By 1750 over 140,000 pounds were being exported annually from the port of Charleston, and planters and merchants were buying up large numbers of slaves and great tracts of land to develop the indigo culture on a vast scale. The disruptive influence of the American Revolution, competition from East India indigo, and a growing cotton production in South Carolina brought about the end of indigo production in the South. A coal-tar product has replaced vegetable indigo in modern times.

One of the major attractions the New World held out to the Europeans was the vast expanse of virgin land stretching westward from the Atlantic. Colonial leaders capitalized on this desire for land to attract settlers to their colonies. The headright system became the principal means of acquiring land in the southern colonies throughout the seventeenth century. A headright grant consisted of 50 acres of land given to anyone who would emigrate to the colony. Headrights were also freely given to members of the emigrants' families as well as to others for whom an emigrant paid the transportation to America. Because of lax standards by which headrights were given, the system resulted in landholdings averaging nearly 200 acres as early as 1632 in Virginia, and by 1670 average holdings were up to nearly 700 acres. The development of tobacco as a successful staple crop and the desire for profits were responsible for the increasing size of the farms in the South. The proprietors of both Maryland and the Carolinas had dreamed of establishing feudal estates of several thousands of acres, but their grand plans for a manorial economy mirroring the English system failed to develop in the seventeenth century. In the following century a number of huge estates existed in the southern colonies, and the average size of all farms continued to increase. Estates of 5,000 acres became common. The Carroll and Dulany families acquired great estates in Maryland. In Virginia, "King" Robert Carter came to control 333,000 acres; the Beverley family owned over 100,000 acres; and the Byrds of Westover possessed giant plantations in the central section of the state. Other families had similar holdings in the Carolinas and Georgia. Along with tobacco, rice and indigo stimulated these large landholdings, but greater sources of wealth were related to land speculation. The land speculator, so important in the westward development of the country, appeared early on the American scene, purchasing or otherwise acquiring undeveloped lands and later selling them to incoming settlers. The first great fortunes in America and in the South were made from the sale of real estate.

But the majority of the landholders in colonial America were content to make their profits from cultivating the land. In order to do this, however, an adequate labor supply was necessary. The principal source of labor for the large farms in the seventeenth century was the indentured servant, usually a white Englishman who voluntarily bound himself by contract to work for a southern landholder for a specified period in return for payment of passage to America. The labor shortage was so great in colonial America that paupers, criminals, drunks, and young people were kidnapped by agents in England and transported against their wishes to work in the tobacco fields of the southern colonies. After their period of forced labor was ended, the white laborers were often able to acquire land for themselves, and many of them became respectable and distinguished members of southern society. In 1632 six of the forty-four members of the Virginia House of Burgesses were former indentured servants, and in 1663 the legislature had thirteen such men. Descendants of former servants also played a role in later years in the politics and society of the southern colonies.

Historians are still debating whether the "twenty Negars" carried in a Dutch ship to Virginia in 1619 were slaves or lifetime indentured servants, but the question is academic. Slavery was gradually established by custom as more blacks were imported to Virginia and as the rapidly increasing tobacco production demanded more unskilled laborers. In 1660 a Virginia statute made the status of an individual legally dependent upon whether his mother was free or slave. The tradition was set by law in other southern colonies and states, and it remained in effect until the passage of the Thirteenth Amendment in 1865. While white indentured servants were the main labor source in the southern colonies before 1660, after that date Negro slavery gradually came to dominate the labor scene. Staple crop production, large landed estates, and chattel slavery thus were inextricably intertwined by the beginning of the eighteenth century, and together they characterized and dominated southern agriculture for the remainder of the century.

The Expanding South

The majority of settlers in the colonial South were from the British Isles, perhaps two-thirds of them from England alone. Besides the attraction of land in America, a variety of conditions in England compelled immigrants to the American shores. Important among these factors were political difficulties, particularly the conflict between the King and the Parliament; the conversion of agricultural lands into sheep pastures, which drove the peasants from the farms into unemployment in the cities; high land rents; soil exhaustion; and the belief that England was overpopulated. Next to the English the largest national group in the colonial South was the Scots. The migration from Scotland increased greatly after 1708 when Parliament passed the Act of Union which opened the

trade of the Empire to Scottish merchants. Scotch-Irish—Scots who had
earlier migrated from Scotland to northern Ireland—also settled in the
South, as did Irish from the southern regions of the Emerald Isle. Small
numbers of Welsh settled in the Pee Dee Valley of South Carolina.

But the South's population was not homogeneous. An important
admixture to the population from the British Isles was provided by settlers from France. The Edict of Nantes, which had granted religious toleration to French Protestants, was revoked in 1685 and after that date
many of these Huguenots fled to other lands, a good number settling in
the New World. The largest concentration of these middle-class Frenchmen settled in South Carolina, and their skills as craftsmen, traders, and
farmers contributed to that colony's development. The French in
Charleston intermarried with the English, gave up their own language,
joined the Church of England, and generally assimilated well into the society. Small groups of Swiss arrived in the Carolinas at the beginning of
the eighteenth century, but more important in numbers were the Germans who settled in all the southern colonies. Many Germans as well as
Scotch-Irish migrated first to Pennsylvania and later moved south. This
migration from the North and Europe continued throughout the colonial
period, but by the end of the eighteenth century the stream of migration
slowed to a trickle, a development directly related to the by then well-
established slave labor system.

As the lands along the Atlantic coast became inhabited by people
from the British Isles and the continent of Europe, and as tobacco growing wore out the Tidewater soil, pressure built up to move westward.
The good lands from the ocean to the fall line, the place where the rivers
became no longer navigable as boats moved upstream, were fairly well
taken up in Virginia by 1676, and considerable settlement in the other
colonies had also occurred by that date. West of the fall line lay the Piedmont, the low-lying foothills of the Appalachian Mountains. Population
pressures and the desire for new land for tobacco-growing helped attract
people to this region in the late years of the seventeenth century, and it
was fairly well settled by the time of the American Revolution. Many of
the non-English immigrant groups moved into the Old West, as the Piedmont region has come to be called. The Germans and Scotch-Irish from
Pennsylvania pushed into the Valley of Virginia, finally spilling over into
the Yadkin and other valleys of the South. Both English and non-English
settlers moved into the interior from such coastal population centers as
Charleston, Wilmington, and Savannah.

The Appalachian Mountains constituted a geographic barrier halting the westward advance of settlers for several years. The Piedmont region to the east of the mountain range filled rapidly because of natural
population increase and immigration, the fertile land in the beautiful
hill country attracting men by the thousands. The mountains could

not contain the westward push of southern men indefinitely. Cumberland Gap, the break in the mountain dike through which thousands of men and their families were to make their way to the New West, was first viewed by white men in 1674 when an illiterate Indian trader named Gabriel Arthur stumbled upon it. The famous pass was rediscovered in 1750 by Thomas Walker, an agent of a land company, and before the outbreak of the American Revolution a number of men in the forefront of the westward advance had made their way through the pass to explore and settle the lands west of the mountains. During the decade of the 1760s, the land soon to be called Kentucky and Tennessee was crisscrossed by the Long Hunters, groups of white men who searched for wild game during extended periods of time in the pristine wilderness. The most famous—but by no means the first nor the most important—of these earlier explorers was the legendary Daniel Boone. Told of the wealth and natural beauty of "Kaintuck" by a fur trader who preceded him into the "dark and bloody ground," Boone and a party of associates filed through Cumberland Gap in the spring of 1769 on a hunting expedition. Boone was much attracted to this wonderful new wilderness, and four years later he led a band of hardy settlers and their families into the region. Indian attacks forced the abandonment of this early village, and the first white man to establish a permanent settlement in Kentucky was not Boone, but James Harrod. Founded in 1774 in central Kentucky, Harrodsburg was temporarily abandoned during Lord Dunmore's War, but it was reoccupied the following year.

Fast on the heels of the original pioneers in the New West were the land speculators. Richard Henderson formed the Transylvania Company, and in 1775 he negotiated a treaty with the Indians for control of all of present central Kentucky. Henderson had hopes of establishing a colony called Transylvania, modeled after Maryland. Other settlers in the region objected to Henderson's grandiose plans, presented their objections to the Virginia government, and received the latter's permission to resist domination by Henderson. In December 1776 the Virginia legislature created the county of Kentucky with boundaries surrounding all of the widely scattered settlements of the region, and Henderson's ambitious plans for a state of Transylvania ended. In less than twenty years Kentucky was to become a state in the new Union.

Many of the pioneers who passed through Cumberland Gap turned south to settle what is now eastern Tennessee. Arriving in the late 1760s these settlers made their homes in the Watauga Valley, and in the early 1770s they petitioned the North Carolina government to establish a local government there. When their request went unheeded, they drew up a constitution providing for a legislature of thirteen men and established the first autonomous government in the New West. This government lasted until 1776, when North Carolina set up Washington County, embracing the Watauga settlements and most of the future state of Tennessee. In 1779 James Robertson founded Nashville in middle Tennessee, and William Blount and other land speculators promoted additional colonization in middle and east Tennessee. To protect themselves against Indian raids, the people of east Tennessee in 1784 organized the state of Franklin. John Sevier, an important figure in the colonization of Tennessee, was named governor of this extralegal government which was motivated in part by land speculation. The Franklin experiment lasted only a few years, after which North Carolina reasserted its authority over the entire region. When Tennessee was admitted to the Union in 1796, the new state's boundaries included the Watauga settlements, the state of Franklin, the Nashville region, and other small palisaded settlements and forts south of Kentucky.

The westward march of the southern frontier was due in no small measure to the activities of land speculators, as many writers in recent years have pointed out. But not to be overlooked are those sturdy pioneers who were attracted to the land for what it was. They moved away from the Atlantic seaboard into the Piedmont and then across the mountains to the valleys east of the Mississippi River as they searched for good land to cultivate and a place to bring up their children. Although it is an oversimplification to say that the frontier created American democracy, it is nevertheless true that the society in the backcountry and beyond the mountains did take on the peculiar American stamp at an early date. The fertile mountain valleys provided homes for small farmers who did not desire to establish great plantations, and their economy and society was more democratic than that along the coast.

And what kind of society was growing up on the coast? In the early years of the southern colonies yeoman farmers were the backbone of the coastal society too. Owner of a few acres and working along with the members of his family and an occasional indentured servant or slave, the yeoman constituted the largest number in any economic or societal grouping in the South. More important in influence, if not in numbers, however, were the families and individuals who acquired large numbers of acres. These planters constituted an upper class in the colonial South, and they lived on an economic level considerably higher than that of the yeoman farmer. The myth that English aristocrats settled and dominated the South has been thoroughly discredited, but this does not preclude the fact that a "native aristocracy" grew up in the seventeenth century. While some reputable historians stress the importance of the yeoman farmers and others the aristocratic elements, it seems reasonable to conclude that the seventeenth-century South was a land of many yeoman farmers with a small number of large planters at the apex of the social pyramid. The presence of large tracts of land quite naturally encouraged a native aristocracy in the eighteenth-century South. The sons and grandsons of the previous generations inherited or otherwise acquired huge estates, increased their slaves to till the soil, and contributed considerably to the myth that the colonial South was composed primarily of these "first family" descendants. Actually, large planters comprised perhaps no more than 10 percent of the population of the colonial South at the beginning of the eighteenth century.

The Maturing South

Both democratic and aristocratic elements were present not only in southern society, but in the colonial governments as well. The seeds for a democratic government in America were planted quite early, beginning with the call for the first assembly in Virginia in 1619. Although the first session of the assembly met in Jamestown upon the order of Sir Edwin Sandys, the treasurer of the Virginia Company, rather than upon the demand of the settlers, the House of Burgesses was intended to be a representative assembly. Representative assemblies were organized in the seventeenth century in all of the other southern colonies except Georgia, and that colony established one soon after its founding in the early eighteenth century. The King and the proprietary authorities clearly intended the governor to be the focus of colonial government, the assemblies being nothing more than subordinate bodies called to meet when taxes needed to be levied, or when local ordinances proposed by the governor needed to be approved. Thus, before 1689 the governor and his council dominated the southern colonial governments, and the representative bodies were subordinate to their rule. Jack P. Greene has elucidated the struggle between the southern colonial assemblies and the executives in the years after the Glorious Revolution of 1689. He contends that a successful "quest for power" by the lower houses of the legislatures resulted in a restriction of the authority of the executive and undermined the system of colonial administration which imperial and proprietary authorities had set up. As a result, on the eve of the American Revolution, the lower houses of the southern colonial assemblies were paramount in the affairs of their respective colonies. Although the evolution of the lower houses to a position of prominence was different in detail and in time in each of the colonies, they moved in the same direction in their demands for increased authority, and they all arrived at approximately the same place. Before 1700 most of the lower houses were still in subordinate positions as they slowly groped for the power to tax and the right to initiate laws. They also demanded and gradually received a separate identity from the governors' councils. As the lower houses bid for political supremacy, great struggles occurred, usually resulting in an accommodation with the executives. These political arrangements paved the way for the ascend-

ancy of the lower houses, and by 1763 the colonial governors had been almost totally stripped of power.

The South Carolina assembly was the first in the southern colonies
to gain considerable power. In the first decade of the eighteenth century,
the colony's lower house came into vicelike control of all areas of South
Carolina's government. After 1730 its attention was directed to the smallest details of local administration. A series of governors offered almost no
significant opposition. The power of the lower houses of North Carolina
and Virginia developed somewhat more slowly. The North Carolina
lower house competed on fairly equal terms with the governor during the
last years of proprietary rule and under the first governors appointed
after the colony was taken over by the King. But not until the 1760s did
the lower house, now meeting regularly, gain the upper hand in the colony's politics. Likewise, the Virginia House of Burgesses worked to establish its control in the second decade of the century, but it did not attain
supremacy until the period of the Seven Years' War, when more regular
sessions were needed.

Maryland's lower house was slower yet in its rise to power. It
made some advances at the turn of the eighteenth century and it aggres-
sively tried to extend its authority in the 1720s with the assistance of the
older Daniel Dulany and in the late 1730s and early 1740s under the
leadership of Dr. Charles Carroll. But these attempts were usually stifled
by the proprietors, and the members of the lower house were unable to
overcome the power of the executive in spite of an all-out effort during
the French and Indian War. Not until the decade prior to the outbreak
of the American Revolution did the Maryland body gain dominance in
that colony equal to the power of the South Carolina, North Carolina,
and Virginia assemblies. Georgia, the youngest of the southern colonies,
was the scene of the latest rise of a lower house to a position of power.
Founded after the other colonial assemblies had begun to make a bid for
colonial power, Georgia was ruled with particular pains by the King and
his royal governors who hoped to prevent the shifting of power to the assembly. A succession of capable governors (excluding Captain John Reynolds) and Georgia's lack of experience with representative institutions
combined to give the Crown an important advantage, and the Georgia
assembly did not play a major role in the government of the colony before the Revolution. The pace of political development quickened when
the colony began to prosper economically, however, and within twenty
years, Georgia made gains which had taken older colonies a century to
accomplish. A group of able politicians emerged in Georgia in the 1760s,
and they were becoming increasingly conscious of the assembly's potential role in the affairs of the colony. They also came to view the assembly
as an agency through which they might attain social and economic, as
well as political, prominence. Inspired by their neighbor South Carolina,

which had one of the most powerful of the colonial lower houses, these Georgians became unusually active after 1763. They further expanded their vision when the debates between the American colonists and the British emphasized the importance of a strong representative legislature. After 1765 these men regularly advanced claims to many of the powers already gained by other colonial legislatures. They often battled the governor to a standstill, but with the coming of the Revolution, the representative element in Georgia at last attained political supremacy.

While the representative bodies and the executive branches of the southern colonies struggled for supremacy at the highest level of government in the colonies, local government was fairly stable. The smallest unit of government was the parish ruled over by vestrymen, usually well-to-do freeholders elected by the parishioners. Vestrymen collected local taxes, appointed Anglican clergymen, investigated moral offenses, and chose the church wardens. The wardens served as prosecutors in morals cases, gave relief to the poor, and audited the parish accounts. Above the parish was the county court, although the parish and the court often overlapped in personnel, boundaries, and responsibilities. The county commissioners (or justices), appointed by the governor, had a heterogeneous array of administrative and judicial functions. These county "squires" arbitrated petty quarrels, administered regulations affecting tradesmen, prices, and wages, supervised the maintenance of roads and ferries, recorded wills and contracts, issued land titles, and appointed or nominated other local officials. Often land-rich planters, the county commissioners were a self-perpetuating oligarchy which dominated local government. Many members of the county courts were elected to the colonial assemblies, and this dovetailing of political positions closely tied local government to provincial government. In many ways the voices of the elected assemblies were the voices of the collective county courts and their interests. The practice of expressing local interest through an oligarchy of leading citizens was thus established quite early in southern history.

Suggestions for Further Reading

Wesley Frank Craven, *The Southern Colonies in the Seventeenth Century, 1607–1689* (Baton Rouge: Louisiana State Univ., 1949) is the best single volume devoted to the early southern colonies. Soon to be published in the same excellent series is Clarence Ver Steeg's *The Southern Colonies in the Eighteenth Century, 1689–1763* which together with Craven's volume will complete the story of the southern colonies before the American Revolution. Louis B. Wright, *The First Gentlemen of Virginia: Intellectual Qualities of the Early Colonial Ruling Class* (San Marino, Calif.: Huntington Library, 1940); Charles Sydnor, *Gentlemen Freeholders: Political Practices in Washington's Virginia* (Chapel Hill: Univ. North Carolina, 1952); and Philip A. Bruce, *Social Life of Virginia in the Seventeenth Century* (Richmond: The Author, 1907) stress the importance of the aristocracy in early Virginia. Robert E. and Katherine B. Brown, *Virginia, 1705–1786: Democracy or Aristocracy?* (East Lansing: Michigan State Univ., 1964) discount the contention that sharp class lines existed in the colonial and revolutionary South, and Thomas J. Wertenbaker, *The Old South: The Founding of American Civilization* (New York: Scribners, 1942) likewise deprecates the concept of a preeminent aristocracy in the colonial South.

Jack P. Greene, *The Quest for Power: The Lower House of Assembly in the Southern Royal Colonies, 1689–1776* (Chapel Hill: Univ. North Carolina, 1964) brilliantly details and analyzes the struggle between the colonists' representatives and the King's men. Ella Lonn, *The Colonial Agents of the Southern Colonies* (Chapel Hill: Univ. North Carolina, 1945) deals with another important topic of interest, as does Richard M. Brown's *The South Carolina Regulators* (Cambridge, Mass.: Belknap, 1963). For information on non-English migrants into the colonial South, see Dieter Cunz, *The Maryland Germans: A History* (Princeton: Princeton Univ., 1948); James G. Leyburn, *The Scotch-Irish: A Social History* (Chapel Hill: Univ. North Carolina, 1963); A. H. Hirsch, *The Huguenots of Colonial South Carolina* (Durham: Duke Univ., 1928). Everett Dick, *The Dixie Frontier: A Social History* * (New York: Knopf, 1948) is a good general history of social conditions on the expanding frontier, as is V. W. Crane, *The Southern Frontier, 1670–1732* * (Durham: Duke Univ., 1929).

Volumes which do not focus on the colonial South but which have much relevant material include: James T. Adams, *Provincial Society, 1690–1763* (New York: Macmillan, 1927); Charles M. Andrews, *Colonial Folkways* (New Haven: Yale Univ., 1921); Lawrence H. Gipson, *The British Empire Before the American Revolution*, vol. 2 (New York: Knopf, 1958); Leonard W. Labaree, *Royal Government in America* (New

Haven: Yale Univ., 1930); Oliver M. Dickerson, *American Colonial Government, 1696–1765* (Cleveland: Arthur H. Clark, 1912). Daniel J. Boorstin, *The Americans: The Colonial Experience* * (New York: Random House, 1958) is a competent, interpretive study with comments on colonists in all regions. Francis Butler Simkins, *A History of the South,* 3rd ed. (New York: Knopf, 1963) and Clement Eaton, *A History of the Old South,* 2nd ed. (New York: Macmillan, 1966) are general surveys which begin with chapters on the colonial period.

* Available in paperback.

CHAPTER II

THE SOUTH AND THE NEW NATION

Between 1607 and 1763 Great Britain did not have and thus could not enforce a consistent colonial policy. Before 1689 the King and Parliament were engaged in a titanic struggle for supremacy within the government. The beheading of Charles I, the English civil war, and the Cromwellian interregnum were all a part of this contest over whether the hereditary monarch or elected representatives would dominate the government of Great Britain. When William of Orange and his wife Mary accepted Parliament's invitation to reign jointly over the nation, the turning point in the struggle was reached, the decision being that ultimately Parliament would rule. From 1689 to 1763 England was involved in a series of four wars which held her undivided attention. After 150 years of neglecting her colonies because of domestic problems and foreign wars, Great Britain in 1763 was at last able to give attention to her colonial appendages. Parliament then began passing and enforcing laws which rankled the colonists, who revolted within a dozen years.

The revolution beginning in 1776 resulted from a desire to conserve both economic and political independence. By 1763 most of the southern colonies were already under the political control of colonists rather than British officials. This was true in other colonies as well, and the Americans were in no mood to relinquish hard-gained political power. But it was the economic policies of the British which in the end created the sparks setting off the Revolution. Southern colonists were much involved in these events, as indeed they were in the Revolution itself and in the crucial events of the postwar period.

Southern Revolutionaries

During the colonial period of American history European peoples and nations took for granted the economic doctrine called mercantilism. For an individual nation the primary goal of mercantilism was to gain economic power through national self-sufficiency—and the quickest way for a nation to achieve this economic independence was to establish colonies from which raw materials could be taken and which in turn could serve as markets for the mother country's manufactured products. Europeans believed that the presence of gold in their national treasuries was a barometer of economic power, and an inherent aspect of mercantilism was the establishment of a favorable balance of trade for the mother country, so that gold would accrue in the national treasury. The regulation of trade between the mother country and her colonies was a natural concomitant to putting the theory of mercantilism into effect.

The English colonies founded in the New World in the seventeenth century were assumed to be under the umbrella of mercantilism. When the British government and commercial companies early encouraged new crops in the southern colonies, for example, they were taking halting steps toward the realization of a self-sufficient empire. The first important act of Parliament which incorporated the principles of mercantilism and which directly affected the southern colonies was the Navigation Act of 1651. With this measure the British attempted to circumscribe the rival Dutch carrying trade, especially since that trade had been expanding all over the world and now included the transportation of tobacco from the English colonies. The act required that English or English colonial ships be used to carry colonial goods to England. The unstable conditions in the British Isles during the aftermath of the English civil war and the Cromwellian Protectorate prevented effective enforcement of this regulation. Colonial tobacco growers indifferently shipped their products in whatever carrying vessels were available.

When Charles II was restored to the throne of England in 1660, Parliament renewed efforts to regulate colonial trade in accordance with mercantilistic theory. Additional acts of trade and navigation were passed. The New England shipbuilding industry approved of these measures which resulted in more carrying trade for colonial ships, but the laws irritated tobacco planters in Virginia and Maryland who were forced to pay higher freight rates because the Dutch competition was being excluded. At the same time, Parliament drew up an "enumerated" list of specific colonial products that had to be shipped to England. Tobacco was the main southern product appearing on the original enumerated list, but later other products were added, including rice, naval stores, and lumber. Southern planters often evaded these laws, because the principal markets for rice and tobacco were on the continent of Europe. Evasion was so common that in 1696 Parliament established vice-admiralty courts in the colonies so that smugglers could be speedily tried and punished. Colonists objected to these courts which tended to deal more harshly with violators of the trade acts than did local juries, who previously had jurisdiction over these offenses.

Reflecting the prejudice of national sentiment, older historians maintained that the trade laws were acts of tyranny deliberately designed to harm the colonies and that they were in large measure responsible for the American revolt. More objective historians have concluded that the trade acts did not seriously restrict the economic progress of the colonies, and they have correctly stressed that none of the laws before 1763 were strictly or consistently enforced. Whether the colonies would have made more money had the laws not existed is difficult to answer, but certainly one fact is clear: the colonies generally prospered.

The southern colonies, more than New England or the middle colonies, grew products well suited to assist in the establishment and maintenance of a self-sufficing empire. The semitropical products of the southern colonies were much-desired in England, while the northern colonies produced grain and other commodities in direct competition with the English farmer. Furthermore, British laws restricting manufacturing fell on the northern colonies more than the southern colonies, since the colonies north of Maryland competed with English industries by producing hats, woolens, and iron manufactures. It should not be forgotten that Maryland and Virginia tobacco growers were granted a monopoly of the British market through tariffs; Spanish tobacco was virtually excluded even though it was a superior product. Indigo producers were awarded a bounty of six pence a pound and paid no duties at British ports. Likewise, producers of North Carolina naval stores received generous bounties, and the Tar Heel Colony had no basis for complaints against the operation of the mercantile system.

The tobacco planters of the Chesapeake Bay region felt the restrictions of the trade and navigation laws most. After tobacco was designated an enumerated product, all of the tobacco legally shipped from the southern colonies was sent to Britain. Although Great Britain purchased the total tobacco crop each year, that country consumed only a small proportion of it. For example, in 1773 the colonies shipped to Great Britain over 100,000,000 pounds of tobacco, but the mother country consumed less than 4 percent of this total. Most of the tobacco was reexported to Holland and Germany. Tobacco planters would have been better off sending the tobacco directly to its ultimate consumers, avoiding the high customs duties at the English ports, as well as additional freight, insurance, commissions, and charges for handling the cargo. While the cost of producing tobacco rose in the eighteenth century, the price remained relatively low; the middlemen's charges often prevented the planter from making any profit at all. In a fluctuating market affected only by supply and demand, the economic squeeze would have been tight enough without mercantile restrictions, and the planters on occasion protested, but little attention was paid to their objections.

When Great Britain emerged victorious from the colonial wars, properly designated by Lawrence Gipson as The Great War for the Empire, her rivals, particularly France, no longer threatened her in the colonial world. Great Britain now turned to administer her long-neglected offspring in America. In a new imperial policy, she proposed to enforce the mercantile system, at the same time modifying it by levying a series of new taxes. Had these policies been advanced and enforced in the seventeenth century, the struggling colonists probably would have accepted them as a matter of course. But after ignoring laws, seeking their own markets, generally prospering by their own efforts, and directing their own political affairs, many colonists refused to accept the new policies. The economically and politically maturing colonies were of no mind to submit to what they now considered arbitrary rule by the mother country. Leaders in England, unable or unwilling to understand that the American scene had changed over the decades, failed to develop the foresight to alter their policies to meet new exigencies, and the course set upon in 1763 led directly to revolution. Colonists in the South contributed their fair share to the discontent of the decade.

Southern colonists expressed unhappiness when the Proclamation of 1763 was announced. Designed to halt temporarily white settlement in the British territory west of the Appalachians, the policy advanced in the proclamation became a permanent policy of exclusion. Land speculators and land-hungry pioneers objected to a policy which severely limited expansion to lands west of the mountain range, and colonial officials feared the loss of right to areas which had been within boundaries specified in colonial charters. More objectionable were the laws passed by Parliament to levy taxes in the colonies to help defray the costs of empire. Superseding the old Molasses Act of 1733, the first of these laws was a new Sugar Act passed in 1764, placing duties on sugar, coffee, wines, and similar products imported directly to the mainland colonies. Duties on foreign molasses were cut in half, but at the same time the British government aimed to enforce this and the other trade laws of the empire which had been violated while Great Britain had been occupied with other matters.

The greatest outcry came when the Stamp Act was passed in 1765.

The measure was designed to raise more revenue in order to pay for the expense of maintaining a British army to defend the colonists. It provided that all newspapers, legal and business documents, and other printed matter bear revenue stamps. This tax offended more than any other, because as a direct, internal tax it touched all colonists. The uproar over it was so great Edmund and Helen Morgan have called the Stamp Act crisis the "prologue to revolution." The first important vocal protest in this prologue was made before the Virginia legislature by Patrick Henry, who vehemently argued that the colonial legislature had the sole authority to levy taxes in Virginia. Other colonial assemblies also raised objections, the Massachusetts General Court proposing an all-colonial congress to formulate and advance the American position. Of the southern colonies only South Carolina and Maryland sent delegates to this Stamp Act Congress, but much support for the stand taken at the meeting existed in the entire South.

The success of the Stamp Act Congress in bringing about repeal of the detested tax inspired the colonists to additional resistance as the British Parliament initiated still more measures to pay for the high cost of protecting an empire. When the Townshend Acts placed duties on certain products being imported into the colonies, New York and New England were most directly affected, but colonial unity was growing and Virginia's assembly adopted a resolution stating that only the colonial legislatures had the right to tax the colonies. Despite objections from the governor, South Carolina took similar action.

When the Intolerable Acts were passed to reprimand Massachusetts for the Boston Tea Party, Virginians sent food to Bostonians whose port had been closed until restitution could be made for the damaged tea. To show sympathy for Boston the Virginia legislature designated the first day of June 1774 as a day of prayer and fasting. When Virginia's governor, Lord Dunmore, dismissed the legislature for this action, the members of the assembly then reassembled at Raleigh Tavern in Williamsburg and called for a general continental congress to gather in Philadelphia to discuss colonial grievances. Only Georgia failed to send representatives to this First Continental Congress, dominated by Virginia and Massachusetts delegates. A Second Continental Congress began sessions in the spring of 1775, as relations between the mother country and her colonies continued to deteriorate.

Although not as famous as the incident at Lexington and Concord, several military skirmishes occurred in the South in 1775 and early 1776. Patrick Henry assumed command of the Virginia militia and won a victory over Governor Dunmore near Norfolk. Soon after that, clashes between Patriots and those loyal to the Crown occurred in North Carolina and Georgia. These and other military events helped convince colonists that they must declare and fight for their total independence. In June

1776 Richard Henry Lee of Virginia offered a resolution at a session of the Second Continental Congress declaring that "these United Colonies are, and of right ought to be, free and independent States." After heated debate, Lee's resolution was adopted on July 2, 1776. In the meantime, a committee of five, led by Thomas Jefferson of Virginia, had been assigned the task of drawing up a formal Declaration of Independence, and on July 4 this declaration was adopted by unanimous vote. The break with the mother country was official and complete.

Revolution in the South

The philosophy espoused and the grievances listed in the Declaration of Independence, despite being written in inimitable Jeffersonian prose, did not reflect the unanimous opinion of the American colonists—North or South. A significant proportion of the colonists had disagreed with arguments used by dissenting Americans in their post-1763 dispute with the mother country. Some of these hesitant colonists joined the side of the Patriots once military skirmishing began, but a large number of them were repulsed when the quickened pace of events led to revolution. The conservatives of the American Revolution, these Loyalists did not believe that the political and economic grievances of the colonists justified revolution. Men who held these views were present in all of the colonies, in every economic class, and in every rank of the social structure.

Loyalism was quite strong in Georgia and the Carolinas. Georgia was a royal colony, her population was small, she had been established more recently in the colony-founding period, and she was relatively late in maturing as a colony. The Carolina colonies were longtime royal colonies, and opposition strong enough to be treasonable had never developed in large segments of the population. The fact that these colonies did not feel the sharpest pinches of the mercantile system may help explain their hesitancy to revolt. Moreover, the great plantation owners, who quailed when they contemplated the loss of property, were inclined to be cautious. The presence of Patriots and Loyalists in these areas made the Revolution take on the character of a civil war.

The military events of the Revolution were concentrated in the northern colonies during the first years of the struggle. With loyalism strong in New York, the British captured the city at the mouth of the Hudson River early in the war and used it as a base of operations for almost the entire duration of the conflict. Placing their faith in the divide-and-conquer theory, the British in 1777 undertook to gain control of the Hudson River Valley from New York to Canada, thus isolating New England from the remainder of the colonies. The grand strategy called for General John Burgoyne to advance southward from Canada, Lieutenant Colonel Barry St. Leger to push eastward from Fort Oswego on Lake Ontario, and General William Howe to sail up the Hudson, the three forces to converge on Albany, New York. Burgoyne was decisively defeated at Saratoga, St. Leger was driven back to Oswego after his movements bogged down, and Howe failed to execute his drive on schedule because he wasted too much time trying to capture Philadelphia first. As a venture in coordinated military tactics, this grand plan was a fiasco.

Other military efforts by the British were equally frustrating. For example, in 1778 the British planned to attack the colonies from the Northwest Territory after filtering in troops from Canada. This plan was foiled when Kentuckian George Rogers Clark and a band of some two hundred Americans harassed the British in the Northwest posts with such success that His Majesty's troops were essentially driven out of the territory. After nearly four years of fighting, the British had won only New York City and had failed in their ambitious plan to divide the colonies. Unsuccessful in the northern and middle colonies, the British decided to transfer military campaigns to the South, anticipating more support from cooperative colonists, since that section apparently had a large share of Loyalists. They expected to move northward if they were successful in the southernmost colonies.

General Henry Clinton was made general director of the southern campaigns. In the fall of 1778 he ordered Lieutenant-Colonel Archibald Campbell and thirty-five hundred troops to invade Georgia. Campbell was to join General George Prevost, who was to move northward from St. Augustine with about two thousand men. Landing near Savannah in December 1778, Campbell attacked that city without waiting for Prevost. Weakly defended, Savannah capitulated quickly. After Prevost appeared from Florida, Augusta fell into British hands in January 1779. The British controlled Georgia after a month of easy fighting. The Americans hurried extra troops into lower South Carolina and made two attempts to recapture Georgia. The first ended in defeat at Briar Creek, fifty miles north of Savannah, and the second was aborted by a swift countermove by Prevost. After his successful maneuver, Prevost moved north, preparing to attack Charleston. When an American force appeared on the scene, Prevost hastily retreated to Georgia, where his position was secure. In the summer of 1779 Americans attacked Savannah by land, and French allies bombarded the seaport from the ocean, but the city remained in the hands of the British.

In the spring of 1780 the British successfully attacked the port and city of Charleston, routing General Benjamin Lincoln and his troops who had been stationed there to defend the area. The loss was a severe blow to the cause of the Patriots, because supply lines from the sea to this finest port south of the Chesapeake Bay region were interrupted. General Charles Cornwallis was left in South Carolina with matters seemingly under British control. The British now occupied all of the settled areas of Georgia and considerable portions of South Carolina. But, refusing to accept British military rule, the Patriots of the region resorted to guerrilla warfare. Replacing Lincoln, General Horatio Gates moved with an army into South Carolina to help the unorganized Patriots. As Gates moved toward Camden, South Carolina, an important British position, Cornwallis scurried to Camden to reinforce the fort. When Gates attacked, he was repulsed, and he and his army retreated to Charlotte, North Carolina. Cornwallis then attempted to take Charlotte, but he was driven back. Part of his force was decisively defeated at King's Mountain in northern South Carolina before the British general retreated to the safety of the fort at Camden.

After receiving reinforcements, Cornwallis in early 1781 decided to attack North Carolina again. By that time General Nathanael Greene had been placed in charge of the garrison at Charlotte, and Greene harassed Cornwallis's movements, confusing the British with puzzling strategy. Although a force of Patriots defeated a contingent of British troops at Cowpens, South Carolina, Cornwallis refused to be cautious; he pursued Greene's army whenever he had a chance. Greene was not afraid to fight, and the two armies collided at Guilford Court House, North Carolina. The British won, but it was almost a Pyrrhic victory with many British troops killed or wounded. Cornwallis realized his victories in North Carolina were costly. His depleted army was beginning to be too weak to risk even defensive war in North Carolina. He decided to move elsewhere, but he chose to go to Wilmington, rather than to Camden or Charleston. He reached Wilmington unmolested in the spring of 1781.

Greene could not resist taking advantage of Cornwallis's absence from South Carolina and Georgia. Cornwallis had left British troops and Loyalists in control of these two states, but their numbers were not great nor their control strong. Greene himself hardly ever won a pitched battle, but other Patriot military leaders were highly successful. In the three-month period of summer 1781, the British were defeated time and again. British occupation in the lower South was reduced to Charleston, Savannah, and small areas near those ports. Greene was not able to take Charleston and Savannah, but he hovered around them so that the British there had no opportunity to take the offensive. The British held these two ports and St. Augustine until the end of the war, but their presence was without purpose or effect.

During that summer Cornwallis considered returning to South Carolina and Georgia, but he correctly judged that the odds were against his success. Deciding to attack Virginia to the north, he moved to Petersburg, Virginia, and gathered around him all available troops. Then there began an exchange of communication between Cornwallis and Clinton as to who should help whom. Cornwallis wanted Clinton, who was stationed in New York, to assist him by coming to Virginia and concentrating some troops there; Clinton wanted Cornwallis to move into Pennsylvania. Faced by a growing American and French army in Virginia, Cornwallis settled down at Yorktown to await supplies which he hoped would reach him from the sea. In July and August he built fortifications without interference. His feelings of assurance under these circumstances would have been justified had the British continued to control the water. But General George Washington, commander-in-chief of the Patriot forces, had persuaded French Admiral Count de Grasse to move his fleet from the French West Indies into the Chesapeake Bay. Arriving in August, de Grasse stationed his well-manned fleet off Yorktown.

Washington moved into the region with an army from New York intent on trapping Cornwallis. The entire operation worked to perfection. Washington's Patriot army with French troops moved to positions surrounding Cornwallis, cutting him off from every avenue of escape by land. If he were to escape, it would have to be by sea. Through September and into October Clinton considered ways to save Cornwallis. With a fleet only two-thirds the size of the French fleet, Clinton finally decided to sail towards Yorktown, but while he was on the voyage, he learned that Cornwallis had surrendered. He wisely returned to New York. The surrender of some seven thousand troops on October 19 at Yorktown signaled the end of the military events of the revolutionary war. With this large military force immobilized, the British abandoned Wilmington in the following January, Savannah in July, and Charleston in December. The fight for independence had been successful.

The Germinal South

When Charles Pinckney in 1787 declared, "When I say Southern, I mean Maryland, and the states to the southward of her," that South Carolinian was expressing a point of view not uncommon in the postrevolutionary period. The terms southern, middle, northern, and eastern were spoken and written without all the users agreeing upon their precise limits, but they were applied during the war and afterwards with a surprising degree of uniformity. Some historians have argued that the South as a section conscious of its own interests first developed during these years. They do not contend that this was the Old South of John C. Calhoun or Jefferson Davis, but they have shown that it was a South which often differed with the North on matters of vital importance, as did the nineteenth-century Old South. Although no one in the eighteenth century predicted that someday the South might attempt to secede from the Union, many of the bases for conflict were present in incomplete and germinal form during the revolutionary era.

The early beginnings of a contest between the South and the North appeared before the Declaration of Independence was signed. Delegates at the First Continental Congress, desiring to use economic pressure to force Great Britain to lift the Intolerable Acts, suggested that colonial goods not be exported to Britain or the British West Indies. Men from South Carolina, whose economy stood to suffer more than others because of long-standing trade relations, requested that rice and indigo not be included in the embargo. Northerners called this a request for favoritism, and a debate on economics began. A compromise was effected when the Congress decided that indigo should be on the boycott list, but rice should not. But the dispute was a portent for the future, since most of the sectional disagreements during the revolutionary era were economic.

While the Second Continental and Confederation congresses were functioning in succession as the legislative bodies of the new nation, many troublesome problems revolving around sectional interests appeared. A dispute beginning as early as the fall of 1775 and continuing during most of the war centered on the use of Negroes as Patriot soldiers. Southerners blanched at the thought of guns in the hands of Negro slaves, and Edward Rutledge of South Carolina introduced a resolution to discharge all Negroes—free and slave—from the continental army. The resolution was defeated, but a few months later the Congress voted to restrict Negro enlistment in the future, although those already in service were not to be affected.

A much more serious early sectional controversy occurred when American leaders began to draw up a national constitution soon after independence had been declared. Fear of a strong central government pervaded the minds of both northerners and southerners at a time when the alleged tyranny of King and Parliament was still strong, and the Articles of Confederation were the written bases for a weak central government. Almost everyone agreed upon the advisability of a central government with limited powers; nevertheless, sectional disputes arose while the Articles were being formulated, and much sectional ill feeling emerged later when attempts were made to revise them. For example, the South bitterly disagreed with the North over how the costs of the central government were to be apportioned among the states, and debate on equitable apportionment of national expenses stretched over several years. An early draft of the Articles provided that the states contribute funds to the national government in proportion to population, excluding Indians. In 1776 the South's population was approximately 50 percent of the colonial total. Although their section was relatively poorer than the North, southerners would pay about one-half of the national expenses, and they objected to this disproportion.

Much of the apportionment dispute focused on the status of the black slave: was he person or property? Southerners argued that the slave was property, and therefore should not be counted in the population for expense-apportionment purposes. Northerners disagreed. A motion to designate slaves as property only was defeated in the Second Continental Congress, at which time several southerners indicated that their states would not ratify the Articles of Confederation, unless Negroes were excluded from the population figures. At that time the Congress voted for a motion calling for the ratio of contributions to the national expense to be made on the basis of private lands and their improvements, rather than population. New England delegates opposed this solution as against their better interests, but middle state representatives believed that southerners had to be placated on this point and voted with the South for passage. Although northerners were not happy with it, this provision was part of the Articles as long as they were in effect.

The central government chronically needed more money because of high expenses and because the states did not always pay their allotted share of requisitions. When the Confederation Congress in 1783 took up the question of how to get more money into the treasury, the old suggestion was made that state requisitions be based upon numbers, including Negroes, rather than property. Naturally southern men opposed this alternative. When it was suggested that national expenses be based on population, counting two blacks as one white for apportionment purposes, men in both North and South acknowledged this as a possible solution to the sticky problem. But many men did not feel the 2 : 1 ratio was the proper one, and in the course of the discussions, a number of other ratios were advanced, including 4 : 3, 4 : 1, 3 : 1, and 3 : 2. When compromise seemed impossible, James Madison of Virginia suggested five Negroes be counted as three white men. This compromise suggestion was accepted by the Congress, and an amendment was sent out to the states for ratification, but it failed to receive unanimous approval, and thus it did not go into effect.

After the French entered the revolutionary war on the side of the Americans, many members of Congress believed that the war would shortly come to an end. When they gave thought to a peace treaty, they all agreed that the terms should be as generous as possible in regard to boundaries and rights. But when specifics were considered, northerners and southerners fell into another quarrel, this time in regard to fishing off the coast of Newfoundland and the right to navigate the Mississippi River. New Englanders wanted the fishing rights to be made a necessary condition for peace, while southerners felt the same way about the right to transport their goods on the Mississippi River. Each section believed the other was asking for too much. After considerable debate which reflected the economic self-interests of the two sections, the New Englanders abandoned their stand that the fishing rights be a *sine qua non,* but they requested that the American peace commissioners consider these rights a desirable—if not a necessary—condition for peace. Shortly, James Madison persuaded other southerners to abandon their demand for absolute free travel on the Mississippi River, Madison reasoning that a less rigid attitude by the Americans might bring about the good will and support of Spain in the American war effort.

When the Treaty of Paris was signed in 1783, New Englanders received the coveted fishing arrangements, but southerners did not obtain the right to navigate the lower portion of the Mississippi River which ran through Spanish territory. Southerners between the Appalachian Mountains and the river looked to the great stream and its tributaries as major trade and traffic routes, and considerable diplomatic maneuvering occurred between the United States and Spain over the right to navigate the river and to deposit goods at New Orleans. Finally, in 1803 the United States solved the problem by purchasing Louisiana and thus controlling both banks of the river all the way to its mouth. New Englanders were never enthusiastic about the South's attempts toward transportation and deposit rights, and acrimonious debate occurred in Congress from time to time because of these differences of opinion.

The location of the nation's permanent capital also generated sectional heat in the Confederation Congress. Each delegate hoped to have the capital as near as possible to his state. It was moved to New York in 1785 when Far South delegates voted with others to move it there, because they could reach New York by water more easily than Trenton, New Jersey, and Annapolis, Maryland, the cities which had been designated to serve alternately as the nation's capital. A later dispute on this question ended in compromise when the permanent capital of the nation was moved to the banks of the Potomac.

Finally, the concern for sectional advantage may be seen in the reaction to proposals to admit new states to the Union. Both Vermont and Kentucky found opponents to their admission in the opposite region, and each was refused admission during the Confederation period. Both states were, however, admitted to the Union within a short time of each other soon after the Constitution went into effect—the admission of Maine and Missouri in 1820–21 was not the first compromise of this sort.

John R. Alden has argued that, because of these sectional disagreements, by the end of the revolutionary era the South had emerged as a distinct section with southerners clearly distinguishable from northerners. While Alden overstated his case, seeds of antagonism ultimately leading to civil war certainly existed during the era of the Revolution and were slowly nourished to maturity in the years to follow.

But a balanced view of the South and its relation to the remainder of the Union during the revolutionary years would not overlook the strong national sentiment present there. It took several years for Englishmen in the American colonies to become conscious of being Americans, and likewise many more years passed before Americans below the Mason-Dixon Line became southerners. Indeed they were very much concerned about their section's economic interests, but a genuine sectional consciousness was not yet present. Basically southern revolutionaries were like their northern counterparts: they were concerned with overthrowing British rule and protecting their economic self-interests after independence had been attained.

"In Order to form a more perfect Union"

By 1787, when economic conditions and a faltering government compelled men to consider ways to save their nation, many southerners were ready to give more power to a central government. A Convention was called to meet at Philadelphia in May of that year to draw up amendments to the Articles of Confederation. Before the men at the Convention were finished, however, they had constructed a completely new frame of government. Many southerners were much in favor of a stronger central government, and they worked hard to strengthen the nation at this Convention. Yet when specifics were considered, they and others could not totally disassociate themselves from the regions they represented, and incipient sectionalism raised its head on more than one occasion. The Constitution has properly been called a bundle of compromises, many hammered out because of North-South differences.

The delegations of Maryland, North Carolina, and Georgia were composed of mediocre men who made few contributions at the Constitutional Convention. South Carolina was more ably represented by Pierce Butler, Charles Pinckney, Charles Cotesworth Pinckney, and John Rutledge. But none of these men matched the towering delegates from Virginia. That state was represented by men such as James Madison, George Mason, Edmund Randolph, George Wythe, and George Washington. Early in the debates these men supported what became known as the Virginia Plan, a frame of government which, if acceptable, would have established a government with vast authority, the states being relegated to a completely inferior position. This strong plan clearly showed that Virginia delegates were more interested in establishing a national government than in stressing sectional differences. But other delegates were less confident of the efficacy of a concentrated central government, and even Madison himself, the Father of the Constitution, wanted to be sure the South would not have its interests too narrowly delimited by a central government. George Mason anticipated John C. Calhoun's later suggestion for a dual executive by proposing early in the debates that a triple executive be established, so that the three major sections would all have a share in controlling the executive branch of the government.

Much more crucial to the southern delegates was the question of representation in the Congress. The now well-known debate between large and small states was not sectional, and the small states obtained their wish in gaining equal voice in the upper house of the proposed bicameral legislature, but representation in the lower house was another matter. Since this body's members were to be elected on the basis of population, should representation be based on the slave as well as the white population? Southerners desired to include slaves when their representation was determined in the House of Representatives, although slaves did not and would never vote. Northerners contended that slaves should not be counted for representation. After brief debate, the convention voted to apportion delegates to the lower house on the basis of each state's free men, plus three-fifths of its slave population. This ratio had been suggested by Madison in 1783 in regard to financial support for the Confederation, and at first it appeared to be an acceptable provision. But several delegates would not let this decision stand. They wanted representation to be based on wealth as well as numbers. When the Convention voted to set aside the previously adopted three-fifths formula, a delegate from North Carolina expressed the sentiment of several southerners when he warned that his state "would never confederate on any terms that did not rate them [the slaves] at least as $\frac{3}{5}$. If the Eastern states meant, therefore, to exclude them altogether the business was at an end."

Another problem facing the Convention was that of advancing a suitable method for direct taxation of the states to support the new government. Southerners desired to exclude slaves from the population count for taxation purposes, while northerners insisted they be counted in establishing each state's share of direct federal taxes. These two problems concerning population were combined and compromised to the satisfaction of all. The three-fifths ratio was to be used for both representation and direct taxation. Since the Congress rarely imposed taxes on the states, the South gained more than it lost in this compromise.

Delegates from South Carolina and Georgia proposed that the new legislature be constitutionally prohibited from levying export duties, interfering with the trans-Atlantic slave trade, or passing navigation acts. Northern delegates accepted the limiting clause against export taxes, but delegates from the upper South and North were bitterly opposed to the slave trade. The Convention finally agreed to authorize the Congress to impose a tax up to ten dollars per imported slave and to regulate the slave traffic beginning in 1808. The Convention refused to prohibit the passage by Congress of navigation acts, nor would the delegates approve a requirement for a two-thirds vote on them. Southerners finally agreed with the North that navigation acts were permissible if passed by simple majority in both houses of Congress.

After these compromises were worked out, the Convention members put the finishing touches on the new document, and by September 1787 they were prepared to present their handiwork to the states for ratification. The Convention declared that the new document was to go into effect after ratification by nine state conventions, chosen especially for that purpose. By having the Constitution presented to special conventions rather than to the state legislatures and by not requiring unanimous consent before it became operative, the Convention delegates were doing what they could to assist with the ratification process. Nevertheless, the document had difficulty securing approval.

As far as the southern states were concerned, ratification varied greatly from state to state. Still a frontier state and looking to a strong central government for military support against hostile Creek Indians, Georgia called a convention which ratified the new Constitution unanimously and quickly early in 1788. The Antifederalists of the South Carolina backcountry sent delegates to the state convention to speak and vote against the Constitution, but because their section was underrepresented in the first place, these men had no chance against the Tidewater aristocrats who favored the Constitution as the best that could be written under the circumstances. Arguments of C. C. Pinckney and Edward Rutledge both inside and outside the convention made South Carolinians more amenable to the Constitution, especially when the two men agreed that the South Carolina members in the Congress-to-be should support amendments to the Constitution, including one that the states absolutely guard "every power not expressly relinquished by them."

In Maryland the Federalists won a five-to-one majority among the delegates to the state ratifying convention. Despite this setback the Antifederalists waged a strong fight against ratification. Many Marylanders who opposed the Constitution were debtors who stood to lose financially if the document was adopted, and they were supported by others who did not want paper money banned. The Federalists at the convention refused to debate the Constitution, since they had an overwhelming majority, and when the vote was taken, the Constitution passed 63 to 11.

The delegates to the ratifying convention in Virginia were fairly evenly divided between supporters of the Constitution and its opponents. Delegates in the south and west of the state were generally against it, while the men in the north and east were for it. The main opposition at the convention clustered around and emanated from delegate Patrick Henry. No longer the ardent American nationalist he had been in the early days of the Revolution, Henry feared a strong central government, and he disliked the prospect of northern control over that government to the disadvantage of the southern people. Henry and others meticulously picked the Constitution apart word by word, raising all the familiar objections to it. They pointed out that personal liberties were endangered because the document contained no bill of rights, and they argued that it would restore monarchy and create a ruling clique of aristocrats. More importantly, they reasoned that the Constitution might work to the disadvantage of the South. Benjamin Harrison forthrightly wrote to George Washington: "If the Constitution is carried into effect, the states south of the potowmac [*sic*], will be little more than appendages to those to the northward of it. . . ." These constituted such grave objections that the Constitution's opponents at the Virginia convention believed the document should be drastically amended if not totally rejected. They announced that if it was not amended, Virginia ought to consider creating a southern federation in which the rights of the individual, a republican government, and southern interests would be protected.

Staunch Federalist George Washington expressed much concern over the criticisms of the Constitution's opponents, and on occasion he questioned their motives: "That there are some writers (and others who may not have written) who wish to see these states divided into several confederacies is pretty evident." To avoid the charge that he was angling for the Presidency of the new government, Washington had not sought election to the Virginia convention, but he did not hesitate to use his influence to bring about ratification. Led by James Madison and Light-Horse Harry Lee, the Federalists at the convention effectively answered the Constitution's detractors, but because of the divided delegation, the fate of the Constitution was in doubt until the final vote, which favored the document 89 to 79. New Hampshire had become the ninth state to ratify the Constitution, and theoretically the new government could have gone into effect shortly afterward. But Virginia's prominence among the states was such that Virginia had to ratify the Constitution if it was to be effective. The new nation could hardly survive without the Old Dominion's leadership. Also, without Virginia the nation would have been divided into two parts geographically. When Virginia became the tenth state to ratify the Constitution, plans were then laid to organize the new government.

North Carolina possessed no powerful Tidewater aristocracy, yeoman farmers dominating the politics of the state. These men were attracted to the arguments of the Virginia Antifederalists, and if Virginia had remained outside the Republic, North Carolina would surely have followed her lead. But hopes for a southern confederation were dashed with Virginia's decision, and North Carolina could not stand alone. The Tar Heel State had rejected the Constitution in 1788, but in 1789 with the new government in operation and with the promise of a bill of rights, North Carolina reconsidered her actions and ratified the Constitution. North Carolina had insisted that her opposition to the Constitution was based upon the menaces to southern interests in the document. In this instance she was reflecting the fears of many southerners, and the South became a part of the new government without the assurance of sufficient constitutional safeguards against the domination of a central government. Yet most American leaders living in the South had supported the new document as superior to the old Articles, and despite the misgivings of many in their region, they did not allow specific sectional interests to prevent them from supporting a Constitution which they hoped would revitalize the economy and government of the entire nation.

The Young Republic

National leaders who hoped to encourage the development of a strong central government dominated that new government and the national scene from 1789 to 1801. Important supporters of the policies and principles of Federalism were southerners such as John Rutledge, Charles Lee, and Richard Henry Lee. George Washington of Virginia served as President of the nation for two terms, and he represented the epitome of southern Federalism. Federalists were generally well-bred and financially secure conservatives who distrusted political democracy, and who believed that "those who own the country ought to govern it."

Those men from all over the nation who stressed liberty over order were attracted to the concept of Republicanism, under the leadership of Thomas Jefferson and James Madison, both Virginians. Republicanism received the support of men from the South such as Edmund Randolph and John Taylor of Caroline. If the Republicans stressed states' rights against a strong government, this does not mean that they opposed the Constitution or the Union. Unlike the old Antifederalists, Republicans in the 1790s upheld the Constitution and spoke of the "beautiful equilibrium" it was designed to maintain between the states and the central government. Republicans professed that their primary goal was to guard this sacred covenant from debased Federalists who desired to twist it and use it to their own ends, namely, for "a consolidation of the union in a Republic *one and indivisible.*"

A two-party political structure, which was to become characteristic of American politics, evolved from conflicting positions in regard to the interpretation of the Constitution, the financial schemes of the first Secretary of the Treasury (Alexander Hamilton), and foreign affairs. Federalists generally held to a liberal (or loose) interpretation of the Constitution; they lent support to Hamilton's proposals to place the nation on a sound financial footing; and they expressed a certain amount of friendliness toward their old mother country, England. Republicans believed in interpreting the Constitution literally (or strictly); they opposed Hamilton's financial plans because the measures gave too much aid to the business and commercial classes; and they were sympathetic to Frenchmen who were advocating liberty during the French Revolution.

While both groups were nationwide in scope, the Federalists began to reflect more and more the image of Alexander Hamilton, and the Republicans came to verbalize the protest of southerners against Federalism. President Washington, more than any other southern statesman, had a national outlook, and he came to rely upon northern Federalists as his administration progressed. Although he spoke out against the rise of political parties, Washington favored strengthening the national government, the first priority of the emerging Federalist party's program. Under the direction of Jefferson and Madison, the Republicans came to be dominated by southerners who were unhappy with the government being run by northerners.

As was true during the Revolution, the Confederation period, and at the time of the drafting of the Constitution, sectional disputes in the 1790s were primarily economic in nature. Madison's attacks upon Hamilton's financial plans were only indicative of the developing economic differences between North and South. When the Hamiltonian program was announced, southerners recalled Patrick Henry's prophecy at the time of Virginia's ratification of the Constitution: "A gentleman has said . . . that there is contest for empire. There is also a contest for money. The states of the North wish to secure a superiority of interest and influence." To be sure, southerners desired the same superiority and influence, but in fact the South appeared to be losing most of the battles. Federalists dominated the Congress during Washington's administrations, and they effected the Hamiltonian program. The central government funded the national debt and assumed the unpaid debts of the states, a national bank was authorized, and a protective tariff was passed. Jefferson and Madison continued their opposition of Hamiltonianism, clinging to a doctrine of states' rights but without apparent effect.

Washington further alienated his fellow Virginians and other southerners by striving for neutrality when England and other European countries determined to intervene in the internal affairs of France after that nation's King had been executed and a French republic had been founded. The French cause was popular with the South and with Jefferson, minister to France during the Confederation, and Washington's stock fell in the region below the Potomac. Jefferson became so alienated from Washington by this time that he resigned from his position as Secretary of State, and in 1796 he ran for the Presidency on a ticket opposed to many of Washington's policies.

Federalism reached its zenith during the administration of John Adams, Washington's Vice President who had defeated Jefferson for the Presidency. Adams essentially carried on the Washingtonian program in both domestic and foreign affairs, and during his administration many Federalist principles were solidified. Republican opposition increased as Federalism became entrenched, and the Adams administration attempted to muzzle effective political opposition by passing the Alien and Sedition Acts. Jefferson and Madison responded with the Kentucky and Virginia resolutions which included the germs for ideas later advanced to help the cause of states' rights. The Alien and Sedition Acts contributed to the decline of the Federalists' political strength. Republicans won the mid-term elections in 1798, setting the stage for Jefferson's ascendancy to the Presidency in 1801. Jefferson and Madison were in the White House for the next four Presidential terms, and the Republicans became so powerful and the Federalists so weak that the latter's power hardly existed by the end of Madison's second term.

But Jefferson's and Madison's rise to the Presidency did not result in a reversal of Federalism or the advancement of states' rights. Jefferson pushed aside his constitutional scruples in order to clinch the purchase of Louisiana, doubling the size of the United States and assuring the national government of more power than ever before. Madison led the nation in the nationalistic War of 1812, and interestingly his greatest opposition came from New England, when representatives from that region opposed the declaration of war and called the Hartford Convention to express objection to Madison and to espouse states' rights for *New Englanders*. Federalist principles continued to be advanced by Virginian John Marshall, second Chief Justice of the U. S. Supreme Court, who served on the Court long after the Federalist party had expired.

Throughout the first twenty-five years of the nation's existence under the Constitution, many southerners continued to contribute to a growing sectionalism by advocating states' rights, while other men from the South were among the most nationalistic of all Americans. Before 1815 hints of incipient sectionalism were present, but southern sectional consciousness had still not fully developed by that date. At that time, the South was possibly the most nationalistic region of the nation. The main roots of sectionalism lay dormant in the years before 1815, and while an occasional shoot crept above the surface of the ground before then, not until after that date did pre-Civil War sectionalism appear.

Suggestions for Further Reading

John R. Alden, *The South in the Revolution, 1763–1789* (Baton Rouge: Louisiana State Univ., 1957) is an excellent survey of the region in a time of crisis. Related to specific aspects of the controversy between England and her colonies are: Edmund S. and Helen M. Morgan, *The Stamp Act Crisis: Prologue to the Revolution* (Chapel Hill: Univ. North Carolina, 1953); Oliver M. Dickerson, *The Navigation Acts and the American Revolution* (Philadelphia: Univ. Pennsylvania, 1951); Lawrence A. Harper, *The English Navigation Laws* (New York: Columbia Univ., 1939); Arthur M. Schlesinger, *The Colonial Merchants and the American Revolution, 1763–1776* (New York: Columbia Univ., 1918); Thomas P. Abernethy, *Western Lands and the American Revolution* (New York: Appleton-Century, 1937); Robert O. DeMond, *The Loyalists in North Carolina During the Revolution* (Durham: Duke Univ., 1940); Claude H. Van Tyne, *The Loyalists in the American Revolution* (New York: Macmillan, 1902). Old but still useful is Evarts B. Greene, *The Revolutionary Generation, 1763–1790* (New York: Macmillan, 1943).

Merrill Jensen has written two volumes of general interest with much pertinent information on the South during the Confederation period: *The Articles of Confederation* * (Madison: Univ. Wisconsin, 1948) and *The New Nation: A History of the United States During the Confederation, 1781–1789* * (New York: Knopf, 1950). For a different point of view see John Fiske, *The Critical Period in American History* (Boston: Houghton Mifflin, 1916). Allan Nevins, *The American States During and After the Revolution, 1775–1789* (New York: Macmillan, 1924) remains unsurpassed in insight and structure. Burnett, "Southern Statesmen and the Confederation," *North Carolina Historical Review*, vol. 14 (1937) is a good survey of a neglected subject. The South's role in the framing of the Constitution may be followed in these volumes: John R. Alden, *The First South* (Baton Rouge: Louisiana State Univ., 1961); Carl Van Doren, *The Great Rehearsal: The Story of the Making and Ratifying of the Constitution of the United States* * (New York: Viking, 1948); Broadus and Louise Mitchell, *A Biography of the Constitution of the United States* * (New York: Oxford, 1964); Charles A. Beard, *An Economic Interpretation of the Constitution of the United States* * (New York: Macmillan, 1913); Forrest McDonald, *We the People: The Economic Origins of the Constitution* * (Chicago: Univ. Chicago, 1958); Robert Allen Rutland, *The Ordeal of the Constitution* (Norman, Okla.: Univ. Okla., 1965); Cecelia M. Kenyon, *The Antifederalists* * (Indianapolis: Bobbs-Merrill, 1966); Fletcher M. Green, *Constitutional Development in the South Atlantic States, 1776–1860* (Chapel Hill: Univ. North Carolina, 1930). William P. Murphy, who was forced to leave the University of Mississippi Law School in 1962 because of his defense of Supreme Court decisions and his attitude on the state sovereignty question, has produced a scholarly work in support of his views: *The Triumph of Nationalism: State Sovereignty, the Founding Fathers, and the Making of the Constitution* (Chicago: Quadrangle Books, 1967). He has amassed much evidence that the framers of the Constitution, including many southerners, consciously and intentionally sought to eradicate the state sovereignty that had prevailed under the Articles.

Thomas P. Abernethy, *The South in the New Nation, 1789–1819* (Baton Rouge: Louisiana State Univ., 1961) is marred because it places too much emphasis on the frontier. Other general works may be read as correctives: John C. Miller, *The Federalist Era, 1789–1801* * (New York: Harper & Row, 1960); Leonard D. White, *The Federalists: A Study in Administrative History* (New York: Macmillan, 1948) and *The Jeffersonians: A Study in Administrative History, 1801–1829* * (New York: Macmillan, 1951); Edward Channing, *The Jeffersonian System, 1801–1811* (New York: Harper & Brothers, 1906). Claude Bowers's *Jefferson and Hamilton* * (Boston: Houghton Mifflin, 1925) and *Jefferson in Power* * (Boston: Houghton Mifflin, 1936) are pro-Jefferson but remain valuable studies of the early years of the new nation. Marcus Cunliffe, *The Nation Takes Shape: 1789–1837* * (Chicago: Univ. Chicago, 1959) is a more recent and well-balanced account of the nation's early years.

* Available in paperback.

CHAPTER III

ANTEBELLUM SOUTHERN CULTURE

Southerners in the antebellum South believed that they enjoyed a superior "culture." They used this term synonymously with enlightenment and refinement of taste acquired by intellectual and aesthetic training. When the sectional controversy deepened as the decades passed, they became more and more convinced that their "culture" was far and away higher, better, and more refined than the North's. In a volume entitled *Culture in the South* (edited by W. T. Couch and published in 1934), a group of southerners has written about such diverse subjects as industry, religion, labor, literature, and the poor whites under the name of "culture." Without engaging in a dispute over semantics, the following pages will discuss the culture of the South as reflected in its religious movements, educational development, and literary trends.

From Orthodoxy to Rationalism

The Puritan ethic was strong throughout the colonial South. If Massachusetts and other New England colonies were founded in part because of discontent in England with the established Anglican Church, it should not be assumed that men with Puritan values migrated only to those colonies. Indeed, vast numbers of Puritans settled in the islands of the Caribbean during the early colonial period, and many if not most Englishmen who settled in the colonial South were influenced by Puritan ideals. In most colonies attendance at church on Sundays was compulsory, and violators of these laws were prosecuted. Authorities frowned equally upon cursing, gambling, games on the Sabbath, sexual excursions outside the bonds of matrimony, excessive drinking, and laziness. The "Blue Laws" of northern colonies were matched by similar statutes in the South, and the Puritan overtones of twentieth-century southern society are the remnants of early colonial regulations and traditions. The Puritan influence, so often related primarily to Massachusetts, permeated all of American society, including the South.

The Anglican Church became the established religious institution in all of the southern colonies. Proprietors, governors, and other rulers of these colonies had close ties with England, and they encouraged the establishment of the church in Virginia, South Carolina, and Georgia. Even Maryland, founded as a refuge for Catholics, was quickly dominated by the Protestants within its boundaries, and by 1702 the Anglicans were able to make theirs the established church in the colony. The Anglican Church was not formally established in North Carolina until 1765, but Anglicanism had been strong in the colony long before that time. In its favored position, the Anglican Church became intertwined with the ruling cliques of the South. While the records indicate considerable conflict between churchmen and government leaders in the southern colonies, a small body of men dominated both institutions for their own purposes. The same men who composed the county courts frequently ran the parish vestries, and the established church was often not so much an agency of God as it was a means for government officials, planters, and merchants to rule both Church and State.

Despite the favored position of the church in the southern colonies, Anglicanism did not thrive in America. Well-suited for the English urban and village society in a small geographic area, the church did not readily adapt itself to the new environment. The concept of the parish, so useful in the British Isles, was not practical when applied in the New World. Scattered settlements along a coastline of hundreds of miles could not be easily served by parish priests, the only persons officially approved to minister the sacraments or conduct religious services. The shortage of parish priests was intensified because new priests were required to travel to England to be ordained. Circuits were set up for priests to travel by horseback to distant churches in their parishes, but this proved to be unsatisfactory. Large numbers of Anglicans were without religious assistance or instruction for weeks or months at a time. This situation necessitated certain alterations in the practices of the Church of England in America, one of the most important being that lay readers were allowed to conduct religious services. Lack of proper vessels used in Anglican services required substitutions, and ministers often failed to wear the proper vestments. Moreover, marriages came to be performed elsewhere than in a church and, contrary to church practice, the dead were often buried in private cemeteries rather than in consecrated churchyards. Just as the English government neglected the political and economic development of her colonies for many years, the Church of England gave little attention to the needs of colonial Anglicans. The Bishop of London was charged with general supervision of the colonies, but his interests were directed elsewhere. It was no wonder that the colonial church gradually grew away from the mother church.

Whatever its shortcomings and problems, the Church of England to some extent met the religious needs of the developing colonial aristocracy, but this was not true for the common people. During the colonial era, various dissenting sects grew up in the South to serve the small farmers and those living on the edge of the frontier. Quakers, Moravians, Mennonites, Dunkards, Lutherans, and various German pietistic sects were evident in the southern colonies, primarily as a result of migrations by colonists from Pennsylvania. More important ultimately in the South's religious history were the Baptists, who spread from Rhode Island to Pennsylvania to the southern colonies fairly early. Also to develop into a major church were the Methodists, introduced into Georgia by John Wesley and George Whitefield early in the eighteenth century. When Scotch-Irish settled in the back country of the South, they brought with them Presbyterianism, based on the teachings of John Calvin. These churches were much closer to the people, were less formal, had fewer liturgical demands, depended less upon a hierarchical structure, and thus met the emotional and religious needs of a colonial population.

Protestant sects greatly increased their numbers and influence in the South as a result of the Great Awakening, a religious movement of the 1730s and 1740s which affected all of colonial America. The back country of the South, populated by dissenters, neglected by the Church of England, and isolated from the coastal society, was fertile ground for a religious awakening. Uneducated men, starved for religious experiences, were ripe for the emotional exhortations of men like George Whitefield, who spent several months preaching the need of salvation to the inland residents. By the time the revival had subsided, the ground had been laid for Baptists, Methodists, and Presbyterians to become the most populous and influential churches in the South.

Baptists especially profited from the revival and its aftermath. Like most of the Protestant dissenters, the Baptists emphasized the necessity of a religious experience. Sinners had to acknowledge their shameful state, believe in Jesus Christ as their Lord and Saviour, and then confess their new faith publicly. The emotional release from such a religious conversion was great. The mass psychology of a revival service assisted individuals with their conversion experiences, and revivals continued after the Great Awakening itself had subsided. Emphasizing emotion over education, faith over reason, a distinctive symbol of baptism by immersion, a congregational form of church government over a highly structured one, and strict separation of Church and State, the Baptist denomination fully suited the dwellers of the back country in the South. In the 1750s and 1760s Baptists increased greatly in numbers as the result of the work of such dedicated revivalists as Shubal Stearns, Daniel Marshall, and Oliver Hart. Virginia alone had a Baptist population of ten thousand when the Revolution began.

Methodists, who remained a part of the Anglican Church until 1784, grew rapidly in the years before the American Revolution. By 1776, revivals were responsible for thirty-five hundred Methodists in Virginia, and almost as many in the Carolinas. The Methodists perfected the circuit-riding system, organized a church structure midway between the Baptists and the Anglicans, continued to preach a democratic theory of salvation, and used printing presses and schools to advance their cause.

Some Presbyterians were not happy with the new methods of evangelism, and "Old Sides" and "New Lights" constituted two opposing factions within Presbyterianism after the 1740s. Presbyterians stressed education and an educated ministry more than the Baptists and Methodists, and this did not appeal to such large numbers, but their secure theology, their opposition to the favored position of the Church of England, and their hybrid church structure placed them in a competitive position for future growth. Needless to say, the leaders of the Church of England were displeased with the move to emotionalism, but the church's influence, which had never been great among the colonial masses, was weak in the eighteenth century, and it had no effect in stemming the tide of non-Anglican Protestantism.

Concurrent with the growth of the dissenting sects in the southern colonies prior to the American Revolution was the development of an intellectual movement in Europe called the Enlightenment. This movement crossed the ocean as American colonists began to read the exciting works of theoretical scientists and others, including Sir Isaac Newton, the genius who expounded upon gravity and the laws of motion. Southern intellectuals responded to the implications of the theories and discoveries made by these men. Instead of living in a world created by a personal God, men began to believe that they resided in a universe based on impersonal, scientific laws that governed the behavior of both animate and inanimate objects. All parts of the magnificent universe seemed to fit perfectly into an immense, intricate, and logically designed machine. God

came to be viewed as the master builder who had conceived and created
the marvelous universe and who continued to watch over it, but who
never interfered or intervened in the operations of his creation.

The Enlightenment, or the Age of Reason, hardly touched the
small frontier farmer in America who continued to believe in a God who
could and did intervene daily in the lives of men, but its impact upon intellectual America was great. Many leaders of the southern colonies and
the American Revolution, such as Thomas Jefferson, became Deists, rejecting the traditional Christian beliefs about Jesus Christ, including his
special relationship to God and his purpose for being on earth. Some of
the skeptics became Unitarians, playing down the traditional view of the
Trinity. While Unitarianism was strongest in the northern colonies, it
was also prominent in the South during the era of the Revolution. Some
Deists did not actually join the Unitarian Church, remaining members of
the orthodox churches or omitting church affiliations altogether. The rational thought of the Enlightenment remained influential in the early
years of the new Republic.

Reaction to Rationalism

If rationalism permeated the society and thought of the intellectual South, it had little impact upon men living in the back country. At
the opening of the nineteenth century, a Second Awakening began, another great crusade to convert the masses to emotional Christianity. Because of the rapid expansion of the frontier across the mountains into
Kentucky, Tennessee, and the Ohio River Valley, thousands of settlers
had lived and worked in the American wilderness without benefit of
church or religious experiences. Religious men east of the mountains saw
this society as fertile ground for new endeavors, and James McGready, a
Presbyterian minister, traveled to Logan County, Kentucky, to hold revival services in the summer of 1800. After their crops were harvested,
country people for miles around came with their families and camped in
tents or lived in covered wagons for several weeks of revival preaching,
praying, and socializing. McGready's successful revival was followed by
others for the next half-dozen years, most of them being "camp meetings"
and all of them well attended by frontier dwellers.

The greatest camp meeting of all was held at Cane Ridge in Bourbon County, Kentucky, in August 1801 with a crowd of over twenty thous-
sand. Numerous preachers from several denominations shared the privilege of orating to the great throng. These evangelists tried to frighten
their listeners into becoming religious by describing the horrors of hell
and the torments of damned souls. More sensitive people in the audience
became so excited that they fell into extravagant physical "exercises."

Some swooned in trances, some shouted for mercy, while others were overcome by the holy laughs or the holy jerks. Some babbled in unknown tongues and others barked like dogs. While the spirit was moving in these wondrous and mysterious ways, a few persons at the Cane Ridge meeting were present for other than religious uplifting. Bringing together this large number of people, normally isolated by their frontier environment, inevitably meant that social contacts would result in physical contact. Intimate, temporary quarters for large numbers of people resulted in some immorality, even necessitating the establishment of a "night watch" to prevent secret meetings between men and women at the campground. A cynic surely overstated the case when he quipped that "more souls were born than saved" at Cane Ridge, but immorality certainly existed. Charles Johnson, the historian of the frontier camp meeting, has pointed out, however, that the excessive physical exercises and the immorality at Cane Ridge did not typify the revivals of the Second Awakening.

The revival meetings at the beginning of the nineteenth century became institutionalized shortly thereafter, and the camp meeting became a traditional part of frontier Protestantism. These revivals had profound results on southern religion and society. Religious orgies unquestionably fulfilled a much needed social outlet; they brought emotional catharsis and social contact to men and women accustomed to living in isolated areas. Yet emotionalism increased intolerance among rural people, and many times religious conversions were not permanent. Camp meetings developed hymns and tunes which affected the American musical tradition, and the evangelists influenced southern oratory toward more emotionalism and the use of biblical illustrations. More importantly, the revivals led to the rapid expansion of the evangelical churches in the South and Southwest. Baptists, Methodists, and Presbyterians, already the numerical leaders, became more evangelistic and larger than ever before. At the same time, sectarianism was accentuated. A new denomination, the Disciples of Christ (sometimes called Campbellites), was formed by Barton Stone and Alexander Campbell. Highly evangelistic, it came to rival the major denominations in the South before the Civil War.

The frontier revivals may also have aided the development of democracy in the South. Central to the revival movements was the democratic concept that an individual could exercise his free will and be "saved." This doctrine was in accord with the frontier psychology of optimism and self-reliance and gave dignity to the humblest human being. Moreover, preachers emphasized the equality of the rich man and the poor man in the light of eternity, and in the church government the common man received training in the practice of self-government. Even though the evangelistic churches stressed emotional experience, they also placed much emphasis on the Bible as the authoritative word of God; therefore, church members were encouraged to read the scriptures, which in turn meant that all men needed to have the rudiments of an education. Seminaries for preachers and colleges for the children of the faithful were established in great numbers in the early nineteenth century. In addition, the denominations purchased printing presses, and church publications encouraged education for the masses, while attempting to expound the dogmas of the denomination.

One of the most important results of the stress on evangelism growing out of the frontier camp meetings was the enforcement of religious orthodoxy and the elimination of skepticism from the South. The Second Awakening had come when religious liberalism was at its height. In the eyes of many southerners, Deism and Unitarianism had attained a level of respectability and accommodation if not total acceptance. Numerous intellectual leaders in the South had embraced the end products of the Age of Reason without fear of reprisal, but in the wake of the revival tradition, religious liberalism declined quite rapidly. Horace Holley, president of Transylvania University in Lexington, Kentucky from 1818 to 1827, was a graduate of Yale University, and as a Unitarian minister and intellectual leader, he exerted a liberal influence in that region. He opposed the doctrine of the depravity of human nature, upheld the Unitarian faith, and believed that man should use his reasoning powers to investigate the mysteries of religion. After disagreements with school and community leaders, Holley was driven from his position at Transylvania. Similarly, Thomas Cooper, president of the College of the City of Charleston from 1821 to 1834, was dismissed, after being charged with advocating religious opinions dangerous to the youth at the college. Cooper's sin was to champion freedom of speech and thought when the discoveries of geology began to disturb the orthodox leaders of the churches and colleges. He did his cause no good when on one occasion he referred to the Book of Genesis as a collection of "absurd and frivolous tales." The University of Virginia abandoned its policy of secular instruction only and introduced courses in religion and the Bible.

Southern clergymen were disturbed by the dangers of skepticism arising from the new science of geology. Geological discoveries pointed out the long age of the earth and the evidence of fossils in the strata of the earth, which seemed to contradict the account of Creation in the book of Genesis. Preachers and orthodox teachers warned their congregations and students against such findings and apparent conflicts, and religious orthodoxy continued to grow in the South as southern leaders strove to regiment thought within the region. This obsession for religious unanimity was most surely related to other events of that time. When the abolitionist crusade was at its height, southerners felt compelled not only to defend slavery but also to protect their section's very civilization from hostile northern attack. The South found support for its defense in orthodox, conservative Protestantism; there was no room for those who did not agree with the majority. By 1860 the reaction against religious liberalism had reached the farthest swing of the pendulum. The Age of Reason was no more. The Unitarian Church in the South was dying if not dead by the time the Civil War began. The Census of 1860 showed few liberal churches in the South, nor was there much liberal religious thinking in the region at that time.

On the eve of the Civil War religion in the South was firmly rooted in medieval traditions. Protestant southerners believed in the Devil as a real person who tempted men to sin at every occasion, and both heaven and hell were actual physical places. The southerner's highest goal was to be "saved," a condition which assured him an eternity in heaven, a blissful place where work was unknown. Men who were not "saved" were to live forever in hell, a hot and sulfurous place of torment. Most southerners believed that God was constantly intervening in human affairs, rewarding the righteous and punishing the wicked. They believed in the miracles of the Bible, and acknowledged the power of a God who could perform similar feats in modern times as well as in ancient days. The Puritan ideal prevailed in regard to personal habits, and churches dismissed members who strayed from the straight and narrow path.

By 1860 the Baptist, Methodist, and Presbyterian churches in the South had become powerful centers for the protection of conservative southern institutions and civilization. The sectional disagreements which were to result in civil war in 1861 were preceded by religious disagreements and the breakup of these three major nationwide denominations. Committed to a conservative theology, when religious liberalism was growing in the remainder of the nation, Presbyterians in the South became disenchanted with the national denomination and in 1838 the southern churches separated from the national group. This move was followed by the southern branches of the other two major churches. In 1844 the Methodist Episcopal Church in general conference asked Bishop James O. Andrew, who had recently married a woman who owned slaves, to stop his work with the church until his family had disposed of the slaves. Andrew refused to abide by the request, and this incident became the last in a series of irritations between the national organization and the southern churches. The southern delegates withdrew from the national denomination, and in 1845 they organized the Methodist Episcopal Church, South. In the same year the Baptists in the South broke with their national group over the slavery issue and immediately organized the Southern Baptist Convention. The split of three major Protestant churches in America was an ominous sign of what the entire nation was to face in 1861.

These southern churches ardently supported secession, the formation of the Confederacy, and the South's efforts to defend herself in war. In 1861 the Southern Baptist Convention passed a resolution indicating its implacable support of the Confederacy and praying that the North's "pitiless purposes" would be frustrated. The following year the southern Presbyterians officially announced that the South's struggle was not only for civil rights, property, and the home, but also "for religion, for Church, [and] for the gospel." Religious leaders preached the righteousness of the southern cause with such zeal that many southerners came to believe that the war was primarily a moral and religious struggle.

The Gates Open Slowly

In keeping with traditions inherited from England, most colonial southerners assumed that education was only for the aristocracy. As a native aristocracy developed in the colonies, many sons of the wealthy planters were educated either by tutor or in English boarding schools. While these arrangements satisfied the colonial elite, the remainder of the colonists generally did not aspire to attain the rudiments of an education. However, contrary to the conventional picture, and even though education was assumed to be a private matter, a few free schools did exist in the colonial South. In Virginia, the Syms School and the Eaton School were in operation by the early 1670s, founded in accordance with the wills of two enlightened Virginians. Furthermore, the Society for the Propagation of the Gospel in Foreign Parts, the missionary arm of the Church of England, had established free schools in a number of southern towns, including Charleston and New Bern. In Maryland the Free School Act of 1694 attempted, however ineffectively, to support education with general taxation. Yet the size and influence of the free schools were miniscule in the face of the task they were trying to accomplish, and education in the colonial South remained primarily a private responsibility.

Below the college level, education in the South between the American Revolution and the Civil War was characterized by its inadequacy. Several factors were responsible. Like their colonial forefathers, antebellum southerners did not believe in educating the masses. Having inherited their educational traditions from England, they thought that only the upper classes and the future leaders of the state and nation needed to be educated. The South generally assumed a laissez-faire attitude toward the government's role in education, believing that the state should not assume a function widely regarded as a private duty. Southerners traditionally paid low taxes, and the upper classes did not want to bear the burden of educating the children of the poor. Many small farmers had no appreciation of "book learning" and did not demand schooling for their children. In a rural region where pupils were widely scattered and where good roads were not always present, the difficulties of establishing a school system were compounded.

Large numbers of southerners in the early nineteenth century were influenced by the educational philosophy of Thomas Jefferson, a strong advocate of selective education. Jefferson favored three years of schooling for all white children, supported by public taxation, because he believed that all men should master the three Rs. He suggested that the most promising children then be selected for additional education at academies where they should receive free tuition. Jefferson then advocated that the most intelligent children be chosen from these schools to attend colleges at public expense. Thus, he assumed that the brightest students would be selected from the masses to be educated for their roles as leaders of the nation. Like most of his countrymen, Jefferson believed that education was basically a private rather than a public responsibility. He felt that the state was obligated to train only its future leaders, not the masses. His plan provided for the selection of a "natural aristocracy of the intelligent" from all ranks of society and for the education of these for the greatest usefulness. The weaknesses of the Jeffersonian system are apparent: the great mass of southern people would be left untouched by anything more than the most elementary educational training, and Negroes would be left out of the educational system altogether. In 1779 Jefferson presented "A Bill for the More General Diffusion of Knowledge" to the Virginia legislature, but it was not adopted at that time. His ideas were written into a statute in 1796, but the state was negligent in implementing the law. Thus, while Jefferson's ideas for educating only the brightest children, who would control politics and state governments in the future, were generally accepted throughout the region, they were not often carried out.

Under these circumstances, what kind of schooling existed in the South before the development of a bona fide public school system? The custom of sending children to England for education declined rapidly after the Revolution, although antebellum planters sometimes followed the example of their colonial ancestors and provided private tutors to give elementary school education to their children. More often, private schools were established by groups of planters who could not afford the expense of tutorial education. Many such schools were established on worn-out soil and thus became known as "old field" schools. Maintained by private money, these schools were always manned by one teacher, responsible for six or eight grades, depending upon the size of the families participating in the joint enterprise. These crude log schools had very informal instruction, normally limited to the three Rs.

Above the elementary schools were secondary schools known as academies, operated under state charters and endowed by private funds. Planters who wanted their sons to be gentlemen often cooperated to establish an academy. The instruction was classical; Latin, Greek, mathematics, grammar, public speaking, and metaphysics occupied most of the

students' attention. It was not unusual for ministers to be the teachers in
these academies, since churches occasionally established them as a service
to a region. The main purpose of the academies was to train young men
in law and politics, the only professions open to gentlemen if they did
not enter the military. Academies ranged from one-room log cabins to
schools with several buildings. Some of them developed into excellent
schools, including Zion-Parnassus in Rowan County, North Carolina, and
David Caldwell's School near Greensboro, North Carolina. The Moses
Waddel School in Willington, South Carolina, which flourished from
1804 to 1819, had as its students such important leaders of the Old South
as John C. Calhoun, William H. Crawford, and George McDuffie.

An educational system built around the academy had two serious
defects. In the first place the schools placed stress on political oratory and
civic patriotism, while neglecting modern literature and criticism. In the
second place, it completely neglected the children whose parents could
not pay the tuition fees. Such an educational system meant that much illiteracy existed in the South. In 1800 at least one-third of all southern
whites and essentially all blacks in the region were illiterate. Fifty years
later nearly one-fourth of the white southerners remained in a state of
ignorance; no headway had been made in educating Negroes. The South
would have fared badly enough if it had conscientiously instituted Jefferson's plan. By accepting his philosophy but not entirely implementing
it, the South lagged seriously in its educational development.

In the early 1800s some of the southern states made small attempts
to rid themselves of some of the illiteracy among the whites. In 1810 Virginia established a Literary Fund, and a few years later interest on this
fund was used to help with the education of the poor. About the same
time, South Carolina established a school fund to be used for the education of children whose parents could not afford to send them to private
schools. Other states made arrangements to send poor children to private
schools with the tuition being paid by the state. A few states set up public schools, free to all white children residing in a given state. Wealthy
southerners were reluctant to send their children to such schools, since
these first meager public schools were generally regarded as charitable
agencies. When the socially conscious southerner stamped these institutions as "pauper schools," even the small farmers, who also had their
pride, were hesitant to send their children to them.

However late the process was begun and however haltingly it proceeded, around 1830 the older states of the South had made definite beginnings in the establishment of public school education. And yet in the
decade of the thirties the South had a significant illiterate white population. Upon the rise of Jacksonian democracy at that time, when the illit-

erate whites received the right to vote, this group came to have considerable influence in politics. Politicians of the Jacksonian era deliberately appealed to the ignorance and prejudice of this segment of the population. If democracy was to operate successfully, southerners reasoned, education must be developed. Thus, in the 1830s many southerners began to respond to the public school movement, a trend that had become nationwide by that time. School reformers such as Horace Mann had been instrumental in leading free school movements in northern states, and southerners studied the work of these northern reformers. They began to advocate public education for their states and to spread the idea that public schools should not be looked upon as schools for paupers. Before the end of the decade, rather good school systems had been developed in cities like Baltimore, Louisville, Charleston, New Orleans, and Natchez. More difficulty was encountered in establishing schools in areas where children were widely scattered; however, the major problem in establishing free common schools in the southern states was the question of finances. The reformers' good intentions were often mislaid in the face of the lack of taxable southern assets and the resistance of public leaders to tax available resources.

The southern states which made the most progress in founding free public schools prior to the Civil War were Kentucky and North Carolina. Louisiana had a progressive system of public schools on paper, but the laws were not implemented in this early period. In 1847 the Kentucky legislature adopted a small property tax to help support the free common schools, this action constituting the beginning of state taxation for schools in Kentucky. This minimal beginning was increased from time to time as the years passed. North Carolina developed free schools under the leadership of Calvin Wiley, Whig lawyer, editor, and member of the state legislature. Wiley inaugurated a one-man crusade to establish better schools in the Tar Heel State. As state superintendent of schools from 1853 to 1866, he accomplished such a revolution that North Carolina had the best system of public instruction in the pre-war South.

While the southern states varied in their progress toward adequate public school systems before 1861, the Civil War shattered much that had been accomplished. The free schools in North Carolina continued to operate during the war, as the educational leaders prevented the state's Literary Fund from being used for war expenses. Other states were unable to resist the demands of war financing, and meager school systems suffered great damage. After the holocaust of war, the southern states had to begin the painful task of laying the foundations once again for reasonably adequate school systems, and not until the twentieth century did they make relative headway in educating their youth below the college level.

Education for Gentlemen

The first institution of higher learning in the South, and the second in the North American mainland colonies, was the College of William and Mary, established in 1693 at Williamsburg, Virginia. Founded by the Reverend James Blair, Commissary of the Church of England in Virginia, this pioneer college had as its original purpose training ministers for the colony and providing education for Indians. Diaries of William Byrd II and Phillip Fithian include comments about the college's professors who spent their evenings drinking and gambling in public taverns, but this is only part of the story. Eminent professors who took their duties seriously taught at the college; they included William Small, who had considerable influence on a tall, red-haired student named Thomas Jefferson, and George Wythe, who had the distinction of being the first professor of law in America. Attended by many of the South's well-known statesmen, among them Jefferson, John Marshall, James Monroe, Edmund Randolph, and John Tyler, it was the only southern college before the American Revolution. Colonial southerners with money sent their sons to be educated in the great English universities, Oxford and Cambridge, although an occasional planter's heir attended Harvard, Yale, King's College, or Princeton in the northern colonies. During the fight for independence, the Episcopal and Presbyterian churches began to operate a few small colleges, but most of them folded soon after opening their doors.

The paucity of colleges and universities in the South before 1800 ended rapidly in the early decades of the nineteenth century, when many institutions of higher learning were founded. One reason southern states devoted so little attention to elementary and high school education prior to the Civil War was that they were bending their educational efforts to develop colleges. The South's interest in educating its future leaders goes a long way toward explaining this concentration of effort in the antebellum period. The first state in the South to establish a university was North Carolina, whose state-supported institution offered instruction beginning in 1795. Franklin College (the future University of Georgia) was chartered earlier than the University of North Carolina, but the Georgia school did not begin instruction until 1801. The College of Charleston was incorporated as early as 1785, but it did not offer college-level instruction by the standards of that day until the first quarter of the nineteenth century. In 1837 the city of Charleston assumed control of the college, making annual appropriations to it after that year. This school thus had the distinction of being the first municipal college in the nation. In 1804 the South Carolina state legislature appropriated money for the establishment of a college at Columbia, the state capital. South Carolina College was the forerunner of the University of South Carolina.

Founded in 1819, the University of Virginia, brainchild of Thomas Jefferson, was to become one of the most influential of the southern universities. As one of the outstanding architects in two hemispheres, Jefferson designed the buildings and laid out the campus of the school. He also drew up the curriculum into which modern languages and scientific courses not offered at other institutions were introduced. Abiding by his concept of a "wall of separation" between Church and State, Jefferson prohibited the teaching of religion at this state-supported institution. He also introduced the elective system, moving away from the large number of strictly enforced compulsory courses characteristic of other schools. Students were allowed to adopt an honor system for examinations, and they were not forced to attend chapel or other religious exercises. Jefferson enticed the first faculty of the University of Virginia from England, and the school had an early tradition of excellence.

Founded in 1780, Transylvania University at Lexington, Kentucky has the distinction of being the oldest institution of higher education west of the Allegheny Mountains. The school's great years came after 1818, when Horace Holley was president. A Boston minister who saw the future of America in the West, Holley dreamed of making this school in the wilderness an American Oxford. During the 1820s Transylvania's medical and law schools flourished, the latter being perhaps the best in the nation in that decade. For a time, Transylvania had as many students as Harvard, its faculty was on a par with the older school, and its instruction was recognized as equal to any in the United States.

As southerners moved westward, expanding the area of the cotton kingdom, additional states joined the Union, followed by the establishment of colleges and universities in the lower South. For example, Louisiana, which became a state in 1812, shortly thereafter began to subsidize the College of Orleans. Soon it had founded the College of Louisiana at Jackson. Catholics dominated the former, while the latter was mainly for Protestants; both institutions received state funds. Alabama entered the Union in 1819, and a dozen years later the University of Alabama was founded at Tuscaloosa. Mississippi attained statehood in 1817, the University of Mississippi at Oxford coming into existence in 1848. In addition to these and other state-supported universities, the South also had several excellent military schools, including Virginia Military Institute, founded in 1839, and South Carolina Military Academy (The Citadel), chartered in 1842 by the state legislature. Louisiana State University at Baton Rouge was originally a military school patterned after VMI. Along with all of these schools, over forty colleges controlled by religious denominations were founded in the South during the first half of the nineteenth century. Not to be forgotten were numerous women's colleges established in southern states prior to the Civil War. Invariably small and poorly financed, these institutions were intended to be nothing more than finishing schools for the daughters of the aristocracy, but their presence illustrated the South's preoccupation with "college" training.

State universities had as their purpose the training of future political leaders, the military schools prepared officers for the army, and the church schools were engaged in educating clergymen, but the curriculum was much the same in all of the schools. Typical courses included Latin, Greek, mathematics, moral philosophy, mental philosophy, political philosophy, natural philosophy, natural history, ethics, general history, English composition, and surveying. The military schools added training in strategy and tactics, but little else. Extracurricular activities at all the schools consisted of literary and debating societies. These societies were concerned with social activities as well as intellectual matters, and many modern-day social fraternities and scholastic societies have their roots in nineteenth-century literary organizations. Phi Beta Kappa, the first Greek-letter scholastic society, was organized in 1776 at the College of William and Mary, and many lesser, similar organizations followed in the next century.

In 1850 the nation had 239 colleges and universities, 113 of these schools within the South. Thus, nearly one-half of the nation's institutions of higher learning served about one-fourth of the population. Furthermore, many sons of planters attended colleges in the North. In 1850 nearly one-half of the students at Princeton University in New Jersey were from the South, and the proportion of the southern student population at the University of Pennsylvania at the same time was almost as great. Approximately two-thirds of the student population in all the nation's schools combined were southerners. The South's commitment to higher education could hardly be more emphasized by any other statistic.

In 1860 the South's educational picture was clearly drawn. By nineteenth-century standards the South had built a good educational superstructure with its colleges and universities, but the foundations were weak. Badly neglecting the solid and essential building blocks of elementary and secondary education, the South had chosen to establish citadels of learning which suffered for lack of earlier training for its youths.

The outbreak of the Civil War disrupted college training and college life in the South as teachers and students alike rushed off to the battlefields. The University of Mississippi halted instruction before the hostilities commenced, and other schools closed shortly thereafter. A few colleges gallantly continued to operate during the war, but they accomplished little in the face of the excitement of war and the shortages of teachers, students, and funds. For lack of use many college buildings deteriorated, while others suffered physical abuse, especially if they were in the areas where fighting occurred. The College of William and Mary and the University of Alabama accumulated such extensive physical damages from invading armies that after the war the United States Congress appropriated money and land to help rebuild those schools. Other institutions were not so fortunate to be reconstructed even partially by federal funds, and along with the public schools they fought a battle of survival in the last years of the nineteenth century.

Romanticism and Realism

Antebellum southern literature was neither great nor abundant. Those who aspired to the field of belles lettres faced formidable handicaps, the combination of which prevented the development of a sizable body of worthy literature. The rural nature of the region militated against a large reading public with cosmopolitan literary tastes. Illiteracy and provincialism were prevalent, restricting the size of a discriminating reading public. In a region where farming was praised as the best way of life, men did not devote undue attention to aesthetics. The practicality of southerners reinforced the barrenness of the literature. Furthermore, in the antebellum years the South's preoccupation with slavery and the southerners' attempts to justify it were at cross purposes with the development of a literature indigenous to a completely free society. But whatever the handicaps and shortcomings, the literature that emerged from the antebellum South did reflect the conditions and values of southern society.

The dominant theme in the South's prewar literature was romanticism. This trend was present in part because these writings appeared at a time when romanticism flooded the literary scene in both Europe and America. But the South was particularly responsive to romanticism in literature. Southern readers found escape from isolation, hard work, and routine of plantation and farm life by entering into a medieval romantic world of knights in shining armor. Moreover, many southerners, especially those at the top of the socioeconomic order, looked upon their region as an actual reincarnation of the literary world created by Sir Walter Scott. Rollin G. Osterweis has pointed out that a cult of chivalry existed in the South, because southerners mistakenly believed that they were the descendants of noble Cavaliers. He believed that this cult of chivalry was so important that it constituted the third leg of the tripod —along with slavery and the cotton-plantation system—which supported the civilization of the Old South.

John Pendleton Kennedy, son of a Baltimore merchant and a Virginia aristocrat, was one of the more important southern writers who helped perpetuate the myth that the southern plantation was a medieval manor somehow transplanted to nineteenth-century America. *Swallow Barn,* published in 1832, presents a pleasant picture of Virginia's plantation society around 1800. The spirit of the novel and Kennedy's attitude toward the social élite are summed up in this passage: "the mellow, bland, and sunny luxuriance of her old-time society—its good fellowship, its hearty and constitutional *companionableness*, the thriftless gaiety of the people, their dogged but amiable invincibility of opinion, and that overflowing hospitality that knows no ebb." Kennedy dwells upon the virtues of the southern gentry, including their devotion to the family, their belief in honor, and their paternalism. His fictional portrait of slavery is primarily that of gentleness on the part of the masters and devotion on the part of the slaves, although Kennedy actually disapproved of the institution. Kennedy added to the myths of the Old South by romanticizing the southern woman. The heroine in his *Swallow Barn* is not concerned with the chores of a plantation household; rather she spends her time training a pet hawk, as if she lives in an age of medieval chivalry.

In 1835 Kennedy wrote *Horse-Shoe Robinson,* a historical romance dealing with both gentry and poor whites. The novel resulted from the author's trip into the back country of South Carolina, when he met an old man who claimed to have been a scout in the guerrilla warfare of the revolutionary war and who filled the novelist with colorful tales of men and war. *Rob of the Bowl* (1838) is set in Maryland during the reign of Charles II, and it casts a romantic glow over that colony's early years. *Quodlibet* (1840) is a good-natured but severe critique of Jacksonian democracy and was Kennedy's final literary work. Kennedy had leaned toward Jeffersonianism in his early years, but in later life he became a political conservative. His writing career ended because of his active interest in politics. His novels reflect his political conservatism, and taken as a whole they constitute an apology for the southern privileged class.

Perhaps the only person in the Old South who was able to make a living from writing alone was William Gilmore Simms. Born in Charleston in 1806, Simms was the son of a Scotch-Irish immigrant who was by no means a member of the ruling class. When his father migrated to Mississippi, young Simms remained in South Carolina, determined to establish himself as a man of letters in his native state and to be accepted by the aristocratic class. After financial difficulties and the death of his first wife, Simms moved to the North and soon thereafter published three novels: *Martin Faber* (1833), *Guy Rivers* (1834), and *The Yemassee* (1835). But he yearned to live in the South, and he soon returned to Charleston. In 1836 he married a woman of wealth and social standing, and therafter he devoted himself to writing sympathetically of the aristocratic tradition. Dividing his time between Charleston and his father-in-law's Barnwell District country estate, Simms produced ten novels within seven years including *Mellichampe* (1836) and *The Scout* (1841). As the sectional controversy began to boil in the 1840s, Simms used most of his literary efforts to defend South Carolina and the South. He wrote essays, edited magazines, and indulged in oratory in reaction to those who were attacking South Carolina and its institutions. In the 1850s Simms wrote apologies for slavery and became an active advocate of secession. At the same time he wrote several romantic novels: *Katharine Walton* (1851), *The Sword and the Distaff* (1853), *The Forayers* (1855), *Eutaw* (1856), and *The Cassique of Kiawah* (1859). When the Civil War came, Simms's country estate was destroyed and his fortune was lost. He spent the last five years of his life attempting to recover his former economic status, although the tragedy of losing nine of his fourteen children was overwhelming.

Romanticism is the dominant theme in most of Simms's novels. *Guy Rivers* is a romance of the southern border, while *The Yemassee* portrays South Carolina Indians as if the novel was written jointly by Sir Walter Scott and James Fenimore Cooper. Simms studied the South's history carefully, and *The Partisan, The Forayers,* and *Woodcraft* (originally, *The Sword and the Distaff*), three of his best works set during the American Revolution in South Carolina, reveal Simms's historical knowledge. All three novels deal with the social conflict between the Loyalists and the Patriots. Simms was able to describe the southern frontier and landscape with accuracy, and his descriptions add a note of realism to his romantic tales. This talent for realism was also manifested when he dealt with the common people of the South. Vernon C. Parrington has referred to Captain Porgy—rowdy fighter, frontier philosopher, and glutton par excellence—as "the most amusing and substantial character in our early fiction." In contrast, Simms's fictitious southern aristocrats were not real, perhaps because Simms himself was an aristocrat by marriage rather than by birth and training, and perhaps because the aristocrats had a misunderstanding of themselves. Simms's versatility is revealed in *Beauchampe* (1842), an almost literal account of a famous crime committed in Kentucky in 1826. Seduction, murder, and death are sensational subjects, and Simms made the most of them in this fictional account, but he was also able to write into his story the elements of a Greek tragedy. Moreover, Simms creates suspense and drama in *Beauchampe,* as well as in his other romantic novels of the southern border.

Simms's old biographer, William P. Trent, made much of the fact that the South Carolinian was a prophet without honor in his own country. Simms himself contributed to this impression when he wrote in 1858: "All that I have [done] has been poured to waste in Charleston, . . . which has steadily ignored my claims, which has disparaged me to the last, has been the last place to give me its adhesion, to which I owe no favor, having never received an office, or a compliment, or a dollar at her hands." Recent critics maintain that Simms and Trent have exaggerated South Carolinians' lack of appreciation for the foremost writer of the Old

South. It is true that Simms received little encouragement or patronage from southern aristocrats, but neither did any other southern writer, for that matter. It is true that Simms received most of his acclaim from the North, but the South was without a literary critic of any moment in the antebellum period. It is true that Simms's volumes made the author money because they were purchased by northern readers, but southerners read few books, whether published in North or South. With all the handicaps facing an author of the Old South, Simms was fortunate indeed to be able to make a living from only pen and paper.

While Kennedy and Simms were two of the better writers who romanticized their region, the South's most talented literary figure was Edgar Allan Poe. Born in 1809 in Boston of actor parents, Poe spent most of the forty years of his life in Baltimore and Richmond. When his mother died while he was still a child, Poe was taken into the home of John Allan, a Richmond merchant, who was responsible for his rearing. Allan sent the young man to England for a few months of college training, after which Poe spent a year at the University of Virginia, but his gambling debts forced his foster father to remove him from that institution. After a brief stint in the army, part of which he spent stationed at Fort Moultrie, Charleston, South Carolina, Poe enrolled at West Point, but he was soon dismissed from that institution because he refused to carry out his duties. After that Poe diligently applied himself to a literary career. In 1835 he became editor of the South's most distinguished magazine, *The Southern Literary Messenger,* published at Richmond. Although he held this post for less than eighteen months, he performed brilliantly, revealing both his critical talents and his ironic wit. Poe was dismissed as editor of the *Messenger* because of his difficult disposition and his independence of mind, not because of his addiction to alcohol or because of an unwillingness to work. After losing this position, which paid fifteen dollars a week, Poe became dissipated and irresponsible, unable to support himself. After renewing a youthful love affair in Richmond, he moved to Baltimore where he died in 1849 after several weeks of heavy drinking.

Poe's brilliance placed him several rungs above the regional writers, and he is seldom classified as a "southern" writer. While it is true that he was generally disinterested in social problems, politics, sectional disputes, or the question of slavery, this does not mean that he was not southern. Jay B. Hubbell has pointed out that Poe was a loyal southerner, when contrasted with New England's moral idealists and democratic optimists. Poe resented the assumption made by New England writers that they had a monopoly on the nation's literature. He saw the shallowness of the works of highly publicized New Englander Henry Wadsworth Longfellow, and he did not hesitate to poke fun at Longfellow and to ridicule New England provincialism. His sharp criticism of

New England's finest and his references to Boston as "the frogpond" did not help advance his immediate literary career. Furthermore, Poe did not like abolitionists, and his penchant for rich rhetoric was very much in the southern tradition.

On the other hand, Poe the artist to a large extent lived apart from his southern environment. He was a romanticist, but his romanticism was totally divorced from those writers who would defend and mythicize plantation society. If his short story "The Gold Bug" has touches of local color based upon his brief residence in South Carolina, most of his technically perfect stories are not related to time and place. His brilliant short stories, including such well-known ones as "The Fall of the House of Usher," "The Purloined Letter," and "The Cask of Amontillado," which emphasize terror or the ingenious, were not intended to speak to social problems. He wrote beautiful poetry for the sake of beauty itself, not to speak a message on the issues of his day. His poems *To Helen, Israfel, The City by the Sea, The Raven,* and *Annabel Lee* are beautiful not only for their lilting meter, but also for the haunting effect they have upon the reader. As a writer and a poet who worked in isolation, Poe was not restricted by environment or age.

If romanticism constituted the major chord in southern literature, minor notes of humorous realism can also be distinguished. The work of the humorists generally took the form of short, short stories or brief episodes published mainly in newspapers for the casual reader. It was regarded as trivial and coarse, and at the time it would have been unthinkable to have it considered as "literature" comparable to the artificial, romantic writing churned out by the Kennedys, the Simmses, and the like. Yet the literary endeavors of the southern humorists reveal a side of southern society neglected by the romanticists. If Kennedy, as Shields McIlwaine has pointed out, "did not allow a playful notice of one lone poor-white to blur the genteel pattern of Squire Meriwether's estate," the southern humorists redressed the balance by writing of Mike Fink, "Big Foot" Wallace, "Cousin Sally Dilliard," and the crackers of Georgia. The humorists have told much about the social history of the common people by writing vivid and often authentic accounts of weddings and funerals, horse racing and horse swapping, country dances and quilting bees, revival meetings and dishonest preachers, grudge fights and shooting matches. The focal points of many of the stories were horses, dogs, and bears; politicians, preachers, and practical jokers; shysters, rivermen, and drunkards. Interestingly the antebellum humorists hardly ever focused upon the Negro for their material.

Augustus Baldwin Longstreet may be considered the founder of the school of southern humorists. After attending Moses Waddel's academy, Yale University, and the law school at Litchfield, Connecticut, Longstreet settled down at Augusta, Georgia, where he was at one time or another lawyer, judge, politician, preacher, college president, newspaper editor, and story writer. This versatile and able man was an advocate of nullification and secession, as well as the leader in establishing a free Methodist church. He also found time to write humorous sketches about southern poor whites and yeoman farmers living on the Georgia frontier, which he published in his newspaper, the Augusta *State Rights Sentinel.* Collected and published in a volume entitled *Georgia Scenes* (1835), these stories reveal Longstreet's own expansive nature as well as much insight into the ways of the Georgia cracker. Ransy Sniffle, a raw-boned poor white, was his favorite character. Longstreet's stories invariably had a moral, which was the author's way of justifying writing about practical jokers, boyish pranks, and grotesque southerners. For all their crude realism and humor, Longstreet's stories describe aspects of Georgia's life and history neglected by the respectable writers.

In the tradition of Longstreet was Joseph G. Baldwin whose *Flush Times in Alabama and Mississippi* (1853) describes the color of the turbulent frontier society of the lower South. Set in the days prior to the Panic of 1837, *Flush Times* reveals the speculative mania, the desire for materialism, and the unwarranted optimism of frontier southerners. Filled with boisterous realism and ludicrous situations, the volume exposes the shortcomings of both the frontier economy and the men who attempted to manipulate it.

While in the prewar era the proportion of southerners who attempted to earn their living by the pen was small, their numbers ran into the hundreds. The writers discussed in the preceding pages were the most representative (or in the case of Poe, the most important) of the literary stylists of their day. If the humorists depicted the lower strata of southern society with considerable realism, the romanticists created and enlarged myths about the upper levels. Southerners in the antebellum South felt the need to envelop themselves and their region in myths as the sectional controversy came to dominate the American scene. They were unable to justify the developments on the political front without these myths. Southern writers greatly contributed to the image the southerner had of himself and his region. The ultimate results were tragic for both the South and the nation.

Suggestions for Further Reading

A reading program on religion in the Old South must begin with William W. Sweet, *The Story of Religion in America* (New York: Harper & Brothers, 1930) and *Revivalism in America* (New York: Scribners, 1944). Ernest T. Thompson, *The Presbyterians in the South, 1607–1861* (Richmond: John Knox, 1963) and Walter B. Posey, *The Baptist Church in the Lower Mississippi Valley, 1776–1845* (Lexington: Univ. Kentucky, 1957) and *The Development of Methodism in the Old Southwest, 1783–1824* (Tuscaloosa: Univ. Alabama, 1933) survey the three most important Protestant groups in the South before the Civil War. Posey has written an essay about another influential religious body: "The Protestant Episcopal Church: An American Adaptation," *Journal of Southern History*, vol. 25 (1959). Charles A. Johnson, *The Frontier Camp Meeting* (Dallas: Southern Methodist Univ., 1955) is an excellent study of the evolution of an institution, with much information on religion on the southern frontier. Des Champs, "Union or Division? South Atlantic Presbyterianism and Southern Nationalism, 1820–1861," *Journal of Southern History*, vol. 20 (1954) and Green, "Northern Missionary Activities in the South, 1846–1861," *ibid.*, vol. 21 (1955) deal with religious questions on the eve of the Civil War.

Frank T. McVey, *The Gates Open Slowly: A History of Education in Kentucky* (Lexington: Univ. Kentucky, 1949) is a study of the slow pace of educational development in the prewar South. Charles W. Dabney's *Universal Education in the South*, 2 vols. (Chapel Hill: Univ. North Carolina, 1936) is now a classic, as is P. A. Bruce's *A History of the University of Virginia, 1819–1919*, 5 vols. (New York: Macmillan, 1920–1922). E. Merton Coulter, *College Life in the Old South* (New York: Macmillan, 1928) focuses on Georgia and is a good case study. Other works on specific institutions are J. H. Easterby, *A History of the College of Charleston* (Charleston: Trustees of the College of Charleston, 1935) and Daniel W. Hollis, *University of South Carolina*, 2 vols. (Columbia, S. C.: Univ. South Carolina, 1951–1956). Two helpful articles are: Ezell, "Southern Education for Southrons," *Journal of Southern History*, vol. 17 (1951) and Hall (ed.), "A Yankee Tutor in the Old South," *New England Quarterly*, vol. 33 (1960).

A good general appraisal of antebellum southern literature is Vernon C. Parrington, *The Romantic Revolution in America, 1800–1860* * (New York: Harcourt, Brace, 1927). Also useful are: C. Alphonso Smith, *Southern Literary Studies* (Chapel Hill: Univ. North Carolina, 1927); Edd W. Parks, *Segments of Southern Thought* (Athens, Ga.: Univ. Georgia, 1938); Shields McIlwaine, *The Southern Poor-White: From Lubberland to Tobacco Road* (Norman, Okla.: Univ. Okla., 1939). William P. Trent,

William Gilmore Simms (Boston: Houghton Mifflin, 1892) treats one of the antebellum South's best-known writers. For a later perspective on Trent, see Welsh, "William Gilmore Simms, Critic of the South," *Journal of Southern History*, vol. 16 (1950). The title of David K. Jackson's *Poe and the Southern Literary Messenger* (Richmond, 1934) indicates its focus. More general is Hervey Allen, *Israfel: The Life and Times of Edgar Allan Poe*, 2 vols. (New York: Dietz Press, 1934). John D. Wade, *Augustus Baldwin Longstreet* (New York: Macmillan, 1924) is an adequate biography. Also relevant to this chapter is Current-Garcia, "Southern Literary Criticism and the Sectional Dilemma," *Journal of Southern History*, vol. 15 (1949).

* Available in paperback.

CHAPTER IV

SOCIETY AND AGRICULTURE IN THE OLD SOUTH

Travelers who toured the South and abolitionists who criticized the region, as well as antebellum southerners themselves, were in large part responsible for the creation of the myth that southern society was comprised of wealthy planters, degraded poor whites, and Negro slaves. The motion picture extravaganza, *Gone with the Wind,* based upon Margaret Mitchell's best-selling novel of the same name, deeply imbedded in the minds of mid-twentieth-century Americans a stereotype of antebellum southern society that historians, for all their efforts, have been unable to correct. When the movie industry refurbished the scratchy old film in the late 1960s, restoring its magnificent color and enlarging it to spread over the new, mammoth screens of modern movie theatres, many historians capitulated, resigning themselves to the fact that the myths of the Old South would be present forever. Actual characters in bona fide history books could not compete for the public's attention in view of the attractions of Clark Gable's handsome, dashing, and debonair Rhett Butler and Vivien Leigh's petulant, capricious, and playful Scarlett O'Hara. Perhaps Americans have a deep-seated need for this stereotype of an era "gone with the wind," but this does not excuse the historian from continually trying to "tell it like it really was."

The Country Gentleman Ideal

A small group of planters sat at the apex of the social pyramid of the Old South. In 1860 the United States Census Bureau arbitrarily classified a planter as one who was engaged in agriculture and who owned at least twenty slaves. By the bureau's standard only 46,274 persons (heads of families) were thus classed as planters. Of this number 43,982 owned fewer than one hundred slaves, and must therefore be considered "small" planters, while the remaining 2,292 who owned one hundred or more slaves may be called "large" planters. Most people in the planter class owned between twenty and fifty slaves, only 10,000 owning more than fifty slaves. The picture may further be clarified by pointing out that only 14 slaveholders owned over five hundred slaves, and only 1 planter owned over one thousand. When one remembers that in 1860, approximately 1,250,000 white families resided in the slaveholding states, the small number of planters in the South becomes more striking.

Usually owning many hundreds of acres of land, along with their property in slaves, the planters to a large extent dominated the economic life of the South. William E. Dodd has calculated that the annual income of 1,000 families in the cotton belt was about $50,000,000, while the combined income of the remaining 666,000 families was only $60,000,000. This favored economic position, along with a tradition extant from colonial days, assisted the planters in dominating the political and social life of the region as well. Like their colonial ancestors, the planters often shared political power with men of lower status, but the elite invariably controlled the political alliances. So smug were these self-appointed aristocrats that they considered themselves as *the* South, and they took the point of view that "what is good for the planter is good for the South."

These southerners believed that they were descended from aristocrats who had migrated from England during the colonial era. Actually, few Cavaliers migrated to the colonies and the aristocracy that developed in America was native to the New World, not to England. The men of the antebellum South, however, liked to think of themselves in the tradition of the eighteenth-century English country squires, living a life of leisure and pleasure on vast landed estates. This concept became ingrained in the minds of both southerners and northerners before the Civil War, but it was an even more powerful concept after the war was over. In a fine volume entitled *Cavalier and Yankee* (1961), William R. Taylor has pointed out that in the postwar humiliation southerners glorified the society of the Old South, partly as a defense mechanism against trying times and partly as a justification for their actions which helped bring on the Civil War. In truth, most planters in America did not inherit large landed estates and many slaves, but rather were self-made men who profited from an expanding market for cotton and tobacco, who speculated in land and slaves, and who were perpetually in debt. Far from being content to live the life of English gentlemen, most planters reflected the hustle and bustle of frontier America, and they commonly moved westward to more fertile land as their old plantation lands became worn out. The moving frontier was no place for a man who desired to stress his landed inheritance and who hoped to have it pass quietly to his sons and grandsons upon his death.

The lands of these southerners were not usually contiguous. The landholdings of the larger planters were always scattered among several plantations, and it was a rare small planter who owned land in only one area. By trial and error these men had come to realize that the most efficient cotton plantation was about one thousand acres, tilled by some fifty or sixty slaves. The largest planters hired overseers to supervise the work of the slaves and to coordinate the production of their several plantations. Small planters or their sons usually served this function for their one or two agricultural units. A small degree of absentee landlordship developed because of the unusually large holdings of some of the wealthier families, but more commonly, the landowner lived on or near his lands.

The southern aristocrat is often depicted as living in a fine two-story mansion, tastefully decorated and containing many of the conveniences of modern homes. Some of his colonial ancestors had adapted the prevailing English styles to their new environment, importing skilled carpenters and bricklayers to construct pretentious homes. The red-bricked, white-trimmed, symmetrically pleasing Georgian architecture, beautifully restored and on display at Colonial Williamsburg, Virginia, is typical of the style of buildings the wealthiest colonists erected in the eighteenth century. This Georgian style gave way to the Greek Revival architecture of the early nineteenth century. Based upon the design of a Greek temple, this type of architecture was developed in America by several architects, one of the best known being Benjamin Latrobe, an Englishman who served as the designer for the Capitol in Washington. Its popularity was related in part to the sympathy southerners had for the heroic struggle of the 1820s in which the Greeks battled to win their independence from Turkey, in part to the classical education in Greek and Latin which planters' sons acquired through formal training. This Greek Revival developed considerable momentum in the thirties and forties, when cotton planters were raising their socioeconomic status. Ordinarily, when one thinks of the "typical" southerner's mansion, it is the Greek Revival image which comes to mind: a two-storied, large, white, wooden structure with Doric or Corinthian columns, circular balustrades on the roofs, and wide piazzas beneath the Greek porticoes. The pleasing Greek temple façades contributed to the myth that quiet dignity and an atmosphere of harmony and leisure always existed in the homes of the planters. While the classic vogue was dominant throughout the antebellum period, Gothic Revival architecture appeared on the scene in the dozen years before the Civil War. Expressing in architecture the romantic mood of the literature of the era, the Gothic Revival was concurrent with southerners' absorption in the novels of Sir Walter Scott. As he read about medieval days, the southerner could view buildings which seemed transported from that earlier era. Many public and private buildings erected in the South in the 1850s were imitations of castles, containing stained glass windows, scalloped walls, and numerous arches and gables. Although the Gothic Revival was a fad, on the eve of the Civil War it contributed to the distorted view of prewar society held by postwar southerners.

Only a comparatively small number of southerners lived in Georgian, Classical, or Gothic homes. Those buildings which have been preserved as a remainder of how the elite of the Old South lived tend to be misleading. For every structure preserved, dozens upon dozens have long since crumbled. And most of the structures which did not survive were a far cry from the architecturally pleasing ones erected for the elite. The typical small planter lived in a simple, one-story, unpainted, wooden house. Some homes were nothing more than one-room log cabins. Often the small planters built "double" log cabins, with a breezeway between the two called a "dog run." This shaded breezeway became the center of household activity, since it was cooler than the rooms themselves in the hot and humid weather of the South. Small planters built such utilitarian homes rather than stately mansions because of the nature of the southern economy. They often considered their homes as temporary, assuming that they and their families would move west when the fertility of the land they were then farming was reduced. The southern frontier was no place for a family primarily interested in architecture, culture, or a leisurely way of life.

To southerners living in a region captured by the aura of romanticism, honor was important. If a southerner was insulted, lied about, or verbally attacked, his honor compelled him under certain circumstances to challenge his adversary to a duel. An elaborate *Code Duello* etiquette developed from the French tradition, and southerners sent written challenges, made excessive preparations, and executed the duel itself in accordance with strict rules. Men of the same class dueled against each other, a southern "gentleman" being unwilling to stoop to duel with a man of lesser rank. The lower classes took up the tradition of dueling too, although without the refinements "gentlemen" insisted upon. Guns, knives, fists, and feet were often used by men in the lower classes, and duels not infrequently turned into brawls. More than one southerner lost an eye from a finger-gouging opponent in what began as a sedate duel. Thousands of southerners engaged in one or more duels in their lifetimes, and few of the region's well-known prewar leaders escaped at least one duel, including Andrew Jackson, Cassius M. Clay, and William L. Yancey. Many in the South saw the senselessness of dueling, and Anti-Dueling Associations were established to help settle differences that might lead to a duel. Furthermore, several southern states passed laws outlawing the practice, although they were difficult to enforce in view of the persistence of the concept of honor and the duel's relationship to it.

Closely connected to the concept of manly honor was the cult of southern womanhood. Southerners who would protect their own honor and reputation were doubly protective of their women. The southern legend had it that the southern white woman was faithful to her husband, a puritan in regard to morals, and the center of the southern Christian family. Anyone who hinted that this might not be true, or who tampered with a southern woman, had to account for his words or behavior to an irate husband or brother who would as soon kill as not. The southerner's image of himself demanded that he not only protect his woman from abuse, but that he should also shield her from profanity and vulgarity. The subject of sex, whether related to animal reproduction or a backroom dirty story, was taboo in front of a southern woman, and if by chance the subject arose in her presence, she was required by tradition to show embarrassment. The romantic ideal of the southern woman pictured her with soft, white hands which knew no work, with leisure time to read romantic novels, with pretty crinoline dresses and elaborate hairdos, and with a spirit of gay abandon which added life and zest to social occasions. No wonder a cult of chivalry developed in the South. What man would not give his comfortable seat in a living room, stage coach, or railroad car to such a beautiful lady?

Even though the romantic tradition was present, most southern women worked very hard. After marrying early, usually in their teens, women spent long hours cooking, sewing, cleaning, and bearing and rearing children. The planter's wife was supposedly relieved of the dreary and heavy tasks of housework by household slaves, but the mistress of the plantation inherited additional responsibilities with the presence of the slaves. She had to supervise their work, including kitchen tasks, the weaving of cloth, and the making of soap, as well as attend to sick slaves and assist with childbirth. If planters' daughters were permitted to enjoy the leisure and fun-loving way of life depicted in the romantic novels which they devoured, the girls were rudely jerked back into reality as soon as they were married.

Another dimension of the romantic legend was the hospitality southerners extended to both friends and strangers. A number of factors contributed to the southerner's hospitableness. While he was happy to live in rural isolation, away from towns and alien urban conditions and values, the southerner did not desire to be lonely, and he was eager to en-

tertain those who passed by his gates. The plentiful supply from his garden and the availability of servants made it easy for the southerner to extend his gracious welcome to one and all. Southerners placed much
emphasis upon the family, including even distant relatives within the
family circle, and he welcomed these "kissing cousins" with open arms.
Such familiarity helped him to extend a warm greeting to strangers willing to partake of his generosity. Finally, the warm climate which characterized the South encouraged a man to live and work out-of-doors, rather
than to restrict himself to the confines of his home for several months
each year, and this encouraged an openness and friendliness less common
in cooler climates. The South's hospitality was well-recognized by northerners during the antebellum period. Frederick Law Olmsted, a reporter
for *The New York Times,* apparently believed that his travels through
the South would cost him little, in view of the South's reputation for hospitality, and he complained that he was charged for food and quarters
during his tours. Olmsted was probably expecting too much, although
there did seem to be considerable truth to that part of the South's tradition which stressed the region's hospitality, and this characteristic was
present in all strata of southern society.

Realities of the Social Structure

If the romantic ideal of the country gentleman dominated the Old
South's image, and if upper-class planters possessed an inordinate amount
of social prestige and economic and political power, the largest group of
white southerners in the prewar South was, nevertheless, the yeoman
farmers. Constituting the bulk of those people who made up the middle
class, these farmers varied greatly in their land and slave ownership;
nevertheless, they had common characteristics which were identifiable. By
far the greatest number of these "plain folk of the Old South" owned relatively small plots of agricultural land which they plowed without the assistance of slave labor. Many—but not all—of these lower-middle-class
folk often owned the less desirable lands in the South, whether they were
abandoned worn-out lands in the Southeast or the lands in the Southwest
which were less fertile than those owned by the planters. Still, and perhaps most important to remember, this mass of southern farmers aspired
to be land and slave owners. Their support of the South's institution of
slavery in the wake of attacks upon it can only be understood in this
frame of reference. Class consciousness was not great on the part of these
people, and they unabashedly moved up the socioeconomic scale when
they were able.

These characteristics were most apparent in the yeoman
farmers at the upper end of the middle stratum. In 1860 approximately

385,000 white heads of families in the South owned one or more slaves. Since only 46,274 of these slaveholders owned twenty or more slaves and thus could be called planters, the remaining slaveholders, constituting approximately 88 percent of the total, were members of the yeoman class. Furthermore, 72 percent of the total number of slaveholders owned fewer than ten slaves, and only slightly less than 50 percent held fewer than five. These statistics reveal that very few family heads in the South were actually slaveholders; they also indicate that the majority of the slaves were held by men who owned relatively few of them. Approximately two-thirds of all the slaves in the South in 1860 were owned by men who held fewer than fifty slaves, and who farmed comparatively few acres of land, in contrast to the legend that the South was covered by sprawling plantations worked by large gangs of Negro slaves. These small land and slave owners did aspire to a higher economic rung, and in numerous instances they moved into the planter class. Marriages between yeomen and planters' children commonly assisted a change in economic status, often blurring distinctions between the two groups. In reality the lines between the upper-middle-class yeoman farmer and the small planters were thin and sometimes nonexistent. Southern class lines generally were not as sharply etched as the conventional theory would indicate.

The emphasis upon the yeoman farmer in the South is relatively recent. Just after World War II Professor Frank L. Owsley and a group of his graduate students at Vanderbilt University began systematic statistical studies of the unpublished census records of the Old South. They discovered not only that slaveholding was more widespread than was popularly believed, but also that landowning in the South was far from restricted to planters. Their research indicated that, contrary to unfounded assumptions, many of these common folk lived among the planters, not relegated to the sidelines of the society. Furthermore, they plowed land comparable in quality to that cultivated by the large plantation owner, rather than being forced to till less fertile land. The Owsley School has also indicated that the economy was expanding rapidly in the 1850s, and that nearly all southerners, especially those in the lower economic brackets, experienced prosperous expansion. Thus, their picture of the South as a dynamic economic democracy has revised former assumptions about the South's social structure and economy. Occasional challenges have been advanced criticizing the Owsley group's statistical methods, but even the critics praise Owsley for documenting and calling attention to the presence and characteristics of this large middle class.

Like his small planter neighbor, the yeoman farmer usually lived in an unpretentious clapboard or log home. Household activities centered around the huge stone or brick fireplace, where the hardworking yeoman's wife cooked a monotonous diet of pork and cornbread, sweetened by sorghum molasses. The family washing was done outside the home, clothes being boiled in a huge black pot over an open fire. In addition to cooking, washing, and mending, the farmer's wife also raised chickens, tended the family vegetable garden, and even helped in the fields at harvest time. Children, who slept on hay in the loft of their modest dwelling, were required to do a multitude of household and barnyard chores, including hauling drinking and washing water from a nearby well, spring, or creek. The yeoman farmer and his children constituted the labor force for their land under cultivation, unless they were fortunate enough to own a few slaves, in which case both whites and blacks worked alongside each other. As with the planters, cotton was the major money crop, although many yeoman farmers grazed cattle on their unplowed lands. Generally the farmer depended less upon the cash crop than the planter did, since he engaged in more subsistence agriculture than the planter. To this extent the farmer was more economically self-sufficient than was his more prestigious neighbor.

While the "respectable" literature of the South dealt mainly with the society of the planting class, southern humorists wrote earthy stories about yeoman farmers. Much of the knowledge of this little-known middle class comes from the accounts of the everyday activities of the common man. Numerous short stories were written dealing with incidents at country dances, camp meetings, barbecues, county court days, and crossroads stores. Ribald practical pranks, gambling, drunkenness, brawling, and skinning the city slicker were common occurrences within the sphere of the yeoman farmer, if the literature about him is an accurate barometer of his daily life. He was a man who worked hard, played hard, laughed loudly, and aspired to improve himself both materially and spiritually. He very much represented not only the norm among southerners but also among Americans in general.

One of the reasons the middle-class yeoman farmer was overlooked in the social structure of the Old South was the fascination observers found in the southern poor whites. The poor white, with all of his degradation, laziness, slothfulness, and idleness, made much better reading material for northerners than did the comparatively bland farmers. Also, abolitionists orated about the great number of poor whites in the South, using this group as an example of the deteriorating effects upon a society which tolerated slaves. Finally, lower-class yeoman farmers made much of the fact that poor whites existed in the South, perhaps as a defense against the alternative that without poor whites, small farmers themselves would be at the bottom of the white social and economic stratum.

More fortunate white southerners referred to these people as "crackers," "sand-hillers," and "hillbillies," while Negroes called them "poor white trash" and "poor buckra." Poor whites probably constituted less than 10 percent of the South's population, although their presence in the region appeared much greater than that to the antebellum observer.

Part of the reason for misjudging the numbers came from the fact that many small farmers were assumed to be poor whites. But the differences between the two groups were striking. While the small farmer aspired to a better life, the poor whites were content to remain in their squalor. The farmer lived and worked land near his more prosperous neighbors, but the poor white was generally relegated to the hills and mountainous regions of the South. Earlier writers theorized that poor whites were the descendants of indentured servants and convicts from colonial times, but historians now believe that they were more likely simply the weakest elements of the frontier population who were forced into the less desirable mountain regions and overwhelmed by their environment of isolation.

The laziness of the poor white may have been less the result of his lack of ambition than lack of proper diet and the presence of enervating diseases. Living in less fertile lands than others, the poor whites had difficulty growing even the basic foods necessary for an adequate diet. Dietary deficiencies sometimes forced the poor whites to eat white "hearth clay," thus attaching to him the stigma "clay eater." More importantly, the poor white was infected with hookworm and malaria, both debilitating diseases. The hookworm parasite thrived in the warm, sandy soil of the South, and was an enemy to nearly all southerners, not just the poor whites, since the majority of southern rural folk did not wear shoes many months each year. The hookworm entered the body through the sole of the foot, passed into the bloodstream, and attached itself to the wall of the intestine by means of a hook on its body. Its eggs were then laid, many of which were passed from the individual through excretion to the soil. In a region where toilets were a luxury, these eggs were thus deposited in wide areas, where the warm sun and soil hatched the larvae. The life cycle of the parasite was then ready to be resumed when a barefooted southerner walked by. The presence of this pernicious parasite within the human body drained it of energy, and the victim became pale and listless. The lost man hours in terms of work for southerners will never be known, but authorities agree that the hookworm was an important factor in holding the South back economically throughout the nineteenth century. Not until the twentieth century was this dissipating disease eradicated from the South. Infected individuals were treated during extensive campaigns financed by both federal and private money, and an education movement to encourage southerners to wear shoes brought the parasite under control. Malaria was also controlled in the twentieth century, but not before it had drained countless southerners of their normal energy. Administering quinine for the infected, draining swamps to reduce the hatch of anopheles mosquitoes, and using screens on doors and windows went a long way toward controlling this disease.

For all of their deplorable conditions, the poor whites refused to work to lift themselves to a higher level. Nor would their pride permit them to beg or accept handouts from governments or individuals. They owned no slaves, and had hardly any contact with black men, yet they were racists and strongly supported the institution of slavery. If nothing else, they had their white skin which they regarded as making them superior to the African descendant.

The traditional view of the Old South's social structure implies that it was composed only of wealthy planters, poor whites, and Negro slaves. Even with the addition of the yeoman farmer, the largest and one of the most important groups, the picture of the class structure of the Old South remains incomplete. While the Old South was primarily an agricultural region, several large cities and numerous small and medium-sized towns existed throughout the South. Charleston, Richmond, Mobile, and New Orleans had populations of significant size when compared with other urban centers outside the region. Not to be overlooked in any discussion of the South's society were the urban dwellers, many of whom were businessmen, traders, shopkeepers, shippers, skilled and common laborers, editors, and professionals, including lawyers, teachers, medical doctors, and ministers. While their numbers were small by comparison to those engaged in agriculture, they were a necessary part of the southern economy, and not infrequently they held high social and economic positions in the towns and surrounding countryside. Furthermore, in the cities and towns were those who made their living indirectly from agriculture. Cotton factors, warehouse owners, slave traders, farm implement dealers, horse and mule traders, and others could not have existed without the vitality of agricultural regions. Whether tied closely or loosely to agriculture and slavery, 7.8 percent of all southerners in 1860 lived in population centers of four thousand or more, and they constituted a significant minority in the region. Their presence lends support to the statement that antebellum southern society was more diverse, dynamic, and democratic than former stereotypes would admit.

The Black Minority

In 1860 approximately 250,000 free Negroes lived in the South. For a variety of reasons these black men had gained their freedom. Some were rewarded because of faithful service rendered to their masters. Wills of southerners reveal that many slaves were freed upon the death of a master, Richard Randolph and Thomas Jefferson being only two better known southerners who freed slaves in this way. Occasionally slaves purchased their own freedom by saving or stealing money or through some stroke of good fortune. Denmark Vesey, leader of an aborted slave revolt in Charleston, South Carolina, in 1822, had previously bought his freedom by holding a winning ticket in a $1500 lottery. Other Negroes had moved out of the bonds of slavery because they were mulatto and had physical characteristics which bore too much resemblance to their master or one of his sons. Many free Negroes in the nineteenth century were the descendants of slaves who had been released during the preceding century. In the later years of the eighteenth century, before the invention of the cotton gin, when tobacco land was wearing out, when slaves appeared to be multiplying too fast for the labor needs of the upper South, when the philosophy of the Declaration of Independence was in vogue, and when groups of Quakers began small antislavery organizations, numerous slaves were emancipated, especially in Virginia and Maryland. By 1860, 58,000 free blacks resided in Virginia, while 85,000 lived in Maryland.

Free Negroes quite naturally gravitated to the towns and cities where they became barbers, skilled mechanics, petty tradesmen, domestic servants, and unskilled laborers. But theirs was a precarious existence. White racism kept free black men at the bottom of the social scale, and instances of white resentment of economic competition from able free Negroes were common. Custom, tradition, and laws were such that the free Negro was in fact a second-class citizen. This was especially true as the nineteenth century progressed, when slave revolts and rumors of revolts stimulated white southerners to pass laws against free Negroes, who were assumed, sometimes correctly, to be agitators among the slaves. The free Negro's right of assembly was limited, he was often subjected to early evening curfew, and meetings of fraternal lodges and churches often required the presence of a white man. Since he was a potential revolutionary, the free black was not to entertain slaves, nor own a gun without a special permit. Some states or localities refused free Negroes the right to go into business for themselves. They could not be itinerant peddlers, since this occupation might place them in positions where they could stir up enslaved blacks. Fearful that they might produce abolitionist literature, whites prohibited free Negroes from being typesetters. Nor were they permitted to own grocery stores, since this would allow them to possess and sell whiskey, which whites did not trust in black hands. If an able-bodied free black did not have a job, he was subject to classification as a vagrant, and he could be sold into servitude for months or even years. In some instances, free Negroes were driven out of certain sections of the South. John Hope Franklin's term "quasi-free" may be the most appropriate designation for this group of black southerners.

Frustrations stemming from attempts to live and work in a supposedly free society may have been primarily responsible for the involvement of free Negroes in numerous slave uprisings. The free black no doubt was sincere in desiring freedom for his enslaved brothers, but he knew that he needed more numbers if he was ever to compete freely with the white man. As a minority group, the free Negroes were in some ways the forgotten men of southern society. The antebellum white south-

erner looked upon them as hardly more than slaves, and his treatment of
the free black expressed these attitudes. Leon Litwack has pointed out
that the Negro in the northern states during the slavery era was also pro-
scribed by customs and laws, much as he was restricted in the South, but
Litwack's volume simply verifies that racial prejudice was not limited to
the region south of the Potomac.

The "mudsill" of antebellum southern society was the slaves themselves (the subject of Chapter V). In 1860 some 3,900,000 Negro slaves
lived in the South, over one-third of the region's entire population. Approximately one-half of all the slaves worked in small groups on the
lands of the yeoman farmers. Class consciousness did not exist
for these slaves who lived in a certain degree of isolation. But such
was not the case on the plantations where upwards of 20 to 100 slaves
lived. Perhaps as the result of the attitudes of the whites and perhaps related to the slaves' growing sense of values, plantation slavery developed
its own rank orders within the black population. At the bottom of the
slave society were the common field laborers. While these young, able-
bodied men were expensive (worth from $1000 to $1500 in the 1850s),
and while their work directly produced the crops which permitted the
plantation economy to survive, they were looked down upon socially by
other blacks. In the eyes of their fellow slaves, long hours, hard work,
and no recognition as individuals relegated these laborers to the bottom
of the social order. These common field hands usually constituted only
about one-half of the total number of slaves on larger plantations. They
not only had the least desirable jobs, but they also lacked the numerical
strength to demand more respect within the slave society.

Above the field hands were the house servants. Their responsibilities entailed cooking, cleaning, washing, and similar chores necessary to
keep the planter's home in reasonable order. Many planters allowed their
older children to have a servant or two to care for them, entertain them,
or to be their companions. Slave women often had a brood of children
who spent their days in the shadow of the "big house" while their mothers worked inside. They played with the planter's smaller children until
they were old enough to be given minimal responsibilities. These household servants and their children were generally treated fairly well. They
ate from the kitchen of the planter, thus having access to better food
than the field hands. Cast-off clothes from the planter's closets gave them
better quality clothing as well as more variety. Because of association
with the white families, some of the domestic slaves learned to read, to
sew, and to acquire other valuable skills. If a plantation had an over-
abundance of slaves, many of them were given small jobs around the plantation home, some planters allowing as many as twenty or twenty-five servants to be available to wait on the white family. These luxury slaves

were an economic waste, but the slaves themselves made much of the fact that they were "favored" by the whites, and they did not hesitate to lord it over the lowly field hands.

At the top of the slave society were the skilled servants. Black-smiths, carpenters, and wheelwrights were indispensable to the successful operation of a plantation, and owners coveted the services of slaves with these necessary skills. These slaves remained in the barns and worksheds, often without a white man present, avoiding the hot sun and drudgery to which common laborers were exposed. They were treated with much more concern by the planter and his subordinates than were other slaves. Social snobbery among slaves was not uncommon, especially on the larger plantations, and those slaves in the more desirable positions often used their status to their own advantage within the slave society.

In a class by themselves were the urban slaves. While the great majority of slaves in the South lived on the farms and plantations, Richard Wade's study of slavery in the southern cities is a necessary corrective, a reminder that city dwellers also owned slaves, and that the institution of slavery in the cities was far different from that in the rural areas. City slaves often lived in the somewhat restrictive homes of their owners, where the slaves gained an intimacy of contact unknown to most rural slaves. In the comparatively cramped urban centers, the slaves also came into contact with whites in the market place, on the streets, and even at social gatherings, and from these conditions and associations the urban slave culturally outdistanced his rural kinfolk. Many slaves were hired or leased to other whites, depending upon specific skills and the needs of the labor market, which to some extent gave blacks a relative degree of freedom. Other urban slaves were permitted to "live out," away from their masters, working, caring for themselves, and generally controlling their own affairs. They were obligated to give their owners a certain percentage of their wages, but if they were working and stayed out of trouble, these slaves often had little contact with their masters. Contrasting his life in Baltimore in the 1830s with his earlier experiences in rural Maryland, Frederick Douglass exclaimed, "A city slave is almost a free citizen. He enjoys privileges altogether unknown to the whip-driven slave on the plantation." Douglass's escape from his Baltimore slave life may indicate the relativity of his statement.

Urban slaves were in many ways less restricted than free Negroes, and because of the protective attitudes of their owners, they often enjoyed conditions considerably more favorable than those of the free black men. Watched over by their masters with a minimum of restraint, permitted to live in family units, and not subject to the laws designed to restrict the free Negro, the urban slave who "lived out" probably had a better life than any other black man in the South. Yet even this favored position was nothing to rejoice over, and black men in the Old South had a long way to go before they would be accepted into the white social structure, and before restrictions, however minimal, would be removed.

Tillers of the Soil

While some whites and blacks lived in the urban centers of the antebellum South, the vast majority lived in the rural areas, devoting themselves, one way or another, to tilling the land. The agricultural scene in the prewar South resulted from the natural evolution of an agrarian economy originally established in colonial days. Tobacco, the main crop of the forefathers of nineteenth-century southerners, remained important. In 1860 tobacco cultivation was centered in Virginia and North Carolina, just west of the Tidewater area. But migrating southerners had discovered that the riverlands of western Kentucky were well suited to tobacco, and considerably before the Civil War, that region was profiting from the "filthy weed." Moreover, as southern frontiersmen continually sought more land, they had moved up the Mississippi and Missouri rivers to grow tobacco in the central counties of the state of Missouri.

While tobacco was important in the westward expansion of the frontier, rice remained behind in the lowlands of Georgia and South Carolina. Requiring large quantities of water, southern rice culture was not easily adapted to inland cultivation. Nathaniel Heyward, the largest slaveholder in the South before his death in 1851, was a Carolina rice planter, and his vast rice plantations on the Combahee River were as valuable as gold mines. He regularly netted $100,000 per year from his rice lands. Other rice planters also grew wealthy from their endeavors. But rice cultivation was not available to large numbers of southerners. Considerable capital was required to build dikes and flood gates and to prepare the lowlands of the Tidewater region for rice cultivation. Also, each rice planter was required to build and maintain his own rice mill in order to remove the husks and polish the grain. Much labor was required, and all rice planters had to own many slaves. If Heyward's 2,087 slaves were amassed partly as "conspicuous wealth," dozens upon dozens of slaves were not uncommon on a typical rice plantation. The fact that rice culture was relatively unimportant in the South after the Civil War is related to the results of that war. Upon emancipation, many blacks fled from the arduous labor in the watery rice fields, and rice planters were unable to entice free men into the fields, for any price. Before the end of the nineteenth century, rice as a farm product on the Atlantic coast was almost nonexistent.

A nineteenth-century product grown with profit in the upper South was hemp. Central Kentucky and central Missouri produced this crop which came to supply much of the nation's rope needs, although competition from quality Russian hemp existed. American hemp was widely used for cotton bagging and for bale rope, but it was less than satisfactory for the tarred rope used by the American navy throughout the antebellum period. James F. Hopkins in *A History of the Hemp Industry in Kentucky* (1951) tells the story of the competition between foreign and domestic hemp in terms of the inflexible bureaucracy of the United States navy and the inertia of the American hemp producers. Henry Clay, who had married into a wealthy hemp-growing family in Kentucky, was an outspoken advocate of tariff protection for the industry. But the American hemp industry never quite met the competition nor overcame inherent obstacles, and its demise soon after the middle of the nineteenth century came as no surprise.

Sugar cane was introduced into Louisiana by way of the West Indies. Violence in the wake of the slave insurrections in Santo Domingo in the early 1790s forced many French sugar planters to flee to Louisiana, bringing with them their knowledge of sugar cane cultivation. These planters were forced to grow Philippine ribbon cane, since the cane in the Caribbean Islands matured late and was killed by frost in Louisiana. But their expertise in growing cane and in turning it into syrup and sugar, which netted them handsome returns, caused others in the region to cultivate that product. By 1850 over fifteen hundred sugar plantations existed in Louisiana. Other southern regions experimented with sugar cane production, but except for a small area along the Texas coast, prewar sugar production in the United States was limited to the southern half of Louisiana. Sugar, like rice, required much capital outlay, great gangs of strong laborers, and much land. Details of the cane cultivation, extractive methods, and the society which developed in the sugar country have been described in essays and in a book by J. Carlyle Sitterson.

Just as tobacco dominated the colonial South so did cotton dominate most of the antebellum South. Small quantities of cotton were grown in the region before the American Revolution, but cotton did not become a major crop there until after 1793, when a mechanical contraption for separating cotton fibers from seeds was put into use. At first, long-staple cotton, necessary for fine fabrics, could be grown successfully only in the sea islands off the coast of South Carolina and Georgia. This excellent strain of cotton was introduced into Georgia about 1786 by migrants from the Bahama Islands. Cultivation of this sea-island variety of cotton was greatly expanded in the nineteenth century, over eleven million pounds being exported annually in the 1820s. Short-staple cotton was a sturdy plant which could be grown in the hill country and the interior of the South. It very rapidly spread over a giant area of land from North Carolina to the south and southwest, all the way to eastern Texas. This cotton belt became the world's largest producer of raw cotton, at the very time demand for cotton cloth rose greatly on the world market.

The key to the expansion of the cotton culture was the invention of a successful cotton engine by Eli Whitney. Unlike sea-island cotton, short-staple cotton lint was difficult to detach from the seed, and until a mechanical device was available to break this bottleneck, cotton culture was strapped. Whitney, a Yankee who was visiting a cotton plantation in Georgia, began to experiment with crude models to overcome this serious obstacle. In the spring of 1793 he constructed a box made of slats, equipped with rotating wooden rollers with wire teeth. When turned by men or horses, the rollers pulled the cotton from the box, the seed remaining in the box. When the wire teeth became clogged with lint, Whitney added another cylinder equipped with brushes revolving in the opposite direction to sweep the lint from the original roller. Whitney patented his machine, but his efforts did not prevent others from building their own cotton engines. It was a simple mechanical device, easily copied by any competent blacksmith. Improvements were also made, and soon the South was filled with "gins." The South was now in a position to produce great quantities of cotton with the assurance that the separation of the lint and the seed would no longer limit production. The following statistics reveal the impact of the cotton gin: in 1790, the South produced 2,000,000 pounds of cotton; in 1800, 40,000,000 pounds; in 1810, 80,000,000 pounds; in 1820, 160,000,000 pounds; in 1830, 350,-000,000 pounds. These reveal not only the impact of the invention of the cotton gin, but also the expansion of the cotton culture westward; yet the two went hand in hand, each affecting the other.

Also important in cotton production was the ever-present slave. Cotton required much cultivation during the growing season, and gangs of slaves spent hours hoeing weeds from around tender cotton plants, a hot and boring task. Harvest time saw as many slaves as possible in the field, for the job of pulling the fleecy fiber from the sharp-pointed dry bolls was a slow task. Furthermore, since the cotton was placed in a long bag to be dragged along the ground until it was filled, slaves found the job a back-breaking one. Even so, a diligent slave could average picking over 300 pounds of cotton a day, and occasionally a slave might pick as much as 400 or 500 pounds a day. The need for laborers in cotton production was the chief factor in the rapid spread of slavery westward. For example, in 1790 the Piedmont region of South Carolina counted only about 20 percent of its population as slaves, but by 1830, after cotton had moved into the region, the number of blacks had risen to about 50 percent.

The Appalachian Mountains did not stop the advance of the cotton domain. As lands in the Piedmont wore out, cotton planters moved with their slaves to the fertile lands of Alabama and Mississippi, and later to Arkansas and eastern Texas. The warm climate and rich lands of the lower Mississippi Valley and the Gulf coast were ideally suited to the cotton plant, and by the middle of the 1830s this area began to produce more cotton than the Atlantic states. In fact, from about 1835 to the Civil War, the Gulf states and Arkansas produced about 75 percent of all the cotton grown in the United States. In 1859 the South produced over 4,500,000 bales of cotton, each bale averaging about 400 pounds. In the years immediately preceding the Civil War about three-fourths of the South's entire crop was marketed abroad, comprising about 60 percent in value of the nation's exports.

While profits from cotton lured men to buy more land and slaves, a fickle market created hazards for the cotton planter. In 1801, cotton sold for 44 cents a pound, but in 1811 it was selling for only 9 cents a pound. When the War of 1812 began, the price fell even lower, as the foreign market was affected by the events of the war. Along with an unstable foreign market went overproduction, as planters expanded the kingdom of cotton too rapidly, and these factors coupled with the lack of government controls caused prices to be depressed. In the 1840s prices fluctuated violently, often dropping below the cost of production. The decade prior to the Civil War saw prices somewhat more stable at around 12 cents a pound, a selling price which was profitable to cotton growers. Despite the vagaries of cotton, southerners were wholly committed to the fleecy product, and Confederate diplomacy during the Civil War later revealed a blind faith in the importance and power of cotton.

Planters who bought up vast lands and large numbers of slaves were not alone in their commitment to cotton. With the westward expansion of the cotton kingdom, yeoman farmers also saw the possibility of profit from the white fiber, and being as enthusiastic about growing cotton as were the planters, they assisted in its advance. While a tobacco farmer could make a living by growing his crop on an acre or less, the cotton farmer needed at least one hundred acres. But this requirement for extensive land was not a great problem on the moving frontier, and farmers easily joined the planters in their westward march. Plantations required gangs of slave laborers, but a farmer with two or more children and perhaps a slave or two could profitably grow a cotton crop, even though he was shorthanded during the harvest season.

While the plantation economy was devoted almost exclusively to the one-crop system, the farmer often reduced his need for a large money crop by engaging in a certain amount of subsistence farming. An extensive vegetable garden, a small plot devoted to hay, some pasturage, and a few hogs and cows, usually taken care of by his wife, went a long way toward supplementing the farmer's basic needs. Sometimes a farmer turned to corn, wheat, and livestock to help maintain his existence, and on occasion he marketed these products for cash. But he invariably grew some cotton, even if only a small amount, so that he could have money to buy such necessities as sugar, salt, gun powder, and lead. Thus, the South did not devote its energies exclusively to the cultivation of staple crops for export. Yet the South's agriculture was not as diversified as it might have been, and both planters and yeoman farmers came to place too much reliance on cotton alone. For the Deep South states, cotton culture became almost synonymous with southern culture, and the society as well as the economy were forever marked by its presence.

Suggestions for Further Reading

Stressing the importance of the aristocracy in the antebellum South is Charles S. Sydnor, *Gentlemen Freeholders* (Chapel Hill: Univ. North Carolina, 1952). For an interesting discussion of the same topic, see Eaton, "Class Differences in the Old South," *Virginia Quarterly Review,* vol. 33 (1957). Although dealing with only one state, the following volume by implication has much to say about the entire South: Roger W. Shugg, *Origins of Class Struggle in Louisiana* (Baton Rouge: Louisiana State Univ., 1939). Challenging the importance of the upper classes in the South is Frank L. Owsley's pathbreaking volume, *Plain Folk of the Old South* * (Baton Rouge: Louisiana State Univ., 1950). Several of Owsley's students have written more limited studies to support their teacher's contention that the yeoman farmer was a major factor in the social and economic structure of the South. For examples, see Blanche H. Clark, *The Tennessee Yeoman, 1840–1860* (Nashville: Vanderbilt Univ., 1942); Herbert Weaver, *Mississippi Farmers, 1850–1860* (Nashville: Vanderbilt Univ., 1945); Coles, "Some Notes on Slaveownership and Landownership in Louisiana, 1850–1860," *Journal of Southern History,* vol. 9 (1943). Critical of the Owsley group's handling of data is Linden, "Economic Democracy in the Slave South: An Appraisal of Some Recent Views," *Journal of Negro History,* vol. 31 (1946). A microcosm of the South can be seen in Bonner, "Profile of a Late Ante-Bellum Community," *American Historical Review,* vol. 49 (1943–44).

In his *Life and Labor in the Old South* * (Boston: Little, Brown, 1929), Ulrich B. Phillips pointed up the importance of the plantation and large gangs of Negro slaves in the economy of the South. For a critique of this position, see Hofstadter, "U. B. Phillips and the Plantation Legend," *Journal of Negro History,* vol. 29 (1944). Buck, "Poor Whites of the Ante-Bellum South," *American Historical Review,* vol. 31 (1925–26) is old but a good place to begin for a study of the lowest class of white southerners. Also useful is Craven, "Poor Whites and Negroes in the Ante-Bellum South," *Journal of Negro History,* vol. 15 (1930). One of the most perceptive volumes written on the South in recent years is William R. Taylor, *Cavalier and Yankee: The Old South and the American National Character* * (New York: G. Braziller, 1961).

Unfortunately there is no volume on the free Negro in the southern states comparable to Leon Litwack's *North of Slavery: The Negro in the Free States, 1790–1860* * (Chicago: Univ. Chicago, 1961). Limited studies which taken together give a reasonably complete picture include: Luther P. Jackson, *Free Negro Labor and Property Holding in Virginia, 1830–1860* (New York: Appleton-Century, 1942); James M. Wright, *The Free Negro in Maryland, 1634–1860* (New York: Columbia Univ., 1921);

John Hope Franklin, *The Free Negro in North Carolina, 1790–1860*
(Chapel Hill: Univ. North Carolina, 1943); England, "The Free Negro in
Ante-Bellum Tennessee," *Journal of Southern History,* vol. 9 (1943);
Fitchett, "The Traditions of the Free Negro in Charleston, South Caro-
lina," *Journal of Negro History,* vol. 25 (1940) and "The Origin and
Growth of the Free Negro Population of Charleston, South Carolina,"
ibid., vol. 26 (1941); Russell, "Colored Freemen as Slave Owners in Vir-
gina," *ibid.,* vol. 1 (1916); Sydnor, "The Free Negro in Mississippi Before
the Civil War," *American Historical Review,* vol. 32 (1926–27); Eaton,
"Slave Hiring in the Upper South: A Step Toward Freedom," *Mississippi
Valley Historical Review,* vol. 46 (1959–60).

Many volumes listed at the end of Chapter V have material relevant to the slave society and classes. In addition, the following are worth
mentioning here: James Hugo Johnston, *Race Relations in Virginia &
Miscegenation in the South, 1776–1860* (Amherst: Univ. Mass., 1970);
Hunter, "Slave Society on the Southern Plantation," *Journal of Negro
History,* vol. 7 (1922); Moore, "Slave Law and the Social Structure," *ibid.,*
vol. 26 (1941). Benjamin Quarles, *The Negro in the American
Revolution* * (Chapel Hill: Univ. North Carolina, 1961) and *The Negro
in the Civil War* (Boston: Little, Brown, 1953) present considerable material on race relations in time of war. The only full length study of urban
slavery is Richard C. Wade's excellent *Slavery in the Cities: The South,
1820–1860* (New York: Oxford, 1964).

Any study of southern agriculture must begin with Lewis C.
Gray's classic work, *History of Agriculture in the Southern United States
to 1860,* 2 vols. (Washington: Carnegie Institution, 1933). A general study
with much information on the South is Paul W. Gates, *The Farmers'
Age: Agriculture, 1815–1860* (New York: Holt, Rinehart & Winston,
1960). More limited studies of value are: J. C. Robert, *The Tobacco
Kingdom* (Durham: Duke Univ., 1938); James F. Hopkins, *A History of
the Hemp Industry in Kentucky* (Lexington: Univ. Kentucky, 1951);
James C. Bonner, *A History of Georgia Agriculture, 1732–1860* (Athens,
Ga.: Univ. Georgia, 1964); J. Carlyle Sitterson, *Sugar Country: The Cane
Sugar Industry in the South, 1753–1950* (Lexington: Univ. Kentucky,
1953); Avery O. Craven, *Soil Exhaustion as a Factor in the Agricultural
History of Virginia and Maryland, 1606–1860* (Urbana: Univ. Illinois,
1926); John H. Moore, *Agriculture in Ante-Bellum Mississippi,
1850–1860* (New York: Bookman Associates, 1958); Cornelius O. Cathey,
Agricultural Developments in North Carolina, 1783–1860 (Chapel Hill:
Univ. North Carolina, 1956). F. P. Gaines, *The Southern Plantation: A
Study in the Development and the Accuracy of a Tradition* (New York:
Columbia Univ., 1924) is still worthwhile reading.

* Available in paperback.

CHAPTER V

HUMAN SLAVERY

For over two hundred years the vast majority of black men living in the United States were enslaved. While the Thirteenth Amendment freed them from bondage, Negroes remained second-class citizens for another one hundred years. The demands for racial equality which reached crescendo proportions in the 1960s grew out of three centuries of overt and covert attempts by whites to control blacks and their activities. Civil rights disorders have stimulated renewed research into the institution of slavery, and numerous books on the subject have recently been published. Ulrich B. Phillips's classic study on *American Negro Slavery* (1918), while based upon manuscript sources, was far too sympathetic to the institution, and in recent years scholars have considerably revised many of Phillips's interpretations. Kenneth M. Stampp's volume on *The Peculiar Institution* (1956) reflected a white liberal's approach to the subject before the current unrest was fully underway. Stampp was antagonistic toward Phillips's pro-southern assumptions, and he criticized the immoral institution at every turn. Other writers have undertaken studies comparing and contrasting slavery in the United States with the institution in the Caribbean, Brazil, and elsewhere, in attempts to shed new light on an old but relevant subject. Slavery as a problem in Western culture has been the subject of another work. These writers have raised new questions, advanced new theories, and presented new insights into an institution which, while peculiar to the antebellum South, directly affected all of American society. Its residual effects are still being felt, and will undoubtedly influence American history for many years to come.

91

The Institution Evolves

Near the end of the fifteenth century Portuguese sailors explored the sub-Saharan coast of western Africa, rounded the Cape of Good Hope, and thus gave their nation claim to exclusive rights to the whole African continent. Two papal bulls issued in 1493 confirmed the claims. By that date Portugal had already built forts on the African coast as centers of national influence and as depots from which black slaves could be shipped. Most of the earliest slaves deported from Africa were sent to Lisbon for resale, and early in the sixteenth century a group of Genoese merchants formed a syndicate to buy slaves from the markets in the Portuguese capital. By the middle of the sixteenth century, Portugal's control of the African trade was being challenged by other nations, including France, England, and the Netherlands, and to a lesser extent by Sweden, Denmark, and Prussia.

The slave trade flourished from the beginning, millions of Africans being transported to all points of the globe. Before 1865 some fifteen million black men had been sent as slaves to the Western Hemisphere, a forced migration that was larger and ultimately more influential than any other such movement in the world's history. Despite losses and dangers, profits were so great that even royalty could not resist the temptation to make quick money. In 1562 Captain John Hawkins of England, who later played an important role in the defeat of the Spanish Armada, made a private voyage to Guinea, acquiring three hundred Negroes "partly by the sword and partly by other means." Hawkins exchanged his cargo in Hispaniola for hides, sugar, ginger, and "some quantitie of pearles." When Queen Elizabeth I heard of Hawkins's slaving venture, she expressed detestation and believed that it "would call down vengeance from heaven" upon the participants. But when Hawkins showed the Queen his profit sheet, she forgave him his unauthorized voyage and became a shareholder in his second effort.

In the seventeenth century English and Dutch traders became the main carriers of slaves to the North American mainland and the islands of the West Indies, although the number of slaves carried to those regions remained comparatively small for many years. As late as 1673 only 9,504 slaves lived on Barbados, the largest island in the Caribbean to use slave labor in the developing sugar economy. The number of slaves on the mainland remained fairly small until the cotton gin was invented. The eighteenth century witnessed a rapid increase of slavery in the Caribbean Islands as the sugar economy began to boom, and by the end of that century the expanding cotton economy on the mainland was demanding a larger labor force.

The African slave trade was legally closed in 1808 in the United States as the result of a compromise at the Constitutional Convention of 1787, although the South's fast growing cotton culture at that very moment needed more laborers than ever before. Smuggling occurred sporadically until the time of the Civil War, although natural increase was a much more important factor in the rising black population. Slightly less than one million slaves lived in the United States in 1808, and they produced the nearly four million black persons present in the country on the eve of the Civil War.

When the upper South came to have a surplus of laborers and the lower South expanded its cotton lands to the Southwest, a lively domestic slave trade came into being. As tobacco lands wore out, surplus slaves in Virginia were shipped to the lower South. In the absence of "fresh" slaves when the foreign supply ended, cotton planters encouraged the domestic trade in their eagerness to acquire more laborers for the growing cotton culture. Slave markets were established in such towns as Alexandria, Richmond, Charleston, Mobile, New Orleans, Natchez, and Memphis. Virginia became the leading exporter of slaves, almost 300,000 leaving the state between 1830 and 1860. Slave traders ranged from itinerants who visited the back counties of the upper South to large-scale entrepreneurs operating giant commercial ventures. Professional slave traders were responsible for most surplus slaves in the upper South being sold to the areas in need of unskilled labor. Armfield and Franklin Company was the largest and most successful slave trading company in Virginia, annually sending over 1,000 slaves to its depot near Natchez. Boston, Dickens, and Company, the largest slave trading company in Memphis on the eve of the Civil War, had branches in Lexington, Kentucky; St. Louis, Missouri; and Vicksburg, Mississippi. Mirabou Lamar of Georgia, Lewis Robards of Kentucky, Isaac Franklin of Natchez and New Orleans, and Nathan B. Forrest, later a famous Confederate cavalry general, were among the more successful traders. Franklin and Forrest made fortunes in excess of $500,000 each by trading in slaves. Slave trading companies sent buyers into Virginia, Maryland, and Kentucky to purchase surplus slaves. These buyers often dealt with "commission agents" or "auctioneers," who sold slaves for planters at a commission of 2½ percent. Sometimes these agents privately bought slaves for speculation and resale. Not infrequently slave traders did both.

Most often gangs of slaves were herded overland in coffles, chained together to prevent runaways. Sometimes slaves were delivered to New Orleans and similar southern ports via the ocean, transported by coastwise vessels. Armfield and Franklin owned three ocean-going vessels to transport their human merchandise, and during the trading season each regularly made the round trip from Alexandria, Virginia, to New Orleans twice each month. The risk involved in shipping slaves via the water was demonstrated in 1841, when slaves seized control of a ship named the *Creole.* They sailed to Nassau, where British authorities freed the blacks, causing an international incident. A significant number of slaves were shipped southward on boats or rafts down the Ohio and Mississippi rivers. ("Sold down the river" is an expression originating in connection with this interstate slave trade.) A trader could make from $150 to $300 gross by buying in Virginia and selling in Louisiana. The cost of transportation reduced the net profit to something less than that, but slave trading was nevertheless a profitable business, and numerous southerners engaged in it.

However, despite the widespread misconceptions spread abroad by abolitionists and in recent years by pulp novels such as *Mandingo,* slave breeding for short-range profits was not deliberately practiced by southerners in the upper South. Their critics have charged that when they came to realize the profits inherent in selling slaves to the cotton regions, tobacco growers in the upper South consciously turned to commercial breeding and rearing of slaves. Comparative statistics indicate that the birth rate among slaves was about the same as whites, and there is little evidence to support the charge that southerners encouraged mating among slaves so that their children could be sold at a profit. On the other hand, a slave woman's known or assumed fecundity influenced her market value. Advertisements commonly used the term "good breeders" when referring to women for sale. The prospect of an owner increasing the value of his slave property through natural increase was a pleasant one, but most owners hoped to keep the slaves as workers for their own lands. Nevertheless, some planters who encouraged the natural increase of their slaves were often forced to sell part of their "capital," and these actions seemed to verify the misconception that commercial slave breeding was a common practice.

Slave auctions were held on the lawns of county courthouses (often when the county court was in session), in dealers' auction rooms, and occasionally in hotel lobbies. Interested buyers inspected the slaves' teeth, arms, fingers, legs, and backs for disease or damage, a practice which degraded the slaves to the position of cattle or horses. The inhumanity of the slave trade was often pointed up when slave women implored their new masters to purchase their small children, usually to no avail. Journals and diaries of those engaged in or observing the sale of slaves poignantly recall such incidents.

Slaves were sold when an estate was settled after the death of a master, or when mortgages on slave property were foreclosed, often resulting in the division of slave families. On occasion a planter was forced to sell some of his slaves to satisfy his debts, and extant diaries relate the soul-searching and grief sometimes accompanying such a decision. Not infrequently owners stipulated in their wills that their slaves should be sold only as families, and others specified that their slaves be sold only to "good" masters. These instructions were not always obeyed.

Prices for slaves fluctuated moderately with supply and demand, which in turn were related to the price of staple crops, especially cotton. Yet at the same time the value of slaves generally rose from 1800 to 1860. In the former year, a prime field hand cost about $400, while cotton was selling for 36 cents a pound. On the eve of the Civil War, with cotton selling for 11½ cents a pound, a choice field worker was valued at approximately $1,500. With cotton prices off by two-thirds, why were slaves worth nearly four times as much after sixty years? Part of the explanation lies in the fact that a slave in 1860 could produce more cotton than one in 1800, but more important was the intense speculation in Negroes in the 1850s. Slaves were property and many men were convinced that it was better to invest their money in slaves than in real estate or businesses. The artificial prices slaves were bringing were not unlike the inflated prices of stocks and bonds in a time of feverish speculation. Furthermore, the events of the antebellum years revealed the growing belief that slave ownership was related to social distinction, and demands for slaves under such circumstances inflated their value.

In view of the large amount of capital invested in slaves, how efficient was the slave as a laborer? Contemporary travelers from the North and Europe generally agreed that slaves did about one-third to one-half the labor of a northern worker. The slave system encouraged an unhurried pace among the blacks, and if left alone, the majority of the slaves worked as little as possible. On the other hand, some planters used various incentives to get more work out of their slaves and in some cases these methods were successful. Promises of days free of work, occasional shorter hours, sweets, small amounts of liquor, and similar bribes were used to encourage field hands to work, especially during the harvesting season. Plantation records indicating the amount of cotton picked reveal that on occasion slaves worked very hard and accomplished much. During harvesting time, the average slave normally picked about 150 pounds of cotton a day throughout the antebellum period. Records of slaves picking over 500 pounds of cotton in a single day indicate the influence not only of rewards, but in all probability the development of a sense of pride of accomplishment, a feeling not usually present in the slaves. Obviously the efficiency of slaves varied from plantation to plantation and from slave to slave. It is surely correct to assume that any given slave was more or less efficient from day to day depending upon a host of constantly changing factors.

By the same token, the profitability of slavery as a business enterprise varied from time to time and on different plantations. Many intangible factors must be considered when discussing the question of slavery and profits, and historians have spent much time trying to sift these fac-

tors and arrive at satisfactory conclusions. Earlier writers, including Ulrich B. Phillips, Charles S. Sydnor, and Charles S. Davis, believed that
slavery was an uneconomical system of labor and that only those planters
who owned especially fertile land, who had good transportation facilities
available, and who had the ability to manage their farming operations
well were able to make a profit using slave labor. Phillips also concluded
that slavery as an economic system—as well as a business enterprise—was
unprofitable to the South.

Recent writers have challenged this view of plantation slavery.
Lewis C. Gray's research revealed that slave labor was fairly efficient on
carefully managed plantations. Gray argued that inducements and punishments probably resulted in more productive work by slaves than was
done by the free Negro laborer in the modern South. He also believed
that slavery had the advantage over free labor because it provided a stable supply of workers. Gray further contended that slave labor had an
"irresistible ability to displace free labor" on rich lands which had easy
access to markets, especially if that labor was under competent management. However, Gray hedged all of his conclusions by writing only about
"well-managed" plantations. A question naturally arises concerning the
number of such plantations in the antebellum South and also concerning
the margin of profit on those plantations which were not so well managed.

Alfred H. Conrad and John R. Meyer conducted a study comparing the earnings of slaves with dividends made from New England cotton
mills, railroads, and municipal bonds. After studying original investments, life expectancies, and the cost of clothing, food, medical care,
taxes, and the supervision of the slaves, these economists concluded that
slave labor engaged in raising cotton was responsible for 4.5 to 8 percent
earnings on average lands in the South. For those planters who earned
money by the sale of slaves, returns between 7 and 8 percent were common. Since municipal bonds paid returns of about 5 percent, railroads
about 7 or 8 percent, and cotton mill dividends fluctuated between 5.75
and 16.76 percent, Conrad and Meyer drew the conclusion that southern
slavery "was apparently about as remunerative as alternative employ-
ments to which slave capital might have been put." They also believed
that slavery did not hamper economic growth in the South. Thomas P.
Govan has carefully scrutinized ledgers and account books of prewar
planters, and he has concluded that slavery was a highly profitable business. Whereas other investigators who viewed planters' books assumed
the planters were losing money, Govan interpreted the data otherwise.
He believed that when figuring a planter's profit, the following items,
usually omitted, should be considered: services rendered by household
slaves, food and other provisions grown on the plantations and used by
the owner, and the increase in the value of land and slaves. Furthermore,

he said that interest on investment was a profit item, rather than an item of expense, as the planter erroneously supposed. With these adjustments, Govan saw slavery as profitable.

The importance of the question of profitability is related to slavery's presence on the political scene. Most exponents of the profitability thesis believe that slaveholders remained solvent only because the cotton culture expanded into the Southwest. Southeastern lands of low or declining productivity were abandoned for the richer soils in the Southwest, and if the slave system had remained tied to the former, it may have suffered a natural demise. Charles W. Ramsdell has argued that slavery reached its natural limits by 1860. The kinds of soils suited for cotton and slave labor gradually ran out beyond eastern and central Texas, and when it was realized that the crop was uneconomical in that region, it would not have expanded farther westward. If Ramsdell was correct, and there is much to be said for his thesis, the question of the expansion of slavery was more closely related to the political scene than to economic conditions. If slavery was not to be a profitable labor system in the West, the entire argument over the expansion of slavery was largely a sham issue. Southerners and northerners were arguing—and ultimately fighting—over an issue that was not relevant. It would be ironic indeed if the issue at stake had already been settled by geography, and if the tragedy of the Civil War came partly because political attitudes of leaders from two sections of the nation had polarized.

If the national leaders had recognized that slavery in the western territories was not a vital issue, and if indeed slavery would not have expanded beyond the 100th meridian, would the institution have died of its own accord in the older southern states? Historians who have argued that slavery was unprofitable would be inclined to answer YES. But even if the system was inefficient, even if it was useful to some planters and not to others, even if it was unprofitable during difficult times and profitable in good times, the likelihood exists that without conflict, slavery would probably have existed in the South for years to come. Slavery as an institution had become a part of the "southern way of life." After the 1830s it came to be defended as all other aspects of southern society and culture came to be defended. It had become intertwined into the economy in such a way that even if it were conclusively proved to be unprofitable, it would have remained for decades. The idea of slavery became more important than the institution. That is, southerners were committed to slavery as much as they were committed to cotton, to a leisurely pace, to a regional allegiance, and to the concept of separateness which developed ever so rapidly in the antebellum period. As Ulrich B. Phillips succinctly stated, "Plantation slavery . . . in the large . . . was less a business than a life." Slavery was in the South to stay, to be torn from the region's breast only by civil conflict.

The Institution in Practice

How were slaves treated in the antebellum South? Since they were valuable property, did their owners see that they were well-housed, well-fed, and well-clothed, or did the slaveholders care little about the welfare of their slaves? Did the planters attend to sick slaves, much the way owners of valuable horses today protect their investments by keeping their animals in good health, or were the slaveholders negligent and unresponsive to slaves desiring medical attention? Did their overseers remember the slaves' value and resist harsh punishment of slovenly slaves, or were whippings and brutality the rule rather than the exception? Did slaves revolt because of harsh treatment? These are questions which historians have long attempted to answer, and the events of the 1950s and 1960s stimulated renewed interest in the care and treatment of slaves.

Records concerning the physical care of slaves are fragmentary and contradictory. Researchers have found support for almost any statement they might make in regard to this subject. Some planters were very much interested in keeping their slaves happy by providing them with reasonably adequate shelter, food, and clothing, while others gave no consideration to the physical or emotional needs of their slaves. Wise planters recognized that if they did not treat slaves who were sick, an investment of upwards of $2,000 might be lost. Others were responsible for slaves' deaths by their casual actions and attitudes. It is not unlikely that on occasion a planter gave considerable attention to his slaves, and that at other times that same planter may have neglected their welfare in the face of other pressing responsibilities. Some overseers believed that punishment and fear best spurred slaves to work hard, while others preferred to use promises of sweets and other inducements to encourage productive slaves. Overseers were not always consistent in their approach to the slaves. Responding to pressures to harvest a cotton crop, they were often harder on slaves in the fall than when the crop was being planted. Generalities concerning the treatment of slaves must be made with care.

In most instances, by any standard of comparison, shelter for the mass of antebellum slaves was inadequate. Slave quarters usually consisted of small, one-room log huts, each with a large fireplace. Sometimes these cabins had attics, and sometimes slaves were permitted to add another small room if they so desired. Clay chinks were used between the logs to form reasonably solid walls, but openings for doors and windows were seldom closed off. Floors were invariably dirt or clay. A slave family occupied each cabin, which served primarily for sleeping and eating.

Although some plantations established modified cafeteria-type feeding arrangements, most slaves ate their meals in their own cabins. Food for slaves consisted of cornmeal, molasses, and hog meat, the main staples on the planters' table. Average rations per slave each week amounted to about 3½ pounds of pork, a peck of meal, and a pint of molasses. While not an abundance of food, this quantity was apparently generally enough. Corn grew easily in most of the South because of the warm climate, and grinding it into meal was a simple process. Also hogs thrived on corn, thus making meat available for the planter and the slave. Pork was salted or smoked, which preserved it for future use, and one of the most important buildings on any plantation or farm in the South was the "smokehouse" where the pork was smoked and stored. Without refrigeration beef was not a practical meat for southerners, and neither whites nor blacks ate much beef before the Civil War. The greatest shortcoming of the slaves' food was its lack of balance. Some slaves tended their own small garden plots in the spring, and their monotonous diet was supplemented for a time by green vegetables and sweet potatoes, but for many months of the year, slaves had nothing more than a greasy, starchy diet of fat pork and cornbread.

The mild climate of the South did not demand that slaves have heavy clothes, and thus their clothing was reasonably adequate. They usually received two outfits per year, one for winter and one for summer use. Most slave clothing was made of linsey-woolsey, a rude, sacklike material similar to present-day gunny bags. An unintentional uniformity in clothes developed as planters came to use this inexpensive material for slave clothing. One pair of shoes per year was the average for each slave, and when that pair wore out, the slaves went barefoot for the remainder of the year. House servants sometimes acquired the cast-off clothings from the master's family, and brightly colored dresses and coats were highly coveted by them. Slave children often went naked for the first seven or eight years of their lives.

Medical books on plantations show that some planters gave medical attention to their slaves. The mistress of the plantation often had charge of the slaves' medical needs, although some plantations were large enough to warrant a full-time doctor, much like great animal farms today hire resident veterinarians. Sickness was fairly prevalent among slaves. Some diseases struck blacks and whites alike: yellow fever, cholera, typhoid, malaria, and hookworm. Diseases most common among the slaves were pneumonia, tetanus, dysentery, tooth trouble, and hernia. Slaves' diseases were related to their living conditions and their work; thus, when little regard was given to slaves who had to work in water, rain, and wind, it is not surprising that pneumonia was the most fatal of all diseases in the slave population. Slaves who worked with rusted tools often contracted tetanus, germs entering the body through wounds and causing dreaded and agonizing lockjaw. Hernia was a condition inherent in a la-

boring force that did much heavy work without the aid of modern machinery and equipment. Dental problems stemmed from improper diet
and lack of care for the teeth of the slaves, and many slave health problems probably stemmed indirectly from this inattention.

Slaves did not suffer greatly from pellagra, a dietary disease caused
by the lack of fresh vegetables. Turnip greens, mustard greens, and col-
lards, a wild variety of kale often called "poke salad," apparently gave the
slaves enough green food to stave off that particular disease. Nor did the
slaves have an abundance of tuberculosis. Working and living out of
doors and in the warm sunshine of the South, slaves and post-Civil War
rural Negroes were amazingly free of this consumptive disease. Very common among the black population in twentieth-century United States,
tuberculosis hit the Negro only after he began to migrate to the northern
cities. Incidents of tuberculars have been disproportionately high in the
city slums, and whatever else was hard about the life of the slave in the
rural South, at least he did not face the slum and its attendant evils. Contrary to popular belief, syphilis was not common within the slave population. While some plantations were plagued by it, most were completely
free. For the most part, syphilis did not seem to strike those plantations
where masters permitted and encouraged close family relationships
among slaves. The fact that most slaves lived and worked in small groups
also tended to control this social disease.

If some planters carefully nursed valuable slaves when they were
sick, far too many records reveal the negligence of other masters toward
their slaves' medical needs. If this is difficult to understand, perhaps it
helps to remember that it is difficult to understand why some twentieth-
century Americans invest thousands of dollars in new automobiles and
then promptly wreck them on the highway. In any event, Negroes' life
expectancies were several years shorter than whites', strengthening the argument that slaves were generally not properly cared for medically.

Plantation health records indicate that severe physical abuse of
slaves was not common, yet letters, newspaper reports, and journal accounts speak of punishments with enough regularity to attest that lazy or
recalcitrant slaves often felt the lash of a rawhide or blacksnake whip.
Whippings usually resulted from a slave not doing his job, and they were
often used by the planter or overseer on one slave as an example to others to spur them to work hard. Occasionally gross brutality occurred, and
reports of slaves dying as the result of sadistic punishment are frequent
enough that not all of them may be discounted. Newspaper advertisements telling of a slave sale or describing a runaway often mentioned a
branding mark upon a slave. While branding was not widespread, it was
extensive enough to verify that many owners considered their slaves as
animals, not hesitating to brand their property with a hot iron. Sometimes ears were cropped as another means of identification.

The overseer was the individual most responsible for punishment of the slaves. Discipline had to be maintained if the overseer was to make the labor force productive, and thus assure the production of a large cotton crop, his main responsibility. Overseers were used by those planters who had upwards of thirty slaves working in the fields. They were poorly paid, usually around $500 per year, although food and shelter were also furnished. If the overseer did not produce an adequate cotton crop, he was not retained the following year, and this resulted in a considerable turnover in the position on most plantations. Furthermore, he held no social position whatsoever, and men of ability avoided such jobs if possible. The overseer had a most difficult position. If he drove the slaves too hard, they rebelled or ran away, causing considerable anxiety and financial loss to the planter. If he did not drive the slaves, they neglected their work, with a consequent decline in productivity. Most overseers erred on the side of too many whippings rather than too few.

How did the slave react to his lowly station in life? Did he passively accept his environment, or did he strike back at the system which oppressed him? Earlier historians who viewed slavery with a certain amount of sympathy stressed the paternalistic attitude expressed by the master toward the slave. If they did not contend that the slave system itself was all good, they implied that an institution which encouraged white men to look after and care for black men could not be all bad. Ulrich B. Phillips and his students made much of the often close contacts between the master and slave. They accepted at face value slave statements appreciating that "massa" took care of them, and that the slaves returned love for this protective care. They asserted that slaves were happy and that revolts seldom happened because of the benign, paternalistic nature of slavery and the childlike characteristics innate in Negroes. A recent writer, Stanley Elkins, has acknowledged that this paternalism existed, but in contrast to the Phillips School, he criticized its effects. Elkins believed that this paternalism was responsible for the happy-go-lucky "Sambo" characteristics in the black man's personality, that the slave was docile because he was beaten down, degraded, and oppressed. Although Elkins carried this concept too far by comparing slavery with World War II concentration camps and their debilitating effects on prisoners, he nevertheless made penetrating observations about the slave system and its effects upon both blacks and whites. He certainly underscored the horrible and dehumanizing quality of slavery in the United States.

By contrast, Kenneth M. Stampp has emphasized the slaves' rebelliousness. Stressing the day-to-day resistance of slaves, he has written in detail about runaways, slave "strikes," work slowdowns, slaves hiding for minutes or hours from a planter or overseer, and deliberate accidents which temporarily or permanently impaired the working ability of a slave. Assuming that Negroes are "only white men with black skins, nothing more, nothing less," Stampp wrote from a point of view that saw the slave tugging at the reins of slavery, yearning to be free, and attempting to free himself as soon as possible. Stampp despised the system of slavery and he assumed that all in bondage also must have despised it. In view of the diversity of the slave system and the millions of persons associated with it, it is surely safe to say that slavery was a social system in which whites and blacks lived in both harmony and antagonism. If some blacks were provoked by the system, others were resigned to it. If not all slaves developed "Sambo" personalities, many did. And there is firm evidence that numerous slaves actually loved their masters, despite the fact that many Americans today find this totally impossible to believe.

Herbert Aptheker, who has written extensively on the subject of slave insurrections, interpreted his research in the framework of his Communist ideology and stated that the slaves were constantly in revolt—like all oppressed classes of peoples. In his *American Negro Slave Revolts* (1943), Aptheker chronicled and analyzed some 250 revolts. Despite Aptheker's attempts to picture the slaves in virtually constant revolution, this is an amazingly low average of about one per year throughout the history of American Negro slavery. And many of these plots never happened, while others were merely small local disturbances of questionable importance. Aptheker admitted that he included insignificant revolts which never matured, and some of the revolts he wrote about were no more than the product of overly imaginative whites who feared the worst. When all such incidents are discounted, it becomes clear that no widespread slave insurrection or rebellion was ever imminent in the United States. Careful research has turned up a mere three uprisings of any significant size, only two of which may be called revolts, and some may question whether even they deserve that name.

In 1800 a slave blacksmith named Gabriel Prosser laid plans to destroy the city of Richmond, Virginia. The plot was discovered before it was carried out, but it frightened the whites of the area, and it led to the formation of a small standing army in Richmond and a move to colonize free Negroes on the western frontier. In Charleston, South Carolina, in the summer of 1822 the Denmark Vesey plot was uncovered. Born in Africa, Vesey was a former slave who had purchased his freedom after winning a $1,500 lottery. This free Negro artisan was accused of organizing a formidable conspiracy among slaves in the area. When one of the slaves revealed the plot to a white man, the people of Charleston were overcome by fear. Vesey and thirty-four followers were hanged, while thirty-five other Negroes were deported. The Vesey incident may have been nothing more than the figment of the imagination of the white people of Charleston, for its existence has not been clearly substantiated. It revealed the fear and panic among whites when rumors of a slave revolt reached them, and it is a reminder that even when slaves were not on the verge of revolt, many whites assumed they always were. This hysteria on the part of whites undermines southerners' statements that Negroes generally loved white folks and that whites in turn treated blacks kindly.

The most important slave revolt in United States history occurred in August 1831 in Southampton County, Virginia. Nat Turner, a fanatical slave preacher who came to control a large number of blacks in that area, conceived and attempted to execute a plot to lead all slaves in a revolt for their freedom. Before the revolt was suppressed, more than sixty whites were killed, as well as many Negroes. While Turner's revolt reached impressive proportions by comparison with others in the United States, fewer than one hundred slaves were actually involved. Compared with the great slave revolts in Brazil at about the same time, involving literally thousands of blacks over a period of several decades, Turner's activities were mild indeed. And it should be pointed out that no major slave revolt occurred between 1832 and 1865, the very years when the slavery issue came to dominate the American political scene, when abolitionism was at its height, and when the accumulation of explosive events was leading the nation directly to a civil war.

Why were the slaves in the United States not prone to insurrection, when revolts in Brazil, Haiti, Jamaica, Cuba, and other countries were so prevalent? Antebellum southerners believed that the absence of revolts verified their contention that slavery in the South was not oppressive and that slaves were contented under it. Eugene Genovese has disagreed with these assumptions, and by contrasting slavery in the United States with Caribbean and Brazilian slavery, he has advanced four other reasons for the lack of a tradition of revolution among southern slaves. First, because of the trade routes, Africans imported to the United States came from Lower Guinea, which had peoples who were accustomed to servitude and domination. By contrast, Angolans and Congolese, who were difficult to control because of their military and cultural past, were shipped in large numbers to Brazil. Second, the United States halted the foreign slave trade in 1808, and the lack of large numbers of newly enslaved Africans militated against uprisings in the South. Slaves born in the United States were less inclined to violence in the absence of encouragement from rebellious fresh slaves. Cuba and Brazil continued to import slaves far into the nineteenth century, and disturbances in those countries were often led by these new arrivals. Third, the white men in Cuba and Brazil did not present a united front to the slaves, nor did they have governmental machinery adequate to cope with slave revolts. Under these conditions, runaway slaves who attempted to establish maroon colonies were more likely to be successful than in the United States where men and laws carefully controlled slaves' activities.

Fourth, a serious revolt presupposed the presence of leaders and an ideology. In Brazil and in the Caribbean, where great sugar plantations encouraged the use of masses of blacks under the control of a few whites, slaves retained much of their African culture and learned to look to leaders who, under proper conditions, nurtured resistance movements. In the United States, where most of the slaves lived and worked in comparatively small units, and where little opportunity existed to preserve the African culture, leaders of revolt did not arise, nor did an adequate ideology develop among southern slaves. Slaves in the United States engaged in strikes and in day-to-day resistance against the system of slavery, but a tradition of recalcitrance is not the same as revolution. The slaves no doubt had a dim awareness of oppression, but cumulative ideological growth did not develop. While most slaves were conditioned to a psychology of dependence because of white paternalism, some expressed opposition to the system of slavery, but this was usually nothing more than individual acts of violence. The fact that no revolutionary tradition evolved among the slaves largely explains why they did not rise en masse to shake off their chains when the abolitionist movement was in full swing. It probably also is the reason why the slaves did not rise up as a body against their masters when the Civil War was raging. Those slaves who rushed to the Union side did not do so in order to aid in defeating the South, but because they believed that northern white paternalism was somehow better than southern white paternalism. This lack of a revolutionary tradition among the blacks also explains why one hundred years passed after the demise of slavery before Negroes in the United States began to expound an ideology and voice collective resentment at the systems of segregation and proscription.

Antislavery Sentiment

Under the influence of the rational ideas of the Age of the Enlightenment, many Americans saw the paradox of slavery within the bounds of a democracy based upon equalitarian principles. Colonists both North and South had opposed slavery, and the establishment of the new nation saw a movement to make *all* men free. A group of Quakers organized the first antislavery society in 1775 in Pennsylvania. The chaos of the American Revolution forced the new society into inactivity, but it was revived in 1787 with Benjamin Franklin as its president. Other local societies were organized north of Virginia as the new nation experimented with a government under a new Constitution, but all of these were small and their methods were conservative. Yet the antislavery impulse was strong enough to bar slavery in the area north of the Ohio River by the famous Northwest Ordinance of 1787, and by 1804 all states north of the Mason-Dixon Line had abolished slavery. Although the new Constitution which went into effect in 1789 recognized slavery, a provision was made for Congress to abolish the slave trade after 1807, and the last victory of the early antislaveryites was the passage of such a law. Many Americans honestly believed that slavery would die of its own accord when the slave trade was halted, and antislavery agitation was not as strong in the early years of the nineteenth century as it had been during the revolutionary era.

A major stumbling block to freeing the slaves was in the mind of the southerner. If Negroes were freed, what was to become of them? Since white men generally agreed that black men were inferior, the thought of the latter mixing freely in society was repugnant. The majority of southerners who favored emancipation invariably linked that concept with deportation. Suggestions were made to colonize the Negroes in the American West, in various Caribbean islands, and in Africa. When the Virginia legislature petitioned Congress to eliminate slavery, Congress in 1817 chartered the American Colonization Society with the expressed task of removing Negroes to Africa. The society purchased a tract of land, which it called Liberia, on the western coast of Africa, and it initiated a campaign for private funds to assist its cause. The American Colonization Society was supported largely by slaveholders of Virginia, Maryland, and Kentucky. John Marshall and Henry Clay were presidents of the society, and it had the support of other national figures from the South, including Andrew Jackson. After a decade of private effort, the society requested a congressional appropriation to aid its cause, but its leaders were unsuccessful in obtaining federal assistance. By 1840 this private society had returned some thirteen thousand Negroes to Africa, but the high birthrate of slaves in America more than offset this figure, and the net number of slaves in America was not reduced by the society's efforts. A shortage of funds, a lack of interest on the part of slaves to return to the unknown continent, and the absence of united support from a significant number of people caused the American Colonization Society to fail.

The Deep South states had not been overly interested in colonizing the slaves. Their rapidly growing cotton culture demanded a large unskilled labor force, and the slave was a natural element in the economics of their region. By the time Andrew Jackson became President, the efforts to remove the slaves had been spent, and most people in the South were apathetic toward any emancipation or colonization plans. At this very time, abolitionist groups in the North began to be organized. A part of the greatest humanitarian reform impulse in the nation's history, these groups were few in number, but they were quite influential. Although antislavery sentiment had existed in both North and South for many years, the abolitionist crusade is usually dated from January 1, 1831, when William Lloyd Garrison published the first issue of the *Liberator*. This Boston newspaper was the mouthpiece of a man who wanted immediate, complete emancipation of slaves without payment to the owners. He made it clear that he did not wish to think, speak, or write with moderation on the subject of slavery. And he fully expected to have his voice heard and his newspaper read. When reminded that the Constitution approved of slavery, Garrison retorted that the Constitution was "a covenant with Death and an agreement with Hell." On one occasion he publicly burned a copy of the document.

Garrison's policy was to publicize the most repulsive aspects and exceptional incidents of Negro slavery. He attacked slaveholders and all who defended them as men-stealers, torturers, and traders in human flesh. He recognized no rights of the masters, acknowledged no color problem, tolerated no delay. But many people in the North did not agree with the extreme abolitionist statements made by Garrison and his followers. On one occasion Garrison was mobbed by a group of Boston businessmen because they believed him to be a public menace, and he had to hide in a jail to protect himself. A preacher named Elijah Lovejoy was killed by a mob in Illinois for expounding Garrison's fanatical views. Garrison's newspaper never had a large circulation, and his followers remained limited in number. Yet the humanitarian impulse of the times resulted in abolition societies popping up in all sections of the North. A society founded in 1833 in New York developed into one of the most significant of these groups. Important leaders of the New York society were wealthy businessmen Lewis and Arthur Tappan, who financed innumerable anti-slavery publications.

From this New York base a number of crusaders moved farther west, Ohio becoming the center for much abolitionism. A young minister named Theodore Weld quickly became an outstanding leader among the western group. Effectively tying together abolition and Christian doctrine, Weld and his "Holy Band" of seventy men who traveled in twos strived to arouse the conscience of the Midwest. They preached abolitionist doctrine on both sides of the Ohio River, convinced that the Ohio Valley was the place where they could be most effective. Weld's converts, including Beriah Green of Western Reserve College of Cleveland, James G. Birney, a former Kentucky slaveholder, and sisters Sarah and Angelina Grimké (the latter of whom Weld later married), were probably more effective than Garrison's group. The western group was much less extreme in its public statements, worked quietly for effective results, and apparently won more converts to abolitionism.

The fact that Weld and his followers went into slaveholding country to preach their doctrine revealed that they were willing to meet the issue on its own terms. A number of southerners—some influenced by Weld—joined in the crusade to abolish the peculiar institution. While southern liberals had been permitted to speak their views in a free climate of opinion at the turn of the century, the northern abolitionist crusade brought a strong protest of disapproval from many southerners, and southern liberals found themselves in a difficult position. James G. Birney tried to establish an antislavery newspaper *The Philanthropist* in his native state of Kentucky, but hostile demonstrations forced him to transfer his paper to Cincinnati. Other southerners voiced their opposition to slavery in the face of growing resentment against abolition. John Hampden Pleasants wrote a number of editorials dealing honestly with the slavery question in the Richmond (Va.) *Whig* before he was shot and killed in a duel in 1846 by a rival editor who had stamped him as an abolitionist. A more colorful southerner who espoused abolition with a vengeance was Kentuckian Cassius Marcellus Clay, distant relative of Henry Clay. Advocating gradual emancipation of slaves, Clay began publishing *The True American* in 1845 in Lexington, Kentucky, fully realizing that many Kentuckians opposed his beliefs. When he began his agitation, Clay fortified his printing office with cannons and rifles in the event of mob attack. Only a few months after his newspaper began, Clay's shop was attacked while he was sick, and the press was dismantled and shipped to Cincinnati.

While humanitarian motives were prominent in the minds of a large number of abolitionists in both North and South, the published documents of leaders of the movement reveal that many arguments against slavery revolved around economics. For example, Clay argued in his paper that slavery depressed land values and worked an economic hardship on the white skilled laborers of the South. He wrote, "We are *provincial,* an agricultural people, without division of labor and without capital, and must remain so while slavery lasts. Slavery is destructive of mechanical excellence. The free states build ships and steam cars for the nations of the world; the slave states import the handles for their axes." Clay anticipated many of the arguments of Hinton Rowan Helper, who in the 1850s laid most of the South's economic ills at the feet of the institution of slavery.

While the intensity of southern feeling and action for seeking a solution to Negro bondage varied with time and conditions, some southerners were always seeking to solve the problem from the era of the Revolution until the outbreak of the Civil War. Colonization or deportation were honest efforts on the part of men who ascribed to the inferiority and superiority of the different races. Southern liberals for various reasons, some of them surely stimulated by northern abolitionists, spoke out against the peculiar institution whenever they had occasion. But many southern liberals, as Clement Eaton has ably documented, were cowed into silence by the growing resentment on the part of those southerners who did not want to free the slaves. Freedom of thought as well as freedom of speech was sharply curtailed. Conservative southerners became increasingly vocal as time passed, especially as the northern abolitionists flooded the nation and the South with inflammatory propaganda not only against the institution of slavery but also against the South itself. These violent attacks from the outside stimulated a considerable reaction.

Proslavery Thought

While some southerners preferred to abolish slavery, many hesitated to make this suggestion or to advocate colonization because they had come to feel that it was a necessary economic evil. This attitude grew especially after Eli Whitney patented his cotton gin. Whereas heretofore numerous slaves had spent countless hours separating the seeds from the cotton, Whitney's gin greatly reduced the requirements for workers and time. The gin freed cotton to expand rapidly from the 1790s onward, and the South prospered greatly from the production of cotton.

In the early 1830s southerners began to argue that slavery was a positive good—rather than a necessary evil. This change in mentality resulted from several factors, some of which will be dealt with in the next chapter. Not the least of these influences was the raw propaganda of the abolitionists. Although a few southerners advocated the positive good theory before 1830, most historians date the inception of this concept from the so-called Virginia Debates in the early 1830s. After the Nat Turner insurrection, the Virginia legislature seriously and freely debated the question of whether that state should emancipate her slaves. Many arguments were given on each side of this great question, as men grappled with the fundamentals of the issue. The records of the debates reveal that these Virginians were genuinely trying to weigh the advantages and evils of the system. After a close vote, they decided that the slaves in the state should not be emancipated. Many were convinced by arguments that emancipation would be worse than slavery for the Negro, that slavery was really not too bad, and that in fact it was a pretty good way of life for the Negro and for the South.

At the same time the Virginia legislature was struggling with these grave issues, Thomas R. Dew, professor at the College of William and Mary, was philosophizing about the social structure of man's society, and shortly after the debates ended, he published a treatise in which he boldly repudiated antislavery views. His basic argument was that the inequality of man was fundamental to all social organizations. Three years later, Governor George McDuffie of South Carolina delivered his now famous message in which he contended that slavery was a blessing to both the white and black races. He argued that it was not a political evil but "the cornerstone of our republican edifice." McDuffie's speech is ordinarily considered the beginning of the South's staunch defense of its institution. The final outcome was a swing to the "positive good" theory.

A large body of proslavery literature appeared in the years following 1835. A heavy tome published in 1852 entitled *The Pro-Slavery Argu-*

ment drew together most of the southern views which had been expressed in speech, pamphlet, sermon, tract, and book in the twenty years prior to that date. Although southerners themselves often did not approach the subject in a systematic or logical way, the proslavery argument had a certain organization to it, despite its verbosity and repetition.

One argument held that slavery was good for the black man. Slavery was justified on the grounds that it was more humane than the free labor system of the North and Europe. Southerners pointed out that the free white laborers in the factories of the North endured worse working conditions than did the enslaved Negro. They recalled the unsanitary living conditions of the poor workers in New York City, and argued that the slaves were better clad, fed, and cared for than such workers. Slave children worked under better conditions than did the children in the northern and English factories, too. Much was made of the great bonds of love between masters and their slaves. Owners of northern factories were not interested in the welfare of their workers, but slaveowners watched over their slaves, giving them the benefit of paternalistic security. Furthermore, the slaves were better off in the South than in Africa. Negroes who were civilized and Christianized were assuredly advanced over the savage idolators on the "dark continent." Readers were reminded that some masters hired clergymen to minister to the black population on the plantations. The conclusion was that the black man was improved by his servitude. Southerners decided that their system of labor was the best organized, most humane, and most efficient ever known to the civilizations of the world.

The slave system was good not only for the Negro, but also for southern society. A well-ordered society gave no occasion for the rise of radical movements, and the society in the South was nearly perfect in this respect, it was argued. As Thomas R. Dew wrote, "It is the order of nature and of God that the being of superior faculties and knowledge and therefore of superior power control and dispose of those who are inferior." Such society was peaceful and calm with none of the poverty, insecurity, discord, and prostitution of a free society. Moreover, slave labor was good for the United States, since it was responsible for the nation becoming a commercial nation. Without slave labor, cotton would never have been grown in this country for export. As one writer put it: "Slavery is not a national evil; on the contrary, it is a national benefit. The agricultural wealth of the country is found in those states owning slaves." But not only was slavery good for the nation, it was also good for the world. "Blot out Negro slavery, and you arrest the trade of the world." "Destroy the production of cotton in the South and you will almost ruin Europe and America." From these arguments, southerners came to believe that slavery was good for the black man, the white man, the South, the nation, and the world.

To support their case, southerners appealed to the Constitution, which recognized slavery. As one writer stated: "We maintain that the slavery of the black race on this continent is the price America has paid for her liberty, civil and religious; and humanly speaking, these blessings would have been unattainable without her aid." When they were reminded of the ideology expressed in the Declaration of Independence, they either denied Jefferson's views or distorted them into conformity with southern thought. While southerners on the one hand criticized the concept of natural law, on the other hand they argued that slavery was in accord with the laws of nature. One writer pointed out that white and red ants made slaves of black ants, and for each Negro in slavery in the South there were 100,000 black ants in slavery; therefore, slavery was not incompatible with the economy of nature.

Numerous writers stressed that the Negro was ethnologically inferior to the white man, and the widespread appeal to ethnology indicated the southerners' belief that their case was strongly supported by that science. Some writers declared that the Negro was organically constituted to be an agricultural laborer in tropical climates, since they inaccurately believed that black skin better endured the rays of the sun. Others believed that the Negro had been provided with a special eye to enable him to withstand the sun's bright rays; surely God meant the black man to work as a slave in the hot fields. Southerners used these arguments to put their position on a scientific basis. A few writers argued the Negro was not just an inferior human being, but that he was somehow subhuman. This clever syllogism circulated in the South:

A. Man is made in the image of God.
B. God, as everybody knows, is not a Negro.
C. Therefore, the Negro is not a man.

Countless books and articles were written defending slavery from a historical point of view. Since slavery existed in ancient civilizations and probably existed since the beginning of time, why should northern abolitionists take it upon themselves to end an institution which had been a part of history since the beginning of the world? George Fitzhugh defended the slave regime not because it was a blessing or a necessary evil, but because it represented the normal historical organization of society. He believed that free society had been a failure, and that a slave society was its logical successor and would not fail.

In a region where orthodox Protestantism was strong, slavery was of course said to be in accord with the Bible. The appeal to the biblical record for proslavery arguments came very early, and as the issue was joined literature continuing the argument poured from the presses. Before the contest was over, the Bible was used more than any other basis for the defense. As early as 1826 Thomas Cooper of the College of the

City of Charleston pointed out that the Bible nowhere specifically forbade slavery. As the debate developed the Holy Scriptures were exhaus-
tively researched, and a great variety of elaborate and systematic proslavery statements were advanced. While not one verse in the Bible
specifically condemned slavery, countless verses sanctioned slavery indirectly. The patriarchs, the Mosaic law, and the teachings of Christ and
his apostles all illuminated the slave system of the South in a new way
when viewed by the proslavery advocates. Job, that steadfast Old Testament servant of God, numbered slaves among his household, and Abraham, the father of God's chosen people, had bond servants, and God criticized neither. Furthermore, provision was made for the bringing in,
buying, inheriting, and governing of slaves in the Promised Land of the
Israelites. One of the Ten Commandments reads: "Thou shalt not covet
thy neighbor's wife, nor his manservant, nor his maidservant, nor his ox
nor his ass, nor anything that *is* thy neighbor's." (Exodus 20:17) When
the word "servant" was interpreted "slave" by southerners, they had a
field day with their arguments. Jesus never condemned slavery in all of
the New Testament, nor does slaveholding appear in any catalogue of
sins in the New Testament. The letters of Peter and Paul do not charge
the sin of slaveholding to anyone. In fact, Paul's letter to Philemon directly involved the ownership of a slave, and the owner is not censored.
The Bible seemed almost a handbook for the relation of slaves to their
masters when preachers exhorted their slave congregations with such
texts as: "Servants, obey your masters"; and "Well done, thou good and
faithful servant." A syllogism based on scripture ran:

A. Whatever God has sanctioned among any people cannot itself be
   a sin.
B. God did expressly sanction slavery among the Hebrews.
C. Therefore, slavery cannot be in and of itself sin.

The defense of slavery became interwoven into the political, economic, social, and intellectual life of the South to such an extent that it
became a part of southern civilization, and slavery came to be justified
and defended along with the right to life, liberty, and the pursuit of hap-
piness. But the South was weak in its defense. The South's comparison of
slaves with northern laborers overlooked the fact that the latter had a
chance to rise on the economic and social ladder, whereas the slaves did
not. Northern laborers owned the *freedom* to improve economically,
whatever their present state of working conditions may have been. The
South was not on firm ground when it argued that slavery was justifiable
for economic reasons. Cotton was a part of the commercial activity of the
nation and the world, but it was not KING. The prosperity of the
United States and Europe resulted from diversified economic activity of

which cotton was only a small part. Huge piles of white cotton during the harvest season in the South misled the southerner as to the national and worldwide importance of the fleecy staple.

The South's appeal to the Constitution was acceptable until others pointed out that the Constitution needed amending; then southern arguments immediately lost their force. Modern anthropology has found that no race is innately inferior or superior to the others. Despite biblical appeals, slavery was not in accord with the spirit of Christianity. Clement Eaton summed up modern scholars' reactions to the proslavery defense when he wrote: "The argument that Southerners evolved to justify the institution of slavery is one of the great rationalizations that the human mind has conceived."

Suggestions for Further Reading

Ulrich B. Phillips, *American Negro Slavery* (New York: D. Appleton, 1918) is the proper point of departure for additional reading on the subject of human slavery. Phillips's overly sympathetic view of the institution is corrected by Kenneth M. Stampp, *The Peculiar Institution: Slavery in the Ante-Bellum South* * (New York: Knopf, 1956). Individual studies of slavery in specific states include: James C. Ballagh, *A History of Slavery in Virginia* (Baltimore: Johns Hopkins, 1902); Rosser H. Taylor, *Slaveholding in North Carolina* (Chapel Hill: Univ. North Carolina, 1926); Charles S. Sydnor, *Slavery in Mississippi* * (New York: Appleton-Century, 1933); Ralph B. Flanders, *Plantation Slavery in Georgia* (Chapel Hill: Univ. North Carolina, 1933); O. W. Taylor, *Negro Slavery in Arkansas* (Durham: Duke Univ., 1958); J. Winston Coleman, *Slavery Times in Kentucky* (Chapel Hill: Univ. North Carolina, 1940); Harrison A. Trexler, *Slavery in Missouri* (Baltimore: Johns Hopkins, 1914); Chase C. Mooney, *Slavery in Tennessee* (Bloomington: Indiana Univ., 1957); Joe Gray Taylor, *Negro Slavery in Louisiana* (Baton Rouge: Louisiana State Univ., 1963); James B. Sellers, *Slavery in Alabama* (University, Ala.: Univ. Alabama, 1950); Frank J. Klingberg, *An Appraisal of the Negro in Colonial South Carolina* (Washington: Associated Publishers, 1941). Innumerable articles dealing with the various aspects of slavery appear in professional journals; those interested in the subject are referred particularly to the *Journal of Negro History*.

A good study of the slave trade is Daniel P. Mannix, *Black Cargoes: A History of the Atlantic Slave Trade, 1518–1865* (New York: Viking, 1962). Winthrop D. Jordan, *White Over Black: The Development of American Attitudes Toward the Negro, 1550–1812* (Chapel Hill: Univ. North Carolina, 1968) and William R. Stanton, *The Leopard's Spots: Scientific Attitudes Toward Race in America, 1815–1859* * (Chicago: Univ. Chicago, 1960) are excellent studies emphasizing the context in which attitudes and ideas toward slavery developed in the United States. Herbert Aptheker, *American Negro Slave Revolts* * (New York: Columbia Univ., 1943) gives an exaggerated list and description of the attempts by slaves to throw off the yoke of bondage.

The most exciting recent works on slavery have been those which have taken a comparative approach to the subject. The pioneer study in comparative history is Frank Tannenbaum, *Slave and Citizen: The Negro in the Americas* * (New York: Knopf, 1947). David B. Davis, *The Problem of Slavery in Western Culture* (Ithaca: Cornell Univ., 1966), the first volume of a projected three-volume study of the antislavery movement in Great Britain and the United States, is a Pulitzer Prize winner filled with insight. Stanley Elkins, *Slavery: A Problem in American Insti-*

*tutional and Intellectual Life** (Chicago: Univ. Chicago, 1959) is requisite reading, although he strains his efforts when comparing the effects of slavery on the personality of American Negroes with the effects of Nazi concentration camps upon their prisoners. Eugene D. Genovese, *The Political Economy of Slavery** (New York: Pantheon Books, 1965) and *The World the Slaveholders Made: Two Essays in Interpretation* (New York: Pantheon Books, 1969) are replete with pregnant ideas. Other volumes and essays whose titles indicate their contents are: Marvin Harris, *Patterns of Race in the Americas** (New York: Walker Library, 1964); Harmannus Hoetink, *The Two Variants in Caribbean Race Relations* (New York: Oxford, 1967); Herbert S. Klein, *Slavery in the Americas: A Comparative Study of Virginia and Cuba* (Chicago: Univ. Chicago, 1967); Gilberto Freyre, *The Masters and the Slaves: A Study in the Development of Brazilian Civilization** (New York: Knopf, 1946); H. Orlando Patterson, *The Sociology of Slavery* [*in Jamaica*] (London: MacGibbon, 1967); Alexander, "Brazilian and United States Slavery Compared," *Journal of Negro History,* vol. 7 (1922); Williams, "The Treatment of Slaves in the Brazilian Empire; a Comparison with the United States," *ibid.,* vol. 15 (1930). Carl N. Degler is currently researching and writing a study of race relations and slavery in the United States and Brazil, and he has presented a brief preview of his efforts in "Slavery in Brazil and the United States: An Essay in Comparative History," *American Historical Review,* vol. 75 (1970).

The question of slavery and profits is discussed from a historiographical view by Woodman, "The Profitability of Slavery, A Historical Perennial," *Journal of Southern History,* vol. 29 (1963). Specific articles on the subject are: Govan, "Was Plantation Slavery Profitable?" *ibid.,* vol. 8 (1942); Russell, "General Effects of Slavery Upon Southern Economic Progress," *ibid.,* vol. 4 (1938); Smith, "Was Slavery Unprofitable in the Ante-Bellum South?" *Agricultural History,* vol. 20 (1946); Conrad and Meyer, "The Economics of Slavery in the Ante Bellum South," *Journal of Political Economy,* vol. 66 (1958); Dowd, "The Economics of Slavery in the Ante Bellum South: A Comment [on the Conrad and Meyer article]," *ibid.,* vol. 66 (1958).

General works on the antislavery movement include Gilbert H. Barnes, *The Anti-Slavery Impulse, 1830–1844** (New York: Appleton-Century, 1933) and Louis Filler, *The Crusade Against Slavery, 1830–1860** (New York: Harper & Row, 1960). Valuable volumes on the abolitionists are as follows: Hugh C. Bailey, *Hinton Rowan Helper: Abolitionist-Racist* (University, Ala.: Univ. Alabama, 1965); Betty L. Fladeland, *James Gillespie Birney: Slaveholder to Abolitionist* (Ithaca: Cornell Univ., 1955); Benjamin Thomas, *Theodore Weld: Crusader for Freedom* (New Brunswick: Rutgers Univ., 1950); John L. Thomas, *The Liberator, William Lloyd Garrison: A Biography* (Boston: Little, Brown,

1963). Benjamin Quarles, *Black Abolitionists* * (New York: Oxford, 1969) explores a neglected aspect of the abolition movement in a scholarly way. P. J. Staudenraus, *The African Colonization Movement, 1816–1865* (New York: Columbia Univ., 1961) is an account of efforts to colonize the free Negro outside the United States.

William S. Jenkins, *Pro-Slavery Thought in the Old South* (Chapel Hill: Univ. North Carolina, 1935) is a good summary of the subject, while George Fitzhugh, *Cannibals All! Or Slaves Without Masters* (Richmond: A. Morris, 1857) reveals the thinking of a contemporary writer. Harvey Wish, *George Fitzhugh, Propagandist of the Old South* (Baton Rouge: Louisiana State Univ., 1943) is an adequate although uninspired study of a proslavery advocate. Clement Eaton, *Freedom of Thought in the Old South* (Durham: Duke Univ., 1940) has much material relevant to this subject. The titles of the following articles reveal the approaches of their authors: Hesseltine, "Some New Aspects of the Pro-Slavery Argument," *Journal of Negro History,* vol. 21 (1936) and Morrow, "The Proslavery Argument Revisited," *Mississippi Valley Historical Review,* vol. 48 (1961–62).

* Available in paperback.

CHAPTER VI

THE SOUTH AND THE UNION, 1815–1860

The contest between the Federalists and the Republicans during the 1790s ended in victory for Republicanism when Thomas Jefferson was elected President in 1800. Republicans from all over the nation were attracted to the principles and the party of Jefferson, and the party solidified its position during Jefferson's and James Madison's four terms in the Presidency. The Federalists survived as the opposition party until the end of the War of 1812, but their influence as a political entity lessened with each passing year. In the decade following the war, when one-party politics was the order of the day, southerners had much influence within the Republican party. James Monroe of Virginia was elected President of the United States in 1816, and three of his cabinet members were southerners, including William H. Crawford of Georgia and John C. Calhoun of South Carolina. Henry Clay of Kentucky was Speaker of the House of Representatives. With southerners having a large share in national affairs, the South in general was satisfied with the way the government of the nation was being managed. But in 1861 the nation was plunged into civil war when eleven southern states attempted to secede from the Union. What happened in the brief span of years between the end of the War of 1812 and the beginning of the Civil War to cause southerners to become unhappy within the Union?

Seeds for Sectional Conflict

A hint of future difficulty came in 1819 when the settlers in Missouri Territory asked Congress to pass legislation to enable their territory to become a state. Missourians had moved from many states in the Union, with a large number migrating from nearby southern states, including Kentucky and Tennessee. Many of these immigrants had taken their slaves with them as they pushed westward in the never ending search for better farm land, and the people of Missouri assumed the legality of slavery within the proposed state. But Representative James Tallmadge of New York introduced an amendment to the Missouri statehood bill to prohibit the further introduction of slaves into Missouri and to provide that all slave children born in the state after admission should be freed when they were twenty-five years old. The voting on the Tallmadge Amendment revealed a definite sectional alignment, all but one southern congressman voting against it. After considerable debate, the Senate struck the House-attached Tallmadge Amendment from the enabling legislation, passing only the original bill. Again the division was sectional, although not so sharp as in the House. But the House refused to pass the measure without the proviso against slaves.

Congress adjourned without agreeing upon the Missouri bill, and the subject of slavery in Missouri was discussed all over the country. The broader question was whether slavery should be confined to the states where it then existed or whether it should be extended into American territories and future states. A corollary was: did Congress have the right to impose restrictions upon a state as it entered the Union? The Missouri controversy also caused men to discuss the morality of slavery. Southerners insisted that this was not the issue, but many northerners expressed opposition to slavery on moral grounds, the Pennsylvania state legislature declaring that the admission of Missouri as a slave state would "open a new and steady market for the lawless venders of human flesh."

When Congress reassembled in 1820 it reached a compromise satifactory to both North and South. Maine, which had been requesting statehood for a number of years, was paired with Missouri, the New England state joining the Union as a free state and Missouri entering as a slave state. Slavery was prohibited in the remainder of the Louisiana Territory above the line 36°30'. Like a fire bell in the night, the Missouri Compromise awakened a retired Virginian named Thomas Jefferson and filled him with terror; he predicted that the Union would eventually split over the slavery question. Although not all Americans could see as clearly into the future as the "Sage of Monticello," many southerners began to have an uneasy awareness of their section as a minority.

But the growing southern sectional consciousness stemmed from more than the slavery issue. During the postwar period of intense nationalism, a number of the country's young political leaders were interested in developing a new economic order. For example, they wanted to construct a large network of roads and canals at national expense, a job that many other Republicans felt belonged to the states. These more conservative Republicans argued that the Constitution did not allow the national government to spend money for such internal improvements. But in 1824 the young enthusiasts pushed a bill through Congress by which the national government assumed some responsibility in this area. The advocates of government-financed roads and canals believed that the parts of the nation would be more closely bound together by better transportation arteries.

The debates in Congress and in the press in the early 1820s over this part of the young Republicans' program served exactly the opposite purpose. Since its rivers and streams flowed toward the Atlantic Ocean and the Gulf of Mexico, enabling cotton to be shipped to the coast relatively easily, the South saw only the North and West profiting from money spent on these projects, and it resented attempts to push the program upon the Congress and the nation. South Carolina's Governor John L. Wilson warned his state's legislature that the Supreme Court and the Congress "have gone [too far] toward establishing a great and consolidated government subversive of the rights of the States, and contravening the letter and spirit of the Constitution and of the Union." He went on to say: "The act of the last session appropriating money to make surveys [for roads and canals] is but an entering wedge which will be followed, no doubt, by the expenditure of millions, unless the people apply the proper corrective. The day, I fear, is not far distant, when South Carolina shall be grievously assessed, to pay for the cutting of a canal across Cape Cod." The South Carolina legislature condemned nationally financed internal improvements and made its views known to Congress. Other southerners and state legislatures agreed with South Carolina and followed that state's lead.

A sectional disagreement also developed over the second Bank of the United States. Chartered in 1816 the Bank was an important aspect of the program of the young Republicans. When the Bank established branches in several states, some state legislatures imposed heavy taxes upon them. These state tax laws could have killed the Bank had they been enforced. Southern and western farmers would not have objected to the Bank's demise because many of them had mortgaged their land with the Bank or one of its branches during the period of rapid westward expansion following 1815. Often seeing their land taken from them when the Bank foreclosed during and following the financial panic of 1819, these men were convinced that their own finances would improve if the Bank were dead. As hostility to the Bank increased, a case before the

United States Supreme Court dealt with the right of a state to tax the Bank. When the Court ruled in *McCulloch* v. *Maryland* (1819) that a state could not tax an agency of the national government, the ill will directed toward the Bank was now heaped upon the Court. The Court's tendency to espouse broad and nationalistic constitutional doctrines caused many people to raise serious questions about the power of the Court and the role of the states in the federal system. They argued that the Court did not have the prerogative to decide all constitutional questions, especially those which involved the rights of the states. Some state political leaders began to look for ways to protect their interests from adverse decisions of the Court.

The young Republicans also proposed tariff protection for American industry. Moderate protection had begun with the tariff of 1816, but the panic of 1819 brought a demand from manufacturing interests for greater protection. Agitation for additional protective measures centered mainly in the states where manufacturing was developing—Pennsylvania, New Jersey, New York, and Ohio. Some regions of the South had a few infant industries in 1816 (Kentucky's hemp industry is an example), and others had hopes for developing manufacturing; therefore, some regions in the South favored the tariff of 1816. When manufacturing did not develop in the South, the agricultural region had more to lose than to gain from protective tariffs. Advocates of the tariff argued that agriculture would benefit from protection because prosperity in the manufacturing population would give the farmer a better market for his corn, wheat, and meat. But this "home market" argument appealed mostly to northern and western farmers who produced foodstuffs for the increasing seaboard population. In the 1820s cotton and tobacco were by far the major cash crops in most of the southern states, and factory and urban populations in the North purchased small shares of these crops. The largest markets for cotton and tobacco were in Europe, and the South came to realize that European countries could also pass protective tariffs. If Europe were to reciprocate by raising tariff barriers against the South's cotton and tobacco, the South could be doubly harmed by American tariff duties. The South as a section did not view the tariff as designed to help all sections, despite the arguments of its proponents.

Under these conditions, southern states' representatives generally spoke and voted against the tariff of 1824 which boosted rates from around 25 percent to new heights of about 37 percent on value of dutiable goods. In the debates on this tariff, southerners raised constitutional objections, and the legislatures of South Carolina, Georgia, and Alabama passed resolutions denying the constitutionality of protective tariffs. Thus, the tariff question was debated from the standpoint of the Constitution just as the issues of a national bank and internal improvements at national expense had been.

Differences between North and South also appeared in conjunction with the westward expansion of the nation. As a result of the land law of 1800 and an amendment to it in 1804, a migrant to the West could buy a minimum of 160 acres at $2 each over a period of four years, with a down payment of $80. Many settlers speculated in western lands under laws which did not require full cash payment for land. When the panic of 1819 struck, these speculators—some large, some small—often could not pay off their debts. Whole communities sometimes defaulted on their installment payments when hard times came. Farmers and speculators alike clamored for relief. Other Americans who wanted land joined in the chorus to demand a revision of the land laws. This demand was greatest in the West, men there arguing that cheap land would help fill out the western regions and thus strengthen the national economy. The Congress obliged by passing a new land law in 1820. Under this act the minimum amount of land to be sold to one individual was cut to 80 acres. Cash was required under the terms of this law, and credit provisions on public land sales were deleted. But even so, for $100 cash a farmer was able to start life afresh in the West, and this law pleased westerners. Northerners were happy that the treasury would receive money from public land sales to help pay for government expenses, particularly internal improvements. But southerners asked: how did all this help the South? A negative response was implicit in the question.

The sale of western lands resulted in a reduction of the national debt, and with money in the treasury Congress began to make special grants of land to states to subsidize roads and canals. It also considered outright gifts of money to states for other internal improvements and for education. Many Republicans continued to oppose the national government's desire to spend public money in this way. More importantly, leaders of southern states were becoming concerned over the growing power of that government.

Paradoxically, the postwar nationalism of 1815 was leading not to national unity but to disunity. Most men apparently looked at the national program from the standpoint of local interest rather than from the vantage of the national welfare. The tendency was for South and North to disagree on major national issues, and the South was on the negative side of practically every one of them. While the South opposed many public measures on economic grounds, it came to argue its position by falling back on a strict construction of the Constitution. The growing realization in the South that it was being hurt by the new trends in national policy is quite significant. It meant that southern political self-consciousness was developing. Extreme sectionalism did not appear in the South overnight, but certainly its seeds were planted in the 1820s, and the nation was to reap a harvest of tares in the 1860s.

Southerners in a Minority

The tendency for South and North to maneuver for political and sectional advantage became more than apparent in 1828. Although the Republican party remained the only major political organization on the scene, two rather distinct groups with different political and economic philosophies were developing within the party. In 1828 when Andrew Jackson and Henry Clay were the two main contenders for the Presidency, supporters of Jackson's candidacy seized an opportunity to play politics with a tariff bill before Congress. Introduced by New England congressmen and designed to increase protection of American industries, the bill was revamped by Jackson men who attached amendments not only to increase duties on certain manufactured items but also to raise them on goods such as molasses, wool, and hemp. New England wanted cheap molasses for the manufacture of rum, low-priced wool for its woolen textile mills, and the better Russian hemp was preferred over Kentucky's hemp. Jackson's supporters assumed that the New England representatives would vote against the entire bill as amended, thus appearing to be against protection. By amending the bill, they hoped to embarrass the New England congressmen, President John Quincy Adams, and the President's choice as his successor, Henry Clay. Clay had recently supported protection, and his political enemies were convinced that he had done this simply to gain votes in New England. Hoping to discredit the Clay candidacy in the North when the New England congressmen voted against the amended bill, the Jacksonites planned to advance their candidate as a true friend of protection. But the New England men realized that they could not afford to be stamped as antiprotectionists and, swallowing hard, they voted for the amended bill, much to the surprise and chagrin of the Jackson men.

The political trick backfired. As heavy consumers of manufactured goods, southerners were shocked by the excessive rates of the tariff of 1828, and they promptly branded the bill the "Tariff of Abominations." Numerous editorials and pamphlets were written in the South expressing opposition to the new law. Except in Kentucky and Louisiana, where there was approval of protection, the southern states' legislatures were almost unanimous in their dissent. The Virginia legislature stated that the protective tariff was "unconstitutional, unwise, unjust, unequal and oppressive." The Alabama legislature said, "Let it be distinctly understood, that Alabama . . . regards the power assumed by the General Government to control her internal concerns, by protecting duties, beyond the fair demands of the revenue, as a palpable usurpation of a power not given by the Constitution." The protest reached its most extreme form in South Carolina. A newspaper editor ventured the guess that no more than 150 South Carolinians living outside the city of Charleston did not regard the tariff as unjust, unequal, and oppressive. At a meeting called to protest protection, South Carolinian Thomas Cooper declared that through the operation of the tariff "wealth will be transferred to the North, and wealth is power." He asked, "Is it worth our while to continue this union of states, where the north demand to be our masters, and we are required to be their tributaries?" He concluded by stating that the alternatives of submission or separation were fast approaching.

The most influential and ominous of the pronouncements from the South was entitled the *South Carolina Exposition and Protest,* written anonymously by John C. Calhoun and published in 1828 by a committee of the South Carolina legislature. Earlier a supporter of the tariff, Calhoun had come to feel that the tariff was of little benefit to his native state. Along with an elaborate statement on the unconstitutionality of the tariff, he marshaled statistics to reveal how the South was being ruthlessly exploited by the North. Calhoun's suggestion to protect a state or minority section against such exploitation is known as the doctrine of nullification. Calhoun reasoned that the states had created the Union; thus, being the agent of the states, the national government was sharply limited in its powers by the Constitution. If difficulty arose between the national government and a state, each state had the prerogative to judge whether the government in Washington had violated the supreme law of the land. Calhoun contended that a single state through a specially elected convention had the legal power to nullify within its boundaries the operation of a law of Congress which the state regarded as unconstitutional. In the so-called "Fort Hill Letter," Calhoun in 1832 publicly restated, refined, and qualified his earlier arguments in the *Exposition.* He pointed out that if a state nullified an act of Congress, three-fourths of the states could make the law operable again in all the states by passing a constitutional amendment. In that event, the disagreeing state had no choice but to submit to the law or secede from the Union.

A now famous debate in the Senate in January 1830 further revealed the developing differences between the North and South. The debate was precipitated when Senator Samuel A. Foot of Connecticut introduced a resolution which had as its object the restriction of the sale of public lands. Since this resolution reflected the attitude of most New Englanders, Foot was acting in behalf of his constituents. But under the leadership of Senator Thomas Hart Benton of Missouri, westerners objected since they were continually agitating for more available land. Men of the South were not particularly interested in the question of land sales, but politically shrewd southerners rushed to the side of the West, hoping to obtain that section's support in the South's fight against the tariff. Western and southern Senators, ably led by Robert Y. Hayne of South Carolina, argued on the Senate floor that the North (particularly New England) was obstructing national development by favoring the Foot resolution. Behind the magnificent oratory of Daniel Webster of Massachusetts, New Englanders defended their position and criticized the South for favoring states' rights against the national interest. They charged the strict constructionist southerners with holding to a constitutional interpretation which injured western interests. They hinted that some southerners apparently wanted not only to weaken the national government but also to destroy the Union. Moreover, they reminded the West that it had frequently been unable to obtain its objectives because of southern zeal for a strict interpretation of the Constitution. Instead of ignoring northern jibes at states' rights, southerners accepted the challenge and rushed to defend their position regarding the Constitution. Thus, the South almost immediately went on the defensive by arguing for states' rights rather than on the offensive by continuing the dispute between the North and West. More significantly, the Webster-Hayne debate clarified the constitutional issues involving states' rights and the power of the national government; both sides assembled a multitude of arguments as bases for debate and action in the future.

As the debate developed, the sectional nature of the political situation became clear. No one of the three sections was able by itself to govern the nation; only by coalition could a working majority be created. No two sections had identical interests. Overly simplified, the North favored high-priced public lands, internal improvements at government expense, and a high tariff; the South favored high-priced public lands, no internal improvements, and a low tariff; the West favored low-priced public lands and internal improvements. The picture was complicated by the fact that the Northwest desired a high tariff, while the Southwest preferred a low tariff.

The recurrent tariff problem brought about a serious sectional crisis in 1832. The "abominable" tariff of 1828 had pleased no one, and in 1832 the Congress debated a bill designed to remove the patently bad tariff provisions. But many undesirable ones were retained, and southern representatives were unable to prevent the passage of the new law. It appeared to the South that this tariff might remain for many years as the law of the land. Leaders in South Carolina were particularly disconcerted over the tariff of 1832. Spurred by the thinking of John C. Calhoun, a states' rights party had already been formed in that state, and with both a philosophy and an organization states' righters were able to implement some of Calhoun's suggestions. A popularly elected statewide convention dominated by Calhoun men was called. There, George McDuffie, an ardent nullifier, declared that the North would not dare push the cotton states to the extremity of secession because the elimination of cotton exports would have a devastating effect upon the national economy. The convention accepted McDuffie's reasoning, and in November 1832 it adopted an ordinance of nullification which declared that the tariffs of 1828 and 1832 were null and void within the state of South Carolina. The ordinance prohibited customs authorities from enforcing these tariff measures in the state, and it required state officers to take an oath under penalty of removal from office to enforce the ordinance and any legislation enacted to support it. Moreover, the ordinance declared that the people of South Carolina would be absolved from their political connections with the people of other states if the national government attempted to implement the new tariff act by armed force, by closing the ports of the state, or in any other way except through civil courts.

President Jackson refused to be badgered by this action, and he was prepared to see that the laws of the national government were obeyed. He declared the action of South Carolina treasonous, and with characteristic vigor he sent ships and soldiers to Charleston in case they were needed. But Jackson was wise enough to realize that armed conflict between the national government and a state would solve few problems. Many national leaders agreed. From this climate a new tariff law, primarily the work of Henry Clay and John C. Calhoun, was passed in 1833. This tariff called for gradual reduction of duties for the next decade, after which time rates were not to exceed 20 percent on any article. When both sides had approved this compromise tariff and it had been passed by Congress, the South Carolina convention reassembled and voted to cancel its nullification ordinance. A serious confrontation was thereby avoided, although many South Carolinians stated that they still believed that a single state had the right to nullify a national law if that law was not in the best interests of the state.

While in the 1820s something like a southern platform had evolved, in the 1830s a charge of emotion was added to the situation. Despite the compromise of 1833 in which South Carolina was able to force its will upon the national government, throughout the remainder of the decade the South felt oppression, desperation, and despair. Difficult to describe, this state of mind unquestionably existed long after the nullification controversy ended. Part of the explanation for it may be found in the South's reaction to the antislavery agitation and abolitionist sentiment rapidly developing in the North after 1830. From then on it would not always be possible to explain southern action and attitudes by a rational analysis of the facts in each new episode. In addition to the facts, this emotional tension and attitude which became apparent in the 1830s must also be considered.

Tension and Compromise

During the 1830s and 1840s the nation experienced a two-party system. Growing out of the old Republican organization, the Whig party developed in the early 1830s with considerable support in the South. Embracing property holders in both North and South, the Whigs claimed to have within their membership about two-thirds of all slaveowners. The Democratic party, the other wing of the old Republican party, led by men like Andrew Jackson, was also strong in the South. As a matter of fact, both parties were nationwide in their membership and influence, each having southern and northern members within its ranks. But the rapid pace of events in the 1840s did much to undermine the national unity of both parties, and they began to be torn along sectional lines.

Even though the nation's political leaders desperately tried to ignore the slavery and sectional issues, the westward expansion of the 1840s forced the subjects upon them. In that decade Texas was the focus of the first of two dramatic struggles between the United States and Mexico. Having been encouraged by the Spanish and later the Mexicans to settle in Texas, many Americans, particularly southerners such as Stephen F. Austin, had migrated there in the 1820s and 1830s. Attracted by the magnet of free or cheap land, thousands of settlers moved to that north Mexican province. The land was particularly suited to growing cotton, and many men who migrated there took their slaves with them. After living under Mexican rule for several years, these white, Anglo-Saxon, Protestant Americans grew restless under the incompetent rule of their brown-skinned, Catholic, Mexican rulers. The successful Texas revolution, climaxing with the battle of San Jacinto in 1836, was led exclusively by Americans dwelling in Texas. Establishing an independent republic, these Texans elected Sam Houston as their first president, initiated diplomatic relations with foreign nations, and expanded their cotton economy.

But Texans were not content with independence, and agitators from the early days of the republic demanded that Texas be attached to the United States. Northerners too readily assumed that the Texans' revolution and demand for union with the United States was a carefully calculated scheme on the part of southerners to expand the institution of slavery. These attitudes affected party politics, and Texas became a major issue in the Presidential election of 1844. Whig candidate Henry Clay, who had been working hard to unify his party, gave much attention to southern Whigs, making an extensive tour of the South early in 1844. His popularity reached its apex as the election approached, with the Whig party attaining a high degree of unity. But before the election could be held, the question of slavery reemerged when the annexation of Texas was debated. Clay confused his followers by modifying an earlier antiannexation pronouncement. Trying to remain neutral at a time when men were demanding that their political leaders take a definite stand, Clay irreparably damaged his Presidential chances. Democratic candidate James K. Polk won the election, primarily because he appealed to the nationalist and expansionist mood of the nation at the time. But Polk was a Tennessee slaveholder, and many northern opponents suspected that he coveted Texas in order to assist slaveholders.

Nationalist and expansionist that he was, President Polk became embroiled in a dispute with Mexico which resulted in the Mexican War, 1846–48. The Treaty of Guadalupe Hidalgo, signed at the end of that war, provided for the cession to the United States of a vast tract of northern Mexican land extending from Texas to the Pacific coast. Polk's opponents charged that he had deliberately provoked the war with Mexico to acquire this land for the expansion of slavery. Provocation of the war for more territory may fairly be laid at Polk's door, but to acquire this land for the extension of slavery was not in the President's mind. Most of the territory in question was unsuited for slavery, and many of the staunchest defenders of slavery were opposed to the war and to the acquisition of more territory. For example, John C. Calhoun voted against the declaration of war. John A. Campbell of Alabama, who later became a justice of the United States Supreme Court, reasoned that any large acquisition of Mexican land by the United States would upset the balance of power in the nation to the disadvantage of the South. He based his conclusion on the belief that the area was entirely unfit for slavery, and that expansion would therefore result in an increase of nonslaveholding states and a corresponding abatement of slave state strength. Even though the war and the acquisition of additional territory were not the products of a proslavery conspiracy, northern Whigs found it good politics to make the charge, and tension between North and South continued.

Directly related to this controversy and assisting in keeping the situation tense was the Wilmot Proviso. Introduced into Congress in 1846 by Pennsylvania Congressman David Wilmot, this resolution provided that slavery be excluded from any land acquired from Mexico. If passed, the Wilmot Proviso would have effectively halted the westward expansion of slavery. More importantly, the proviso was supported by northern Whigs and northern Democrats, while southerners of opposing party affiliations rallied against it. Debated over a period of years, the proviso was never adopted by Congress, leaving the question of slavery in the Mexican territory for future settlement, but the debates on it widened the breach between the sections. The fact that the Wilmot Proviso remained an issue even though the land in the Southwest was not suited to slavery reveals how the opposing camps were willing to quarrel when little or nothing was at stake. The tendency for party lines to become unimportant whenever the question of slavery was raised resulted in a loss of national strength for the Whigs in the late 1840s, and the Democratic party developed well-defined northern and southern wings. Since national parties help hold the nation together, it was unfortunate for the country when the two parties began to lose their national unity. But loyalty to section was becoming more important than loyalty to party by the late 1840s, and the Union was to suffer as a consequence.

A major crisis was reached when Americans in newly acquired California asked for formal territorial status as a prelude to statehood. Although California preferred to enter the Union as a free state, under the prevailing conditions southerners could not acquiesce in the request. With the virtual breakdown of the parties, the question was strictly sectional as the extension of slavery remained an issue on the national scene. Tempers rose as northerners and southerners accused each other of bad faith. Resenting northern attempts to restrict the progress of slavery, southern congressmen caucused in 1849 and called for the people of the South to unite in one party. Upon Calhoun's suggestion, a Mississippi gathering requested a convention of the slave states to meet in Nashville, Tennessee in June 1850 to plan strategy against the North. Nine states sent delegates, among them Robert Barnwell Rhett, outspoken editor of the Charleston (S.C.) *Mercury*. The convention adopted resolutions asserting that all Americans had equal rights to migrate to the territories without congressional interference, and fire-eating delegates advocated secession if the North did not respect the South's rights within the Union.

Several problems relating to the general controversy between free and slave states had plagued the nation's leaders over the years, and the men who favored compromise came to the fore again in a difficult situation. Collectively called the Compromise of 1850, five resolutions were passed by Congress to ease the critical situation facing the nation. California was admitted as a state with a constitution outlawing slavery, but the remaining territory acquired from Mexico in 1848 was organized as the territories of Utah and New Mexico without mention of slavery. The tacit understanding was that when the territories applied for statehood, they could decide the slavery issue for themselves. In a boundary disagreement between Texas and New Mexico, most of the disputed land was acknowledged as New Mexico's, but Texas was compensated from the United States Treasury to the tune of $10,000,000. Northerners were able to have a resolution passed abolishing the slave trade in the District of Columbia, while southerners in turn pushed through an effective fugitive slave law. Except for the final resolution southern congressmen did not generally feel that the Compromise of 1850 was to their section's advantage. While some of them had spoken openly of secession on the floor of the House and the Senate, they did not threaten this drastic move as did

the fire-eaters of the Nashville convention. When the choices were na-
kedly reduced to secession or compromise, the southerners in Washington
felt they had no alternative at that time. Extremists in the South denounced the compromise, and attempts were made to bring about secession in some states, particularly South Carolina, but the movement for
southern rights collapsed in the face of the number of moderates who favored compromise and in view of the lack of agreement among extremists
as to how secession should come.

Tensions were eased as most of the nation's leaders accepted the
Compromise of 1850. A crisis had been passed. But the compromise dealt
with specified cases, not with principles or values. The conditions which
had produced the critical situation were still present, as were the interests
and ideals behind the contending groups. The basic issues had to do
with matters which men would not compromise. Even some of the terms
of the compromise resolutions could not be accepted without damage to
consciences on both sides. Perhaps a Georgia editor was correct when he
wrote in January 1851: "The elements of that controversy are yet alive
and they are destined to outlive the government. There is a feud between
North and South which may be smothered, but never overcome."

Prologue to Secession

The relative calm following the Compromise of 1850 was short-
lived, as a series of events occurred which led rapidly to secession and
armed conflict. The twins, slavery and westward expansion, were responsible for opening the wounds once again. In 1854 Senator Stephen A.
Douglas of Illinois introduced a measure to organize the Territory of Nebraska. Since the territory was wholly within the Louisiana Purchase area
and above the line 36°30', slavery was prohibited there by the terms of
the Missouri Compromise, but southerners had voted down previous bills
to organize the plains area for this very reason. Under pressure from his
constituents to organize the territory, thus increasing the odds for a proposed transcontinental railroad routed across the central plains, Douglas
ignored the compromise of thirty years by suggesting that the residents in
the territory decide whether slavery would exist in it. This suggestion of
popular (or squatter) sovereignty appealed to southerners who saw an opportunity to extend slavery into heretofore forbidden territory. When
southerners suggested that Douglas's measure provide for two new territories, Nebraska and Kansas, Douglas readily agreed. Implicit in the discussions was the double intention that Nebraska would be organized by freeholders and that Kansas would be settled by slaveholders.

Northerners accused the South of having originated the drive to
organize Nebraska. The Sandusky (Ohio) *Commercial Register* editorial-

ized the opinions of many northerners: "As every intelligent man knows, it is the South alone who . . . is the instigator of all the excitement that may result from this unexpected reagitation of the slavery question." Even though the charge was without foundation, northerners were suspicious of a sinister slave power trying to dominate the Union. Over considerable northern opposition the Kansas-Nebraska Act was passed in 1854, and the idea of southern aggression grew steadily in northern circles during the next half dozen years. Northerners were not about to accept the reversal of the long-standing Missouri Compromise and allow slaveholders to dominate Kansas Territory simply because southerners assumed that Kansas was to be slave. Out of the Kansas-Nebraska debates had come a notion, widely accepted in the North, that popular sovereignty meant a race between free settlers and slaveholders for control of Kansas. Victory would belong to the side that was there first with the most. With both free men and slaveholders pouring into Kansas, conflict was virtually inevitable as each group vied for control of the territorial government. A bloody civil war followed in Kansas; it reached all the way to the halls of Congress when South Carolina Congressman Preston Brooks personally assaulted Massachusetts Senator Charles Sumner on the floor of the Senate, after the latter had made a speech on "The Crime Against Kansas." "Bleeding Kansas" was a prologue to the major conflict which started in 1861.

Further adding to the sectional flames, the new Republican party was formed just after the Kansas-Nebraska Act was voted in Congress. Filling the vacuum created by the recent death of the Whig party, the new party was an almost wholly northern organization, comprised of former northern Whigs, abolitionists, and free soilers. Controlled by seasoned politicians and dedicated to the proposition that slavery should not expand into the territories, the new party grew rapidly. When the Republicans nominated John C. Frémont as their Presidential candidate in 1856, southern extremists foresaw the ruin of the South if Frémont was elected. They expressed fears that the Missouri Compromise would be restored, Kansas would become a free state, the fugitive slave law would be repealed, insurrection and war would be kindled in the South, and the amalgamation of the races would be permitted. Some southerners voiced the belief that a Republican victory would result in the burning of southern homes and the slitting of southerners' throats. Faced with these misgivings, the South could say but one thing: if Frémont should be elected President, honor and interest demanded that the South withdraw from the Union and establish an independent confederacy. When Frémont was not elected in 1856, the South did not have to make good its threats, but fire-eating southerners vowed at the time that if a purely northern party ever elected a President, the South would have no alternative but to leave the Union.

The hostility southerners held for Republicans was due in part to their belief that all Republicans were in reality abolitionists in disguise. While political disputes were simmering, a number of popular books were published, further engendering southern dislike of abolitionists. The most celebrated of these publications were Harriet Beecher Stowe's *Uncle Tom's Cabin* and Hinton Rowan Helper's *The Impending Crisis in the South.* Originally published in serial form in the *National Era,* a rather obscure religious magazine, Mrs. Stowe's story appeared as a book in 1852. The novel was an immediate publishing success, and thousands upon thousands of copies were printed and read all over the nation and the world. The fact that Mrs. Stowe had never seen slavery from personal observation did not harm the sale of the novel; indeed, sales may have increased because of the author's lack of firsthand knowledge. The importance of *Uncle Tom's Cabin* lay not in whether it was an accurate account of the institution of slavery. Rather the novel was important because it supplied northerners with concrete stereotypes. In Uncle Tom, Simon Legree, Topsy, Little Eva, Ophelia, and George Harris slavery was personalized. It was no longer an abstraction toward which morally conscious northern men could be indifferent. Contrarily, the South knew that Mrs. Stowe had grossly misrepresented its social system, and it sneered at northern jeers.

While northerners were agreeably devouring Mrs. Stowe's sentimental story and southerners were yelling distortion, a book of a different sort increased sectional animosities. Helper, a widely traveled nonslaveholding North Carolinian, published his book in 1857 with the thesis that the South's backwardness as contrasted with northern progress was due to Negro slavery. Piling up page after page of statistics, Helper believed that anyone who could read could see how slavery was responsible for the South's lowly condition. His remedy for the South's ills was singularly simple: abolish slavery immediately. Helper's analysis was erroneous, but northerners were in a mood to accept his conclusions without question. His remedy was too extreme and southerners repelled by it said as much. The book added fuel to the impending conflagration.

Another giant step along the sectional path was taken when the Supreme Court handed down the Dred Scott decision in the year Helper's book was published. Concerned with the right of a slave to be free because his master had taken him to live in a free state and territory for a short time, the Dred Scott case resulted in a technical victory for the South. The Court ruled that, as a Negro, Scott did not have the right of a citizen to sue in a federal court. The Court could have stopped at this point and dismissed the case for lack of jurisdiction, but Chief Justice Roger B. Taney and his four southern associates dominated the Court, and they welcomed the opportunity to speak on the question of slavery in the territories. Although reaching the same conclusion by different legal and logical routes, a majority of the members of the Court believed that Congress had gone beyond its authority when it passed the Missouri Compromise in 1820, and that slavery could not be prohibited from any American territory by Congress or a territorial legislature. Northerners saw the Dred Scott decision as more evidence of an aggressive slavocracy. Pro-southern though the Court's decision was, the South found it a hollow victory in the quickening pace of events.

In October 1859 John Brown and a small group of northern fanatics crossed the Potomac River at Harpers Ferry, intending to incite a slave rebellion in Virginia. Brown's band carried arms for itself and for anticipated slave sympathizers. The town of Harpers Ferry was seized, and unsuccessful attempts were made to induce slaves to join the attackers. After a few innocent lives were taken in the first hours of the surprise attack, most of the invaders were killed or captured by the Virginia militia. Brown was wounded and seized, pronounced sane, given a hasty trial, and promptly hanged for treason against the Commonwealth of Virginia. Simpleminded in conception and inadequate in execution, the fiasco amounted to hardly more than an isolated, local disturbance, but its meaning was tragically national. News of the event spread like wildfire across the country. In the eyes of the South here was an intolerable northern attack on southern property and lives, all the more reprehensible when southerners learned that Brown's raid had been financed by northern abolitionists and businessmen. The South blamed the Republican party for the outrage, even though conservative Republicans condemned Brown's harebrained scheme. This violent episode, which should have been looked upon as the misguided act of a mad man, was important in destroying the last bonds of sentiment holding the Union together; southern emotions reached fever pitch. With an accumulation of distrust and fear which had been forming for a generation, southerners asked, "How much more can the South take before it is compelled to secede?"

Before the bitterness produced by the raid on Harpers Ferry had subsided, the Presidential campaign of 1860 brought the sectional dispute to a final crisis. For their candidate, Republicans turned to Abraham Lincoln who had been thrust into the political spotlight in 1858 by his unsuccessful bid to unseat Illinois Senator Douglas. Douglas was chosen at a convention in Baltimore as the Democratic party's Presidential nominee, but his nomination came only after southern delegates had walked out of a convention at Charleston when the party's platform did not include a statement that the national government should protect slavery in the territories. Two other candidates also ran for the Presidency in 1860. Holding their own convention, the disgruntled Democrats, who were mostly from the cotton states, nominated John Breckinridge of Kentucky. They adopted a platform favoring the annexation of Cuba and the extension of slavery into the territories. The hastily formed Constitutional Union party, a reaction to almost everything that had transpired politically since the middle of the 1840s, nominated Senator John Bell of Tennessee as a compromise candidate. The reactionaries who led this party hoped to avoid the forces and issues which were about to cause a division of the Union by turning the clock back and starting all over again. Bell and Breckinridge battled for support in the southern states. When the votes were counted, Bell had carried Virginia, Kentucky, and Tennessee; the remaining slave states had gone to Breckinridge. Douglas and Lincoln found most of their supporters in the North. Although Douglas received 1,376,957 popular votes, he won only the nine electoral votes of Missouri and three of New Jersey's seven, as Lincoln swept the North. Lincoln's popular vote of 1,866,452 comprised only 40 percent of the total cast, but his majority in the electoral college was substantial. With fire-eaters having constantly proclaimed that the South could not remain in the Union if an exclusively northern party won the Presidency, the South moved rapidly after November to effect secession.

This brief résumé of the South's relation to the remainder of the nation from 1815 to 1860 reveals that by the 1820s the South was in the early stages of becoming an economically and politically distinct section of the United States. During the 1820s a kind of political platform evolved based on opposition to many national policies. This was illustrated by the South's attitude toward the Bank, tariff, internal improvements, and western land expansion. The decade of the 1830s saw this opposition charged with emotionalism as the South came to realize that it was fast developing into a political minority in the nation. The rise of the antislavery crusade in northern quarters reinforced this realization and imbedded automatic defense mechanisms into southern responses concerning politics and slavery. The spirit of sectionalism intensified in the 1840s with both North and South jockeying for political and economic power as slavery and the expansion of the nation westward were focal points for disagreement. The Compromise of 1850 brought a breathing spell, but the 1850s saw slavery and westward expansion come once again to the fore. By this time the South had become so defensive and afraid of what the future held for it in the national balance of power that many southerners were developing a southern national consciousness beyond simply a strong feeling of sectionalism. Southerners began to sense that their region could not remain as a part of the Union and that they would have to establish their own nation. The event which triggered the secession movement was the election of Abraham Lincoln as President.

Suggestions for Further Reading

Good general coverage of the South from 1819 to 1861 can be found in Charles S. Sydnor, *The Development of Southern Sectionalism, 1819–1848* (Baton Rouge: Louisiana State Univ., 1948) and Avery O. Craven, *The Growth of Southern Nationalism, 1848–1861* (Baton Rouge: Louisiana State Univ., 1953). Additional general volumes are: Henry H. Simms, *A Decade of Sectional Controversy, 1851–1861* (Chapel Hill: Univ. North Carolina, 1942); Charles H. Ambler, *Sectionalism in Virginia from 1776–1861* (Chicago: Univ. Chicago, 1910); J. T. Carpenter, *The South as a Conscious Minority, 1789–1861* (New York: New York Univ., 1930); Avery O. Craven, *Civil War in the Making, 1815–1860* (Baton Rouge: Louisiana State Univ., 1959). William W. Freehling, *Prelude to Civil War: The Nullification Controversy in South Carolina, 1816–1836** (New York: Harper & Row, 1966) has superseded C. S. Boucher, *The Nullification Controversy in South Carolina* (Chicago: Univ. Chicago, 1916). Studying the process by which moderates became radicals is Harold Schultz's *Nationalism and Sectionalism in South Carolina, 1852–1860* (Durham: Duke Univ., 1950). Allan Nevins, *Ordeal of the Union*, 2 vols. (New York: Scribners, 1947) is a detailed and highly readable account of the years from 1846 to 1857. Theodore C. Smith, *Parties and Slavery* (New York: Harper & Brothers, 1906) is valuable for the political aspects of the sectional struggle, as is Arthur C. Cole, *The Whig Party in the South* (Washington: American Historical Association, 1913).

Also available are Ulrich B. Phillips, *The Course of the South to Secession* (New York: Appleton-Century, 1939) and Arthur Y. Lloyd, *The Slavery Controversy* (Chapel Hill: Univ. North Carolina, 1939). Sharply contrasting interpretations may be found in Arthur C. Cole, *The Irrepressible Conflict, 1850–1865* (New York: Macmillan, 1934) and Avery O. Craven, *The Repressible Conflict, 1830–1861* (Baton Rouge: Louisiana State Univ., 1953). Glover Moore, *The Missouri Controvery, 1819–1821* * (Lexington: Univ. Kentucky, 1955) and Holman Hamilton, *Prologue to Conflict: The Crisis and the Compromise of 1850* * (Lexington: Univ. Kentucky, 1964) are sound studies of two of the three major compromises during the era of rising sectionalism.

Margaret L. Coit, *John C. Calhoun: American Portrait* * (Boston: Houghton Mifflin, 1950), Gerald M. Capers, Jr., *John C. Calhoun, Opportunist: A Reappraisal* (Gainesville: Univ. Florida, 1960), and Charles

M. Wiltse, *John C. Calhoun,* 3 vols. (Indianapolis: Bobbs-Merrill, 1944–1951) are interpretive biographies of the South's foremost political leader prior to the Civil War. Two one-volume studies of Henry Clay also deserve mention: Clement Eaton, *Henry Clay and the Art of American Politics* * (Boston: Little, Brown, 1957) and G. G. Van Deusen, *The Life of Henry Clay* * (Boston: Little, Brown, 1937).

Valuable articles on the sectional conflict include: Ramsdell, "Natural Limits of Slavery Expansion," *Mississippi Valley Historical Review,* vol. 16 (1929–30); Stenberg, "The Motivation of the Wilmot Proviso," *ibid.,* vol. 18 (1931–32); Durden, "J. D. B. De Bow: Convolutions of a Slavery Expansionist," *Journal of Southern History,* vol. 17 (1951).

* Available in paperback.

CHAPTER VII

THE SOUTHERN CONFEDERACY

"'A house divided against itself cannot stand.' I believe this government cannot endure, permanently half *slave* and half *free*. I do not expect the Union to be dissolved—I do not expect the house to *fall*—but I do expect it will cease to be divided. It will become *all* one thing, or *all* the other." Abraham Lincoln had expressed these sentiments from a public platform during a political campaign in 1858, and while this Whig-turned-Republican edged nearer to the front door of the White House during the next two years, southerners continually recalled what they considered to be the fanaticism of this tall, awkward, and sometimes uncouth man. Lincoln's election in November 1860 climaxed forty years of events which had been building up pressure against the South within the Union. Southerners were convinced that the President-elect would cooperate with Senator Charles Sumner, Indiana Congressman George W. Julian, and other antislavery radicals of the Republican party. They could not overcome their fear that this Republican's primary goal was to use the office of the Presidency to destroy slavery. Lincoln's election amounted to the moment of conception for the Southern Confederacy.

The Months of Gestation

After the South Carolina legislature met in November 1860 to choose Presidential electors, it remained in session to see whether the outcome of the national election necessitated its taking any action. When news reached South Carolina that its preferred candidate, John C. Breckinridge, was a poor third in the popular-vote totals and that Abraham Lincoln had gained a runaway victory in the electoral college, the state legislature immediately passed a resolution calling a convention to meet in December to consider the question of secession. Afraid of being stamped as "submissionists" if they tried to stem the hysterical tide, many South Carolinians who opposed the rapid pace of events refused to stand for election to this convention; a much larger number expressed their unhappiness by not voting. Thus, the delegates elected to the convention favored secession overwhelmingly. At the convention an ordinance of secession was passed 169 to 0. Pointing out that a convention in South Carolina had ratified the Constitution of the United States on May 23, 1788, the ordinance declared that now on December 20, 1860, the Constitution and its amendments were hereby repealed, and that "the union now subsisting between South Carolina and other States under the name of 'United States of America' is hereby dissolved." News of the action created a mighty wave of exultation in Charleston, the city in which the convention had met. As word spread quickly to the rest of the state, church bells rang the glad tidings, businesses closed their doors, and Palmetto flags were unfurled.

South Carolina's action was not unanticipated, because secession had been discussed and threatened for years in the state and throughout the other southern states. In fact, southern leaders had conferred from time to time on the possibility of a southwide secession convention, and some charged that South Carolina's rapid action showed little respect for the interests of other slave states. A newspaper editor in Arkansas chided South Carolina for having "whirled herself" out of the Union "without even passing the compliments of the season with her sister slaveholding States. . . . [S]he has passed us by without even saying 'good morning, d——m your sowl.' "

But South Carolina's action was not unpremeditated. Ever since the abortive Nashville Convention of 1850, many secessionists despaired of achieving success at an all-South secession convention. Thus, South Carolina fire-eaters had determined to "go it alone." They had been assured by the governors of three or four other states that their action would be followed, and the general feeling over the South lent psychological support to the South Carolinians. But they were taking a calculated risk. The other states might not have followed suit, because many people in the South remained loyal to the Union. The possibility existed that South Carolina's action might have completely isolated that state.

Subsequent events proved that South Carolina's leaders had gauged the sentiment in the southern states correctly—at least in the lower South. Their decision set off a chain reaction shortly after the Christmas holidays. Mississippi, Florida, and Alabama passed ordinances of secession on January 9, 10, and 11, respectively. Georgia followed on January 19, but not until after Unionists had made strong efforts against secession. Alexander H. Stephens, Benjamin H. Hill, and Hershel V. Johnson were not convinced that the time for separation had arrived, but Georgia followed Robert Toombs, Howell Cobb, and Thomas R. R. Cobb who believed that "each hour that Georgia . . . remains a member of the Union will be an hour of degradation, to be followed by certain and speedy ruin." The vote on separation in that state's convention was 208 to 89. Louisiana had a large number of citizens committed to the Union, but many were convinced that their voices would not be heard above the loud clash of events, and they did not trouble themselves to vote for delegates to the secession convention. Under the circumstances secessionists easily dominated, and Louisiana's ordinance of secession was passed on January 26 by a vote of 113 to 17. Texas Governor Sam Houston was unalterably opposed to secession, and Texas separatists were forced to override the governor. They finally cast the stern old patriot-nationalist out of office for refusing to take an oath to support the Confederacy. On February 1 a state convention passed an ordinance of secession, and the Texas voters supported this action in a popular referendum three weeks later.

The leader of public opinion in the upper South was Virginia, whose action in regard to secession probably influenced neighboring states decisively. The Virginia legislature called a convention to meet in Richmond on February 13 to determine the state's future in view of the Confederacy then being established. In session for two months, this convention had many delegates who favored delay and compromise. The majority apparently preferred an upper South convention to consider the amendments to protect the rights of the southern states within the Union. It was abundantly clear that Virginians were not willing to secede simply because Lincoln had been elected President, although they were concerned about their security within the Union. Secessionists used various means to garner support for their movement. They organized torchlight parades to stir up enthusiasm for secession, they spoke eloquently for the South's cause, and they invited men from the lower South to address the convention to explain their grievances and recent actions. After southerners fired upon the Union's Fort Sumter in April, President Lincoln called upon the states to furnish troops to maintain federal authority in the seceded states. Lincoln's appeal added to the snowballing of secession sentiment in Virginia, and the convention passed a secession ordinance 88 to 55 later that month.

Virginia's act led to the creation of a new loyal state. Many of the votes against secession at the April convention had been cast by men from Virginia's western mountains. The people of western Virginia held no brief for the large slaveholding and landowning aristocrats of the east, and they feared that secession would bring war to their region sandwiched between Ohio and Virginia. Western Virginia refused to go along with the state's leaders, and in 1863 the state of West Virginia was admitted to the Union. Tennessee also had a region not in sympathy with the Confederacy. The mountainous eastern portion was occupied chiefly by small farmers with few slaves who had little in common with the men and economy in the remainder of the state. Although Unionists were present throughout the state, secession gained support in middle and west Tennessee after the firing on Fort Sumter and Lincoln's call for troops. Soon thereafter the secessionist governor called the legislature into a special session which adopted an ordinance of separation. In June the document was put to the people of the state who voted 2 to 1 for it. East Tennesseans tried to imitate the West Virginians, but their efforts to secede from the state were stifled by armed force.

A state with many small farmers, North Carolina had a large share of Union sympathizers. When Lincoln had been elected in November 1860, most North Carolinians favored giving his administration a fair trial, but secessionists along the eastern coastal regions beat the drums for the Confederacy, and again Lincoln's call for military support helped crystallize the secessionists' appeal. A convention called by a special session of the legislature met in May and passed a secession ordinance unanimously. Although many Unionists lived in North Carolina, they were quashed by the weight of overpowering events. Nevertheless, the convention's action probably represented the will of a majority of North Carolinians. In Arkansas the governor led the secession faction, opposed by the state's western counties which did not want to join the Confederacy for fear of the federally controlled, strong Indian tribes to the west. But a convention met and quickly passed an ordinance of secession soon after the first shot of the Civil War was fired.

Kentucky was the most important upper South state from a military standpoint, because control of the Ohio River was militarily essential to victory for either side. The people of Kentucky had conflicting loyalties, the legislature expressing this when it proclaimed the state neutral in the battle shaping up between North and South. Lincoln recognized the ticklish situation in Kentucky and avoided taking any action that would alienate that state. As he irreverently said, "I hope to have God on my side, but I must have Kentucky." He hoped to win the support of that important state by patient diplomacy. The Confederates were not so cautious. A Confederate army moved into the Bluegrass State to capture Columbus, a key point on the Mississippi River which the Confederates believed the Union was about to take over. As far as the Kentucky legislature was concerned, this act constituted an invasion; the legislature abandoned its neutrality and declared its loyalty to the Union. Ambivalence continued in Kentucky despite this act of the legislature. Families were tragically divided in their loyalties to or support for the two sides. Some thirty-five thousand Kentuckians fought in the Confederate army, while about seventy-five thousand joined the Union army. Sentiment for the Confederacy increased in Kentucky during and after the war, and the closing of bank doors on Confederate memorial day remained a common practice in Kentucky in the twentieth century.

Like Kentucky, Maryland was divided in sentiment about secession. The slave and plantation owners of the eastern shore were pro-southern, while the small western farms were plowed by men inclined to remain with the Union. If Maryland joined the Confederacy, the Union's capital would be surrounded by Confederate territory. This would be an intolerable situation for the United States. It was essential that Maryland remain in the Union, and President Lincoln took strong action against Confederate sympathizers, many being imprisoned in violation of their civil liberties. Secession activity subsided in Maryland, but the eastern counties were held in the Union by force.

The secession movement in Missouri led to bloody conflict. The state's leaders were divided on secession, troops lined up behind the leaders of each side, and guerrilla warfare broke out. Two governments were operating in Missouri, each claiming to represent the people. The government at Neosho sent representatives to the Confederate Congress, but most historians hold that Missouri did not secede from the Union.

The Confederacy had reason to believe that it could win the allegiance of the tribes in the Indian Territory. Most of the Indians there had been removed from the South in the 1830s, taking with them their slaves and a knowledge of cotton culture. They had affiliations with southern churches, and the federal superintendent of the Indians and most of his agents were southerners. Confederate officials promised to continue equally generous financial payments which the Indians were receiving from the federal government, if they would support the South's war effort. The South also held out the bait of applying a strong fugitive slave law to the Indians' slaves and promised to grant statehood in the Confederacy to the Indian lands. Some Indians responded to these overtures, but the majority of them retained their allegiance to the Union.

The Confederacy temporarily acquired territories in the Southwest. After a Confederate army from Texas invaded New Mexico, the western part of the region, pro-southern in sentiment, was organized as the Territory of Arizona and admitted into the Confederacy in January 1862. But federal troops converged on the region from Colorado and California and recovered control of the territory in the summer. After that time Confederate jurisdiction was confined to the eleven states which had seceded, although the Confederacy continued to claim Missouri and Kentucky and the Confederate battle flag sported stars for thirteen states.

The Birth of the Confederacy

On February 4, 1861, delegates from South Carolina, Mississippi, Florida, Alabama, Georgia, and Louisiana met in Montgomery, Alabama, to form the Confederate States of America. Joined by a delegation from Texas a few days later, these fifty men were some of the most outstanding leaders in the South. Seventeen were planters, and only one delegate was not a slaveholder. Forty were lawyers, many of whom had been active in politics or had served in judicial capacities in their respective states. Medical doctors, businessmen, teachers, college presidents, newspaper editors, and preachers were also present. Nearly half of the men had served in the national Congress, and two had held cabinet posts. Recent historians have contended that these men as a group were political moderates, and their actions in convention tend to support this conclusion.

The delegates readily agreed that they must act in haste and with unanimity. Their desire for speed was understandable. Lincoln was to be inaugurated on March 4, and they reasoned that the sooner they agreed upon a constitution and officers for their new republic the better were their chances of survival. Their desire to show the world their total consensus was less reasonable, and the "mania for unanimity" stifled honest differences of opinion, sowing seeds for later dissatisfaction. On February 5 a committee was charged to draw up a provisional constitution. Two days later the committee brought forth a document, and after one day's debate which resulted in only a few minor alterations, a provisional constitution based on the Constitution of the United States was adopted without dissent. On February 9 a committee was appointed to write a permanent constitution, and during the next three weeks the committee rushed through its task. On the last day of the month the convention began its deliberations on the committee's handiwork, and on March 11 it unanimously adopted a permanent constitution.

This permanent constitution of the Confederate States of America was a curiously interesting document. The delegates at the convention almost to a man revered the U. S. Constitution. What they did not like was the perversion of that sacred document by northerners who were using it to their own ends. Thus, the Confederate constitution resembled the U. S. Constitution, establishing a government with separate executive, legislative, and judicial functions and embracing the concept of checks and balances. But the new document contained clarifications, additions, and alterations, some of which were distinct improvements. For example, the substance of the twelve amendments to the old document was incorporated into the text of the new one. The President and Vice President were to serve for six-year terms, the President being ineligible for reelection. The President had the power to veto individual provisions of appropriation bills. If Congress approved, the President's cabinet members could sit with the Congress to discuss measures involving their departments.

Some of the innovations of the Confederate constitution reflected the agrarian interests of the southern people. Protective tariffs, bounties, and appropriations for internal improvements were outlawed. A two-thirds majority in Congress was necessary to levy export duties or admit new states to the Confederacy. Moreover, a two-thirds vote in each house of Congress was required for any appropriation of money, except requests of a cabinet officer who was required to submit an estimate through the President. The general welfare (or elastic) clause of the federal Constitution was pointedly omitted. Whereas the U. S. Constitution spoke of "those bound to Service for a Term of Years," the Confederate instrument avoided euphonious phrases and referred specifically to slavery. It forbade Congress to pass any bill impairing the right to own slaves, it guaranteed the right to slavery in the territories, and it prohibited the foreign slave trade. The three-fifths ratio concerning slaves for apportioning representation in the lower house of Congress was retained.

The new constitution did not overtly provide for secession from the Confederacy. The implication of the right to separate can be read into the preamble ("each State acting in its sovereign and independent character"), but the delegates who had been crying states' rights for years could not bring themselves to write into their document the basis for destruction of their own government. Later in the life of the Confederacy frequent demands were made to include the right of secession in the constitution, but the leaders of the Confederacy both early and late were painfully aware of the dangers inherent in secession.

To expedite the establishment of the new government, the men at Montgomery served not only as a constitutional convention, but also as the Congress of the provisional government. Each state had one vote in this makeshift unicameral legislature, but when the permanent bicameral assembly came into being, it was structured and it functioned almost exactly as its Union counterpart. The provisional Congress assumed the responsibility of electing a temporary President and Vice President. Everyone recognized that whoever filled these offices would probably be reelected under the permanent constitution (which proved to be true), and thus the task was a solemn one.

The South had many able leaders who for one reason or another could legitimately seek her highest office. A number of these potential candidates were either participants at the Montgomery convention or were on the scene as observers. At least three Georgians were serious contenders for the position. Howell Cobb, popular president of the assembly and the epitome of southern society and statesmanship, was perhaps the most logical choice. An affluent slaveowner, Cobb had much political experience as former governor of Georgia, Speaker of the House of Representatives in Washington, and Secretary of the United States Treasury. In addition to Cobb, Georgia offered Robert Toombs—rotund, affable, and militantly secessionist—and sickly Alexander Stephens, an ambivalently mixed Unionist and states' righter. Other possibilities were two great fire-eaters, Robert Barnwell Rhett, who bore primary responsibility for leading South Carolina out of the Union, and William L. Yancey, silvery-tongued Alabamian who had stirred secession sentiment in his native state for years. Broad experience in both civil and military administration brought Jefferson Davis's name to the front as a possibility, although Davis was not at Montgomery.

The demand for haste and unanimity was an important factor in the election of Jefferson Davis and Alexander Stephens as President and Vice President, respectively. The usual political maneuvering was kept to a minimum, subordinated to the consuming desire to establish a new government without delay. Moderate attitudes of the members of the convention militated against extremists like Rhett and Yancey. The Georgia delegation was split between Cobb and Toombs for the Presidency, and when several states, especially South Carolina, indicated that Davis was their choice, Georgia accepted him, but that state received the consolation prize when Stephens was named for the second post. On February 9 Davis and Stephens were unanimously elected on the first ballot. Less than two weeks later they were inaugurated as provisional leaders of the new government. Elected under the permanent constitution in November, they were inaugurated for their full terms the following February.

The son of a yeoman farmer, Jefferson Davis attended Kentucky's Transylvania University and West Point. When a wealthy brother gave him a Mississippi plantation, Davis became a successful cotton planter. After spending much time reading and preparing for political leadership, in 1845 he became a member of the United States Congress. During the Mexican War he commanded a volunteer regiment, promptly becoming Mississippi's best-known soldier. In 1847 he was elected to the United States Senate, and for the next four years he was an important leader in the proslavery cause. When Davis was defeated for the governorship of Mississippi on a platform opposing the Compromise of 1850, his political fortunes fell, but they were quickly revived when President Franklin Pierce appointed him Secretary of War. Later he reentered the Senate, where he championed southern interests. By the time of the secession crisis of 1860–61 Davis had moderated his southern extremism, and although he was a sincere believer in secession and the Confederacy, he took a more balanced view of these subjects than did some southern leaders. His moderate stand was not overlooked when he was designated President of the new republic.

Jefferson Davis possessed many qualifications for his high position. His years in Washington had given him both legislative and executive experience, his cabinet position being a particularly valuable apprenticeship. As Secretary of War, he dominated the Pierce administration, making a solid record for himself. Davis was deeply devoted to the Confederacy, and he was a tireless worker in its service. He made considerable sacrifices for the Confederacy, and he encouraged others to do the same. Perhaps his greatest service to the South's cause was his selection of superior military officers at the outset of the war; President Lincoln wasted much valuable time experimenting with incapable men. But in other ways, Davis was inferior to Lincoln as a wartime President. He was thin-skinned in the face of criticism, he had a sense of pride dangerously out of proportion to his other qualities, and he did not have Lincoln's relaxing sense of humor. For Davis to read from Artemus Ward at a meeting of his cabinet before considering a military crisis was not only highly improbable but also well-nigh impossible.

Davis's shortcomings accentuated discord in the Confederacy, particularly as the tide of events began to inundate the South. He was not a robust man, and his poor health made him irritable and tense. An able military commander who preferred to be in the field rather than at the head of the government, Davis often quarreled with his leading generals over both strategy and tactics. A most serious fault was that of attending to details of government which he should have delegated to subordinates. He lacked the ability to discriminate between major and minor matters —a first requisite for a good administrator. He tried to answer all his mail, even responding to a complaining letter from a widow whose hogs had been stolen by Confederate cavalrymen.

If Jefferson Davis loved the Confederacy, Alexander Stephens did not. A sixteen-year veteran of the U. S. Congress, Stephens had great respect for the American Constitution and the Union. His interpretation of the Constitution included a place for states' rights and secession, but in 1860 he refused to support the candidacy of John C. Breckinridge, and he opposed the withdrawal of Georgia from the Union. He agreed to be a delegate to the Montgomery convention only after others assured him that the Confederate constitution would closely follow the one he revered. The politics of the Montgomery convention pushed him into the

Vice Presidency, probably the greatest mistake of the convention. The diminutive and dyspeptic Stephens could never quite back the Confederacy wholeheartedly, and his pessimism and bitterness did much harm to the Confederate cause. As "Little Ellick" came to oppose Davis's policies, he engaged in obstructionist tactics of the most vicious sort. His opposition turned to hatred, and after 1863 Stephens attacked the President publicly. He became obsessed with what he believed were Davis's plans to establish a military dictatorship, and he did all within his power to hinder Davis. At a time when the infant Confederacy needed united leadership, it did not receive it.

The Life of the Confederacy

As soon as Jefferson Davis was elected provisional President, he began to establish a stable administration, including a cabinet. Some of the politicians who would have been most useful to the Davis administration preferred the battlefield to a civil post; thus, Davis was unable to tap the brains of men such as John C. Breckinridge, Howell Cobb, and Henry A. Wise. But appointments went to men of ability, generally, although the Chief Executive took into consideration a prospective appointee's state in an effort to give as wide a representation as possible. Robert Toombs became Secretary of the Treasury; Leroy P. Walker of Alabama, Secretary of War; Stephen R. Mallory of Florida, Secretary of the Navy; Judah P. Benjamin of Louisiana, Attorney General; and John H. Reagan of Texas, Postmaster General. At the time of their appointments, these selections were applauded throughout the South. Southerners were confident that the right men were in the right positions at the right time. But only Mallory and Reagan remained at their posts for the life of the Confederacy, a total of fourteen appointees holding the six cabinet positions. No fewer than six men served as Secretary of War during the four-year period. A more stable cabinet would have benefited a harassed President and a struggling new nation.

The leaders of the Confederacy faced many bewildering problems at the time of their appointments, and indeed, throughout their tenure of office. A workable government had to be established based upon the permanent constitution. Statutory chaos was avoided when the Confederates declared that all United States laws in effect in November 1860 were to be operative in the Confederacy, unless they were not compatible with the Confederate constitution or unless they were specifically repealed by the Confederate Congress. The Supreme Court provided for in the Confederate constitution was never established, and lesser courts meted out Confederate justice, generally on the principle of *stare decisis,* by basing their rulings on previous decisions of the United States courts.

Other problems proved more difficult in the life of the Confederate government. The permanent Confederate Congress did not contain
men of the same high caliber who sat in the provisional legislature; con-
sequently, it was weak throughout its lifetime. The glory and honor accompanying a military command in a land with an aristocratic tradition
attracted able leaders away from both congressional and executive posts.
Besides offering mediocre leadership, the Congress harmed the cause of
the Confederacy and its own effectiveness by carrying on much of its
business in secret. Neither the Congress nor the President admitted that
this policy undermined the morale of the southern people, even though
critics of the administration pointed it out many times. The prestige of
the Congress was further lessened when large regions of the South were
captured and controlled by Union forces, resulting in some members of
the Congress representing only "imaginary" constituencies. More importantly, the artificial unanimity of the Montgomery convention melted
rapidly in the warmth of difficult times, and the Davis administration
found exasperating critics both in and out of Congress. While pressing
problems in dire need of solution languished, the administration's supporters and their opponents engaged in hours of fruitless talk. Administration leaders in the Senate were Benjamin H. Hill and Howell Cobb of
Georgia, James Phelan of Mississippi, Clement C. Clay of Alabama, and
Robert M. T. Hunter of Virginia, while in the House of Representatives
there were Jabez L. M. Curry of Alabama and Ethelbert Barksdale of
Davis's home state. Besides Vice President Stephens, the President's opponents included Senator Louis T. Wigfall, a Texas fire-eater, and Tennessee Congressman Henry S. Foote, whose longtime opposition to Davis
was bitter. Stephens's tongue-lashing tirades against Davis caused violence
in Congress, and fists, bowie knives, and pistols were occasionally used to
settle quarrels. Although the opposition was not organized or united, it
interfered with the functions of the government, and it lowered the morale of the southern people. A congress filled with second rate men deeply
divided on the policies of President Davis could hardly have been expected to accomplish a great deal. So much needed to be done, but as
Stephens remarked, "The mountain labors and brings forth a mouse."
He could have added that his contribution to this paradox was notable.

Southerners believed that diplomatic recognition by European nations, especially Great Britain and France, would assure their nation's
survival, and Confederate diplomacy was directed toward that end. Having become convinced that cotton was the link pin in the world's trade
chain, the Confederates based all of their diplomacy on the supposed supremacy of their staple product. But that confidence was ill-founded;
King Cotton was not that important to world trade, and it was a grave
mistake for the South to base its entire diplomatic efforts upon it.

The southern leaders had such confidence in the power of cotton that they took for granted that their potential allies would uphold their cause. Instead of adopting a policy of persuasion, they attempted one of coercion to gain the support of France and England, whose great textile industries consumed about three-fourths of the South's crop and whose lifeblood supposedly depended upon it. In the summer and fall of 1861 Confederate leaders unofficially urged cotton planters and shippers to hold back their produce. When Europe thus came to realize its virtually total dependence upon cotton, it would then support the Confederacy, southerners reasoned. Although eschewing an official embargo, the Confederate leaders were pleased that their call for a voluntary one was heeded. The cotton crop of 1861 was one of the largest on record, but an infinitesimal portion of it reached European ports. The supremacy of King Cotton was about to be tested.

Jefferson Davis and his Secretaries of State had the difficult task of pressuring England and France to assist the newborn nation. Robert Toombs was a man of ability, but he was likely to make violent and dramatic statements, and he had none of the polish expected in a successful diplomat. Overcome by the frustrations of his job, Toombs resigned from the State Department within a few months after assuming office, accepting instead an appointment in the army. Frustration continued to dog him, he began to drink heavily, and before the war ended he engaged in obstructionist tactics against the Davis administration. The abilities of this man were wholly lost to the Confederate cause. Judah P. Benjamin assumed the post of Secretary of State in March 1862, and he ultimately became Davis's most important cabinet member, "the brains of the Confederacy," as this able Jew was called.

Davis was less shrewd in the choices of men he sent to Europe to carry on personal diplomacy for the Confederacy: the Alabama fire-eater William L. Yancey; Judge Pierre Rost, a French-speaking Louisiana Creole; and A. Dudley Mann, a Georgian who had had diplomatic experience serving for the United States. Yancey was the foremost orator of the antebellum South, but he did not understand the subtleties of diplomacy. Nor were the other two delegates particularly distinguished in the affairs of state.

Soon after these men arrived in London, the Confederacy won its greatest diplomatic triumph, but it was a windfall rather than the result of the work of the southern representatives. In May 1861 as a reaction to Lincoln's formal proclamation blockading southern ports, the British government announced its neutrality, thus recognizing the Confederacy as a belligerent. A few weeks later, the French Emperor Napoleon III also recognized the belligerent status of the Confederacy. This action gave Confederate interests the right to market their goods freely in England and France, an economic advantage of considerable magnitude. But Confederate diplomats could not take credit for this turn of events, and they failed totally in the object of their mission. The Confederate emissaries were instructed to appeal to the British on the basis of law and economics. On the one hand, they were to present secession as the exercise of a constitutional right; on the other hand, they were to make "delicate allusion" to the role of cotton in the world's economy, especially British dependence upon it. But these representatives were not "delicate," and they were recalled or reassigned to other posts.

In the fall of 1861 President Davis designated James M. Mason of Virginia and John Slidell of Louisiana as commissioners to England and France, respectively. Mason was a warm, intelligent man, but he was a curious choice for a representative to England. As author of the Fugitive Slave Act of 1850, he was anathema to British liberals. Furthermore, he was provincial in speech and manners, and many feared the worst for the Confederacy with an envoy at the Court of St. James who was somewhat careless when he spit tobacco juice. Mrs. Mary Chesnut recorded in her diary: "My wildest imagination will not picture Mr. Mason as a diplomat. He will say 'chaw' for 'chew' and he will call himself 'Jeems,' and he will wear a dress coat for breakfast." On the other hand, Slidell was a well-known and astute politician. A former United States Senator with diplomatic experience in Mexico, he spoke French and was married to a girl from a Louisiana Creole family. He was easily the ablest diplomat the South sent abroad.

Mason and Slidell sailed for Europe in November on the British ship *Trent*, but they were taken from the vessel on the high seas by Captain Charles Wilkes of the Union navy and placed in a Boston prison. The North crowed over this "diplomatic" triumph, but the British were affronted at this blatant violation of the rights of their neutral ship, and they demanded that the two Confederates be released. The trespassing upon British property by a Union naval official so offended John Bull that a serious threat of war occurred. Eight thousand British troops were hastily ordered to Canada, and Lincoln and his cabinet wisely allowed the diplomats to continue their voyage. Ironically, Mason and Slidell may have come closer to gaining foreign intervention in the war while in prison at Fort Warren than at conference tables in Europe.

Mason and Slidell were instructed to stress the commercial advantages to be obtained by Europe from an independent Confederate States of America. They challenged the legality of the northern blackade, arguing that it was not effective and therefore not legal under international law. Their main goal was diplomatic recognition, and in the beginning they did not seek European alliances or intervention. But neither the British nor the French were eager to extend recognition to an infant nation that might not survive. When cotton supplies in both England and France dwindled, those governments were more inclined to consider recognition. But when military battles were won by the Union, both nations' leaders got cold feet. The ebb and flow of military events in America proved to have more influence upon the decision-makers in Europe than any other factor.

Besides the desire for special considerations for southern cotton, another selfish goal motivated Napoleon III in the diplomatic game. He coveted Mexico, but as long as the United States was not divided, he feared to act. The American Civil War gave him new courage; during that time he established a protectorate over Mexico, installing as emperor his brother-in-law, the Archduke Maximilian of Austria. If the Confederacy survived, Napoleon reasoned, United States power would be diminished, and his chances of permanently extending French hegemony over Mexico might materialize. Yet Napoleon could not bring himself to support the Confederacy unless the British did, and the latter's stance in the final analysis kept him from taking the plunge.

Economic distress in the British cotton factory areas of Lancashire, Cheshire, and Derbyshire was severe in the face of the cotton famine. Even though the lack of cotton for the mills threw thousands of workers out of jobs, the British people were not inclined to favor southern independence. Moral indignation has been advanced as the reason for the English workers' refusal to bow to the economic pressures of cotton shortages, but a more likely explanation is that the workers sensed that somehow their long-range economic well-being was more nearly related to the Union than to the Confederacy. Perhaps the laborers doubted that the Confederacy would survive. Certainly doubt influenced the British leaders who negotiated with the visiting diplomats.

Such attitudes placed the Confederacy in an undesirable paradox. The South required British support to win the war, but the British government would not extend aid until the South proved that it would win. When the South won battles at the beginning of the war—in the Shenandoah Valley, on the Virginia Peninsula, at Second Manassas—the British perked up their ears to Confederate diplomatic overtures. But Confederate military reverses dulled the enthusiasm of Queen Victoria's government, and a policy of "wait and see" remained in effect, much to the disappointment of the Davis administration. When the battles of Vicksburg and Gettysburg in July 1863 ended in Union victories, the prospects of British (and thus French) recognition of the Confederacy fell to a new low. Nor were Confederate diplomatic fortunes revived after that time. For all practical purposes, King Cotton had been dethroned.

The South had based its diplomacy on the hope of receiving British and French recognition. Actually recognition without assistance would not have been of great benefit. Only if recognition had prodded the North into declaring war on the two European nations, thus making them allies with the South, would recognition have had any effect. The South needed supplies, trade, loans, and military assistance which recognition alone would not bring. Unfortunately for the South, the southern people and their leaders had overestimated the power of King Cotton.

Some of the South's economic problems grew out of a shortage of money, one historian of the Confederacy observing, "If I were asked what was the greatest single weakness of the Confederacy, I should say . . . that it was in this matter of finances." Certainly the military power of the new nation could not long endure without adequate financing. Davis entrusted the Confederate Treasury to Christopher G. Meminger, whose task would have been extremely difficult with a most helpful Congress; with a Congress reluctant to levy the necessary taxes or to establish a sound fiscal policy Meminger's task was close to impossible. The Secretary of the Treasury was responsible for converting the assets of an agricultural economy—land, slaves, and cotton—into cash and credit necessary to carry on total war.

Despite the obvious problems facing Meminger, he strove to establish a sound national financial system. The bases for his system were loans, taxes, and paper money. Following Meminger's recommendations, Congress in February 1861 floated a bond issue of $15,000,000, paying 8 percent interest and secured by a nominal tax on cotton exports. Redeemable in ten years, the bonds were eagerly gobbled up by loyal Confederate citizens when they were first made available, but the shortage of cash in a credit economy slowed the sale noticeably after the first wave of enthusiasm. Ultimately, banks bought most of the bonds. To provide money until these bonds were purchased, $1,000,000 worth of treasury notes was made available.

After the war began, Meminger asked Congress for a loan of $50,-000,000, a war tax of $15,000,000, an import tariff of 12½ percent, and $20,000,000 more in treasury notes. Because of the slow sales of the first bonds, the so-called Produce Loan was extended to planters and farmers as an inducement to buying the bonds. They were allowed to pledge for these bonds money they hoped to receive from their unharvested crops. Chief Commissioner J. D. B. De Bow publicized this scheme and at first it appeared successful, but it soon became clear that this was not a valid source of revenue. The Union blockade and the southern embargo on cotton threatened cotton farmers with no market in the fall of 1861. They feared that they might have to sell their product at low prices in a flooded domestic market in order to honor pledges to buy the bonds, a fear not without some foundation. More ominously, many southerners hesitated to buy long-term Confederate bonds, thus expressing a lack of confidence in the basic financial soundness of the southern nation. Because of the snail's pace in the sale of bonds, Meminger suggested that Congress authorize another $100,000,000 in paper currency, which it did in the summer of 1861.

As the war progressed, the government needed larger and larger

sums of money, and the job of acquiring it became more and more difficult. Since taxes and loans did not pay for the immense cost of military
necessities, the Treasury Department turned increasingly to paper currency to solve its money shortage. Flooding the inflated southern economy with treasury notes, especially after the summer of 1863, the government gave impetus to the runaway spiral of inflation. Treasury notes
became the primary medium of exchange in the South, but they depre-
ciated so rapidly that they were worth no more than four cents on the
dollar during most of the war period. It took a wheelbarrow full of paper
money to purchase a small bag of groceries. Meminger has been criticized
for turning to paper currency to subsidize the South's war effort, but the
criticism is unjust. He had no other alternative. On several occasions
throughout the war he pleaded with Congress to enact stringent fiscal
measures, but Congress was generally unresponsive. When it did pass taxing or funding measures, the laws were usually filled with loopholes and
did not greatly assist the war effort. Furthermore, these inequitable laws
were opposed by those who felt they were being taxed unfairly. The laws
invited and received evasion. Even the most generous cooperation between the Congress and Meminger (and his successor George A. Tren-
holm) would not have solved the South's serious economic and fiscal
troubles. The old maxim "you can't squeeze blood from a turnip" was
never more applicable than to the South and her limited resources.

In comparison with the North, the South was extremely poor in
both manpower and material resources. The population of the twenty-
three northern states was 22,700,000 in contrast to 9,000,000 southerners
in eleven states. Included in this latter number were a docile slave population of some 3,900,000 and unknown thousands of white southerners
who sat on their hands or actively fought against the Confederacy, further stacking overwhelming odds against the South. On the battlefield
the ratio was not so great, but there also the South was at a distinct disadvantage. The Union sent two soldiers for each one the South placed in
the field. Those soldiers needed to be adequately fed, clothed, and
armed, and the South's economic resources were clearly second best. Military historians have concluded that in many specific battles, the southern
soldiers were as well equipped with guns and ammunition as the northern men, but in the long run the South felt the pinch of trying to fight
the war without the basis of a modern industrial economy.

The beginnings of a great industrial economy and society were
present in the North but not in the South. In 1860 northern factories
produced nearly six times as much as did those in the South, and once
the war was under way, the disparity widened. Uniforms, shoes, socks,
blankets, guns, and ammunition were generally in short supply in the
South throughout the war. The South looked in vain outside its boundaries for the tools and machines to step up its industrial production. Fac-

ing an impossible task, the famous Tredegar Iron Works of Richmond, Virginia, alone produced nearly all the South's cannons until near the end of the war, while scores of factories in the North early turned out heavy military equipment of all kinds for the Union. The South was ostensibly the most agricultural region in the nation, and this was true in regard to the number of acres under the plow, but northern farms produced more per acre and had a larger total land value. Beginning with a circumscribed economic base in all areas and by any standards, the Confederacy was soon bankrupt.

The Death of the Confederacy

The crumbling of the South's economic structure was a major consideration in the ultimate defeat of the Confederacy. Assisting with the economic disintegration on the one hand, and growing out of it on the other, was an intangible factor which also hastened that defeat. Historian Edward Channing called this invisible but nonetheless substantial element the loss of the "will to fight." The ebullient enthusiasm of southerners at the beginning of the war rose and fell with victories and defeats on the battlefield for the first two years of the conflict, but after mid-1863 a gathering gloom slowly enveloped the southern people, despite the efforts of their leaders to dispel it.

Several factors contributed to the lowering of southern morale. One of these was the pervasive and disruptive influence of the doctrine of states' rights. While a strong central government with much power over the states needed to be established in order to assist with the prosecution of the war, the framers of the Confederate constitution deliberately deemphasized the powers of the central government. Many state leaders who had orated in favor of states' rights before the formation of the Confederacy continued to stress this doctrine after the Confederacy was born. Georgia's Governor Joseph E. Brown, an ardent secessionist at the beginning of the war, led obstructionists against Davis's policies on the ground that they violated states' rights. Brown was particularly vocal in his opposition to the conscription law, which he stamped as unconstitutional, unnecessary, and in violation of the rights of Georgians and Georgia. He refused to allow the draft to be implemented in his state until Georgia's legislature and highest court gave the law their approval. Even then Brown obstinately hindered the operation of the draft law. His actions and words bordered on treason. Equally obstreperous toward the central government with which he regularly quarreled was Zebulon Baird Vance, governor of North Carolina. An example of the provincialism of the latter was his refusal to send uniforms and shoes to Robert E. Lee's troops in Virginia who sorely needed them, even though Vance had a stockpile of over ninety thousand uniforms and large supplies of leather and blankets. Vance insisted on saving these articles for North Carolina soldiers. The actions of these and other southern state leaders and their followers hastened the declining fortunes of the Confederacy.

Closely related to the concept of states' rights was a peace movement, especially strong in Georgia and the Carolinas, which weakened the Davis administration and gave false hope to many southerners. Leader of the secession movement, South Carolina was the unlikely spearhead of this drive. After major military defeats in 1863, the peace movement picked up momentum throughout the South as southerners looked for ways to hasten the end of the war and to avoid the South's total defeat. Southerners who had opposed or reluctantly supported secession in the first place gave impetus to the movement. Also, it was affected by internal state politics and the personal ambitions of men opposed to Jefferson Davis. In December 1864 the anti-Davis states' rights men in South Carolina elected Andrew G. Magrath to the governorship. A few months before, these same men had proposed that both northern and southern states send delegates to a convention to discuss a peaceful settlement of the war. Part of the reason for the request for this convention was political. The peace leaders hoped their actions would help northern Democrats elect a peace candidate to the U. S. Presidency in November 1864. The hopes of the peace-seekers were dashed when Lincoln was reelected.

By this time the war had reached the stage where the North's superior economic and military resources were wearing down the South. Diplomatic efforts to gain economic assistance had failed miserably, and the southern populace knew it. Newspapers became increasingly critical of President Davis, contributing to the growing belief that the South could not win the war. War weariness dampened the spirits of the civilian population which suffered inestimable physical suffering and mental anguish in the face of diminishing supplies of necessities and the relentless military endeavors of northern generals like William T. Sherman and Philip Sheridan. Added to these developments was the daily news that additional southern boys had lost their lives in battle; hardly a family seemed not to have lost one or more sons or husbands, the abundance of black mourning dresses being a sad reminder of this. Mounting desertion from Confederate armies were discouraging not only to battlefield commanders, but also to southern morale generally. So serious was the lack of manpower late in the war due to desertion, declining enlistments, and death that the South in desperation considered using Negro troops. As the South's military forces were repeatedly defeated, the morale of the southern people deteriorated accordingly.

Economic disintegration, repeated reverses on the battlefield, and sagging morale were the major ingredients in the death of the Confederacy. Each affected the other, and they singly and in combination contributed to the failing cause. The next chapter will be devoted to a brief account of the military history of the Civil War, ending with General Lee's surrender which was simultaneous with the expiration of the short-lived Confederate States of America.

Suggestions for Further Reading

Volumes enlightening the secession movement include: Dwight L. Dumond, *The Secession Movement, 1860–1861* (New York: Macmillan, 1931); Henry T. Shanks, *The Secession Movement in Virginia, 1847–1861* (Richmond: Garrett & Massie, 1934); J. Carlyle Sitterson, *The Secession Movement in North Carolina* (Chapel Hill: Univ. North Carolina, 1939); Percy L. Rainwater, *Mississippi: Storm Center of Secession, 1856–1861* (Baton Rouge: Louisiana State Univ., 1938); C. P. Denman, *The Secession Movement in Alabama* (Montgomery: Alabama State Dept. of Archives & History, 1933); W. M. Caskey, *Secession and Restoration of Louisiana* (University, La.: Louisiana State Univ., 1938); Kenneth M. Stampp, *And the War Came: The North and the Secession Crisis, 1860–1861* * (Baton Rouge: Louisiana State Univ., 1951). Ralph A. Wooster, *The Secession Conventions of the South* (Princeton: Princeton Univ., 1962) is a carefully documented study of times of crisis and decision in the southern states. Accounts of the secession crisis can also be found in Roy F. Nichols, *The Disruption of American Democracy* * (New York: Macmillan, 1948) and Allan Nevins, *The Emergence of Lincoln,* 2 vols. (New York: Scribners, 1950). Much information may also be gleaned from David M. Potter, *Lincoln and His Party in the Secession Crisis* * (New Haven: Yale Univ., 1942) and Oliver Crenshaw, *The Slave States in the Presidential Election of 1860* (Baltimore: Johns Hopkins Univ., 1945). Articles which may be profitably read on the subject are: Cole, "The South and the Right of Secession in the Early Fifties," *Mississippi Valley Historical Review,* vol. 1 (1914–15) and Venable, "William L. Yancey's Transition from Unionism to States Rights," *Journal of Southern History,* vol. 10 (1944).

The best single volume on the Confederacy is Clement Eaton's *A History of the Southern Confederacy* * (New York: Macmillan, 1954), although Charles P. Roland's briefer volume, *The Confederacy* * (Chicago: Univ. Chicago, 1960) and E. Merton Coulter's longer study, *The Confederate States of America, 1861–1865* (Baton Rouge: Louisiana State Univ., 1950) are also good. Not to be overlooked are two volumes by Clifford Dowdey, *Experiment in Rebellion: The Southern Confederacy* * (Garden City: Doubleday, 1946) and *The Land They Fought For: The Story of the South as the Confederacy, 1832–1865* * (Garden City: Doubleday, 1955). Charles Robert Lee, Jr. has studied *The Confederate Constitutions* (Chapel Hill: Univ. North Carolina, 1963), and Frank L. Owsley has surveyed Confederate diplomacy in *King Cotton Diplomacy* (Chicago: Univ. Chicago, 1931). Owsley analyzes the weaknesses of the Confederacy in his *States Rights in the Confederacy* (Chicago: Univ. Chicago, 1925), and the decline and fall of the southern monetary system is revealed in

Richard C. Todd, *Confederate Finance* (Athens, Ga.: Univ. Georgia, 1954). Difficulties in regard to southern industry, finance, and daily living are discussed by Charles W. Ramsdell, *Behind the Lines in the Southern Confederacy* (Baton Rouge: Louisiana State Univ., 1944), while Mary E. Massey, *Ersatz in the Confederacy* (Columbia, S. C.: Univ. South Carolina, 1952) writes of shortages and substitutes during wartime. Richard D. Goff, *Confederate Supply* (Durham: Duke Univ., 1969) argues that the bungling of supply management by Jefferson Davis and his associates contributed in large measure to the defeat of the Confederacy. Charles H. Wesley, *The Collapse of the Confederacy* (Washington: Associated Publishers, 1937) majors on societal flaws which harmed the South's ability to carry on a successful war. Case studies of Confederate governments in operation at the state level may be found in the following: Jefferson Davis Bragg, *Louisiana in the Confederacy* (Baton Rouge: Louisiana State Univ., 1941); John K. Bettersworth, *Confederate Mississippi* (Baton Rouge: Louisiana State Univ., 1943); Charles E. Cauthen, *South Carolina Goes to War, 1860–1865* (Chapel Hill: Univ. North Carolina, 1950).

Jefferson Davis has been interpreted from widely differing points of view, as illustrated by William E. Dodd, *Jefferson Davis: Statesman of the Old South* (Philadelphia: G. W. Jacobs, 1907) and Hudson Strode, *Jefferson Davis: American Patriot,* 2 vols. (New York: Harcourt, Brace, 1955–1959). Rembert W. Patrick, *Jefferson Davis and His Cabinet* (Baton Rouge: Louisiana State Univ., 1944) is a study of personal relationships, while the following two volumes concentrate on specific members of the Confederate cabinet: Ulrich B. Phillips, *The Life of Robert Toombs* (New York: Macmillan, 1913) and Robert D. Meade, *Judah P. Benjamin: Confederate Statesman* (New York: Oxford, 1943). The Confederate Vice President has been the subject of volumes by Louis Pendleton (Philadelphia: G. W. Jacobs, 1908) and Rudolph von Abele (New York: Knopf, 1946), the latter being a skillful Freudian interpretation. Biographies of other influential southern leaders include: Laura A. White, *Robert Barnwell Rhett: Father of Secession* (New York: Century, 1931); John W. Du Bose, *The Life and Times of William Lowndes Yancey* (Birmingham: Roberts & Son, 1892); Henry H. Simms, *Life of Robert M. T. Hunter* (Richmond: William Byrd Press, 1935); W. A. Cate, *Lucius Q. C. Lamar: Statesman of Secession and Reunion* (Chapel Hill: Univ. North Carolina, 1938).

* Available in paperback.

CHAPTER VIII

THE CIVIL WAR

The formation of the Southern Confederacy in 1861 did not necessarily mean that a bloody civil war was inevitable. Many Americans on both sides of the Mason-Dixon Line favored southern separation from the Union without conflict. Such an attitude was openly expressed by men in prominent positions, Horace Greeley of the *New York Tribune* editorializing that the "wayward sisters" should be allowed to "depart in peace." War would occur only if Union leaders insisted upon the South remaining in the Union. But if one group of states could disengage itself from the Union without compunction, so could others. A tradition could have been established for the ultimate dissolution of the entire Union. The new President of the United States realized this; therefore, he took a strong stand against recent events in the South in his March 1861 inaugural address. Lincoln gently but firmly reiterated the constitutional doctrine that the Union was older than the states and that the contract drawn up by the states could not be revoked. He restated his position that he had no intention of interfering directly or indirectly with the institution of slavery, as southerners had come to fear. He insisted that the southern states had no valid reason for attempting secession, and he must have spoken more slowly in order to be clearly understood when he said: "In your hands, my dissatisfied fellow countrymen, and not in mine, is the momentous issue of civil war. The government will not assail you. You can have no conflict without being yourselves the aggressors. You have no oath registered in heaven to destroy the government, while I

shall have the most solemn one to 'preserve, protect, and defend' it."
Charles Sumner believed the inaugural address was well described by Napoleon's simile of "a hand of iron in a velvet glove."

Actually Lincoln had not taken as firm a stand as his words would imply. The Confederates had already seized much United States property in the South, and the new President quite frankly admitted that he would not attempt to regain it. A few places in the South remained in loyalist hands, including two rather inconsequential forts at Pensacola, Florida, and on an island in Charleston harbor. Because of national publicity directed toward forts Pickens and Sumter, Lincoln hesitated to allow them to fall under Confederate control, yet he feared a show of force would make reconciliation impossible. After temporizing for several weeks, he ordered food delivered to the beleaguered Sumter soldiers.

When Pierre G. T. Beauregard on April 12 gave the order to fire upon Fort Sumter, while the supply ships were on the way, Lincoln had no alternative but to protect federal property and to make war against those who would destroy the Union. With an indignant populace behind him, he issued a call for seventy-five thousand volunteers to defend federal property and men. As a consequence, both northern and southern men rushed to arms, and the American Civil War was on. After decades of tension and compromise, the nation made the undesired but compelling decision to settle the sectional controversy by force.

Conflict: Round One

To win the war the South had only to hold the territory in those states which had seceded. Defensive strategy called for the separated regime to arm its young men and station them on the perimeter of the South to repel hostile armed forces. To maintain the integrity of the Union, officials of the United States government had the task of making offensive war. Northern soldiers had to be sent into the South to conquer the seceded land. The Union's general strategy to heal the ugly schism was not worked out overnight, and it was not executed with particular precision or dispatch when it was settled upon; nevertheless, a sound plan to defeat the South was evident fairly early in the war. The Union's blueprint for victory may be summarized under four points: (1) a blockade of southern ports; (2) seizure of the Mississippi River, separating western Confederate states and territories from the main body of the South; (3) attacks upon southern lines from the north and west, pushing them back, constricting the area which the South controlled; and (4) the capture of the Confederate capital, which had been moved from Montgomery, Alabama, to Richmond, Virginia, a few weeks after the Old Dominion voted to secede.

President Lincoln proclaimed a blockade all along the southern coastline shortly after the war began. The federal navy was small and widely scattered in 1861, and for several months the blockade was a joke because of its ineffectiveness. The Confederate seacoast extended some thirty-five hundred miles from Virginia to Texas and contained hundreds of inlets, bays, and river openings. Not even a drastically enlarged navy could completely blockade this lengthy coastline. But Lincoln believed that the Confederacy would be weakened if its chief ports were effectively patrolled, and as the war progressed, the number of federal ships in waters off the southern coast increased. The sievelike blockade was never 100 percent effective, but it seriously hurt the South's ability to make war, and it must receive due credit in the ultimate Union victory. Those who favored the South's cause or who were attracted by the profits to be gained from a successful entry into a southern port tried running the blockade. The best-known fictional blockade runner was Rhett Butler, the dashing hero of *Gone with the Wind*. The real blockade runners may not have been as glamorous as Clark Gable's Butler, but they were helpful to the South's cause.

The Confederacy was born without a navy, and it was unable to develop a fleet that could contest the ever-increasing Union navy. Lack of funds, shortage of shipbuilding facilities, and effective northern diplomacy overseas restricted the Confederates' efforts to build or buy additional vessels of war. Primarily due to the absence of naval protection, a number of southern ports were captured by Union amphibious forces in 1861. The South rallied and slowed this process down, however, and by 1863 it was managing to hold its remaining coastal areas, particularly the important port of Charleston, South Carolina. Northern frigates continued to apply pressure along the southern coastline, and southerners in port cities had to contend with the naval forces of Union officers such as Admiral David Farragut—the greatest naval figure produced by the war —who launched attacks on important southern seaport cities, including New Orleans and Mobile Bay. The latter was the site in 1864 for the tough admiral's famous response "Damn the torpedoes! Full speed ahead!" after a subordinate had reminded Farragut that the waters of the bay were filled with "submarines," crude forerunners of today's mines.

Although the Confederacy had few ships, several southern raiders were successful throughout the course of the war. The *Florida* captured thirty-four ships before being seized in 1864 near Brazil. The English-built *Alabama* took sixty-two ships on the high seas before being sunk off the coast of France in a duel with a Union ship. The *Shenandoah* bagged over forty ships, including eight seized two months after the war on land had ended. The Confederate fleet on the Mississippi River should not be forgotten. Headed by the *Louisiana* and the *Manassas*, two well-built river boats with powerful iron prows which served as battering rams, the

South's river fleet was later strengthened with the completion of the *Mississippi,* the most powerful warship in the world at that time. These and other sloops and gunboats delayed the Union's plans to control the river from New Orleans north to federal territory.

One of the most famous southern attempts to build a navy occurred when Confederate engineers raised from the bottom of a harbor in Virginia the burned hulk of the *Merrimack,* a Union frigate which had previously been sunk. Rechristened *Virginia,* this old wooden ship was converted into a metal-clad vessel with sloping iron plates four inches thick to protect her decks. Carrying a battering ram weighing fifteen hundred pounds, this Confederate man-of-war was launched in Virginia waters in March 1862, and promptly cleared five Union frigates from the estuary near Norfolk. Two wooden Union ships sailed to do battle with the strange vessel. One went down in deep water with blazing but ineffective guns, and the other was hopelessly grounded and set aflame. The three others were grounded in their attempts to escape; the following day one of the disabled ships was an easy target for the cumbersome but powerful iron monster. To neutralize this ominous weapon the Union sent its own iron-clad vessel into the Virginia coastal waters. The *Monitor,* designed by a Swedish engineer named Ericsson who sold Lincoln on it, was a low-lying vessel completely covered with iron plates, with one iron turret on top of an almost flat deck. A three-hour battle between the two ended in a draw, since neither ship could pierce the plating of the other. A revolution in naval craft design and manufacture had begun, and within a brief span of years the all-wooden warship was as obsolete as the sailboat was when the steamship was perfected. Discussions of the war on land should not minimize the importance of the naval forces on the high seas, in the coastwise waters, and on navigable streams, especially the Mississippi River.

During the Civil War the land movements of both northern and southern military forces were complicated. Two separate areas of military operations existed during most of the war. The Appalachian Mountains served as a giant geographic barrier, keeping armies from moving freely from eastern states to the western area, and vice versa. The armies on each side of the mountains thus fought independently of each other. Not until 1864 were the campaigns of the two areas effectively coordinated by the Union government, and this was never successfully accomplished by Jefferson Davis and his military and civilian advisors. Then, too, in the nineteenth century an invading army seldom moved directly against an enemy force. Its primary target was usually an important city, railroad junction, or command post on a river. Once the invading army was in motion, the defending force then maneuvered to place itself between the invader and his objective, thus setting the stage for battle. These military tactics explain why so many major land battles occurred near large cities rather than in them. Richmond (the Confederate capital), New Orleans and Vicksburg (strategically located on the Mississippi River), and Chattanooga and Atlanta (vital railroad centers) became the principal targets for federal troops, and major battles near each of these cities reveal nineteenth-century military thought.

Few battles occurred in 1861, when neither the North nor the South had highly organized, efficient armies. But Lincoln and his Congress hoped to end the war quickly by capturing Richmond, and Union military forces made three thrusts into Virginia in that year. The first move was from Ohio into the pro-Union counties of western Virginia. In a series of small battles, Confederate sympathizers were subdued or driven out of this mountainous region, and Confederate control was never reestablished; in fact, in 1863 this area entered the Union as West Virginia. The other two federal invasions of Virginia were less successful. In one, Union troops tried to take Richmond by approaching that city from the peninsula to the east, but Confederate soldiers chased the invaders out without difficulty. The third and main Union push into Virginia in July resulted in the largest battle fought in 1861. Under the command of General Irvin McDowell, a federal army of nearly thirty-five thousand troops marched toward Richmond, but to be successful it had to capture an important railroad junction at Manassas, some twenty miles south of Washington on a tributary of the Potomac called Bull Run Creek. When Confederates got wind of the movements, the newly formed Army of Northern Virginia containing fewer than thirty thousand men was moved to Manassas. Here McDowell's men attacked the Confederate forces under the leadership of General Beauregard, the "Napoleon of the South." McDowell's green recruits pushed back the Confederate left flank, and a Union victory seemed imminent. At the last moment a brigade of Virginians under the Bible-quoting, lemon-sucking infantry genius, Thomas J. Jackson, was rushed to the area by rail from the Shenandoah Valley. Tenaciously clinging to a strategic hill, Jackson's men caused the flanking movement to fail. Jackson received the nickname "Stonewall" at this time when a South Carolina general, seeking to rally his own faltering columns, shouted that Jackson and his troops were "standing like a stone wall" against enemy fire. When the southerners counterattacked, the inexperienced Union troops were forced to fall back, and retreat soon became rout. As the northern troops ran toward the security of Washington north of the Potomac, they threw down their guns, upset supply wagons, and brushed aside curious sightseers who had come out to view the fight.

Although the casualties were light on both sides, this first battle of Manassas had several important effects. Southerners were convinced that Yankees were poor fighters and that the war would be brief and end in victory for the South. Northerners realized that the defeat of the Confederacy would take longer than they had originally estimated. While the South celebrated its victory, the North began a naval building program, reconditioning old vessels and laying down keels for new ones. This battle convinced Lincoln that a tight naval blockade needed to be clamped on all major southern ports. While southerners prided themselves on superior manpower, the North began raising and equipping large armies for full-scale war. In the short run Manassas was a psychological victory for the South; in the long run it aided in the South's defeat.

The Confederates also won a few lesser battles during the first year of the war. But President Lincoln and his government did not feel despondent. General George B. McClellan was named commander of the Union's eastern army, and during the winter of 1861–62 he began building an army at Washington ultimately to total nearly 150,000 men. This force was to be the largest ever amassed in the Western Hemisphere up to that time, and its mobilization spelled ultimate doom for the South. The South was misled in 1861 when it thought the war nearly over. The war's full fury was yet to come.

"In All Its Fury"

In 1862 a thin line of Confederate soldiers guarded the 600-mile stretch from the Appalachian Mountains to the Mississippi River. General Albert Sidney Johnston commanded Confederate forces in Kentucky, his authority extending into Arkansas and over an army there under General Earl Van Dorn. Southern troops in this western theatre totaled about 70,000. Northern troops numbering nearly 100,000 were gathered to attack these limited defenses. General Henry W. Halleck commanded Union troops in Missouri and western Kentucky, and General Don Carlos Buell headed forces in eastern Kentucky. With Halleck's blessing, northern forces led by an unkempt, cigar-chewing West Pointer named Ulysses S. Grant attacked southern lines at weak spots, several forts falling into the invaders' hands. In February from a base at Cairo, Illinois, Grant moved down the Mississippi River with armored gunboats, easily capturing forts Henry and Donelson, supposedly strong Confederate positions on the Tennessee and Cumberland rivers in northwestern Tennessee. When Grant moved against Fort Donelson, the Confederate commander, General Simon Bolivar Buckner, requested "the best terms of capitulation." "No terms except an unconditional and immediate surrender can be accepted," was Grant's terse reply. The squat, laconic general gained the name "Unconditional Surrender" Grant as a result of this statement and was thus catapulted to national fame. By taking these forts and over fifteen thousand prisoners, Grant assured Union control of nearly all of western Kentucky and much of western Tennessee. This successful action placed Union forces in a good position to attack Mississippi and Alabama. The loss of these forts was therefore a severe blow to southern morale, as well as a penetration of the southern defense perimeter. Within a few months skirmishes and battles in Arkansas also resulted in federal victories. Both Arkansas and southern Missouri were either occupied by federal troops or effectively separated from Confederate military forces east of the Mississippi River. The South seemed impotent to prevent the Union from carrying out its divide-and-conquer plan.

In April 1862 General Halleck, now commander of the Union's total western forces, ordered Grant and a large army of federal troops into southwestern Tennessee near the Mississippi border, in preparation for an attack on Corinth, Mississippi, an important railroad junction; control of the junction would permit a deeper thrust into Confederate territory. General Buell was ordered to join Grant. To check Grant's invasion generals Johnston and Beauregard hurriedly amassed forty thousand troops and attacked Grant's men at an encampment at Shiloh, a country church twenty miles north of Corinth. Hoping to destroy Grant's army before Buell and his men arrived and before the combined army made its attack on southern-held territory, the Confederates in this early morning surprise attack caught many soldiers in the middle of boiling their morning coffee, others only half-dressed, and still others yet in their blankets. Grant's men brought a semblance of order out of the original chaos and managed to hold their lines on the first day. Buell's fresh troops poured into the area during the night, and by the end of the second day, the tide of battle favored the federals. Grant's counterattack forced the exhausted and demoralized Confederates to retreat to Corinth, but not until after they had lost thirteen thousand men (including General Johnston). The federals lost ten thousand. Grant was visibly shaken by this unexpected battle, and he failed to pursue the enemy in its retreat. This oversight tarnished the solid reputation he had won when he captured forts Henry and Donelson. General Halleck assumed command of Grant's and Buell's forces, and by early June as he pushed cautiously southward, Halleck controlled the Mississippi River as far south as Memphis. At the same time, northern forces had been moving up from the mouth of the river, after a naval squadron under Farragut had steamed through the weak Confederate defenses, forcing the surrender of New Orleans in early May. While a Union land force under General Benjamin F. Butler occupied the city of New Orleans, additional pressure was placed on Baton Rouge and Natchez, and by the end of the summer these two river towns were also in Union hands. Except for the strong fortress at Vicksburg, Mississippi, Union forces controlled the Mississippi River. The fact that this control was not complete lay at the door of Grant's field tent, and the Union had to wait until the following summer before it successfully cleared the river of all Confederate power.

Meanwhile, General McClellan, commander of the Army of the Potomac, was busy in the east making preparation to attack Richmond. McClellan had many solid qualifications for responsible military command, one of which was experience. He had served in the Mexican War after his graduation from West Point, and during the Crimean War he had spent a year in Europe studying fortifications and the classical theories of warfare. "Little Mac" had a flair for the dramatic which he used to good advantage to inspire his troops; moreover, he was a good administrator, and he had supreme confidence in his own destiny. He enjoyed concocting bold plans, and he dreamed of bringing the war to a quick end by capturing Richmond. But he drilled his troops instead of attacking. He always overestimated his enemy's strength and underestimated his own, and he repeatedly asked for more troops.

After many unaccountable delays, McClellan at last decided to move against Richmond, and some of the most bitter and deadly fighting of the war resulted. Believing that a frontal attack over the difficult terrain of northern Virginia was foolish, McClellan had his army transported by water to the tip of the peninsula at the mouths of the York and James rivers. He intended to move against Richmond to the northwest. It was a sound battle plan because it lessened supply problems for a large army in hostile country, but McClellan soon revealed his total lack of understanding of the developing concepts of modern warfare. McClellan viewed the Civil War not as a titanic struggle between two peoples who disagreed over fundamental issues. Rather he saw it not unlike a gigantic chess game which generals played at a leisurely pace and for limited objectives. He was more concerned about capturing Richmond, for example, than in trying to destroy the army protecting it. His peninsula campaign of March 1862 revealed these concepts.

Proceeding cautiously, McClellan and 112,000 men floated down the Potomac to Fort Monroe on the coast. Taking plenty of time, McClellan occupied Yorktown, and by mid-May he had set up a base on a tributary of the York River about twenty-five miles from Richmond. A rapier thrust might have broken the resistance of the Confederates in Virginia, but McClellan delayed, even though he had 80,000 men up front and many reserves in the rear. Constantly calling upon Washington for more troops, McClellan pushed slowly toward the Confederate capital. General Joseph E. Johnston commanded the Confederate forces in Virginia, and he placed his relatively small army between McClellan and Richmond, cautiously retreating in the face of McClellan's giant force. The Army of the Potomac advanced to within six miles of the Confederate capital, the stately spires of the city in sharp outline against a clear sky, but there the advance halted. McClellan's army had been divided by the flooding of the Chickahominy River, and Johnston took advantage of this to attack one segment of the Union force. In May Johnston halted

McClellan's advance at the indecisive two-day battle of Seven Pines, but the general himself was seriously wounded in the fighting, and his army fell back toward Richmond.

Shortly after the battle of Seven Pines, President Jefferson Davis placed General Robert E. Lee in command of the Army of Northern Virginia. Although Lee had not been enthusiastic for secession and did not like war, he was a brilliant military leader. His gallantry under fire and his favorable intuitive reactions to new conditions during the Mexican War had brought praise from both superiors and troops. As an individual he could hardly have been more unlike McClellan. While McClellan was full of swagger and vainglory, Lee was gentle, courteous, and tactful. McClellan was egotistical to the point of failure, while Lee was self-deprecating to the point of embarrassment. Yet as a military tactician, Lee was crafty, decisive, and relentless in the defense of his homeland and in searching out his enemy on the field.

Fearing that McClellan might receive reinforcements from Washington, the Confederate high command instructed General Stonewall Jackson in the Shenandoah Valley of Virginia to launch an apparent attack on the Union capital. Between May 4 and June 9 Jackson advanced northeastward in the valley in a series of brilliant moves. Three different federal armies were sent into the valley solely to destroy him, but after four major battles Jackson was still alive and his army intact. He drove as far north as the Potomac River and then retreated, but he had accomplished his purpose. He had forced the Union government to retain a large guard in Washington, preventing powerful reinforcements from reaching McClellan.

After the battle of Seven Pines, Jackson moved to Richmond to help Lee against McClellan. Before Jackson's arrival, McClellan had held a clear numerical majority, but he had managed to move only at a snail's pace. With Jackson's troops, Lee held the advantage with eighty-five thousand men. The day after Jackson arrived—June 26—Lee in a massive surprise attack struck at the Union forces still straddling the Chickahominy River. In a campaign which lasted seven days, Lee forced McClellan, who believed his troops were hopelessly outnumbered, to retire from the area and to establish a new base on the James River, where Union naval guns could protect him. McClellan's position was good, his supply lines were secure, and his large force was ready for battle again. Lee's brilliant but complicated battle plan had not been executed well by his untested army, and he had not been able to hit the Union army with the full force of his weight at any one time. Lee had absorbed heavy losses but had gained no particular advantage. Exasperated with McClellan when he surrendered the initiative, the deliberative Lincoln at last took the decisive action of placing McClellan under the supervision of General Henry Halleck. Halleck promptly ordered McClellan's men to join General John Pope, who was organizing a new army on the Potomac near Washington.

Lee's actions during Lincoln's time of leadership troubles reveal the Virginian's military genius. With considerable daring he moved his army toward Pope, before McClellan's slow-moving force joined him. Lee's and Pope's men faced each other across the Rappahannock River. Without McClellan's troops, Pope headed an army of sixty-five thousand men as against Lee's fifty-four thousand, but this did not deter Lee. Coolly dividing his forces, he sent Stonewall Jackson and twenty-five thousand men in a wide circle to the west and north of Pope's position. In order to move swiftly, these troops did not take wagons or knapsacks. Moving across the headwaters of the Rappahannock, they rapidly filtered through Thoroughfare Gap in the Bull Run Mountains and seized Manassas junction. This move cut off Pope's rail connection to Washington and resulted in large quantities of Union arms and supplies falling into Confederate hands. Pope sent an army of men to chase Jackson, but Jackson evaded the trap set for him. At the same time, the other half of the Confederate army marched toward Thoroughfare Gap. The Confederates met Pope's army at Bull Run, where the first major engagement of the war had been waged, and they drove the Union forces from the field. Pope and his beaten army retreated to Washington in a heavy rain, the general licking his wounds and nursing his crushed pride. Virginia was temporarily free of federal forces because of the effective fighting of Confederate soldiers under generals Lee, Jackson, and James Longstreet, the latter having led men at Seven Pines, in the Seven Days' campaign, and at Second Manassas.

Lee concluded that the time was ripe to invade the North. He reasoned that success in battles on Union soil might secure Maryland for the Confederacy and bring official recognition to the southern nation from England and France. He hoped that both foreign powers would then send supplies, and possibly troops, to aid the southern cause. He also hoped that a dramatic blow struck on northern soil would harm the morale of the northern populace and persuade it that military victory was impossible. Accordingly, his army waded across the Potomac River in September 1862 and moved hastily northwestward away from the defenses of Washington.

Acting boldly again, Lee divided his army into several units, one overwhelming Harpers Ferry and another pressing north to Hagerstown, Maryland, nearly into Pennsylvania. Lincoln's dismay with Pope's incompetence had led him to turn back in desperation to McClellan, and the latter cautiously watched Lee's movements. When a captured dispatch revealed Lee's plans, McClellan acted decisively, forcing Lee to a fight on September 17 near Sharpsburg, Maryland. Seventy thousand Union troops encountered forty thousand Confederates on the banks of Antietam Creek, and by the end of the day the two sides counted twelve thousand and nine thousand casualties, respectively. Although Lee's lines had held, the Virginian's position was untenable. His troops were exhausted, while McClellan was receiving fresh men hourly. The cautious McClellan did nothing the following day when a forceful attack might have annihilated the Army of Northern Virginia. That night the Confederates crossed the Potomac into Virginia, happy to slip out of a slack noose which if tightened would have strangled Confederate military strength in the upper South.

Lee's invasion of the North, the most serious threat to the Union in the war, had ended in failure. The responsibility for Lee's army not being totally wiped out lay with McClellan, and Abraham Lincoln relieved the colorful but ineffective general of his command. Lee returned to the defenses of Richmond to rebuild his army for another day.

The battle at Antietam Creek was a signal to Lincoln for the issuance of an emancipation proclamation. Lincoln had insisted all along that the war was being fought to preserve the Union, but pressures were building from various sources for him to acknowledge that the war was also one to free the slaves. Political pressures were among the strongest with which Lincoln had to contend. In April 1862 Congress had abolished slavery in the District of Columbia, and shortly thereafter it took similar action against the institution in the territories. Lincoln personally favored gradual emancipation with compensation to the slaveowners, but by the summer of 1862 he had become convinced that his administration should assume a strong antislavery position. He believed this would help both the military effort and the Union's attempts to win European support for its side. But Lincoln did not want a proclamation of emancipation to be misconstrued as a sign of northern military weakness, and thus he waited until after the victory at Antietam Creek to make his announcement. On September 22 he publicly proclaimed the Emancipation Proclamation which stated that after January 1, 1863, all slaves in the areas in rebellion against the United States "shall be then, thenceforward, and forever free." Lincoln insisted he had larger motives in mind, but southerners considered the proclamation an invitation to slaves to revolt, and they resolved to fight harder. Jefferson Davis announced that the restoration of the Union was "forever impossible." If the war was not a fight to the death in the beginning, it most assuredly was now.

The Critical Year

When Lincoln dismissed McClellan for the last time, he passed the baton to General Ambrose Burnside, of whom a military historian has written: "He was a pioneer in the art of personal salesmanship, simply oozing elusive charm and sterling worth from every pore; the only general in history to have a barber's specialty named after him." Lacking the basic self-confidence necessary for a military leader, he accepted the major post with honest reluctance. But once in command, Burnside was the antithesis of McClellan. He was a general of action, not caution, and he immediately made plans to march on Richmond. Bad weather and supply problems delayed his march until mid-December 1862, however, and by that time Lee had been able to concentrate his army south of Fredericksburg, Virginia, on the Rappahannock River, where Burnside planned to cross into Confederate-held territory. Despite his numerical superiority (120,000 to 75,000), the overly aggressive Burnside should have called off his proposed attack, because Lee's men occupied impregnable positions behind the town in fortified hills called Marye's Heights. But Burnside refused to be intimidated, moving his men across the river and occupying the town of Fredericksburg. All day long on December 13, waves of Union troops stormed the Confederate defenses only to be thrown back time and again. Losses mounted frightfully in this futile assault with more than 12,000 Union soldiers killed or wounded. On the following day the northern army retreated, and shortly thereafter Burnside requested to be relieved as commander of the Army of the Potomac.

With great reservation but hardly any other choice, Lincoln replaced Burnside with General Joseph ("Fighting Joe") Hooker, an ill-tempered, foul-mouthed man of intrigue who occasionally allowed his own ambitions to override his superior's orders. Hooker amassed 125,000 troops in the spring of 1863, and in late April he forded the Rappahannock near Fredericksburg, concentrating his men about ten miles west, near Chancellorsville. With a 2 to 1 numerical advantage, Hooker might have forced a battle immediately, but he chose not to—perhaps convinced that Lee would not fight against such unfavorable odds. When cavalryman J. E. B. Stuart reported that Hooker's right flank was unprotected, Lee sent Stonewall Jackson and 28,000 men across a portion of an area called the Wilderness, broken terrain tangled by one huge mat of second growth and chaparral, to a position directly opposite the Union troops. Beginning at midnight, Jackson's force marched through the night and all the next day to reach its destination. Never hesitating, Jackson and his men attacked the Union lines at evening twilight. The Union right flank was caught completely by surprise and promptly collapsed. Upon hearing the first shots on the right, Lee dispatched his troops toward the Union lines along the entire front, hoping to prevent troops from being moved over to shore up the right flank defenses. The northern army was almost cut in two, and the Confederates undoubtedly would have won a decisive victory if the battle had commenced earlier. But as darkness enveloped the area a lull came—welcomed by exhausted men who had traveled hard and fought hard for over eighteen hours.

Union forces were able to organize and dig in before the sun rose the next morning, and hard fighting continued for three long days that first week in May 1863, before Hooker finally ordered a retreat. After his initial attack on May 2, Jackson had hoped to strike at daybreak the blow that would drive the last nail in the Union army's coffin, and he had ridden forward in the night to locate the weak spot. As he returned to his own lines, his men shot him down, mistakenly assuming that the shadowy form moving along the front belonged to the enemy. His left arm had to be amputated, and Lee wrote to Jackson's chaplain: "He has lost his left arm, but I have lost my right." Jackson died a week later of pneumonia and complications of the amputation, and that death was an incalculable loss to the Confederate cause. Besides Jackson, the Confederates lost about twelve thousand men—a costly victory from any view. Union losses were about the same, but they were more easily replaced. The North's problem was more critical at the leadership level. Could it ever find a competent general to lead the Union to military victory?

Recognizing this psychological advantage, Lee mapped out a second invasion of the North. He hoped to capture an important northern city, while the morale of the northern people was low. He retained the belief that a great Confederate victory on Union soil might cause England to offer to act as mediator. Furthermore, he desired to transfer the war from his own ravaged native state, and he sought to acquire supplies for Confederate soldiers. In June with his army at peak strength of seventy-five thousand men, Lee moved out of the Fredericksburg area and into the Shenandoah Valley, heading north. When Union scouts reported the huge army was spread out over a fifty-mile arc, Lincoln, increasingly impatient with timid and inept generals, wrote to Hooker, "If the head of Lee's army is at Winchester and the tail at Fredericksburg, the animal must be slim somewhere. Could you not break him?" Hooker's response: "Impossible. I cannot divine his intentions as long as he fills the country with a cloud of cavalry." In a postscript reminiscent of McClellan, Hooker added, "I am outnumbered. I need a reinforcement of 25,000 men." Hooker already had an army of ninety thousand men but he was content to move north at a safe distance as Lee made his way across the Potomac into Maryland. By the end of the month, Lee's army had moved into Pennsylvania, strung out over nearly fifty miles from Chambersburg through Carlisle and York to a point near the Susquehanna River. Still Hooker kept his distance, moving in a concentric circle to Lee's advance with Washington as the pivot, watching particularly carefully Lee's right flank. On June 27 Hooker penned a note to Washington offering his resignation if he were not sent reinforcements. If Hooker was bluffing, his strategy failed. His resignation was accepted, and General George Meade was appointed commander of the Army of the Potomac.

Lee was in a position to attack either Baltimore or Philadelphia,

but while contemplating the situation, he received word that the whole
Union army was north of the Potomac River and edging westward toward his communication lines. Lee knew that the rich countryside would
provide food for his men, but powder and arms must be shipped to the
troops from Richmond. Without a second thought, Lee shifted his plans.
The three major divisions of the Army of Northern Virginia were ordered to converge upon Gettysburg, a small village to the east and south
of the Cumberland chain, after which the entire army would move south
along the Monocacy River, drive through the scattered federal corps and
attack Washington, D. C. James Longstreet, R. S. Ewell, and A. P. Hill,
commanders of the army's three corps after Jackson's death, moved with
their men respectively from Carlisle to the north, Chambersburg to the
west, and York to the east. At the same time a sleepless and harried
Meade was striving to understand the situation suddenly thrust upon
him. He correctly reasoned that the threat to Lee's communications
would draw the southerners down the Monocacy, and he ordered his engineers to fortify a strong position along Pipe Creek where he fully expected battle to be enjoined. Early on the morning of July 1, a division of Hill's corps bumped into a Union cavalry picket west of Gettysburg. Shots were exchanged, and the Confederates at first thought
the opposing cavalry was being supported by nothing more than a few
Pennsylvania militiamen. But they soon realized that they were in battle
with tested soldiers of the Army of the Potomac, and both sides sent out
calls for reinforcements. Northern and southern troops converged on the
little city as if they were iron filings drawn by a powerful magnet. The
greatest battle ever fought in the Western Hemisphere was underway.

On July 1, 1863, Lee's army occupied Gettysburg, but Meade's
army settled in a strong defensive location on Cemetery Ridge, a fish-
hook-shaped stretch of high ground to the south of the town. Culp's Hill
and Cemetery Hill formed the barb of the hook. Meade's front extended
for three miles along Cemetery Ridge, ending at a hill called Little
Round Top. Lee ordered his men to occupy Seminary Ridge, a parallel
position a mile to the west. Confederates rammed the Union lines for the
next two days from every angle and with every conceivable kind of attack
—heavy artillery, direct infantry attacks, flanking cavalry movements—
but all to no avail. On July 2 Lee concentrated his attacks on the flanks
of the Union lines. Hood led a Confederate contingent against Little
Round Top, the highest peak of the enemy defenses at the south end of
the Union lines. At the same time, Ewell had been sent to attack Culp's
Hill on the outskirts of Gettysburg and near the northern end of the
Union lines. The best federal troops were exhausted after their right had
been effectively turned by Ewell and their left splintered by Hood. At
that evening's planning session, Lee knew that Union soldiers had been
pulled from the center of the Union defenses to stave off these attacks.

He reasoned that the center of Meade's defense must now be weak—probably guarded by inferior troops, perhaps only militia. He then planned an attack for the next day. With concentrated artillery cover, fifteen thousand men under the leadership of General George E. Pickett were to storm the Union's weak center, dividing and crushing the enemy with the help of Longstreet on the Confederate right flank and Ewell on the left. On July 3 Pickett's men, marching in parade formation, swept across an open field and up the sides of Cemetery Ridge, facing murderous enemy fire. A fraction of Pickett's troops reached the crest of the ridge, and for twenty long minutes they fought to remain. But the Confederates were not fighting militia; rather they were battling some of the Union's most seasoned soldiers, and these men plus hastily called-for reserves pushed the sourtherners back before they could consolidate their position. Forced to fall back, one Confederate soldier astutely observed, "It ain't so hard to get to that ridge. The hell of it is to stay there." Union artillery and infantry had savagely broken Pickett's frontal assault. Often called "the high-water mark of the Confederacy," Pickett's now-famous charge revealed the fruitlessness of direct attacks across open ground against a strongly entrenched enemy. When night came that evening the Confederate army was exhausted, and the Union lines remained intact. The previous evening Longstreet had doubted the wisdom of the plan, but Lee had not listened, and Lee now cried in anguish, "It's all my fault." On July 4, weary from the fatigue of battle, the two giant armies rested. If Meade had ordered his men to attack at that time, it is possible that the Confederate army would have been overwhelmed. But like other northern generals before him, Meade hesitated to follow up, much to Lincoln's disgust, and this day of grace saved the Confederate army to fight again. On July 5 Lee began a successful retreat to the safety of Virginia. For the first time, Lee had been beaten in a major battle. Losing more than twenty thousand men dead or wounded, Lee would never again have the strength to launch a major offensive. Ironically, the Army of the Potomac won its first clear-cut victory on northern soil.

While these crucial events were transpiring in the east, developments of almost equal magnitude were underway in the west. The one remaining Confederate-held point on the Mississippi River preventing Union control from the mouth of the river all the way north was Vicksburg, Mississippi. The importance of the river for the Union in regard to supplies alone justified all-out attempts against Vicksburg. Furthermore, the fact that this would finally and completely cut the western part of the South from the east, thereby preventing the trans-Mississippi region from shipping men, livestock, grain, or foreign imports across the river, was added incentive to Union forces to take Vicksburg—at almost any price.

When Lincoln had called General Halleck east in July 1862, U. S. Grant had once again been given command of Union troops in western

Tennessee. Now, in 1863 Grant's orders were to capture Vicksburg, completing the task he had previously left undone. Since that city sat on a high bluff overlooking a sharp bend in the river, Grant discovered it was not approachable from the west or north. At first he tried to move directly against the city from the north, with naval support from Captain David D. Porter. But the army bogged down in the low and marshy ground north of Vicksburg. On one occasion Grant ordered engineers to cut a canal to divert water from the Mississippi so that his troops could move downstream and yet bypass the city. None of these approaches proved feasible.

In April 1863 Grant launched a new plan. Under cover of darkness Union gunboats and supply ships slipped past the Confederate river guards, setting up a base at a point on the river south of Vicksburg. Then Grant floated his large army down the Mississippi to within a few miles of the city. After leaving a contingent of troops there to give the impression that an attack from the north was in the making, he moved with his remaining sixteen thousand troops to the west bank of the stream, marching them rapidly southward. Aided by the Union boats, Grant's army recrossed the river at Hard Times, several miles below Vicksburg. This maneuver meant that Grant had cut his communication and supply lines, but he was now on dry ground on the east bank of the river. Confederate General John C. Pemberton had fifty thousand troops in Mississippi, many more than Grant's total, but they were widely scattered. Some were at Haines' Bluff, north of Vicksburg, where Grant had ordered General William T. Sherman to make a feint; some were in Jackson, fifty miles east of Vicksburg; the main force was at Vicksburg; and a small corps was at Port Gibson across the river from Hard Times. Upon crossing the river, Grant had driven the Confederates out of Port Gibson. When Pemberton learned of Grant's position, he called all his troops to Vicksburg, except those in Jackson. Assuming that Grant would move directly north along the river to attack Vicksburg, Pemberton was confident that Grant could not successfully storm Warrenton, located on fortified bluffs south of Vicksburg.

But Grant did the unexpected. He had heard that Confederate General Joseph Johnston had a force of twelve thousand men at Jackson, and Grant determined to knock that army out of commission before attacking Pemberton and Vicksburg. Grant, Sherman, and James B. McPherson surrounded Jackson and struck so suddenly that Grant stepped into a textile mill to find looms still spinning army cloth with "C.S.A." woven into each bolt. By capturing Jackson, Grant at the same time prevented Confederate reinforcements from reaching Pemberton at Vicksburg. When Pemberton learned that Grant was heading toward Jackson instead of Warrenton, he had a touch of inspiration: move south, sever the communication line between Grant and Hard Times, and then

surround the Union army in need of supplies and food. Pemberton was
dismayed to learn that Grant had no supply or communication lines, and
that the latter was already attacking Jackson.

After overwhelming the Confederate army at the Mississippi capital, Grant then moved east toward Vicksburg. Pemberton attempted a
stand at Champion's Hill, high ground on the main road between Vicksburg and Jackson and about midway between the two cities, but he
could not derail the Army of the Tennessee. He retreated to Vicksburg
which Grant immediately laid under siege. Grant tried assault after assault from the east and south, as heavy guns came down the river to rain
shells upon the city. Every house in the city was shot through, the inhabitants reduced to eating mule meat and hiding in caves in the clay hillside
upon which the city sat. The siege continued through most of May and
all of June. General Johnston strove to round up an army of relief, and
he finally got some thirty thousand additional men, but they shied away
from battle when Sherman's troops turned to face them. Also, more men
were being rushed to Grant on every boat that sailed down the river.
Pemberton's men ran out of food. On July 1 this note was left on the
general's doorstep: "I tell you plainly men are not going to lie here and
perish. Hunger will compel a man to do almost anything.—One of your
soldiers." A council of war was held, and the Confederate leaders agreed
that it was futile to continue to resist. On July 4, 1863, after seven weeks
of siege, Pemberton surrendered, along with thirty thousand Confederate
soldiers. A few days later the steamer *Imperial* traveled unmolested from
St. Louis to New Orleans, and Lincoln exuded, "The Father of Waters
again flows unvexed to the sea." Upon the loss of the Mississippi River,
Texas and Arkansas were isolated from the remainder of the Confederacy.

The defeat was a forceful blow to Confederate defenses against the
increasing strength of the federal military machine. Coupled with the retreat from Gettysburg, the fall of Vicksburg brought southern morale to
a new low. In retrospect, the dual defeats of July 3 and 4 constituted the
turning point of the war. But this does not mean that Union forces were
any less relentless; indeed, these defeats signaled stepped-up activity.

While Grant was preoccupied with the siege of Vicksburg, General
William Rosecrans was drawing together a Union army of seventy thousand at Nashville. After Vicksburg capitulated, Rosecrans in August
began an advance against Confederate General Braxton Bragg who was
protecting Chattanooga, a key railroad center and Confederate strong-
hold in southeastern Tennessee. Rosecrans moved his army across the
Tennessee River at Bridgeport, Alabama, advancing toward Chattanooga
from the south. Chattanooga was situated on a large bend in the Tennessee River and surrounded on all sides by mountains, peaks of the western
edge of the Appalachian chain. Signal Mountain reached skyward on the

west across the river, Missionary Ridge was on the north and east, and Lookout Mountain, ignoring the state boundary line, sloped off southward into Georgia.

After General Burnside had occupied Knoxville, Bragg expected and prepared for an attack from the north. But when Rosecrans appeared determined to cross over Lookout Mountain, Bragg's communications with Atlanta were threatened, and he was compelled to move out of Chattanooga. Rosecrans and his men occupied the city, but they did not remain. They rashly tailed Bragg, catching up with him and his army in September on the banks of Chickamauga Creek. Bragg had over sixty-six thousand men, while Rosecrans commanded fifty-eight thousand, one of the few times during the war that the Confederates held a numerical advantage in battle. When a vague order on the battlefield was misunderstood, the center of the Union lines was inadvertently weakened, and General Longstreet was wise enough to take the advantage, rushing into the breach. The Union lines were broken, and the panicked army fled in confusion to the safety of Chattanooga. General George H. Thomas protected the retreat, halting several charges against his position at Rossville Gap. "The Rock of Chickamauga" became Thomas's lifetime nickname. Unable to pursue the Union soldiers through the gap, Bragg positioned his men on Missionary Ridge, Lookout Mountain, and other heights south of the city, where they kept the defeated army under surveillance in the valley below. The two-day battle of Chattanooga had resulted in success for the Confederates, but it may have been a Pyrrhic victory— twenty-three thousand men killed or wounded. Bragg moaned, "One more [victory] like this and I am ruined." By holding Lookout Mountain, the Confederates prevented the federals from receiving supplies by either railroad or water. Since necessary goods could come in only across the mountain roads from the west, the Confederates held clear strategic advantage and settled down to starve the enemy into submission.

After the brilliant victory at Vicksburg, Lincoln reorganized the Union army, placing Grant in command of all federal operations in the west. Grant journeyed to Chattanooga in late October, finding the Army of the Cumberland on the verge of starvation. Acting immediately, Grant ordered a corps of men under cover of darkness and fog silently to cross the river to the Confederate outpost at Kelly's Ferry. The maneuver went exactly as planned, the outpost taken and secured before the Confederates could send in enough men to prevent it. The river was thus opened for food to be shipped in from the Union base at Bridgeport. The Confederate siege of Chattanooga had been broken by a simple but brilliant move. When foodstuffs arrived to give sustenance to his men, Grant then ordered Sherman's newly arrived corps to march to the north end of Missionary Ridge. His plan was to have Sherman cross the river and force the enemy soldiers down the ridge, while having Joe Hooker strike at the south end of Missionary Ridge near Rossville Gap. When the Union forces began to put the plan into effect on November 24, the Confederates quickly realized what was happening, rushing troops from Lookout Mountain to assist on the ridge. Both Sherman and Hooker were slow to implement their assignments, but northern soldiers who were eager to redeem their defeat at Chickamauga swept up Missionary Ridge without orders. This frontal assault upon the center of the Confederate line on the ridge was overpowering as Thomas's men charged like savages up the side of the mountains. The battle was over within an hour. The break in the Confederate center routed the southern soldiers, and Bragg's army was in danger of being completely annihilated. Bragg ordered a hasty retreat to the safety of Georgia. But that safety was short-lived. The Chattanooga-Chickamauga campaigns cleared the way for a not-too-distant invasion of Georgia which was to split the eastern Confederacy in two.

"Ring Down the Curtain, Boys"

In 1864 the federal war machine shifted into high gear. The two men most responsible for this stepped-up military effort were Abraham Lincoln and U. S. Grant. Lincoln had almost despaired of finding a general-in-chief who would prosecute the war with vigor. But the more Lincoln learned about Grant's leadership in the west (Lincoln's best-known statement concerning Grant was, "I like that man. He fights."), the more he came to believe that Grant could coordinate the fighting in both east and west and lead the Union to victory. After the Chattanooga-Chickamauga campaigns, the U. S. Congress passed a law reviving the grade of Lieutenant-General, unused since George Washington. In March 1864 Lincoln named Grant to the position, giving him command of all armies of the United States. The new commander immediately began to make plans for the strangulation of the Confederacy.

Grant's master plan was simple: attack. He ordered federal forces to advance simultaneously at all points, applying constant pressure on the faltering South. He correctly believed that the Confederacy could not withstand this continual onslaught. After accepting the Washington position, Grant personally took charge of the Army of the Potomac, while General William T. Sherman took command of the North's western forces. Federal military operations in both east and west now proceeded from one consistent strategy, much to the detriment of the South.

As 1864 opened, the constricted Confederate defenses extended from Richmond southwestward to southern Virginia, along the eastern edge of the Appalachian Mountains to northwestern Georgia, ending at Atlanta. In May Grant and Sherman struck at the outer edges of this defense perimeter, Grant heading south toward Richmond and Sherman moving from Chattanooga southeasterly toward Atlanta. Both armies had rough going. Grant realized that he could not take Richmond by approaching it directly, and he moved his army back and forth in the area north of Richmond probing for a soft spot in Confederate defenses. With fewer men, Lee in May forced Grant into a fight in the Wilderness area. Lee hoped that the rough terrain in the forested area would constitute an equalizing factor for his outnumbered army. The battle of the Wilderness resulted in great losses for Grant (eighteen thousand casualties), but he did not withdraw to Washington as his predecessors had. Rather he shifted a few miles to the southeast in an effort to outflank his enemy. A few days after the struggle in the Wilderness, the two armies again clashed, this time near Spotsylvania Court House. After a five-day battle, Grant had lost about twelve thousand men and Lee's position remained strong. But Grant would not stop; like a bull dog he pushed southward, determined to smash Lee. He announced, "I propose to fight it out on this line if it takes all summer." In June Grant attacked strong Confederate defenses at Cold Harbor, about nine miles from Richmond. The Army of the Potomac once again was repulsed with staggering losses. Murderous fire killed six thousand men in sixty minutes. The North had fifty-five thousand casualties in a single month, but "butcher" Grant (as he was being called in both North and South) remained convinced that the South would ultimately collapse from the constant pressure. Grant could replace his lost men and equipment; Lee could not.

Grant next moved around Richmond on the east, preparing to take Petersburg, directly south of the Confederate capital. Since all railroads supplying Richmond passed through Petersburg, Grant determined to seize these roads and force Lee into a showdown fight in the open. A small Confederate force under Beauregard harried Grant so that Lee had time to rush troops to Petersburg, and when Grant arrived he realized his only alternative was to place the city and the Confederates under siege. Both sides wearily dug miles of trenches on the outskirts of the city at the beginning of the deadening siege, which dragged on for nine long months. The Union forces slowly but methodically weakened the Confederates, even cutting their rail connections, thus aborting the supply system into the beleaguered city. Lee's army at last seemed pinned down. If it moved again, it would necessarily be away from Richmond, which would mean the abandonment of the capital.

In the meantime, Sherman with ninety thousand men had been inching his way toward Atlanta, not only a vital railroad center but also an indispensable center for much of the South's heavy industries, cannons, powder, and other war necessities. Joseph E. Johnston had replaced Bragg as the commander of a defensive Confederate force of some sixty thousand troops. In May the Union army moved toward Dalton, Georgia, but Sherman did not attack the strongly entrenched Confederates.

Instead he threatened to disrupt Johnston's rail connection with Atlanta by passing around Dalton and attacking Resaca to the south. Whenever Johnston prepared for a fight, Sherman stretched out his lines farther than the Confederates were able to do, and Johnston was compelled to retreat. After a month of this military chess game, Sherman struck at Johnston at Kennesaw Mountain in June, but he was thrown back with heavy losses. After that Sherman continued his flanking operations, and by July 9 he was within six miles of Atlanta.

Confederate politics and personality clashes were responsible for a change in Confederate military command at this crucial time. Jefferson Davis, who had quarreled with Johnston throughout the war, had been forced after the Chattanooga campaign to appoint Johnston to replace Bragg, his favorite military commander. Still Davis's principal military adviser, Bragg now suggested that Johnston be removed from his command, and on July 17 Davis replaced Johnston with John B. Hood, whose reputation as a fighter was well known. The defense of Atlanta lay in his hands, and Hood did the best he could, but it was not enough. Sherman besieged Atlanta for nearly a month, but he did not want to be delayed longer. He sent part of his army south of the city to seize its only railroad and thus cut Hood's supply line. Hood evacuated Atlanta on September 1, and Sherman occupied the city the following day. This victory was a plus factor in Lincoln's reelection two months later.

Since Sherman's lines of communication reached to Chattanooga and on northward to Nashville, Hood reasoned that if he could break this long link, Sherman would be isolated. George Thomas had been placed in command of the Union army of sixty thousand at Nashville, and he had the responsibility of dispersing Hood's forces when the latter moved into Tennessee to sever Sherman's contact. On December 15 and 16 Hood and Thomas met south of Nashville, where Hood's army was overwhelmingly smashed. After the inglorious battle, Confederate soldiers retreating to Mississippi sang these bitter words to the tune of "The Yellow Rose of Texas":

> "You may talk about your Beauregard
>   And sing of General Lee
> But the gallant Hood of Texas
>   Played hell in Tennessee."

Sherman had been unconcerned with Hood's attempt to break his communication line with Nashville. Confident that Thomas could handle Hood and nonchalant if he could not, Sherman—who believed that the war had to be carried to the southern people themselves before the Confederacy would collapse—was busy devising a bold scheme. Receiving Grant's reluctant permission, Sherman burned Atlanta on November 15, abandoned his communication link with Nashville, and slashed through the heart of the South in his famous "march to the sea." Living off the land (the corn had not yet been harvested), Sherman's men took what food and livestock they needed, burning or killing the remainder. A swath of land 30 to 60 miles wide and nearly 225 miles long was totally decimated as Sherman's men marched unopposed from Atlanta to the Atlantic coast. Nothing of military value remained as they laid to waste everything that might help the South continue the fighting. Stragglers, known as *bummers,* tore up railroad tracks and made bonfires with the ties. Then they heated the rails until they were red-hot and wound them around nearby trees, making "Sherman's hairpins." The area was so blackened that a crow had to carry its own rations when flying over it, and Sherman estimated that his men destroyed $100,000,000 worth of property. He reasoned that this horrible destruction would crush the South's will to fight longer. For three weeks Lincoln knew where Sherman was only because southern newspapers reported his position. On December 10 Sherman communicated with Union naval vessels in Savannah harbor anxiously awaiting his arrival. A siege against Savannah began, and on December 21 Sherman entered that seaport city, after Confederate General William J. Hardee had withdrawn. "General Sherman makes the American people a Christmas present of the city of Savannah with 150 heavy guns and 25,000 bales of cotton," was Sherman's message to Lincoln.

The South trembled in the wake of Sherman's success. Another large chunk of the Confederacy had been lopped from the government at Richmond. Just as the Confederacy had been divided when Union forces gained undisputed control of the Mississippi River, another vital division was made when Sherman occupied Savannah. Only Virginia and the Carolinas remained of the soon-to-be-defeated Confederacy. Sherman's successful march had much to do with the diffusion of political opposition in the North, as anti-Lincoln forces were expressing disenchantment with the President's war efforts, and it was a major factor in boosting northern morale. But while Lincoln and the North were emotionally lifted by the march to the sea, the Confederacy felt the shock of the traumatic blow.

Confederate leaders agreed that Sherman must be destroyed. But how? The Confederate Congress was in continual session now, but it was harmed by vague rumors of defeat, divided over petty issues, and handcuffed by the South's inability to defend itself. Grasping at straws, the Congress voted to have built twenty ironclad warships, but the region had no functioning shipyard and no foundry to cast cannon. It also passed a bill to purchase 200,000 slaves to serve in the army, but southerners would not tolerate this move. Congress voted to compel Texas and Louisiana to fulfill their conscription quotas, but Confederate leaders in the region west of the Mississippi had not been in communication with the Congress for over a year—since the fall of Vicksburg, to be exact.

In January 1865 the Congress took one concrete, attainable action.

A bill was passed making Robert E. Lee the supreme military commander (the word was dictator) of the Confederacy. Confidence in Jefferson Davis as commander-in-chief of the Confederate forces had reached its nadir. The act was a blow to him, but it seemed essential. Lee remained a gentleman in his relationship to Davis, but he recognized that the most immediate military problem was to stop Sherman, and he began to work on it. He recalled General Johnston from retirement, giving him the task of containing Sherman. Correctly assuming that Sherman planned to march northward through the Carolinas and Virginia to link up with Grant and the Army of the Potomac, Johnston made plans to gather some thirty-four thousand men at Columbia, South Carolina: the remnants of Hood's army, Georgia and Carolina militiamen, and fragments of forces from wherever they could be found. Johnston sent a corps under Hardee to Charleston, South Carolina, and another corps under Bragg to Augusta, Georgia, not knowing which of these cities Sherman might strike. Once the Confederates determined where Sherman was headed, the other force was to move to assist the one in the path of the northern army. Johnston remained in Columbia, the northern apex of a defense triangle with Augusta on the west and Charleston on the east.

The plan was sound, but it did not work. On the morning of February 7 Johnston learned that Sherman's army of sixty thousand men had waded across the low-lying swamps in the face of hostile armies, and was on the outskirts of Columbia, having bypassed both Augusta and Charleston. Since Hood's army had not yet reached Johnston, Columbia was defenseless. Sherman plundered and burned the city and continued his northward march. As his men stomped across South Carolina they left behind "a broad black streak of ruin and desolation—the fences all gone; lonesome smoke stacks, surrounded by dark heaps of ashes and cinders, marking the spots where human habitations had stood." By striking at the center of Confederate defenses, Sherman had driven between the two flanks of the opposing army, neither of which was powerful enough to attack him. Johnston ordered the forces into North Carolina, where he vainly hoped to draw together enough manpower to halt the intruders. But Johnston was driven back at Averysborough and Bentonville, and he abandoned Raleigh and Greensboro as Sherman moved forward.

In the meantime, General Philip H. Sheridan had been given the job of permanently clearing Confederate troops out of the Shenandoah Valley, which he did with the same methodical approach Sherman was taking farther south. Early in March Sheridan moved east to join forces with Grant. At the same time, Lee and Davis were debating whether Petersburg should be abandoned, both leaders giving serious consideration to having Lee's army move out of Virginia to help Johnston in North Carolina. Lee and Davis agreed that it was politically necessary that Richmond be defended, and Lee's army remained in Virginia. In late March

Sheridan won a minor victory at Five Points, and the news spurred Grant to order an attack along his own lines. The Confederates were too weak to resist on all fronts, and they finally abandoned Petersburg. Richmond could no longer be defended under the circumstances, and on April 3 the Confederates evacuated their beloved capital.

The end was in sight. Lee's men moved westward but the outnumbered army found federal troops wherever it turned. On the morning of April 9, Lee sent a message to Grant requesting a meeting. In a farmhouse at the little country community called Appomattox Court House, Lee and Grant agreed upon the surrender terms, which were generous. The twenty-eight thousand Confederate officers and soldiers were to receive a full day's rations and were released on parole. They were to stop fighting and return to their homes. They were allowed to keep their horses, and officers retained their side arms. Die-hard Jefferson Davis had wanted Lee to resort to guerrilla warfare in the final weeks of the conflict, but Lee realized the futility of this suggestion and refused to sacrifice more southern lives in a lost cause.

Davis was not ready to give up the fight. After a conference in Danville, Virginia, he and members of his cabinet hurried to Greensboro, North Carolina, where he consulted with Johnston. Johnston agreed with Lee that the cause was hopeless, and on April 18 at Durham he surrendered to Sherman. Sherman's terms were broader than Grant's, providing for southern state legislatures to reassemble and making other political arrangements. Washington authorities revoked these provisions, substituting conditions similar to Grant's terms with Lee. On May 4 General Richard Taylor surrendered a good-sized Confederate army in Alabama, and the remnants of Confederate forces in the west under the command of General Edmund Kirby-Smith gave up the fight shortly thereafter. In all, about 175,000 soldiers laid down their arms. The final shot of the war was fired on May 26 by the *Shenandoah,* and in November that vessel hauled down its Confederate flag at Liverpool, England.

After a final meeting with his cabinet in the village of Washington, Georgia, Jefferson Davis recognized the hopelessness of the cause and tried to escape, intent on reaching South America. On May 10 he was captured at Irwinville, Georgia and placed in prison at Fort Monroe, Virginia. The South's military efforts had collapsed, and its highest officer was in chains. The Confederate States of America was dead.

Suggestions for Further Reading

No other subject in American history has received more attention than the Civil War. Books by the thousands have been published, and the bulk continues to be increased by several hundred more each year. Allan Nevins, James I. Robertson, Jr., and Bell I. Wiley (eds.), *Civil War Books: A Critical Bibliography*, 2 vols. (Baton Rouge: Louisiana State Univ., 1967–1969) contain approximately five thousand entries on the military aspects of the war, prisons, the Negro, naval operations, diplomacy, and government and politics, and the editors admit that they have probably listed only about 8 or 10 percent of the total books on these and related subjects. The following highly selected list is intended to be only an introduction to the subject. The reader is referred to the volumes listed above or to the bibliographies of the following works if they themselves do not satisfy his interest in that great conflict. The best single volume on the military aspects of the war has been written by the dean of Civil War historians, Bruce Catton, entitled *This Hallowed Ground* * (Garden City: Doubleday, 1956). Catton's trilogy, *Mr. Lincoln's Army* * (Garden City: Doubleday, 1951), *Glory Road* * (Garden City: Doubleday, 1952), and *A Stillness at Appomattox* * (Garden City: Doubleday, 1953), combines solid historical research with a journalist's flair for writing to produce a masterfully detailed account of the war. Also valuable is Catton's *The Centennial History of the Civil War*, 3 vols. (Garden City: Doubleday, 1961–65). Other short histories of the war which deserve to be mentioned are: Alan Barker, *The Civil War in America* * (Garden City: Doubleday, 1961); Roy P. Basler, *A Short History of the American Civil War* (New York: Basic Books, 1967); Harry Hansen, *The Civil War* * (New York: New American Library, 1961); George F. Milton, *Conflict* (New York: Coward-McCann, 1941); Earl S. Miers, *The Great Rebellion* * (Cleveland: World Publishing Co., 1958); Fletcher Pratt, *A Short History of the Civil War* [*Ordeal by Fire*] * (New York: H. Smith & R. Haas, 1935).

Douglas S. Freeman, *R. E. Lee: A Biography*, 4 vols. (New York: Scribners, 1934–35) and *Lee's Lieutenants*, 3 vols. (New York: Scribners, 1942–44) brilliantly detail much military history of the war. Good one-volume biographies of the South's greatest military leader are Clifford Dowdey, *Lee* (Boston: Little, Brown, 1965) and Earl S. Miers, *Robert E. Lee: A Great Life in Brief* * (New York: Knopf, 1956). Much of the writing on the Civil War must necessarily deal with Abraham Lincoln. The best one-volume biography is Benjamin P. Thomas, *Abraham Lincoln* (New York: Knopf, 1952), but Reinhard H. Luthin, *The Real Abraham Lincoln* (Englewood Cliffs: Prentice-Hall, 1960) is also good. J. G. Randall, *Lincoln the President*, 4 vols. (New York: Dodd, Mead, 1945–55) is a critical, multivolumed biography, while Carl Sandburg, *Abraham Lincoln: The Prairie Years,** 2 vols. (New York: Harcourt, Brace, 1926) and *Abraham Lincoln: The War Years,** 4 vols. (New York: Harcourt, Brace, 1939) constitute a detailed, human interpretation of the President.

* Available in paperback.

CHAPTER IX

RECONSTRUCTION

Commenting upon the conditions of the southern state governments and their leaders during the time of radical Reconstruction, Lord Bryce wrote in 1888: "Such a Saturnalia of robbery and jobbery has seldom been seen in any civilized country. . . . The position of these adventurers was like that of a Roman provincial governor in the latter days of the Republic. . . . [All] voting power lay with those who were wholly unfit for citizenship, and had no interest as taxpayers, in good government. . . . [Since] the legislatures were reckless and corrupt, the judges for the most part subservient, the Federal military officers bound to support what purported to be the constitutional authorities of the State, Congress distant and little inclined to listen to the complaints of those whom it distrusted as rebels, greed was unchecked and roguery unabashed." Three quarters of a century later, Kenneth Stampp concluded his volume on Reconstruction with these words: "The Fourteenth and Fifteenth Amendments, which could have been adopted only under the conditions of radical reconstruction, make the blunders of that era, tragic though they were, dwindle into insignificance. For if it was worth four years of civil war to save the Union, it was worth a few years of radical reconstruction to give the American Negro the ultimate promise of equal civil and political rights."

Lord Bryce anticipated the general interpretations of the Dunning School of Reconstruction which dominated the writing on the subject from the 1890s to the 1940s. Stampp's volume, a synthesis of two and

This chapter is similar to the organization and interpretation of *The Era of Reconstruction* by Kenneth M. Stampp.

one-half decades of reinterpretation of the era, concluded on a note which many revisionist historians would not accept; nevertheless, it demonstrated the wide gulf between the most recent interpreters of Reconstruction and those in the older tradition. Properly called the bloody battleground of historians, Reconstruction history continues to be revised and refined, and a general consensus has by no means been reached. There remain only tentative conclusions about this period so important in southern history and so influential for the entire nation.

"With Malice Toward None"

While the Civil War was raging, the nation's leaders considered the question of what to do to restore the Union and the South after that section had been defeated. Since the United States Constitution and the laws of Congress did not anticipate a secession crisis and a civil war, naturally no provision had been made to reconstruct the Union or the disaffected section. Throughout the war President Lincoln operated on the assumption that the Union was indestructible, that the southern states' ordinances of secession were illegal, and that the war was nothing more than a domestic rebellion. Lincoln's occasional inconsistencies—for example, when he proclaimed a blockade of southern ports and by so doing extended to the South the status of a belligerent power under international law—did not keep him from stating time and again that the Union was engaged in suppressing a rebellion. The President reiterated this theme in his last public address when he observed that the southern states were "out of their proper practical relation with the Union" and that it was the government's responsibility to restore that relationship. Lincoln believed that the reconstructing of the Union should entail nothing more than refurbishing the old relationship between the southern states and the remainder of the Union. To Lincoln the establishing of loyal state governments as quickly and as painlessly as possible was the federal government's major responsibility. Because the President was commander-in-chief of the nation's armed forces, and because he had the constitutional power to grant pardons and amnesty to rebellious southerners, Lincoln assumed that it was his responsibility to carry on this reconstructing process.

A number of Republican leaders in Congress disagreed. Since the Constitution grants to Congress the right to accept or reject members sent to it by the several states, and since the Congress must guarantee a republican form of government in each state, many congressional leaders argued that Congress should assume the responsibility of reconstructing the South. If Lincoln and the Congress had agreed upon how Reconstruction was to be carried out, the question of jurisdiction would probably not have arisen. But the fact that they did not agree created friction between the President and the Congress well before the end of the war.

Long before the South was defeated, Lincoln began to devise and implement a Reconstruction program without consulting congressional leaders. As early as 1862 he began designating provisional governors in conquered states, and in December 1863 he announced his policy on Reconstruction. In a formal proclamation he stated that he would grant pardons to all who would take an oath of loyalty to the United States. Exceptions to this generous gesture included high-ranking Confederate army officers and southerners who had resigned from Congress or the United States army to aid the Confederacy. Special pardons were possible for those excluded. When one-tenth of the qualified voters of 1860 in any state had taken the oath of allegiance, a government might be formed, and Lincoln promised to recognize it. A more charitable plan to bind the Union together after civil war could hardly have been devised.

The fact that Lincoln was a kind and compassionate man was a factor in his advancing such a mild Reconstruction plan. Also, when Lincoln announced this plan, the war was far from over; his scheme was a war measure as well as a postwar one. The President hoped to break down southern support for the Confederate war effort by establishing a small loyal group around which others could rally as the South drew closer to defeat. Richard Current has pointed out another reason for Lincoln's conciliation: the political implications of any plan of Reconstruction implemented in the South. Lincoln was aware that the Republican party was only a few years old, that it did not exist in the South, and that it needed to expand if it was to become a truly national party. A former Whig, Lincoln logically reasoned that prewar southern Whigs, many of whom had doubted the wisdom of secession in the first place, were prospective Republican party members. These southern Whigs had not rushed into the Democrats' embrace when the party of Henry Clay disintegrated in the 1850s.

Even though the northern Republican party was prosecuting the war against the South, Lincoln reasoned that southern conservatives might join a national conservative party once the slavery controversy had been settled and if a mild Reconstruction plan was put into effect. The solid Democratic South had not yet developed; the ex-Whigs were fair game to be enticed into the Republican fold.

Members of Congress were unimpressed by the President's reasoning and liberal policy, and they were displeased that Lincoln had assumed that the restorative process was the President's prerogative. After refusing to accept representatives elected from the loyal minority governments which Lincoln had recognized in Louisiana, Arkansas, and Virginia, Congress in July 1864 passed its own Reconstruction plan. Asserting its right to control the Reconstruction process, the Congress in this

Wade-Davis bill demanded that over 50 percent of the qualified voters take an oath of allegiance before a civil government could be established. Congress drew up a list much longer than Lincoln's of people to be excluded from political activity, including those persons known "to have held any office, civil or military, State or Confederate, under the rebel usurpation, or to have voluntarily borne arms against the United States." When the required number was enrolled, a state could then call a constitutional convention at which it must abolish slavery and repudiate its ordinance of secession. While this process was being carried out, the state would be ruled temporarily by a military governor. Clearly this scheme would take more time to be put into effect than Lincoln's, and it was severe in comparison, but it was not a harsh plan under the circumstances.

After Lincoln pocket-vetoed this bill, Senator Benjamin Wade and Representative Henry W. Davis issued an angry statement castigating the Chief Executive and declaring that in regard to Reconstruction "the authority of Congress is paramount and must be respected." In January 1865 a pro-Union government was set up in Tennessee under the Lincoln plan, but the President could not persuade Congress to accept members elected to that body from the state. Thus, when the war ended in April 1865, a stalemate existed between the President and Congress. Whether the two sides could have worked out an acceptable compromise program if Lincoln had not been assassinated is a moot question. The President was concerned about a possible rupture in the Republican party, and to forestall that likelihood he might have been willing to negotiate with Congress. Whether such negotiation would have been successful is even more speculative.

Troubled Tennessean

When Andrew Johnson was elevated to the Presidency, many so-called radical Republicans, who wanted the process of Reconstruction to proceed fairly slowly, were happy, because the new Chief Executive had often indicated his displeasure with the aristocratic planters who had led the South out of the Union. Some ten months before Lincoln's death, Johnson had declared: "I say the traitor has ceased to be a citizen, and in joining the rebellion has become a public enemy. . . . Treason must be made odious, and traitors must be punished and impoverished. Their great plantations must be seized, and divided into small farms, and sold to honest, industrious men." Not surprisingly, Senator Wade confidently addressed the new President: "Johnson, we have faith in you. By the gods, there will be no trouble now in running the government." Despite Johnson's well-known devotion to a united nation, the radical Republicans mistakenly expected his full cooperation to effect the slow Reconstruction of the Union they preferred. Yet within a few weeks after Johnson assumed the nation's highest office the radicals began to suspect he was not their friend, and three years later they impeached him in a desperate attempt to remove him from office. What happened in the meantime to cause this rapid deterioration in the friendship between Johnson and the radicals is a vital part of Reconstruction history.

Congress was not in session when Johnson moved into the White House in April 1865, and it was not scheduled to convene until December. The radicals expected the new President to call a special session to help with Reconstruction or perhaps delay it until after the Congress began meeting in regular session. Johnson did neither. He decided to complete Reconstruction within the next few months, presenting Congress with an accomplished fact when it convened. Like Lincoln, Johnson proposed to act alone, but his decision was political suicide. President by accident, he had no mandate from the American people. More importantly, as a Democrat elected primarily by Republican votes on a thinly disguised wartime coalition ticket, Johnson had no power base in either political party. Although head of the nation, the Chief Executive was quickly separated from the body politic.

In principle, Johnson accepted Lincoln's policy, and in practice he continued and extended it. The new President recognized the four state governments established under Lincoln, and he promptly appointed native southerners as provisional governors in the other seven. These governors were instructed to call state conventions, the delegates to be chosen by "loyal" citizens. The conventions were required to declare illegal their ordinances of secession, repudiate all debts incurred during the war, and abolish slavery. Also, the conventions were charged with prescribing such qualifications for voting and officeholding as they deemed desirable. Johnson announced that when a state had taken these steps, he would revoke martial law and withdraw the federal troops, the process of political Reconstruction then being complete.

Johnson's requirements as announced in May 1865 were minimal, and by autumn regular civil governments were functioning in ten of the former Confederate states. Texas completed the process early the following year. When Congress assembled in December, President Johnson proclaimed that Reconstruction was finished. Members of Congress—radicals and others—had watched with growing annoyance as Johnson's plan was implemented in state after state during the summer of 1865. A large minority in Congress officially protested Johnson's actions as soon as the session began. Eventually Congress threw out the Johnson governments in the southern states and drew up its own Reconstruction plan, putting it into effect in 1867.

Did repudiation of Johnson's Reconstruction program stem from vindictiveness on the part of the radicals? On the surface, Johnson had successfully completed his announced program, and now Congress was kicking out the established governments in southern states and starting all over again. The radicals have been accused of sinister motives for this reversal, but the truth is that Johnson had not put his original goals into effect. Johnson had earlier stated that the prewar leaders of the South should be disfranchised, prohibited from office, and relegated to political insignificance. He wanted new men to be found to run the southern governments. Also, he had hoped that the large plantations would be confiscated, partitioned into small farms, and sold to hardworking, small white farmers. But the President's dream of an ideal agrarian society for men of his own class did not become fact. When Johnson realized that he would be unable to effect his desired economic program, he then committed himself to a rapid termination of political Reconstruction. In the name of states' rights, he resorted to a strict interpretation of the Constitution to defend a policy which he did not originally favor.

Why did Johnson give up so readily? Hating the planter aristocracy, he had assumed that all men of his class shared his hatred. But many small farmers had a certain amount of respect for the large planter and had aspirations of moving into the planter class. When Johnson was prepared to establish new state governments with new men, he found no significant grass-roots movement demanding a change in political leadership. As the various states elected governors and other officials under the Johnson scheme, scores of men were elevated to office who were not entitled to take the amnesty oath or who had not yet been granted Presidential pardons. This made the President unhappy, but he was not willing to confront the states on the issue. In fact he cooperated with the trend by issuing Presidential pardons in wholesale lots to the very southerners he had hoped to see relegated to political unimportance after the war.

These men not only came into power in the South during Johnson's ascendancy, but they also maneuvered the President into a position in which he was compelled to align himself with them against the radical Republicans. If Johnson had refused to cooperate with these men who were making a shambles of his plan of Reconstruction, for all intents and purposes he would have been inviting Congress to take charge of Reconstruction. Johnson did not want this to happen. For this reason, he announced in his opening address to the new Congress that his Reconstruction program was finished and was a complete success. He stated that the southern governments were being run by men who were now both repentant and loyal. He said that they were acting in good faith, that they were dealing uprightly with their former slaves, and that they were not hostile toward northerners. If Johnson's statements had been true, the President would have held a strong hand in his dealings with the Congress; the latter might have been forced eventually to accept the

Johnson governments. But Johnson's statements were not true. The very men whom Johnson was defending were at the same time discrediting him by their irresponsible actions. The southern political leaders, with the expressed or tacit consent of the white masses, must share a large part of the responsibility for defeating Johnson's Reconstruction plans, for driving opponents into league with the radicals, and for finally bringing on a harsh Reconstruction program for the South.

To generalize about the attitude of six million white southerners is next to impossible, but rumors of widespread support for a planned continuation of the rebellion in 1865 were without foundation. Apparently most southerners acknowledged their total military defeat, although many rapidly recovered from the state of shock and humiliation brought on by that defeat. The southern majority did not accept the premise that their actions in 1861 were morally wrong. Touring the South soon after the war, Carl Schurz reported, "Treason does not appear odious in the South. The people are not impressed with any sense of its criminality." Other observers confirmed this view. The southern press assisted in the development of a state of mind free from guilt. Encouraged by this support and the liberality of Lincoln and Johnson, former secessionists had begun to speak about their constitutional "rights," entering into debates about how the Union should be restored. Under these circumstances, old Confederate leaders succeeded to positions of power in the Johnson governments. Reflecting the attitudes of the southern people, these political leaders often took actions which displeased northerners and helped increase sympathy for a more stringent Reconstruction program. For example, northerners reacted adversely when several southern conventions merely repealed—rather than declared illegal—their ordinances of secession. Other actions were equally irritating. Arkansas handed out pensions to its Confederate veterans; the Mississippi legislature voted not to ratify the Thirteenth Amendment; South Carolina failed to cancel its Confederate debt; several state legislatures refused to fly the American flag over their capitols. These errors were compounded when no laws were passed by any state restricting the political activity of ex-Confederates in any way. In 1865 the former Confederate states elected the following to represent them in the national Congress: the Vice President of the Confederacy, six Confederate cabinet officers, fifty-eight members of the Confederate Congress, five Confederate colonels, four generals. Not a single one of these men was qualified to take the oath of office even under the liberal Presidential policy.

Not wholly reconciled to the free status of the Negro, the white masses in the South supported policies of the Johnson governments in regard to the blacks. The President had urged that literate or property-owning Negroes be allowed to vote, but no southern state heeded this suggestion. Furthermore, the Johnson rulers planned to relegate the black man to an inferior economic role in the South, expecting him to remain an uneducated, unskilled, rural laborer. This attitude of the southerner toward the Negro brought about the enactment of the so-called Black Codes by the Johnson legislatures. These laws were drawn up to replace the defunct slave codes and were based upon the old slavery statutes, northern laws regulating vagrants and apprentices, and laws in the British West Indies dealing with emancipated slaves. On the positive side, the new laws permitted the recently freed Negro to own property, to sue and be sued, to make contracts, and to marry. But the laws were also discriminatory. No state gave the Negro the right to vote, and interracial marriages were forbidden. Blacks were not allowed to serve on juries or testify in court against a white person, they were prohibited from carrying guns, and they were restricted in owning or renting land in some states. More importantly, the laws required the black man to work, forbade him to quit his job, and by so doing denied him the freedom of economic mobility. Vagrancy provisions were especially restrictive. Southerners defended the codes as a temporary but necessary expedient to help the Negro make the transition from slavery to complete freedom. But to many northerners they appeared to be a ruse to saddle blacks with unofficial slave status or second-class citizenship. Rather than being designed to help the Negro through a transitional stage, they actually were put into effect to keep him under control politically, socially, economically, and legally for as long a time as possible. President Johnson had not spoken against the Black Codes while they were being passed, and they constituted an important spur to the radicals' efforts to convince northerners that southern institutions needed congressional renovation.

The Radicals Assume Command

Three major political groupings were apparent in the Congress which convened in December 1865. The first was a combination of a small band of Democrats and a rather weak clique of conservative Republicans who were committed to Johnson. The radical Republicans comprised a second group, larger in number than the Johnson supporters, but clearly a minority. Moderate Republicans constituted the third and largest bloc in the Congress. Most of the moderates leaned toward Johnson at the beginning of the session, but many of them were soon vacillating between the radical and Johnson camps. Whichever side the moderates supported would ultimately control the Congress and Reconstruction. The moderates were aware that the radicals had increasingly criticized the President's Reconstruction program as the summer and autumn of 1865 came and went, but they held out hope that conflict between the President and the Congress would not occur. If the President wanted to win or maintain a friendly majority in Congress, he would have to be circumspect and facile, and those men who controlled the Johnson state governments would have to have a large measure of good judgment. But Johnson proved to be tactless, stubborn, and violent toward those who opposed him, and the southern political leaders ignored northern public opinion. Johnson and his followers eventually forced the moderates into the arms of the radicals. By the summer of 1866, the radicals with moderate support controlled the Congress and were in the driver's seat of the Reconstruction wagon.

Between the time the Congress began meeting in December 1865 and President Johnson's impeachment trial in the spring of 1868, the radicals and Johnson verbally sparred with each other. Each side levied irresponsible insults and false accusations, but much of what was said was a serious discussion of the basic problems confronting them. One of these problems concerned the abstract question of whether the southern states had successfully seceded from the Union. Like Lincoln, Johnson believed that it was impossible for a state to leave the Union; therefore, he said that all he needed to do was establish loyal governments in them. The radicals contended that by attempting to secede, the southern states had fundamentally altered their relationship with the remaining states and the Union. The most extreme position was taken by Pennsylvania's Representative Thaddeus Stevens who argued that the states had seceded and that they were now conquered provinces to be rebuilt and admitted to the Union by Congress. Senator Charles Sumner of Massachusetts accepted the argument that the states did not succeed in seceding, but he theorized that when they made the attempt they had committed suicide as states and had regressed to territorial status. Thus, he believed they were subject to whatever rules Congress might establish for them and could regain statehood only after meeting congressional requirements.

The most crucial problem discussed by the radicals and the President related to the position of black men in American society. The research of LaWanda and John Cox has revealed that Johnson believed that white men should dominate his native region. The radicals disagreed with the President, and the primary goal of their Reconstruction program was to give the free Negroes equal rights under the law. Many northerners did not agree with this objective of the radicals, and the latter managed to win support of the northern populace only after broadening their program's appeal to include areas besides civil rights for Negroes. The conservatives in Congress did not believe that the radicals were sincere in their demands for Negro equality. They believed that the radicals were mouthing words like equality, democracy, and civil rights as a disguise to cover up their real motives. They suspected that the typical radical was out to exploit the black man and had no honest desire to help him whatsoever.

The question of motivation of the radicals is a vital one in the Reconstruction story. The radicals have been criticized for their desire for revenge, and they have even been referred to as the "Vindictives." They have been accused of wanting to punish the South to make her pay for her treason, and there is no doubt that many radicals felt contempt, bitterness, and even hatred toward the South. Some radicals admittedly desired to elevate the Negroes in order to punish the white southerners. Critics of the radicals have stressed that the latter were out to gain political advantage for themselves and their party. This accusation was undoubtedly true. The Republican party was hardly more than ten years old, and they wanted to assure the success of the party by giving the southern Negro the vote and by encouraging him to vote Republican. But the conservative Republicans also thought in terms of politics. They wanted the Republican party to be a nationwide organization too, but they concluded like Lincoln that the party's appeal in the South should be made to conservative whites rather than to blacks. They knew that Negro suffrage was unpopular in the North, and that if they advocated it, they would assist in the defeat of their own party at the polls. Party unity was uppermost in their minds when they feared that a break with Johnson would split the party and give the reins of government to the Democrats again. The radicals were less cautious on this score.

Another motive their critics attributed to the radicals was the desire to advance the interests of northern businessmen. The Congress which overthrew the Johnson Reconstruction governments gave more than nominal attention to economic matters. It dealt with tariff legislation, proposals to subsidize commercial firms, laws for the benefit of railroad promoters and builders, and policies to guard investors in national banks and government securities. In the eyes of some Republican congressmen, the party had become to some extent the political arm of northern business interests. The radicals' call for Negro suffrage was undoubtedly related to these practical political and economic matters. The radicals feared that if southern and northern Democrats ever gained control of the national government, the result would be political and economic policies hostile to the Republican party.

Besides wanting revenge and political and economic advantages, the radicals had another motive for their behavior. Some of them were moral idealists who believed that Negroes should have the rights entitled to all Americans simply because they were Americans. The Republican party was formed in the mid-1850s by a number of groups and combinations, including an important coterie of idealists who had been active in the prewar reform movements, notably abolitionism. These moralists hated slavery, and they had joined the Republican party because they believed it was to become a political agency for moral reform. Prior to the Civil War the term radical Republican was a label often stamped on these reformers. During the war these men were partly responsible for making the fight one to end slavery as well as one to save the Union. They helped influence Lincoln's decision to issue the Emancipation Proclamation, and they were in large measure responsible for the passage of the Thirteenth Amendment abolishing slavery.

Radical Republicans supplied much of the idealism of the Union cause during the Civil War, and this idealism continued after the war. When they insisted that the federal government support the cause of the free Negro, they were being wholly consistent. Many of the idealistic radicals were men like Charles Sumner who had been active in the abolition movement, while others were the moral heirs of the prewar reformers. The violent reaction of the radicals to the passage of the Black Codes by the Johnson governments can best be understood in terms of idealism.

This idealism coupled with disappointment in Johnson's political and economic restoration program was a major factor behind congressional action when the Congress met in December 1865. On the first day of the session, radical and moderate Republicans voted together to prevent the seating of senators and representatives elected from the southern states. The two groups then established a Joint Committee on Reconstruction to investigate conditions in the South and to recommend appropriate action to the Congress. This bipartisan committee of fifteen, dominated by moderate Republicans, wrote most of the Reconstruction legislation passed by Congress.

President Johnson strengthened the Committee's hand by early vetoing two congressional measures. One was passed to prolong the life and extend the powers of the Freedmen's Bureau, an agency created near the end of the war to aid the displaced Negroes; the other, accepted a few weeks later, was a civil rights bill. Moderate Republicans had joined with the radicals to pass these two measures, and they made the point to Johnson that they expected him to sign the bills into law if he desired to retain their support. Johnson's impolitic vetoes drove some of the moderates into the radical camp. In April and July 1866 Congress passed over Johnson's vetoes the civil rights bill and a revised version of the Freedmen's Bureau bill. More and more members of Congress were deserting Johnson, but the President seemed not to care or understand.

Johnson alienated more moderates in June when he responded to the Congress's passage of the Fourteenth Amendment, designed to define American citizenship and clearly including black citizens. Even though the amendment did not need the President's signature or comment, Johnson attacked it and suggested that southern states not ratify it. Of the eleven former Confederate states, ten took the President's advice, three legislatures unanimously rejecting it. When Tennessee's legislature ratified the amendment in July, Congress readily agreed to seat senators and representatives elected from that state. If the Fourteenth Amendment and a series of civil rights acts had been passed immediately upon the end of the Civil War, southerners—in the shock of military defeat—probably would not have openly opposed them. But after receiving such generous treatment in the summer of 1865, they felt that these proposals amounted to the imposition of new conditions near the end of the game. By the summer of 1866 they were inclined to resist these measures, especially since the President also opposed them.

The growing differences between the Congress and the President were more than apparent in the political campaign preceding the congressional elections of 1866. Johnson's famous "swing around the circle" campaign in which the President attempted to win support for candidates disposed to support his Reconstruction program was a disaster. Johnson damaged his cause when he indulged in intemperate remarks, responded to hecklers who did not deserve his attention, and generally carried on the campaign at a low level. But Republicans were no mean campaigners themselves. They revived earlier charges of Johnson's being a drunkard, accused him of keeping a harem in the White House, and implied that he was a party to the assassination of Lincoln. In this campaign Republicans began "waving the bloody shirt"—that is, orators attempted to saddle the Democratic party with the onus of treason and with the onset of civil war.

The anti-Johnson Republicans won hands down. Capturing every contested governor's seat in the northern states and winning every northern state legislature, they controlled more than a two-thirds majority in both houses of the national Congress. Many explanations have been given for this utter defeat of the President and his party, but the most logical one is that the voters honestly feared that Johnson might lose the peace. Genuine fear existed that if Johnson men won, southern ex-Confederates might come into control of the South, reenslave the Negro, and undo the positive results of the Civil War. To allay this fear, northern voters in effect told the Republicans that the time had come for them to try their hand at Reconstruction.

The Radicals Try Their Hand

The congressional elections of 1866 cast the radicals in a new role. No longer were they a minority biting at the heels of the decision-makers, but rather they were in control of the government with responsibility for blueprinting and implementing a Reconstruction plan of their own. They made mistakes, they misjudged their opponents, and they faced formidable problems which they often could not fully comprehend or solve. One of the most important forces with which they had to contend was the southern aristocrats who dominated the Johnson governments. This old ruling class continued to hold economic and political power, and the radicals were compelled to turn to the blacks in the South for political support against the strength of this opposition. Indeed, they quickly realized that Negro backing was vital to the success of their program.

How best to involve the blacks in the political process? The radicals might have worked out a well-organized program to carry the Negro through a transitional period after which time he would exercise civil and political rights he then fully comprehended. But this they did not do. Instead, they preferred to give the Negro these rights immediately and teach him to live as a free man while he enjoyed full citizenship. They believed that the Negro could not learn to live as a free man without being given complete freedom. They realized the black man would make mistakes with his new freedom, but they expected him to profit from them and soon play more than a passive role in the life of the nation. Kenneth M. Stampp has called this attempt to revolutionize the relations of the races by giving full citizenship to southern Negroes the great "leap in the dark" of the Reconstruction period. He contends that it was this aspect of their program that justifies the designation "radical" for certain Republican members in the Congress.

Many radicals realized that civil and political rights in the hands of the Negroes would be without value unless they were given some economic assistance too. The Negro was a free man, but no steps had been taken to help him help himself. Since the uneducated Negro was destitute and had nothing but his labor to offer, the best way to make him economically independent was to provide him with land. In this way, he could plow his own plot of ground, profit from hard work, and learn to manage his own affairs. Since four million former slaves were now free, a tremendous amount of land was needed to effect the Negroes' economic independence. After considerable deliberation, the radicals concluded that the property of wealthy Confederates should be confiscated and made available to black men. They argued that seizing the land of the former slaveholders and redistributing it to the Negroes would be good penalty to the whites who had committed treason, and fair compensation to the blacks who had nothing to show for their years of work under a slave regime.

But the moderates in Congress refused to support the radical proposal. When several Reconstruction measures were passed in 1867, a program of confiscation was not among them; even some radicals had expressed opposition to the deleted proposals. The defeat of confiscation was a severe blow to the radicals' Reconstruction plans. It meant that their program would include few economic benefits for the Negro, which in turn would mean that Negro civil and political rights would be limited. The failure of land reform probably resulted in the ultimate collapse of the entire radical program.

Land reform was the most ambitious plan devised by the radicals to reconstruct the South, but other better-known schemes to assist the Negro were also advanced. For example, the Freedmen's Bureau, first established in March 1865, was commissioned to look after Negroes, refugees, and abandoned lands. General Oliver O. Howard ran the Bureau with competence, but it was severely criticized by white southerners. Some of the charges against the Bureau were true. Bureau agents were sometimes corrupt and often incompetent; the Bureau was used to win Negro votes for the Republicans; the Bureau on occasion became involved in matters not properly within its jurisdiction. Despite the valid criticism of the Bureau's opponents, the agency achieved much good. It provided emergency relief for many needy people, at the same time trying to make the blacks self-supporting as quickly as possible. It put over $5,000,000 into schools for black pupils; it supervised the signing and carrying out of labor contracts to keep Negroes on the job and to keep employers from taking advantage of them; it set up special courts to handle cases involving Negro civil rights. When Congress decided that the Bureau's activities should end in 1869, it halted a small but important effort by the federal government to come to terms forthrightly with some of the postwar social and economic problems facing the South. When the Bureau ceased to exist, Congress had no ad hoc agency interested in defending Negro civil and political rights.

The Congress passed several measures in attempting to guarantee civil rights for Negroes. Besides the Civil Rights Act of 1866 and the Fourteenth Amendment (ratified by the required number of states in 1868), both of which dealt with citizenship, the Congress in 1869 passed the Fifteenth Amendment (ratified in 1870), which was to guarantee the right to vote to all citizens regardless of "race, color, or previous condition of servitude." In 1875 Congress passed another civil rights act, designed to grant to all persons, whatever their race or color, "the full and equal enjoyment of the accommodations . . . of inns, public conveyances, theatres, and other places of public amusement." This public accommodations law was declared unconstitutional in 1883 in a series of civil rights decisions, when the Supreme Court ruled that Congress did not have the authority to regulate the social relationships of the races.

On March 2, 1867, Congress enacted the First Reconstruction Act, containing the general outline of its plans for political Reconstruction of the South. Three later acts clarified nebulous wording in this measure and structured the program as it was put into motion. Also, laws were passed to limit the powers of the Chief Executive, preventing him from obstructing the effectiveness of the earlier laws. All of these measures went into effect only after Congress passed them over Johnson's veto. The radical Reconstruction program was advanced on the premise that neither legal state governments nor adequate protection for life and property existed in ten of the former Confederate states. This meant that the Lincoln and Johnson civil governments were abolished in all of the states except Tennessee. The remaining unreconstructed states were organized into five military districts, ruled by military commanders who were given wide powers to protect life and property, to restore peace and order, and to punish disturbers of the peace. Military courts were established even though civil courts existed, and the commanders could use either as they pleased. Thousands of citizens were arrested and hundreds were tried in military courts where basic civil liberties were not protected. Over five hundred convictions by military tribunals were handed down in North and South Carolina in fewer than fifteen months of military rule. The commanders were empowered to remove from office any state or local official, and while they ruled, five governors and scores of lesser officials were suspended.

The primary task of the district commanders was that of effecting the radicals' program of political Reconstruction. They were to enroll all "loyal" male voters over twenty-one, including Negroes but excluding those southerners disfranchised for participating in the rebellion. Under their supervision, delegates were to be elected to conventions charged with drawing up new state constitutions. When a state constitution, which had to provide for Negro suffrage, was approved by the voters and by Congress, a governor and legislature could be elected. The first legislature had to ratify the Fourteenth Amendment. When that amendment was made a part of the federal Constitution, the state was then entitled to send representatives to Congress. In the meantime, the civil governments in the states were to be considered provisional. Southerners not allowed to vote under the terms of the Fourteenth Amendment were prohibited from voting in elections held under these provisional governments.

By March 1868 new constitutions had been drawn up in all southern states except Texas. Provisional civil governments had begun to operate, and by June the legislatures of North and South Carolina, Georgia, Florida, Alabama, Louisiana, and Arkansas had ratified the Fourteenth Amendment, as required. Northern states were also ratifying this important amendment, and after it had been approved by three-fourths of the state legislatures, the national Congress accepted members from the seven former Confederate states, this act officially readmitting them into the Union. Virginia, Mississippi, and Texas completed the process for admission in 1870. By that time Congress had passed the Fifteenth Amendment and these three tardy states had to ratify that amendment too before they were restored to their former places in the Union. Because of untoward events in Georgia, that state was also required to ratify the Fifteenth Amendment. Thus, by 1870 congressional political Reconstruction requirements had been fulfilled by all of the states of the Confederacy.

Brown Reconstruction

The Reconstruction Era did not end when acceptable constitutions were drafted or when elected senators and representatives took their seats on Capitol Hill. Each of the eleven ex-Confederate states was ruled by a radical Republican regime for a part or all of the decade between 1867 and 1877. Why did southerners not take over the governments of their states as soon as congressional political Reconstruction requirements had been met? A common misconception is that conservative white southerners were disfranchised in such large numbers that they could not outvote their opponents. Actually the lack of voting strength among southern conservatives stemmed from the fact that the conservatives were not well organized and that many qualified white voters failed to go to the polls, either out of protest or indifference. Thus, radicals and their supporters dominated southern state governments until the southern conservatives could organize and marshal the support of the masses to vote the radicals out of office.

Many charges—some true, some exaggerated, and some false— were made against the radical governments and their leaders. Yankee carpetbaggers, southern scalawags, and Negroes collectively dominated these governments, and they have been called incompetent, corrupt, and inexperienced men who replaced the South's experienced statesmen and "natural" leaders. Some of the officials in the radical governments fitted the stereotype, but the majority did not. Many men known as carpetbaggers migrated to the South in order to buy cotton lands or enter business. Some were interested in promoting railroads. Others were Union army veterans who liked the southern climate and desired to make the South their permanent home. Others went as school teachers, clergymen, or officials of government agencies or benevolent organizations set up to aid the Negroes. Many of these people moved south before they were permitted to be involved in politics, and they went into politics only after living in the South for several years. Certainly the great majority of them were not conniving political adventurers who invaded the South solely for premeditated plunder. Nor were all white southerners who aligned themselves with these governments necessarily corrupt opportunists whose main interest was in the spoils of office. Some of the so-called scalawags were Unionists who had been persecuted during the war by Confederates, and now they were vindictive toward the former Confederates. Others were poor yeoman farmers who joined with the radicals because they were repelled by the ruling planter class. Business-minded southerners who stood to gain from the economic policies of the Republican party sometimes became scalawags. They liked protective tariffs, a national banking system, and federal support of internal improvements. A small group of scalawags were upper-class southerners who had been active in prewar Whig politics. These men did not like the Democrats, and they joined with the radicals hoping to build the Republican party in their native region. Thus, on the one hand the scalawags consisted of small farmers who disliked planters, and on the other hand they comprised large landowners and businessmen whose Whiggish tendencies made them rivals of the Democrats. The trite expression "politics makes strange bedfellows" was never more true.

Southern Negroes constituted the third large group in the radical coalition. The Negroes were charged with being the ignorant dupes of white Republicans who used the black men for selfish purposes, while at the same time, the Negroes were said to dominate these governments so much that this period has been called "black" Reconstruction. Neither charge is entirely accurate. Many Negroes were ignorant and illiterate, and they were often the puppets of white Republicans, but as John Hope Franklin has pointed out, others were quite responsible as voters and as elected officials. Although Negroes were politically influential in each state in the South, at no time did they ever control one of them. Every state legislature had black members, but only in South Carolina did they comprise a majority, and then only briefly. No Negro was elected governor and only a few served as lieutenant governors. Fourteen Negroes served in the United States House of Representatives, and two represented Mississippi in the Senate for a brief time. But as a rule, they held lesser offices in the radical governments, while white men generally dominated the higher offices.

Although native whites opposed "outsiders" ruling their governments and held in contempt those southerners who cooperated with the carpetbaggers, the most distasteful aspect of the radical governments was the Negro as voter and officeholder. It mattered not that the black man had little political power. That he was involved in politics at all was enough to throw consternation into the southern people. Whatever southern fears, however, the Negroes seldom used their political positions to take advantage of the native whites. No responsible Negro leader suggested that the freedman try to gain complete political control. No attempts were made to establish a "Negro man's party." No Negro shouted "Black Power."

It has often been assumed that radical Reconstruction was the same as military rule. Generally speaking, the end of military rule did coincide with the date when Congress admitted each state to the Union. This means that military rule ended in 1868 in seven southern states and by 1870 in the other three. On occasion state militia (including Negro guards) or federal troops were utilized to support the radical civil governments, but this does not mean that an extraconstitutional government existed. And when the military was present, the number of troops actually stationed in the South was quite small. Approximately twenty thousand troops constituted the "army of occupation," seven thousand of these concentrated in Louisiana and Texas. Only two garrisons numbered more than five hundred men. For most of the time, southern states were under civil—not military—government during radical Reconstruction.

Not surprisingly, radical supporters dominated conventions called by the military governors to write new state constitutions. Although sharply criticized by white conservatives, these men drew up politically orthodox constitutions containing no novel economic provisions. Nor was there experimentation with social policies. These essentially conservative documents often did institute modest but much-needed reforms, lagging a full generation behind northern states. They departed from the old state constitutions by providing for more equitable legislative apportionment, more elective—as opposed to appointive—offices, enlarged rights for women, fairer tax structures, reformed penal codes, additional improvements in state systems of public education, and improved facilities for eleemosynary institutions. To the men writing these constitutions must go the credit for introducing universal male suffrage in the South, for abolishing property qualifications for officeholders, and for making available generous homestead exemptions. Granting the shortcomings of these documents, they contained many democratic provisions. They proclaimed the equality of all men by referring to the Declaration of Independence, and blacks were guaranteed the same civil and political rights as whites. Most of the constitutions were vague on the subject of social relationships of the races, but even so, the constitution-makers must be credited with actually attempting to extend American democracy to include the Negro.

What kinds of civil governments did the radicals run? Since some of the governmental officials were ignorant and others unscrupulous, much corruption existed in these governments. School funds were embezzled with regularity and other state moneys were wasted or stolen with uncommon frequency. Bond issues were tainted with fraud, land sales and purchases were often made with graft uppermost in the minds of men on both sides of the bargains, and contracts for public works went to the largest briber. Henry Clay Warmoth, carpetbagger from Illinois, settled in Louisiana and in 1868 was elected governor of his adopted state. He admitted making $100,000 during his first year in office, although his salary was only $8,000. When a committee of the South Carolina legislature was appointed to investigate reports of the misuse of a contingency fund by Governor Franklin J. Moses, the scalawag governor took money from the fund to bribe the committee members to soft-pedal the investigation. The end result was that the legislature exonerated Governor Moses of any wrong and increased his contingency appropriations. While these larger and smaller corrupt practices flourished, public debts increased and the credit of the southern states was harmed. State officials were forced to levy more taxes to finance both legitimate expenses and shady deals, the tax rate quadrupling in most states in less than a decade.

But the corruption of the radical governments must be viewed in perspective. At that same time, President Grant's administration was suffering from corruption at the national level. State and municipal rings were present in many northern areas—the Tweed Ring which fleeced the taxpayers of New York City of millions of dollars was one of the most notorious. During the postwar period a moral laxity was apparent all over the country, not just in the South. More significantly, national economic expansion was a force being felt in the South. If a primary corrupting influence existed, it was expanding capitalism, and all leaders in the nation and the South were greatly influenced by it. The Johnson governments before radical Reconstruction had had their share of corruption, waste, and extravagance. So did the white conservative governments which followed. Although the radical governments deserve criticism, they should not be singled out for incompetence and corruption.

End of an Era

Many white conservative southerners were bitter and often violent in their reaction to carpetbag-scalawag-Negro political domination of the South. Unable to overthrow these governments by legal means during the first years of radical rule, some southerners resorted to extralegal ways to curb the power of their opponents. Several secret societies were formed, the most famous of which was the Ku Klux Klan. These organizations broke up Republican meetings, threatened radical leaders, whipped black militiamen, and intimidated Negro voters. Many Negroes, carpetbaggers, and scalawags were promised reprisals; some had their property plundered; others were murdered. When the Klan went to excesses, respectable southerners withdrew their support from it, but it continued unabated as a vehicle of vengeance for others. After an investigation, the Congress in 1870 and 1871 adopted legislation designed to suppress organized terrorism. Additional federal troops were sent to the South, and after numerous arrests, fines, and imprisonments, the Klan's power was finally broken. By 1872 it had run its course. But the breakup of the Klan did not mean the end of violence or the threat of it. Southerners used various other methods in their efforts to kick out the radical governments. Economic coercion against the Negro was often as effective as terrorism. So much violence, intimidation, and coercion occurred in Mississippi that these methods became known collectively as the "Mississippi

Plan," and Democrats in several other southern states followed the Magnolia State's lead in their attempts to oust the radicals.

Racial demagoguery was closely related to physical violence or the threat of it, and white southerners freely used it in their drive to unseat the radicals and gain control of their state governments. Southern Democrats made concerted appeals to white farmers and lower-class workingmen who looked upon the Negro as a potential economic competitor. White men in both North and South generally considered black men innately inferior, and many whites in both sections had nagging doubts about political power in the hands of Negroes. Scalawags began to desert the radicals when whites played upon racial fears, and the Republican party in the South became mainly an organization of carpetbaggers and Negroes. The cry of white supremacy struck a responsive chord in most white southerners' breasts, and it became an effective tool to rid the South of these political interlopers.

National political events also assisted southern conservatives in their drive to gain control of their state governments. By the time U. S. Grant became President in 1869, many Republicans were beginning to feel that the party had done all that could reasonably be expected of it. The secession movement had been crushed, the Union had been preserved intact, slavery had been abolished, and civil and political guarantees for Negroes had been written into the Constitution. Although much more needed to be done to assure equal protection under the Constitution and the laws of the nation, Republicans began to feel that the federal government had no further responsibility. These changing attitudes were related to the changing scene. Many of the older radical leaders were dead or retired from public office by 1869, and with this leadership gone, most of the force of the movement for social reform was spent. The new leaders who replaced the old radicals were called stalwarts, and they dominated Grant's two Presidential terms. Not reformers or radicals, these men favored the status quo. The radical-stalwart struggle within the Republican party had much to do with undermining the radical governments in the South. At the same time, the psychological and numerical strength of the Democrats in the South was increased when Congress finally removed the political restrictions from most of the wartime leadership. By 1872 only a few hundred former Confederates remained disqualified to vote. More importantly, previously apathetic southerners tired of radical rule and began to respond to appeals to "throw the rascals out."

Under these circumstances, conservative southerners gained control of the state government of Tennessee as early as 1869. During the next two years radical officeholders were voted out in Virginia, North Carolina, and Georgia. Southerners gained political ascendancy in Alabama, Arkansas, and Texas in 1874, and Mississippi came to be domi-

nated by native whites a year later. Louisiana, Florida, and South Carolina came under the control of conservative southerners in 1877, and the
Reconstruction Era closed in the early summer of that year when the remaining federal troops were removed from these three states.

The official end of Reconstruction was intertwined with the disputed Presidential election of 1876. In that election which required 185
electoral votes for a victory, Democratic candidate Samuel J. Tilden garnered 184 votes to Republican candidate Rutherford B. Hayes's 166, with
the 19 votes of Louisiana, Florida, and South Carolina in dispute. Tilden
had apparently won the closely contested elections in these three states,
but when national Republican leaders realized Hayes could capture the
Presidency if all of these states were awarded to their candidate, they encouraged Republicans in control of the states' election machinery to
throw out sufficient Democratic ballots to alter the final results. When
state officials followed this suggestion, invalidating Democratic ballots in
wholesale lots, Democrats immediately challenged this action and filed returns indicating Tilden had won. The Congress established an Electoral
Commission to decide the disputed cases, and in every instance the contested ballots were awarded to Hayes. Violence, intimidation, and ballot-
box stuffing had been present in the elections in all three states, both Republicans and Democrats tampering with the voting process, but most
historians agree that Tilden should have been awarded Florida and thus
the election.

Hayes won the election, however, not because of fraud, but because his northern Republican supporters were able to obtain a satisfactory compromise with conservative southern Democrats. Northern Democrats were prepared to fight for Tilden's election, but southerners were
willing to accept Hayes if northern Republicans would agree to a bargain. In his brilliantly researched volume, *Reunion and Reaction* (1951),
C. Vann Woodward has exploded the myth that the compromise was
reached on February 26 in a smoke-filled room at the Wormley Hotel in
Washington, D.C.; rather it was the result of several informal conferences
and conversations held over a period of months between representatives
of the southern Democrats and northern Republicans. Overly simplified,
southerners agreed to Hayes's election, while the Republicans promised
that Hayes would remove the federal troops from the South, thus permitting southerners to rule all their states; that Hayes would appoint a
southerner to his cabinet; that the Republican-dominated Congress
would be more generous toward the South in regard to internal improvements; and that the Congress would vigorously press for federal support
of the Texas and Pacific Railroad, a transcontinental rail project long desired by the South. Republicans did not honor all features of the compromise after southerners permitted the peaceful inauguration of Hayes, but
the new President did remove the federal troops, permitting southern

Democrats to control their state governments and setting the stage for a new chapter in the South's and the nation's political history. Furthermore, the economic aspects of the compromise, which aligned southern conservative leaders with northern Republican business interests, had an untold effect upon the nation's and the region's history.

What was the political, economic, and social heritage of Reconstruction? The Republican party emerged from the era in a position of national preeminence. From that time until 1912 the Democrats only once (in 1892) won the Presidency and both houses of Congress at the same time. But the Republicans had bargained the South away politically in the compromise of 1877, and the South was fastened with a stagnant single-party arrangement which influenced both regional and national politics in a variety of ways for the next century. For the South's part, it had little influence in the national political equation. The national Republican party did not woo southern voters because it would have been futile, and the national Democratic party did not have to woo them because it would have been superfluous.

Reconstruction came at a time when the American capitalistic system was expanding, and undoubtedly the era assisted in consolidating the position of that industrial system. Economic arrangements between northern and southern business interests were made then, and the years following Reconstruction revealed the profit of these arrangements for both sides.

The tragedy of Reconstruction was that it failed to provide for Negroes to share fully and equally in the promise of American life. In fact, the idealism of the radicals exacerbated the South's fear, and southerners determined to control the Negro when they returned to political power. Both the South and the North shared the responsibility for the incompleteness of this aspect of Reconstruction. The northern idealists were unable to translate their equalitarian ideals into reality—and bungled as they made the attempt—and southern whites refused to cast aside the memories of military defeat or their feelings about the inferiority of black men. The passage of liberal laws and constitutional amendments did not result in immediate gains for the Negro; on the contrary, the very presence of this legislation spurred opposition to the reality of racial equality. The century following Reconstruction still did not see the full implementation of these laws or amendments, and the American nation and the South were the less because of it. Yet, the third quarter of the twentieth century witnessed forces at work to carry out the implications of the Declaration of Independence and the Constitution, and black men were nearer than ever before to grasping the ultimate promise of equal civil and political rights available to all Americans.

Finally, the tragic events of the Reconstruction Era were responsible for the glorification of the Civil War as a "lost cause" and for the romanticizing of the Old South by southerners. United in defeat and threatened by northern domination during the postwar readjustment, southerners shrouded themselves and their region in myths. The trauma of military defeat and postwar humiliation affected the southern psyche so much that later southerners themselves did not always understand why they acted and reacted as they did. Reconstruction and its long aftermath laid a heavy burden upon the South.

Suggestions for Further Reading

This chapter generally follows the outline and arguments of Kenneth M. Stampp, *The Era of Reconstruction, 1865–1877* * (New York: Knopf, 1965), an outstanding synthesis of revisionist writing on Reconstruction. While by no means in total agreement with each other, volumes in the revisionist tradition are: John Hope Franklin, *Reconstruction: After the Civil War* * (Chicago: Univ. Chicago, 1961); John and LaWanda Cox, *Politics, Principle and Prejudice, 1865–1866: Dilemma of Reconstruction America* (New York: Free Press of Glencoe, 1963); James B. McPherson, *The Struggle for Equality: Abolitionists and the Negro in the Civil War and Reconstruction* (Princeton: Princeton Univ., 1964); W. R. Brock, *An American Crisis: Congress and Reconstruction, 1865–1867* * (New York: St. Martin's, 1963); Eric L. McKitrick, *Andrew Johnson and Reconstruction* * (Chicago: Univ. Chicago, 1960); James S. Allen, *Reconstruction: The Battle for Democracy, 1865–1876* (New York: International Publishers, 1937); Francis B. Simkins and Robert H. Woody, *South Carolina During Reconstruction* (Chapel Hill: Univ. North Carolina, 1932); Vernon L. Wharton, *The Negro in Mississippi, 1865–1890* * (Chapel Hill: Univ. North Carolina, 1947); Richard N. Current, *Three Carpetbag Governors* (Baton Rouge: Louisiana State Univ., 1968); Henderson Donald, *The Negro Freedman* (New York: H. Schuman, 1952); Thomas B. Alexander, *Political Reconstruction in Tennessee* (Nashville: Vanderbilt Univ., 1950); Robert Cruden, *The Negro in Reconstruction* * (Englewood Cliffs: Prentice-Hall, 1969); J. G. Randall and David Donald, *The Civil War and Reconstruction,* 2nd ed. rev. (Boston: D. C. Heath, 1961). Donald has taken a quantitative approach to the subject in his *The Politics of Reconstruction, 1863–1867* (Baton Rouge: Louisiana State Univ., 1965). Anticipating the revisionist approach was W. E. B. Du Bois, *Black Reconstruction in America* * (New York: Harcourt, Brace, 1935). For excerpts from the major revisionists see Kenneth M. Stampp and Leon F. Litwack (eds.), *Reconstruction: An Anthology of Revisionist Writings* (Baton Rouge: Louisiana State Univ., 1969).

The revisionist interpretation of Reconstruction may be said to have begun officially with an article by Beale, "On Rewriting Reconstruction History," *American Historical Review,* vol. 45 (1939–40). Other general revisionist essays include Hesseltine, "Economic Factors in the Abandonment of Reconstruction," *Mississippi Valley Historical Review,* vol. 22 (1935–36); Simkins, "New Viewpoints of Southern Reconstruction," *Journal of Southern History,* vol. 5 (1939); Williams, "An Analysis of Some Reconstruction Attitudes," *ibid.,* vol. 12 (1946); Bond, "Social and Economic Forces in Alabama Reconstruction," *Journal of Negro History,* vol. 23 (1938); Franklin, "Whither Reconstruction Historiography?" *Journal of Negro Education*, vol. 27 (1958); McWhiney, "Reconstruction: Index of Americanism," in Charles G. Sellers, Jr. (ed.), *The Southerner as American* * (Chapel Hill: Univ. North Carolina, 1960); C. Vann Woodward, "The Political Legacy of Reconstruction," in *The Burden of Southern History* * (Baton Rouge: Louisiana State Univ., 1960). Additional revisionist essays on specific subjects include: Donald, "The Scalawag in Mississippi Reconstruction," *Journal of Southern History*, vol. 10 (1944); Alexander, "Persistent Whiggery in the Confederate South, 1860–1877," *ibid.*, vol. 27 (1961); Scroggs, "Southern Reconstruction: A Radical View," *ibid.*, vol. 24 (1958); Cox and Cox, "General O. O. Howard and the 'Misrepresented Bureau,'" *ibid.*, vol. 19 (1953); Sproat, "Blueprint for Radical Reconstruction," *ibid.*, vol. 23 (1957).

The revisionists first began their writings in reaction to the Dunning School of Reconstruction, a pro-South, anti-Negro, anti-radical group which had dominated Reconstruction historiography for half a century. Examples of works in the Dunning tradition are: William A. Dunning, *Essays on the Civil War and Reconstruction* * (New York: Macmillan, 1898) and *Reconstruction, Political and Economic, 1865–1877* * (New York: Harper & Brothers, 1907); Claude G. Bowers, *The Tragic Era* * (Boston: Houghton Mifflin, 1929); John W. Burgess, *Reconstruction and the Constitution, 1866–1876* (New York: Scribners, 1902); Walter Fleming, *The Sequel of Appomattox* (New Haven: Yale Univ., 1919) and *Civil War and Reconstruction in Alabama* (New York: Columbia Univ., 1905); H. J. Eckenrode, *The Political History of Virginia During the Reconstruction* (Baltimore: Johns Hopkins Univ., 1904); William W. Davis, *The Civil War and Reconstruction in Florida* (New York: Columbia Univ., 1913); John R. Ficklen, *History of Reconstruction in Louisiana (through 1868)* (Baltimore: Johns Hopkins Univ., 1910); Ella Lonn, *Reconstruction in Louisiana after 1868* (New York: Putnam, 1918); James W. Garner, *Reconstruction in Mississippi* * (New York: Macmillan, 1901); J. G. DeRoulhac Hamilton, *Reconstruction in North Carolina* (New York: Columbia Univ., 1914); Charles W. Ramsdell, *Reconstruction in Texas* (New York: Longmans, Green, 1910); Thomas S. Staples, *Reconstruction in Arkansas* (New York: Columbia Univ., 1923); C. Mildred Thompson, *Reconstruction in Georgia* (New York: Columbia Univ., 1915). Recent works in the Dunning tradition include Robert S. Henry, *The Story of Reconstruction* (Indianapolis: Bobbs-Merrill, 1938); W. C. Nunn, *Texas Under the Carpetbaggers* (Austin: Univ. Texas, 1962); E. Merton Coulter, *The South During Reconstruction, 1865–1877* (Baton Rouge: Louisiana State Univ., 1947); Avery O. Craven, *Reconstruction: The Ending of the Civil War* * (New York: Holt, Rinehart & Winston, 1969); and a popular account by Hodding Carter, *The Angry Scar: The Story of Reconstruction* (Garden City: Doubleday, 1959).

Essays summarizing Reconstruction historiography include: Don E. Fehrenbacher, "Division and Reunion," in John Higham (ed.), *The Reconstruction of American History* * (New York: Humanities Press, 1962); Vernon L. Wharton, "Reconstruction," in Arthur S. Link and Rembert W. Patrick (eds.), *Writing Southern History: Essays in Historiography in Honor of Fletcher M. Green* * (Baton Rouge: Louisiana State Univ., 1965); Taylor, "Historians of Reconstruction," *Journal of Negro History,* vol. 23 (1938); Weisberger, "The Dark and Bloody Ground of Reconstruction Historiography," *Journal of Southern History,* vol. 25 (1959).

A well-balanced, scholarly summary of the era is Rembert Patrick, *The Reconstruction of the Nation* * (New York: Oxford, 1967). C. Vann Woodward's *Reunion and Reaction: The Compromise of 1877 and the End of Reconstruction* * (Boston: Little, Brown, 1951) is a detailed analysis and reinterpretation of the end of the Reconstruction Era. John Samuel Ezell, *The South Since 1865* (New York: Macmillan, 1963) and Thomas D. Clark and Albert D. Kirwan, *The South Since Appomattox: A Century of Regional Change* (New York: Oxford, 1967) are general surveys of the recent South which begin with chapters on Reconstruction.

* Available in paperback.

CHAPTER X

BOURBONS AND AGRARIANS

Reconstruction governments and military occupation disappeared in the southern states beginning with Tennessee in 1869 and ending with South Carolina in 1877. The native southerners who gained control of their state governments from the 1870s to the end of the century have been called Redeemers or Restorationists (because they rescued and restored their states after Reconstruction), Brigadiers (because a large number of them were former Confederate military leaders), or Bourbons. The last designation was applied by their political detractors after they took office, with the implication that, like the ruling monarchs of France, they were so wedded to the ideas and practices of the past that they forgot nothing and learned nothing. None of these names is satisfactory. It is debatable how much redeeming and restoring was done, some of the leaders were not military men, and it is patently false to say they learned nothing. Despite its limitations, the term Bourbons will be applied here because it is the most used of the four appellations.

The abortive attempts to drive the Bourbons from office were made by farmers from the middle and lower social and economic strata of southern society. Because they favored agricultural relief and reform, these Bourbon opponents have traditionally been called Agrarians.

The Politics of Bourbon Democracy

Upon the end of Reconstruction, many southerners who had assisted in driving radical and Negro rule from their states disappeared from the political scene. Their main objective of home rule accomplished, they returned to the daily task of making a living, remitting control of the southern states to a small group of native white politicians. Playing upon bitter memories of war and Reconstruction, this coterie of planters, merchants, and lawyers dominated southern state politics for a generation. Because so few men were seriously interested in the political process, the professionalization of political careers became one of the more obvious characteristics of these Bourbon governments. Courthouse rings evolved in which men held the same offices continuously for years. If a limitation existed on the number of times one might be successively elected to a single office, rotation of men among the offices at the local level was common. More than one petty officeholder moved regularly from one county office to another—auditor, treasurer, tax collector, and sheriff. Appointive positions were filled on the basis of party loyalty rather than ability. If a man was particularly ambitious and aspired for higher office, with the blessing of party leaders he might move to a statewide post after serving his apprenticeship at the county level.

County politics and officeholding was a miniature of statewide political practices. In state after state a small group of men controlled the governmental machinery. In Georgia a famous triumvirate from Atlanta ran the state politically for nearly two decades. John B. Gordon, Joseph E. Brown, and Alfred H. Colquitt shared Georgia's highest offices on a rotating basis during the eighteen years immediately following the end of Reconstruction. Either Gordon, who had been a Confederate general in his twenties, or Brown, a former war governor of the state, occupied one of the state's seats in the United States Senate, and after 1883 Colquitt, a wealthy cotton-raiser, held the other. For most of this period either Colquitt or Gordon served as governor. Their monopoly of Georgia's choice offices reflected their political power in all of the state's political activities. Wade Hampton, wealthy planter and former owner of over three thousand slaves, was the most important political leader in South Carolina in the late nineteenth century. After serving as governor for two terms, he moved to the Senate for twelve years during which time he continued his political domination of the state, personally designating the choices for governor. Leading political forces in Mississippi were Lucius Q. C. Lamar, Edward C. Walthall, and James Z. George, all of whom at one time or another were in the United States Senate. John M. Stone and Robert Lowry were the only men to sit in the governor's chair in Mississippi for over twenty years of Bourbon rule. George S. Houston, George F. Drew, and Arthur S. Colyar, governors of Alabama, Florida, and Tennessee, respectively, represented less powerful but quite successful Bourbon governments in their states. No one leader stood out in Virginia, but all of the state's governors during the period were Confederate veterans.

One of the reasons for the Bourbons' ascendancy in their states in the 1870s was their attacks upon the radicals' political use of Negroes during Reconstruction. Negroes in office were anathema to the southern whites, and Bourbon politicians promised, if elected, to relegate the black man to a minor political role. Political campaigns based upon appeals to white supremacy were notably more successful than those which played down the race issue. Once in power the Bourbons carried out their promises, employing various methods to suppress the Negro vote. Extralegal means to reduce the weight of the black vote included gerrymandering, requiring the payment of poll taxes well in advance of election day, making some elective offices appointive, and holding a tight rein on political party machinery. Complex election laws were used to confuse the politically unsophisticated Negro voters, the most notable being South Carolina's Eight Box Law requiring a separate voting box for each office. Ballots placed in the wrong receptacle were not counted. White election officials were in charge of the boxes, and the illiterate black man was often the victim of disfranchisement when the boxes were moved around with purposeful intent to confuse him.

Whites resorted to subterfuge and trickery to eliminate the Negro voter because this was a means whereby the Fourteenth and Fifteenth Amendments could be bypassed. Race was not mentioned in these extralegal restrictions, and the United States Supreme Court sanctioned these efforts at voter control in 1883, when it ruled that since these regulations were not technically directed toward black men, the federal courts could not protect Negro rights supposedly guaranteed by the constitutional amendments. But the Bourbons were not satisfied; they wanted greater disfranchisement. Several states added amendments to their constitutions providing that all qualified voters must be able to read a passage of the United States Constitution or give a reasonable interpretation of a portion of it after it was read to him. Election officials were vested with the power to apply this literacy test, and the end result was a rapid decline in the Negro vote. Along with a literacy test, after 1895 some states also set up minimum property qualifications for voting.

While the Bourbons were intent upon sharply reducing Negro voting totals, some southerners criticized them for allowing blacks to vote at all. And they began to ask embarrassing questions. Since many of the laws and actions of the Bourbons to disfranchise the Negroes were equally restrictive upon the poorer farming classes, was this not an indi-

rect but effective way to suppress white political opposition? Most Negroes lived in the black belt counties, the historic centers of southern
wealth and influence and bulwarks of Bourbon support. Could it be that
the Negroes in those counties were being used in behalf of Bourbon domination? In recent years impressive historical evidence has been
unearthed to support the suspicions raised by the yeoman farmers. But
whether those suspicions were well founded is not as important as the actions taken by agrarian leaders when they became firmly convinced that
the Bourbons were willingly disfranchising the small farmer. This became one of many factors in the agrarian revolt of the 1890s.

Bourbons were often referred to as Bourbon Democrats because
Democrats comprised the majority of the group's leaders and adherents.
But to equate Bourbonism with the Democratic party is misleading.
Southern Whigs, who had been left without a political home when their
national party was broken asunder in the 1850s, attempted to maintain
their identity as a separate party immediately after the war, but they
were unsuccessful. However much they may have been at odds with their
Democratic opponents in the past, the political facts of life demanded
that they join forces with the Democrats to control the South after the
sectional crisis ended. The Democrats welcomed the alliance with the
Whigs and for a time several states' dominant political organizations
were called Conservative parties, a name designed to appeal to southern
voters in general who despised the radical label; also it was insisted upon
by the Whigs who resisted the term Democratic in their adopted party's
title. As the image of the Democrats was rehabilitated, the term Democratic gradually replaced the Conservative designation.

Historical conditions dictated that the Democratic party—by
whatever name it may have been called—was really the only place for
men with political ambition to turn. The Republican party was in disfa-
vor in the South because of the taint of abolition and the scars of Reconstruction, and independent movements simply did not have the numerical strength to compete with the Democrats until the 1890s. This is not
to say that Republicans and independents did not exist in the South
in the seventies and eighties. They were both significant in numbers
and power, and they belie the term Solid South during those decades.
Although every southern state supported the Democratic Presidential
nominee in 1800, it was not true that the Republicans were totally
impotent in the South during the last twenty years of the nineteenth century. Republican voting strength was over 40 percent in the eleven ex-
Confederate states in 1880, a slightly higher percentage than that in 1876.
The Republican Presidential candidate in 1884 received a larger propor-
tional vote than in 1880 in eight of the former Confederate states. A
general decline of Republican percentages occurred in 1888, but most of
the states in the South did not experience a great drop below the pre-

vious election. Republicanism remained a strong factor in southern politics in the 1890s, and not until after 1900 did it descend sharply throughout the region. The Republicans' progressive loss of support in the black belts during the decade of the 1880s reflected the successes former Whigs were having in carving out places for themselves in the Conservative (i.e., Democratic) party. One of the old-line Democrats of the Bourbon years was later quoted as saying: "We had to get the old Whigs in by using a good deal of soft soap, but after we got them in, they were better Democrats than we were and got most of the offices." This Whiggish element in the Democratic party during the Bourbon period was vital in shaping the principles and actions of the party, particularly those related to finances, economics, and industry.

Bourbon Economic Policies

Financial frugality characterized the Bourbon governments. After viewing with alarm the wasteful spending of the Reconstruction Era, the new rulers made economy in government a cardinal virtue. Retrenchment being their watchword, they sharply reduced taxes. As a result, many state offices were abolished outright, some departments were run by skeleton staffs, and salaries were reduced for officials who were retained. Public service agencies were starved, with care for state prisoners, the insane, and the blind becoming more inadequate than ever. Public school education suffered from lack of funds. Cost-conscious politicians showed little concern for the long-range negative results of their economy drives, and the states' public service bureaus and eleemosynary institutions suffered for years as a result of their policies.

In view of the penny-pinching of the Bourbons, one might expect that no financial underhandedness existed. But C. Vann Woodward has shown that such was not the case. Gaining office in part by decrying the graft and corruption of the radicals, these unscrupulous officials in turn systematically raided state treasuries. In 1883 the Tennessee, Alabama, and Arkansas state treasurers were discovered to have embezzled funds totalling nearly $1,000,000. Major E. A. Burke, a state treasurer in Louisiana, earned $1,777,000 for himself by falsely selling state bonds which he had been commanded to destroy. By the time this thievery was discovered, Burke was safely and serenely living in Tegucigalpa. State treasurers in Virginia, Kentucky, and Mississippi likewise failed to uphold standards of honesty, although they profited to a lesser degree than did Burke. The state comptroller in Georgia was convicted of larceny, and that state's commissioner of agriculture was forced to resign in view of shady deals in his department. A host of lesser county and local officeholders all over the South were discovered with their hands in the till. Despite the corruption, the Bourbons were not harshly criticized by their contemporaries who were more inclined to overlook stealing by native white southerners than by carpetbaggers or Negroes. One reason for the average southerner's lack of concern stemmed from the relatively small amounts of money the Bourbon legislators appropriated for state use. Contemporaries falsely assumed there was not a sufficiently large supply of state funds to be handled recklessly. Historians have compared the dishonest handling of funds during the Reconstruction and Bourbon periods and have found the Bourbons to have been less dishonest because they had less money to steal, but in both eras a virtuous politician was a rarity.

When the Bourbons assumed office most state debts consisted of three parts: prewar debts, Confederate debts, and Reconstruction debts. Every southern state except Mississippi and Texas repudiated all or a major portion of their Reconstruction debts, and all but these two states and Kentucky "readjusted" (scaled down) the other debts as much as they dared. The total extent to which the state debts were reduced is impossible to determine with accuracy, but the best estimates place it in the neighborhood of $150,000,000. North Carolina repudiated all of its Reconstruction debt, and paid only 40 percent of its other obligations. Georgia, Alabama, South Carolina, and Louisiana indicated that they would pay all "honest" debts, but after considerable financial maneuverings in the four states over several years, they finally repudiated virtually all of their debts. A political battle involving Bourbons, Negroes, and small white farmers developed over debt repudiation in Virginia. Under the leadership of former Confederate Major General William Mahone, a Negro faction called for readjustment of the state debt by force, if it could be accomplished no other way. After compromising with the Readjusters, the Bourbon legislature in 1890 reduced the $43,000,000 Virginia debt to about $19,000,000.

Needless to say, wholesale repudiation of debts ruined the credit of most of the states. But the Bourbons were unconcerned. Bitter recollections of war and Reconstruction, the desire for political power through officeholding, and a conservative attitude toward taxation and the role of government in society were more important in the minds of the Bourbons than the credit of their states.

The belief that the Bourbons who controlled the South after Reconstruction were the same men who dominated the region before the Civil War has been established as a myth. Some of the men who ruled the post-Reconstruction South were of the old planter class, but the majority were not. These new leaders were unanimous in their rejection of the Old South's reliance upon agriculture for regional salvation. Although they appealed to southerners when they recalled nostalgic antebellum days and identified themselves with the romantic cult of the Confederacy, these men were committed to economic progress through industry as the solution to the South's problems, and they became ardent advocates of industrial development in the South. Realizing that industry could come to the region only in so far as northern industrialists cooperated, the Bourbons were staunch supporters of sectional reconciliation. The compromise of 1877 was only the beginning of an economic alliance between the North and the Bourbons which went far to undermine the old agrarian traditions before the end of the century. That they were fastening upon the South a colonial economy to be dominated by northern money and men bothered the Bourbons not one moment.

The Bourbons have been accurately characterized as preeminently commercial-minded men who purposely aligned themselves with the Republican-industrial North in order to exploit the manpower and resources of their section. Since many of the Bourbons, even though members of the dominant Democratic party, were former southern Whigs with a predisposed friendliness to business, it was not difficult for them to emphasize the South's need for industry. Many old-time Democrats willingly sacrificed long-held tenets of agrarianism and states' rights for the great wave of industrialism sweeping all sections of the nation. The Bourbons eagerly joined the hungry throng at "the great barbecue."

Political leaders in the South did not favor industry for their region because of unselfish altruism. Basically self-seeking, they filled their own pockets with silver and gold through their connections with business and industry. The Georgia threesome of Gordon, Colquitt, and Brown collectively or separately owned interests in insurance, publishing, mining, manufacturing, real estate, railroads, textiles, and shipping. Brown grew quite wealthy as president of the Western and Atlantic Railroad, the Southern Railway and Steamship Company, the Walker Coal and Iron Company, and the Dade Coal Company. Wade Hampton of South Carolina helped organize the Southern Life Insurance Company, and George F. "Millionaire" Drew owned several saw mills, great tracts of timber, and the largest mercantile business in Florida. William D. Bloxham, Drew's successor as governor of Florida, granted much public land to speculators. Tennessee's first governor after Reconstruction was John C. Brown who later became president of the Bon Air Coal Company. Brown, Arthur S. Colyar, and a succession of other Tennessee governors worked while in office to gain favors for railroads in which they had investments. The Bourbons in Virginia passed a law providing that the state's valuable holdings in railroads be sold, at a low price, to private interests, and they funded the state debt in such a way as to be advantageous to the moneyed interests. The Louisville and Nashville Railroad won favors of all kinds through the hiring of legislators and public officials, the result being that Kentucky politics and railroad interests had become inseparably intertwined before the end of the century. Governor George S. Houston of Alabama received considerable financial support for his political campaigns from northern capitalists who were amply repaid when the governor adjusted the state debt in a manner highly pleasing to the railroad interests. Mississippi governors John M. Stone and Robert Lowry were both conservative railroad lawyers who resisted regulatory legislation while in office. Lowry became a close friend of owners of factories, railroads, and textile mills who sought tax exemptions and less stringent regulations.

These examples reinforce the argument that the Bourbons desired industry in the South for strictly personal and selfish reasons. Their attentiveness to industry and its leaders and the resulting lack of concern for the problems of agriculture was another factor leading to the most serious attempt to drive the Bourbons from the political temples.

Bases for Agrarian Discontent

During the supremacy of the Bourbons, southern farmers experienced economic frustrations of considerable magnitude. Although minor fluctuations occurred, the price of cotton generally declined throughout the period from an average of 15 cents a pound in 1870 to slightly less than 8 cents a pound in 1890. The cost of producing the South's cotton remained constant at about 7 cents a pound. Although these figures theoretically show the farmer making at least a small profit, the grower always seemed to receive less than the stated market price for his product, and the truth was that he was perpetually in debt. Necessary expenses, including the minimum of food, shelter, and clothing for his family, forced even the most frugal and penny-wise cotton farmer into chronic economic deprivation. Other farmers in the South lived under equally marginal conditions, and thousands spent every waking hour struggling with the impossible task of trying to make ends meet.

The farmer refused to acknowledge that overproduction, disregard of scientific methods of farming, and failure to diversify were in part responsible for his economic plight. Nor was he able to see himself properly in view of the powerful economic forces at work over which he had no control. Since colonial days the southern farmer had looked upon himself as essential to the economy of the nation. Those who tilled the soil were God's chosen people, and the southern farmer had always believed he had a special relationship with his Maker and the American economy. When he suffered, he was not introspective, objectively analyzing why he was a failure. Rather he placed the blame for his condition on others. As he looked around, several possible villains were conspicuous. The farmer expressed discontent with the railroads whose high discriminatory rates took money directly from the pockets of the growers. Farm magazines and newspapers were particularly critical of railroad activity, reminding their readers that the roads were owned by northern capitalists. Farm publications often charged that the railroad owners and the Bourbons were in league with each other and that the Bourbons, who received special considerations from the railroads, failed to pass forceful railroad regulations because of conflicts of interest. The jute-bagging trust, the cottonseed-oil trust, the fertilizer trust, and the tobacco trust were also blamed for farm failures. Because credit was difficult to secure, the farmer singled out bankers—especially northern bankers—for special criticism, and bankers and politicians were held responsible for the shortage of currency in circulation, a shortage which became particularly acute for the debtor as the years passed. Furthermore, the agrarian producer was unhappy with high tariffs, an unfair marketing system, and a tax structure which placed a disproportionate burden on small landowners. Residing in states where crop mortgage laws favorable to the Bourbon merchant class were in effect, the small farmer saw himself at a distinct disadvantage.

The farmer chafed when social services were curtailed as a result of the Bourbon fetish for governmental economy, and his unhappiness increased when the Bourbons refused to provide such services as state boards of agriculture and agricultural experimental farms and colleges. Social problems were not uppermost in the mind of the unredeemed farmer, but they were always just beneath the surface of his consciousness, and they added to his general uneasiness. While he continued to express his belief in individualism, the farmer in the South became aware of his social and physical isolation, a feeling especially strong in farmers' wives who seldom left the farm on which they lived. The paucity of social diversions irritated the farmer as he brooded upon his low economic status.

Many of the problems which the farmers were experiencing in the 1870s and 1880s were apparent to Oliver H. Kelley in 1866 when that United States Bureau of Agriculture clerk toured the South. Distressed by the southern farmers' poverty and isolation, Kelley organized the National Grange of the Patrons of Husbandry, an association to promote agricultural welfare throughout the United States, but particularly in the South. Even though Kelley had the highest motives in establishing the Grange, southerners were suspicious of this organization headquartered in the nation's capital and founded at a time when the South was under northern political control. Since the organization admitted women on an equal basis with men, patriarchal southern men viewed it as contrary to the established way of life. But the problems overwhelmed misgivings, and by 1871 the Grange had gained a foothold in South Carolina, Mississippi, and Kentucky, and soon thereafter it had spread throughout the remaining southern states. By 1873 Grange membership totaled 210,000 in the former Confederate states.

The Grange's avowedly social function was one of the reasons for its growth in the South. Southern women saw that local chapters of the organization met frequently to relieve the loneliness and isolation often felt by both the farmer and his wife. Picnics, box suppers, barbecues, and dances were only a few of the ways the Grangers entertained themselves. Agricultural education of the southern farmer was another purpose of the Grange, and monthly meetings were held at the local level to study economic problems, to read agricultural material, and on occasion to listen to one of several dozen full-time speakers hired by the national organization to discuss topics such as animal breeding, crop rotation, and the value of fertilizers. As the farmers gathered for social and educational purposes, they naturally discussed economic ills, including their dislike of "middlemen" who siphoned off farm profits and capitalists who overcharged for retail goods. Out of these discussions came moves to appoint purchasing agents and to establish cooperative stores so that Grange members could bypass the middlemen and the capitalists. The farmers were not qualified to run business enterprises properly, their efforts were generally undercapitalized, and they tried to pass along the benefits derived from cooperative action too rapidly. The venture into cooperative wholesaling and retailing proved to be a total failure for the Grangers.

The southern Grange declined precipitately after 1875, the victim of powerful landlords and merchants who could not afford organized opposition to the crop mortgage system and who violently opposed the cooperative ventures. Also contributing to the Grange's death was the lack of competent and aggressive leadership and the abject apathy on the part of thousands of farmers who made no effort to support the Grange, not because of opposition to it, but because they simply spent all of their time and energy in day-to-day existence. But the Granger movement was not without its successes and influence. The Bourbons passed mild railroad rate regulations because of Grange pressures, and small farmers came to realize that they could effectively use legislation to fight poverty and injustice. This developing attitude was an important facet of the revolt of the 1890s. The Granger movement also stimulated the small farmer's consciousness of his class status, a consciousness which was to become quite strong by the nineties and which also played a role in the uprising of that decade.

While the Granger movement addressed itself primarily to economic and social problems, political overtones were also evident, as is witnessed by its influence upon railroad rate regulation. But the movement was not overtly political and was never intended to be. The small white farmer expressed his desire for political influence through other means. While independent political movements were generally not successful in unseating the Bourbons in the southern states, they along with the Grange built a solid base for the agrarian revolt of the 1890s. Taking a variety of names—Independent, Greenbacker, Laborite, and Anti-Bourbon—these independent organizations usually reflected the Agrarians' antagonism toward the rule of the black belt Bourbon aristocrats. When these independents threatened to unite with the Republicans in a given region, the Bourbons wisely took the combined political leverage seriously. Bourbons often made efforts to solidify southern white men under their banner, and these efforts were intensified or relaxed in direct proportion to the political strength of the independents at a particular time and place.

One of the most significant of these earliest independent political movements expressed itself in the Readjuster party in Virginia. While the readjustment of the state's debts was the avowed reason for the rise of the new party, the differences between the Bourbons and the Readjusters were much more. The Readjuster party arose in the 1870s when times in Virginia were ripe for a political upheaval. Economic conditions were grave, inequitable taxes weighed against the poor farmer, and schools were suffering from inadequate funds. The Republican party was out of favor in the state, and the Bourbons were faced with a number of perplexing problems, only one of which was the disposition of the state debt. As criticism of the conservative Bourbon leadership increased, small farmers from the upcountry became aware of the political implications of the Granger movement. At that time William Mahone appeared on the scene to forge the most successful of the independent parties to oppose the Bourbons before 1890.

Mahone's party reflected the geographic and social differences in Virginia. It appealed to the small white farmers in the western areas of the state and to a substantial number of Negroes in the lowlands of the eastern areas, welding these two groups into a powerful political organization. Numerically superior in the Virginia state legislature in 1879, the Readjusters controlled Virginia politics for a brief time. They filled both United States Senate seats (one being taken by Mahone himself), as well as six posts in the House of Representatives. During their four-year supremacy, the Readjusters revised the tax structure, abolished the poll tax, outlawed the whipping post, made liberal appropriations for education, passed laws favorable to labor, and readjusted the state debt. At the national level Mahone received the blessing of the Republican party, the latter hoping to use Mahone as a vehicle for reviving the minority party in the state. But while out of office the Bourbons played upon fears of Republican and Negro domination, and in 1883 they regained control of the state from Mahoneism.

Virginia was the only southern state where independents actually ousted the Bourbons from office for a time, but all of the former Confederate states witnessed evidence of independent revolt in the decade of the eighties. The independent movement was based upon more than disagreement over Bourbon fiscal policies and how or whether state debts should be repudiated. Along with the usual complaints about inequitable taxes, unequal division of educational funds, and the lack of public services, the independents expressed dissatisfaction with machine politics, courthouse and statehouse rings, and election frauds. Neither were they happy with the apportionment of state legislatures nor the Bourbons' use of Negroes to maintain political power. The convention system for nominating and selecting party leaders was often tied to the system of representation, and this meant that black belt counties had delegations at the party conventions in greater proportion than their actual voting numbers. Unhappiness with these conditions added strength to the Bourbons' political opposition.

When economic conditions improved slightly in the middle of the 1880s, the edge of the independent movement in the southern states was briefly dulled. But the improvements were temporary, and in the final years of the decade growing agricultural adversity appeared. The stage was being set for the independent movement's final act.

The Failure of the Independents

Agrarian dissatisfaction of the late 1880s expressed itself in a number of agricultural societies similar to the old Grange. Farmers' Alliances, Agricultural Wheels, and Farmers' Unions were typical names given to these organizations, the most important of which was the Farmers' Alliance founded in Lampasas County, Texas, as early as 1875, when a group of cotton farmers organized to protect themselves against cattlemen and land syndicates. This local group grew slowly at first, but after reorganizing in 1879 it rapidly became a statewide farmers' movement and claimed 50,000 members in 1885. Under the leadership of Dr. Charles W. Macune, several lesser farmers' groups in Texas joined with the Farmers' Alliance, and Macune determined to organize all cotton farmers of America for their self-protection. The original Texas organization successfully consolidated many lesser but similar groups from all over the South into one large Alliance dedicated to general farm reform. Desiring financial benefit, southern farmers flocked in great numbers to the organization which came to be known popularly as the Southern Alliance. The Alliance developed a solid national organization with offices in Washington, D.C., claiming some 3,000,000 members by 1890. Another 1,250,000 Negro farmers were members of the Colored Farmers' National Alliance, organized in 1886. Efforts were made to merge the southern groups with similar ones which had sprung up in the Middle West to protect the interests of the plains farmers, but there were not successful.

The ostensible purposes of the Farmers' Alliance were social, economic, and educational—like the old Grange. But the Alliance men soon realized that if they were to institute a successful reform movement, they must resort to political methods. In 1886 Alliance men in a number of southern states openly supported candidates for the state legislatures who were sympathetic to the farmers' needs. When little benefit was gained from these elected officials, some Alliance men talked of organizing a third party, and Alliance parties were formed in Texas and Arkansas but with little success. The majority of the Alliance men preferred to gain political power for farm reform by attaining ascendancy in the states' Democratic parties. These preferences were channeled into a plan of action when North Carolinian Leonidas L. Polk, editor of the *Progressive Farmer,* became president of the Alliance. In his early years as editor, Polk had devoted editorials to improved farming techniques, but having been active in politics during the Confederacy and Reconstruction, he easily turned to politics as the most effective means to help the farmers. After advocating political action for several years, upon his election in 1889 Polk led the Alliance to front center on the political stage.

Making no official announcement of its move into politics, in 1890 the Alliance in several southern states wrested control of state Democratic nominating conventions from the Bourbons. In North Carolina, for example, Alliance men forced that party's state convention to extend verbal support to the farmers who suffered under the "yoke of Bourbonism," and they elected legislators and congressmen sympathetic to agrarian reforms. In other states Alliance men running as Democrats were successful in the November elections. Fifty-two seats in Florida's one-hundred-seat legislature were captured by Alliance men, and in Tennessee the Agrarians named J. P. Buchanan as governor and filled slightly less than half of all posts in both branches of the state legislature. Reuben F. Kolb, the Alliance's state leader in Alabama, failed in his bid for governor, but the farmers elected 75 of 133 Alabama legislators. James S. Hogg and Benjamin R. Tillman landed the gubernatorial posts in Texas and South Carolina as the result of the uniting of their political machines with Alliance forces. In all, the Alliance was victorious in more than half of the contests for legislative seats in eight states, it elected six governors, and it placed the organization's stamp of approval on over fifty congressmen elected to the U.S. House of Representatives.

The Southern Alliance synthesized a philosophy and a platform from the inchoate miscellany arising from agricultural depression and revolt. Aside from local demands peculiar to a given region, the Alliance sponsored a host of reform measures, including government regulation of trusts and railroads, land reform, government-based credit, an inflated currency, a more equitable tax structure, and fairer representation in the state legislatures. It also advanced the Sub-Treasury plan, a scheme calling for the national government to construct warehouses for temporary storage of nonperishable farm products. The plan sought for the government to loan to individual farmers using the warehouses up to 80 percent of the market value of the products stored. This loan could then be repaid at a low rate of interest when the farmer sold his crop. The advocates of the plan hoped that this arrangement would keep the market from being glutted with a product at a particular time, thus keeping up the market price for farm products. Whatever the merits of these demands, the Alliance was notably unsuccessful in putting them into effect after their 1890 victories. Obtaining campaign endorsements from Democratic politicians proved even less difficult than securing legislative reforms. The Southern Alliance produced the economic and political ideas from which the Populist movement was launched.

Farmers in other parts of the nation, especially the West, were also in the mood for political action. Neither of the two major parties was attentive to the problems of the farmers, and by the end of the 1880s westerners were moving in the direction of forming a new party to compete with the Democrats and Republicans in order to satisfy farmers' demands. Many southerners, including Hogg, Tillman, and others, believed that a third party was not the solution to their problems. Overriding in this attitude was the fear that an overt split in the Democratic party in the South might result in political power falling into the hands of the Negro minority. But other southern leaders were more desperate. Upon the formation of the nationwide Populist party in the early 1890s and with economic conditions worsening, a number of important Alliance men bolted to the new organization. Leonidas L. Polk of North Carolina, Thomas L. Nugent of Texas, Thomas E. Watson of Georgia, Reuben F. Kolb of Alabama, and other Alliance leaders used the press and the platform to argue that the southern farmer's salvation lay with the Populists and not within the Bourbon-dominated Democratic party. Numerous southern farmers took the plunge and joined the new party, but most southerners remained loyal to the Democratic party, unwilling to accept the pain of breaking ancient party loyalties and clinging to the hope that the Democrats who approved of Alliance demands would not fail the small farmer.

The southern Populists knew that they were not numerous enough to contest the Bourbon Democrats on even terms in the voting booths; therefore, they sought support from southern Republicans. Republicans jumped at this chance to have real political influence, and "fusion" tickets were entered against the Democrats in nearly every southern state in 1892, the first election year in which the Populist party officially ran candidates at the national level. Politics in the South was enormously invigorated as a result of this "fusion" (as it developed, "accommodation" would have been a more appropriate term), and from 1892 to 1896 the South experienced the operation of a genuine two-party system as the

Populist-Republican combination battled the Democrats blow for blow.

In addition to this alliance of necessity with the Republicans, the southern Populists based their political strategy upon three other combinations related to regional, class, and racial lines. By aligning themselves with western Populists, they hoped somehow to halt the exploitation of their region by the Northeast, an exploitation which had been painfully obvious to Bourbon critics since the compromise of 1877. The southern Populists, like the old Alliance men, favored uniting farmers with city and factory workers, seeing no incongruity in farmers championing organized labor and the right to strike. The most difficult of the combinations was an attempt to form a political union between white farmers and Negro farmers and laborers. Racial feelings were strong on the part of the middle- and lower-class southerner who comprised the backbone of the Populist movement, and the small white farmer had long criticized the Bourbons' political alliance with Negroes. Why, then, did these white southerners make an appeal to the Negro for his political support? Long suppressed politically and economically, these men were determined to have power, and they were willing to go to any extreme to obtain it. Little concrete evidence remains to substantiate the Populist appeal to the Negro voter—Populist newspapers in the South were conspicuously silent on the Negro question—but there is no doubt that the appeal was made. As a matter of fact, both the Bourbons and the Populists made sub rosa appeals for the Negro vote, all the while advocating white supremacy when orating before white audiences.

Noticeably unsuccessful in the elections of 1892, the Populists used the panic of 1893 to aid their cause. Depression prices for cotton and tobacco were lower than in the economic crisis of the 1870s. Debts, mortgages, and bankruptcies piled up with uncommon frequency. Nature added to the woes of the southern farmers as floods and droughts alternately plagued the land. In 1893 southerners hoped to receive sympathy and aid from the Democrats who, for the first time since 1860, controlled the Presidency and both houses of the national Congress. But President Grover Cleveland and his administration disappointed the South. They refused to inflate the currency to help the debtors; instead, Cleveland requested and obtained repeal of the Sherman Silver Purchase Act, a step looked upon with favor by the business interests of the Northeast. Adding fuel to the fires of Populism, the Democrats took other actions revealing that the national party had little or no sympathy for the plight of the southern farmer. New Populist clubs were organized, more newspapers espousing the cause were founded, and converts by the thousands deserted the Democratic party for the new movement. Reaching high tide in 1894 the Populists (with the aid of Republicans) gained control of both houses of the North Carolina legislature. That state sent a Populist and a Republican to the United States Senate and three Populists to the national House of Representatives. Populists in Alabama elected one congressman to Washington, barely failing to win the governor's chair for Reuben Kolb. In Georgia the Populist-Republican combination polled over 44 percent of the total vote cast, and it made strong bids in almost all other southern states. Expectations ran high for victory in 1896.

Opposition to Cleveland's conservative administration crystallized in 1895 within the ranks of southern and western Democrats. Those Democrats who were sympathetic with Populist demands but who did not favor third-partyism determined to make an all-out bid for control of the Democratic party's Presidential nominating convention the following year. When those liberal Democrats successfully took over their party in many southern and western states and in large part adopted the Populist goals, including currency inflation (symbolized by the free silver crusade), prescient southern Populists came to realize that their earlier optimism was ill-advised. The liberal wing of the Democratic party delegated its supporters to the national convention, subsequently controlling the nominating process and naming William Jennings Bryan as its candidate.

When the Populists met in convention they had no choice but to support Bryan, a western Democrat who had sincere sympathy for Populist demands. Two Presidential candidates running on almost identical reform platforms would have been political folly; the Republicans would surely win in view of a divided vote. The Populists nominated Tom Watson as their Vice-Presidential candidate to run with Bryan on the third party's ticket, probably to appeal to southern Populists to support Bryan, but the circumstances in 1896 were wholly intolerable for the southern Populists. Called upon to support the Democratic Presidential candidate at the national level, the Populists in the South were committed to "fusion" with the Republicans against Democrats at the local level! The consequences were immeasurably bitter and confusing. To southern Populists it appeared that those Agrarians who had not left the Democratic party had stabbed the Populists in the back. They had forced the Populists into a position where the third party was compelled to accept the Democratic Presidential candidate, they had appropriated the Populist program, and they had weakened the numerical strength of southern Populism by encouraging small farmers to remain within the traditional party. Under such circumstances, countless southerners became disgusted with the political maneuverings. Not surprisingly, many did not vote in the elections of 1896.

Southern Populism's cruel and baffling dilemma, Bryan's defeat for the Presidency, and improved economic conditions after 1896 brought about the rapid disintegration of the national Populist party. The short-lived attempt of the southern Agrarians to withdraw from the Democratic party and to use Republican and Negro voters to assist them in their fight with the old Bourbons had failed miserably. Embarrassed and without fanfare most of the southern discontents drifted back into the Democratic party. Some migrated to other states to begin new political careers where their rampant Populist pasts were less well known. For example, Thomas P. Gore, a totally blind Agrarian who migrated to Indian Territory after a flamboyant career in Populist politics in Mississippi and Texas, became one of Oklahoma's two Democratic senators when the new state joined the Union in 1907.

Although a failure in the short run, the Populist party was not without lasting influence. Its espousal of positive governmental responsibility, control of business, and further political democracy vitally influenced twentieth-century America. Farmers made another step toward the abandonment of their traditional individualism. Future requests for government economic aid for the farmer went far beyond the Sub-Treasury plan, a radical proposal at the time it was first advanced. Demands for the regulation of railroads were heeded, and a graduated income tax, popular election of United States senators, and free rural mail service became law. Farm credit reform, new marketing techniques, better farming methods, minimum prices for farm products combined with programs to limit overproduction, and soil conservation programs were outgrowths of the heritage of Populism. Perhaps as important was the development of a class consciousness on the part of the small farmers, to the extent that they were to become one of the most class conscious groups in the nation.

One of the chief results of Populism in the South was the stimulus it gave to Negro disfranchisement. Both the Populists and the Bourbons agreed that the political corruption of the decade must not be permitted to continue. The Bourbons were shocked by the possibility of a political alliance based on the common economic interests of small white farmers and Negroes. Agrarians, contending that the Negro had been used by the Bourbons to usurp their political power, abandoned their fair play principles and turned against the black man in the mid-nineties. While both groups had appealed to the Negro for votes at the beginning of the decade, they came to realize and fear that the Negro could easily become the political balance of power in the South, and both determined to deny him the vote. A major objective of southern politicians in the twentieth century was the maintenance of white supremacy. Upon Populism's death, the South returned to one-party politics. The independent movement, Republicanism, and internecine struggles had reached their climax with Populism, and by withstanding the assaults of Populism, the Solid South became institutionalized. Having seen the results of a third-party movement, southern Democrats would long hesitate before leaving the established party again.

Suggestions for Further Reading

A good general study of the Bourbon period in southern history is needed. In its absence, these works may be read: C. Vann Woodward, *Origins of the New South, 1877–1913* (Baton Rouge: Louisiana State Univ., 1951); Allen J. Going, *Bourbon Democracy in Alabama, 1874–1890* (University, Ala.: Univ. Alabama, 1951); William B. Hesseltine, *Confederate Leaders in the New South* (Baton Rouge: Louisiana State Univ., 1950); V. P. DeSantis, *Republicans Face the Southern Question: The New Departure Years, 1877–1897* (Baltimore: Johns Hopkins Univ., 1959); C. C. Pearson, *The Readjuster Movement in Virginia* (New Haven: Yale Univ., 1943); W. A. Sheppard, *The Red Shirts Remembered* (Atlanta: Ruralist Press, 1940); J. F. Doster, *Railroads in Alabama Politics, 1875–1914* (University, Ala.: Univ. Alabama, 1951). W. A. Mabry, *The Negro in North Carolina Politics Since Reconstruction* (Durham: Duke Univ., 1940) and the more general volume by Paul Lewinson, *Race, Class, and Party: A History of Negro Suffrage and White Politics in the South* (New York: Oxford, 1932) have much material on post-Reconstruction southern politics. A valuable state study is Margaret Law Callcott, *The Negro in Maryland Politics, 1870–1912* (Baltimore: Johns Hopkins Univ., 1969). Excellent essays on the Bourbons are Grantham, "Southern Bourbons Revisited," *South Atlantic Quarterly*, vol. 60 (1961) and Halsell, "The Bourbon Period in Mississippi Politics, 1875–1890," *Journal of Southern History*, vol. 11 (1945). Valuable, but not limited to the Bourbons, are Dewey W. Grantham, Jr., *The Democratic South* * (Athens, Ga.: Univ. Georgia, 1963) and Albert D. Kirwan, *Revolt of the Rednecks: Mississippi Politics, 1876–1925* * (Lexington: Univ. Kentucky, 1951). *Bourbonism and Agrarian Protest: Louisiana Politics, 1877–1900* (Baton Rouge: Louisiana State Univ., 1969), by William Ivy Hair, is an in-depth political study of a single state, while Olive Hall Shadgett, *The Republican Party in Georgia from Reconstruction through 1900* (Athens, Ga.: Univ. Georgia, 1964) details the story of the political have-nots and their attempts to cooperate with the Populists and the Negroes in the decade of revolt.

Three old but still valuable volumes dealing with the agrarian revolt, with some material on the South, are: John D. Hicks, *The Populist Revolt* * (Minneapolis: Univ. Minnesota, 1931) and Solon J. Buck, *The Agrarian Crusade* (New Haven: Yale Univ., 1921) and *The Granger Movement* * (Cambridge, Mass.: Harvard Univ., 1913). Theodore Saloutos, *Farmer Movements in the South, 1865–1933* * (Berkeley: Univ. California, 1960) is a penetrating study which demonstrates conclusively that the Southern Alliance was the intellectual precursor of the Populist movement. Not to be overlooked is Carl C. Taylor, *The Farmers' Movement, 1620–1920* (New York: American Book Co., 1953). C. Vann Woodward's *Tom Watson: Agrarian Rebel* * (New York: Macmillan, 1938) is a solid study of one of the movement's leaders. Biographies of other agrarian leaders are: Francis B. Simkins, *Pitchfork Ben Tillman* * (Baton Rouge: Louisiana State Univ., 1944); Stuart Noblin, *Leonidas L. Polk: Agrarian Crusader* (Chapel Hill: Univ. North Carolina, 1949); Daniel M. Robison, *Bob Taylor and the Agrarian Revolt in Tennessee* (Chapel Hill: Univ. North Carolina, 1935); Robert C. Cotner, *James S. Hogg* (Austin: Univ. Texas, 1959). State histories of the agrarian revolt include: Francis B. Simkins, *The Tillman Movement in South Carolina* (Durham: Duke Univ., 1926); R. C. Martin, *The People's Party in Texas* (Austin: Univ. Texas, 1933); A. M. Arnett, *The Populist Movement in Georgia* (New York: Columbia Univ., 1922); R. P. Brooks, *The Agrarian Revolution in Georgia, 1865–1912* (Madison: Univ. Wisconsin, 1914); W. D. Sheldon, *Populism in the Old Dominion* (Princeton: Princeton Univ., 1935). T. Harry Williams, *Romance and Realism in Southern Politics* * (Athens, Ga.: Univ. Georgia, 1961) is applicable to the material in this chapter, and Helen G. Edmonds, *The Negro and Fusion Politics in North Carolina, 1894–1901* (Chapel Hill: Univ. North Carolina, 1951) is a well-documented study of a complicated story concerning politics and race. Two general essays on the subject are Abramowitz, "The Negro in the Populist Movement," *Journal of Negro History*, vol. 38 (1953) and Lewis, "The Political Mind of the Negro, 1865–1900," *ibid.*, vol. 21 (1936). Robert F. Durden, *The Climax of Populism: The Election of 1896* * (Lexington: Univ. Kentucky, 1965) deals with the apogee of the agrarian movement.

* Available in paperback.

CHAPTER XI

TOWARD A
NEW SOUTH—
AGRICULTURE

After the conference at Appomattox Court House in April 1865, when Grant informed Lee that southern soldiers could keep their horses because they would be needed for the spring plowing, countless Confederate veterans straggled home that desolate spring to start life anew. The South had been an agricultural civilization before the war, and the men of the South assumed that they could return to farming as an occupation with some assurance that they would be able to make a living from the soil. But conditions in many parts of the South were not conducive for spring plowing. Fields not leached or eroded by water were tangled with briars, or overgrown with sassafras bushes and new scrub pines. Fences had fallen down or rotted away, farm animals had wandered away or had been stolen, and barns and buildings still standing revealed the neglect of four war years. The worst of these discouraging physical conditions were overcome by the southern farmer within a few years after the end of the war, but they symbolized the frustrations, heartaches, and economic bondage which he faced for generations to come.

General Characteristics to 1900

Devotion to single money crops characterized southern agriculture after 1865. Tobacco and cotton had been the upper and lower South's economic mainstays before the war, and southern farmers quite naturally turned to growing these staple crops after the war. The disruption of normal markets and the shortages created by reduced production during the war created a maldistribution and scarcity which temporarily guaranteed high prices for cotton and tobacco. The worldwide demand for cotton to make cheap textile fabrics and the revived tobacco trade related to the popularity of the cigarette seemed to portend long-range profits for the southern farmer. But certain disadvantages accompanied the growing of a single money crop. The farmer was compelled to import food for himself and his animals, his implements and tools were made outside the South, he tended to exhaust his land with a single crop year after year, and his economic status was geared to worldwide prices. Equally important was the fact that staple crop production made the farmer less independent in financial matters.

Closely related to the one-crop system was the presence of tenancy, another important aspect of postwar southern agriculture. Slave labor had been tied to the farms and the plantations before the war, but with forced labor no longer legal, how were the land and the laborers to be brought together again? Attempts were made in the first year after the war to operate farms with wage-earning laborers, but this proved wholly unsatisfactory because the landowner did not have ready cash to pay wages, and laborers often left fields and crops uncultivated and unharvested when wages were not forthcoming.

The solution to this problem was the growth of tenancy, a multivaried system in which the landowner generally made land available for cultivation while the tenant and his family supplied the labor, the tenant receiving a share of the crop as payment for his work. This system not only overcame the disruption of the labor supply, but it also helped solve problems resulting from a lack of cash, since no money changed hands between the landowner and the tenant. Tenancy contracts normally called for the profits of the money crop to be split evenly between tenant and owner, but the percentage for either party might be lower or higher depending upon whether the tenant contributed something other than his own labor, such as a wagon, mule, or farm implements. Those tenants who had only rough hands and strong bodies to offer were called sharecroppers, while share tenant was the name given to those who supplied some equipment along with their labor. There was also a group of cash tenants who rented land for a fixed sum, who furnished not only labor but also all necessities for growing a crop, who were free to grow what they pleased, and who farmed without restrictions, but this class remained quite small. The vast majority of the tenants had no cash, and they had no alternative but to become sharecroppers or share tenants. Since most tenants were engaged in cotton or tobacco farming, they worked the land so as to get as much income from it as possible in one growing season. Only the unusual tenant considered his presence on a farm in terms of more than one year's investment of his labor. Farm tenancy added its bit to the process of soil exhaustion.

Countless Negroes and landless whites entered into tenancy arrangements as a temporary expedient, but as time passed the system proved self-perpetuating, and escape from it seemed difficult if not impossible. Each year saw the number of tenants increase, while soil exhaustion continued and profits dwindled. While in 1880 only some 30 percent of all farmers in the lower South were tenants, that percentage was more than doubled over the next forty years.

Without question nearly one hundred years of farm tenancy hurt the South. The landowners were not able to insist upon scientific farming, tenants had no feeling of responsibility toward the land, and until the mid-twentieth century tenants had little chance to move into the landowning class. The system was pitted with weaknesses, but it appeared to be the only means to bring together farm land and a low grade of labor in a region where cash was in short supply.

Contrary to popular belief, the plantation system did not disappear after the Civil War. The federal government reported a larger number of farms in the South with each passing decade, but these figures have been misunderstood. The land in the South was retained by its prewar owners or their heirs, but in order to use the labor available after the war, the landowners subdivided their acreages into small farm plots for tenants to work. The presence of many small farms did not mean a redistribution of land ownership. Rather it was an indication of a change in the labor system. In 1860 there were 750,000 farms of all sizes in the South, but in 1880 that figure had jumped to 1,500,000, and by 1900 the total was up to 2,500,000. The opening of new lands was responsible for some of this increase, but the rising totals were mainly due to the subdividing of the large plantations. When times became especially hard, some landlords sold their lands, but the new owners were hardly ever from the tenant class which continued to play "catch-up" in the game of survival.

The most common type of landlord was the one who lived on his own land, working part of it himself and contracting with one or more sharecroppers or share tenants to work the remainder. Propinquity allowed these resident landlords to supervise their tenants' work to some extent, and this made these lands reasonably productive. The least productive lands were controlled by absentee landlords who made only occasional trips to the country; tenants usually produced little without the careful eye of a landlord watching over their shoulders. The most productive lands were those controlled by company landlords. As time passed and for a variety of reasons, great company-owned plantations developed, especially along the lower reaches of the Mississippi River. Divided into small tracts for individual cultivation, these plantations were worked by tenants, usually Negroes, who often contracted to be paid with part of the crop rather than with cash. Resident superintendents were hired to oversee the work of the tenants, and the companies usually managed their land in a businesslike manner. A final type of landlordship developed when southern merchants foreclosed mortgages which they held on farmers' lands; a few merchants became large landholders when farmers were unable to meet their financial obligations.

Why did these merchants have mortgages on farmers' land in the first place? When the farmer wanted to borrow money, why did he not go to a bank? The shortage of banks and scarcity of capital existing in the Old South were accentuated by the war, and the postwar South found both banks and capital severely limited. These partial statistics indicate the plight of the entire South. In 1870 only 36 national banks capitalized at $7,000,000 existed in Virginia, North Carolina, South Carolina, and Louisiana. Twenty-five years later 417 national banks were open in the former Confederate states, but almost half of these were in Texas and almost all of them were quite small with limited resources. In 1895 the South had a mere 118 state banks located in 66 counties, but 123 counties had no banking facilities at all. By 1905 national banks in the ex-Confederate states numbered 477 with capital assets amounting to more than $50,000,000, but these dollars were far too scarce to support major farm financing. Even if banks had the funds to loan, many farmers and tenants were unable to give assurances that they could repay the borrowed money. A reckless financier might have made cash loans to white and black tenants, but southern bankers were not inclined to be reckless. Nor were they eager to make a loan to a landowner when the note was to be secured by a run-down farm.

Because of the limitations of banks and the lack of cash, the farmer was forced to look to other sources for readily available credit, an absolute necessity for his farming operation. He thus turned to the southern country merchant. While some merchants made a few direct loans secured by the land of the farmers, most of them did not have so much cash handy. Instead, they granted credit to the farmer, this credit loan to be secured by a lien against the crop to be planted during the coming season. The first state law permitting liens to be taken on ungrown crops was passed by the Georgia legislature in December 1866, and other southern legislatures quickly followed suit. Some of the statutes allowed landlords to take liens against their tenants' future crop in order to protect the owner against a defaulting tenant. As the system developed, both landowner and tenant usually made credit arrangements with the local merchant so that they had some means of existence while their crops were being grown.

As the crop lien system became institutionalized, the country store merchant came to play a vital role in postwar southern agriculture, serving much the same function as the prewar factors by supplying both commodities and capital to the farmers. At the beginning of the growing season the tenant and the landlord bought on their credit from the storeowner items needed to plant the crop: seed, fertilizer, tools, and occasionally work animals and farming implements. While the crop was being grown they depended upon the merchants for items necessary for survival: meal, bacon, flour, molasses, clothing, as well as tobacco and other goods for personal use. Once a crop lien was made, the debtor was required to make his credit purchases from the merchant who held the lien. In addition to those already existing, hundreds of small town and crossroads furnishing stores sprouted in the South, the owners willing to extend credit to landowners and tenants alike, hoping to make a profit from their credit loans once the crop was harvested and sold. Because the country merchant was taking a greater risk by extending credit based upon an ungrown crop rather than upon real estate, he necessarily charged a high rate of interest, customarily from 8 to 15 percent. He also charged more for an item when it was sold under a credit arrangement than when it was sold for cash. Mark-ups on items needed by the farmers varied with individual storekeepers and with the particular item in question, but it might cost from 10 to 200 percent more to purchase some items on credit rather than for cash. Merchants justified these markups because they had to cover expenses such as taxes and interests and bad debts resulting from tenants who disappeared without settling accounts at the store. Besides charging excessive prices and exacting usurious interest rates, merchants were criticized for other practices which weighed against the farmer: selling inferior goods, dishonest bookkeeping procedures, and stiffling the advance of agricultural progress. No doubt some merchants were guilty of all of these charges, but careful studies have revealed that they did not willfully falsify customers' accounts; the merchant appeared to lose as often as he gained due to bookkeeping errors. It is difficult to distinguish between grades of merchandise from the records now extant, but the charge that the merchant sold low-quality goods must be viewed in the light that the furnishing merchant was in many ways at the mercy of the big wholesale mercantile houses, fertilizer manufacturers, and meatpacking companies in much the same way the farmer was subservient to the merchant.

There is no doubt that the merchants must share a large part of the blame for the evils resulting from the crop lien system. They insisted that their customers plant money crops—cotton or tobacco—so that the liens could be repaid. The further exhausting of southern soil was a result. But the merchant did not become wealthy at the expense of the landowners and tenants. Droughts, floods, or the abandoning of fields in mid-season by irresponsible tenants frequently reduced harvests so that the merchants could not be paid for the credit extended. For those crops which reached the market, lower and lower prices were paid over the years. When the landowner and the tenant did not clear enough to pay for their loans, they were often bound by contract to trade with the same merchant the following year. But the system did not result in great profits for the merchants, and it was a straight and narrow road to tenancy for many yeoman farmers. Those who were already tenants were trapped by an economic system which was not thrown off when they fled to another community and which instilled a sense of fatalism in them. As one perceptive historian has written, "A chain of debt bound tenant, planter, merchant, and banker together, and in their efforts to extricate themselves the banker exploited the merchant, the merchant exploited the tenant, and the tenant exploited the land."

Because of the financial and economic conditions in the South immediately after the war, there seemed to be no alternative to the crop lien system if southern agriculture was to get on its feet. Once established it could not be thrown off. In the long run the enactment of lien laws inaugurated a prolonged and debilitating era of farm economics in the South. The crop lien laws, the devotion to single money crops, the presence of tenancy, and the exhaustion of the soil through ill-usage and erosion saddled the South with poverty and economic insecurity well before the end of the nineteenth century.

Will the Government Help Us, Please?

The first decade and a half of the twentieth century saw southern farm tenancy on the increase, more farmers deeper in debt, continued adherence to single money crops, and a frightening pace of soil exhaustion. Whereas four southern states in 1900 had a majority of their farms operated by tenants, the number had increased to eight by 1910. One-half of the tenants in the nation resided in the Cotton Belt. On the bottom rung of the economic ladder, the marginal farmer in the new century was no better off than he had been in the 1890s. These baffling economic conditions were inseparable from other problems of the South, and the region at the turn of the century became the focus of great sociological experiments financed by northern philanthropy. Eager to obtain outside assistance, southern school leaders, churchmen, and editors were instilled with humanitarian zeal and a passion to uplift the Forgotten Man. While the philanthropists and their supporters directed most of their money and attention to the South's educational deficiencies,* they gradually came to realize the interrelationship of education, poverty, and apathy. They asked how southerners could support their schools if their earning power was not greatly increased. Accordingly, philanthropists worked with previously established land-grant agricultural colleges to persuade the farmer to adopt more efficient methods of cultivation in order to increase his productivity. Agrarian agitators and newly formed farm organizations, such as the Farmers' Union, argued for more scientific farming in the South. But it was impossible to educate the southern farmer into prosperity. Farm demonstration efforts were stepped up, exorbitant claims being spoken in their behalf, and while demonstration work recorded astonishing achievements, debt-ridden farmers remained realistically pessimistic about their future. The task of overcoming the complex economic conditions engulfing the southern farmer was beyond the limited resources of northern philanthropists, farm organizations, and agitators, and beyond minimum government assistance.

The political reformers who strove to improve the nation's urban slums during the Progressive Era were not concerned with poverty-stricken rural slums. Southern reformers reflected the concerns of the national leaders by expressing interest in "busting" the trusts, regulating the railroads, and strengthening public-utilities commissions, but they were generally blind to the more basic needs of their rural constituency. A small group of southern reform governors—including Napoleon Bonaparte Broward of Florida, William Goebel of Kentucky, Braxton Bragg Comer of Alabama, and Hoke Smith of Georgia—championed the farmers against the predatory railroads, made efforts to save public lands from the "land pirates," and worked to secure better labor laws, but their efforts proved to be of little direct benefit to the lowly farmers, the most overlooked of the Forgotten Men. Only near the end of the Progressive period was minimal attention directed toward the needs of the rural areas. Finally, through the combined efforts of legislators from the nation's farming areas, two pieces of national legislation to assist agricultural education were passed during the Woodrow Wilson administration. The Smith-Lever Act of 1914 created a generous federal grant-in-aid system for agricultural education by establishing university and governmental extension work in farm communities, while the Smith-Hughes Act of 1917 provided federal grants-in-aid for vocational education, resulting in liberal subsidies for states that taught agricultural and industrial arts in secondary schools.

The national movement to improve agricultural conditions resulted in increased interest in rural credit reform. During the first years

* See Chapter XIII for details of northern philanthropy and southern education.

of the twentieth century, farm leaders and supporters had come to believe that the commercial banks on which the farmers depended were not
adapted to their needs, that the financial machinery enjoyed by other
classes of borrowers was inadequate for the farmers, and that the farmers'
rates of interest were higher than the rates paid by others. In 1912 the
major political parties endorsed rural credit reform in their national conventions, and President Wilson expressed the need for reform in this field
in his first inaugural address. Agitation for a scheme to reduce the farmer's rate of interest thus grew rapidly after 1913. Emerging from these efforts was the Federal Farm Loan Act of 1916, the "Magna Charta of
American farm finance." This act established a system composed of
twelve federal farm loan banks capitalized at $500,000 each, the essential
function of which was to provide credit for farmers at a low rate of interest on a long-term basis. This was a distinct victory for the representatives of agrarian interests in the nation's capital, and it helped many regions of the country, including the South, but it was not enough, and it
attacked only one aspect of the South's multi-faceted problem.

Of more immediate consequence was the impact of World War I
upon the southern economy. Wartime inflation and demands for southern products brought a brief period of unprecedented prosperity, and the
southern farmer held high hopes of climbing out of his economic slough
of despond. The cotton crop of 1919 sold for a satisfying $2,000,000,000,
and postwar prices continued to rise in the early months of 1920. But
farmers who had expanded their operations and gone further into debt
in order to capitalize on inflation and the increased demand for products
found themselves victims of the "cotton cycle." Cotton prices rose to a
high of 42 cents a pound in New Orleans in April 1920, and southern
farmers that spring planted their largest crop since 1914. Prices held
steady until the middle of the summer, when they began to decline. By
December the price had fallen to 13½ cents and the great 1920 crop
proved to be a disastrous financial failure. The crisis of 1920–21 inflicted
near fatal wounds. The first opportunity since the Civil War for cotton
farmers to accumulate enough capital to pay off their oppressive debts
ended in tragedy, and the farmers' financial and psychological supports
were abruptly undercut. Tobacco farmers and others suffered similar
boom and bust conditions during and immediately following World War I.

The price break in the cotton market resulted in demands to cut
production in 1921, and a Cotton Acreage Reduction Convention met
in Memphis to encourage reduced planting in the spring of that year.
The Memphis convention, the boll weevil, and bad weather combined to
keep the cotton crop down, but a short cotton crop did not solve the
farmers' basic problems. Concerned about the future of cotton, L. S.
Wannamaker of South Carolina and Harvie Jordan of Georgia formed
the American Cotton Association. Convinced that cotton's problems

stemmed mainly from unscientific farming, the crop lien system, and a less than satisfactory marketing system, the Association went on record favoring rural credits, holding operations, crop limitations, and diversification. It emphasized the need for good business operations, including cooperative marketing, direct selling, better warehouse facilities, the control of pests, improved seeds, and more foreign markets. The Association stimulated a cooperative marketing movement of considerable proportions in the early 1920s. The Association promoted state cooperative laws, and in 1920 the first statewide cotton cooperative was formed in Oklahoma. Other states set up cotton growers associations, and while they did not secure a monopoly on the marketing of cotton, as many had hoped, they marketed as much as 10 percent of the crop in several states. The state associations federated in 1921 under the American Cotton Growers Exchange in Memphis, the Exchange maintaining sales offices and accounting, financing, and advisory services for farmers.

But the farmers' problems were not confined to marketing procedures. Rupert Vance in 1929 stated flatly, "Today the world's largest consumer of raw cotton is the boll weevil." Certainly the boll weevil's impact upon the cotton economy and the farmer was both widespread and depressing. The following statistical story reveals the stark and devastating effects of the boll weevil: Greene County, Georgia, ginned 20,030 bales of cotton in 1919, 13,414 in 1920, 1,487 in 1921, and 333 in 1922. The weevil invaded Texas in 1892, moved eastward across Louisiana and Mississippi and half of Alabama by 1913, across Georgia by 1916, into South Carolina in 1917, and was present throughout the South by 1923. Attempts to evict the weevil were unsuccessful, although experimental insecticides were used against him with some degree of success. Eventually the weevil became just another risk which the farmer assumed, along with all the other unseen variables in farm production. Harmful though the boll weevil was, his presence undoubtedly accelerated crop diversification in those areas where his damage was the greatest. From this point of view the weevil was not an unmixed blessing, but crop diversification was a costly move when accomplished at the expense of several years of crop losses due to the insect.

Farmers' persistent problems in the 1920s were accompanied by the rise and decline of numerous farm organizations. The farmer alternately joined or abandoned organizations designed to help with his problems, depending upon his mood, financial condition, or state of mind. The revived National Grange, the Farmers' Union, and the American Farm Bureau used various methods to gain support for their organizations and to agitate for better farm conditions. Inevitably farm problems invited political solutions, and the Farm Bloc, formed during the agricultural crisis of 1920–21, probably accomplished more for the farmer for a brief period than did the agricultural organizations. Between 1921 and

1923 Farm Bloc senators and representatives from the rural states successfully supported agrarian legislation in the tradition of the Wilson period.
They backed or led the fight for these measures: the Emergency Tariff of
1921, which protected farm products; an extension of the War Finance
Corporation to aid storage and export operations; the Grain Futures
Trading Act; the Capper-Volstead Cooperative Marketing Act, which ex-
empted agricultural cooperatives from the antitrust laws; a move to include a "dirt farmer" on the Federal Reserve Board; and the Intermediate Credit Act of 1923, extending credits under the Federal Reserve
system and establishing intermediate credit banks for medium-term loans.

The Farm Bloc declined in influence after 1923, but the battles in
the legislative halls during the remainder of the decade attested to the
fact that farm representatives were still out to help the farmer. For example, in 1924 the first McNary-Haugen bill was introduced into the Congress, designed to secure "equality for agriculture in the benefits of the
protective tariff." Relatively simple in conception, the bill was a plan to
dump American farm surpluses abroad at the lower world prices, with
the farmers assuming the loss through an "equalization fee." Theoretically, on a specific crop the farmers would have profited by rises in the
domestic price which was supposed to reach a level of the world price
plus the tariff on the crop. This plan constituted the western farmers' solution to the farm problem throughout the 1920s, but southern cotton
farmers were unenthusiastic. The plan would not help cotton farmers
who were to pay the equalization fee, while at the same time dumping
over one-half of their total crop into the world market. They realized
that the domestic price on the remainder of the crop would not rise
enough for them to recover their losses. Thus, southern congressmen assisted in the defeat of the first McNary-Haugen bill in 1924. A second bill
in 1925 did not reach the floor of either house. When bumper cotton
crops created another price crisis for southern farmers in 1925 and 1926,
they became less critical of the proposed solution offered by their western
friends. A third bill in 1926 was favored by the South, when western
leaders wrote into it a provision for a more orderly handling of exports, a
proposal designed to appeal particularly to cotton growers. But even with
southern support, this bill failed to pass in the House of Representatives.
Momentum had been developing, however, and a drastically revised
McNary-Haugen bill was introduced in 1927. In a bold effort to raise cotton prices, this new plan proposed that cotton farmers pay equalization
fees which, when accumulated, were to be used to support a holding operation to limit production. Southerners supported this bill which passed
both houses of Congress, but President Coolidge vetoed it. A similar bill
was vetoed in 1928.

Clearly the farm leaders had moved away from the concept of
dumping American surpluses abroad in favor of some kind of orderly

marketing through cooperative efforts. Their goal had become that of stabilizing production and markets. While the McNary-Haugen bills all failed, the debates on them forced the nation to consider the farm problem as a major issue on the national scene. When a national program finally emerged in the 1930s, acreage reduction and holding operations were basic features.

Depressed Farmers and the Great Depression

When the Great Depression of the 1930s brought hard times to all Americans, the long-suffering farmer said "welcome to the club." During the 1930s other groups and regions of the nation felt the economic pinch the farmer had experienced in the previous decade, and the farmer's position dropped another notch nearer the bottom of the economic ladder, at a time when he had assumed that he was already on the lowest rung. In 1932 farm incomes dropped to 39 percent of the 1929 level, while the general decline caused all incomes to fall to an average of 58 percent of that level. Cotton farmers received only $374,000,000 for their crop in 1932, after having made $1,245,000,000 in 1929. As conditions worsened, innumerable rural dwellers, landowners, and tenants alike fled from the farms. The Okies who migrated to California, as depicted in Steinbeck's *The Grapes of Wrath* (1939), were fortunate; they were able to scrape together enough money and will power to take their rattletrap Fords or Chevys on trips of many hundreds of miles. Others could flee only as far as the nearest town or city, there to find that the depression was curtailing employment of all kinds. But those who suffered the most were the ones who stayed on the land.

The farmers had looked to the national government for support from time to time in the past, but the government had taken little cognizance of their needs. Herbert Hoover had long possessed a humanitarian interest in the problems of the farmer, and farmers held out hope that the President would alleviate their deteriorating conditions. The Hoover administration passed two measures to deal with the farmer's fundamental and perennial maladies of low prices and inadequate markets. The first was the Agricultural Marketing Act of 1929. Passed before the great stock market crash, this act embodied President Hoover's concept of "orderly" cooperative marketing of agricultural products. The Federal Farm Board created by this act was funded with $500,000,000 to assist cooperatives and "stabilization corporations" in buying surpluses and thus to keep the market price for farm products at a reasonably high level. The Farm Board's efforts, limited mainly to wheat and cotton, got

under way just as the Great Depression began in October 1929. Prices
did not respond to the Board's activities, and in the summer of 1930 the
Board asked the governors of fourteen cotton states to use their influence
to reduce production. A movement for crop reduction was apparent in
the following months, but it proved unsuccessful. In the meantime, the
Farm Board had stopped purchasing surpluses, helplessly watching cotton sink to lower and lower prices. But the Farm Board and the crop reduction efforts did help prepare southerners for a more meaningful reduction movement during the coming Roosevelt era.

The second measure passed by the Hoover administration,
designed in part to assist the farmer, was the Smoot-Hawley Tariff of
1930. President Hoover had recommended that tariff rates be raised
slightly on agricultural products, but the final bill proved to be one generally revising the tariff upward, including factory goods as well as farm
products. That this tariff measure received spotty support in the South is
unimportant. It did not stem the decline of farm commodity prices, and
southern agriculture descended into the lowest depths of the depression.
King Cotton was near death and the disease which had felled him infected southern manufacturing and business as well as farming.* All of
the South suffered miserably. Other meager attempts by the Hoover administration were no more helpful to the South than were the tariff and
the Farm Board. Southerners turned to state and local agencies for relief,
but they found these governments beset by debts, unable to retain traditional public services, and totally unprepared to cope with widespread
distress. The Hoover administration had been unsuccessful in its efforts
to alleviate farm adversity, and the nadir of the agricultural depression
occurred.

Responsibility for improving the lot of the agricultural South was
thrust upon the national government, controlled after 1933 by the administration of President Franklin D. Roosevelt. Farm relief was high on
the Democrats' plan to improve the economic situation, and Roosevelt
and his assistants boldly prepared to solve agriculture's problems. Extreme poverty and economic depression in the rural South forced the nation to focus its attention on the region. Many of the New Deal measures
passed during the early months of Roosevelt's administration were directed toward the agricultural South, and he was to label the South the
"Nation's no. 1 economic problem." Tenancy, inadequate marketing procedures, lack of capital and credit, and the pitfalls of the single crop system constituted the basic problems southern agriculture had faced since
the Civil War, and New Deal legislation attempted to solve those prob-

---

* Tobacco was to some extent a depression-proof industry, since Americans were
reluctant to give up smoking even during hard times. Nevertheless, tobacco growers
were only slightly better off than their very depressed cotton neighbors.

lems by extending credit, adjusting debts, instituting soil conservation efforts, and placing acreage controls on major crops.

In consultation with the nation's farm leaders, the Department of Agriculture wrote an omnibus farm bill which the President submitted to Congress on March 16, 1933. Among other features it included a crop limitation program, and—at the insistence of southern senators—a scheme for inflating the currency, to be used at the President's option. In the same year the Federal Farm Mortgage Corporation was established to relieve the rural credit problem somewhat by making available low interest loans on agricultural land. The New Dealers also passed the Farm Credit Act to provide loans for both the producers and marketers of farm products. A law setting a five-year moratorium on farm foreclosures was designed to help the embattled landowners. The Farm Security Administration Act of 1937 created a government bureau to loan money to tenants to buy animals and equipment. The Resettlement Administration attempted to withdraw from cultivation many acres of marginal land in the South and to resettle the residents elsewhere, but these efforts were not highly successful.

One of the most important of the New Deal agricultural measures for the South and the nation, both for the depression and the years to follow, was the Agricultural Adjustment Act of 1933. Containing nearly every major device previously suggested for farm relief, this measure had as its primary objective the raising of farm prices. It sought voluntary crop and acreage restrictions mainly by means of government contracts which provided attractive benefit payments to cooperating farmers. The payments were designed to restore the farmers' purchasing power to parity, that is to the relative level of buying ability the farmers had held from 1909 to 1914. The act was originally directed toward seven basic commodities, including southern staples cotton, tobacco, and rice. Soon cattle, peanuts, sugar cane, and six more crops were included, and the list was steadily expanded as time passed. An element of McNary-Haugenism was also present in this act, when it authorized the government to subsidize exports and make marketing arrangements with food processors.

The Agricultural Adjustment Act was not passed until May, after many thousands of acres of cotton and tobacco had been planted and after the spring's pigs and calves had been born. Artificial scarcity and resultant higher prices could be obtained only by slaughtering the excess animals and plowing under the rows of cotton and tobacco which would produce surpluses. Farmers who voluntarily cooperated with the government's program for crop reduction found benefit payment checks in their seldom-used mailboxes. The federal treasury sent millions of dollars to southern farmers under these programs. Many farmers were unhappy that crops and animals were being destroyed when people in the nation and the world were unclothed and starving, but the prospect of a government check helped them overcome their reservations as they contemplated their own lowly estate. Secretary of Agriculture Henry A. Wallace admitted that it was "a shocking commentary on our civilization" to kill newborn animals and destroy growing crops, but he favored it "as a cleaning up of the wreckage from the old days of unbalanced production."

An example of the effects of the program can be seen in regard to cotton. Nearly 10,500,000 acres of cotton lands were taken out of production, reducing the 1933 crop to about 13,000,000 bales, some 4,000,000 below what could have been expected without the plowing-under programs. Cotton farmers received over $112,000,000 in benefit payments, and for a time sagging cotton prices were given a significant boost (with parity at 12.7 cents, prices reached 11 cents in July). But long before the total annual crop was marketed, prices were again low (fluctuating between 8 and 10 cents) and farmers were justifiably complaining. Effective relief for the nation's cotton farmers finally came from a massive holding program supported by government loans. President Roosevelt in October 1933 set up the Commodity Credit Corporation which made loans to farmers so that their income from cotton plus the loans was equal to 10 cents a pound in 1933 and 12 cents a pound in 1934. Later this government corporation extended price supports on other nonperishable farm products, including southern-produced naval stores, tobacco, and peanuts. In 1939 the Department of Agriculture absorbed the agency after which time it became the general administrator for all of the government's price support programs.

When the first AAA was declared unconstitutional in 1936, a temporary Soil Conservation and Domestic Allotment Act was passed which omitted acreage quotas and the unconstitutional processing taxes. This measure was designed to place money in the hands of rural dwellers, paying farmers for practicing soil conservation by planting soil-building legumes on land formerly planted with soil-depleting crops. The hope was that crop limitation would be accomplished through soil conservation. Farmers were also encouraged to take other measures to slow down soil erosion and restore fertility. This act was in keeping with the Soil Conservation Act of 1935 by which the national government assumed major responsibility for a nationwide program of soil conservation. A federal Soil Conservation Service cooperated with state and local agencies to establish soil conservation districts. The SCS made contracts with tenants and farmers to encourage crop rotation, contour plowing, terracing, strip cropping, and the free planting of legumes. Southerners were as eager as others to participate in this program, and by 1940 all the southern states had established cooperating districts.

While soil conservation was highly successful in regard to its primary purpose, it was a total failure as a means of limiting production. Farmers took their poorer lands out of production, but by intensive farming they could produce as much from their better lands as when all their land was in extensive production. Calls for controls were again expressed, and in February 1938 the second Agricultural Adjustment Act was passed. This basic act essentially reestablished and codified the various acts passed between 1933 and 1936 to establish a national farm program. Acreage allotments for the basic farm commodities were reinstituted on a voluntary basis, compulsory marketing quotas were established subject to the approval of two-thirds of the farmers affected, parity payments were to be made, and crop insurance was available first for wheat (1939) and then for cotton (1941). The concept of parity included in this measure remained basic to government agricultural programs after that time.

To what extent the agricultural programs of the New Deal helped the South remains a disputed question. Not a few farmers survived the depression years only because of government subsistence. But survival does not correspond with prosperity, and at the end of the 1930s the chief occupation of the South was still in distress. Hardest hit was the man at the bottom of the economy: the tenant. If some landlords received benefit payments for crop reduction, the tenant often did not. Always a marginal farmer, the tenant profited little from the government's various plans and proposals to assist agriculture. Because fewer acres were being planted, fewer laborers were required to cultivate and harvest them. Thousands of tenants, the majority of them Negroes, were made jobless, adding to the already lengthy relief roles of counties and towns. David Conrad has told the bitter, tragic story of these "forgotten farmers" who were evicted from the land under policies which clearly favored the landlords. One of the great millstones around the neck of the South, tenancy reached its peak between 1930 and 1935. But statistics heralding the decline of tenancy after 1935 were no cause for rejoicing by those who had long deplored the presence of the system. The circumstances which inaugurated the decline were as unwelcome as the continued existence of the system itself.

After the worst conditions of the Great Depression began to subside, unemployed southerners sought to return to their old jobs, but they were usually unwanted. Unable to find employment as tenants, thousands permanently joined the ranks of the seasonal migrant workers, those members of the agricultural economy who moved from area to area to assist with the harvesting of perishable crops. These migrants became an important part of the southern labor force during World War II and after. Blacks and poor whites gathered tons of tomatoes, lettuce, onions, potatoes, peaches, and similar products grown along the Gulf and Atlantic coasts, as well as lemons, oranges, and grapefruit in Florida. Mexican-Americans and "wetbacks" harvested similar crops on the Texas side of the Rio Grande. Although most Americans in the postwar period experienced a rising standard of living, the migrant laborer did not. Wages remained stable while temporary living quarters deteriorated with each passing year.

In the summer of 1970 a Senate subcommittee listened to testimony concerning this most disadvantaged group in the nation. The painful stories about the plight of the nearly one million migrants moved Senator Walter F. Mondale to say, "The capacity of our society to mangle people who lack the power to stand up for themselves is virtually limitless." Mondale was not exaggerating when he observed that the conditions of life among the migrants were "undoubtedly the worst in America today." Four medical doctors catalogued for the committee an endless parade of illness, deformity, disability, and human suffering. Quoting from their recently completed study of conditions in Texas, the doctors told the committee that the life expectancy of migrants was forty-nine years, twenty years less than that of the average American. The doctors reported that a hospital in McAllen, Texas, bluntly informed migrant mothers: "Pay the bill or we keep the baby." One person testified that "you can't walk without stepping on roaches and scorpions," and there was firm evidence to support the charges concerning the hard conditions and squalor under which the migrants worked and lived. Poverty workers and farm laborers angrily criticized the cold-heartedness of the big agri-corporations in general and in particular of the Coca-Cola Company, whose subsidiaries— Minute Maid, Hi-C, and Snow Crop— employed more than one thousand migrants in their Florida citrus groves. J. Paul Austin, president of Atlanta-based Coca-Cola, appeared before the panel to acknowledge that conditions in the migrant camps were "deplorable," and he offered ambitious corrective measures which his company planned to implement. Mondale replied, "The test will not be whether we talk about improving housing, but whether there *is* improved housing." Past experience, unfortunately, indicated that the prospect for improved working and living conditions for thousands of workers and their families from west Texas to south Florida were not bright at the outset of the new decade.

The Agricultural Revolution

Just as World War I brought a measure of better income for the southern farmer, so did World War II. In truth, the second war must be viewed as a major turning point in the life of southern agriculture. Every pound of almost every product from the farmer's land was gobbled up at rising prices during the war, even bumper crops finding purchasers in the marketplace. Although the farmer faced the consumer shortages which all Americans experienced during the war years, he was still better off than he had ever been before. When the global conflict ended, the farmer's lot did not decline precipitately as it had following World War I. Mainly responsible for the improved conditions were the continued demands for farm products, the national government's commitment to price supports,

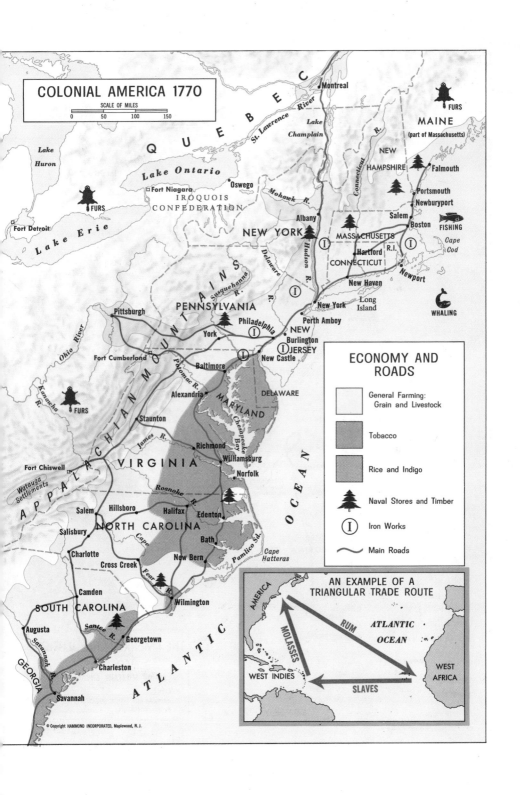

COLONIAL AMERICA 1770

SCALE OF MILES

0   50   100   150

QUEBEC

Montreal

St. Lawrence River

Lake Champlain

MAINE
(part of Massachusetts)

FURS

Lake Huron

Lake Ontario

Oswego

Fort Niagara

IROQUOIS CONFEDERATION

Mohawk R.

NEW HAMPSHIRE

Falmouth

Portsmouth
Newburyport

Albany

Connecticut R.

Salem

Boston

FISHING

FURS

Fort Detroit

Lake Erie

NEW YORK

MASSACHUSETTS

Cape Cod

Hudson R.

Hartford

R.I.

CONNECTICUT

Newport

New Haven

Long Island

WHALING

Susquehanna R.

Delaware R.

APPALACHIAN MOUNTAINS

PENNSYLVANIA

New York

Pittsburgh

Philadelphia

Perth Amboy

NEW

Ohio River

York

Burlington

JERSEY

Fort Cumberland

New Castle

Baltimore

Potomac R.

Alexandria

DELAWARE

Kenawha R.

FURS

Staunton

MARYLAND

Chesapeake Bay

James R.

Richmond

Williamsburg

Fort Chiswell

VIRGINIA

Norfolk

Watauga Settlements

Roanoke R.

Salem   Hillsboro   Halifax   Edenton

OCEAN

Salisbury

NORTH CAROLINA

Bath

Cape Hatteras

Charlotte

Cape Fear R.

New Bern

Pamlico Sd.

Cross Creek

Camden

Wilmington

SOUTH CAROLINA

Santee R.

Augusta

Georgetown

Savannah R.

GEORGIA

Charleston

ATLANTIC

Savannah

© Copyright HAMMOND INCORPORATED, Maplewood, N. J.

ECONOMY AND ROADS

General Farming:
Grain and Livestock

Tobacco

Rice and Indigo

Naval Stores and Timber

Ⓘ Iron Works

Main Roads

AN EXAMPLE OF A TRIANGULAR TRADE ROUTE

AMERICA

MOLASSES

RUM

ATLANTIC OCEAN

WEST INDIES

SLAVES

WEST AFRICA

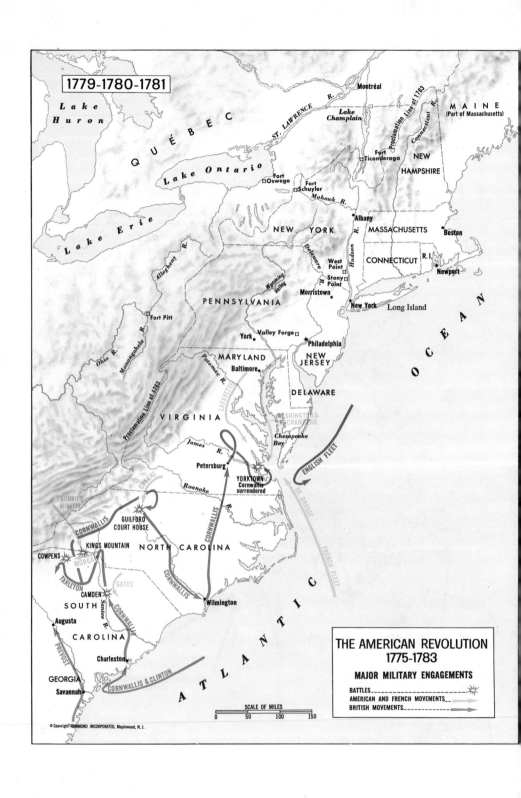

1779-1780-1781

Lake Huron

Montréal

QUÉBEC

Lake Champlain

St. LAWRENCE R.

Proclamation Line of 1763

MAINE
(Part of Massachusetts)

Connecticut R.

Lake Ontario

Fort Oswego

Fort Schuyler

Fort Ticonderoga

NEW HAMPSHIRE

Lake Erie

Mohawk R.

Albany

NEW YORK

MASSACHUSETTS

Boston

Allegheny R.

NEW YORK

Delaware R.

Hudson R.

CONNECTICUT

R.I.

Newport

West Point

Fort Pitt

Monongahela R.

PENNSYLVANIA

Wyoming Valley

Morristown

Stony Point

New York

Long Island

O C E A N

Ohio R.

Proclamation Line of 1763

York

Valley Forge

Philadelphia

NEW JERSEY

MARYLAND

Potomac R.

Baltimore

DELAWARE

LAFAYETTE

VIRGINIA

WASHINGTON & CHAMBEAU

Chesapeake Bay

James R.

Petersburg

YORKTOWN
Cornwallis surrendered

ENGLISH FLEET

GREENE

Roanoke R.

CORNWALLIS

DE GRASSE

FRONTIER MILITIA

GUILFORD COURT HOUSE

CORNWALLIS

FRENCH FLEET

COWPENS

KINGS MOUNTAIN

MORGAN

NORTH CAROLINA

CORNWALLIS

TARLETON

GATES

CAMDEN

SOUTH

Santee R.

CORNWALLIS

Wilmington

Augusta

CAROLINA

PREVOST

Charleston

GEORGIA

Savannah

CORNWALLIS & CLINTON

A T L A N T I C

THE AMERICAN REVOLUTION
1775-1783

MAJOR MILITARY ENGAGEMENTS

BATTLES_____
AMERICAN AND FRENCH MOVEMENTS___
BRITISH MOVEMENTS_____

SCALE OF MILES
0   50   100   150

© Copyright HAMMOND INCORPORATED, Maplewood, N. J.

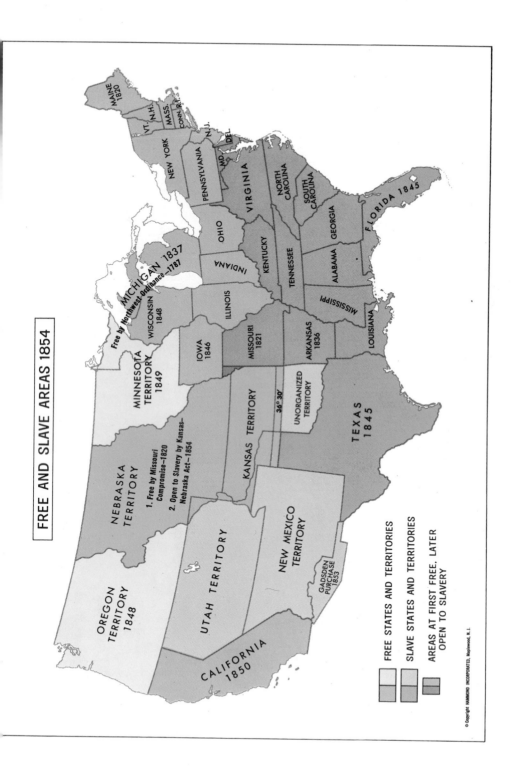

FREE AND SLAVE AREAS 1854

MAINE 1820

VT. | N.H. | MASS.

CONN. | R.I.

NEW YORK

N.J.

PENNSYLVANIA

MD. | DEL.

VIRGINIA

NORTH CAROLINA

SOUTH CAROLINA

FLORIDA 1845

OHIO

KENTUCKY

TENNESSEE

GEORGIA

ALABAMA

INDIANA

ILLINOIS

MISSISSIPPI

LOUISIANA

MICHIGAN 1837

Free by Northwest Ordinance –1787

WISCONSIN 1848

IOWA 1846

MISSOURI 1821

ARKANSAS 1836

MINNESOTA TERRITORY 1849

1. Free by Missouri Compromise–1820
2. Open to Slavery by Kansas-Nebraska Act–1854

KANSAS TERRITORY

36° 30'

UNORGANIZED TERRITORY

TEXAS 1845

NEBRASKA TERRITORY

UTAH TERRITORY

NEW MEXICO TERRITORY

GADSDEN PURCHASE 1853

OREGON TERRITORY 1848

CALIFORNIA 1850

FREE STATES AND TERRITORIES

SLAVE STATES AND TERRITORIES

AREAS AT FIRST FREE, LATER OPEN TO SLAVERY

© Copyright HAMMOND INCORPORATED, Maplewood, N.J.

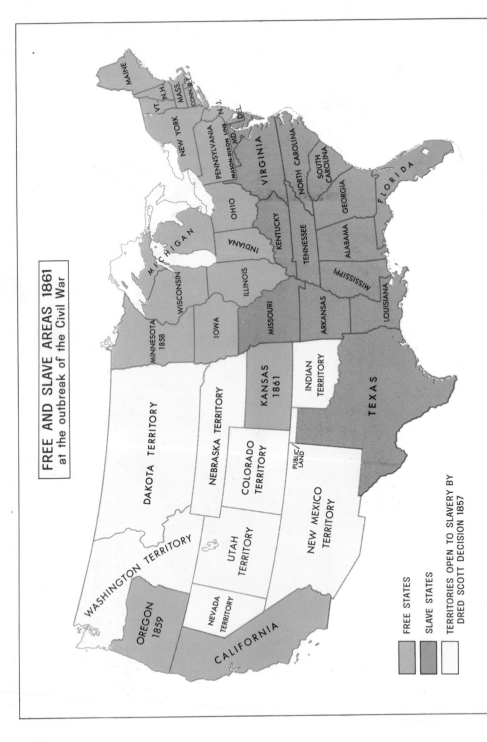

FREE AND SLAVE AREAS 1861
at the outbreak of the Civil War

FREE STATES

SLAVE STATES

TERRITORIES OPEN TO SLAVERY BY
DRED SCOTT DECISION 1857

© Copyright HAMMOND INCORPORATED, Maplewood, N.J.

MAINE

VT. N.H. MASS.
CONN. R.I.
N.J.
DEL.

NEW YORK

PENNSYLVANIA

MASON-DIXON LINE
MD.

VIRGINIA

NORTH CAROLINA

SOUTH CAROLINA

FLORIDA

OHIO

KENTUCKY

TENNESSEE

GEORGIA

ALABAMA

MICHIGAN

INDIANA

ILLINOIS

MISSISSIPPI

WISCONSIN

IOWA

MISSOURI

ARKANSAS

LOUISIANA

MINNESOTA
1858

DAKOTA TERRITORY

NEBRASKA TERRITORY

KANSAS
1861

INDIAN
TERRITORY

TEXAS

COLORADO
TERRITORY

PUBLIC
LAND

WASHINGTON TERRITORY

UTAH
TERRITORY

NEW MEXICO
TERRITORY

OREGON
1859

NEVADA
TERRITORY

CALIFORNIA

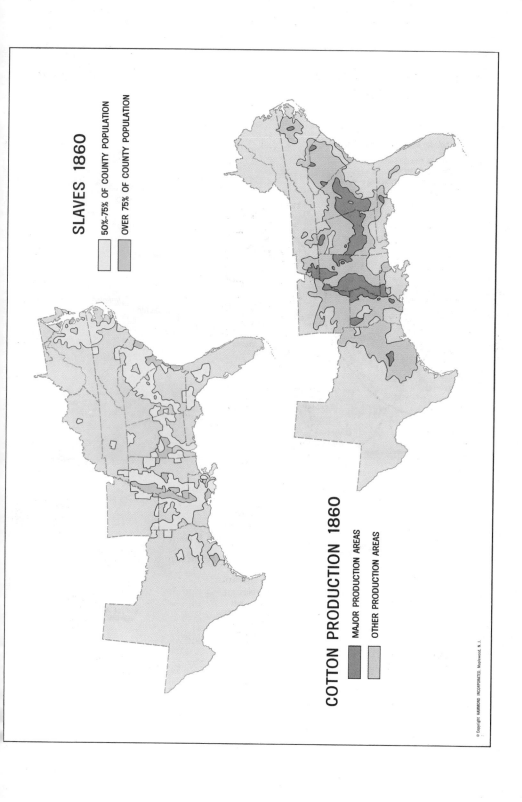

SLAVES 1860

☐ 50%-75% OF COUNTY POPULATION

☐ OVER 75% OF COUNTY POPULATION

COTTON PRODUCTION 1860

☐ MAJOR PRODUCTION AREAS

☐ OTHER PRODUCTION AREAS

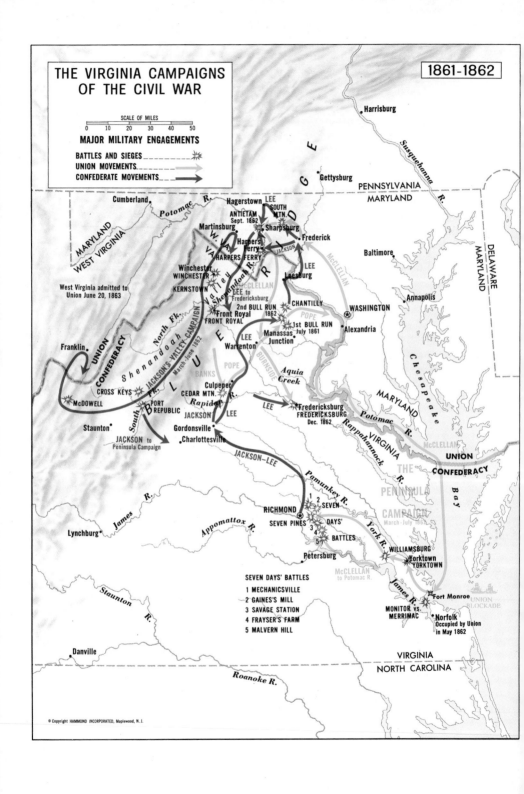

THE VIRGINIA CAMPAIGNS
OF THE CIVIL WAR

1861-1862

SCALE OF MILES

0   10   20   30   40   50

MAJOR MILITARY ENGAGEMENTS

BATTLES AND SIEGES

UNION MOVEMENTS

CONFEDERATE MOVEMENTS

Harrisburg

Susquehanna R.

Gettysburg

PENNSYLVANIA
MARYLAND

Cumberland

Potomac R.

Hagerstown   LEE

ANTIETAM   SOUTH
Sept. 1862   MTN.

Martinsburg   Sharpsburg

Frederick

MARYLAND

WEST VIRGINIA

Harpers
Ferry

HARPERS FERRY

JACKSON

Baltimore

LEE

Leesburg

McCLELLAN

Winchester
WINCHESTER

KERNSTOWN

West Virginia admitted to
Union June 20, 1863

McCLELLAN

LEE to
Fredericksburg

Annapolis

WASHINGTON

CHANTILLY

2nd BULL RUN
1862

Front Royal
FRONT ROYAL

POPE

1st BULL RUN
July 1861

Manassas
Junction

Alexandria

Franklin

UNION

CONFEDERACY

Shenandoah   North Fk.

JACKSON'S VALLEY CAMPAIGN
March-June 1862

LEE

Warrenton

LEE

BANKS

POPE

BURNSIDE

Aquia
Creek

Chesapeake

McDOWELL   CROSS KEYS

South Fk.   PORT
REPUBLIC

Culpeper
CEDAR MTN.

Rapidan R.

JACKSON   LEE

LEE

Fredericksburg
FREDERICKSBURG
Dec. 1862

MARYLAND

Potomac R.

Rappahannock R.

VIRGINIA

McCLELLAN

UNION

CONFEDERACY

Staunton

JACKSON to
Peninsula Campaign

Gordonsville

Charlottesville

JACKSON–LEE

Bay

THE
PENINSULA
CAMPAIGN
March-July 1862

James R.

Lynchburg

Appomattox R.

Pamunkey R.

1 2
SEVEN

RICHMOND   3
SEVEN PINES   4
5

DAYS'

BATTLES

York R.

WILLIAMSBURG

Williamsburg
YORKTOWN
Yorktown

Petersburg

McCLELLAN
to Potomac R.

SEVEN DAYS' BATTLES

1 MECHANICSVILLE
2 GAINES'S MILL
3 SAVAGE STATION
4 FRAYSER'S FARM
5 MALVERN HILL

Staunton R.

James R.

Fort Monroe

MONITOR vs.
MERRIMAC

Norfolk
Occupied by Union
in May 1862

UNION
BLOCKADE

Danville

VIRGINIA

NORTH CAROLINA

Roanoke R.

© Copyright HAMMOND INCORPORATED, Maplewood, N.J.

BLUE   RIDGE

Shenandoah Valley

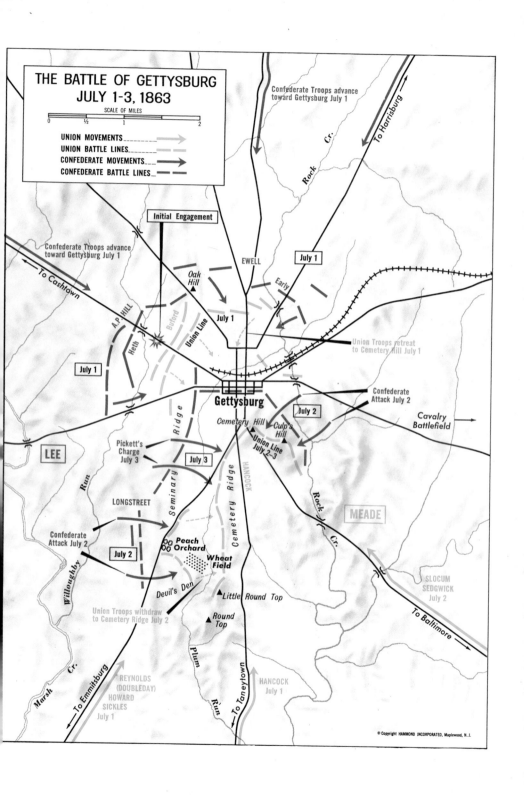

THE BATTLE OF GETTYSBURG
JULY 1-3, 1863

SCALE OF MILES

0   ½   1   2

UNION MOVEMENTS_____
UNION BATTLE LINES_____
CONFEDERATE MOVEMENTS____
CONFEDERATE BATTLE LINES__

Confederate Troops advance
toward Gettysburg July 1

To Harrisburg

Rock Cr.

Initial Engagement

Confederate Troops advance
toward Gettysburg July 1

EWELL

July 1

To Cashtown

Oak Hill

Early

A.P. HILL

Buford

July 1

Union Line

Union Troops retreat
to Cemetery Hill July 1

Heth

July 1

Gettysburg

Confederate
Attack July 2

Ridge

Cemetery Hill

Culp's Hill

July 2

Cavalry
Battlefield

LEE

Pickett's
Charge
July 3

Seminary

July 3

Union Line
July 2-3

HANCOCK

Rock Cr.

Run

LONGSTREET

Cemetery Ridge

MEADE

Confederate
Attack July 2

July 2

Peach
Orchard

Wheat
Field

Willoughby

Devil's Den

Little Round Top

SLOCUM
SEDGWICK
July 2

To Baltimore

Union Troops withdraw
to Cemetery Ridge July 2

Round
Top

Plum

Marsh Cr.

To Emmitsburg

REYNOLDS
(DOUBLEDAY)
HOWARD
SICKLES
July 1

Run

To Taneytown

HANCOCK
July 1

© Copyright HAMMOND INCORPORATED, Maplewood, N.J.

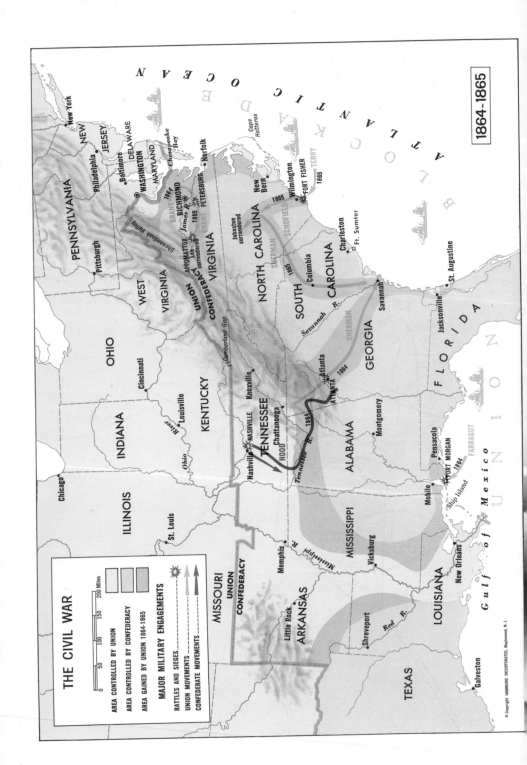

THE CIVIL WAR

0 50 100 150 200 Miles

AREA CONTROLLED BY UNION

AREA CONTROLLED BY CONFEDERACY

AREA GAINED BY UNION 1864-1865

MAJOR MILITARY ENGAGEMENTS

BATTLES AND SIEGES

UNION MOVEMENTS

CONFEDERATE MOVEMENTS

1864-1865

ATLANTIC OCEAN

BLOCKADE

New York

NEW JERSEY

Philadelphia

PENNSYLVANIA

Pittsburgh

DELAWARE

Baltimore

MARYLAND

WASHINGTON

Chesapeake Bay

Norfolk

Cape Hatteras

GRANT

1864

RICHMOND

James R.

GRANT

1865

APPOMATTOX
Lee surrendered

Shenandoah Valley

UNION

CONFEDERATE

VIRGINIA

WEST VIRGINIA

PETERSBURG

New Bern

Wilmington

FORT FISHER

1865

1865

SCHOFIELD

Johnston surrendered

NORTH CAROLINA

SHERMAN

1865

Columbia

Charleston

Ft. Sumter

SOUTH CAROLINA

St. Augustine

OHIO

INDIANA

Cincinnati

Louisville

Ohio River

KENTUCKY

Knoxville

Cumberland Gap

Savannah R.

SHERMAN

Savannah

Jacksonville

FLORIDA

Chicago

ILLINOIS

St. Louis

Nashville

NASHVILLE

Chattanooga

1864

HOOD

Tennessee R.

TENNESSEE

Atlanta

ATLANTA

1864

GEORGIA

Montgomery

ALABAMA

Pensacola

FORT MORGAN

1864

FARRAGUT

Mobile

Ship Island

Gulf of Mexico

MISSOURI

UNION

CONFEDERACY

Memphis

Mississippi R.

Vicksburg

MISSISSIPPI

New Orleans

LOUISIANA

Little Rock

ARKANSAS

Shreveport

Red R.

TEXAS

Galveston

UNION

© Copyright HAMMOND INCORPORATED, Maplewood, N.J.

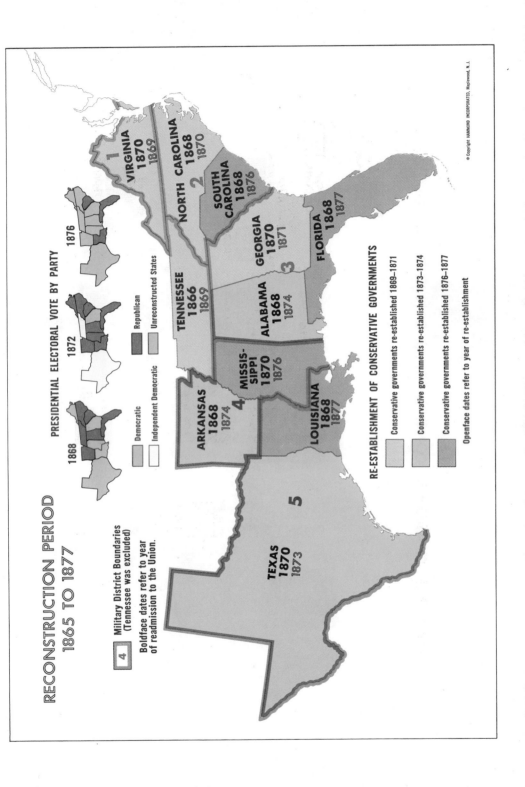

RECONSTRUCTION PERIOD
1865 TO 1877

PRESIDENTIAL ELECTORAL VOTE BY PARTY

1868   1872   1876

Democratic   Republican

Independent Democratic   Unreconstructed States

4 Military District Boundaries
(Tennessee was excluded)

Boldface dates refer to year
of readmission to the Union.

VIRGINIA
1870
1869
1

NORTH CAROLINA
1868
1870
2

SOUTH
CAROLINA
1868
1876

GEORGIA
1870
1871
3

FLORIDA
1868
1877

TENNESSEE
1866
1869

ALABAMA
1868
1874

MISSIS-
SIPPI
1870
1876
4

ARKANSAS
1868
1874

LOUISIANA
1868
1877

TEXAS
1870
1873
5

RE-ESTABLISHMENT OF CONSERVATIVE GOVERNMENTS

Conservative governments re-established 1869–1871

Conservative governments re-established 1873–1874

Conservative governments re-established 1876–1877

Openface dates refer to year of re-establishment

© Copyright HAMMOND INCORPORATED, Maplewood, N.J.

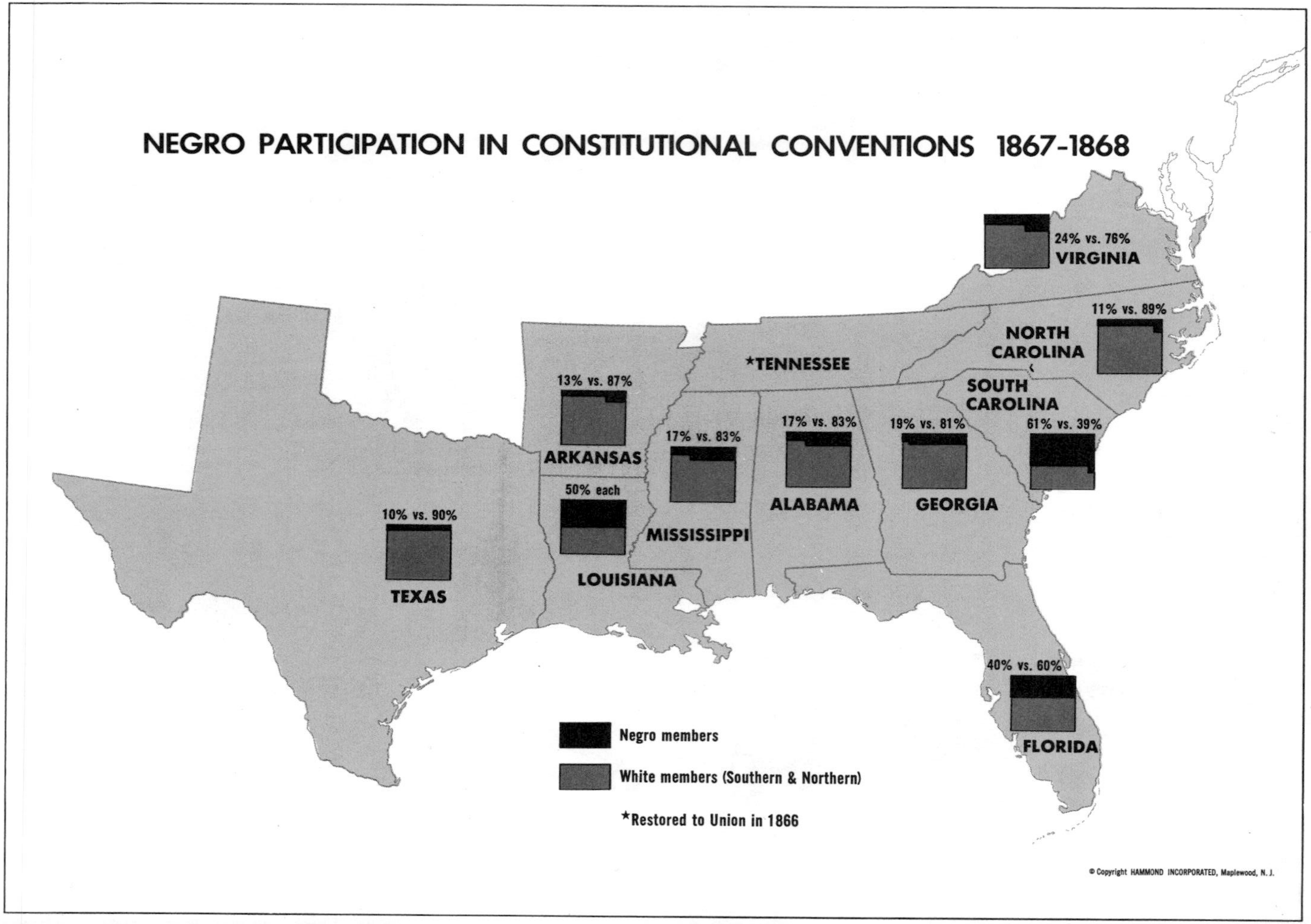

NEGRO PARTICIPATION IN CONSTITUTIONAL CONVENTIONS 1867-1868

VIRGINIA 24% vs. 76%

NORTH CAROLINA 11% vs. 89%

SOUTH CAROLINA 61% vs. 39%

FLORIDA 40% vs. 60%

GEORGIA 19% vs. 81%

ALABAMA 17% vs. 83%

*TENNESSEE

MISSISSIPPI 17% vs. 83%

ARKANSAS 13% vs. 87%

LOUISIANA 50% each

TEXAS 10% vs. 90%

Negro members

White members (Southern & Northern)

*Restored to Union in 1866

© Copyright HAMMOND INCORPORATED, Maplewood, N.J.

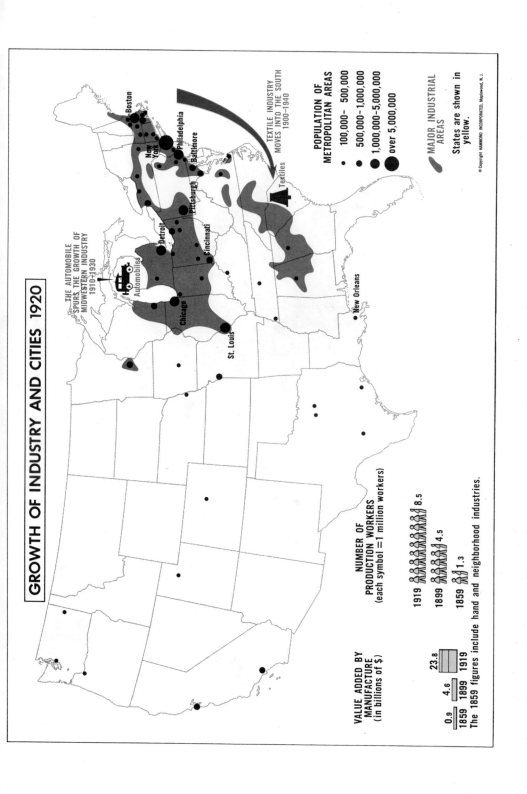

GROWTH OF INDUSTRY AND CITIES 1920

THE AUTOMOBILE
SPURS THE GROWTH OF
MIDWESTERN INDUSTRY
1910-1930

Automobiles

Boston
New York
Philadelphia
Baltimore
Pittsburgh
Detroit
Cincinnati
Chicago
St. Louis
New Orleans

TEXTILE INDUSTRY
MOVES INTO THE SOUTH
1900-1940

Textiles

POPULATION OF
METROPOLITAN AREAS

- 100,000– 500,000
- 500,000–1,000,000
- 1,000,000–5,000,000
- over 5,000,000

MAJOR INDUSTRIAL
AREAS

States are shown in
yellow.

© Copyright HAMMOND INCORPORATED, Maplewood, N.J.

VALUE ADDED BY
MANUFACTURE
(in billions of $)

0.9	4.6	23.8
1859 1899 1919	1859 1899 1919	1859 1899 1919

NUMBER OF
PRODUCTION WORKERS
(each symbol = 1 million workers)

1919 &&&&&&&&&& 8.5
1899 &&&&& 4.5
1859 && 1.3

The 1859 figures include hand and neighborhood industries.

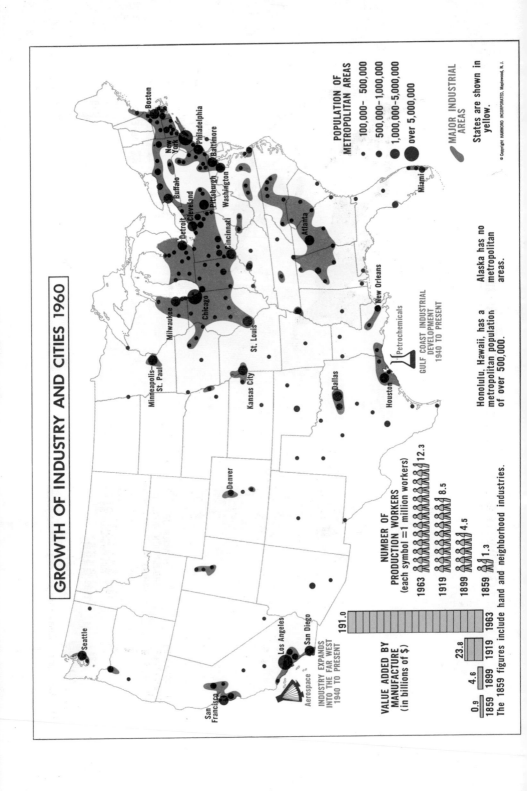

GROWTH OF INDUSTRY AND CITIES 1960

POPULATION OF
METROPOLITAN AREAS

· 100,000– 500,000
• 500,000–1,000,000
● 1,000,000–5,000,000
● over 5,000,000

MAJOR INDUSTRIAL
AREAS

States are shown in
yellow.

© Copyright HAMMOND INCORPORATED, Maplewood, N.J.

Alaska has no
metropolitan
areas.

Honolulu, Hawaii, has a
metropolitan population
of over 500,000.

GULF COAST INDUSTRIAL
DEVELOPMENT
1940 TO PRESENT

Petrochemicals

NUMBER OF
PRODUCTION WORKERS
(each symbol =1 million workers)

1963 &&&&&&&&&&&& 12.3
1919 &&&&&&&& 8.5
1899 &&&& 4.5
1859 && 1.3

INDUSTRY EXPANDS
INTO THE FAR WEST
1940 TO PRESENT

Aerospace

VALUE ADDED BY
MANUFACTURE
(in billions of $)

0.9 4.6   23.8   191.0
1859 1899 1919   1963

The 1859 figures include hand and neighborhood industries.

Seattle
San Francisco
Los Angeles
San Diego
Denver
Minneapolis–
St. Paul
Kansas City
Dallas
Houston
New Orleans
St. Louis
Milwaukee
Chicago
Detroit
Cleveland
Cincinnati
Pittsburgh
Buffalo
Washington
Baltimore
Philadelphia
New York
Boston
Atlanta
Miami

CONSERVATION OF NATURAL RESOURCES

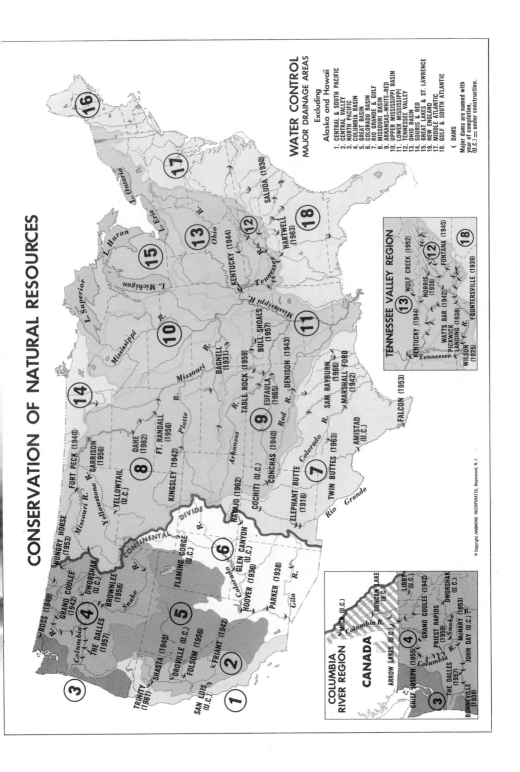

WATER CONTROL
MAJOR DRAINAGE AREAS
Excluding Alaska and Hawaii

1. CENTRAL & SOUTH PACIFIC
2. CENTRAL VALLEY
3. NORTH PACIFIC
4. COLUMBIA BASIN
5. GREAT BASIN
6. COLORADO BASIN
7. RIO GRANDE & GULF
8. MISSOURI BASIN
9. ARKANSAS–WHITE–RED
10. UPPER MISSISSIPPI BASIN
11. LOWER MISSISSIPPI BASIN
12. TENNESSEE VALLEY
13. OHIO BASIN
14. SOURIS & RED
15. GREAT LAKES & ST. LAWRENCE
16. NEW ENGLAND
17. MIDDLE ATLANTIC
18. GULF & SOUTH ATLANTIC

(DAMS

Major dams are named with year of completion.
(U.C.) = under construction.

© Copyright, HAMMOND INCORPORATED, Maplewood, N.J.

TENNESSEE VALLEY REGION

WOLF CREEK (1952)
NORRIS (1936)
KENTUCKY (1944)
WATTS BAR (1942)
PICKWICK LANDING (1938)
WILSON (1925)
GUNTERSVILLE (1939)
FONTANA (1945)

Tennessee

COLUMBIA RIVER REGION

CANADA

MICA (U.C.)
DUNCAN LAKE
ARROW LAKES (U.C.)
LIBBY (U.C.)
GRAND COULEE (1942)
PRIEST RAPIDS (1959)
CHIEF JOSEPH (1955)
DWORSHAK (U.C.)
THE DALLES (1957)
McNARY (1953)
JOHN DAY (U.C.)
BONNEVILLE (1938)

Columbia R.
Snake R.

Main map labels

ROSS (1949)
GRAND COULEE (1942)
HUNGRY HORSE (1953)
DWORSHAK (U.C.)
BROWNLEE (1958)
TRINITY (1961)
SHASTA (1945)
THE DALLES (1957)
OROVILLE (U.C.)
FOLSOM (1956)
SAN LUIS (U.C.)
FRIANT (1942)
FORT PECK (1940)
GARRISON (1956)
YELLOWTAIL (U.C.)
OAHE (1962)
FT. RANDALL (1956)
KINGSLEY (1942)
FLAMING GORGE (U.C.)
GLEN CANYON (1936)
HOOVER (1936)
PARKER (1938)
NAVAJO (1962)
COCHITI (U.C.)
CONCHAS (1940)
ELEPHANT BUTTE (1916)
TWIN BUTTES (1963)
AMISTAD (U.C.)
FALCON (1953)
BAGNELL (1931)
TABLE ROCK (1959)
BULL SHOALS (1957)
EUFAULA (1965)
DENISON (1943)
SAM RAYBURN (1966)
MARSHALL FORD (1942)
KENTUCKY (1944)
SALUDA (1930)
HARTWELL (1963)

CONTINENTAL DIVIDE

L. Superior
L. Michigan
L. Huron
L. Erie
L. Ontario

Columbia
Snake R.
Colorado R.
Gila R.
Rio Grande
Colorado R.
Missouri R.
Yellowstone R.
Platte R.
Mississippi R.
Missouri R.
Arkansas R.
Red R.
Ohio R.
Tennessee R.
Mississippi R.

CONSERVATION OF NATURAL RESOURCES

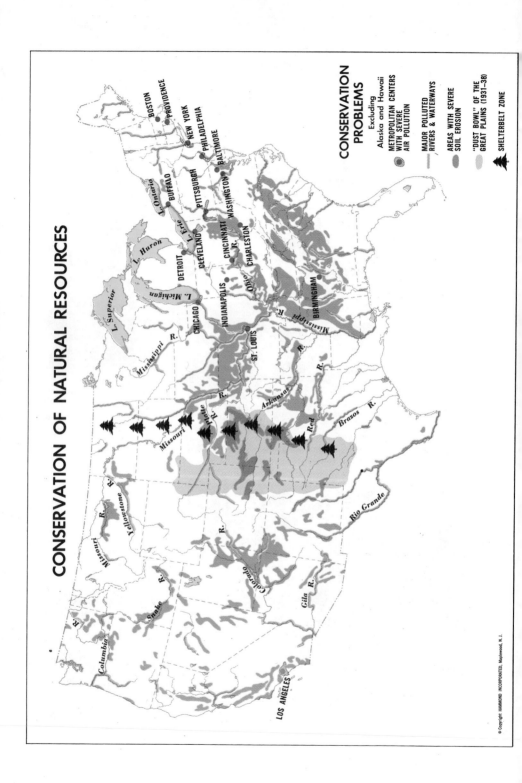

CONSERVATION PROBLEMS

Excluding
Alaska and Hawaii

- ● METROPOLITAN CENTERS
  WITH SEVERE
  AIR POLLUTION
- ⁓ MAJOR POLLUTED
  RIVERS & WATERWAYS
- AREAS WITH SEVERE
  SOIL EROSION
- "DUST BOWL" OF THE
  GREAT PLAINS (1931–38)
- 🌲 SHELTERBELT ZONE

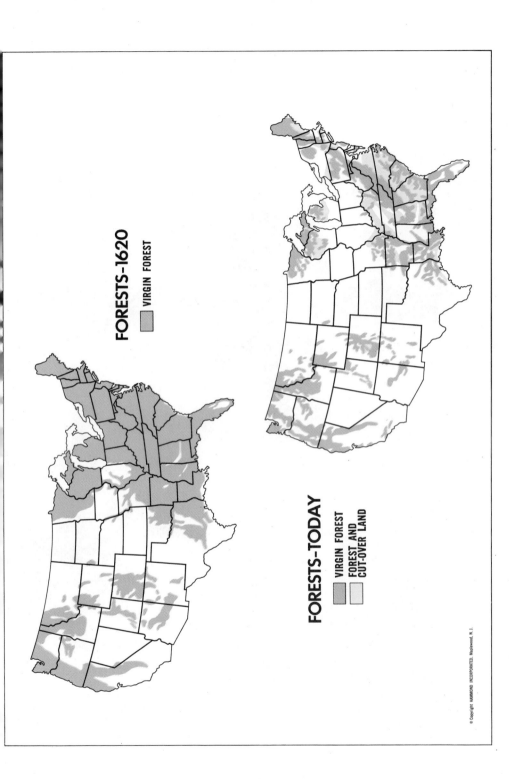

FORESTS—1620

VIRGIN FOREST

FORESTS—TODAY

VIRGIN FOREST

FOREST AND
CUT-OVER LAND

© Copyright HAMMOND INCORPORATED, Maplewood, N. J.

POLITICAL SECTIONALISM
PRESIDENTIAL ELECTORAL VOTE BY STATES AND PARTIES

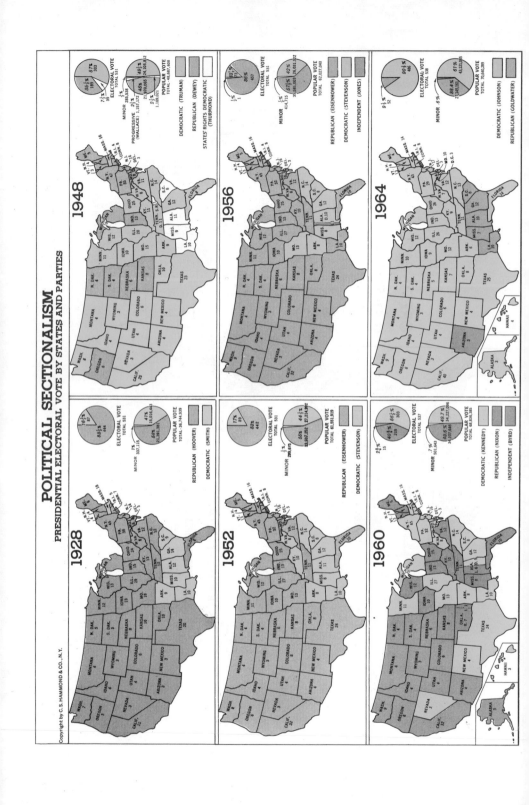

and the inflationary tendencies of the economy. But these alone were not enough. Without basic changes on the southern agricultural scene itself, the farmer's condition after World War II would not have been significantly different than it had been for the past one hundred years.

Many factors contributed to the agricultural revolution in the South after 1945, not the least of which was mechanization. The history of the development of machinery for agricultural production is, of course, a long one, but the South's willingness and ability to adapt to mechanization are recent. The mainstay of mechanized farming was the tractor, and a few statistics will suffice to dramatize its crucial role in recent southern agriculture. The successful development of the gasoline combustion engine resulted in an appreciable increase in the number of tractors in the South between World War I and World War II. While motorized farming still does not totally dominate the modern South, its growth has been fantastic. For example, when World War II began, the mule was the primary source of plowing power in the state of Alabama. Only 7,638 tractors existed in that state—the heart of Dixie. Five years later more than twice that number were being used in the fields, and by 1950 over 45,000 tractors were in operation. The number jumped to over 65,000 in 1955, and by 1970 the figure was conservatively estimated at 200,000.

The story was much the same in other Deep South states. Between 1945 and 1950 the number of tractors in the South doubled, and totals continued to skyrocket in the fifties and sixties. Other kinds of farm machinery and implements became commonplace on southern farms, and a farmer who did not have ability to make minor mechanical repairs was a rarity. In some communities the farm implement dealer vied with the local banker for supremacy on the socioeconomic scale.

The traditional picture of a tenant farmer leaning against a broken-down plow and encouraging a balky mule to move ahead was becoming hazy. Mules were fast vanishing, and mule breeders and traders, so much a part of the South's past, were all but ignored in the postwar era. Mississippi counted 358,000 mules in 1930, but the number had dropped to less than 200,000 by 1955. During the same quarter-century, the value of mules in Mississippi shrunk from about $32,000,000 to just over $9,000,000. Within a three-year period in the 1950s eleven southern states lost nearly 300,000 horses and mules. Mule barns were becoming a thing of the past; tractor sheds were commonplace. Moreover, mechanization had in many instances replaced the tenant, playing a major role in the social revolution sweeping the twentieth-century South. While in 1900 some 2,750,000 farms existed in twelve southern states, fifty-nine years later the number had shrunk to 1,460,000, and by 1970 the figure was just over 500,000. Machinery, the decline of tenancy, and larger farming units went hand in hand to alter the face and body of the South.

The tractor was used not only for plowing but for general farm use as well, and its importance cannot be overemphasized. But the mass production and widespread use of many other types of farm machinery must not be overlooked. The South's number one crop, cotton, was the recipient of countless labor-saving devices, not the least of which was the mechanical picker. No matter how much progress was made in planting and cultivating this basic crop, its harvesting remained a considerable bottleneck between field and gin until a successful cotton picker was invented. The idea of picking cotton mechanically had stimulated the imaginations of Americans since before the Civil War, but the early experimental machines were unsuccessful. By the turn of the century a number of inventors had tinkered with mechanical contraptions, but it was not until the 1930s that worthwhile progress was made. Mack and John Rust of Memphis, Tennessee, invented a machine which proved to be practical. But it took the South many years before it was willing or able to accept the Rust invention or the innumerable variations of it. Much land in the South was laced with gullies which prohibited the easy movement of the large and cumbersome machines. Furthermore, cotton was a temperamental plant, bolls on the same stalk ripening at different times, and the mechanical picker could not distinguish between green and ripe bolls. Most importantly, the widespread use of the machine had grave implications for the social structure of the South if thousands of human cotton pickers were put out of work.

Despite the problems and resistance to the mechanical picker, it has become essential to production in parts of the South, especially in the Mississippi Delta and the plains of Texas. In recent years as more compact machines have been built, as more hybrid plants which ripen consistently have been developed, and as the out-migration of the Negro tenant has increased, the cotton picking machine has come to be used widely throughout the region. A tourist during harvest time may still see Negro tenants picking cotton by hand and stuffing it into large canvas bags pulled along the ground behind them, but more likely he will see a mechanical monster roaming the fields gobbling up the matured fluffy cotton. As more and more of the South's cotton crop is mechanically picked each year, the visitor will be hard pressed to find gangs of laborers in the cotton fields anywhere in the South, except perhaps in the foothills of the Appalachian highlands.

Along with mechanization has gone scientific farming. While large numbers of Southern farmers continued to plant and harvest in the postwar years as their forefathers had, many were coming under the influence of educational programs designed to increase the quality and production of farm products and the income and the standard of living of the farmer. Soil conservation practices, the use of pesticides and fertilizers, crop rotation, contour plowing, and land reclamation were unknown to the southern farmer of an earlier generation. Encouraged by a variety of government programs, many southern farmers came to see that their salvation lay in cooperating with federal agencies. Dating from the days of the New Deal the federal government had placed much emphasis on soil conservation. Earlier emphases upon crop experiments and reports were accelerated until, in the postwar period, the farmer was literally inundated with valuable materials from the Government Printing Office. Perhaps the most influential of the government's activities was effected by the Tennessee Valley Authority. This agency's great regional experiment along the banks of the Tennessee River became a showplace for what could be done in a formerly depressed agricultural region with the aid of government support and some level-headed planning on the part of the individual farmer. A new day had dawned for those living near the TVA project, and others saw prospects for improving their estate.

Suggestions for crop diversification began in the Jamestown colony when the price of tobacco dropped due to surplus production. While the South had gradually accepted other crops, cotton and tobacco had remained as the basic staples throughout the region's long history. At no time in the past, however, had so many serious inroads been made upon the supremacy of these two crops as in the middle years of the twentieth century. Ironically, at the very time the South was relegating the mule and the horse to the sidelines, many southern farmers began to find profit from grasslands. Farmers who had spent a lifetime hoeing undesirable grass from around young cotton plants did not adapt easily to the sea of green which soon covered former cotton lands. But grass has come to be a vital factor in the regional economy, and the growing of grass has prompted an entirely new concept of land care in the South. Grasslands today absorb a large percentage of all chemical fertilizers used there. Farmers have found that growing grass entails less uncertainty than any other type of southern agriculture. A North Carolina experiment recently demonstrated that grass required far fewer man-hours of labor to produce comparable digestible livestock nutrients than wheat, corn, or oats.

During the dozen years immediately following World War II, over twenty million acres of southern farmland were returned to pasturage and hay production. In 1950 Alabama, Georgia, Mississippi, and Tennessee saw 37 percent of their farm lands in pasturage, and this percentage was increased as the decade passed. Furthermore, the quality of southern hay has risen. Legumes, greatly improved grasses, and scientifically tested fertilizer have meant a more nutritious forage. Finally, corn, wheat, sorghum, oats, peas, and beans for feeding purposes constitute a significant percentage of southern land currently devoted to cultivated crops.

Directly related to this attention to grass, hay, and pasturage was the South's renewed interest in cattle. Cattle had been raised in the nineteenth-century South, but lack of scientific breeding and pointed attention to cotton as a staple crop prevented them from assuming great importance. Furthermore, the cattle tick took its toll of southern herds, and southerners manifested little interest in cattle raising at the beginning of the twentieth century. Shortly thereafter the government began a campaign to eradicate the deadly tick by subjecting cattle to the dipping vat. Opposition to this program of tick control resulted not only from lack of education on the part of the farmers but also from a vague notion that somehow programs of this sort had wider implications for the South—as indeed they did. The campaign against ticks continued with varying degrees of success for three decades before victory was achieved. With tick-control accomplished and with the introduction of selective breeding, southern cattle herds of quality animals rapidly multiplied. Local livestock sales barns, animal clinics, and veterinary medicine have become as much a part of southern agriculture as cotton wagons and tobacco barns. The developing of local markets for southern-raised animals has assured cattle a relatively permanent place in southern agricultural pursuits. Dairying as well as the raising of beef cattle has also become common throughout the region.

Another semi-agricultural product which saw rapid growth in the twentieth-century South was the chicken. With its center in Georgia, the chicken industry had its early beginnings in the 1920s, but it did not expand greatly until the Great Depression. The broiler industry in Georgia and neighboring regions of the Appalachian foothills was well established by the beginning of World War II, and the industry was accelerated in the postwar period. Stepped-up grain production for chicken feed, modern refrigerated trucks, and improved highways aided the southern chicken grower in overcoming his production and marketing problems. In 1954 Georgia's total income from poultry was nearly $150,-000,000, while her cotton production grossed $132,000,000. "Who'd ever thought a dad-blamed chicken would scratch cotton off the land!" was the startled observation of a native of the state who recognized a revolution in agriculture of great import to the region.

Rice had been an important crop in colonial South Carolina, and it continued to be produced there on a limited scale into the twentieth century, but it had long before taken a back seat to cotton and tobacco. Enterprising southerners began a new rice culture in the 1880s in the coastal areas of east Texas and southwestern Louisiana. In the next decade central Arkansas farmers also began production. By 1903 the prairie lands in these three states accounted for 99.2 percent of the nation's rice acreage. Although American eating habits leaned more toward the potato than to rice, the market was enough so that the neglected, low-lying coastal area was profitably reclaimed, and the Arkansas farmers were also making money. Transportation facilities, mechanization, up-to-date milling processes, increased knowledge of rice cultivation, scientific farming, abundant water plus effective utilization of it, and improved varieties of grain contributed to the amazing growth of this enterprise in the twentieth century. Statistics show that southwestern rice production increased from 836,000 bushels in 1879, to 28,000,000 bushels in 1919, to over 200,-000,000 bushels in 1969.

More widespread than the rice culture was what may generally be called truck farming. The warm and long growing seasons of the Deep South, especially along the Gulf coast and the southerly regions of the Atlantic coast, early encouraged the growing of fruits, nuts, and vegetables. The development of improved transportation and better marketing facilities was responsible for this diversity in agriculture, and truck farming was fairly well established before the twentieth century. As with many other southern endeavors, truck farming became big business by the mid-twentieth century. Florida citrus fruits came to rival those of California, and a multimillion dollar business developed from the orange alone. The Orange Bowl sports stadium in Miami has never quite reached the prestige of the Rose Bowl in California, but it serves as a not too subtle reminder to the nation's television viewers of the importance of that industry to Florida.

In 1970 cotton and tobacco remained the South's primary crops, but that primacy no longer existed in many areas in the South, and it was clearly in jeopardy in others. Mechanization, scientific farming, and crop diversification joined with other forces to alter the southern landscape. A flight across the South today reveals a strikingly different view from yesteryear. If over one-sixth of the South's total area by 1900 had been laid bare by decades of overuse and misuse, half a century later much of that land had been revitalized by deliberate processes. Patches of green now dot the landscape where gullies and canyons once existed. The South still has a long way to go in the 1970s before it can completely overcome the gross mismanagement of the land by illiterate farmers, but much progress has been made. What the future holds for southern agriculture is speculative. Undoubtedly farming will continue to be of great importance, but it will in all probability reflect less and less a regional pattern as it moves toward the national norm.

Suggestions for Further Reading

Although they deal with many topics, C. Vann Woodward, *Origins of the New South, 1877–1913* * (Baton Rouge: Louisiana State Univ., 1951) and George B. Tindall, *The Emergence of the New South, 1913–1945* (Baton Rouge: Louisiana State Univ., 1967) have much material on southern agriculture between Reconstruction and the end of World War II. Good for background material for this chapter is Lewis Gray, *History of Agriculture in the Southern United States to 1860*, 2 vols. (Washington: Carnegie Institution, 1933). Howard W. Odum, *Southern Regions of the United States* (Chapel Hill: Univ. North Carolina, 1936) is a classic study which focuses on agriculture. Charles S. Johnson and others, *The Collapse of Cotton Tenancy* (Chapel Hill: Univ. North Carolina, 1935) and Arthur F. Raper, *Tenants of the Almighty* (New York: Macmillan, 1943) and *Preface to Peasantry* * (Chapel Hill: Univ. North Carolina, 1939) emphasize twentieth-century agricultural problems. A more recent publication on the subject is Morton Rubin, *Plantation County* * (Chapel Hill: Univ. North Carolina, 1951). Valuable chapters on the South are included in Fred A. Shannon's *The Farmer's Last Frontier: Agriculture, 1860–1897* * (New York: Farrar & Rinehart, 1945). Other works include: H. H. Bennett, *The Soils and Agriculture of the Southern States* (New York: Macmillan, 1921); A. M. Tang, *Economic Development in the Southern Piedmont, 1860–1950: Its Impact on Agriculture* (Chapel Hill: Univ. North Carolina, 1958); Arthur F. Raper and I. D. Reid, *Sharecroppers All* (Chapel Hill: Univ. North Carolina, 1941); T. J. Woofter, Jr. and A. E. Fisher, *The Plantation South Today* (Washington: U. S. Govt. Printing Office, 1940); Victor Perlo, *The Negro in Southern Agriculture* * (New York: International Publishers, 1953).

Two of the three essays in *Three Paths to the Modern South: Education, Agriculture, and Conservation* (Athens, Ga.: Univ. Georgia, 1965) by Thomas D. Clark relate to this chapter, as do many of the pages in that author's *The Emerging South,* * 2nd ed. (New York: Oxford, 1968). General studies are Joseph C. Robert, *The Story of Tobacco in America* * (New York: Knopf, 1949) and *The Tobacco Kingdom* (Durham: Duke Univ., 1938). John Leonard Fulmer, *Agricultural Progress in the Cotton Belt Since 1920* (Chapel Hill: Univ. North Carolina, 1950) and James H. Street, *The New Revolution in the Cotton Economy: Mechanization and its Consequences* (Chapel Hill: Univ. North Carolina, 1957) reveal a changing agricultural South. David E. Conrad has poignantly told the plight of *The Forgotten Farmers: The Story of Sharecrop-*

pers in the New Deal (Urbana: Univ. Illinois, 1965). Also of importance is Willard Range, *A Century of Georgia Agriculture, 1850–1950* (Athens, Ga.: Univ. Georgia, 1954).

* Available in paperback.

CHAPTER XII

TOWARD A NEW SOUTH— INDUSTRY

If a southern Rip Van Winkle had fallen asleep at the close of the Civil War and awakened one hundred years later to view the intervening industrial developments within his native region, he would have been many times more astonished by the changes than the original Rip who arose after a long sleep to view the new society in the Catskills. No sane prophet would have dared predict in 1865 the economic advancements to occur in the southern states in the century following the war. The progress in business and industry was slow to start and moved at a snail's pace for several years, but the tempo was noticeably stepped up by the end of the century, and the term "New South" became the equivalent of "industrial South." The twentieth century saw the industrial floodgates opened wide and the South almost inundated by industrial development.

The Northern Invasion

In the stillness following Appomattox, reflective southerners pondered the shortcomings of their civilization. Was it possible that the Civil War had proved that the South could not live by cotton alone? Could it

250

be that the prewar ills of the South were due to slavery and cotton? Was the current poverty due not only to the ravages of war, but also to the shortcomings of southern society itself? Should the South seriously consider turning its back upon its agricultural past and following in the footsteps of the victorious North by placing its faith in an industrial economy? These questions were answered in the affirmative by numerous southerners, not the least influential of which was F. W. Dawson, editor of the Charleston (S.C.) *News and Courier.* Zealously preaching the South's need for more industry, Dawson argued that the great significance of the Civil War was the *white* man's emancipation. No longer restricted by an outmoded labor system nor tied to cotton culture, the South was now emancipated and there was a chance for a new beginning, Dawson believed. Using his daily newspaper and the lecturer's platform, this South Carolinian was an early prophet of the New South concept. Some southerners were receptive to Dawson's pleas. Upon reflection they were somehow convinced that their past was sinful, and during the Reconstruction Era a sort of moral regeneration occurred. They were determined to disavow the past and face the future as new men.

Also influential and well known among those who advocated the growth of industry in the South was Henry W. Grady, longtime editor of the Atlanta (Ga.) *Constitution.* Grady orated to northern audiences as well as southern ones in his pursuit of an industrial economy for his region, and his editorials in the late nineteenth century preached this theme with vigor. The following editorial appearing in his paper in the late 1880s revealed his hard-hitting approach to the South's lost opportunities as he described a funeral in Georgia:

> The grave was dug through solid marble, but the marble headstone came from Vermont. It was in a pine wilderness, but the pine coffin came from Cincinnati. An iron mountain overshadowed it, but the coffin nails and screws and shovels came from Pittsburgh. With hardwoods and metals abounding, the corpse was hauled on a wagon that came from South Bend, Indiana. A hickory grove grew near by, but the pick and shovel handles came from New York. The cotton shirt on the dead man came from Cincinnati; the coat and breeches from Chicago; the shoes from Boston; the folded hands were encased in white gloves from New York, and round the poor neck, that had borne all its living days the bondage of lost opportunity, was twisted a cheap cravat from Philadelphia. All that the South contributed to the funeral of one of its sons was the corpse and the hole in the ground.

More than implicit in such writings was a call to southerners to give up regional laziness and embrace the national tradition of accomplishment through hard work and willpower.

The South's political leaders were receptive to the development of industry in the postwar South. Southern political and economic leaders not only advocated this economic turn, but actively pursued the moneyed interests of the North and Europe to assist the South in its endeavors. Northerners were at first somewhat skeptical that industrial profits could be had in the South, and southerners were compelled to begin the process alone. But when northerners were convinced that they could make money, they poured investments into the South at an alarming rate, especially after 1879, at the end of a great depression when both northern and foreign capital were seeking outlets for investments. The industrial revolution in the South was thus closely related to powerful economic forces outside the region, as well as to southern remorse for past mistakes and to the pledge to recover as quickly as possible.

While some southerners made disparaging remarks about Yankee money, others forgot or sublimated old animosities as they enticed the northern financier and entrepreneur southward. But the South got more than it bargained for. If southerners hoped to retain control of an economy supported by outside funds, they were sorely misled. Northern money meant northern control, and the South quickly became an economic appendage to the North. This colonial status of the southern economy was well established in several industries before the end of the nineteenth century, and it continued to exist and expanded in the years following. This is not to say that the South did not profit from the presence of new industrial plants. Indeed, it did. While the total value of farm, manufactured, and mine products in the South in 1870 amounted to $1,153,396,760, by 1920 that figure had risen to $15,195,871,512, an astonishing 1500 percent increase! Paralleling this economic growth, southerners' standards of living improved, purchasing power increased manyfold, and public services were expanded. But there was still the gnawing feeling inside many sons of the South that all was not right. On the one hand, they had strongly encouraged the investment of large sums of northern capital in their region, but on the other hand, they had qualms that they were somehow being exploited by these northern invaders. Like Esau in the Old Testament, they had sold their birthright for a mess of pottage, and their misgivings were legion.

If some southerners desired to drive the northern intruder out, it was too late by the end of the 1870s. Northern capitalists and industrialists had by that time warmly accepted the proffered and famed southern hospitality, and they were not about to withdraw. Rather they were on the verge of gigantic expansion activities in the region south of the Potomac. Exploitative aspects of northern economic policy were well illustrated by speculators' activities in regard to the public domain in the South. In 1876 the Congress repealed limitations formerly placed upon the timber, coal, and iron lands owned by the national government, and soon the lands were placed for sale on the open market. The excitement among northern investors was so great that special trains were run from Chicago to Mississippi and Louisiana to accommodate the interested speculators. Huge timber and mineral domains were established in the lower South. Purchases encompassing over 100,000 acres were common, and in one case a group of investors acquired over half a million acres of desirable land. Between 1877 and 1888 over 5,500,000 acres of southern federal lands were transferred to private hands. Bourbon governments, eager for progress and profit, encouraged this gigantic land steal.

The amount of land acquired from the national domain was a drop in the bucket compared with the state lands practically given away to speculative enterprises. In 1881 Florida sold 4,000,000 acres at 25 cents an acre to a Philadelphia syndicate led by Hamilton Disston. By 1885 Texas had virtually exhausted its vast public domain, including much land which had supposedly been reserved for the benefit of the public schools. Twelve railroad companies acquired over 32,000,000 acres of Texas land, an area as large as the state of Indiana. Other states had less land to dispose of, but dispose of it they did. Speculators, railroads, and lumber syndicates made profitable business ventures throughout the wooded lands of the South.

Southern railroad development proved to be even more attractive to northern and foreign capital than southern lands. While some railroad construction occurred in the South during the Reconstruction Era, the boom did not begin until 1880. Railroad mileage increased from 16,605 miles in 1880 to 39,108 in 1890, resulting in a 135.5 percent increase in comparison with an 86.5 percent increase for the nation as a whole. In the decade of the eighties, over 180 new railroad companies instituted activities in the region. Many of these companies were quite small, but they revealed the faith various states and the region were placing in railroad building. In some cases, dreams came true. For example, in 1882 the Southern Pacific was extended from New Orleans to San Francisco, completing a transcontinental railroad which southerners had hoped for since the early 1850s.

Following a national trend, consolidation came to characterize railroaders' activities in the late years of the nineteenth century. The Richmond and West Point Terminal Company, within a period of a few years, came to control over 8,500 miles of rail and water lines, making it the largest in the South and the forerunner of the later J. Pierpont Morgan transportation empire. In its drive to root out competition and to take over near-bankrupt companies, the Terminal in three years acquired the Richmond and Danville Railroad (which had previously taken over twenty-six lines), the East Tennessee, Virginia and Georgia Railroad (which had developed as the result of earlier mergers), and the Central Railroad and Banking Company (which had over 2,000 miles of rails).

Other consolidations occurring in the eighties were responsible for placing over half the railroad mileage of the South under the control of
about twelve large rail companies. They were invariably controlled by
northern hands. Nearly four hundred other companies divided the remaining rails, some with less than 40 miles of usable tracks.

In the nineties J. Pierpont Morgan and New York banking firms
ushered in an even greater period of rail consolidation. The depression
following the panic of 1893 was too great for many rickety railway companies to survive, and into the breach hurried the House of Morgan. By a
series of large-scale consolidations, Morgan created the Southern Railway
out of the ruins of the Richmond and West Point Terminal Company.
Two other great systems, the Atlantic Coast Line and the Seaboard Line,
were consolidated near the turn of the century, and northern control over
the railroad system of the South was essentially complete. Symbolic of
this northern octopus in southern regions was the Atlantic Coast Line's
purchase of the controlling stock in the Louisville and Nashville Railroad, one of the South's oldest and strongest systems. Southerners generally welcomed these changes, and rather than being imposed upon the
South, these developments had been desperately sought by some people.
The South had placed its faith in Progress.

The story of southern iron and steel followed the railroading pattern in a general way. The South's three largest producers—Alabama,
Tennessee, and Virginia—felt the impact of great quantities of northern
and English capital. Birmingham, sitting beside an iron mountain, experienced particularly rapid expansion. Alabama's iron production in 1889
amounted to ten times the state's output a decade earlier, and it was
more than twice the total production of Tennessee and Virginia. In
fact, Alabama produced more than all the other southern states combined.

During the eighties the South made a counter-invasion of the
North, when southern iron began to compete successfully in northern
markets. The South was producing more pig iron than the entire nation's
output before the Civil War, and in the final quarter of the nineteenth
century, the South's pig-iron production increased seventeen-fold, more
than twice the national rate. Great iron deposits, their proximity to coal
and limestone, the rapidly developing transportation system, and northern investment capital all combined to give the South a decisive edge in
the sectional competition in the iron and steel industries. As in the railroad industry, the panic of 1893 toppled numerous smaller iron and steel
companies organized during the boom of the eighties, but recovery was
reasonably rapid when New York bankers seized control of the failing enterprises, reorganized them, consolidated them, and underwrote the new
larger companies with investment capital.

By World War I, the southern iron and steel industries—with

their centers in the bustling and growing Birmingham—were on solid footing. Yet despite advantages of cheap materials and labor, these industries remained under sharp check by northern capitalists in the twentieth century. The Tennessee Coal and Iron Company, subsidiary of United States Steel Corporation after 1907 and the giant in the field in the South, was carefully controlled. Northern steel men could not tolerate the competition of southern mills, and they carefully regulated the industry's expansion in the South. Furthermore, pricing policies to protect established plants prevented expansion in the South. From 1900 to 1924 the steel industry set prices in such a way that Pittsburgh steel plants could successfully compete with others anywhere in the country. Whatever the competitive position of Birmingham's mills might have been, it was effectively nullified by these practices. The Federal Trade Commission's investigations revealed many occasions when southern plants were operating under this disadvantage, and even after the price-leadership practice was officially outlawed in 1924, Birmingham continued to operate under a system which placed it at a disadvantage with Pittsburgh producers.

Southern iron and steel industries at mid-twentieth century remained subordinate to northern control. Basic to the entire American economy, these industries had been crucial to the late nineteenth-century economic revolution, and they remained in a paramount position in the twentieth century. Competition was minimal, federal regulations were stringent, and production was controlled. Under the circumstances, southern mills were integrated into the industry so that the South had little or nothing to say about its progress or direction. Iron and steel were completely nationalized, and the South was of necessity a part of the total industry.

Old Standbys: Cotton and Tobacco

The most important southern industry before the Civil War had been cotton textile manufacturing, and worldwide demand for coarse cotton cloth assisted the rapid recovery of this major industry in the postwar years. Between 1860 and 1880 North Carolina, Georgia, and South Carolina, respectively doubled, tripled, and quadrupled their prewar production. Thus, the three leading cotton-manufacturing southern states were seemingly unaffected by the disruptive years of the war and the supposedly economically oppressive Reconstruction Era. But the gains of the immediate postwar decades were only a small indication of the acceleration to come after 1880. Growth and production after that date were so great that both historians and promoters of textiles have inaccurately assumed that 1880 marked the beginning of the industry in the South.

After 1880 the textile industry entered a dizzy period of expansion, at the same time manifesting the stamina which was to make it the basis of the southern industrial economy. The number of mills in the South rose from 161 in 1880 to 400 in 1900. The rate of growth in the nineties was 67.4 percent compared with the national increase of 7.5 percent. Almost all of the South's production occurred in four states—Alabama, Georgia, and the Carolinas—and U. S. Census figures from those states starkly revealed the expansion of the industry. In 1880 each mill averaged 3,553 spindles; in 1900 the figure was 10,651. Stated another way, in 1880 the total number of spindles in the same states was 422,807; in 1900 that number had increased to 3,791,654. During the two decades, the total number of workers in all southern mills rose from 16,741 to over 97,500. Production increased from 182,349 bales to 1,479,000, while capital investments went from just over $17,000,000 to $124,500,000. Capital investments in southern cotton mills increased by 131.4 percent during the two decades, while investments in New England mills had increased by only 12.1 percent.

Undoubtedly the profit motive was a primary factor in this unparalleled expansion of the cotton industry. In the 1880s investments in southern mills generally returned about 22 percent profit, and sometimes as much as 30 to 75 percent. Even though many mills were saddled with bad management and reduced profits (some even failed), it was a wise man who was "in" southern cotton textiles at this time. At first, the chief source of capital for the expansion of the industry came from within the South. Northern investors, reluctant to ship their money to the South before the depression years of the 1890s, rushed in after seeing southerners making good returns on their investments. A common practice was for a small amount of local capital to be raised for the establishing of a new mill, with the majority of the stock issue being purchased by northern textile machinery and commission firms. Thus, both northern and southern money were involved, but northern control was great and a sizable share of the resultant profits was drained into northern pockets.

Another factor in expansion of the industry was civic pride. Southerners saw not only an opportunity for economic development, but also a hope for social salvation. Small towns as well as major cities inaugurated campaigns to entice more mills into their regions, readily acknowledging the rehabilitation value of their presence. Chambers of commerce, businessmen, public officials, preachers, and newspaper editors led the chorus for their village or city to acquire more mills. A town's status in a region was to a large extent determined by its ability to attract mills to its vicinity. The total efforts to draw mills to specific regions, especially in the Piedmont area, amounted to a crusade. The advantages of mills were espoused at every turn, and the region was firmly committed to the crusaders' zeal.

The southern cotton textile industry did not suffer serious setbacks during the depression of the 1890s, primarily because of the continued demand of foreign markets for coarse cloth. If the hurrying pace to construct new mills was somewhat slackened in the early years of the decade, lost time was made up in later years, and the mills already in operation continued to run at full capacity throughout the decade. Between 1890 and 1897 the number of spindles in the South increased 151 percent, while New England's increase was a minimal 20 percent. As a matter of fact, New England had been aware of southern textile production for a number of years, and textile interests in the Northeast began to sense that *their* salvation lay in the South. After 1895 millions of New England dollars were invested in southern branch mills.

Textile corporation owners saw the South in a new light when they realized that mills could be operated more cheaply there than in New England because of an abundance of willing laborers, lower taxes, proximity to cotton fields (resulting in reduced transportation costs), plentiful water supply, favorable climate, inexpensive land, nearness to coal deposits for steam power, and a large supply of lumber for building purposes. Furthermore, the existing mills in the South were newer, cleaner, and more efficient. The cheap labor supply and the efficiency of newer equipment proved to be the most important advantages of the southern mills, but the other arguments often tipped the scales for northern financiers to invest in southern mills and for New England owners to establish branch mills south of the Potomac. The trend toward colonial subservience was clearly present in regard to cotton textiles.

World War I caused southern textile production to experience a boom period which did not end when the war was over. Throughout the 1920s mill promoters continued their crusade for economic salvation for particular regions in the South. Gaston County, North Carolina, sloganized, "Organize a mill a week," and even though this was a dream, it indicated the high hopes of mill men.

In the twentieth century, many New England mills with southern branches moved their major operations to the South, causing much economic and social distress for some areas of the Northeast. The decade following 1923 saw New England lose 40 percent of its mills and over one-half of its 190,000 laborers. At the same time the number of southern mill workers rose from 220,000 to 257,000. If the dismantling of mills in New England caused problems for that region, the development of the mill town had equally important consequences on the society of the South. Tenants left the farms to supply the needed labor in the mills. Rural families by the hundreds moved to the mill towns, and many times all members of the family gained jobs in the mills. In the mill towns the corporation owned the workers' houses, recreational facilities, stores, churches, and (later) community swimming pools and common television antennas. The benevolence of the masters gave security to the workers, but it also kept them in a subservient position, and in the long run the towns probably created more problems than they solved. Recently many industrial villages under company management have been discontinued.

The southern textile manufacturing industry has changed greatly in recent years. Mills which once produced only bolt cotton cloth and limited numbers of spools of thread now produce tire cord, special fabrics, and other goods combining textiles and synthetics. For a time the competition of synthetic fibers seemed to endanger the cotton textile industry, but by combining the synthetics with the cotton fibers, new products have emerged which have revitalized a historic southern industry. Chemical plants in Virginia, North Carolina, and Tennessee produce tons of materials to be used by the mills in the production of the modern fabrics demanded by the twentieth-century American.

Tobacco manufacturing has been almost exclusively a southern monopoly throughout the nation's history. The South led in tobacco manufacturing before the Civil War, and it was able to take the lead early in the postwar period. Virginia, North Carolina, and Kentucky, for years the center of the tobacco industry, quickly recovered their losses from the war, and they soon overtook and outstripped their prewar production. Within four years after the end of the war, it was evident that this southern industry was recovering rapidly, and by the end of the decade, losses had been recouped. Another decade saw an approximate doubling of both capital and output over the late antebellum years.

These developments came about largely through the use of manufacturing methods common in the prewar period. Then in the decade after 1885 advances in mechanization revolutionized the entire industry. In addition to a successful cigarette-making machine, patented in 1880 by James A. Bonsack, a Virginian, many other devices related to the cigarette industry were invented and put into use. The manufacturing of cigarettes, smoking tobacco, and chewing tobacco, heretofore hand operations, was so totally mechanized that by the turn of the century only 5 percent of the cost of manufacturing was due to labor. This revolution was not only related to mechanization, but it was also based upon the rapidly developing market which demanded cigarettes, to a large extent a postwar development in consumer tastes. Concurrent with the popularity of the cigarette was the expansion of bright-tobacco production. A mild, comparatively sweet plant which flourished in the sandy soil of the Carolinas, bright-tobacco became the essential ingredient in the cigarette. The shifting of the locus of the tobacco industry from Virginia to North Carolina revealed the developing importance of this product.

Inseparably linked with mechanization, the popularity of the cigarette, and the expansion of the bright-tobacco culture was a group of dynamic young southerners comparable to northern entrepreneurs who came to the forefront of American economic history at the same time. Men like R. J. Reynolds, William T. Blackwell, James R. Day, Julian S. Carr, and Washington and James Buchanan (Buck) Duke were not bound by the traditions of the South nor the Puritan ethic. Through their leadership North Carolina surpassed Virginia as the center of tobacco manufacturing. Winston, Salem, and Durham, brash new towns in a state with a future, ignored the old rules of growth and stability in their headlong plunge for Progress and Industry. While these aggressive businessmen led the way, the city fathers (more often the sons of the fathers) willingly followed. As they came into their own, these new leaders rightfully looked upon themselves as the new southern aristocracy. Washington Duke, of Durham often signed his name with an intentionally misplaced comma: Washington, Duke of Durham.

Washington Duke's son best illustrates the successful southern entrepreneur. Buck Duke was determined to dominate the tobacco industry as John D. Rockefeller was coming to control the petroleum industry. Beginning with a small corporation, Duke developed a magnificent trust. The big fight for control of tobacco production began in the 1880s when Duke began trying to take over or squeeze out his competitors. Using methods typical of the era, Duke was highly successful in crushing his opponents. He gave rebates to wholesalers who bought only his products, he undersold his competitors in their own marketing areas until the weaker companies went bankrupt, he monopolized products such as glycerin and licorice used in the production of tobacco, and he was accused of placing inferior tobacco in his competitors' packages. By 1890 Duke had combined the five leading tobacco companies into one trust called the American Tobacco Company. This giant corporation ruthlessly continued to root out all independent companies. By 1896 Duke had gained almost total control of cigarette production. In 1901 Duke formed Consolidated Tobacco, a holding company, in order to gain control of other forms of tobacco manufacturing. By 1905 Duke also controlled almost all of the production of chewing tobacco, snuff, and stogies.

In 1904 Duke's vast holdings and interests were combined into the new American Tobacco Company, capitalized at $300,000,000, with almost complete monopoly of the American market. The European market was small by comparison and not so important to Duke, although he was not unaware of the international implications of his gigantic empire. In 1911 the United States Supreme Court ruled that Duke's holdings must be broken up, and four companies (American Tobacco, R. J. Reynolds, Liggett and Myers, P. Lorillard) resulted from that decision. The decision, however, did not noticeably impinge upon Duke's economic empire. Perhaps it should be noted that Duke and most of the other tobacco leaders were native southerners. Here was a major southern industry not under the tutelage of northerners, although Buck Duke's empire became so large that it had a national rather than a regional perspective.

R. J. Reynolds was determined to compete with the Duke empire, but since cigarettes had become so uniform in content and taste, the rivalry centered around a gigantic advertising campaign. In 1913 Reynolds introduced a brand named Camel, launching it with a multimillion dollar advertising pitch. Reynolds' success with his promotion encouraged Liggett and Myers in 1915 to introduce Chesterfield. American Tobacco first produced Lucky Strike as a popular competitor in 1916. These domestic blends were marketed during World War I when demand was high, and consumption continued after the war emergency was over. Reynolds spent $19,000,000 in 1926 for advertising. American Tobacco spent over $12,000,000 on a campaign for Lucky Strike alone, and in one week in 1931, despite the economic crisis of the nation, Reynolds spent $1,000,000 promoting a new cellophane wrapping. In that year the entire tobacco industry spent about $75,000,000 for promotion. Cigarette production was concentrated in the hands of American Tobacco, Reynolds, and Liggett and Myers, these three companies producing about 90 percent of all cigarettes at the onset of the Great Depression.

The Big Three, plus P. Lorillard and Brown and Williamson Company, were the major producers of American cigarettes after 1930. For the next four decades they were the chief benefactors of the rising demands for tobacco products in the United States. The annual per capita consumption of tobacco in the nation in 1870 had been two pounds. By 1900 the figure had risen to five pounds, and by 1960 it had reached an astounding twenty pounds. In 1967, 545,000,000,000 cigarettes were smoked in the United States, or an average of 220 packs for every man, woman, and child over 18 years of age. In that year the tobacco industry spent $198,000,000 on television advertising alone, while Americans responded by spending over $9,000,000,000 for tobacco products.

After 1953 cigarette consumption decreased steadily, and at the end of 1969 the U. S. Department of Agriculture happily reported that the average American smoked fewer than 202 packs of cigarettes that year, the lowest per capita rate in more than ten years. This drop was probably due to increased publicity concerning a causal relationship between cigarette smoking and lung cancer. While tobacco companies' analysts continued to report that no direct evidence had been found to link cigarettes and lung cancer, the United States Surgeon General's office in 1964 issued a searing report of disagreement. A host of private investigators also insisted that the connection was definite, and while the mounting evidence was not conclusive, it could not be ignored. In 1966 the Congress decreed that each package of cigarettes carry the statement: "Caution: cigarette smoking may be hazardous to your health." Responding to mounting public pressure, in April 1970 Congress passed an anti-cigarette bill that strengthened the statement on cigarette packs to read: "Warning: the Surgeon General has determined that cigarette smoking is dangerous to your health." The bill also banned all radio and television cigarette commercials as of January 1, 1971.

Whatever the relationship between cigarettes and disease, some smokers switched to pipes, others quit altogether, and still others tried to stop but could not break the habit. In the meantime, tobacco companies recognized the health problem as a serious threat, and they introduced a variety of products to allay the smoker's fears. Filters, cigarettes lower in "tars," cigarellos (to be rid of suspect paper), and cigarette holders (to prevent mouth cancer) were designed and marketed in the face of rising hostility to cigarettes. The health scare undoubtedly influenced the American Tobacco Company to step up its diversification efforts, and in 1969 it changed its name to American Brands, an appellation designed to reflect the company's varied interests.

The tobacco industry had a combination of advantages which greatly assisted the producers. First of all, tobacco had no competition from any other industry in the country. While cotton in the twentieth century feared the future uses of nylons and rayons, no tobacco substitutes or synthetics were successfully marketed. Second, tobacco had no real competition from other countries. Again, the cotton industry had some cause for concern about competition from India and Egypt, but the small amounts of Turkish tobaccos produced in no way diminished the sales potential of American varieties. Third, tobacco was an industry hardly affected by the economic cycle. It was a poor man's luxury, and men bought it in equal amounts in times of prosperity and depression. Habit-forming products had a way of being placed high on the purchaser's priority list, even when food and other necessities had to come second. Last, tobacco was a totally consumable product. While the automotive manufacturers came to be conscious of the used-car market, when they discussed production figures and schedules, tobacco men knew that the demand for new tobacco products would remain high. Such advantages as these, despite the health scare, helped this southern-controlled industry give the South one of its most important economic assets.

A Colonial Economy

While southern industry slowly but steadily increased its proportion of the national output before World War I, the war itself quickened the forces of economic advancement. In addition to the nation's increased demands for cotton cloth, tobacco, and iron and steel during wartime, the South became the site for many improvised training camps for the

American army. Shipbuilding and naval installations brought a stir of activity in numerous coastal cities and towns. The need for explosives stepped up the South's heretofore small interest in hydroelectric power and chemical manufacturing, and after the war these industries retained their momentum. An unfinished wartime nitrate plant at Muscle Shoals, Alabama, on the Tennessee River became the focal point for the development of the Tennessee Valley Authority in the 1930s.

The South's industrial advancement helped the region survive the brief postwar depression of 1920–21, and in the 1920s when businessmen and their ideas dominated the government in Washington, the South continued to expand and diversify its industries. Nowhere was the growth of southern industrial development more apparent than in the lower Appalachian Mountains, especially in the Piedmont region from Virginia to Alabama. The South's fast-flowing rivers were ideal for the development of electric power, and power companies were formed and dynamos built at a rapid pace throughout the decade. Generating capacity in the southern states increased by 156 percent in the 1920s, while the increase was 58 percent for the remainder of the nation. The availability of this power was a factor in the crusade for textile mills in the Piedmont. It also provided energy for lumber mills.

Because of the South's great forests, lumbering ranked second to cloth manufacturing in the antebellum South, and not surprisingly it constituted a major industry after the Civil War. Land speculators in the immediate postwar era were primarily interested in timber, and they did not wait long to exploit their newly purchased lands. In the 1880s northern lumber syndicates stripped southern forests of desirable stands. Louisiana's lumber production rose in value from $1,700,000 in 1880 to $17,-400,000 in 1900. In those two decades five Gulf states increased their production value from $13,000,000 to $73,000,000. Concerns about overcutting were brushed aside as unwarranted. The greedy lumbering interests did their job thoroughly. A government forestry expert stated that "probably the most rapid and reckless destruction of forests known to history" had occurred in the twenty-year period following 1886.

Lumber production in the twentieth century continued to increase with each decade. When production from the Great Lakes region declined at the beginning of the century, the South took the lead in value of lumber produced. Exploitation continued, with little concern for selective cutting or reforestation and none for soil damage or flood control. By 1920 the total cutover area in the South was over 156,000,000 acres, an area equal to 60 percent of the whole state of Texas. Economic damage resulting from Sherman's march to the sea was miniscule compared with the wasteful harvest of southern virgin timber lands before 1920. In the 1920s some efforts were made to conserve the South's forests, to cut out in a consistent and protective way, and to replenish the trees. Trained foresters joined the staffs of the largest lumber companies, and in 1928 seven million pine seedlings were planted by the Great Southern Lumber Company. The South led the nation in lumber production from 1909 to 1925, regaining the lead in 1940. By that date five southern states counted more than a thousand lumber mills each.

This trend toward reforestation and conservation was aided by the Civilian Conservation Corps during the 1930s when thousands of unemployed young southern men were used by the government to preserve the region's natural resources. Lumber and paper companies began to realize the importance of reforestation and timber care, as county agents, editors of farm journals, and state foresters preached conservation of the region's natural resources. The wasteful butchery of the South's virgin timber stands was virtually put to an end. The inefficient "peckerwood" mills continued with their small fly-by-night operations, but as time passed evidence of their wastrel methods was less apparent. The attitude of "get in, get as much as possible, and get out" diminished as landowners came to realize that with scientifically managed forests they could receive steady income over many years.

After World War II many acres of former cotton lands were planted with fast-growing pine seedlings, some crops being harvested for pulpwood within ten to fifteen years. Many of the South's poorer lands have been planted in trees, and in 1970 about 40 percent of the South's acreage was growing trees. By that year southern timberlands were supplying some 39 percent of the nation's lumber and 56 percent of its pulpwood. Thanks to the foresighted lumber men and the efforts of forestry schools' educational programs, by 1970 the annual growth and harvest figures were nearly equal. Lumbering and its allied industries continued to constitute a major source of southern income and employment.

Naval stores had been important to the economy of the American Southeast since colonial days, and the great pine trees of that region continued to yield their valuable products in the nineteenth and twentieth centuries. Southern companies developed new techniques for manufacturing softwood distillation products (primarily turpentine), gum products, charcoal natural dyestuffs and natural tanning materials, tall oil and rosin, and rosin acid products, until the South had a virtual national monopoly on naval stores production by 1930. In that year pine tree products contributed some $40,000,000 to the region's economy and in 1963 the figure had risen to nearly $89,000,000. Southern furniture-making, closely related to the South's great forests and the lumbering industry, had its beginning in the 1880s but it came into its own in the 1920s. While every southern state had furniture factories, Virginia, North Carolina, and Tennessee were the leaders in the industry which centered around High Point, North Carolina, where the ten-story Southern Furniture Exposition Building was erected in 1922. By 1930 southern furniture production constituted over 15 percent of the nation's total, and furniture and fixtures manufactured in the South in 1963 were valued at $1,030,247,000. Furthermore, the South provided non-southern manufacturers with maple, walnut, cherry, and other popular woods used to produce chairs, couches, and reproductions of antique furniture.

Important to both southern industry and agriculture were the beginnings of the paper and chemical industries. In the early years of the twentieth century, some twenty-five paper mills were operating in the eleven former Confederate states, but their processes were not well suited to the southern pine, a resinous wood, and they produced only small amounts of quality paper. In 1909 the Roanoke Rapids Paper Company in North Carolina began mass producing brown kraft bags and wrapping paper by successfully employing a German-invented sulphate process which could be used with both resinous and nonresinous woods. Paper plants in Texas and Mississippi quickly adopted the new process, and by 1930 seventeen southern kraft mills had been established. By that date forty-eight southern paper mills were in operation, producing almost one-half of the nation's paper. In the meantime, related industries were manufacturing insulating and building boards from sugar cane waste and wood chips. The Celote mills in Louisiana and the Masonite Corporation of Laurel, Mississippi, were two examples of these minor industries.

The southern chemical industry may be dated from World War I. Foundations for the industry had already been established in oil, sulphur, woodpulp, and fertilizers, and after the war chemical development was both rapid and diverse. Wood chemical plants established in Tennessee during the war continued in the postwar years, producing methanol, acetic acid, and ethyl acetate. In 1927 Allied Chemical Corporation built a $50,000,000 air-nitrogen plant near Hopewell, Virginia. By that same year the South was engaged in over twenty types of major chemical production, producing about one-fourth of the total national value.

In 1917 the American Viscose Corporation plant at Roanoke, Virginia began producing rayon, a product made from cellulose. Until 1941 this plant had the world's largest rayon production capacity. Other wartime plants established to manufacture cellulose for explosives converted to rayon production after the war ended. Moreover, in the 1920s new plants arose in Tennessee, North Carolina, Georgia, and Virginia. By 1930 the South was manufacturing almost 80 percent of the nation's rayon. Perhaps the most successful and best known of the companies exploiting the new product was Burlington Mills, which began in 1923. Within four years sales reached nearly $2,000,000, and by 1935 Burlington had fourteen plants manufacturing $20,000,000 worth of products.

The Great Depression of the 1930s did not noticeably impede developments in the chemical and paper industries. In fact, a dynamic expansion began in both industries in the middle of the depression. In

1936 the chemical industry spent $33,000,000 on plant construction in the South, about twice the amount expended in the remainder of the nation. Texas and Louisiana were the focal points for this new expansion. In 1935–36 an $8,000,000 Solvay plant to produce soda ash, caustic soda, and chlorine was built near Baton Rouge by Consolidated Chemical. During the 1930s a large chemical plant using gas and oil by-products was established at Texas City, and both Dow Chemical Company and the Monsanto Company soon entered the new field.

In 1932 Charles H. Herty, a disciple of Gifford Pinchot, set up a crude laboratory in a Savannah, Georgia, warehouse with the hope of producing newsprint from young slash pine. His experiments to perfect a process for removal of rosin from pine pulp were successful, and by December 1933 he had prepared enough woodpulp to supply sulphate-bleached newsprint for several days' runs of a newspaper. The process to remove the troublesome rosin and natural discoloration was improved and enlarged, and in 1939 the Southland Paper Mills Company erected a plant near Lufkin, Texas. Supported by a loan of $3,425,000 from the Reconstruction Finance Corporation and a stock subscription of $1,615,000 by thirty-two southern newspapers, whose publishers had contracted for 853,754 tons of paper before the first roll of paper was produced, this plant began production in 1940 with an annual capacity of fifty thousand tons of newsprint. The following year it initiated plans to double its production in the face of an acute shortage of newsprint. In 1948 another newsprint mill was erected near Chilesburg, Alabama, and in 1954 the Bowater Paper Company of Newfoundland constructed a $55,000,000 plant near Calhoun, Tennessee. By that date the South furnished 70 percent of the nation's sulphate-bleached pulp paper, and the southern newsprint industry was expanding rapidly.

In 1940 the Ecusta Paper Corporation began producing cigarette paper in western North Carolina, and in 1936 the Union Bag and Paper Company built a plant near Savannah, Georgia. By 1938 twelve new kraft mills had been erected in the South (making a total of twenty-nine), and the South's percentage of national production rose from 12.4 to 17.2 in two years. By the end of the thirties paper mills of all kinds in the South represented over $200,000,000 in capital investment. Nearly one-half of this investment was poured into the South after 1935. In 1958 twelve southern states netted nearly $405,000,000 from paper and pulpwood products. Georgia and Alabama led in production, but every county in the old cotton states of Mississippi and South Carolina profited from this young and thriving industry.

The expansion of the paper industry can be seen by comparing statistics for 1930 and 1955. In the former year, southern paper mills used about 1,500,000 cords of pulpwood, and in the latter year they consumed over 16,000,000 cords. In 1955 the industry produced nearly 10,000,000 tons of pulp paper. By 1970 the South produced more than half of the nation's chemical woodpulp, the total exceeding all of Canada's production. More than $2,000,000,000 was invested in the southern paper industry, and over half a million southerners received all or part of their income from the industry.

Raw bauxite in Georgia, Arkansas, Alabama, and Tennessee was the basis for the southern aluminum industry. In 1914 the Aluminum Company of America (Alcoa) established a plant near Maryville, Tennessee, which produced nearly thirty thousand pounds daily. By 1929 Alcoa had added carbon, sheet, and aluminum bronze powder plants, employing over three thousand workers. Blount County advanced from near the bottom of the list of Tennessee's counties in taxable wealth to one of the top ten. After World War II Alcoa established a $40,000,000 plant near Charlotte, North Carolina, and Kaiser Aluminum Company constructed a $177,000,000 plant on 280 acres just south of New Orleans.

Oil lubricated the economy of the western edge of the South— Texas, Oklahoma, and Louisiana. A fantastic oil boom was set off in 1901 when exploratory drilling at Spindletop, near Beaumont, Texas, resulted in a gusher of unprecedented capacity. This discovery and production was the beginning of the great Southwest oil boom. Drillers stepped up their efforts to locate the liquid gold and bring it to the surface. In the following years new oil fields were opened in Texas and Oklahoma, making these two states the nation's top producers, and in 1919 Louisiana assumed third place when the Homer field was opened. Fields in Oklahoma included Cushing, Healdton, Doyle, and even the state's capitol grounds in Oklahoma City. Texas fields included the Ranger boom, as well as those at Desdemona, Sour Lake, Humble, Goose Creek, and Burkburnett. The latter field saw both Texans and Oklahomans drilling at a feverish pace along the banks of the dry Red River and in some instances in the river bed itself. Texas rangers were used for a time to keep law and order in the Red River area, when disputes over land and drilling rights arose. The 1920s witnessed an oil find in Arkansas, and in 1929 these four states represented about 60 percent of the major crude oil production in the United States. By 1944 the South was producing over a billion barrels of crude oil annually.

A natural concomitant to crude oil production was the development of the oil refining business. In 1931 the South had over 150 refineries, handling approximately 40 percent of the nation's total crude petroleum. While many large and growing refineries were established in the South, particularly along the Gulf coast of Texas, much southern crude oil was piped north to be "cracked" (to use the industry's term) into various refined products and by-products. The Southwest became interlaced with pipelines as oil was shipped from the place of exploration to the place of refining.

The major oil companies dominated both crude oil production and oil refining. As early as 1924 twenty-three companies accounted for over half the production in Texas and Oklahoma. While Phillips Petroleum Company and Humble Oil & Refining Company, both southern-owned, were able to remain independent and began to compete with the major companies, most local companies were absorbed, until a few giants in the industry came to dominate it. Outside capital brought absentee control, but it also made money available for expansion, new payrolls, and construction contracts, all profitable to the South.

Petrochemicals became big business for the region. By World War II the South, including Texas and Oklahoma, was producing 80 percent of the nation's petrochemicals and nearly as much of its chemical fertilizer. American Cyanamid Company established a $110,000,000 petrochemical plant north of New Orleans, while the largest chemical warfare plant in the nation was based near Huntsville, Alabama. Industrial development along the coast of Texas and Louisiana made Houston (fifty miles inland but connected to the Gulf by a salt water canal deep enough for ocean-going vessels) and New Orleans two of the nation's busiest and largest seaports.

From 1919 to 1939, the fastest-growing industries in the South were clothing (values increased by 383 percent during the interwar period), paper and printing (up 210 percent), furniture (up 131 percent), and chemicals (up 123 percent). Chemicals and paper ranked highest in the numbers of additional employees, but textile mills continued to employ the greatest number of actual workers. Lumber and timber products and food products were second and third behind textiles with numbers of employees. In terms of value added to the southern economy chemicals ranked third behind textiles and food products, followed by lumber, tobacco, petroleum and coal, printing and publishing, paper, and clothing. Each of these categories added more than $100,000,000.

By 1939 total southern industrial production had regained all it had lost because of the Great Depression. Wages in the South were still down about 10 percent from their pre-1929 levels, but they averaged twice that figure outside the South. Still poor by American standards, the South in 1940 had a per capita income of $340 contrasted with $575 for the nation. But the South had come a long way toward achieving parity with the nation, and at the beginning of World War II the region was on the verge of its greatest economic surge.

While World War I stimulated industrial and economic development in the South, World War II and its aftermath greatly quickened the pace. Industries related to warfare, atomic energy, and the space age changed the southern landscape, stimulated the region's economic development, and gave southerners added purchasing power. Billions of dollars worth of war contracts were awarded to companies in the southern states during the war years, and many army posts and camps were established or enlarged to accommodate the training of hundreds of thousands of fighting men. When the war was over, universal compulsory military training dictated the maintaining of a majority of the army-training centers, and the Cold War atmosphere prevented the closing of many wartime plants. In addition, the advent of space exploration added a new dimension to the South's economy. Oak Ridge, Tennessee, Paducah, Kentucky, and Cape Canaveral (renamed Cape Kennedy), Florida, became household words for all Americans in an era when atomic developments and space exploration played a large role in the nation's life.

By mid-century the South had clearly passed beyond the initial stages of modern industrialization. Textiles, lumbering, petroleum, chemical manufacturing, and many other industries basic to a modern and complex economy expanded or were established in the postwar period. In the 1950s some three thousand plants totaling millions of dollars in capital investment were erected in the South, and the pace did not slacken in the following decade. State industrial boards and local chambers of commerce bombarded industrial decision-makers with materials depicting the attractions of a particular state or locality. Competent specialists and public relations men pointed out local opportunities for manufacturers, supplying them with pertinent technical information. Attractive lures were dangled before the eyes of industrialists considering the establishment of plants in the South: tax inducements, cheap land, unorganized (and thus cheap) labor, water power, less expensive building materials, and improved rail and highway arteries.

Mississippi's efforts to attract industry constitute one of the most interesting attempts of a southern agrarian state to pump money into its sluggish economy. The Great Depression brought Mississippi face to face with an economic crisis which demanded drastic action. The old system of agriculture had totally failed. Mississippi laborers could not all be absorbed by farming, nor could agriculture provide enough capital for new economic endeavors. Something had to be done. In 1936 the Mississippi legislature passed a law creating an agricultural and industrial board and provided money for an advertising campaign to attract industry. Billboards, ads in nationally circulated magazines, and news stories trumpeted Mississippi's industrial future. Local communities and counties were encouraged to vote special bond issues to assist with the financing of plant construction. Other inducements were also used. From 1936 to 1955, 138 industries located in Mississippi as a result of that state's efforts. Local bond issues ranged from the $10,000 given to the Pasgagoula Decoy Company to the $4,750,000 made available in 1951 for the construction of the Greenville Mills. The Armstrong Tire and Rubber Company located a large plant at Natchez as a result of a generous subsidy. The company gave a new look, a new smell, and a new economic stimulus to that famous old cotton and river city. Plants in Mississippi now manufacture clothing, ladies' stockings, furniture, paper, glassware, light bulbs, building goods, farm implements, and many other items. Assembly plants have also been established, using parts shipped from outside the state to create finished products. In 1939 items manufactured in Mississippi were worth $175,000,000; in 1952 those items were valued at $1,060,000,000, a 509 percent increase within a dozen years.

Other states had similar stories to tell about their success with industrialization, and literally hundreds of southern communities witnessed amazing changes. Richmond, Louisville, Nashville, Charleston, Atlanta, Birmingham, Memphis, New Orleans, and Houston were hardly stereotyped southern cities. Vestiges of the past continued to recede as oil men, engineers, chemists, economists, and other industrial-minded men remade these and other cities. In the decade following World War II more than $2,000,000,000 was spent on twelve new industrial plants on the banks of the Tennessee River, including a $1,700,000,000 gaseous diffusion plant built for the Atomic Energy Commission. Later a research triangle was developed in the Piedmont of North Carolina, comprising a four thousand acre site for nuclear, chemical, and industrial research laboratories. Guided missiles were produced in northern Alabama and western North Carolina, powder and explosives were manufactured in Alabama, and hydroelectric power was in evidence throughout the South as additional dams were built on the many fast-flowing rivers there. In 1965 eight states attracted some $3,300,000,000 in new and expanded plants.

Southerners embraced industrialization in the postwar period as they sought solutions to their economic problems. Imperceptible in some regions, clearly evident in others, industrialization has radically changed the South. Old ways have been submerged or blurred by the presence of the great plants with towering smokestacks and walls of glass. Conservative southerners reacted negatively to the destruction of old culture patterns, and economic reorganization stimulated sharp emotional struggles within the life of the South. Many southerners gave lip service to the old southern values, but few actually desired to return to the plodding agrarianism of the rural South. Regional characteristics were modified by the presence of industry, and the products manufactured by southerners and purchased by northerners and southerners alike proved the axiom that the South was moving toward the mainstream of American life. Henry W. Grady's late nineteenth-century statement that there is "a new South not through protest of the old, but because of new conditions, new adjustments, and, if you please, new ideas and aspirations" was perfectly applicable to the South facing the last quarter of the twentieth century.

The Southern Laborer

One of the major attractions of the South from industry's point of view was the large supply of readily available cheap labor. After 1865 the South's shattered agricultural economy produced an artificial labor surplus; a permanent, large labor supply was available after the turn of the century, when the boll weevil reduced the cotton crop year after year, driving tenant farmers from the land. Thousands of blacks and whites who could no longer subsist by farming moved to the cities and factories within their native region in search of livelihood. Except for the periods of the two world wars, the South in the twentieth century has always counted far too many laborers available for regional job opportunities. An accompanying development has been the migration of southerners seeking employment outside the South—Detroit, Cleveland, Chicago, New York, and Los Angeles—but with all these migrants a seemingly inexhaustible supply of labor remained in the South. While these laborers constituted one of the powerful forces enticing industry there, industrial plants in turn pulled tenants from their marginal farms. Inevitably when a new plant began operating, job applications ran far in excess of positions available. With such a supply, factory managers were in the enviable position of never being required to hire the less desirable workers.

Besides its abundance, an important characteristic of southern labor was that it was generally unskilled. Thus, many industries followed the pattern of importing its own executives and plant managers from the North, relying upon unskilled southern laborers to tend the machines. Some southerners were trainable and rose to supervisory capacities in the plants, but the majority of them were employed in jobs requiring few or no skills. If poor white men constituted the major source of such labor, women, children, and black men also found work in the factories. Newer types of industries and modern conditions in manufacturing plants seemed specifically designed for these laborers, especially women. In numerous plants in the South the majority of the unskilled workers were women tending machines that were becoming more and more automated. With thousands of women in the factories, the South began to experience a significant social revolution.

This abundant unskilled labor force, along with other factors, had much to do with the fact that southern laborers.were invariably paid less than their northern counterparts. Low wages may have been the foundation of industrial growth in the region, and the regional wage differential was a reality apparently impossible to overcome. During the first thirty years of the twentieth century, the average annual wage for ten

southern states was approximately two-thirds of that for the remainder of
the nation, and while southerners generally received more during the
next thirty years, the percentage did not perceptibly rise. In 1920 the National Industrial Conference Board announced that an annual "minimum American standard" for a family of three in Charlotte, North Carolina, was $1,438; the average textile worker's income in the state was
hardly half that amount. Conditions improved somewhat as years passed,
but even in the inflationary postwar period after 1945, southern workers
were not much better off comparatively than they had been in 1920.

A combination of an abundant labor supply and the desire of employed laborers to have at least a subsistence income resulted in long
working days and weeks for all of southern industry. Ten- and twelve-
hour working days and six- or seven-day weeks were common until recent
years in many industries. Not until Congress passed enforceable legislation did industrial leaders bow to workers' demands that shorter hours
and better working conditions were needed. One of the forces behind federal regulation was the labor leader.

Organized labor made little enough headway in the nation as a
whole during its first decades of activity, but it was even less successful in
the South. In addition to the surplus of labor, which lessened the probability that those laborers with jobs would make demands to alienate employers, labor unions in the South had to fight hostility (on the part of
some laborers and many other southerners), apathy, tradition, ingrained
individualism, poverty, and northern suspicions. Under the circumstances, southerners were not eager to bargain collectively, to demand
higher wages, or to strike for better working conditions. Their traditions
had not prepared them for such "foreign" attitudes or activities. Furthermore, industrial owners had undercut the possibility of organized unions
by adopting a paternalistic attitude toward laborers, not unlike the position southern plantation owners had taken toward black laborers in
the pre-Civil War days. Since many laborers in the early twentieth century, especially in the textile industry, lived in company towns, where
homes, stores, streets, utilities, churches, and schools were owned by
the mill, they were not in position to make demands upon the
mill managers.

Despite these handicaps and traditions, labor unions attempted to
organize in the South, although their successes were limited when compared with the North. Feeble is the proper word to apply to labor
unionism in the South prior to 1930. By that date, some six thousand
regional local unions were affiliated with various larger unions, including the American Federation of Labor. Needless to say, a very small
number of southern workers were unionized by 1930, and those who were
organized were members of skilled craft unions. World War I and the
1920s witnessed a limited growth of these old-line craft unions, but at this

time thousands of southern industrial workers were also attracted to unionism. Much union activity—some of it carried on by outsiders—occurred in the twenties as the United Textile Workers, the Tobacco Workers International Union, the United Mine Workers, the International Timber Workers Union, and others strove to organize laborers within their respective industries.

The late 1920s witnessed a series of bloody strikes and violence in several industries as a result of conflict between management practices and demands of workers for better wages and working conditions. The most famous and perhaps most influential of the strikes in the decade occurred in 1929 in Gastonia, North Carolina. Faced with sharper competition and dropping prices, the Loray Mill introduced the "stretch-out," which meant that workers were required to tend a larger number of machines in the course of a day's work. Resentment among workers rose in response to these increased work loads, and an explosive situation developed as discontent increased in the mill. At that very time national labor unions were initiating new and concerted efforts to penetrate the antilabor Solid South. A group of northern labor organizers rushed to Gastonia, quickly developing a nucleus for a local chapter of the Communist-dominated National Textile Workers Union (NTWU). The newly established local demanded a minimum wage of fifty cents an hour and a maximum work week of forty hours, abolition of the stretch-out, equal pay for women and children, better houses with lower rents, and union recognition. When the mill managers rejected these demands, the union organizers dropped their specific economic proposals and initiated "revolutionary" activity. Leaders of the national Communist party, including party secretary William Z. Foster, hurried to Gastonia in the interests of "the class struggle." Loray Mill management capitalized on the presence of the Reds in Gastonia. Advertisements, brochures, and handouts warned against world revolution, racial mixing, free love, and atheism. Under this barrage of propaganda, Gastonia County residents withdrew their support from the strikers, and many of the strikers themselves refused to engage in Communist-led agitation. By the end of the summer many early strikers were actively opposing the NTWU.

The Communist leaders and their few but loyal followers were determined to continue their strike, the result being turmoil and tragedy for Gastonia. After a strikers' parade was aborted by law officers, a shooting incident resulted in the wounding of a unionist and four policemen, one of whom, the city's chief of police, later died. A mob was stimulated to bomb the strikers' headquarters. The Communists responded by calling for a mass protest rally, but angry opponents prevented the meeting from being held by firing upon a truckload of workers on the way to the meeting place. A woman striker was killed as the labor violence reached its climax. Although Ella May Wiggins was murdered in broad daylight, with at least fifty first-hand witnesses, the five Loray workers who were indicted for the murder were acquitted. Shortly thereafter seven labor union leaders accused of killing Police Chief D. A. Aderholt were convicted of "conspiracy to murder," after the trial had turned into a battle between Americanism and Communism, between the Stars and Stripes and the hammer and sickle, between loyalty and heresy. The results of the two trials foreshadowed the demise of the NTWU in Gastonia. Wilbur J. Cash has written that this strike's chief achievement was "to fix solidly in the minds of the great mass of southerners the equation: Labor unions + strikers = Communists + atheism + social equality with the Negro."

Other towns of the South in the 1920s were linked to violence in the labor movement: Henderson, Marion, Pineville, and Bessemer City, North Carolina; Ware Shoals, Pelzer, Woodruff, Greenville, and Anderson, South Carolina; Elizabethtown, Tennessee; Thompson, Georgia. At all the points of tension, strikers were invariably routed by local police or state militia, and if brought to trial they were in all cases convicted. Public opinion supported strikebreakers, and they were always freed of charges. Law enforcement agencies generally viewed their job as one of breaking the strikes, and juries and judges were swayed more by southern traditions than by workers' conditions or wages. Unionism made little headway not only because of strong public opposition, but also because prounion southerners looked upon unions as instruments for immediate protest rather than as agencies for farsighted collective bargaining.

Unionism advanced markedly in the nation in the 1930s because of the AFL's drive to organize American laborers and because of the tacit or overt support of the New Deal administration. Section 7(a) of the National Industrial Recovery Act set minimum wages, shortened hours, prohibited child labor, and guaranteed workers' right to bargain collectively through their own representatives. The Fair Labor Standards Act of 1938, passed after the NRA was declared unconstitutional, established a minimum wage of twenty-five cents an hour and a maximum work week of forty-four hours, with provisions for future wage raises and shorter hours. Through these and lesser laws, Franklin D. Roosevelt and the New Dealers revealed their interest in the laboring man. Some of these laws were particularly beneficial to southern workers, since they were designed to wipe out regional wage and hour differentials and to assist marginal industries directly.

The formation of the Committee for Industrial Organization in 1935 meant a renewed interest in labor organizing in the South. For the first time a strong national labor union specifically attempted to organize the Negro and the unskilled, the South's two largest laboring groups.

From the beginning, the CIO had strong support in the southern mining districts, but its early drives to organize southern automobile and steel workers were not notably successful. Nor was the CIO any happier with its efforts to organize workers in such fields as oil refining, tobacco, or textiles. Union activity in the late New Deal period was on the whole unsuccessful in the South. During World War II both the AFL and the CIO increased organizing activity, but southerners were not responsive. In 1943 approximately 54 percent of the nation's industrial workers were organized, but only 30 percent of southern workers were union members. While 44 percent of the nation's black industrial workers were unionized, this was true of only 12 percent of southern Negroes.

"Operation Dixie," an all-out effort by the CIO to unionize the textile industry after World War II, was a colossal failure. After spending over $11,000,000 in this effort, the CIO counted only a handful of new members as it struggled against the forces of inflation and prosperity. In fact, authoritative reports indicated that in 1951 union membership among textile workers had actually declined 10 percent since World War II. In the postwar period, however, a few unions—United Steelworkers, United Mine Workers, Railway Clerks, Textile Workers' Union of America, Carpenters and Joiners, National Maritime Union, Teamsters, and Longshoremen—had a total of several thousand southern members, and unionism had been firmly established in several specific industries: aluminum, cement, electrical utilities, transit systems, pulp and paper, and shipbuilding. In 1952 the CIO had approximately 500,000 members in the South, and the AFL boasted nearly 2,000,000 members. Counting the independent unions, including the United Mine Workers (125,000 members), some 2,750,000 out of an industrial work force of 9,300,000 southerners were dues-paying union members. This figure included a pitifully small number of Negroes (700,000). After the passage of the Taft-Hartley Act, designed to place at least minimal controls on Big Labor, several southern states passed "right to work" laws, legislation guaranteeing nonunion laborers the right to work in the same plants with union laborers. This legislation hampered the growth of unionism in the region.

In the 1960s the South remained basically nonunionized and antiunion. In that decade the rate of increase in union membership did not keep pace with the growth of industry in the South. But as old ways of life and behavior are eroded, as industry becomes an integral part of the South's socioeconomic matrix, and as southern laborers become more aggressive, the prospects are that unionism will become stronger in the South. The speed of that growth will depend to a large extent upon how long a full reservoir of workers continues to exist and upon the rate at which southern traditions diminish. In the meantime, the prospects are that organized labor will continue to make only minor gains.

Suggestions for Further Reading

There has been much writing on southern industry since the Civil War, but little synthesis of these materials. Volumes by Woodward, Tindall, and Clark (mentioned at the end of Chapter XI) are excellent for surveys of southern industry. Broadus Mitchell, *The Rise of the Cotton Mills in the South* (Baltimore: Johns Hopkins Univ., 1921) and Broadus and George S. Mitchell, *The Industrial Revolution in the South* (Baltimore: Johns Hopkins Univ., 1930) constitute the best general histories of the textile industry. John F. Stover, *Railroads of the South, 1865–1900* (Chapel Hill: Univ. North Carolina, 1965) is a solid study of one major industry in the region, while J. Carlyle Sitterson deals with a more limited but nonetheless important industry in *Sugar Country: The Sugar Cane Industry in the South, 1753–1950* (Lexington: Univ. Kentucky, 1953). Nannie May Tilley, *The Bright-Tobacco Industry, 1860–1929* (Chapel Hill: Univ. North Carolina, 1948) and John K. Winkler, *Tobacco Tycoon: The Story of James Buchanan Duke* (New York: Random House, 1942) bring much understanding of an industry closely related to the South. Other important southern industries are treated in: Stanley F. Horn, *This Fascinating Lumber Business* (Indianapolis: Bobbs-Merrill, 1943); Max W. Ball, *This Fascinating Oil Business* (Indianapolis: Bobbs-Merrill, 1940); Charles A. Warner, *Texas Oil and Gas Since 1543* (Houston: Gulf Publishing Co., 1939); Walter H. Voskuil, *Economics of Water Power Development* (Chicago: A. W. Shaw, 1928).

Robert Duffus, *The Valley and Its People: A Portrait of TVA* (New York: Knopf, 1944), David E. Lilienthal, *TVA: Democracy on the March* (New York: Harper & Brothers, 1944), Preston J. Hubbard, *Origins of the TVA: The Muscle Shoals Controversy, 1920–1932* (Nashville: Vanderbilt Univ., 1961), and G. R. Clapp, *The TVA: An Approach to the Development of a Region* (Chicago: Univ. Chicago, 1955) tell the story of one of the most important efforts for regional change ever attempted.

Glenn E. McLaughlin and Stefan Robock tell *Why Industry Moves South* (Washington: National Planning Association, 1949), and the South's changing industrial scene is related by Allan P. Sindler (ed.), *Change in the Contemporary South* (Durham: Duke Univ., 1963); Melvin L. Greenhut and W. Tate Whitman (eds.), *Essays in Southern Economic Development* (Chapel Hill: Univ. North Carolina, 1964); Robert B. Highsaw (ed.), *The Deep South in Transformation* (University, Ala.: Univ. Alabama, 1964); R. P. Brooks, *The Industrialization of the South* (Athens, Ga.: Univ. Georgia, 1929); A. E. Parkins, *The South: Its Economic-Geographic Development* (New York: J. Wiley, 1938); William H.

Nicholls, *Southern Tradition and Regional Progress* (Chapel Hill: Univ. North Carolina, 1960); J. M. MacLachlan and J. S. Floyd, Jr., *This Changing South* (Gainesville, Fla.: Univ. Florida, 1956); H. L. Herring, *Southern Industry and Regional Development* (Chapel Hill: Univ. North Carolina, 1940). Calvin B. Hoover and Benjamin U. Ratchford, *Economic Resources and Policies of the South* (New York: Macmillan, 1951) is a mine of valuable information. Also useful is E. Q. Hawk, *Economic History of the South* (New York: Prentice-Hall, 1934).

Most studies of organized labor include passages on labor in the South, but few works focus specifically on that region. Exceptions are F. Ray Marshall, *Labor in the South* (Cambridge, Mass.: Harvard Univ., 1967) and G. S. Mitchell, *Textile Unionism in the South* (Chapel Hill: Univ. North Carolina, 1931). The Negro and southern unionism is dealt with in S. D. Spero and A. L. Harris, *The Black Worker: The Negro and the Labor Movement* * (New York: Columbia Univ., 1931). L. R. Mason, *To Win These Rights: A Personal Story of the CIO in the South* (New York: Harper, 1952) is an account by a union organizer. Other volumes with information about the southern worker include: Carl Kelsey, *The Negro Farmer* (Chicago: Jennings & Pye, 1903); Clarence Herr, *Income and Wages in the South* (Chapel Hill: Univ. North Carolina, 1931); Herbert J. Lahne, *The Cotton Mill Worker* (New York: Farrar & Rinehart, 1944); Jennings J. Rhyne, *Some Southern Cotton Mill Workers and Their Villages* (Chapel Hill: Univ. North Carolina, 1939); E. H. Davidson, *Child Labor Legislation in the Southern Textile States* (Chapel Hill: Univ. North Carolina, 1939); H. L. Herring, *Passing of the Mill Village* (Chapel Hill: Univ. North Carolina, 1939).

* Available in paperback.

CHAPTER XIII

TOWARD A NEW SOUTH—EDUCATION AND LITERATURE

Two Rs—revival and renaissance—best characterize the development of education and literature in the South from the Civil War to the mid-twentieth century. In each instance, a long-lived impartial observer would have been amazed at the change and progress of one hundred years. If southern educational progress was virtually nil before the turn of the century, great strides to abolish illiteracy and to upgrade public school education were made in the first half of the twentieth century. These advances were no cause for complacency since the South remained behind the other regions of the country by almost every standard, but by mid-century, the region had gone a long way toward overcoming the educational poverty of its children and future adults.

The literary renaissance was even more striking. A few dim lights shone in the southern literary world in the immediate decades after the Civil War, but if brighter ones existed, the South had kept them hidden. In the twentieth century, however, particularly after the mid-twenties, southern writers came to have an impact upon the literature of the nation that was impossible to judge; and the end was not in sight in the 1960s. In no other endeavor had talented southerners so impressed the "outside world."

Public School Education before 1900

Developments in the South's educational system after 1865 were related to attitudes and conditions before the Civil War. The belief that education for the masses was a luxury rather than a necessity remained, as did the contention that education was the responsibility of the individual not the state. Taxable assets were limited, southern families were larger than the national average, and the South remained overwhelmingly rural, some 80 percent of its school-age children residing in rural areas. After the war, the freed Negro constituted a new factor in the southern educational equation. Insistence upon separate systems for the two races added serious financial and administrative problems. Moreover, the South came out of the war impoverished. School buildings had been destroyed or had deteriorated; pupils and teachers had been scattered; funds and organizations did not exist. Such were the powerful deterrents to those who attempted to build school systems in the southern states.

The short-lived Johnson governments made initial efforts to improve the lamentable educational conditions immediately after the Civil War. Arkansas, Alabama, and Georgia passed laws establishing public schools, but these schools were not adequately supported financially, and no public school systems were operating when congressional Reconstruction began. During the latter period, good school systems were written into the new constitutions adopted by several states, notably South Carolina, and the legislatures of the states passed laws to enforce the constitutional provisions. But most of the legislation was hastily drawn by ill-informed politicians, and fraud and misappropriation of school funds were all too evident in Reconstruction education. For lack of money the public schools in Georgia, South Carolina, and Alabama were closed for long periods of time in the early 1870s. Furthermore, an army of northern missionaries and educators, bent upon educating the recently freed black and the illiterate white southerner, had invaded the South at the end of the war, and southerners resented these Yankee attempts. Coupled with the southerner's traditional resistance to mass education, the combined private and public efforts were not highly successful, but neither were the accomplishments altogether nonexistent. Illiteracy was somewhat reduced, particularly among the Negro population, and the constitutional and statutory provisions for public schools provided a base to build upon in later years. Equally important was the development of the principle of universality, if not equality, of educational opportunity. Education was coming to be accepted by some southerners as a local and state governmental responsibility.

The Bourbon governments' policies of retrenchment slowed down the developing concept of the responsibility of the state for educating its youth. Many state governments felt that their obligations to holders of state bonds took precedence over their obligations to the public schools, and in an era of penny-pinching, the schools suffered. In 1878 the Virginia state auditor, ruling that the state's obligation to its bondholders was of first importance, helped the funding of the state debt with money which had been appropriated by the legislature for exclusive use by the schools. Such lack of financial support crippled the Virginia school system. Other states' schools likewise suffered from curtailed appropriations. The amount of money spent for each pupil enrolled in the schools of eight South Central states in 1880 was only 60 percent of that expended in 1870, and this had increased to only 80 percent in 1890. In the latter year the per capita expenditure for education in the South was about 97 cents, while the average for the entire nation was $2.24. But inadequate financial support for southern schools was the result of more than the Bourbons' policies of retrenchment. The paucity of taxable assets in the region precluded large sums flowing into the state treasuries in a period when debt and depression were permanent guests in the majority of southern households. The combined taxable wealth of all the southern states in the 1880s was less than New York's alone. The South's greatest educational problem was not the opposition of politicians. Rather it was the general poverty of the region.

Under such adverse circumstances, northern philanthropists offered assistance to the southern educational cause. John F. Slater, a Connecticut textile manufacturer, established a million-dollar fund in 1882 to assist with the manual and vocational education of southern Negroes, and from 1867 to 1897 George Peabody, a Massachusetts merchant, banker, and financier, poured over $2,000,000 into education for both races in the South. The trustees of the Peabody Educational Fund, recognizing that their objective of free schools for everyone was beyond their financial resources, carefully selected the states, cities, and local school districts to which they contributed. Believing that the most good could be done by helping those who helped themselves, they frankly gave the most assistance to the least backward areas. Most of the Peabody money was spent on establishing model schools, providing subsidies so that existing schools could be upgraded, and improving teacher-training facilities. George Peabody College for Teachers in Nashville, Tennessee, was the most conspicuous evidence of emphasis on adequate teacher preparation.

The trustees of the Peabody Fund named Barnas Sears, former president of Brown University, as their general agent. After Sears's death in 1880, native Alabamian Jabez L. M. Curry, Baptist minister and college professor, served in that capacity for some two decades. Although Sears and Curry came from opposite sides of the Mason-Dixon Line, both of them clearly understood the South's educational problems. They traveled widely over the South propagandizing for better schools, helping state and local officials to plan school systems, and distributing money where they felt it would be most beneficial. Building upon Sears' efforts, Curry was particularly effective. As a southerner he helped dispel supicions of Yankee money. His persuasive oratory and appealing personality combined with his dedication to the cause of education made Curry the single most important man to further education in the South before his death in 1903.

The Peabody Fund has been properly credited with keeping the spark of education alive in the South. But the South needed more help than was available from private and local sources, and sentiment arose for the national government to aid education. As early as 1878 delegates from nine southern states gathered in Atlanta at which time they requested that money from the sale of federal lands be distributed to the states for educational purposes, each state being assisted in direct proportion to its illiterate population. The rationale for this suggestion was that Negro emancipation was a national policy and that the nation should accept the responsibility for educating the freedmen, relieving an already financially overburdened South. Hope for national aid for the South was raised in 1883 when New Hampshire Republican Senator Henry W. Blair introduced a bill providing for ten annual appropriations, ranging from $15,000,000 to $1,000,000 each year, to be distributed among all the states on the basis of illiteracy. Having the most illiterates, the South would have been the recipient of over one-half of the total appropriations. Enlightened southerners, especially educators, almost unanimously favored the Blair bill. But those southerners who believed in states' rights, favored low taxes, opposed education for blacks, or feared national control of education objected to the bill. Northerners who disliked seeing the larger share of the money earmarked for the South also opposed the scheme. The Blair bill passed the Senate several times, but it was never voted upon in the House of Representatives.

When efforts to assist southern education at the national level were not successful before 1890, a small but heroic group of southerners who had battled for better schools since the Civil War kept the issue in the political arena. These zealots, more than any others, were responsible for Farmers' Alliance and Populist candidates appealing for votes on the basis of the Bourbons' poor record in state aid to education. Alliance and Populist orators criticized the Bourbon regimes for educational negligence, and Populist newspapers were filled with demands for better schools. When the dirt farmers' plunge into politics in the 1890s fell short, many hopes for education in the South fell with it.

There were many reasons to be downhearted. By any standards

the status of public schools in the South in 1900 was bad. Schools were miserably supported, incompetently staffed, and totally inadequate for the education of the people. The 1900–1901 school year saw $21.14 as the national average for per pupil expenditure, but Alabama spent only $3.10, North Carolina $4.56, and South Carolina $4.62. Not a single southern state expended as much as one-half the national average. The racial differential made the statistics more revealing. Only $2.21 was spent for the average black child, while for the average white child the figure was $4.92. The instruction was generally meager, less than 20 percent of all elementary school teachers having a high school education and less than 50 percent even a modicum of professional training. Teachers in the South were paid an average of $159 per school year, compared with the national average of $310.

By 1900 all but two states outside the South had compulsory attendance laws, but Kentucky was the only southern state to have one. Of approximately eight million school-age children in the South, less than one-half attended school regularly. The percentage of white children in daily attendance ranged from 37 in Virginia to 56 in Texas; black children's attendance percentages ranged from 23 in Texas to 46 in Tennessee. While the national average for school terms was 145 days in 1900–1901, the southern states averaged only 96 days, and in the rural districts the average daily attendance was considerably less than that. To make matters worse, the dropout rate was appalling. For every seventy pupils who enrolled in the first grade, only seven reached the fifth grade and only one achieved the eighth. In no way was the South's educational system meeting the needs of its people.

Public School Education after 1900

Hope for the improvement of southern schools appeared with the beginning of the twentieth century. One of the important reasons for some degree of optimism was the increase of taxable wealth resulting from the development of industry in the South. In the 1890s this taxable wealth jumped by 50 percent, and it increased greatly by irregular spurts in the years following the turn of the century. The impact of this new wealth for southern education can hardly be emphasized too much, although additional factors were also significant.

One of the most important of these other factors was a series of annual conferences held to point up southern educational needs. Called by New York philanthropist Robert C. Ogden, the first of the meetings convened in the summer of 1898 at Capon Springs, West Virginia. Attended by both northerners and southerners, this and two additional conferences resulted in much talk but no action. At the fourth meeting held in 1901 in Winston-Salem, North Carolina, great enthusiasm was generated for immediate improvement of southern education, and the delegates agreed that the time had arrived for action to replace words. The conference resolved to promote "a campaign of education for free schools for all the people," regardless of race. As a result, the Southern Education Board was established, endowed with a nest egg of some $80,000 and authorized to carry on a campaign "exclusively for the purpose of stimulating public sentiment in favor of more liberal provision for universal education in the public schools." Through publicity and propaganda the Board was to encourage state and local districts to adopt or strengthen compulsory school attendance laws, to set longer school terms, to consolidate schools, to provide agricultural and industrial education, and to make more tax money available for education.

For all practical purposes this Board was merged with the General Education Board, created in 1902 to help education in the United States as a whole and endowed by the Rockefeller family with some $53,000,000 over the next eight years. Since the Rockefellers had indicated special interest in southern educational needs, much of this money was used in the South. Intensive statewide campaigns focused on North Carolina (1902), Tennessee (1903), Georgia (1904), Alabama, South Carolina, Virginia, and Mississippi (1905), Louisiana (1906), Kentucky and Arkansas (1908), and Florida (1909) with amazing results. Reminiscent of the textile-mill crusade of the 1880s, all the southern states were caught up by the zeal to attain educational utopia—or the next thing to it. Newspaper editors, churchmen, and educational leaders all shared this enthusiasm. Walter Hines Page of North Carolina, Henry W. Grady and Atticus G. Haygood of Georgia, and Edgar Gardiner Murphy of Alabama stung the public to action. Supported by political leaders such as Governors Charles B. Aycock (North Carolina), Hoke Smith (Georgia), Andrew Jackson Montague (Virginia), Napoleon B. Broward (Florida), and Braxton B. Comer (Alabama), state legislatures revised their constitutions, passed new school codes, reorganized their educational systems, hired new administrators, and appropriated more money from state treasuries. School revenues from 1900 to 1910 increased by 100 percent on the average, some states enlarging educational funds by nearly 200 percent. During the decade illiteracy declined from 27 to 18 percent, the average school term was lengthened from 96 days to just over 121, and the estimated value of public school property more than tripled. Teachers' salaries rose, school consolidation was accelerated, and by 1918 compulsory attendance laws, though imperfectly enforced, were added to the statute books of all southern states. The principle of universal education was finally being accepted by the entire South.

Educational progress made in the first decade of the twentieth century affected both white and black school systems, the poorer Negro schools being singled out for special aid in some instances. In 1905 Miss Anna T. Jeanes of Philadelphia contributed $200,000 to the General Education Board's coffers to assist with the improvement of Negro schools in rural areas, and two years later she gave $1,000,000 to pay salaries of industrial education and extension teachers in those schools. In 1910 the Caroline Phelps Stokes Fund was set up to provide $1,000,000 for research in educational problems, and a year later Julius Rosenwald, president of Sears, Roebuck and Company, pledged millions of dollars to help build some five thousand Negro schools in fifteen states over two decades. But schools for blacks remained considerably behind those for whites, despite the extra money from northern philanthropists.

The impetus of the educational awakening of 1900–1910 in the southern schools continued into the following decades. Annual appropriations for public schools multiplied from $24,000,000 in 1900 to $415,000,000 in 1930. By the latter date, most southern states were spending a greater portion of their total revenues for education than the states in the remainder of the nation. Furthermore, over the years the South received a disproportionate share of money for educational purposes disbursed from the national treasury. Between 1933 and 1935 nearly 80 percent of the $21,000,000 spent by the New Deal to improve public school facilities went to the South. A similar proportion of over $200,000,000 later made available for rural school construction was designated for the region, since the money was distributed on the basis of need and the South's need continued to be maximum. By 1940 the percentage of school-age children actually attending classes in the South was slightly higher than the national average, and by 1945 southern states were spending a larger percentage of their total income for education than were non-southern states. Because of lower incomes and larger numbers of children, however, the South was investing in each pupil only $72.21 per year, compared with $137.87 for the nation.

After World War II the South and the nation became acutely aware of two glaring discrepancies in the educational systems of the southern states. The first of these was the differences in the schools for blacks and whites. Many of the early crusaders had made Negro education their prime consideration, but the Negro had a long way to go to become a functional citizen after years under the handicap of slavery and post-Civil War racism. Education for the Negro was a matter of continuing public concern, but gross discriminations were present at mid-century. The separate-but-equal fiction was bombarded relentlessly after World War II as racially desegregated schools came to be focal points for attack. The story of the successes and failures of the desegregation of southern schools will be reserved for a later chapter.

The other discrepancy which caused many averages, statistics, and generalizations to lose their meanings was the rural-urban dichotomy in southern schools. While the South could boast of schools (including high schools, an important educational development in the twentieth-century South) equal to any in the nation in cities like Louisville, Richmond, Atlanta, Memphis, and Austin, large numbers of other schools, both urban and rural alike, were exceedingly poor in comparison. This was especially true of the schools in the rural areas. While a veritable revolution occurred in the twentieth century when the highway and the school bus combined to make school consolidation feasible in many areas of the South, other regions were so isolated, backward, financially insolvent, and sparsely settled that the transportation revolution and the resultant better schools bypassed those areas as fast as the speeding automobile on the hard-surfaced highway passed the dilapidated cabin of the rural hillbilly.

The rural-to-urban migration evident in the South after 1945 resulted in many children receiving better education, but with declining populations those people who remained in the rural areas had more trouble than before financing their schools. Moreover, an aggressive leadership which might campaign for improved schools in rural communities was often lacking. State aid to education was designed as an equalizer in those pockets of poverty and near-poverty, but theory did not always correlate with practice. The disparity between urban and rural schools was almost as discriminatory as that which separated schools racially.

In the 1960s the South, like the remainder of the nation, was involved in a losing battle to provide classrooms, equipment, and trained teachers to keep abreast of the demands of a burgeoning school-age population. After 1945 the South's problems were compounded by the population shifts which required considerable sums of money to be spent for relocating and rebuilding school plants. Even before 1954 southern anxieties over Negro demands for school integration resulted in belated attempts in some states to build equal facilities for Negro pupils, and these efforts placed additional strains on state budgets.

While the great battle against mass illiteracy was won by the 1960s, the South had another equally difficult battle to wage: that of overcoming functional illiteracy. In a developing society their grandfathers never dreamed would come to the South, southerners faced the complexities of urbanization and industrialization. A fourth-grade education received in a one-room school from a teacher who had scarcely more training than his pupils was no longer adequate in an economy which needed skilled laborers for both industry and mechanized agriculture. If education was the South's greatest challenge throughout the century following Appomattox, in the third quarter of the twentieth century it remained the region's greatest concern—and its greatest hope.

Higher Education

The history of higher education in the South after 1865 closely paralleled that of the public schools. Southerners had put much time, energy, and money into building a large and satisfactory system of colleges and universities in the three decades prior to the Civil War, but many of these gains were lost during the wartime emergency, when colleges had closed their doors. When the conflict ended, some colleges attempted to operate immediately, but few were able to do so in the face of shortages of money, buildings, professors, and students. The University of Alabama opened in 1865, but having only one student it quickly closed. Louisiana State University began classes with four students, and both the University of South Carolina and the University of Virginia opened in 1866 with limited enrollments. But neither these nor other state institutions could count upon more than token financial support in the difficult years following the Civil War. Colleges supported by religious groups before the war attempted to reopen after 1865, but these institutions, dependent upon gifts from church members, also suffered from the general poverty of the postwar period. During the congressional period of Reconstruction a number of Negro colleges were established, the American Missionary Association alone maintaining eight, the best known of which was Hampton Institute in Virginia. Every southern state created normal (teacher-training) schools for Negroes within a few years after the end of the war.

The Morrill Act of 1862, which granted public land subsidies to all states establishing or designating at least one college to offer instruction in agricultural and mechanical training, was a great help to southern states. The first state university in Arkansas was begun in 1872 in response to this act. Negroes shared in the federal money. In 1873 the South Carolina Agricultural College and Mechanics Institute for Negroes was established, and Georgia designated Atlanta University (a Negro school) as well as the state university for white students to be recipients of the Morrill Act generosity. But grants from the national government, churches, and northern groups were not enough to support the higher educational systems in southern states, and the schools suffered from lack of state and local support.

The schools were no better off under the Bourbons when restrictive financial policies and economic depression adversely affected them. When the push for industry was at its height during the Bourbon ascendancy, the old classical curricula, the backbone of the colleges of the antebellum South, were altered or discarded, as educational and political leaders stressed practical training at the college level. This applied not only to agricultural and mechanical training, but also to the training of scientists, engineers, and business leaders who appeared to be the hope of the South. Universities added departments of chemistry, applied mathematics, journalism, and the like to replace or go along with the study of ancient languages, philosophy, and ethics.

Inasmuch as most state universities were for men only, a number of colleges for women were established by the end of the century. Many of these did not warrant being called institutions of higher learning, but they nevertheless existed to be supported, however inadequately, by states or religious denominations.

By 1900 the South counted 216 institutions of higher learning, whatever their degree of excellence may have been. These schools enrolled 28,000 students, had an aggregate income of $2,500,000, and possessed a total of 1,500,000 volumes in their combined libraries. In 1906 the United States Commissioner of Education reported libraries of 50,000 books in only four southern universities. In the early years of the new century the region had but two universities (Vanderbilt and Tulane) with endowments over $1,000,000, while the rest of the nation had twenty-eight such institutions. College buildings and grounds in the South comprised only 14 percent of the total national investment in such real estate. No matter how it was viewed, higher education in the South at the end of the nineteenth century was most inadequate.

Like public school education, higher learning in the South began to emerge from the doldrums in the early 1900s. The General Education Board and other philanthropic organizations gave millions of dollars to raise endowments of southern schools. In 1919 Emory College was moved to Atlanta's Druid Hills section and transformed into a university with an endowment of about $1,000,000 from the Candler family, heirs to the fortune made by the sale of Coca-Cola. More spectacular action was taken by James B. Duke in 1924 when the Duke Endowment of $40,000,000 was set up. Trinity College in North Carolina was designated to receive both principal and income from this fund, and before his death in 1928 Duke gave another $17,000,000 to the school, plus 10 percent of his estate. Duke University became the new name of the fortunate little Methodist college, and the Gothic buildings west of Durham housed one of the best endowed universities in the South in the 1960s.

State-supported colleges and universities shared in the improved financial conditions of the South due to increased taxable wealth. Legislative appropriations increased by surprising amounts in the first two decades of the twentieth century so that by 1930 many southern states were spending about 20 percent of their total income on higher education. But this did not obscure fundamental weaknesses characteristic of these schools before 1930. Money was perennially in short supply and the consequences affected every aspect of the schools. Libraries remained generally inadequate, laboratory facilities and equipment were minimal and outdated, and professors' salaries were often fully one-third less than the national average while faculty teaching loads were one-third more.

If facilities of southern colleges for whites were generally less adequate than the nation, the status of the Negro college was another notch lower. Negro colleges before 1900 were overpowered by a paucity of resources, teachers, and leadership, and the thirty-four institutions for Negroes in the South at the turn of the century offered educational opportunities far inferior to most non-Negro schools. During the first decades of the twentieth century, a number of funds and foundations, including the General Education Board, helped selected Negro schools improve their libraries and faculties and provided scholarships to worthy black students. By 1930 some ninety Negro colleges and universities existed in the South, with endowments totalling nearly $25,000,000 and a student enrollment of around twelve thousand. Approximately thirty more schools were founded during the next four decades, most of them with weak faculties, small enrollments, and limited funds. Fisk, Howard, and Atlanta universities were three of the better-known Negro schools which offered quality education, but most black institutions usually did not approximate the best white southern schools.

The presence of the denominational college in the South after the Civil War reflected the strong religious tone of southern society. Next to preaching the gospel, the southern churches gave their first attention to the education of their youth. Although a religious atmosphere permeated most of the campuses of the state and privately endowed colleges, many church members had grave reservations about sending their children to schools where they might be exposed to the temptations of a worldly campus. Furthermore, they looked to the church-related school for training their children's minds so that they would not "lose their faith" when they became educated. This conservative attitude in the churches resulted in the establishing of dozens of schools controlled by denominations. As early as 1906 the Methodist Episcopal Church was supporting twenty colleges, Baptists had already founded forty, and the largest southern Presbyterian denomination supported over a dozen. This trend continued strong in the twentieth century, and by 1965 some 268 church-related or religiously oriented colleges existed in sixteen southern states.

Many new denominational colleges were founded after World War II, often justified on the grounds of the population explosion which demanded additional space for the education of college-age youth. But the new colleges were usually built because of the impact of a changing society on older educational institutions. The old taboos against dancing, smoking, and drinking were being shattered by the pleasure-seeking, mobile youth on the denominational as well as state-supported campus, and new colleges and "Bible Institutes" were set up to discourage young people from straying from the fold. A brochure announcing the opening of a denominational college in a Deep South state in 1965 stated that the school was planned as "a church-related, liberal arts institution, dedicated to academic excellence and spiritual development in every aspect of collegiate life. In all our learning and daily living, we shall seek to make Christ pre-eminent. Believing in the Faith of our Fathers, we shall pursue research in every area of knowledge, and seek to integrate these findings with the Truth as revealed in Jesus Christ."

A problem unique to the South and compounded with the founding of every new school was the predilection for establishing too many schools of higher education. The South overemphasized the importance of higher education before the Civil War when southerners first became seriously interested in education, and in the 1960s this one-sidedness was still present. In 1965, 456 institutions (universities, senior colleges, teachers colleges, and technical and professional schools) existed in sixteen southern states. Adding another 190 junior colleges, this averages slightly over 40 institutions of higher learning per state. This preponderance of schools in the South, causing duplication of administration, unnecessary competition for students, inefficient use of buildings, and shortage of money for libraries and faculties, added to the already great problems of educational financing in the southern states. A few of the private schools remained well endowed, but most of them, especially those dependent upon the support of denominations and individual church members, struggled with inadequate budgets as they tried to maintain minimum educational standards.

With all of its multiplicity of institutions, the South had no one prestigious university serving as a center for higher education in the region. Tulane, Vanderbilt, Duke, Rice, and Emory were good schools, but they did not serve as outstanding symbols of learning in the South as did Yale and Harvard in New England. No impartial study had equated a single southern state university with the University of Wisconsin at Madison or the University of California, Berkeley, even though the University of Texas ranked first in total endowment among the nation's state institutions. While the Midwest looked to Chicago as its center of higher education, no city below the Ohio River could receive similar attention from southerners. A Carnegie Foundation study of graduate education in the late 1950s ranked no southern university among the top twenty-two institutions in the nation, despite the fact that the South experienced a great growth of graduate and professional education after World War II. Southerners had to look outside their region to find postdoctoral centers such as the Institute of Advanced Study at Princeton University or the

Center for Advanced Study in the Behavioral Sciences at Stanford University. On balance, however, whatever the many shortcomings of southern higher education, much progress had been made in the twentieth century. This was particularly true after World War II when southern legislatures significantly increased their financial support of most state institutions. As a consequence, southern universities were brought closer to the national norm respecting minimum standards, faculty salaries, and teaching loads. It remained to be seen whether southern colleges and universities could meet the challenges of the last quarter of the century.

The Literary Renaissance

After the surrender at Appomattox, many southerners looked at their devastated region and correctly surmised that it would be difficult to make a living by plowing southern soil. Without capital, animals, credit, or land, they realized the inherent problems of survival. But the pressures of poverty or near-poverty demanded that some kind of work be done if they were to earn even a meager income. Under these conditions, hundreds of nameless southerners sought to gain income by writing. Needing only pen, ink, and paper, these men and women wrote countless words as they attempted to make a living by producing potboilers which violated all the standards of good literature. Some of these writers saw that contemporary northerners were writing the history of the Old South and the Civil War, and they were spurred to write to counteract a view of the past intolerable to southerners who were rapidly developing myths about their beloved region. Many wrote to justify the South in the past thirty years of the nation's history. But their appeal was limited, and without contacts with northern publishers upon whom they had to depend for the publication of their works, much of their writing went unprinted. Since a limited market existed for this literature of the 1860s and 1870s, even published works made little money for the writers.

Of the writings of these southerners in the immediate postwar years, only those of Sidney Lanier and Paul Hamilton Hayne are worthy of note. A native of Georgia, Lanier had zealously supported the Confederate cause. His health was permanently impaired after a stint in a prisoner-of-war camp, but he did not develop bitter sectional feelings and he refused to follow many of his contemporaries in their staunch defense of the defeated Confederacy. He gained national notice in 1875 when his poem "Corn" was published in *Lippincott's Magazine,* and his ability to combine his poetic and musical talents was revealed in the same year in "The Symphony." Lanier published only one book of poems before his death in 1881, but he is acknowledged as one of the better poets of post-

Civil War America because of his mastery of sound and his imaginative poetic experiments. Paul Hamilton Hayne was also a Georgian poet who suffered from ill health. In the tradition of Henry Thoreau, Hayne retreated from society to live in a crude shack, determined to make a living as a poet. But Hayne was not Thoreau and his poems were not comparable in literary quality to *Walden*. Most critics agreed that Hayne spent too little time polishing his literary endeavors and that he was out of step with the changing times.

Southern literary endeavors reached a higher plateau in the 1880s, when more competent writers took up their pens. At this time in the North "local color" literature was being produced, and southerners capitalized upon the reading public's interest in local themes. Local colorists realized that the South and its way of life provided fertile sources for their stories, and they exploited the romantic Creoles in Louisiana, the red-necked Georgia Crackers, the mountaineers of the southern Appalachians, and the innumerable varieties of other white and black southerners. These groups were viewed in settings which included swamps and marshes, mountains and back country, cotton fields and small towns, cabins and verandas, and muddy rivers and sea islands. The negativeness which permitted life in a cultural thraldom constituted local color.

Northern publishers and the northern reading public responded favorably to the local color writing. Declining to preach regional prejudice, these writers successfully strove to present southern life in a manner acceptable to the general American reading public. Although they assumed the racial inferiority of the Negro and revealed a trace of regional defensiveness from time to time, they concentrated on other subjects. They introduced into the fictional world a host of new characters: dashing sons and demure daughters of the prewar southern gentry, faithful Negro servants, picturesque poor whites, hard-drinking and feuding mountaineers, enigmatic Creoles, and talking animals with earthy philosophical messages. Northerners who wanted to escape from the worries and harassments of the developing industrial age eagerly read about an almost unreal region seemingly untouched by the ills of an urban society.

Although these authors wrote successfully of southern customs, scenes, and traditions, they did not produce lasting masterpieces. Their most important contribution was to set the stage for later southern writers by demonstrating the permanency of southern themes in literature. They paved the way for the more able writers of the twentieth century who surely had a wider audience because of the northern reading public's acceptance of these earlier writings.

Thomas Nelson Page, Joel Chandler Harris, and George Washington Cable were three of the most typical of these late-nineteenth century southern writers. Page became known for a volume about his native state entitled *In Ole Virginia* (1887). In this nationally acclaimed work, he writes of the idyllic days in Virginia before the war, his chief characters being wealthy planters and faithful Negro slaves. His descriptions of the utopian existence on the plantation for both whites and blacks stir sympathy for the Old South as he overemphasizes the attractive side of antebellum society. The myth of the Old South's pleasant days was continued if not created by Page and others, but Page also wrote well-constructed plots and he skillfully re-created the Negro dialect.

Joel Chandler Harris, a Georgian who worked as a typesetter and humorous writer for newspapers in his state, developed the most authentic and artistic reproduction of Negro dialect ever achieved. Published as *Uncle Remus: His Songs and his Sayings* (1880), these collected stories about animated animals intrigued readers both North and South. Children in the twentieth century continue to find fascinating the escapades of Br'er Rabbit who invariably outwitted Br'er Fox. *Old Creole Days* (1879), one of several volumes by George Washington Cable, portrays life among the French-speaking residents of Louisiana. His descriptions of the exotic but dying Creole culture are yet unsurpassed. Before his career ended, Cable became an important social critic of the southern scene. He argued for prison reform, better election laws, and the abolition of the convict-lease system, and he spoke out against injustices toward the Negro. He became known as a "southern Yankee."

Southern writers at the end of the nineteenth century ignored the trend toward naturalism which was sweeping the world's literary front. They continued to exploit the charming past and except for Cable they were generally blind to the rapidly changing region about which they wrote. When the era of progressivism came, no southern muckrakers appeared to write about the evils of an industrialized age or to criticize the shortcomings of American democracy. Instead, southern writers led in the vogue of historical novels which flooded the nation in the years following the Spanish-American War. These writers were so badly out of touch with the mainstream of American literary endeavor that Henry L. Mencken was able to say in 1917 that the South was an intellectual and literary desert from which came no great literature, art, or music.

Ironically, at the very time Mencken was broadcasting his barbed aspersions against the South, a literary renaissance was in its early beginnings; the result was a truly great era of southern letters. The naturalism or realism which had spread from Europe to America in the late nineteenth century reached the South in the 1920s, and with remarkable suddenness Mencken's cultural Sahara became a literary hothouse germinating abundant vegetation. This new school of writers was intent on holding a mirror to southern society. The prolific southern members of the "lost generation" designed to reveal the South as they saw it; they dwelled upon the ugly and the evil as well as the unusual and the picturesque. They wrote of landlords and country store merchants, avaricious bankers and small-time money lenders, hack politicians and dangerous demagogues, decadent old families and a vast horde of nameless poor folk. Over three hundred volumes of various kinds and on numerous subjects were produced during this flowering of southern literary talent. Among the best of these pre-1930 works were Ellen Glasgow's *Barren Ground* (1925), James Branch Cabell's *Jurgen* (1919), Thomas S. Stribling's *Birthright* (1922) and Julia Peterkin's *Scarlet Sister Mary* (1928). DuBose Heyward's *Porgy* (1925) was the basis for a successful American opera, and Roark Bradford's *Ol' Man Adam and His Chillun* (1928) became a highly acclaimed play entitled *The Green Pastures*. *In Abraham's Bosom* was a 1927 Pulitzer Prize winning play written by Paul Green. These works were succeeded in the 1930s by a virtual explosion of outstanding, brilliant literary works.

The two major southern figures whose literary careers began in the twenties and who were a part of the high tide of southern letters in the thirties were Thomas Wolfe and William Faulkner. Wolfe was a brilliant but erratic North Carolinian who was always at odds with his environment which both bewildered him and charmed him. Born in Asheville in 1900 he had an unhappy and misunderstood childhood. He later attended the University of North Carolina where he became a member of the Carolina Playmakers. After receiving a Master of Arts degree from Harvard, this physically large, bushy-haired young man became an instructor at Washington Square College of New York University, where he began writing the first of four novels which taken together comprise a "fictional autobiography."

Although the first of these volumes, *Look Homeward, Angel* (1929), was about his own family and friends in Asheville, Wolfe was not writing a southern novel in the deepest sense. He did not yearn nostalgically for the Old South; nor did he advance a program for improving the South of his day. Rather he wrote of the conflict of his own spirit with his environment. It is a novel universal in its tragic appeal, set above time and place. It is a spiritual epic. It is also of epic size, over 600 pages long; his second book was nearly 1,000 pages: his main fault was his verbosity. Much of what Wolfe wrote was trivial, rhetorical, and immature. He violated the artistic principle of selection, the narrative often being repetitious and confused. But Wolfe's great literary virtues offset these defects. His humor, vitality, originality, and gusto, along with a sense of grandeur, helped him rise to portray the turbulent struggle of man in quest of himself. Had he lived longer than his thirty-eight exhausting years, Wolfe might have developed the discipline necessary to produce even greater works. William Faulkner ranked Wolfe at the top of the novelists of his day because he "made the best of failure." Faulkner stated, "My admiration for Wolfe is that he tried his best to get it all said; he was willing to throw away style, coherence, all the rules of preciseness, to try to put all the experience of the human heart on the head of a pin, as it were."

Towering over the other major writers during the southern literary renaissance was Faulkner himself. Born in 1897 of a prominent family of Mississippi politicians, Faulkner attended the University of Mississippi at Oxford not far from his family home, but he soon became a dropout, worked at odd jobs, wrote poems and stories, and wandered aimlessly. After a stint in the Canadian Royal Air Force and brief expatriation in Europe, Faulkner settled down in Oxford where he affected an aristocratic disdain for the opinions of others, became something of an eccentric, and was soon being called "Count No-Count" by his neighbors. Between 1924 and 1926 he published two novels and a book of poems, none of which was well received. When it occurred to Faulkner that his "own little postage stamp of native soil was worth writing about" and that he "would never live long enough to exhaust it," he began his writing career in earnest. Characteristic of his later works was *The Sound and the Fury* (1929), the first in a series of brilliant volumes depicting the region he knew so well.

Faulkner was much more of a southerner than was Wolfe. While the latter's Altamont (Asheville) could have been located in any region of the United States, most scenes in Faulkner's works could have occurred only in the South. He created his own literary world in an imaginary Mississippi county named Yoknapatawpha. From Faulkner's novels this county, obviously a rural slum area, can be reconstructed: where the countyseat, Jefferson, was located; where certain key families and individuals in his stories lived; where the rivers flowed; where the railroads crossed the county; and where the Negroes lived. The Yoknapatawpha chronicle encompasses three progressions. First, there is the settling of Yoknapatawpha, the county's period of power, and the catastrophe for both people and county at mid-nineteenth century. Next, in the last decades of the nineteenth century the great landed families of the county are toppled from their place of prominence. Finally, the chronicle deals at length with the twentieth century, when new families took over the holdings and the power of the former aristocracy.

Faulkner's stories are concerned primarily with four families: the Sartorises, the Compsons, the Sutpens, and Snopeses. The first three of these families had previously owned many square miles of Mississippi soil, had furnished leadership for the community, and were the recognized elite. Paralleling the downfall of the Old South, their stature and role diminished after the Civil War until in the twentieth century they were both economically and spiritually bankrupt. Speaking of the deterioration of the Compson family but with broader meaning for southern traditions, the Negro cook Dilsey in *The Sound and the Fury* says, "I've seed de first en de last. I seed de beginnin', en now I sees de endin'."

Faulkner is unmistakably prophesying the extinction of things southern when he depicts these families in a decayed, fiberless shell of their former glory and when he writes of the Snopeses, poor white southerners on the rise. Not bound by a code of honor the Snopeses freely used ruthless and unscrupulous methods to advance themselves economically and socially as the commercial ethic came to dominate Yoknapatawapha County. Thus, while *The Sound and the Fury* reveals the corruption within the Compson family, the novel is basically concerned with conflict between the decaying landed aristocracy and the rising commercial classes.

In order to depict a South in the midst of its own changing values, Faulkner wove the themes of violence and horror into his novels. *As I Lay Dying* (1930), written at a power plant while the author was a coal shoveler on the night shift, is an account of a pilgrimage of a man who, despite repeated obstacles, was grimly determined to honor his promise to bury the decaying corpse of his wife in the site she had requested. Faulkner wrote *Sanctuary* (1931) admittedly because he wanted a money-maker, and his literary devices brought about the desired response of shock and revulsion from his readers. The principal events of the novel are two murders, a rape, a lynching, and an execution. Important characters include a nymphomaniac and an impotent man who perpetrated rape with a corncob. Other Faulknerian novels are filled with half-wits, lower class moonshiners, prostitutes, and perverts who live in a world of violence, debauchery, and sex.

Faulkner experimented with style, and his narratives are often difficult to follow. The opening pages of *The Sound and the Fury*, for example, thrust the reader into the mind of an idiot as the latter and the reader view people and surroundings. Other stylistic devices make Faulkner's works difficult for the less patient, but despite this shortcoming, critics have acclaimed him as the outstanding twentieth-century American novelist. He was awarded both Nobel and Pulitzer prizes.

Erskine Caldwell of Georgia wrote in much the same vein as Faulkner, although he did not rise to Faulkner's greatness. While Faulkner's South was ravished and tortured, high tragedy was also present. But Caldwell's South was plainly bestial, ribald, and shallow. He wrote of the now degenerate poor whites who lived on the exhausted Georgia land which had once been the prosperous farms of their ancestors. Caldwell was denounced for making his stories unnecessarily sordid and sex-ridden, but his works actually featured the deadening of normal emotions by poverty, and he wrote with simplicity, imagination, and humor. His novel *Tobacco Road* (1932) was turned into a highly successful Broadway play and later into a less than satisfactory motion picture. In contrast with Caldwell's works, Margaret Mitchell's *Gone with the Wind* (1936) centered on the beautiful women and handsome men of the plantation South, the nostalgia of bygone days, and the efforts of a determined woman to rebuild her family estate after the destruction of the Civil War. While many events of the novel were depicted with considerable realism, the volume's underlying theme was romantic. Published in the mid-thirties, its romantic flavor appealed to a nation growing weary of a long economic depression. The appeal proved lasting, however, for over thirty years later Americans were still thronging movie theatres to see Clark Gable and Vivien Leigh as Rhett Butler and Scarlett O'Hara. The novel and the movie did much to advance the legend of the Old South in all regions of the nation.

In the 1920s, John Crowe Ransom, Allen Tate, Robert Penn Warren, and Donald Davidson—all poets associated with Vanderbilt University in Nashville, Tennessee—published a magazine entitled *The Fugitive* which came to have considerable impact on American belles lettres. The poetry and the criticism of poetry written by these Fugitives rank with the work of their contemporaries T. S. Eliot and Ezra Pound, and the works of all these poets helped revolutionize the craft in this country. At first the Fugitives did not identify themselves as southerners, but by the end of the decade they were coming to be hostile to American materialism and critical of the South's interest in mass culture and industrial development as opposed to artistic and aesthetic matters. They came to believe that the South's future lay with agriculture, not industry, and they feared that the South was turning away from its time-tested customs, traditions, and attitudes. The Fugitives were thus transformed into Agrarians, and they were quickly supported by others who shared their concern for the direction their region appeared to be taking. The four original Fugitives were joined by another poet, John Gould Fletcher; two novelists, Stark Young and Andrew Nelson Lytle; a professor of English, John Donald Wade; one historian, Frank L. Owsley; one political scientist, Herman C. Nixon; journalist Henry Blue Kline; and Lyle Lanier, a psychologist. In 1930 these twelve southerners published a book of essays destined to become a classic in southern writing. *I'll Take My Stand: The South and the Agrarian Tradition* was a ringing defense of the South's agrarianism as juxtaposed with the industrial tradition of the remainder of the nation. But these men of letters were not economists, and their concern went far beyond economic matters. Dedicated to humanistic values they reacted against the Idea of Progress—so much a part of the American dream—and dedicated themselves to protecting and defending a way of life which transcended the dehumanizing process of a modern industrial society. They held up the image of the Old South as the ideal for southerners, who seemed to be tempted by materialism, and for northerners, who had clearly succumbed to commerce, industry, profits, and degeneracy. If southerners of the 1930s and following did not heed the warnings of the Nashville Agrarians, at least they were made aware of the direction their region was taking.

Other writers of the 1930s, including T. S. Stribling, Hamilton Basso, Olive Tilford Dargan, Katherine Anne Porter, and Grace Lumpkin, exposed the vacuity of southern rural and small town life, depicted the problems of mountain people when they went to the mill villages to work, and agonized with young men who were torn between the old ways and the new. A new generation of writers, such as Eudora Welty, Carson McCullers, Truman Capote, Tennessee Williams, and Peter Taylor, extended into the post-World War II period the southern literary renaissance begun in the late 1920s. While their contributions were varied, without question they may be called the children of the "southern Gothic" school. Perhaps the most permanent contribution of these writers was that they all but destroyed the last vestige of the genteel tradition. The southern renaissance became the most extraordinary literary development of twentieth-century America, a regional development comparable to the flowering of the New England literati one hundred years earlier.

Suggestions for Further Reading

Historians have written surprisingly little on education in the South after the Civil War. A good place to begin reading on the subject is Charles W. Dabney, *Universal Education in the South*, 2 vols. (Chapel Hill: Univ. North Carolina, 1936). Edgar W. Knight, *Public Education in the South* (Boston: Ginn, 1922) and *The Influence of Reconstruction on Education in the South* (New York: Columbia Univ., 1913) are both helpful. The first chapter in Thomas D. Clark, *Three Paths to the Modern South: Education, Agriculture, and Conservation* (Athens, Ga.: Univ. Georgia, 1965) is worthy of attention. Edwin Mims, *The Advancing South: Stories of Progress and Reaction* (Garden City: Doubleday, 1926) includes material on educational approaches in the region. Valuable for the Reconstruction years is Henry L. Swint, *The Northern Teacher in the South, 1862–1870* (Nashville: Vanderbilt Univ., 1941).

Edwin A. Alderman and Armistead C. Gordon, *J. L. M. Curry, A Biography* (New York: Macmillan, 1911) and J. P. Rice, *J. L. M. Curry, Southerner, Statesman and Educator* (New York: King's Crown Press, 1949) tell the story of a courageous battler for better education in the South. Louise Ware, *George Foster Peabody* (Athens, Ga.: Univ. Georgia, 1951) discusses at length the great philanthropist's interests and activities in southern education. Not to be overlooked is Vaughn, "Partners in Segregation: Barnas Sears and the Peabody Fund," *Civil War History*, vol. 10 (1964). Howard Beale, *Are American Teachers Free?* (New York: Scribners, 1936) addresses itself to a question relevant to the South as well as the entire nation. Louis R. Harlan, *Separate and Unequal: Public School Campaigns and Racism in the Southern Seaboard States, 1901—1915 ** (Chapel Hill: Univ. North Carolina, 1958) reveals the inequalities in southern schools at the turn of the century.

Volumes dealing with specific institutions of higher learning in the South include: Walter L. Fleming, *Louisiana State University, 1860–1896* (Baton Rouge: Louisiana State Univ., 1936); James F. Hopkins, *The University of Kentucky: Origins and Early Years* (Lexington: Univ. Kentucky, 1951); Charles G. Talbert, *The University of Kentucky: The Maturing Years* (Lexington: Univ. Kentucky, 1965); Nora Chaffin, *Trinity College, 1839–1892: The Beginnings of Duke University* (Durham: Duke Univ., 1950); Dan Hollis, *University of South Carolina*, 2 vols. (Columbia, S. C.: Univ. South Carolina, 1956). General volumes of value are M. B. Pierson, *Graduate Work in the South* (Chapel Hill: Univ. North Carolina, 1947) and R. S. Suggs, Jr. and G. H. Jones, *The*

Southern Regional Education Board: Ten Years of Regional Cooperation in Higher Education (Baton Rouge: Louisiana State Univ., 1960). Fidler, "Academic Freedom in the South Today," *AAUP Bulletin,* vol. 51 (1965) is a brief survey of academic freedom in higher education.

A great deal of writing has been done on the major southern literary figures. Especially valuable for those who desire to place those writers in historical perspective are: Hyatt H. Waggoner, *William Faulkner: From Jefferson to the World* * (Lexington: Univ. Kentucky, 1959); Cleanth Brooks, *William Faulkner: The Yoknapatawpha Country* (New Haven: Yale Univ., 1963); Andrew Turnbull, *Thomas Wolfe* * (New York: Scribners, 1968); Richard S. Kennedy, *The Window of Memory: The Literary Career of Thomas Wolfe* (Chapel Hill: Univ. North Carolina, 1962); Louis D. Rubin, Jr., *Thomas Wolfe* (Baton Rouge: Louisiana State Univ., 1955); C. Hugh Holman, *Three Modes of Southern Fiction: Ellen Glasgow, William Faulkner, Thomas Wolfe* (Athens, Ga.: Univ. Georgia, 1966); Aubrey H. Starks, *Sidney Lanier* (Chapel Hill: Univ. North Carolina, 1932); Julia Harris, *The Life and Letters of Joel Chandler Harris* (Boston: Houghton Mifflin, 1918); Arlin Turner, *George W. Cable* * (Durham: Duke Univ., 1956); Louis M. Field, *Ellen Glasgow: Novelist of the Old and New South* (Garden City: Doubleday, 1923). Robert Spiller (ed.), *Literary History of the United States,* 2 vols., 3rd ed. rev. (New York: Macmillan, 1963) treats the contributions of many southern writers to the nation's literature.

Much less attention has been devoted to southern writing as a whole, but an exception is John M. Bradbury, *Renaissance in the South: A Critical History of the Literature, 1920–1960* (Chapel Hill: Univ. North Carolina, 1963). Dealing with more recent writers and writings are: Louis D. Rubin, Jr., *The Faraway Country: Writers of the Modern South* * (Seattle: Univ. Washington, 1963); Donald Davidson, *Southern Writers in the Modern World* (Athens, Ga.: Univ. Georgia, 1958); Louis D. Rubin, Jr. and Robert D. Jacobs, *South: Modern Southern Literature in Its Cultural Setting* (Garden City: Doubleday, 1961). Additional good general accounts may be found in: J. B. Hubbell, *The South in American Literature, 1607–1900* (Durham: Duke Univ., 1954); Gregory Paine, *Southern Prose Writers* (New York: American Book Co., 1947); R. C. Beatty and others, *The Literature of the South* (Chicago: Scott, Foresman, 1952); Louis D. Rubin, Jr. and Robert D. Jacobs (eds.), *Southern Renascence: The Literature of the Modern World* * (Baltimore: Johns Hopkins, 1953); Carl Holliday, *A History of Southern Literature* (New York: Neale, 1906). An excellent, interpretive article is Van Auken, "The Southern Historical Novel in the Early Twentieth Century," *Journal of Southern History,* vol. 14 (1948).

* Available in paperback.

CHAPTER XIV

TOWARD A NEW SOUTH— RELIGION

To write of the South since 1865 without stressing the importance of religion in that region would be akin to describing the sun without any mention of heat or light. Religion permeated the South's social, cultural, and intellectual history after the Civil War, also having an impact on politics and economics. No institution in the New South so completely reflected conditions of regional life as did the church. Bishop Atticus Haygood noted in 1880 that since the Civil War "the controlling sentiment of the southern people in city and hamlet, in camp and field, among the white and the black, has been religious." Although this is an overstatement, observers since that time both inside and outside the region have been struck by southern religiosity.

Reconstruction and Reaction

The mid-nineteenth-century rupture between North and South had come earliest in the large Protestant denominations, and the wounds of the churches were slow to heal. During the Civil War both northern and southern churchmen had looked upon the conflict as a holy crusade, and when the war ended many northerners cried that the end verified their contention. Despite their military defeat, southerners felt that somehow their cause remained just, even though they could not understand why they had lost the war. These attitudes interfered with a possible re-uniting of northern and southern churches.

During the Reconstruction Era, northerners assumed that religious reconstruction—like political and economic reconstruction—would be on their terms, and northern branches of some churches imitated the government by using force to bring about reunion, occasionally seizing southern churches and their funds. Many northern missionaries went to the South determined to "reconstruct" southern churches and churchmen. Southern-ers objected to these northern "invaders" just as they opposed the arrival of businessmen and politicians. With northern churchmen supporting the war effort and the radicals' congressional Reconstruction program, south-erners championed home rule and easily rationalized that their churches should remain apart from the northern branches. Even though the Southern Baptists, Methodists, and Presbyterians had gone their separate ways before the war primarily because of the slavery issue, they used northern-ers' confiscations of property and hypocritical "holier-than-thou" atti-tudes to justify their continued independent existence. If they could not prevent northern control of their state governments and their economic resources, at least they could keep their churches free. In 1879 the Southern Baptist Convention pointedly voted to remain separate from its northern counterpart. In the immediate post-Reconstruction period only the Episcopal Church among the major denominations was success-fully reunited. This occurred because the national organization, which had never acknowledged the withdrawal of the southern churches, discreetly and without fanfare encouraged a return to the fold.

In some instances, the churches opposed political reconstruction, especially when carpetbagger church leaders appeared to conspire with the political and military occupying forces. As a result, southern clergy-men were outstanding spokesmen for the southern cause during Recon-struction, and for a time the churches led the resistance to the invasion of northern culture of any kind. Thus, just as the churches had been princi-pal antebellum supporters of the status quo, they often were postwar foci of resistance to northern innovations. Growing out of the war and Recon-struction, the South's religious solidarity against Yankeeism was so strong in the last quarter of the nineteenth century that the term Solid South more aptly applied to religion than to politics. Speaking for the common man, the churches were a powerful influence for southernism. Preserva-tion of the southern culture became one of their most important—although sometimes tacit—functions.

Under such conditions, the Protestant clergy achieved an almost unchallenged position of leadership in the region soon after the Civil War. Giving spiritual sanction to the established social order, these clerics were partially responsible for the southern churches' basic characteristic—conservatism. They espoused exactly what southerners wanted in a time of uncertainty: a conservative social and intellectual philosophy buttressed by an orthodox theology. The belief in the unchanging character of God, the church, and the Bible gave the southerner strength to face postwar realities. It was no surprise, therefore, when the South went seemingly untouched by the three forces which greatly influenced American religion during the final years of the century: biblical criticism, Darwinism, and the Social Gospel movement.

Biblical criticism (sometimes called "higher criticism") was an intellectual movement which began among German theologians in the second quarter of the nineteenth century. For the first time in the history of Protestantism scholars applied literary and historical criticism to the Bible. Scholars who were not afraid of what their investigations might reveal raised questions about biblical authorship and authenticity. This criticism began to make a significant impression in theological circles in the United States after the American Civil War. In the North this literature caused considerable rethinking on the part of many theologians, and to some extent it affected lay church members. Not so in the South. Southern churchmen, both leaders and masses, rejected literary and historical criticism. To the southern Protestant the Bible was the literally inspired Word of God to be accepted on faith in toto. Scientific investigation was acceptable in its proper place, but that place did not include the pages of the Sacred Book. Indeed the greater the accumulation of evidence casting doubt on the literal interpretation of the Scriptures, the more ardently did southerners hold to the Word as they knew it.

Darwinism as an intellectual movement in the United States likewise bypassed southerners. When Charles Darwin published his *Origin of Species* and *Descent of Man* in 1859 and 1871, respectively, he sparked the imaginations of many Americans to an unprecedented extent. The concept of evolution was by no means original with Darwin but his scientific approach in his thoroughly documented volumes attracted the attention of a large segment of the population. As Darwin's ideas were popularized, they became the basis for one of the most important intellectual movements in the western world. But, accustomed to accepting the Bible as authority in all areas of the world's and man's existence, the conservative Protestants could not reconcile Darwinism and the Bible; thus, they rejected Darwinism without a hearing. For example, they could not accept the implications of evolution in view of the biblical story of the Creation. The Genesis chapter relating how God had created man in his own image had always been crucial in a religion which stressed the uniqueness and importance of every individual, and Darwin's explanations for the creation of man especially lodged in the conservative Protestants' throats.

Other investigators in the mid-nineteenth century raised questions about the age of the earth which contradicted conclusions conservatives drew from the Bible. Nowhere were the views of the Darwinists and these early day geologists less acceptable than in the South. The Rock of Ages stood fast while scholars debated the age of rocks. As evolutionary theories came to be understood—and misunderstood—more and more, southern Protestants did not simply reject them; instead, they became staunch defenders of the faith of their fathers. Many southern preachers denounced anyone who questioned the conservative point of view. More than one college and seminary professor lost positions for advancing the views of Darwin and Charles Lyell; these included Alexander Winchell of Vanderbilt University, James Woodrow of South Carolina Presbyterian Seminary, and Crawford H. Toy of Southern Baptist Theological Seminary.

Besides biblical criticism and Darwinism, the Social Gospel movement, growing out of the desire to improve social conditions in the United States, was a third great force in the life of American churches before the beginning of the twentieth century. Traditionally, Protestant Christianity had stressed the importance of the salvation of the individual from eternal damnation. Devoted to this single objective, Protestants in the past had not concerned themselves with social conditions. But with the coming of industrial America, the church examined conditions affecting the individual on this earth. Churches and their leaders became conscious of undesirable factory conditions, the rights of laborers to organize, and slums which spawned prostitutes, drunkards, and juvenile delinquents. They felt an obligation to educate the illiterate hordes of immigrants pouring into the country, to issue used clothing to the needy, and to establish soup kitchens for the hungry. In short, the churches were concerned with man in his present environment, not just his soul after this life.

The Social Gospel movement had its greatest impact in the growing urban centers of the North, and its force was not unknown in other places. But again the South was basically outside a major American movement, for on the congregational level it refused to admit the churches' responsibility in social matters. The fact that the South had few large cities was not the basic explanation for this position. Conditions in mill villages in the New South often were in desperate need of attention, but in an individualistic agrarian society no advocate stepped forth to demand better employment conditions or housing for mill workers. Nor did the social problems of the Negroes and sharecroppers receive the criticism of more than an occasional voice. Charles Otken, a Populist and Baptist minister in Mississippi, dealt with the evils of tenant farming in his *Ills of the South* (1894), but his work commanded little contemporary attention or respect. The South's elementary orthodoxy prevented the populace from becoming aroused, and southerners were not prepared to change their basic social philosophy to embrace another northern movement. Instead of trying to solve social problems, southern churches devoted themselves to preaching the need for individual redemption. Sin was a personal—not a social—matter, and the exorcising of personal sins occupied much of the clergy's attention.

"Give Me that Old-Time Religion"

The emphasis upon a personal rather than a social gospel explains the rural South's continuation of the camp meeting and the development of the revival (or protracted meeting) in the towns. The entire community often attended the revivals, which usually lasted two weeks. Normally held indoors, revival services were peculiarly suited for congregational singing and for the development of emotionalism. Sometimes the local minister did the preaching or at other times a nearby pastor was invited to preach, but a church attained a certain amount of status in the vicinity if it could attract a "visiting evangelist," a traveling professional revivalist. Many of these professionals developed special talents for this kind of service, and some of them became well known regionally and even nationally. Samuel Porter Jones, a native of Georgia and one of the best-known traveling evangelists, spent most of his adult years aiding villages all over the South and the nation in their annual ingatherings of souls. His dramatic pulpit oratory enhanced his reputation, and he eventually received invitations to preach in the larger cities of the Ohio and lower Mississippi valleys, including Louisville, Memphis, Cincinnati, and Nashville. Before his death in 1906, "Sam" Jones had also preached in northern urban centers like Chicago and Brooklyn, but throughout most of his career he concentrated on the South. Many early twentieth-century revivalists imitated Jones's preaching techniques, among them Mordecai F. Ham of Kentucky, Baxter ("Cyclone Mack") McLendon of South Carolina, and Robert ("Fighting Bob") Shuler of Virginia. Some revivalists from outside the South were successful in the region below the Ohio River (notably Billy Sunday), but southerners responded more sympathetically to one of their own. These men all emphasized individual regeneration, and for those listeners who did not repent, they depicted a literally fiery and sulphurous hell of eternal damnation.

The revivalists helped perpetuate a puritan tradition in the South as they and other ministers of the gospel orated against dancing, smoking, cursing, card playing, gambling, divorce, sexual immorality, drunkenness, and violations of the Sabbath. The influence of the church was so great that many states and towns passed blue laws to regulate morality. An editor in morally lax New Orleans denounced "the medieval bigotry and religious tyranny" of Sunday blue laws in neighboring states, and one scholar has accurately concluded that Sunday observance prevailed "to a greater extent in the South than in any other section." The South became more puritan than Puritan New England, manifesting through laws hostility toward the prizefight, the theatre ("one of the ante-chambers of hell," according to a Methodist publication), and the bottle. Since the churches and the churchmen were united as one against strong drink, the Anti-Saloon League and the Women's Christian Temperance Union gained a powerful ally in the region. Before the Civil War all of the southern states except Virginia and Tennessee had passed state laws providing for local prohibition of saloons, and in 1874 Arkansas, Kentucky, and North Carolina supplemented their special state statutes with township local option laws. Texas followed suit in 1876, even before the quickening of activity against strong drink in the 1880s. In that decade county local option laws were adopted in Arkansas, Florida, Georgia, Mississippi, North Carolina, and Louisiana, and local option for townships was provided in Virginia and South Carolina. Because the churches were absorbed in crusades for temperance, a majority of counties and townships in the southern states were dry through local option long before the passage of the Eighteenth Amendment.

One reason for the powerful influence exerted by the churches in the South was the phenomenal growth of Protestant church membership following the Civil War. Having declined during civil conflict, membership in the southern branch of the Methodist Episcopal Church doubled in the fifteen years following the war. While revivalism was at its height in the 1880s, the Methodists in 1885 made their greatest annual gain ever, and a rapid rate of growth continued into the twentieth century. A similar story may be told for the Southern Baptists. These two denominations very nearly held a monopoly of church membership in the South when the religious census of 1906 was taken. Baptists and Methodists accounted for about 47 percent of the church membership in the country as a whole at that time, and together they comprised almost 85 percent of the church membership in the South. In those southern states east of the Mississippi River, total Protestant numbers reached almost 95 percent, ranging from 99.4 percent in North Carolina to Kentucky's 80 percent, Kentucky being the only state with a percentage below 90. In the states of the trans-Mississippi South, Protestants were less impressive but easily dominant nonetheless, since they comprised nearly 68 percent of the church members. The South was not misnamed when it was labelled "the Bible Belt," for Protestantism was the controlling religious force in all the southern states except Louisiana.

In Louisiana Catholicism reduced the Protestant totals to less than

50 percent of the church population. Membership in the Roman Catholic Church dated from the Spanish and French periods in Louisiana's history, and Catholicism continued to be strong in the twentieth century. The presence of a significant minority of Catholics in Kentucky, particularly in Louisville, made that state less Protestant than its neighbors. Louisiana, Kentucky, and Texas contained 1,120,045 out of the 1,398,676 southern Catholics in 1906. The great hordes of European Catholics who immigrated to the United States in the late nineteenth and early twentieth centuries generally avoided the South. Small pockets of Catholicism existed in urban centers, such as Mobile and Charleston and in a few cities in Florida, but on the whole, the South did not respond positively to the Catholic church. Nor did the South embrace such sects or religions as Judaism, Unitarianism, Christian Science, or Mormonism.

On the other hand, the South was the seedbed for the sprouting of hundreds of sects which were closely akin to orthodox Protestantism. These groups mushroomed all over the South, many having their beginnings in the Appalachian Mountains where their appeal to the isolated southerner was strongest. Almost all of them accepted one of the numerous variations of premillennialism, a standard doctrine of orthodox Protestantism that the Second Coming of Jesus Christ would precede a thousand-year period during which faithful Christians were to reign over the earth. That the literal, physical, Second Coming of Christ was imminent appealed to the poor, the illiterate, and the culturally isolated. Sects stressing this doctrine gave refuge to those who looked forward to a cosmic cataclysm which would strike down the rich and mighty, while exalting the poor and humble. Many of these sects' members believed in divine healing, and almost all of them genuinely believed in the imminent end of the world. These latter-day millenarians continually read the Old Testament books of prophecy and the book of Revelation in the New Testament as they searched for divinely inspired insights into future events. Given to emotional outcries and physical contortions as they struggled with the forces of good and evil, members of these sects were derisively called Holy Rollers. It made no difference if the more respectable churchgoers looked down their noses at the antics of the Holy Rollers; these sects cropped up in large numbers among the depressed masses of the South at the turn of the century.

In 1898 premillennialist leaders, who also believed in divine healing, met in South Carolina and founded the Pentecostal Holiness Church. During the next decade numerous other similar cults were formed, including the Holiness Church (in Tennessee), the Free Christian Zion Church of Christ (in Arkansas), and the Churches of the Living God (in Texas). Because of its rapid growth and semirespectability, the most important of the holiness sects was the Church of God, organized in

1907 in Tennessee. Many of the lesser sects continued to call themselves Baptists, Methodists, or Presbyterians, although they may have stressed their uniqueness by following the example of Jesus Christ literally when he washed the feet of other believers (Duck River Baptists), or by using only the words of the Psalms in their songs of praise (Associate Reform Presbyterian Church).

Negroes were responsible for much of the growth of religious sects specifically and church membership generally in the southern regions. The Church of God in Christ was founded in Mississippi in 1895, and in less than thirty years it had over 700 congregations. In 1896 the Church of God and the Saints of Christ was founded, growing to over 200 congregations by 1936. Organized in Atlanta in 1914 was a group called the Churches of God, Holiness which soon claimed nearly five thousand converts. Alabama in 1926 embraced thirteen congregations of the Apostolic Overcoming Holy Church of God, while Texas reported fifty-four Churches of the Living God, the Pillar and Ground of Truth. Negro sects multiplied endlessly.

More important in the life of southern blacks were the larger and more respectable churches established by Negro leaders during Reconstruction. Just after the Civil War southern white churches had tried to maintain religious control over the Negroes by providing for "associate" congregations, but the Negroes had spurned the unequal status of biracial fellowships. Southern Methodists, who counted 208,000 black members in 1860, could claim only 49,000 at the end of the war. Freedmen preferred not to be religiously dominated by their former masters, and well before the end of the century Negroes had organized their own churches, taking pride in their independence. As early as 1865 a church called the Colored Primitive Baptists in America had been organized, followed in 1870 by the Colored Cumberland Presbyterian Church. Eager to join the one social institution which they could control, Negroes had flocked to these churches in large numbers. Near the end of the century the National Baptist Convention was organized in Montgomery, Alabama, and by 1915 Negro Baptists in the South numbered nearly 3,000,000. The African Methodist Episcopal Church counted over half a million, and other important Negro churches were named African Methodist Episcopal Zion, Colored Methodist Episcopal, Reformed Episcopal, Protestant Episcopal, and Afro-American Presbyterian. Besides providing an outlet for religious expression, the church was a vital force in the life of black men. It was the center for many secular activities in Negro communities, including recreation and politics, and it often became the focal point for group cohesion. Small wonder that many of the important leaders of Negro progress in the twentieth century, such as Martin Luther King, Jr., were Negro ministers or lay church leaders.

From *1900* to *World War II*

When writing of religion in the United States from 1900 to World War II, historians have invariably noted three trends: a continued emphasis on the Social Gospel, an increasing liberalization of theology, and a movement toward church unity. Casual observers of the southern scene have assumed that these forces had no discernible influence in the South in the twentieth century. It is true that the South did not respond to these trends as freely as did the North, but the South's reaction was different from the North's in degree and intensity rather than kind. The southern churches relegated these movements to the back pew, but even from that disadvantageous position, they had more than passing influence upon the churches' activities.

Although outspoken factions in all the major southern denominations opposed social reform endeavors, the churches could not totally resist the impact of the Progressive movement and its aftermath. Recognizing that political, industrial, and social conditions could not be ignored, Southern Methodist bishops in 1902 declared it to be the mission of the church to work to change those conditions. But the bishops themselves revealed the narrow sense in which they construed this mission when, after expressing concern for city slum residents, they concluded that "nothing can cleanse and purify these breeding grounds of anarchy and vice but the ethical and vital principles of the gospel." All the major denominations denounced lynching, but in every instance qualifying phrases were added to make the denunciations palatable to their constituencies.

Feeling the impact of the Social Gospel movement, the Southern Methodist General Conference in 1910 organized a Standing Committee on Temperance and Other Moral and Social Questions, and in 1908 and 1913, respectively, the Southern Baptists created a permanent Committee on Temperance and a Social Service Commission. The two groups were merged in 1914 into the Temperance and Social Service Commission, and the new commission condemned sweatshops, the misuse of child and woman labor, overpopulated tenements, graft in politics, and "heartless greed in corporate wealth." Similar committees and commissions were established by other denominations.

Southern Presbyterians acknowledged the relevance of Christian principles to human society and affirmed that the churches should work to improve social relations, and Southern Methodists went on record favoring the regulation of child and woman labor and the right of laborers to organize. The Methodists allocated substantial sums to the work of their aggressive Temperance and Social Service Board. Concerned with prohibition, race relations, conditions of labor, and other social ills, the board's liberal views appeared in Sunday-School literature, the church's press, and in the programs of retreats and study conferences. Reflecting the mood of the pre-World War I Progressive Era, the large denominations in the South became advocates of social justice, proclaiming the Christian churches' obligation to fashion the kingdom of God on earth. These efforts continued during the 1920s and 1930s. For example, when the Methodists' Temperance and Social Service Board was discontinued with the end of prohibition, its remaining activities were reassigned to other bureaus so that industrial, racial, and international relations still received attention.

But many lay church members were displeased with the work of the denominations' committees and commissions. And top-level resolutions, pronouncements, and proclamations, when passed, were not always effected. Below the denominational level little attention was given to social problems, and more than one denomination found itself torn by conservative and liberal factions as the southerners wrestled with the question of the role of the church in modern society.

The southerner's struggle was related to a larger conflict growing out of a nationwide religious reaction which had set in at the beginning of the twentieth century. At a time when the Progressive movement was at its height, when the nation was experiencing the growing pains of a gigantic industrial and technological age, and when religious liberalism seemed to be making progress, many Americans drew back in revulsion. They feared change and the possibility of change, and they voiced a need for a return to absolutes. Therefore, at a national convention in 1910, conservative religious leaders in the United States delineated five doctrines which they held to be fundamental to the Christian faith: the infallibility of the Bible, the virgin birth of Jesus, the physical Resurrection of Christ, the substitutionary view of the Atonement, and the imminent physical Second Coming of Christ. This convention introduced the word fundamental into American religious nomenclature, and many southerners after this time called themselves Fundamentalists, to be distinguished from the Modernists, those liberals who would prostitute the basic Christian faith. These believers sang with meaning a rollicking ditty that went, "Give me that old-time religion, it's good enough for me."

Although the Fundamentalist movement was national in scope, southern churches, both cult and denomination, had long clasped the basic tenets upon which it was founded, and the American South was the region of the movement's greatest vitality. Southern clergymen publicly assented to the five fundamental doctrines, fulminating against liberals who raised subtle questions about any of them. Southern Baptist J. Frank Norris became a self-appointed high priest for the movement in Texas. A perennial crusader against apostates and malfeasance in high places, Norris became the center of numerous controversies both within and without the Southern Baptist Convention. Although agreeing basically with Norris's theology, many Southern Baptists were annoyed with the Texan's sensationalism and his attacks on denominational organizations. For years a bitter struggle raged in the Southern Baptist Convention between Fundamentalist Norris and his ilk and the more moderate leaders of the denomination. After several years of infighting, the convention by unanimous vote in 1926 acknowledged that Genesis taught that man was the special creation of God, rejecting every theory which taught that "man originated in, or came by way of, a lower animal ancestry." Shouts of elation arose from the Fundamentalists when the convention requested missionaries, boards, and institutions under its control to accept this resolution. Other denominations also spoke out against Darwinism, the Southern Presbyterian General Assembly in 1924 categorically affirming that "Adam's body was directly fashioned by Almighty God, without any natural parentage of any kind." The Fundamentalists of the South in the 1920s, whether a part of the independent movement or members of the region's major denominations, were a powerful deterrent to liberalizing social and theological influences.

No large religious denomination officially requested state assemblies to legislate against the teaching of evolution in the public schools of the southern states, but the religious milieu was so pervasive in the 1920s that antievolution laws were natural in the sequence of events. Supported by what was probably a majority of church members in the South, powerful elements of the southern religious press played up the need for this legislation. Adding fuel to the antievolution fires were the leaders of the World's Christian Fundamentals Association whose attempts to mobilize public opinion fell on responsive ears in the South. From 1921 to 1929 the drive for statutory enactment of antievolution concepts was a major political issue in almost every legislative session in every state in the South except Virginia. While some of the Fundamentalist efforts ended in frustration, five southern states—Oklahoma, Florida, Tennessee, Mississippi, and Arkansas—passed measures to prevent either the teaching of evolution in the public schools or the adoption of textbooks which propounded the theory of evolution.

The Tennessee statute produced a bizarre trial in 1925 when John T. Scopes, a high school biology teacher in Dayton, Tennessee, deliberately violated the law in order to create a test case. With William Jennings Bryan as chief prosecutor engaging in verbal battles with Clarence Darrow, a well-known northern lawyer and freethinker who led the defense, the sensational trial received worldwide publicity from the horde of newspapermen who descended on Dayton. Scopes was convicted and the courts upheld the constitutionality of the law. More importantly, the trial and the antievolution crusade from which it came dramatized more

than any other episode of the twentieth century the conservative theological temper of the South. Further, northern ridicule of the South at the
time solidified southern opinion and activated defensive psychological
mechanisms which remained beyond mid-twentieth century.

While the ecumenical movement was receiving support from
church groups across the nation in the first half of the twentieth century,
the Southern Methodists were the only large church body in the South to
participate in the formation of the Federal Council of Churches in 1908.
The southern churches generally advocated separation—not unity—
by demanding denominational loyalty. Increased stress on numbers
made for sharp competition among the denominations for prospective
members, and once an individual joined a particular church, he was in-
doctrinated to insure his denominational allegiance. Children growing
up under the aegis of a denomination were often encouraged not to
marry "outside the church" (meaning the denomination). Intense allegiance to each denomination existed even in small cities and towns.
Quite common in the South were towns of a few hundred souls with a
half dozen or more Protestant churches, and any town of five hundred or
more invariably had at least one Baptist, Methodist, and Presbyterian
church. Many also had a congregation (called the Christian Church) of
the Disciples of Christ. Frequently these churches erected buildings only
a few hundred yards apart, each struggling to exist in order to spread essentially the same Christian gospel but with inadequate facilities, a shortage of funds, and mediocre leadership. Little thought was given to uniting or federating the congregations into a community church large
enough to support a better-paid and better-qualified minister. The
churches seldom entertained consideration of minimal cooperative efforts at the local level. Nor did the denominations encourage such thinking. Agreements to divide territories to lessen overlapping efforts were
not suggested, much less adopted.

Denominational competition and jealousy were important factors
in this situation, but theological differences also kept the churches from
uniting. Baptists insisted upon baptism by immersion only. (The Greek
word *baptizo* means to immerse, not to sprinkle, pour, or dip, Baptist
preachers reminded their congregations regularly.) Presbyterians held to
the Westminster Confession, Methodists had a special doctrine of holiness and sanctification, and other churches embraced similar cherished
beliefs which they contended set them apart. In the main they were all
strongly orthodox Protestant churches with more similarities than differences, but preachers in all denominations made much of minor ecclesias-
tical distinctions.

The history of attempts at denominational unity or cooperation at
the national level also reveals the continued separation of the southern
churches. Only the Methodists were able to unite. After trodding their

separate paths during the Reconstruction, Northern and Southern Methodists from time to time had considered uniting their denominations, but they had entered the twentieth century with little accomplished. Serious talks continued and in 1911 a unification proposal was drawn up by a commission representing both churches. In 1939 Southern Methodists joined with their Northern Methodist Episcopal brothers to form the Methodist Church. Two big stumbling blocks had stood in the way of the merger. The Southern Methodists considered themselves more orthodox on the fundamental doctrines of the faith, and they flinched at the idea of joining with a group which included Negroes. The theological problem was resolved when the southerners became convinced that Methodism was large enough for more than one approach to the Christian faith, and the racial obstacle was overcome when the new union provided for five geographical jurisdictions in the United States, one of which grouped the Negro conferences of the northern church into a segregated Central Jurisdiction.

Unlike the Methodists, the Northern and Southern Baptist conventions were unable to effect a reconciliation. In the late nineteenth century some cooperation between northern and southern *state* conventions occurred in regard to mission work among Negroes in the South, and an effort was made to formalize a cooperative agreement between the two conventions at the denominational level. From 1895 to 1900 an endeavor known as the New Era Plan for jointly sponsored Negro missions was in effect, but this effort failed when Southern Baptists insisted on approving all missionary appointments to work with Negroes. Little cooperation or talk of unity between the two denominations took place in the twentieth century. The Southern and Northern Baptist conventions met concurrently in the same cities in 1933 and 1936 with the appearance of amity, but the same year that the Methodists were uniting, the Southern Baptist Convention voted not to join any merger movements. Occasional efforts for cooperative activity after that time were generally not successful. For example, in 1959 the two denominations joined with other Baptist groups in a nationwide evangelistic effort known as the Baptist Jubilee Advance, but disagreements over the meaning of evangelism and the administration of the program interfered with the success of this all-Baptist program. Viewing the Northern (American) Baptist Convention with suspicion, the Baptist multitudes of the South spurned any and all suggestions of unity with those whom they believed to be contaminated by a dangerous liberalism in social and theological matters.

Similar misgivings permeated the Southern Presbyterians who were convinced that their northern neighbors had strayed from the orthodox theological fold. Serious merger negotiations had begun between Southern and Northern Presbyterians in 1937, and prospects for unification remained bright through the 1940s. But when a specific proposal was brought forth in 1954, it was defeated by the southern body. On the threshold of the 1970s chances for unity of either of these denominations with their northern counterparts remained essentially nil.

Religion since World War II

At no time in their history had southern churches been assailed so persistently by the forces of change as in the years following World War II. Industrialization, urbanization, the growth of suburbia, a rising standard of living, increased social mobility, the changing status of the Negro, improved education, better transportation and communication facilities, and the demands of society all had their separate and combined impact upon the religious institutions in the South in the third quarter of the twentieth century.

The South's great industrial development drew tens of thousands of southern rural folk to the urban centers. A lesser influx of northerners to serve in administrative capacities for the new industries also occurred. The northerners joined with affluent urban southerners to demand more liturgy and ritual in the churches, as well as a more rational behavior to replace the revivalistic emotionalism of an earlier day. Choirs donned colored robes and marched in processionals and recessionals at worship services. Lighted candles became an integral part of the worship experience. But these church services did not meet the spiritual needs of the poor and semiliterate farmers who thronged to the cities to work in the shiny new industrial plants. Thousands of these new urban dwellers who were accustomed to simple, informal church services found refuge in the holiness sects. The gathering of these former rural dwellers into compact masses aided the rise of urban sects specifically formed to appeal to them. One of the most important of these was the Church of Christ, a fundamentalist group with evangelistic enthusiasm and a penchant for literal interpretations of biblical texts. Offering stability, refuge, and social acceptance on earth, as well as eternal rest in the hereafter, these churches relieved somewhat the bleakness and hardness of near-poverty existence experienced by uprooted rural-to-urban migrants.

In cities and towns church membership became an index of social status. Members of holiness sects were near the bottom of the social scale, Episcopalians were at the top, and the Presbyterians, Methodists, Baptists, and Disciples fell in between. Class distinctions also existed within the denominations, and membership in a "First" Baptist Church usually meant more socially than membership in churches named "Immanuel," "Calvary," or "Trinity." As southerners improved their economic levels, they were not averse to using the churches to assist their rise on the social ladder. Vacillating between their responsibilities to the masses and their desire for social status, many churches followed the middle and upper classes to the suburbs, abandoning the downtown areas to the holiness groups. The suburban church with its new wealth, its new buildings, and its new ritualism was often dominated by industrial managers, business executives, and other economic leaders of the community.

Pressure for change struck a most sensitive area following World War II when the Negro's revolution of rising expectations was accelerated by a complex of technological, moral, economic, and political forces moving swiftly to alter old traditions of apartheid. Of all the problems in the social arena, race relations was the one which most challenged and endangered southern churches. Before the end of World War II the southern churches had often reflected the prejudices of their members. Now, at the top levels, the major denominations tried to deal honestly and forthrightly with the Negro question. In 1946 the Southern Baptist Convention took a historic step by designating a committee to draw up a race relations statement. In the following year, the convention ratified the committee's statement of principles, acknowledging its responsibility for the promotion of good will among the races and urging Southern Baptists to express racial attitudes consistent with Christian love. The committee also recommended long-range educational efforts in race relations. In 1947 and 1949 the Southern Presbyterian General Assembly exhorted its members to support those seeking to uphold civil and constitutional liberties for all classes, and urged Presbyterians not to abdicate their racial responsibilities. The quadrennial General Conference of the Methodist Church in 1952 proclaimed that there was no place in Methodism for racial discrimination or segregation, and pledged its efforts to free the denomination of these evils. In 1960 and 1964 significant steps was taken by the Methodists to abolish the all-Negro Central Jurisdiction gradually.

Every major church body in the South supported the Supreme Court's 1954 epochal decision on public school segregation. Meeting in St. Louis in June 1954, the Southern Baptist Convention became one of the nation's first large religious organizations to adopt resolutions agreeing with the Court's decision. Among other things, the resolutions recognized the decision as harmonious with Christian principles of equal justice and love for all men. The 1956 General Conference of the Methodist Church admonished its members to help effect the inevitable adjustments. The Southern Presbyterian General Assembly of 1954 implored Presbyterians to assist in the implementation of the Court's ruling. The assembly declared enforced segregation out of harmony with Christian theology and ethics, and it requested local congregations and church colleges to admit all races. In 1957 the General Assembly broadly indicted discrimination in employment and politics as well as in religion and education.

These were unusually strong statements coming from the South's major church bodies, but they did not necessarily reflect the attitudes of the average member, and they were seldom carried out at the local level. Vast numbers of church people in the South, if they did not actively oppose the racial pronouncements, did or said nothing to assist integration in the public schools or in their churches. On occasion ministers were dismissed by their congregations for publicly supporting the Supreme Court decision or for preaching that the Christian concept of the brotherhood of man included the *black* man. In all of the upper South states and a few of the Deep South states Negroes were allowed to attend the worship services of a sizable number of churches, especially those in college and university towns where desegregation had occurred on the campuses, but few churches welcomed the Negroes to their social gatherings or as members. In the late 1960s indicators were few that the barriers of the southern churches would soon be lowered to admit black members.

Continuing a long-established trend of growing faster than the whole population, southern church membership in the decades following World War II climbed rapidly. Southerners attended church in greater numbers and with greater regularity than did Americans in other sections of the nation. Membership in the Methodist Church in the South grew from 2,837,262 in 1940 to over 4,000,000 in 1965. The Southern Presbyterian Church (officially the Presbyterian Church in the U. S.) rose from 450,000 in 1936 to nearly 1,000,000 in 1965, and by that date the Disciples of Christ counted 1,834,206 members, although not all of these were in the southern states. The Church of Christ was no longer a sect in 1965. With the majority of its members in the southern states, this new denomination claimed 2,250,000 members in that year and was one of the most rapidly growing churches in the South. Other groups with relatively large membership rolls in the South in 1965 included the Missouri Synod Lutheran Church (2,591,762), Church of the Nazarene (342,-000), Church of God in Christ (413,000), and Assemblies of God (543,-003). Numerous lesser bodies—holiness, pentecostal, Free Will Baptist, Evangelical Methodist, and others—added to the Protestant totals.

But none of these churches compared in influence, power, prestige, size, or growth rate with the Southern Baptists. The spectacular increase of Southern Baptists was one of the most conspicuous trends in American Protestantism in the postwar period. With 2,700,155 members in 1936, this mighty church body grew to 10,393,039 members in 1965. Baptizing almost 800 new members every day from 1950 to 1965, it was the fastest growing major denomination in the United States. Moreover, it had eclipsed the nationwide Methodist Church (with 10,234,986 in 1965) to become the nation's largest single Protestant denomination. It had a majority of all church members in nine of the eleven former Confederate states, with near majorities in seven other southern states. The Southern

Baptists in 1965 had over thirty-two thousand churches valued at more than $2,000,000,000. In addition, they administered six seminaries, fifty-one colleges and universities, twelve academies and Bible schools, forty hospitals, and fourteen homes for the elderly. They published twenty-eight weeklies and dozens of monthly and quarterly magazines, and claimed fifteen hundred missionaries in foreign countries.

Many factors contributed to the amazing growth of the Southern Baptists, not the least of which was their continued stress on evangelism. Revivalism remained the basic method by which new church members were gained, and hardly a Southern Baptist church in the land passed a year without at least one two-week evangelistic effort. North Carolinian Billy Graham, who has gained an international reputation as an evangelist, is a Southern Baptist, only one of hundreds of professionals working full time to build the kingdom of God. Using well-planned promotional techniques, these revivalists often had teams consisting of a dozen or more men and women who carefully planned and executed each series of evangelistic services. Advance publicity, prayer meetings, commitment cards, transportation, choir members, seating arrangements, and microphones, each in turn received proper notice. If an occasional voice of protest was raised, it was drowned out by local church members and ministers who measured success in round numbers. Besides, many of the churches used contrived appeals, catch phrases, canvasses, quotas, and pledges in their year-round programs, and this local promotionalism did its bit to increase church membership, Sunday-School enrollments, budgets, and church property values. But the stress on numbers and wealth does not mean that the evangelistic efforts of the churches and the revivalists were insincere. The Baptists' professional leaders were often deeply committed to the spiritual uplifting of their congregations, and they endeavored to see that the spiritual lives of their parishioners were not neglected.

Another factor accounting for Baptist upsurge was the denomination's eagerness to spread wherever southerners settled. In a highly mobile society, southerners lived everywhere by mid-century, and churches were established across the nation: in New York and New England, in California and Oregon, in Iowa and Illinois. Colorado became a spawning ground for new churches in the great Middle West, and sparsely populated states like Wyoming and South Dakota claimed small Southern Baptist congregations. This territorial aggressiveness was symbolically demonstrated when the convention held its annual meetings in Chicago and San Francisco in 1950 and 1951, respectively. At the annual convention in Kansas City in 1956 the convention's president charged his hearers to double the denomination's congregations by 1964. The setting of this staggering goal to be reached in less than a decade seemed to reemphasize Baptists' unadulterated boosterism. By 1965 as many Southern Baptist state conventions existed outside the former Confederate states as within them. In the light of this fervid activity suggestions were made to change the name of the convention, but no proposal was found to be suitable, and Southern Baptists proudly clung to a regional nomenclature for their now national organization.

Other denominations also expanded their memberships in regions outside the South, but perhaps a more significant reason for the growth of the southern churches was the developing concept that the church should be the most important institution in each parishioner's daily life. Church administrators took it upon themselves to keep large numbers of their flock busy at one task or another every day of the week. Weekdays and evenings were given over to Sunday-School teachers' meetings, church board sessions, prayer meetings, visitation and soul-winning activities, Bible study groups, choir rehearsals, and training programs for youth. But the churches' finances also had to be cared for; financial campaigns and monthly business meetings became a regular ritual. With southerners sharing in the "affluent society," the Lord's business became high finance. All the churches encouraged giving (the Baptists loudly trumpeting tithing), and magnificent church edifices were built in the postwar period. Besides the customary sanctuary (called an auditorium), every church of any size boasted an educational building, parlor, small chapel, administrative quarters, kitchen, dining hall, and recreational facilities for the youth (some even had swimming pools and basketball courts). Boards of elders, deacons, trustees, and stewards had come to look upon the church buildings in the same functional sense with which they regarded a factory. Calling their buildings "plants," they wanted them used a certain amount of the time to justify their original cost.

With buildings designed for more than simply worship on Sunday morning, churches increasingly conducted social and fellowship activities which, along with religious and business meetings, kept their doors standing open virtually all the time. Recreational programs engrossed the youth of the churches, and congregations worked up almost as much enthusiasm over church league softball and basketball teams as college students had for their football teams. Some churches allowed dancing in their recreation halls, and dating and mating often evolved under the purview of the church. Opportunities for the parents were not neglected. Ladies' circle meetings, couples' clubs, brotherhood fellowships, informal "family-night" gatherings, suppers, and banquets all had their places on the church calendar. Thomas D. Clark, well-known historian of the South, observed: "A church without a modern kitchen of hotel proportions and a dining hall large enough to serve a banquet to Belshazzar is an antiquated institution. A stranger visiting a southern church could easily get the impression that a gorged stomach is a necessary part of the religious rite; in fact, he would have difficulty at times in knowing whether he was in a church house or an unusually convivial country club." And Harry Golden wrote in *The Carolina Israelite* that archeologists excavating the ruins of our civilization in the distant future may wonder what kinds of sacrifices were offered in the huge bake ovens and barbecue pits discovered in our churches.

Beneath the deftly blended spiritual and worldly spheres and amidst new modes and outlooks, the southern churches clung tenaciously to religious concepts of the past. As keepers of old traditions and guardians of old truths the southern churches loomed large in the survival of a distinctive regional culture in the South in the 1960s, while at the same time the forces of change were returning those churches, however imperceptibly, into the mainstream of the nation's religious history.

Suggestions for Further Reading

Hunter D. Farish, *The Circuit Rider Dismounts: A Social History of Southern Methodism, 1865–1900* (Richmond: Dietz Press, 1938) is a model of the blending of social and religious history. For a similar volume for Southern Baptists, see Rufus B. Spain, *At Ease in Zion: Social History of the Southern Baptists, 1865–1900* (Nashville: Vanderbilt Univ., 1967). W. W. Barnes has written a sympathetic history of the largest Protestant denomination in the United States: *The Southern Baptist Convention, 1845–1953* (Nashville: Broadman Press, 1954). Samuel S. Hill, Jr. and Robert G. Torbet, *Baptists: North and South* * (Valley Forge, Pa.: Judson Press, 1964) contrasts Baptists on both sides of the Mason-Dixon Line. Archie T. Robertson, *That Old-Time Religion* (Boston: Houghton Mifflin, 1950), Jesse M. Ormond, *The Country Church in North Carolina* (Durham: Duke Univ., 1931), N. F. Furniss, *The Fundamentalist Controversy, 1918–1931* (New Haven: Yale Univ., 1954), and Stewart G. Cole, *The History of Fundamentalism* (New York: R. R. Smith, 1931) stress the basic conservatism of southern churches. A recent volume by Kenneth K. Bailey, *Southern White Protestantism in the Twentieth Century* (New York: Harper & Row, 1964), although restricted to Baptists, Methodists, and Presbyterians, is a firmly documented study which reveals the reactions of these groups to such trends as the Social Gospel movement. Flynt, "Dissent in Zion: Alabama Baptists and Social Issues, 1900–1914," *Journal of Southern History,* vol. 35 (1969) supports Bailey's conclusions.

Also useful is Willard B. Gatewood, Jr., *Preachers, Pedagogues and Politicians: The Evolution Controversy in North Carolina, 1920–1927* (Chapel Hill: Univ. North Carolina, 1966). Ray Ginger's *Six Days or Forever?* * (Boston: Beacon Press, 1958) is a brief but excellent account of the famous Scopes trial, while L. Sprague de Camp, *The Great Monkey Trial* (Garden City: Doubleday, 1968) is a good longer version of that famous event. Liston Pope, *Millhands and Preachers* * (New Haven: Yale Univ., 1942) is an instructive account of the interrelationship of religion, society, and economics in the New South. W. G. McLoughlin, Jr., *Modern Revivalism: Charles Grandison Finney to Billy Graham* (New York: Ronald Press, 1959) has much material on the South.

Mohler, "The Episcopal Church and National Reconciliation, 1865," *Political Science Quarterly,* vol. 41 (1926) recounts the healing efforts within a national church rent by the great sectional dispute. The reconciliation of the major branches of the Methodist Church is effectively recounted in Paul N. Garber, *The Methodists Are One People* (Nashville: Cokesbury Press, 1939). The best account of the agonizing change and the resistance to it which southern churches have experienced in recent years is Samuel S. Hill, Jr., *Southern Churches in Crisis* * (New York: Holt, Rinehart & Winston, 1967). Carter G. Woodson, *History of the Negro Church* (Washington: Associated Publishers, 1945) is a good study of a subject which deserves more attention from social historians. For a survey of the latest volumes published on American Protestantism, see Carter, "Recent Historiography of the Protestant Churches in America," *Church History,* vol. 37 (1968).

* Available in paperback.

CHAPTER XV

DEMAGOGUES AND PROGRESSIVES

Two themes dominated southern politics throughout the first third of the twentieth century: progressivism and opposition to the Negro in politics. Paradoxical though they were, the themes coexisted during these three decades, and no southerner took the trouble to rationalize the South's peculiar position. The region embraced the Progressive movement as did other sections of the nation. It was caught up in the traditional demands of that reform era: direct primary elections, initiative, referendum, recall, municipal reform, and direct election of senators. But if the South expressed a preference for broadening the base of American democracy, it expressly forbade black participation in the democratic political process. Ironically, the South's preoccupation with restricting the Negro from voting, thus holding down his influence, so dominated southern politics that in fact the Negro came to have more influence upon the course of politics than he would have had if he had been actively involved.

"Lily-White" Progressivism

In the South in the 1890s political events, which included a larger measure of black participation, convinced white southerners that the

Negro could become the political balance of power in the early twentieth century. Misgivings, prejudices, and fears compelled whites to vote for those candidates upon whom they could most depend to prevent this possibility. Quick to recognize that an anti-Negro stand was a sure road to victory in the aftermath of the political upheaval of the previous decade, southern political aspirants could not speak loudly enough against the black man in politics. The politician who won local, state, or national office in those early years of the new century made opposition to the Negro in politics an important campaign pledge, and he often won only because he had "out-Negroed" his opponents.

In the light of these circumstances, the South not surprisingly spawned a new generation of demagogues at the turn of the century. Often possessing more than average oratorical ability, able to identify with the common man through simple or ungrammatical speech, and sometimes affecting unusual dress or mannerisms, these politicians appealed to uneducated and prejudiced white southerners. In their campaigns they orated against Wall Street, bankers, and the rich, as well as city dwellers, Jews, Catholics, immigrants, and northerners. But their greatest vituperation was directed against the black minority within their midst. The list of state and national politicians from the South whose demagoguery came to be equated with early twentieth-century southern politics is long, including Thomas Watson (Georgia), J. Thomas Heflin (Alabama), James E. and Miriam Ferguson (Texas), William ("Alfalfa Bill") Murray (Oklahoma), and Robert L. Taylor (Tennessee).

Jeff Davis of Arkansas in many ways led the procession of these southern demagogues. Elected state attorney general in 1899, Davis climbed the political ladder to serve for six years as governor of Arkansas, topping his career with a senatorial term in Washington. Identified by his Confederate gray Prince Albert coat, Davis intensified class and racial antagonisms in campaign speeches and official pronouncements. In South Carolina, Coleman L. Blease appealed to the common man with his frank assaults on Negro education. First elected governor in 1910, Blease succeeded in awakening the political consciousness of South Carolina's underprivileged white class. Heir to Pitchfork Ben Tillman, Cole Blease directed his appeal to the rising number of town dwellers in industrially developing South Carolina, as well as to Tillman's constitutents. Both villagers and farmers responded to Blease's prejudicial oratory.

In Mississippi, James K. Vardaman was elected governor in 1903, mainly by playing upon whites' deep fears of a resurgent black minority. He accentuated his appeal for white supremacy by campaigning in the Mississippi countryside from the bed of a whitewashed lumber wagon, drawn by white oxen, while he himself, with long-flowing white mane and beard was clad in an immaculate white linen suit. The symbolism could not have been more obvious even to an illiterate. He advocated schools for Negroes only if funded by their race, he advocated different levels of justice for whites and blacks in the state's courts, and he favored economic suppression of the Negro. Vardaman was succeeded by Theodore G. Bilbo who served as governor of Mississippi for eight years between 1916 and 1932, before being elected United States senator in 1935. Bilbo's gubernatorial and senatorial careers, especially the latter, were characterized by some of the worst manifestations of racial prejudice emanating from high offices. Bilbo's obscene clowning aroused the ire of the Negro press and northern public opinion which in turn only spurred "The Man" to greater oratorical heights against the Negro. He advocated sending all blacks—he usually called them "coons"—back to Africa, but in the meantime he would "keep them in their place." He believed all Negroes were ignorant and debased, not capable of educational improvement. He often stated that they were biologically inferior, more related to simians than to the human race. He loudly advocated lynching as punishment for blacks accused of raping white women. His foulmouthed invectives from the governor's chair and the Senate floor were not muted by critical comments from others, and Bilbo thrived as the leading anti-Negro politician in the nation. Offended by his crudeness, many people believed it was poetic justice—if not divine retribution—that Bilbo died of cancer of the mouth.

The impact of these and similar politicians can be seen not only in their oratory and their political campaigns, but in their actual efforts to restrict Negro political activity. They continued to use many of the extralegal devices originated during the Bourbon ascendancy (such as the poll tax, gerrymandering, and complex election machinery), and they expanded upon the literacy tests and property qualifications which were coming into widespread use in the late 1890s. But these were not enough in a period when white supremacy was the loudest emotional political battle cry. In Louisiana a "grandfather clause" was added to the state constitution in 1898 to protect whites who might lose suffrage as a result of literacy laws or property requirements. Specifically the clause provided that anyone whose grandfather had voted before 1867 was not required to submit to the literacy test or meet the property qualification stipulation. Thus, suffrage was open to poor white illiterates but closed to Negroes, since the latter did not vote in Louisiana before the passage of the Reconstruction Acts of 1867. Other states enacted similar clauses or laws, including Oklahoma in 1910. In *Ginn* v. *the United States* (1915), the Supreme Court declared the Oklahoma law unconstitutional, announcing that a state could not reestablish conditions existing before the ratification of the Fifteenth Amendment, which assured the black man his legal right to vote.

These southern leaders were also responsible for inaugurating the white primary. The direct primary system for nominating party candidates was an important part of the national Progressive movement, but it was supported nowhere in the nation so strongly as in the South. By 1903, when Wisconsin first installed the direct primary, a majority of southern states were already using the system, and by 1915 the remaining states in the region had adopted it. Since the primary election was *the* election in states where the one-party system prevailed, party leaders in the southern states adopted rules for voting in the Democratic primaries which effectively disfranchised many Negro voters. In the South the *direct* primary was the same as the *white* primary.

Local regions and conditions dictated the issues early twentieth-century southern politicians emphasized during their campaigns and while they were in office or in control of party politics, but the anti-Negro theme was always present, whether in the spotlight or in the wings waiting to move onto center stage.

In their prejudicial appeals and bizarre efforts to identify with the masses, these Dixie demagogues have been assumed to have had completely negative administrations. Nothing could be further from the truth. Recent research has discovered that these politicians made significant and tangible contributions while in office. Although the contributions varied within each state and with each politician, many state administrations passed legislation controlling the activities of powerful insurance companies, railroads, and other corporations not acting in "the public interest." They established educational institutions and provided free textbooks and expanded building programs for public schools. They built bridges and public highways. In some cases they abolished poll taxes and rid state governments of much graft and corruption. Many spoke out in favor of direct election of senators. In the most religious section of the nation, these leaders generally favored prohibition, a long-standing cause which tied itself to progressivism and which began to see the dim light of success in the early decades of the new century. Demagogic though they were on the race question, these southern politicians were very much a part of the Progressive movement sweeping the country at the very time they were in office. If progressivism was stronger in the North, it by no means bypassed the South. And while southern progressivism had its own peculiarities, it was essentially an urban and middle class movement, as was its national counterpart, and these southern leaders must be called "Progressive" on many issues.

But a balanced picture of southern politicians and politics cannot be drawn by focusing only on the so-called demagogues, whether upon their racial attitudes or their progressivism. Concurrent with them during the Progressive Era was a group of southern leaders who do not fit the stereotype of the southern politician, but who nevertheless were just as southern, and who also made significant contributions at the state and national level during the Progressive Era. In line with national Progressive thought and action, these men from gubernatorial chairs and senatorial seats advocated direct primaries, initiative, referendum, recall, control of corporations, abolition of the poll tax, municipal reform (both city-commission and city-manager plans originated in the South), prohibition, abolishment of the convict-lease system, and better schools and roads. Their accomplishments included strengthening commissions regulating railroads and public utilities and passing unfair-practices laws, safety and inspection laws for mills and mines, pure food and drug bills, and penal reform measures. A roll call of these leaders includes Carter Glass (Virginia), Hoke Smith (Georgia), Joseph T. Robinson (Arkansas), Oscar W. Underwood and Braxton B. Comer (Alabama), and Robert B. Glenn, Henry Clayton, and Furnifold M. Simmons (North Carolina).

Napoleon Bonaparte Broward, elected governor of Florida in 1904, championed the "little man" in the face of the power of the railroad interests, slowed the process whereby the state's public lands were being acquired by speculators, and became a folk hero by loudly advocating an ambitious scheme to drain and reclaim the swampy Everglades. William Goebel rose to a place of prominence in the reform wing of the Kentucky Democratic party and in 1899 won the gubernatorial nomination, despite ruthless opposition from the powerful Louisville and Nashville Railroad political machine. In a hard-fought contest with the Republican candidate, who was openly supported by L & N money and leaders, Goebel in every speech lambasted the railroad interests and called for increased power for the state railroad commission. Conditions were strained when the election results were disputed, and Goebel was shot by an unknown gunman a few days before he was inaugurated governor. He died four days after taking office. Goebel's career served to illustrate southern progressivism's unsuccessful determination to control powerful railroading interests at the state level.

Since most successful southern politicians were in the mainstream of progressivism in the early years of the twentieth century and since most of them were race-baiters, it may not be entirely accurate to distinguish between demagogues and Progressives. The demagogues played heavily upon racial fears while they were campaigning, but once in office, they focused upon Progressive legislation. Progressives placed just enough stress upon racial distinctions to make sure the white voters recognized them to be "on the right side" of the white-black issue, and once in office they too generally ignored the subject of skin color. In view of the circumstances, the major distinction between the two groups was their emphasis upon race during their campaigns, and even that distinction was a difference in degree rather than kind.

The New Freedom

Southern Progressive Democrats came into their own on the national scene upon the election of Woodrow Wilson as President in 1912. Although Wilson had long been a resident of New Jersey when he was elevated to the Presidency, southerners claimed him as their own. Born in Virginia and spending his childhood days in Georgia and the Carolinas, while his Presbyterian minister father moved from one parish to another, Wilson was indeed in many ways a southerner. He once said that "the only place in the country, the only place in the world where nothing has to be explained to me is the South." Five of the members of the new President's Cabinet were born in the South: William Gibbs McAdoo (Secretary of the Treasury), James C. McReynolds (Attorney General), David F. Houston (Secretary of Agriculture), Josephus Daniels (Secretary of the Navy), and Albert Sidney Burleson (Postmaster General). Two other members had close ties with the South, and new Secretary of State William Jennings Bryan, although a midwesterner, had been idolized by southerners since Populist days. Wilson's unofficial but close adviser and alter ego was Colonel Edward M. House of Texas. In addition, the South received a larger than usual share of other administrative and diplomatic posts in the Wilson administration.

The South's influence was not limited to the executive branch of the government. In the Senate, southerners constituted over one-half of the Democrats, who held a substantial majority. In the lower house, about two-fifths of the majority party were from the South. More important was southern domination of the leadership of the national legislature. In 1913 southerners chaired twelve of the fourteen major Senate committees and eleven of the thirteen major House committees. Oscar W. Underwood of Alabama was the Democratic majority leader in the House of Representatives until 1915, when he was succeeded by Claude Kitchin of North Carolina. John W. Kern of Indiana, a native of Virginia, was the majority leader in the Senate until his death in 1917, at which time Thomas S. Martin of Virginia assumed that important position. In view of the southern strength in both executive and legislative branches of the government, it is not surprising that men of the South rejoiced as Wilson's new administration got under way.

Wilson's New Freedom legislation—in many ways the capstone of the Progressive Era—was generally supported by southerners because they, like Wilson, desired to regulate special privilege and restrain the growth of trusts. Southerners were in complete accord with Wilson's desire for downward tariff revision. While his suggestion for a "competitive tariff" was not as extreme as some southerners preferred, they were still happy to cooperate in bringing about the first significant reduction in United States tariff laws since the Civil War. Underwood, then chairman of the House Ways and Means Committee, and Furnifold M. Simmons, chairman of the Senate Finance Committee, guided the bill through the Congress, and the 1913 tariff measure was made law with a minimum of difficulty. The only significant opposition from the South came from Louisiana congressmen who were unhappy that sugar cane interests were to be afforded no protection.

Another important piece of New Freedom legislation which southerners helped shape was the Federal Reserve Act. Carter Glass (Virginia) and Robert L. Owen (Oklahoma), chairmen of the House and Senate banking committees respectively, were responsible for some of the specific characteristics of this law. Despite heavy pressures from bankers and businessmen, who advocated a strong and highly centralized reserve system in private hands, Glass insisted upon a decentralized system with twelve reserve banks under federal control. Owen, one of the leaders of the southern agrarians, was able with support from others to insist that banker representatives be excluded from the Federal Reserve Board, that Federal Reserve notes be obligations of the United States government, and that short-term farm and commercial credit facilities be provided.

The Federal Trade Commission Act and the Clayton Anti-Trust Act were the Wilson administration's answer to those who demanded stronger antitrust laws. Southerners were generally not intimately involved in the passage of these two acts, although they favored the antitrust principle, and although Henry D. Clayton, the Alabamian who served as the House Judiciary Committee chairman, drafted the Clayton Act. Perhaps this lack of large-scale participation stems from the fact that many southern congressmen were devoting their energies to legislation designed specifically for their constituencies. For example, southern agrarian congressmen were active in the passage of the Smith-Lever Act of 1914, sponsored by Georgia Senator Hoke Smith and South Carolina Congressman Asbury F. Lever. Likewise, southerners supported the Smith-Hughes Act of 1917, sponsored by Smith and Georgia Congressman Dudley M. Hughes.

Most important to the southern leaders in their move to improve agricultural conditions was the growing demand for rural credit reform. By the opening of the twentieth century, the nation's commercial banking system was not serving the farmer's needs. The financial machinery which aided certain classes of borrowers was inadequate for the farmer, and the farmer's rate of interest was higher than that paid by others. The Democratic party had endorsed rural credit reform in the national convention of 1912, and President Wilson expressed the need for this change in his inaugural address. Even before the new administration was in office, rural leaders were laying plans to provide long-term credit at low-interest rates for the farmers of the nation.

On inauguration day, March 4, 1913, under the direction of
Senate Agriculture Committee chairman Thomas P. Gore of Oklahoma,
a bill was approved which made possible the creation of the United
States Rural Credit Commission. This commission was given the power
to investigate and study European cooperative land-mortgage banks, cooperative rural credit unions, and similar organizations and institutions
devoted to the promotion of agriculture and the improvement of rural
conditions. Senator Duncan U. Fletcher (Florida) was made chairman of
this committee, and in conjunction with the Southern Commercial Congress, the commission made a three-month tour of Europe. From the data
gathered abroad, Senator Fletcher framed and introduced a bill in August 1913 to establish a system of privately controlled land banks to operate under federal charter. After being revised by a joint committee of
Congress, the bill included a provision requiring the government to operate the proposed system and to furnish capital for the land banks. Called
the Hollis-Bulkley bill, this measure set off a controversy in 1914, when
the clause for government support was made public. President Wilson
and Secretary of Agriculture David F. Houston argued that this provision
constituted special legislation for a particular group and was not in the
tradition of New Freedom principles. The spokesmen for the bill disagreed, and a stalemate existed for the next two years.

In 1916 President Wilson at last yielded to the agrarian pressures.
The culmination of several years of efforts on the part of southern and
western agrarian leaders, the Federal Farm Loan Act established a system
of twelve federal farm loan banks, each capitalized at $500,000, the essen-
tial function of each being to provide credit for farmers at a low rate of
interest on a long-term basis. Called the "Magna Charta of American
farm finance," this act was a distinct victory for the Progressive agrarian
leaders, and it represented their major achievement under the Wilson administration during the final years of the Progressive Era.

President Wilson was not always as responsive to the needs and
demands of the southern representatives as they would have liked him to
be, and southerners were not as influential during the New Freedom Era
as their numbers would indicate, but certainly no administration since
before the Civil War had been as consciously "southern" as Wilson's.

Wartime Politics

When World War I began in 1914, southern politicians reflected
the sentiments of their constituents by showing immediate concern for
the effect the war might have on the cotton trade. Their concern was justified. At the outbreak of the war cotton prices fell sharply, and agricultural leaders recognized that the bumper crop then in the fields would be

disastrous for the South unless something could be done quickly. They trotted out panaceas which had been suggested in past cotton crises, but most of them were rejected and many of them would not have been effective anyway. The agrarian leaders hoped that the federal government would find relief for the cotton South, but they were disappointed. Brazen suggestions that the government purchase surplus cotton at a predetermined price were rejected out of hand. Other schemes offered in Congress were opposed by the Wilson administration because they smacked too much of "special privilege" legislation, not in keeping with New Freedom principles. The South's problem was finally solved when British firms began to buy more cotton, stabilizing the price of the South's money crop. As the war progressed cotton prices continued to climb, and southern politicians were not required to fight for cotton supports on the legislative battlefront.

Of considerable concern to southern leaders in Washington was the British blockade of German ports, even though cotton was not originally listed as contraband of war. When the British decided to place cotton on the contraband list, they realized that they were unwise to antagonize the South and so worked closely with the United States government to soften the blow to that region. Southern leaders such as Hoke Smith, Asbury F. Lever, and John Sharp Williams still denounced the action, but as the months passed and the price of cotton rose, the South's anger and anti-British feeling subsided.

Despite the South's concern with its own economic well-being during the war, it directed its attention to subjects closely related to the prewar Progressive movement. The increasing momentum of nationwide prohibition apparent before the war received a mighty boost forward during the war when the Congress voted temporary national prohibition, as an expedient to save food resources. National prohibitionists stepped up their propaganda efforts, and Senator Morris Sheppard of Texas, who had introduced a constitutional amendment for prohibition in 1913, brought forth his proposal again in 1917, and with minor changes this became the Eighteenth Amendment. Southerners cast only a handful of the 128 nay votes in the House of Representatives against this amendment, and out of a total of 8 nay votes in the Senate on a standing roll call, observers professed to see no southerners in opposition. These representatives in Washington were reflecting the majority opinion in their states. After passage by Congress in December 1917, the amendment was almost immediately ratified by the legislatures of Mississippi and Virginia, and within a month two other southern states had voted for it. Except for Missouri, the remaining southern states approved the amendment before Nebraska's action completed ratification on January 16, 1919, and Missouri took affirmative action later that same day.

While the South was the region which distilled the largest quantities of illegal alcohol after national prohibition went into effect in January 1920, many religious southerners were sincere in their efforts to dry up the nation. As much cannot be said for all the political supporters of prohibition. Eight months after the Eighteenth Amendment had gone into effect, a still with a daily capacity of 130 gallons was discovered on a Texas farm owned by Senator Sheppard, the "Father of National Prohibition." Moreover, numerous other expedient southern politicians voted "dry" but were personally "wet."

Like the prohibition movement, demands for woman suffrage dated from the nineteenth century. A few midwestern states had permitted women the right to vote in state and local elections by the end of the century, but southern states had been more reluctant, and the drive for women's right to vote in national elections seemed bogged down at the opening of the twentieth century. But woman suffrage was in tune with the Progressive mood, and pressures built rapidly causing various state legislatures to yield. Southern states joined the parade when Arkansas (1917) and Texas (1918) permitted women to vote in statewide primaries. Oklahoma capitulated to statewide woman suffrage in 1918, and Tennessee and Kentucky granted Presidential woman suffrage in 1919 and 1920. Momentum was now in their favor and the suffragettes compelled Congress to approve what became the Nineteenth Amendment. During the ratification process, only the five previously mentioned southern states formally approved the amendment. The other southern states either rejected it or refused to act.

Almost from the outbreak of World War I, the Wilson administration embarked upon a program of defense. Those southerners in the Progressive-pacifist tradition criticized military preparations because they directed attention away from Progressive legislation and because they might lead the nation into war. These critics of military preparation reflected the suspicions of the rural South that munitions and armament manufacturers were unduly profiting from the preparedness program, and they were very much opposed to this. But the majority of southern politicians on the national scene favored the President's preparedness actions, and this became true of southerners in general.

The controversy over preparedness was only one aspect of the larger problem of neutrality facing the nation's and the region's political leaders. Central to this problem was the Germans' reliance upon the submarine as a weapon of war, contrary to international laws concerning the rights of neutrals. President Wilson believed that all of international law would be jeopardized if the United States did not stand up for its rights as a neutral. When Americans were killed or injured by submarine attacks, tensions increased between the United States and Germany, and a number of congressional leaders began to press for Congress to express its belief that American citizens should not exercise their rights to travel on vessels which might be sunk. Resolutions with this intent were introduced into the House of Representatives by Jeff McLemore of Texas and into the Senate by Thomas P. Gore of Oklahoma. A number of southerners supported these resolutions of their colleagues as did other congressmen from across the nation. After a legislative struggle which resulted in the President using his position of strength against the resolutions, each house of Congress finally rejected the McLemore and Gore resolutions. While southerners introduced both resolutions, when the final votes were taken many southern Democrats were forced into line by pressures from the White House, and most of them voted with the President.

When the United States Congress considered a war declaration, which passed both houses overwhelmingly in April 1917, five southern congressmen and one senator (Vardaman of Mississippi) voted against it, although Senator Gore later indicated he would have voted nay had he been present. This minority spirit continued for the duration of the war. While a majority of southerners in Congress generally supported the war effort and voted for such important legislation as conscription, the Espionage Act, the Sedition Act, the Lever Food Control Act, and the Railroad Act of 1918, a vocal minority expressed its opposition to these and other war measures, proving to be an embarrassment to the nation and the administration throughout the war. Senators Vardaman, Gore, Blease, Watson and Thomas Hardwick of Georgia, and Claude Kitchin of North Carolina were among the leading southern opponents of many of Wilson's policies. Although they varied in their intensity and opposition to specific war measures, they particularly disliked conscription, food control, and the espionage bills.

While this southern agrarian-Progressive group was generally ineffective in its opposition to most wartime legislation, it was somewhat successful in its attempts to tax war profits and rising corporate wealth to help pay for the costly war. Most rural southerners gave solid support to their President on such matters as conscription and the control of seditious activities, but they had a strong distrust of the great financial interests and they believed that munitions makers wanted war in order to increase profits. Thus, they sided with Kitchin, Gore, and Vardaman in their demands for higher levies on war profits. Because of these congressional efforts, the war revenue acts of 1917 and 1918 reduced certain tax exemptions and raised tax rates generally. Surtaxes and increased inheritance taxes as well as higher levies on excess profits were also passed because of the pressure from these men.

But basically these southern legislative leaders were out of step with their constituents. The Wilson administration had made determined efforts to cultivate the support of the American people for the war effort, and southerners no less than northerners responded positively to the patriotic appeals. As southerners generally came under the influence of the government's anti-German propaganda, these men came to be stamped as pro-German, an ironic label since few Germans had migrated to the South. Because of his opposition to the war, Vardaman became known in Mississippi as "Herr Von Vardaman." Gore, who believed that conscription was un-American and who was a strong critic of food control, became involved in a running verbal battle with Oklahoma's leading newspapers for his non-support of Wilson's policies. In the midst of the controversy when Gore's studied opposition to the war was greatest, one newspaper editorialized, "It does seem to us . . . [we] have been Gored enough." Another paper headlined "620 More Days of Gore" and periodically announced the number of days left in the Senator's term.

Southern response to Wilson's management of the war can be gauged by what happened to the President's detractors in their next political campaigns. The Democratic primaries of 1918 spelled disaster for most of those who had opposed Wilson's policies. In Texas's Seventh District, Jeff McLemore failed to win a majority in any county. Senators Hardwick and Vardaman were both defeated for renomination, neither ever managing a political comeback after these reversals. Blease and Watson attempted to reenter politics in that fateful year for political mavericks, but neither was successful. In 1920 Gore was defeated in the Democratic primary, his antiadministration stand during the war years still fresh in the minds of the Oklahoma voters. These political defeats pointed up the South's almost total support for Wilson during the war. They indicated the South's willingness to have the central government strengthened in order to prosecute the war. The South's patriotic support of the nation in time of emergency was even more powerful than the region's traditional emphasis upon states' rights.

"Business Progressivism"

National politics in the 1920s was dominated by conservative Republicans, and Progressive southern Democrats were relegated to the back seats in Washington. But this lack of influence in the halls of Congress or within the White House did not prevent southern Progressives from operating successfully in their states. In the postwar decade southern progressivism at the state level placed less emphasis upon social and political reform and more upon efficiency in government and economic development. The South's affinity for industry permeated every aspect of southern life and thought, including both business and politics. Businessmen with a "New South" philosophy were often closely allied with "progressive" state politicians to advance the interests of themselves and their states. "Progressive" states and communities were those which had good government, solid churches, better schools, sound businesses, and thriving industrial plants. George B. Tindall has referred to this trend as "business progressivism" and has pointed out that the concept embraced the old Progressive themes of public services and efficiency. This philosophy elevated industry, education, and good roads as the trinity to be idolized by progressive businessmen and state leaders. If these men did not root out entrenched "privilege," they did espouse and implement the concept that public services were to be provided by the states. By "good government" these men implied that they favored economy in government, but their administrations revealed that they really desired to reduce waste and corruption rather than cut back public services. The programs of selected governors illustrate these generalizations.

North Carolina's governor, Thomas W. Bickett, 1917–21, created a state public welfare system, inaugurated a minimum six-month school term, raised state employees' salaries, and increased expenditures for public health and state institutions. Bickett also sponsored wide-ranging tax reforms, which resulted in more state income for public use as well as a more equitable tax schedule. This tradition was continued by Governor Cameron Morrison, who allocated millions of dollars for highways, education, and charitable institutions. Angus W. McLean succeeded Morrison and expanded his programs, adding an executive budget system and other sound policies to insure the wise expenditure of state funds. The administrations of these three governors in the 1920s did much to cause North Carolina to outdistance her neighbors in educational development and the building of hard-surfaced roads.

John M. Parker was elected governor of Louisiana in 1920 and immediately set upon a program of business progressivism for the state. He instituted constitutional and administrative reforms, expanded the schools, and built highways. After four years in office Parker was defeated, and the state government was returned to the hands of more conservative leaders. But the people of Louisiana had tasted the sweet fruits of business progressivism, and they were dissatisfied with complacency. Into this milieu stepped Huey Long, a young activist who had a long record of warring against vested interests. As a member of the Louisiana Railroad Commission, Long had orated against business monopoly, and he had successfully reduced railroad, streetcar, telephone, and gas rates in the state. Defeated for governor in 1924, he had run well in the state's northern parishes. After politicking for four years in the southern French parishes, promising an extension of the Parker program, Long had substantial support all over the state, and he won the gubernatorial post in 1928. Once in office, Long made good his expansive campaign promises. He pushed through a $30,000,000 bond issue for roads and bridges, he distributed free textbooks to school children, he funneled more money to the state's schools and charitable institutions, and he secured lower natural gas rates for New Orleans. Long's crude methods for getting his program accomplished rubbed many people the wrong way, and he found formidable opposition to his developing political control of Louisiana. But Long was enough of a demagogue and intuitively astute enough to survive the political attacks of his opponents. Before he was assassinated in 1935, he had remolded Louisiana politics until they were never to be the same again, and he had inaugurated a Long dynasty whose influence was felt far beyond the state's borders.

Thomas E. Kilby, William W. Brandon, and Bibb ("Little Colonel") Graves were governors of Alabama during the 1920s. In their political campaigns each professed to favor economy, reduction of taxes, the abolishment of useless state offices, and reduction of state salaries, but when they were safely in office they consistently supported progressive programs. Public schools and colleges were better financed; road bond issues were promoted; and support for hospitals, charitable institutions, and child welfare was increased. They also assisted in the development of the port of Mobile. After campaigning on a platform to reduce government activity and expenditures, Tennessee's Governor Austin Peay poured more money into improving the state's highway system than was saved from his governmental reorganization efforts. Westmoreland Davis, governor of Virginia from 1918 to 1922, led an administration marked by economy and efficiency, his most significant achievements being the adoption of an executive budget, the establishment of a new highway department, the institution of a central purchasing system, and the passage of long-needed prison reforms. Harry F. Byrd, governor of Virginia from 1926 to 1930, carried through an extensive reorganization of the state government, at the same time spending millions of dollars for surfaced roads. Arkansas's Governor John E. Martineau became identified with the slogan "better roads and better schools."

Some progressive governors did not receive the support of their legislators, but progress was made nevertheless, and every southern state was affected by the progressivism of the 1920s. South Carolina in 1921 had the lowest public school expenditure per pupil in the nation; by 1929 it had the highest rate of increase. In 1929 South Carolina also voted a $65,000,000 highway bond issue. Almost every southern state inaugurated administrative and tax reforms, and whatever their leaders said about economy, the states entered upon ambitious public service programs by the dozens. Between 1918 and 1929 every southern state had installed a budget system, and most of them had adopted general reorganization plans.

Increased services resulted in greater debts and additional taxes. The southern states in the 1920s far exceeded the remainder of the nation in the rate of increase in both revenues and debts. Southern legislatures adopted state income taxes, sales taxes, gasoline taxes, and tobacco taxes in their efforts to provide services and at the same time hold debts in line. Despite these efforts, the South trailed the nation in revenues received. In 1932 state and local governments in thirteen southern states grossed $33.26 per capita in general revenues, while the rest of the states averaged $69.63. Yet business progressivism was responsible for much material progress in the southern states in the decade.

While business progressivism was in its ascendancy, southerners gave less attention to the age-old problem of race relations. But the events of the twenties were a part of the trends before and after that decade, and the shadow of the black man was never far away. Before 1920 political parties had set up primary election machinery in such a way as to exclude most Negroes, but without specific reference to race. Desiring to give the force of law to the Texas Democratic party's decisions and concerned over the fact that some Negroes were not disfranchised, the Texas legislature in 1923 enacted a law providing that "in no event shall a negro be eligible to participate in a Democratic primary election held in the State of Texas." The United States Supreme Court in *Nixon* v. *Herndon* (1927) declared this statute a violation of the Fifteenth Amendment, but Texans were not to be deterred. The state legislature then passed a resolution authorizing the state Democratic executive committee to prescribe the specific qualifications of the party's members. The executive committee immediately barred Negroes from the party, a device as effective as a state statute, until this action also was invalidated by the Supreme Court. After this ruling the state party convention assumed authority to establish membership rules for the organization. The convention voted that only white Texans were eligible to belong to the party and thus vote in the primary elections. In 1935 the Supreme Court in the Grovey case held this decision legal, since no state action was involved. The Court overruled its own decision in *Smith* v. *Allwright* (1944), when it acknowledged that the primary was "an integral part" of the election process; therefore, the Texas Democratic party's decision to exclude Negroes from the primaries was unconstitutional. This legal skirmishing in Texas was followed closely by other southern states in the 1920s and 1930s, all of them in one way or another trying to reduce Negro voting.

Concern over the importance of the Negro in politics was revealed by patterns of voting in the South in the 1928 Presidential election. Those areas in which few blacks lived bolted the Democratic ticket to vote for Republican Herbert Hoover, while heavily populated Negro areas remained loyal to the dominant party. The possible future role of the Negro in the political equation was undoubtedly a major factor in this voting behavior. But other factors in the election results must not be overlooked. Democratic candidate Al Smith was a Catholic and an advocate of repeal of prohibition. Smith's religion and his stand against a moral and social issue close to southerners' hearts were important factors in his loss of six southern states, heretofore always assumed safely Democratic. Many political prophets saw this split in the Solid South as a sign pointing to an immediate two-party South, but their predictions were somewhat premature. However, the campaign of 1928 and its aftermath did inaugurate a new era in southern politics. Dominated by prohibition, religious fundamentalism, and business progressivism, southern politicians who supported the national Republican party in 1928 were discredited when the Hoover administration ran afoul of economic forces beyond its control. The way was cleared for loyal Democratic southerners to participate in a new progressive coalition forged by Franklin D. Roosevelt.

Suggestions for Further Reading

Every study of southern politics in the twentieth century must begin with the classic by V. O. Key, Jr., *Southern Politics in State and Nation* * (New York: Knopf, 1949). Key's volume, *American State Politics* (New York: Knopf, 1956) is also valuable for studying southern politics. Reinhard H. Luthin, *American Demagogues: Twentieth Century* (Boston: Beacon Press, 1954) and Allan A. Michie and Frank Rhylick, *Dixie Demagogues* (New York: Vanguard Press, 1939) are sharply critical of the South's political leaders, while Charles W. Collins, *Whither Solid South?* (New Orleans: Pelican, 1948) is written from a southern conservative's point of view. A highly interpretive work with many references to the South is Richard Hofstadter, *The Age of Reform: From Bryan to F. D. R.* * (New York: Knopf, 1955).

Political biographies of southern leaders in the early twentieth century include: Dewey W. Grantham, Jr., *Hoke Smith and the Politics of the New South* * (Baton Rouge: Louisiana State Univ., 1958); Francis B. Simkins, *Pitchfork Ben Tillman* * (Baton Rouge: Louisiana State Univ., 1944); William E. Larsen, *Montague of Virginia: The Making of a Southern Progressive* (Baton Rouge: Louisiana State Univ., 1965); Monroe Lee Billington, *Thomas P. Gore: The Blind Senator from Oklahoma* (Lawrence: Univ. Kansas, 1967); Samuel Proctor, *Napoleon Bonaparte Broward: Florida's Fighting Democrat* (Gainesville, Fla.: Univ. Florida, 1951); Josephus Daniels, *The Editor in Politics* (Chapel Hill: Univ. North Carolina, 1941); Charles Jacobson, *The Life Story of Jeff Davis* (Little Rock: Parke-Harper, 1925); A. S. Coody, *Biographical Sketches of James Kimble Vardaman* (Jackson: A. S. Coody, 1922); G. C. Osborn, *John Sharp Williams* (Baton Rouge: Louisiana State Univ., 1943); A. M. Arnett, *Claude Kitchin and the Wilson War Policies* (Boston: Little, Brown, 1937); J. F. Rippy (ed.), *Furnifold Simmons, Statesman of the New South* (Durham: Duke Univ., 1936); J. E. Palmer, Jr., *Carter Glass, Unreconstructed Rebel* (Roanoke: Institute of American Biography, 1938); Jack Temple Kirby, *Westmoreland Davis: Virginia Planter-Politician, 1859–1942* (Charlottesville: Univ. Virginia, 1968); T. Harry Williams, *Huey Long* (New York: Knopf, 1969). The Long dynasty has received attention from Allan P. Sindler, *Huey Long's Louisiana: State Politics, 1925–1952* (Baltimore: Johns Hopkins Univ., 1956) and Stan Opotowsky, *The Longs of Louisiana* (New York: Dutton, 1960). An early revisionist essay on the southern demagogues is Robison's "From Tillman to Long: Some Striking Leaders of the Rural South," *Journal of Southern History*, vol. 3 (1937). Verifying Robison's thesis that many demagogues were progressive leaders is Albert D. Kirwan's *Revolt of* *the Rednecks: Mississippi Politics, 1876–1925* * (Lexington: Univ. Kentucky, 1951).

C. Vann Woodward, *Origins of the New South, 1877–1913* * (Baton Rouge: Louisiana State Univ., 1951) has chapters on the southern Progressives, and Mowry, "The South and the Progressive Lily White Party of 1912," *Journal of Southern History*, vol. 6 (1940) deals with a related phase of that subject. Link, "The Progressive Movement in the South, 1870–1914," *North Carolina Historical Review*, vol. 23 (1946) is instructive. Devoting attention to prohibition during the Progressive Era are James B. Sellers, *The Prohibition Movement in Alabama, 1702–1943* * (Chapel Hill: Univ. North Carolina, 1943) and D. G. Whitener, *Prohibition in North Carolina, 1715–1945* (Chapel Hill: Univ. North Carolina, 1946).

A dispute has risen over the influence of southern congressmen upon the Wilsonian New Freedom program. For several approaches to the subject, see Link, "The South and the 'New Freedom': An Interpretation," *American Scholar*, vol. 20 (1950–51); Grantham, "Southern Congressional Leaders and the New Freedom, 1913–1917," *Journal of Southern History*, vol. 13 (1947); Abrams, "Woodrow Wilson and the Southern Congressmen, 1913–1916," *ibid.*, vol. 22 (1956); Allen, "Geography and Politics: Voting on Reform Issues in the United States Senate, 1911–1916," *ibid.*, vol. 27 (1961).

George B. Tindall, *The Emergence of the New South, 1913–1945* (Baton Rouge: Louisiana State Univ., 1967) contains superb chapters on southern politics and politicians during the decade of the 1920s. E. A. Moore, *A Catholic Runs for President* (New York: Ronald Press, 1956) has much to say about the South and the 1928 Presidential election. The South's preoccupation with the role of the Negro on the political scene is well recounted in Paul Lewinson, *Race, Class, and Party: A History of Negro Suffrage and White Politics in the South* (New York: Oxford, 1932). Frederick D. Ogden, *The Poll Tax in the South* (University, Ala.: Univ. Alabama, 1958) is a thorough study of a method for Negro disfranchisement. An informative study is E. L. Tatum's *The Changed Political Thought of the Negro, 1915–1940* (New York: Exposition Press, 1951).

* Available in paperback.

CHAPTER XVI

SOUTHERN POLITICS IN TRANSITION

The middle decades of the twentieth century witnessed a politically changing South. The Great Depression and the New Deal divided southern Democratic solidarity as no other events since Populism, and this rending of the southern wing of the party continued in the postwar years. The most judicious observer of the South's political development had difficulty unwinding the tangled threads, but three important trends were discernible: more sharply etched lines between conservatives and liberals, a steady growth of the Republican party at both state and local levels, and increased numbers of Negro voters. These developments placed alongside a continuation of race-baiting, strident factionalism, and an ingrained loyalty to the Democratic party made for confusion which both fascinated and confounded the student of southern politics.

New Deal or Raw Deal?

The agricultural South, like the industrial North, suffered as the great economic depression deepened during President Hoover's four years in office. Southerners no less than northerners were eager for a change of Presidential administrations in view of the old order's lack of success with its rather cavalier fight against the economic crisis. At the Democratic nominating convention of 1932, more than one southerner aspired to the Presidential nomination, including James Nance ("Cactus Jack") Garner, wealthy lawyer and chicken farmer from Texas and at that time Speaker of the House of Representatives. A number of southerners opposed New York's Governor Franklin D. Roosevelt, who entered the convention as the leading contender. Mainly through the efforts of Huey Long of Louisiana, several southern delegates were persuaded to support Roosevelt, who won the nomination on the fourth ballot. Garner, who had released ninety pledged delegates, assuring Roosevelt the nomination, became the Democrat's Vice-Presidential candidate. The southern masses voted for the Roosevelt-Garner ticket, hoping to receive economic relief after the Democrats won the election.

The Roosevelt administration also had the support of a significant number of southern leaders in Washington. Joseph W. Byrns (Tennessee), William B. Bankhead (Alabama), and Sam Rayburn (Texas) used their positions as committee chairmen and as majority leaders and speakers of the House to help with the passage of many basic economic reform measures, including the Securities Act of 1933, the Securities Exchange Act, the Public Utility Holding Company Act, and the Rural Electrification Act. Congressman Robert Lee Doughton (North Carolina), as chairman of the powerful House Ways and Means Committee, helped with the passage of the National Industrial Recovery Act, the Social Security Act, and many New Deal fiscal measures. In the Senate, Majority Leader Joseph T. Robinson of Arkansas, who pushed the Emergency Banking Act through the Senate in less than a day, was diligent in his support of New Deal bills. Alben W. Barkley of Kentucky, who replaced Robinson as majority leader in 1937, proved to be even more effective than his predecessor in behalf of New Deal legislation. As chairman of the Senate Finance Committee, Mississippi's Pat Harrison was influential in the passage of such bills as the National Industrial Recovery Act, reciprocal trade agreements, social security, and revenue measures. Almost as important was South Carolina's James F. Byrnes, a close personal friend of the President's and a valuable liaison between Roosevelt and the Senate.

In the opening days of the New Deal, southern opposition to Roosevelt was almost nil. Senators Carter Glass and Harry F. Byrd of Virginia and Thomas P. Gore of Oklahoma expressed alarm at the New Deal's economic innovations and constitutional violations, raising questions about the first Agricultural Adjustment Act, the NRA, crop limitations, federal relief, old-age pensions, and the growing power of the central government. Other southerners were skeptical of New Deal measures, mainly on economic grounds, but in the early months of the New Deal, they were not willing to speak out directly against Roosevelt and his program. Among this group were Josiah W. Bailey (North Carolina), Walter

F. George (Georgia), Tom Connally (Texas), and Ellison D. ("Cotton Ed") Smith (South Carolina).

The greatest criticism of the early New Deal came not from the conservative right, but from the liberal left. Although Louisiana's Huey Long had assisted with Roosevelt's nomination in 1932 and had voted for such New Deal measures as home loans, farm relief, the Tennessee Valley Authority, prohibition repeal, and regulation of the stock market, the independent senator had opposed the new banking laws, NIRA, income taxes, and government purchase of silver. Said Long frankly on the Senate floor, "Whenever the administration has gone to the left I have voted with it, and whenever it has gone to the right I have voted against it." Long presented the Roosevelt administration with a serious threat when he unveiled his Share-Our-Wealth program, a rather nebulous and continually altered proposal which included confiscating the bank accounts of the wealthy and redistributing them so that all Americans would have money in the bank. The New Deal's Social Security Act and a "soak-the-rich" tax, both passed in 1935, were in some measure Roosevelt's attempt to steal Long's thunder.

While a few were openly critical of the New Deal's beginnings, most southern leaders before 1935 held their peace, realizing that an open break with the President would probably mean political suicide. The implementing of the so-called Second New Deal, which stressed reform over against relief and recovery, increased the grumbling of many southern Democrats. The Social Security bill, a far-reaching labor proposal, a new banking bill, a public-utility holding company measure, and the "soak-the-rich" tax scheme were more than many southern politicians could stomach. Furthermore, when the Supreme Court began striking down some of the major New Deal measures, including the NIRA and the first AAA, southern opponents were encouraged to speak out more bluntly against the administration. Roosevelt's overwhelming reelection in 1936, coupled with the Supreme Court's devastating attack upon his programs, spurred the President to suggest a reorganization of the Court, and this led to a showdown struggle between the President and southern Democrats. Had Senate Majority Leader Robinson of Arkansas not died just as the congressional battle over the court-reform bill began, Roosevelt might have won approval for his suggestion to add as many as six judges to the Supreme Court and to make seventy the mandatory retirement age for the entire federal judiciary. Robinson had enough southern votes pledged to assure passage of the bill, but his death released the pledges and the southerners were free to vote against "packing the Court." The bill went down to inglorious defeat as southerners expressed fear of constitutional violations in Roosevelt's apparent drive for power.

This surprising setback soon after the great election victory in 1936 stunned the President. He pledged to drive into oblivion those

Democrats who had failed to support him on the crucial court-reform scheme. The leaders of an opposition group which had coalesced during the maneuvering on court reform were anathema to him. The group consisted of Vice President Garner, senators Glass, Byrd, Smith, Harrison, Bailey, George, Richard Russell (Georgia), Robert Reynolds (North Carolina), Millard Tydings (Maryland), and Congressman Howard W. Smith (Virginia). In the 1938 congressional elections, Roosevelt attempted to purge the Democratic party of these defectors, and he boldly came out in favor of opponents of those men up for reelection. Southerners resented Roosevelt's interference in state primary elections, and George, Smith, and Tydings, three very painful thorns in the President's side, were returned to Washington by their constituencies. For the remainder of the New Deal, a behind-the-scene struggle was carried on between the New Deal administrators and southern congressmen, effectively neutralizing the final years of the New Deal. Thomas P. Gore had failed to win another term in 1936, but Carter Glass and Walter George continued to lead the vehement opposition to all the New Deal stood for. Despite the critics, Roosevelt garnered the support of other southerners such as William B. Bankhead and Lister Hill of Alabama; Sam Rayburn, Maury Maverick, and Lyndon Johnson of Texas; and Claude Pepper of Florida.

Those senators and congressmen who favored the New Deal were happy to have federal subsidies for farmers in a time of economic crisis, higher wage rates for laborers, regulation of industry and business for the benefit of the consumer, and public assistance to the needy, the sick, and the aged. Those who opposed the President often did so for political and personal reasons, but they were also concerned about issues long-revered in the South: states' rights, weakening of the nation's constitutional foundations, federal influence in the states, the crumbling of southern traditions, and alterations of the "southern way of life." If election results were an accurate barometer, the mass of southerners did not share their representatives' concern about the disappearance of the old way of life in the South. After supporting Roosevelt without undue enthusiasm, the South voted overwhelmingly for the President in 1936. In the depth of the nation's greatest depression, southerners were more concerned about food, clothing, shelter, and jobs than about preserving an old way of life. Conditions were such that some admitted that it was time for the old way to die. In any event, that was happening.

Southern Negroes also expressed confidence in Roosevelt. While most southern black voters cast their ballots for Hoover in 1932, continuing to align themselves with the party of Abraham Lincoln, they soon began to sense that a new protector of Negro interests occupied the White House. Despite his party label, Roosevelt was looked upon by Negroes as a saviour, especially by the poverty-stricken black tenant. If the

New Deal did not help the Negro farmer and tenant as much as it promised, the Negro nevertheless gained a measure of hope from the flurry of activities carried on by the New Deal in his behalf. The New Deal coalition, which included an uneasy alliance between northern urban voters and southern rural folk, was also based upon Roosevelt's appeal to black men. His economic programs assured him the support of the masses of Negroes in the North, and they also enveloped the southern voter. If few Negroes actually voted in the South in the 1930s, national Democratic politicians were aware of the potential vote of this minority group.

For several reasons, many white southerners felt uneasy within the New Deal coalition of which they were a part, and the role of the black in the alliance perturbed them most. Lily-white attitudes of the past continued to dominate, and the New Deal coalition foundered more than once on the shoals of the Negro in politics. Although Roosevelt was wise enough not to antagonize his white southern brethren deliberately, many of his northern followers were less concerned with southern feelings. They pushed particularly hard in the 1930s and early 1940s for a federal antilynching law as well as for revocation of the poll tax. Southerners successfully filibustered against these suggestions, but the fact that the Negro became a focal point for disagreement made southerners wary of the New Deal.

The President would have preferred not to face the Negro question, but the rising tide for minority rights coupled with an emergency on the international scene could not be ignored. In June 1941 Roosevelt issued an executive order which declared racial discrimination in defense industries to be contrary to the public interest and established a five-man Fair Employment Practices Committee to receive and investigate complaints of discrimination and to take appropriate steps to redress valid grievances. During World War II concerted efforts were made in Congress to enact legislation to establish a permanent Fair Employment Practices Commission. By parliamentary maneuvering in committees and on the floor of both houses, including several filibusters, southern Democrats were able to prevent the establishment of a permanent FEPC. Even though the war itself demanded prime attention from the entire nation, southerners were not so preoccupied that they sublimated their prejudices toward black people. They were much concerned about the Negro's role in the economic structure of the nation, and they were not eager to see the Negro break out of the economic bonds which had held him down for generations.

Southerners expressed displeasure toward various aspects of the Rooseveltian program by voting in large numbers for Republican candidate Thomas E. Dewey in the 1944 Presidential campaign, but in the electoral college the South remained solidly behind the President. How much additional opposition to Roosevelt might have developed in the South in view of the region's commitment to racial discrimination probably would have been related to how hard the President pushed the civil rights theme. The possibility of a more serious and open conflict between the South and the President was cut short by Roosevelt's death in 1945.

Democrats versus Dixiecrats

Pressures for Negroes to share in the promise of American life began to affect national politics in the 1930s to a greater extent than ever before, and they intensified during World War II. When the war was over, politicians were more than ever mindful of the presence of the largest minority in the nation. President Truman was receptive to the needs of Negroes, and from his earliest days in the White House he indicated his position on the subject. Less than two months after taking the Presidential oath in April 1945, Truman urged the House of Representatives Rules Committee to allow the House to vote upon a long-pending bill providing for a permanent Fair Employment Practices Commission. At the same time the new President also protested recent action by the House Appropriations Committee cutting off funds for the continuation of the wartime Fair Employment Practices Committee.

Southern members of Congress were outspokenly opposed to the temporary FEPC, and they only reluctantly agreed to an appropriation large enough to extend its life until June 1946. Even though this concession was made, the southerners had no intention of allowing the committee additional funds, nor would they permit the establishment of a permanent FEPC. Senator Bilbo and Representative John E. Rankin, both of Mississippi, led the emotion-laden attack against the FEPC. When Bilbo heard of a petition circulated in Georgia favoring the FEPC, he assumed that "the great majority of these petitioners, representing Negroes, Quislings of the white race, and other racial minorities, hail from the city of Atlanta, the hotbed of Southern Negro intelligentsia, Communists, pinks, Reds, and other off-brands of American citizenship in the South."

Despite this reaction, Truman delivered a comprehensive postwar message to Congress in September 1945 in which he suggested twenty-one guidelines for action on pressing social and economic matters, one of his recommendations being that the FEPC be made permanent. When administration leaders in Congress introduced a bill early in 1946 to establish a permanent FEPC, Mississippi's Senator James Eastland announced that if the bill became law he would recommend to his state's legislature that it protect the sovereignty of Mississippi by passing a nullification proclamation. Bilbo insisted that the FEPC was "nothing but a plot to put niggers to work next to your daughters and to run your business with niggers." A three-week filibuster prevented a vote on the measure.

In December 1946 Truman appointed the President's Committee on Civil Rights composed of fifteen prominent Americans, two of whom were southerners. In 1947 the committee issued a formal report in which it declared that the time had come to create a permanent nationwide system of guardianship for the civil rights of all Americans. Published under the title *To Secure These Rights,* the widely distributed report listed thirty-five specific recommendations for improving and protecting the civil rights of American citizens. In February 1948 Truman included ten recommendations of the committee in a special message to Congress. The four proposals most directly affecting the South included a permanent FEPC, an antilynching law, an anti–poll-tax law, and the prohibition of discrimination in interstate transportation facilities.

Southern reaction to the President's suggestions was immediate. Senator Byrd of Virginia asserted that the civil rights program constituted a "devastating broadside at the dignity of southern traditions and institutions" and that its passage might lead to bloodshed in the South. Representative John Bell Williams of Mississippi believed that Truman "has seen fit to run a political dagger into our backs and now he is trying to drink our blood." Many southern members of Congress accused Truman of playing to the northern Negro vote in view of the forthcoming Presidential election in November, and hints of a southern revolt in the 1948 election were made in both the House and the Senate within hours after Truman had delivered his message. Whatever Truman's motives may have been, and there are indications that the President was indeed politically motivated, there is no question concerning the motives of his detractors.

Mississippi's Governor Fielding Wright denounced the President's proposals and called upon southern Democrats to break away from the national Democratic party, which appeared to desire the destruction of southern institutions and traditions. At a special meeting of the Southern Governors Conference in March a resolution was passed asking that all southern state Democratic conventions pledge their Presidential electors to vote against any candidate in the November elections who favored civil rights legislation. Moreover, they specifically requested that southern delegates to the Democratic national convention be instructed to oppose Truman's nomination. By this time Truman had requested that his civil rights recommendations be turned into law, and he had pointedly stated that if Congress failed to act, he would make civil rights a central issue in his campaign for reelection.

Local Democratic party organizations in the southern states were divided by the collision course set by Truman and his opponents. Most state and local party leaders hoped to maneuver within the party framework to express their dissatisfaction with Truman and his drive for civil rights, and they were too deeply imbued with Democratic loyalty to leave the party, even over such an emotional issue as Negro rights. Other Democrats were willing to break with the party if it ignored their stand on civil rights. Alabama delegates to the forthcoming national convention were pledged to vote against any Presidential aspirant who favored civil rights, and some members of the delegation publicly announced that they would withdraw from the national convention if a strong civil rights statement was adopted there. The Mississippi Democratic executive committee meeting in Jackson in February resolved that Mississippi's Presidential electors and delegates to the national convention should vote against any candidate who favored the President's proposals. They also instructed the delegates to walk out of the convention if they were dissatisfied with the civil rights plank in the national platform. The committee then invited southern Democrats ("all true white Jeffersonian Democrats") to meet in Jackson in May to deal on a regional basis with the trend of the national party. At this meeting, dominated by the delegations from Mississippi and South Carolina, resolutions were passed urging all southern states to select delegates to the forthcoming convention pledged against any candidate who favored civil rights legislation. This group agreed to meet again in Birmingham after the national convention, if at the convention the national party came out in favor of a strong civil rights program.

When the Democratic convention met in Philadelphia in the summer of 1948, the national leaders of the party and the majority at the convention were not bluffed by recent southern actions. Led by Minneapolis's Mayor Hubert H. Humphrey, the convention rejected a mild civil rights plank recommended by the platform committee and instead adopted a strong one praising Truman and urging civil rights laws which would prevent discrimination in voting and employment and which would protect the civil liberties of all Americans. In response to the convention's action, all of Mississippi's delegates and about half of those from Alabama—a total of thirty-five—walked out as a band played "Dixie." Those southern delegates who remained supported Richard B. Russell against Truman, but their efforts were in vain. Senator Alben Barkley of Kentucky was named the Vice-Presidential nominee, but his support of the national party platform identified him with the national party, not with the South.

On July 17, two days after the adjournment of the national convention, the disgruntled southerners convened at Birmingham as planned, where they expressed the view that the Democratic party was anti-southern, disinterested in the South's traditional stands on such matters as states' rights and the role of the Negro in American society. This group of southern conservatives formed a third party named the States' Rights party, its members coming to be called Dixiecrats. The major leaders of this dissident southern faction were Governor J. Strom Thurmond of South Carolina and Governor Wright of Mississippi. Surprising no one, these men were unanimously nominated as the Presidential and Vice-Presidential candidates for the new party to run on a platform decrying national interference in state affairs.

The Dixiecrats had no hopes of winning the election. Their strategy was to take enough votes away from Truman so that neither he nor his Republican opponent, Thomas E. Dewey, could win a majority in the electoral college. With the election thrown into the House of Representatives, where each state delegation would have one vote, the southerners would have a political bargaining position strong enough to force the Democrats to promise support for southern demands. If the Democrats would not cooperate, the Dixiecrats would not hesitate to bargain with the Republicans. It was a grand and ambitious scheme with just enough possibility to intrigue many southerners.

The emergence of the Dixiecrats forced Democrats in the South to make a difficult choice. The Dixiecrats tried to appeal to southerners by arguing that they were "true Democrats," but they did not convince those who considered party regularity the highest of the political gods. Other Democrats who placed states' rights and civil rights at the top of their list of priorities bolted to the Dixiecrats, but in the end their numbers were not enough. The Dixiecrats won majorities in only South Carolina, Alabama, Mississippi, and Louisiana for a total of thirty-nine electoral votes. In the other southern states, where Negro populations were smaller and where a split in Democratic ranks might have given the states to the Republicans, Truman was the victor. Even in the states where the Dixiecrats won, they did so probably only because they had been able to have their candidates placed on the ballots as the regular Democratic nominees, thus binding the Democratic electors to Thurmond rather than Truman. If the Dixiecrats had been able to carry Texas, Arkansas, Georgia, and Florida their plan to cast the election into the House of Representatives would have succeeded. But their efforts met with failure, and the influence of southerners in the national Democratic party reached a new low.

After his upset victory over Dewey, Truman in his next State of the Union message emphatically demanded action on his whole civil rights program. The southern bloc in Congress stymied Truman's legislative plans for advancing civil rights during his second term in office by parliamentary maneuvering and filibustering, but it appeared to be only a matter of time before civil rights legislation would be passed.

At the end of the Truman era, the national Democratic party strove to bind up the wounds opened by the civil rights issue. The national convention in 1952 drew up a moderate plank on civil rights, and pointedly refused to bind all delegates to support the party's nominee in advance. Furthermore, Senator John J. Sparkman of Alabama was nominated for the Vice Presidency, in an effort to placate the South, to run with Illinois's liberal Governor Adlai E. Stevenson, the party's Presidential nominee. But the disaffected southerners were not to be appeased. General Dwight D. Eisenhower, the Republican nominee, carried Virginia, Tennessee, Florida, Texas, and Oklahoma, narrowly missing the electoral votes in Louisiana, Kentucky, and South Carolina. Eisenhower's great personal appeal was primarily responsible for his landslide victory, but in the South his vote totals were increased because of the alienation of southern Democrats from their own party. "Democrats for Eisenhower" clubs were formed, barbed reminders to the regular Democrats that the Dixiecrats were not yet willing to return to the fold, but revealing the Dixiecrats' reluctance to join the Republican ranks permanently. Unhappy with the New and Fair Deals, losing political power on the national scene, and admittedly fighting only a holding battle on the civil rights front, conservative southern Democrats girded up their loins for future battles, perhaps sensing that they had already lost the war.

Recent Presidential Elections

President Eisenhower was one of those rare Chief Executives whose popularity increased the longer he was in office, and this rising personal appeal was evident in the South as well as in the remainder of the nation. Southerners expressed their continued satisfaction with Eisenhower in the Presidential election of 1956, when Texas, Oklahoma, Louisiana, Tennessee, Kentucky, West Virginia, Virginia, and Florida cast their electoral votes for the President. In sixteen southern states Eisenhower won 6,367,208 popular votes compared to Stevenson's 5,824,084 votes. Political observers began to suspect that the Solid South had been broken, since Eisenhower had won so many southern votes in both 1952 and 1956. A close look, however, revealed that southerners were splitting their ballots. While voting for Eisenhower for the Presidency, they continued to support Democratic candidates for congressional seats and in state and local elections. Republican registrations did not rise appreciably during the Eisenhower years; southerners retained their traditional party allegiance, but they were more discriminating in casting their ballots.

While President Eisenhower was in office, two momentous steps were taken in the field of civil rights. In 1954 the Supreme Court handed down the famous *Brown* v. *Board of Education* (*Topeka*) decision, declaring segregated schools unconstitutional, and in 1957 the Congress finally passed a civil rights act, the first since the days of Reconstruction. Southerners expressed regret over both actions, but they rightly saddled the President with neither of these objectionable developments. The civil rights act was the work of Democrats under the leadership of Senate Majority Leader Lyndon Johnson of Texas, and the Supreme Court decision was made independent of the resident in the White House. When violence flared in Little Rock, Arkansas, following Governor Orval E. Faubus's use of the National Guard to prevent Negro students from entering an all-white high school, Eisenhower hesitated. Widely known for his humanitarian impulses, he preferred to let Arkansas solve its own problems. But the Little Rock situation became more acute, and the President was persuaded to provide the Negroes with federal military protection. Southerners sensed that Eisenhower was not eager to intervene, and they supported him even in the face of bayoneted paratroopers in Little Rock.

When the Democrats nominated John F. Kennedy for the Presidency in 1960, they realized that religion might become a factor in the election, since Kennedy was a Catholic and the Protestant South had reacted against a Catholic candidate in 1928. Naming Lyndon Johnson of Texas as Kennedy's running mate was a calculated move to hold southern voters in line. The strategy paid off in a razor-thin victory for the Democrats. Kennedy outpolled Republican candidate Richard M. Nixon by only 118,550 votes in over 68,000,000 cast. In the electoral college, Kennedy received 303 votes to Nixon's 219. Nixon carried Oklahoma, Tennessee, Kentucky, Virginia, and Florida, and the switch of Texas and two or three other southern states to him would have put the Republican candidate across. Johnson's presence on the ticket and his identification with the South may have been the difference between victory and defeat for the Democrats. By way of a footnote, fifteen Presidential electors in Mississippi, Oklahoma, and Alabama cast their ballots for Senator Harry F. Byrd of Virginia, a sign that some Democrats remained unhappy with the national Democratic party and the path it seemed to be following.

After the assassination of President Kennedy in November 1963, Lyndon Johnson assumed the Presidency, the first native southerner elevated to that position since Woodrow Wilson, and the first southern resident at that level since Andrew Johnson. The Democrats chose Johnson as their candidate in 1964, while the Republicans selected Barry Goldwater, senator from Arizona. Even though Johnson was a southerner and had not hesitated to appeal to voters in earlier days by opposing civil rights legislation, in recent years he had become more and more identified with a moderate position on that issue. Furthermore, he had risen in politics during the New Deal days as an ardent admirer of Franklin D. Roosevelt, and his concept of the Presidency and the role of the federal government in the nation's life was in a mold unacceptable to the South. By contrast, Republican Goldwater was a rock-ribbed conservative whose philosophical beliefs were closer to the South's than any candidate since

William McKinley. In his book, *The Conscience of a Conservative* (1960), and in his campaign speeches, Goldwater urged the curtailment of federal programs in the interest of greater freedom for the individual and the states. He opposed federal aid to education, federal price supports for agriculture, and federal expenditures for public projects. While claiming that he was personally against racial discrimination, he indicated that he would leave to the states the protection of civil rights. This was music to southern ears.

The early months of the 1964 Presidential campaign were confused by the candidacy of George Wallace, governor of Alabama. Governor Wallace had gained national notoriety a year before, when he took a public stand against the racial integration of the University of Alabama. Like the Dixiecrats of 1948, Wallace had become disenchanted with the national Democratic party's recent stands on civil rights, and he set out to throw the 1964 election into the House of Representatives, where he would have considerable bargaining power. Unlike the Dixiecrats, Wallace did not restrict his campaigning to the South. He set upon a nationwide campaign, entering a number of Democratic primaries in northern states. At first most observers looked upon Wallace's campaign as a joke, until the Alabamian polled 34 percent of the votes cast in the Wisconsin Democratic primary. A few weeks later he received 30 percent of the votes in the Indiana Democratic primary. As Wallace suspected, his segregationist platform appealed to voters outside the South, and regular Democrats were forced to take his candidacy seriously. But Wallace's candidacy was a more serious threat to Goldwater, whose political goals were not far from those of Wallace. Believing that he had accomplished his mission to "conservatize" the candidates of both major parties and that he did not need to continue as a candidate, Wallace withdrew from the race before the national conventions. Since he and Goldwater had similar political beliefs, Wallace was convinced that his continued candidacy would only assure that the "liberal" Johnson would be reelected.

Under these circumstances, Goldwater carried his home state of Arizona, plus Louisiana, Mississippi, Alabama, Georgia, and South Carolina, the five Deep South states which in the past had been most committed to the Democratic party. Unquestionably Goldwater's stand on the role of the states in regard to Negro rights was an important factor in this redrawing of the political map. Had Wallace remained in the race, he might well have carried these five states, with the Republican candidate winning only Arizona in the electoral college. As it was, Lyndon Johnson rode to victory on a popular and electoral landslide.

When President Johnson announced that he would not be a candidate in the 1968 election, Vice President Hubert H. Humphrey and Senator Robert F. Kennedy, brother of the late assassinated President, quickly emerged as the major contenders for the Democratic nomination.

When the second Kennedy was assassinated in June on the night of his victory in the California state primary, Humphrey became the leader, although he was challenged by Minnesota's Senator Eugene J. McCarthy, who had first entered the race against Lyndon Johnson to protest his Vietnam policy. Humphrey received the Democratic nomination and the chance to run against Richard M. Nixon, to whom the Republicans had turned after the Goldwater debacle.

By now a seasoned professional who had been on the political scene since the early 1950s, Nixon sensed that the South remained disenchanted with the Democratic party. Carefully calculating his campaign, he reasoned that he could win the election if he could carry the South and the West, acknowledging that the urban eastern states would as usual line up in the Democratic column. While Nixon undoubtedly considered many factors when he tapped Maryland Governor Spiro T. Agnew as his Vice-Presidential running mate, observers were quick to note that Agnew was attractive to southerners because of his residence and political beliefs. Newsmen assumed that Agnew's selection and Nixon's desire to win the South were closely related, and they began to refer to Republican campaign efforts as the "southern strategy." Although Nixon never publicly admitted the existence of such a strategy, he campaigned more in the South than any other Republican Presidential candidate in recent times.

During the campaign Nixon stated that if elected he would appoint a conservative judge to fill a vacancy on the Supreme Court. When he became President, he nominated U. S. Fourth Circuit Court Judge Clement F. Haynsworth, Jr. of South Carolina for the position. The Senate refused to consent to the appointment after hearings revealed that a possible conflict existed between Haynsworth's business interests and his role as a jurist; furthermore, the southern judge had drawn attacks from civil rights groups for his conservative decisions in that area. The Senate also rejected Nixon's second nominee, Judge G. Harrold Carswell of the Fifth Circuit Court. Although Carswell disavowed racist statements he had made twenty years earlier, investigation of his record led to charges that the Floridian was a mediocre judge, and after a close vote the Senate rejected Carswell too. Nixon stated that since the Senate apparently would refuse to confirm *any* southerner for this post, he was forced to turn to a northern judge for the appointment. Because of this geographical emphasis in the selection, many of the President's political opponents were more than ever convinced of the existence of a "southern strategy."

A possible hindrance to Republican efforts in the 1968 campaign had been the Presidential candidacy of George Wallace. Unable to succeed himself as governor, Wallace had successfully run his wife for the post in 1966, blatantly admitting that a "vote for Lurleen is a vote for George." With Alabama as his base and segregation as his major theme,

Wallace began campaigning early in 1968, drawing large crowds wherever he spoke, both in and out of the South. After several legal battles, he was able to place his name on the ballot in all fifty states in the Union. While race-baiting was Wallace's forte, the name of his new party—the American Independent party—indicated that he was interested in appealing to the patriotism of Americans as well as in trying to entice them away from the traditional parties. He orated against Communists ("little pinkos and left-wingers"), against both Democrats and Republicans, against federal intervention in states' affairs, against the crumbling of established American institutions, and against the "Warren Court," but most of all he played upon white American fears and dislike of the black man. Wallace insisted that he was for segregation but against racism. In an era of the "white backlash" against recent Negro gains, few of his supporters dwelled on semantics. Both major-party candidates took Wallace's campaign seriously, and rightly so.

The exciting campaign saw Nixon's early lead in the opinion polls fade in the final two weeks as Humphrey's campaign finally got rolling, ending with Nixon and Humphrey in a virtual dead heat. Of the total votes Nixon received 43.5 percent, Humphrey 43 percent, and Wallace 13.5 percent. Nixon polled only 350,000 more popular votes than Humphrey in an election in which 72,000,000 votes were cast; Wallace drew more than 9,000,000. Nixon won 302 electoral votes to Humphrey's 191 and Wallace's 45. In the South the Republican candidate captured South Carolina, Virginia, Florida, North Carolina, Tennessee, Oklahoma, Missouri, and Kentucky. Wallace carried Arkansas, Louisiana, Mississippi, Alabama, and Georgia. Humphrey won West Virginia, Maryland, and Texas, the latter probably only because of his association with the Johnson administration. Nixon's victories in the southern states were enough to assure him of national victory. The shifting of a few crucial votes could have given Humphrey the election, or put the contest in the House of Representatives where Wallace would have become the kingmaker. Most observers agreed that Wallace's candidacy probably hurt Nixon more than Humphrey. Without Wallace in the race, Nixon might well have carried most of the states that went to the Alabamian. In view of the voting patterns in the Presidential elections since 1952, it seemed safe to say that by 1968 the Republican party had become a formidable factor in southern politics, at least in the Presidential contests.

Wallace influenced the outcome of the election in several states; his support ranged from 1 percent in Hawaii to 65 percent in Alabama. More importantly, because of the closeness of the contest, he came within a whisker of his minimum aim of denying victory to the major-party candidates and forcing them to bargain for his support. This possibility frightened many national leaders, and his announcement soon after the November election that he intended to run again in 1972 stirred sluggish legislative machinery to alter the antiquated electoral system in such a way that a Presidential election could not end in a deadlock, that is, that a third-party candidate like Wallace could never be in a position to name the next President.

Civil rights had become one of the dominant issues in Presidential elections since World War II, and politicians on both sides used it to win votes. Many of those who favored civil rights were looking for support not only from white liberals, but from black voters as well. In 1948 Truman received approximately 70 percent of all votes cast by Negroes. In 1952 Stevenson won about 60 percent of these votes, although his Negro supporters dropped to about 50 percent in 1956, undoubtedly the Negro's response to favorable events during the Eisenhower administration. In 1960 both Kennedy and Nixon courted the Negro vote. Nixon had often made appeals to the Negroes, having his picture taken with prominent black leaders and generally attempting to reveal his friendliness to the Negro. During the campaign Kennedy made a sympathetic telephone call to Mrs. Martin Luther King, Jr., when her husband was put in jail after leading a civil rights demonstration in Atlanta. Kennedy was a sincere supporter of Negro civil rights, but this action dramatized his interest as no other event in the campaign. Kennedy received about 85 percent of the Negro votes, and Nixon later claimed, perhaps correctly, that he could have won had he campaigned harder for the Negro vote.

In 1964 Johnson, by now solidly identified with the civil rights movement, appealed to the Negro voter with strong statements about the need for more civil rights legislation, while Goldwater and his supporters made covert and overt appeals to racism. In Virginia, North Carolina, Florida, and Tennessee the Negro vote was greater than Johnson's majorities over Goldwater, and blacks could fairly claim that Johnson would not have won those states without their support. In 1968 Nixon reasoned that he had a better chance to win the election by appealing to whites in the South, than by trying to win the Negro voter. Liberal candidate Hubert Humphrey, long identified with civil rights, outwardly solicited Negro votes, and about 90 percent of the voting blacks supported Humphrey, the high percentage undoubtedly related to Nixon's overtures to white southerners. Southern blacks voted for candidates in about the same proportions as the national Negro voting patterns throughout most of the period from 1948 to 1968, although the number of Negroes voting in the South was fairly small.

If white southerners suspected at times during the post-World War II period that their influence was waning in Presidential elections, they found comfort in the fact that their representatives held powerful positions of leadership in the Congress. One-party politics and the seniority system had for years placed southern representatives in the mainstream of power on Capitol Hill, and this situation continued to prevail in every Congress controlled by the Democrats after the war. For example, of the thirty-six standing committees in the Senate and House of Representatives in 1963, twenty-three had southern Democrats as chairmen, and on twenty-three committees the second ranking member was a southerner. These southerners had much power over committee investigations, hearings, and the progress of both major and minor legislation. And when the Democrats were out of power, southerners were the leading members of the minority opposition. On occasion they joined with conservative Republicans against northern, liberal Democrats on issues involving states' rights, property rights, and civil rights, and although this informal coalition did not always win the battles, when it did, many southerners cheered. Several important civil rights acts were passed in the 1950s and 1960s, but southern congressional representatives delayed and watered down these acts and prevented the passage of others.

State and Local Politics

Since colonial days the county had been central to local government and politics in the South, and in the middle years of the twentieth century county politicians continued to play a major role in regional politics. Self-perpetuating oligarchies, usually composed of land-rich planters, had dominated local government in the South before the Civil War. After the war the political center of gravity moved from the countryside to the county seat, and before 1900 county residents had replaced the planters as the governing class. When these cliques of local politicians came to dominate county politics, "courthouse rings" developed in most of the more than fifteen hundred counties in the southern states in the twentieth century. If laws prohibited a person from serving more than one or two terms as county treasurer, in the next election he ran for county sheriff or court clerk. Some petty officeholders spent a lifetime rotating from one county position to another. In a region dominated by one-party politics, party affiliation was unimportant as voters continued to elect the members of the local oligarchies to office.

Local merchants, small businessmen, and lawyers normally controlled the courthouse offices. In tune with the old Bourbons' interest in attracting business and industry to the South, these men matched those efforts in behalf of "progress." In cooperation with the local chambers of commerce, they unabashedly contacted industrial decision-makers in their attempts to entice industry to their little urban centers. The great textile crusade of the late nineteenth century was a forerunner of these efforts in the twentieth century. No town of more than a few hundred souls was immune to the "industrial fever," as businessmen and local politicians came to believe that an industrial plant would solve economic problems as well as add prestige to the community. "Looking for an industrial site? Consider Abbeville, Alabama" was typical of dozens of signs erected along the right-of-ways of the South's modern highways.

Even though the small town booster-businessman and lawyer had replaced the landowner in county politics, the philosophy of the new leaders was not far different from the former rulers. They were generally conservative in political and social outlook, viewing with suspicion social change and liberal concepts. Getting ahead in business and the professions, making money, and enjoying the benefits of material possessions were often personal goals. Though these new leaders preached the doctrine of hard work, they did not hesitate to use economic or political "pull" for their own benefit. The county seat leader was usually suspicious of intellectuals, and a part of his folklore was a belief in God, the United States, and democracy. Offering lip service to the democratic credo of liberty, equality, and majority rule, he did not extend these concepts to cover Republicans or people with black skins. Jasper B. Shannon has written that the ghost of the antebellum landed gentry hovered over Cottonton, Millville, and Tobaccoburg.

Better known than the thousands of nameless county seat politicians were the politicians who controlled the large urban municipalities of the recent South. A coalition of interests to be called "The Crump Machine" gained control of Memphis in 1932, and Ed H. Crump came to dominate not only that Mississippi River metropolis but Tennessee state politics as well until a reversal occurred at the state level in 1948. Even after that date, "Boss Crump" still controlled every important office in Memphis and Shelby County, as well as one U. S. congressman and one U. S. senator. For over a decade and a half, Crump's grasp of Memphis was so great that his candidates for state office usually received over 85 percent of the Shelby County vote. Crump came into power in Memphis on a reform ticket, and his studious dissemination of a picture of himself as a reformer gave him unparalleled support. Critics generally conceded that Memphis was a cleaner city and had a more efficient government under The Crump Machine, but these blessings came without complete freedom or liberty. Crump used the traditional weapons to discipline those who considered opposing him: threats of increased tax valuation, the overly technical enforcement of a little-used city ordinance, the loss of city business. Businesses and businessmen kowtowed to Crump or they were smashed. Crump was accused of corruption, but no instances of stealing from the public till were found. The main basis for his success lay in general voter apathy. With a well-honed political machine, he was able to get out the affirmative votes when needed, and he laid the basis for machine rule of Memphis for years after his political demise.

If not as powerful, well entrenched, or well known as The Crump

Machine, other political organizations from time to time held unusual control over southern municipalities such as New Orleans, Atlanta, and Louisville. As with The Crump Machine, many of them were not content to rule a city, and they influenced if not controlled state politics as well. Often these statewide machines were closely associated with a well-known politician. The Robert S. Maestri organization of New Orleans is a case in point. Elected to the United States Senate in 1900, Furnifold M. Simmons obtained a vicelike grip over North Carolina state politics. His re-election in 1912 against strong opposition showed who was boss of North Carolina, as he used county cliques and federal patronage to his political advantage. Simmons broke with the national Democratic party in 1928 over the prohibition issue, and he was ousted from power in 1930. In the 1930s a clique led by O. Max Gardner, Clyde R. Hoey, and Otis M. Mull replaced Simmons. Their successors in the postwar years built upon the organization of these men, and whatever their shortcomings, they provided North Carolina with satisfactory state government.

Harry F. Byrd become governor of Virginia in 1926, building upon a base laid by Thomas S. Martin and others, and soon dominating the state's politics. After gaining the confidence of Virginia voters by espousing and inaugurating "business progressivism," Byrd consolidated his position so that he remained in power into the post-World War II period, and his machine was not totally wrecked when he died in 1966. Byrd's conservative politics in the United States Senate was the despair of liberals, but most Virginians were happy with his stands and the way his lieutenants ran the state government. Virginia became a model for others who aspired to run a state efficiently, without apparent corruption, and without burdensome taxes.

Not all southern states were controlled by boss rule, however, and in many of them voters were able to choose their own leaders. After World War II, gubernatorial candidates frequently stressed economy in government, lighter tax burdens, and industrial development, concepts which held great appeal for southerners. State legislators were often elected on the same kinds of platforms, and except in the field of education, legislatures were usually fairly tight-fisted with state monies. Along with conservative spending, state administrations had an overriding devotion to the gospel of industrialization and business favoritism. To this extent they were carbon copies of county seat political leaders. Although the Supreme Court's "one-man, one-vote" decision in 1962 was a giant step in overcoming antiquated legislative apportionment practices which had exaggerated the weight of conservative rural areas, in 1970 southern state legislatures were still dominated by the political philosophy of an older South. Migration, urbanization, the growth of suburbia, industrialization, and many other factors would no doubt ultimately break ruralism's stranglehold on southern state politics.

A Two-Party South?

In the first half of the twentieth century the South was to a large extent a one-party region. After the abortive Populist revolt in the 1890s, the Democratic party commanded the political scene. The South did not always express its political solidarity in national Presidential elections, but Democrats generally reigned supreme in congressional elections as well as in state and local contests. Between 1900 and 1950 over 95 percent of all congressional contests in the South were won by Democrats, and the percentage was almost as high for state and local contests. This does not mean, however, that there were no political battles. On the contrary, factionalism among Democrats was inevitably present, and Democratic primaries were invariably knock-down-drag-out battles among several contenders. Sometimes the primaries were fought on the basis of personalities, other times they were battles over issues between conservative and liberal aspirants, but always they were looked upon by southerners as *the* important political races. The traditionally lower voting ratios of southerners in general elections attest to this fact, as well as to weak Republican party opposition.

Arguments for a one-party system in the South were persuasive to southerners. A genuine two-party system might have resulted in Negroes holding the political balance of power, and this was a possibility to be prevented at all costs. The specter of the Negro as a threat to white supremacy was by itself enough to justify a one-party system. If Democrats controlled elections, restrictions on voting could be enforced, preventing the majority of blacks from being active in the political process. Another argument for a one-party system was that it insured long tenure to southern congressmen who in turn secured influential committee assignments in the House and Senate. Throughout the twentieth century, when the Democrats were in the majority in the House and the Senate, southerners generally held over one-half of the chairmanships of the committees of Congress, and they often occupied other leadership positions: Speaker of the House, presiding officer of the Senate, and majority leader. Once a man was elected to Congress, he used the rule of seniority as one of his main arguments for his perpetual return. Long-tenured southerners were supposedly in a position to speak up for the South and protect its interests on the national scene. Certainly they often had a disproportionate influence upon national legislation because of their favored positions. Perhaps equally important were the indirect consequences of long and powerful tenured positions. In modern times South Carolina's Representative L. Mendel Rivers controlled military appropriations by virtue of his chairmanship of the House Armed Services Committee.

This favored position forced the armed services to court Rivers, and South Carolina had millions of dollars poured into its economy through the establishment or enlargement of military bases and defense installations, and through the awarding of government contracts to South Carolina-based firms.

Despite the benefits derived from a one-party system, the Democratic stranglehold on southern politics began to lessen at mid-twentieth century. The southern wing of the Republican party, which had existed primarily for federal patronage when the Republicans controlled Washington, was revitalized after World War II. The growth of business and industry gave more southerners a feeling of kinship to the traditional philosophies of the Republican party. Furthermore, the industrial development had attracted many northern Republicans to the South as executives and managers, and they desired to remain in their accustomed political home. As urbanization raced ahead in the South, more and more southerners moved up into middle class affluence: suburban homes, two automobiles, private swimming pools, and conservative values reflective of the Republican party. Long-time conservative Democrats, who in the past had no place to turn when they were frustrated by the national Democratic party, began to move into the Republican ranks. The prime example was Senator Strom Thurmond, leader of the abortive Dixiecrat revolt, who moved into the Republican fold in 1964. The agony of jumping the political fence was hard for some Democrats to take, but once the decision was made, they worked to refurbish their new political home. These new individuals and groups within the party were not content with only the plums of patronage for the local party leadership. They wanted to be viable opponents to the Democrats.

As a result of the growth of the Republican party, general election contests were less and less automatically won by Democrats, and by the 1950s Republicans began to run candidates with more than occasional hopes of winning. In fact, Republicans began to win enough elections that the feat was no longer considered a fluke. In 1962 Oklahoma elected Henry Bellmon as governor, the first Republican to win that post since statehood, and he was followed in 1966 by Dewey Bartlett, another Republican. Bellmon moved on to the Senate in 1968, only the third Republican ever to represent Oklahoma in the Upper House. In 1960 John Tower was elected to the Senate from Texas, the first time that state had sent a Republican to the Senate since Reconstruction days. In 1962 the Republican gubernatorial candidate in Texas received 45 percent of the votes, and Republicans ran close contests in eighteen of the state's twenty-three congressional districts. In that same year, former Confederate states sent four new Republican congressmen to Washington to join the seven others already there. Furthermore, Republicans began to win local offices in the Deep South, such as the mayor's position in Mobile, Alabama, and the public prosecutor's post in Lowndes County, Mississippi. In 1964 the Deep South sent seven new Republican congressmen to Washington five of whom were from Alabama, the first in ninety-two years. Republican state legislators, constables, justices of the peace, and other petty officers won scattered elections across the South. By 1970 it was not uncommon for Republicans to win both major and minor offices in the South, or at least for them to give the Democrats real contests many times. These examples of growing Republicanism in the South do not mean that a two-party system has developed or will develop overnight. Breaks in the Democratic ranks will no doubt continue, but generations of tradition, past voting patterns, and party allegiances are not easily overcome, and Republicans will have to work hard for their gains.

The crucial factor in how fast a two-party system develops in the region is the Negro, the basis for the one-party system. Civil rights acts passed in 1957 and following * usually contained provisions designed to aid Negroes to register and vote, and while they were far from totally effective, this legislation was responsible for the addition of thousands of Negroes to the South's political world. For example, after the passage of the Voting Rights Act of 1965, nearly 200,000 blacks were immediately added to the voting rolls in the South. Registration of black voters in eleven southern states rose from 25 percent of eligible voters registered in 1956 to 46.5 percent in 1966. Negro voter registration jumped 50 percent in five Deep South states within twelve months after passage of the voting rights legislation. In 1965 Negroes comprised 6.7 percent of the registered voters in Mississippi; in Alabama, 19.3 percent; in Louisiana, 31.6 percent; in South Carolina, 37.3 percent. By 1968 Negroes constituted a *majority* of the registered voters in these four Deep South states: Mississippi (59.8), Alabama (51.6), Louisiana (58.9), South Carolina (51.2). In Mississippi, Negro registrations rose from 20,000 in 1965 to 236,000 by 1969.

Divergent forces tugged and pulled at the prospective southern Negro registrant. Some blacks attempted to organize third parties based upon race, but these were not widely supported. Many Negroes were inclined to join the Republican party because of their hatred for the Democrats who had dominated the southern political scene, often using fear of the black to strengthen their political power base with whites. Furthermore, the Democrats' emphasis upon states' rights offended Negroes who were coming to look to the national government in Washington for assistance with their cause. On the other hand, the Goldwater campaign of 1964 tended to alienate the Negro registrant and voter, and the Nixon administration appeared not to appeal widely to the Negro. In 1964 the Supreme Court ruled that separate black and white voter lists were illegal, and it is impossible to state with accuracy the Negroes' political preferences. The best estimates are that after 1965 southern Negroes preferred

* For details of these acts, see Chapter XVIII.

the Democratic party over the Republicans by a ratio of about two to one. Apparently Negroes believed that they could have more influence by joining the majority party in the South rather than spending energy refurbishing the minority organization.

In the voting booth, party label meant less to black than to white. Negro Democrats did not hesitate to vote for candidates, whatever their label, who refused to espouse racial hatred. In Alabama thousands of Negroes voted in Democratic primaries in May 1966, the first major election in the South after the passage of the Voting Rights Act of 1965. In the June 1966 primaries, some 35,000 Mississippi Negroes cast their ballots, the largest number of blacks to vote in the state in the twentieth century. In the general elections in November 1966 Negroes supplied the winning margin for a U. S. senator's campaign victory in South Carolina, the election of Arkansas's Republican governor, Winthrop Rockefeller, and victories in at least two U. S. congressmen's races in other southern states. In 1967 Republican gubernatorial candidate Rubel Phillips openly campaigned for Negro support in Alabama, perhaps a portent of the changing political scene in the Deep South.

Blacks were not content only to register and to vote. Much to the chagrin of white southerners, they began to run for political office. Leading the political parade was Julian Bond, publicity director for the Student Nonviolent Coordinating Committee and son of Horace Mann Bond, well-known historian and dean at Atlanta University. When Bond garnered 82 percent of the vote in one of Atlanta's largely Negro districts, he was elected to the Georgia House of Representatives in June 1965. The state legislators seated seven other Negroes at the beginning of the session in January 1966, the first to serve in the assembly since 1907, but they denied Bond a seat, allegedly because of his opposition to United States involvement in Vietnam. While one thousand demonstrators marched on the state capitol in Atlanta to protest this action, Bond filed suit in federal court to obtain his seat, but the court upheld the right of the legislators to refuse to admit him. The following year he was re-elected and admitted to the state assembly. As a delegate to the national Democratic convention in 1968, Bond received nationwide television publicity when his name was suggested for the Vice-Presidential nomination, but because he was only twenty-nine years old, he was compelled to withdraw. This handsome, articulate, young politician served as inspiration to other Negroes aspiring to political office.

In the 1966 elections a number of blacks entered various local elections held throughout the South. L. D. Amerson won the sheriff's race in Macon County, Alabama, the first Negro to hold an elective office in a southern county in the twentieth century. In that same summer, sixteen blacks won local offices in five heavily populated Negro counties in Mississippi, and ten others won places in runoff primaries, only to be defeated by slim majorities. In 1967 New Orleans House District No. 20 elected a Negro to the Louisiana legislature; Mrs. Georgia Davis of Louisville was elected to the Kentucky senate; and Dr. W. Ferguson Reid of Richmond was sent to the Virginia state legislature. Holmes County, Mississippi, elected Robert G. Clark to the state legislature, and twenty-one other Negroes won elections to local offices in the state, including district constables, justices of the peace, district and county supervisors, members of boards of education, and deputy sheriffs. In 1969 Charles Evers, brother of Medgar Evers who only recently had been shot and killed from ambush because he had urged voting rights for blacks, was elected mayor of Fayette, Mississippi, the first Negro mayor elected in Mississippi in one hundred years. In 1969 eighty-one Negroes held elective offices in Mississippi. Approximately five hundred Negroes had been elected to political posts in the southern states between 1965 and 1970. At its state convention in March 1970 the South Carolina Democratic party elected a Negro as its vice chairman and rejected a platform plank which Negro delegates regarded as an indirect endorsement of separate school systems. These victories indicated the Negro's determination to be involved actively in the political process.

White determination to ban Negro political activity was still present in the South in 1970, and it was not likely to end soon even though the barriers continued to fall. Economic pressure, custom, fear on the part of the Negro, and white administration of primary machinery still prevented many blacks from voting. In the heat of the civil rights movement, the greatest detriment to Negro voting was the Negro himself. In a region not known for high voting ratios, even among whites, blacks were not trained in their responsibilities in citizenship. If all barriers to Negroes were suddenly removed, large percentages of the qualified blacks would still fail to vote. The southern Negro had a long way to go yet before he could or would become a significant part of the American democratic political process. Even so the growth of the Republican party and the increased number of Negro voters and officeholders were enough to alter old relationships and forewarn the South of major political changes in the future.

Suggestions for Further Reading

Many of the volumes listed at the end of the previous chapter may be profitably read for the period after 1933. Key's volumes should be supplemented by Alexander Heard's *A Two-Party South?* (Chapel Hill: Univ. North Carolina, 1952). Avery Leiserson (ed.), *The American South in the 1960's* * (New York: Praeger, 1964) is a collection of recently written, informative essays with much political information. John Fenton, *Politics in the Border States* (New Orleans: Hauser Press, 1957) and Jasper B. Shannon, *Toward a New Politics in the South* (Knoxville: Univ. Tennessee, 1949) are thorough studies. Ellis G. Arnall, *The Shore Dimly Seen* (Philadelphia: Lippincott, 1946) contains the comments of a twentieth-century politician on southern conditions. James T. Patterson, *Congressional Conservatism and the New Deal* (Lexington: Univ. Kentucky, 1967) necessarily devotes an unusual amount of attention to southern congressmen. Frank Freidel, *F. D. R. and the South* (Baton Rouge: Louisiana State Univ., 1965) is brief and disappointing. The best one-volume work on the New Deal is William E. Leuchtenburg, *Franklin D. Roosevelt and the New Deal* * (New York: Harper & Row, 1963), but several chapters in George B. Tindall, *The Emergence of the New South, 1913–1945* (Baton Rouge: Louisiana State Univ., 1967) focus specifically on southern politicians and the New Deal and are therefore more valuable. Much work still needs to be done on the relationship of Roosevelt, the New Deal, and the South.

Southern political behavior has been studied by the following: Cortez A. M. Ewing, *Primary Elections in the South: A Study in Uniparty Politics* (Norman, Okla.: Univ. Oklahoma, 1953) and *Congressional Elections, 1896–1944: The Sectional Basis of Political Democracy in the House of Representatives* (Norman, Okla.: Univ. Oklahoma, 1947); Taylor Cole and John H. Hallowell (eds.), *The Southern Political Scene, 1938–1948* (Gainesville, Fla.: Univ. Florida, 1948); Joseph L. Bernd, *Grass Roots Politics in Georgia: The County Unit System and the Importance of the Individual Voting Community in Bifactional Elections, 1942–1954* (Atlanta: Emory Univ. Research Committee, 1960); Alexander Heard and Donald S. Strong (eds.), *Southern Primaries and Elections, 1920–1949* (University, Ala.: Univ. Alabama, 1950); L. M. Holland, *The Direct Primary in Georgia Politics* (Norman, Okla.: Univ. Oklahoma, 1953); Frederick D. Ogden, *The Poll Tax in the South* (University, Ala.: Univ. Alabama, 1958).

Books on southern politics since World War II are limited, but numerous articles in scholarly journals help fill the void: Ader, "Why the Dixiecrats Failed," *Journal of Politics,* vol. 15 (1953); Carleton, "The Fate of Our Fourth Party," *Yale Review,* vol. 38 (1948–49); Lemmon,

"Ideology of the 'Dixiecrat' Movement," *Social Forces,* vol. 30 (1951–52); Grantham, "Politics Below the Potomac," *Current History,* vol. 35 (1958); Strong, "The Presidential Election in the South, 1952," *Journal of Politics,* vol. 17 (1955); Prothro and others, "Two-Party Voting in the South: Class vs. Party Identification," *American Political Science Review,* vol. 52 (1958); Lerner, "The Outlook for a Party Realignment," *Virginia Quarterly Review,* vol. 25 (1949); Cosman, "Presidential Republicanism in the South, 1960," *Journal of Politics,* vol. 24 (1962); Dauer, "Recent Southern Political Thought," *ibid.,* vol. 10 (1948); Harris, "States Rights and Vested Interests," *ibid.,* vol. 15 (1953); La Palombora, "Pressure, Propaganda, and Political Action in the Elections of 1950," *ibid.,* vol. 14 (1952). Theodore H. White, *The Making of the President, 1960* * (New York: Atheneum, 1961) is a fascinating account of the campaign and election of John F. Kennedy to the Presidency. White's volume * on the 1964 election (New York: Atheneum, 1965) is less skillfully done, but it also contains much information about the South's role in the national campaign. Comments upon Richard Nixon's "southern strategy" are numerous in that author's volume * on the 1968 election (New York: Atheneum, 1969). Recently published is Harold M. Hollingsworth (ed.), *Essays on Recent Southern Politics* (Austin: Univ. Texas, 1970).

Margaret Price, *The Negro Voter in the South* (Atlanta: Southern Regional Council, 1957) and *The Negro and the Ballot in the South* (Atlanta: Southern Regional Council, 1959) are written by an expert on southern politics. Hugh D. Price, *The Negro and Southern Politics: A Chapter of Florida History* (New York: New York Univ., 1957) covers the period from 1944 to 1956 in a specific state and is a good in-depth study, as is Andrew Buni, *The Negro in Virginia Politics, 1902–1965* (Charlottesville: Univ. Virginia, 1967). Donald R. Matthews and James W. Prothro, *Negroes and the New Southern Politics* (New York: Harcourt, Brace & World, 1966) is a more general study. Bernard Taper, *Gomillion Versus Lightfoot, The Tuskegee Gerrymander Case* * (New York: McGraw-Hill, 1962) is a brief description of attempts to prevent Negroes from voting in Tuskegee, Alabama. Two volumes which focus upon Negro leadership in the South are Margaret E. Burgess, *Negro Leadership in a Southern City* * (Chapel Hill: Univ. North Carolina, 1962) and Lewis M. Killian and Charles Grigg, *Racial Crisis in America: Leadership in Conflict* * (Englewood Cliffs: Prentice-Hall, 1964). Eli Ginzberg and Alfred E. Eichner, *The Troublesome Presence: American Democracy and the Negro* * (New York: Free Press of Glencoe, 1964) is an excellent summary of earlier studies on the Negro in American politics. Penetrating essays on the Negro in twentieth-century politics are contained in Samuel Lubell, *White and Black: Test of a Nation* * (New York: Harper & Row, 1964). Essien U. Essien-Udom, *Black Nationalism: A Search for an Identity in America* * (Chicago: Univ. Chicago, 1962) and Harold Isaacs,

The New World of Negro Americans * (New York: John Day, 1963) relate the impact of the rise of new African nations upon the American Negro.

A symposium on the southern Negro voter, published in the *Journal of Negro Education,* vol. 26 (1957), details the rising influence of the Negro voter in southern elections. Also worthy of attention are these essays: Alilunas, "Legal Restrictions on the Negro in Politics," *Journal of Negro History,* vol. 25 (1940); Hainsworth, "The Negro and the Texas Primaries," *ibid.,* vol. 28 (1943); Overacker, "The Negro's Struggle for Participation in Primary Elections," *ibid.,* vol. 30 (1945); Van Deusen, "The Negro in Politics," *ibid.,* vol. 21 (1936); Bernd and Holland, "Recent Restrictions upon Negro Suffrage: The Case of Georgia," *Journal of Politics,* vol. 21 (1959); Swisher, "The Supreme Court and the South," *ibid.,* vol. 10 (1948).

* Available in paperback.

CHAPTER XVII

THE RISE OF JIM CROW

In the year slavery was abolished in the United States, approximately 4,440,000 Negroes constituted the nation's largest racial minority, the overwhelming majority of these being former slaves residing in the southern states. By 1900 the black population had doubled, and in 1960 the figure had doubled again, standing at nearly 20,000,000. During the same period the white population was also rising rapidly, and the percentage of blacks in the country dropped slightly from 14 in 1860 to 11 in 1960. The South's proportion of the nation's total Negro population declined relatively during the same years. From 1860 to 1900 over 90 percent of the nation's blacks lived in the South, and while that percentage dwindled with each decennial census in the twentieth century, in 1960 over 50 percent of American Negroes still lived in the South. In 1860, 37 percent of the residents in the South were Negroes, with black majorities in Mississippi and South Carolina and near majorities in three other states. In 1960 the South's population remained 20 percent black, although no southern state had a Negro majority, the ratio in Mississippi and South Carolina having been reduced to 37 and 32 percent respectively. While the falling percentages in the twentieth century are a story in themselves, for one hundred years the great majority of the Negroes in the United States lived in the South. The presence of the black man, his influence upon the region, his relationship to the whites, how he acted and was acted upon, and his role in the society constituted an important facet of the South's history.

The Infancy of Segregation

Because the Thirteenth Amendment prohibited involuntary servitude, millions of black slaves were legally freed, a crucial step in the history of freedom in the United States. But for most of the century to follow, Negro Americans were second-class citizens, with little participation in the political, economic, and social activities of the majority population. True, slavery was gone and the Negro was no longer a marketable chattel object, but except for a brief period during radical Reconstruction, when the Negro experienced a degree of freedom, progress toward the level of freedom enjoyed by white Americans was minimal. At times, the Negro's position was so low and his isolation so great that he appeared to be more degraded than when he was in slavery. As a slave he at least had value as property.

The primary reason for the lowly condition in which the slave found himself stemmed from the racial attitudes of the dominant white majority. Americans in general, and southerners in particular, had long believed in the innate inferiority of the Negro. Years before the blatant proslavery arguments of the antebellum period, southerners had assumed that the Negro was not the equal of the Anglo-Saxon. Many writers have stated that the southerner's low estimate of the Negro evolved because of the presence of the institution of slavery. They have assumed that the southerner reasoned this way: slaves were in an inferior position; Negroes were slaves; therefore, Negroes must be inferior. Recent writers have questioned these assumptions, and Carl Degler has argued cogently that American whites' feelings of superiority over the Africans were not the result of the blacks being enslaved, but that these feelings preceded the institution of slavery and aided in its development. There is much to be said for this point of view. Examples of attitudes of racial superiority may be found throughout the world's history, but they are especially plentiful in the Western world. When Europeans found their assumptions supported by what appeared to be biblical evidence in the Old Testament story, telling how races were formed, racial feelings were intensified, and Europeans traveling to the New World carried these basic assumptions with them. Africans with black skins were usually considered human beings, but they were so degraded that they were looked upon as congenitally inferior.

In the late nineteenth century these views were sustained by the weighty, scholarly opinion of historians, philosophers, scientists, and psychologists in both Europe and America. Affirmers of the doctrine of Negro inferiority included such distinguished Europeans as Charles Darwin, Francis Galton, Thomas Carlyle, and Cesare Lombroso. They were joined in their racial beliefs by Americans such as Nathaniel S. Shaler, Albert Bushnell Hart, Madison Grant, and William McDougall. Regarding Negroes as more closely related to the ape than to man, biblical scholars, anthropologists, anatomists, and biologists advanced as a solid front to give racial prejudice intellectual support in the nineteenth century. Almost alone in this intellectual jungle was a young anthropologist named Franz Boas who maintained that innate racial distinctions were inconsequential, but his voice was lost in the din of racial ignorance.

After years of enslavement, Negroes appeared to be good examples to support the southerners' assumptions. Torn from his African home and enslaved, the black man lost his cultural background and substituted nothing in its place. Prevented from gaining an education, whipped into submission, sold like cattle, and with minimum contact with whites, Negroes revealed little initiative, little culture, and little ability. To the southerner the slave's traits proved not that slavery was degrading, but that the Negro was degraded, and this supported southerners' basic assumptions. Thus, by the time emancipation occurred, the southerner was instilled with the attitude of white supremacy and black inferiority.

At the end of the Civil War, many white people in the South favored strict control of the despised black man. Railroads, steamboats, and public carriages in the South denied first-class accommodations to Negroes. Passenger trains of that time usually had only two coaches, one called the "ladies car," in which both men and women rode if they paid the fare, and the other called the "smoking car." Essentially these amounted to first- and second-class accommodations, the latter being very poor facilities indeed. Immediately upon the end of slavery, Negroes were regularly denied seats in first-class railway coaches, even though they could afford them. These common practices were legalized in 1865, when the Mississippi legislature forbade "any freedman, negro, or mulatto to ride in any first-class passenger cars, set apart, or used by and for white persons. . . ." Negro nurses traveling with their mistresses were acknowledged as exceptions. The law did not refer to the mingling of the races in second-class coaches, nor did it require the railroads to provide an extra car for the exclusive use of Negroes. In the same year the Florida legislature forbade whites to use railroad facilities set apart for the use of Negroes only, and vice versa. But the Florida law also did not require the railroads to make separate cars available for each race, and it did not specifically prohibit the mixing of races in "smoking cars." In 1866 Texas passed a law reqiring all railroads to "attach to passenger trains one car for the special accommodation of freedmen." These three laws were repealed as soon as radical Reconstruction began, but the practice of relegating the black man to separate or inferior facilities continued.

Southern whites expressed displeasure toward many activities permitted blacks during radical Reconstruction, and when they gained control of their states in the 1870s, they passed numerous local ordinances requiring racial segregation in public accommodations. The enactment of these local laws stimulated the national Congress to pass the Civil Rights Act of 1875. This broad piece of legislation provided that all persons, whatever their race, were entitled to equal accommodations in all public conveyances, as well as in inns, theatres, and other places of public entertainment. While some state legislatures passed laws supporting this public accommodations statute, many southerners continued to stress the inferiority of the Negro and they disliked the possibility of social contact with him. The Supreme Court reflected this intellectual milieu, when in 1883 it declared the Civil Rights Act of 1875 unconstitutional. It ruled that states could not abridge the privileges of American citizens, but it pointedly excluded individuals and private corporations from this restriction. This loophole in the decision assisted in the establishment of practices and customs which discriminated against the black man.

In the area of education, where the black race was most deficient and most needed the assistance of the whites, segregation was greatest. Informal arrangements for giving the blacks a modicum of education under segregated conditions began during Reconstruction, and these customs continued after the conservative Bourbons regained control of the southern states. Discounting the three abortive railway laws passed in Mississippi, Florida, and Texas prior to radical Reconstruction, southern state statutes requiring segregation first came in the field of education, and by 1878 most of the southern states had legalized the universal practice of separate schooling for whites and blacks, the remainder following in the 1880s and 1890s.

An act passed in 1881 by the Tennessee legislature required railroads operating within the state to furnish "separate cars, or portions of cars cut off by partitioned walls" so that Negroes with first-class tickets could enjoy the same accommodations as whites who paid comparable fares. This law was not enforced, and most railroad companies in the state continued the previous practice of assigning Negro passengers with first-class tickets to the grossly inadequate second-class cars. The law did not attempt to enforce segregation of the races in second-class coaches.

Negroes who could afford to purchase first-class tickets often objected to being relegated to inferior smoking cars filled with second-class ticket holders. In 1887 W. H. Councill, president of an Alabama state college for Negroes, filed suit with the newly established Interstate Commerce Commission in which he charged discrimination in railroad rates after he was forced to accept second-class accommodations while holding a first-class ticket. The ICC ruled on this and similar complaints by requiring the railways to provide equal facilities for members of both races. In view of this decision, nine southern states passed laws providing for "equal" Jim Crow railway cars. In practice, the railroads usually did not provide separate coaches for blacks, refined Negro ladies with first-class tickets often being relegated to unsegregated second-class coaches where cigar smoke and profanity prevailed. Even though Negro facilities were never equal and often not separate, the Supreme Court in 1896 upheld the validity of a separate-but-equal transportation law in the famous *Plessy* v. *Ferguson* decision. Although the decision involved the issue of separation of the races in public transportation, the Court pointed to segregation in public schools at that time as an indication of the tradition and the reasonableness of the separation of the races in public conveyances. Specifically, the Court held that a segregation law in Louisiana was a valid exercise of the police powers of the state and that the statute did not violate the equal protection clause of the Fourteenth Amendment. The plaintiff said that enforced separation of the two races stamped the colored race with a badge of inferiority. The Court replied, "If this be so, it is not of anything found in the [segregation] act, but solely because the colored race chooses to put that construction on it." By 1900 all southern states had enacted similar statutes.

C. Vann Woodward in a perceptive little volume entitled *The Strange Career of Jim Crow* (1966) has pointed out that a hard and fast system of segregation of the races did not develop immediately upon the end of the Reconstruction Era. On many occasions the two races commingled in virtual equality until near the end of the nineteenth century. Blacks were commonly admitted to theatres, exhibitions, lectures, circuses, "shows under canvas," camp meetings, and other public functions, although whites usually avoided sitting with them, if possible. Upon occasion Negroes ate in public dining rooms, without objections from white patrons. Saloons served both whites and blacks at the same bar, and many jobs were open to both races. Despite the disapproval of the vast majority of southerners, a few instances of intermarriage between the races occurred, usually between white men and Negro women.

While plenty of examples have been found illustrating racist practices by white southerners, relationships of the races were to some extent fluid during the post-Reconstruction years. This is not to say that southern whites were softening their preconceived views of Negro inferiority. Nor does the evidence point to a willingness on the part of whites to accept the black man as a social equal. But in an age of change and uncertainty and before the new role of the freedman had been clearly defined in southern society, proscription of the Negro was somewhat limited.

A partial explanation for white attitudes of accommodation toward the Negro stemmed from the ideologies put into practice by Booker T. Washington, the leading Negro spokesman at the turn of the century. Washington was born into slavery on the eve of the Civil War and was one of thousands of illiterate blacks who were eager for education after obtaining their freedom. Admitted to Hampton Institute in Virginia, where he worked his way through the school, Washington was grateful for the education this institution provided for him, and he resolved to establish a similar school to help Negroes in the lower South. Accordingly, in 1881 Washington founded Tuskegee Normal and Industrial Institute in Alabama. The curriculum at Tuskegee reflected the rising interest in "industrial education," a general term which included manual training, home economics, and preparation for farming, as well as training for skilled jobs such as shoemaking, printing, carpentry, and bricklaying. Philanthropists who supported the institute looked upon Tuskegee's curriculum with favor, as did southern whites who saw such training as a means of keeping Negroes in a subordinate position by having them work with their hands rather than engage in professional careers.

Booker T. Washington was well aware that his school and his philosophy did not provide for a liberal education for members of his race nor for the establishment of a professional class. He advocated that Negroes must first learn skills, work hard, and make their limited contributions to the general economy and society. He hoped that his school and others like it would create a class of self-sufficient artisan-entrepreneurs skilled in the crafts and in farming. Thus, he believed that his race's problems would be solved through an application of the gospel of work. He opposed migration, urging blacks to stay in the South where he believed their opportunity for economic welfare was greatest. He received much southern white support for his views by arguing that his program would help lift not only the Negro but also the region. He expressed unhappiness over the Reconstruction experience, and he advised black men to shun politics. He favored literacy tests and property qualifications, reasoning that Negroes who insisted upon being involved in politics should be required to have both an education and financial earning power. He used conciliatory phraseology when speaking to whites, and he often appealed to them by criticizing blacks who permitted their grievances to overshadow their opportunities. His appeal to white support reached its apex when he declared, "In all things that are purely social we can be as separate as the fingers, yet one as the hand in all matters essential to mutual progress." He asked only for justice for the Negro and an end to racial animosities. He believed that these two things, combined with material prosperity, would bring "our beloved South" into a new age.

This conciliatory and gradualist philosophy caused Washington to declare that the southern whites were the Negro's best friends and that discrimination and prejudice were basically the fault of the Negro. Since poor and illiterate blacks naturally alienated white people, they must also be mainly responsible for their own advancement. "Through the dairy farm, the truck garden, the trades, and commercial life . . . the negro is to find his way to the enjoyment of all his rights," he declared. This stress on self-improvement did not mean that Washington discouraged racial pride; on the contrary, he insisted that Negroes should be proud of their race and loyal to it.

Washington's philosophy was therefore an admixture of industrial education, accommodation, self-help, racial solidarity, noninvolvement in politics, and economic advancement. He expressed most of these concepts in a speech in 1895 at the Cotton States and International Exposition in Atlanta, Georgia. The speech vaulted the Tuskegean to international fame, and from that time until his death in 1915, he was the most important symbol and the recognized leader of the black race in America. He served as adviser on Negro affairs to Presidents Theodore Roosevelt and William H. Taft, Roosevelt appointing no black men who were not recommended by Washington, and most of Taft's black appointees being recommended or approved by him. Within the Negro community, Washington came to exert more power than any other leader. His relationships with the Presidents and his popularity with white philanthropists added to his stature. Negro schools desiring philanthropic support received money only if Washington nodded his approval. Negroes and Negro institutions desiring advancement vied for his support.

While Booker T. Washington spoke publicly about accommodation, privately he often used his contacts with high officials to bring about change more rapidly. While he publicly urged Negroes to accept the separate-but-equal concept in regard to transportation facilities, behind the scenes he led the fight against railroad segregation. Through intermediaries he helped defeat a law designed to encourage segregation on northern interstate lines. At the same time he was urging Negroes not to press for the right to vote, he was surreptitiously fighting disfranchisement laws, and his contacts with political figures, including the Presidents, led him to be the most influential Negro politician in the nation's history. Washington's activities behind the scenes indicate that he was a tireless worker for the advancement of his race—and not always on the white man's terms. Given the racial climate of the turn of the century, Washington's covert activities, diplomacy, and emphasis upon thrift and industry may have been the only realistic approaches to uplifting the black man at that time.

Jim Crow Attains Maturity

While the last quarter of the nineteenth century was far from idyllic for the black race in the South, neither was it nearly so harsh as the early decades of the twentieth century, when the era of genuine segregation was at its height. After about 1898, white southerners took many calculated and deliberate measures to circumscribe all areas of contact between the races; the transitional period from slavery to total segregation came to an abrupt end. Why this "capitulation to racism?" The move toward extreme racism resulted not from a change of mind on the part of the South but rather because of a relaxation of the opposition. Southern whites who suppressed their fears, jealousies, hatreds, and fanaticism toward the Negro after Reconstruction were held in check to some extent by the restraining forces of northern liberal opinion, the courts, the federal government, and moderate southerners. These forces were dissipated when the nation became involved in international affairs. Taking up the White Man's Burden in an age of imperialism and entranced by the doctrine of Anglo-Saxon superiority, liberal northerners were inclined to be less vocal in their criticism of southern racial attitudes. The courts and the federal government fell under the sway of theories of white superiority, as the nation acquired and ruled its empire. Southern white supremacists took advantage of the new national emphasis upon racism to overwhelm moderates who had heretofore prevented blatant racists from dominating the southern scene. Southern extremists gained support from northern public opinion when they proclaimed not only that Negroes were innately inferior, immoral, and criminally inclined, but also that the race had reverted to barbarism because of its freedom. Southern polemicists publicized a rash of ultraracist books which advanced their point of view. *The Negro a Beast* (1900) and *The Negro: A Menace to Civilization* (1907) were indicative titles. Perhaps no book reflected the thinking of white Americans toward the black man as much as did the popular movie *Birth of a Nation,* a racist melodrama which glorified white superiority and stressed black racial degradation. Southern racism rode to power on the crest of a wave of national racist sentiment.

Another factor in the South's capitulation to racism grew out of the regional political battles of the 1890s. When the Populists, who had formed a tenuous alliance with Negroes in order to gain political office, were defeated, many of them blamed the minority race for their failure. The Negro became a convenient scapegoat for the accumulation of two decades of bitterness and frustration. Furthermore, conservative Democrats, even though they had allowed a small number of "safe" Negroes to vote during the Bourbon ascendancy, were appalled at the prospect of black men having real political power. Both reformers and conservatives, for different reasons, concluded that the Negro must be controlled as a political force. Extending this to economic and social arenas, these white southerners determined to proscribe the Negro's activities as had never been done before. The net result of the Populist movement was increased racial hatred and embittered race relations. The efforts toward political disfranchisement of the Negro have already been dealt with; there were also restrictions placed upon him in the social and economic spheres.

While the southern states had passed laws prior to 1900 directed toward segregating the Negro aboard passenger trains and while a few states in the 1890s had enacted laws for streetcar segregation, no other statutes of this nature had been added. After the turn of the century, in the context of tension, frustration, and unabashed racism, many more laws were passed to segregate and discriminate against the Negro, the principle of Jim Crow being applied with inexorable logic. City governments joined with the state legislatures to adopt ordinances prohibiting certain activities by Negroes. Unwritten laws, regulations, customs, and traditions restricting the freedom of the Negro also developed. From 1900 to the beginning of World War II, the Age of Segregation prevailed, the injustices, the inequities, and the subtleties of racial discrimination being present in almost every area of human activity in a modern society. Additional state laws regulating railway service, both on the trains and in the depots and waiting rooms, were passed, as were laws separating the races in other forms of public transportation—streetcars, buses, and taxis.

Beginning in 1910 several cities, including Baltimore, Richmond, Louisville, New Orleans, and Atlanta, passed ordinances which prohibited blacks from living in residential districts reserved for whites. In 1917 the Supreme Court declared these laws unconstitutional, but de facto residential segregation increased after that time. Some southern towns refused to allow Negroes to reside within their city limits, thus becoming known as "sundown towns," because Negroes who worked or visited there could not remain after sunset. Public parks, golf courses, swimming pools, and beaches were segregated. Marriage between the races was made illegal in most southern states. As the years passed, entrances and exits to many buildings were designated for the separate races, and dual drinking fountain and toilet facilities were arranged. "White only" became a sign which illiterate black children recognized and obeyed, if they did not want to suffer physical and verbal abuse. Most southern hotels, motels, restaurants, and theatres refused the patronage of blacks, while movie houses reserved separate sections or balconies for them. Sports and recreational activities and facilities were segregated, and separate facilities were provided by most hospitals, orphanages, prisons, asylums, mental institutions, funeral homes, morgues, and cemeteries.

If the South had followed the *Plessy* v. *Ferguson* decision to the letter, the separate facilities for the Negroes would have been equal. But in every instance, Negroes were compelled to tolerate inferior and inadequate accommodations and conditions. This inequality extended beyond public facilities. Sections in the cities and towns set aside for Negroes were invariably unlighted, unpaved, and underserviced, and the police and the courts did not provide equal protection for Negroes. Although the Supreme Court had ruled that blacks were eligible to serve as jurors, in practice they seldom did. Negroes who had been convicted of petty crimes were often discriminated against by being forced to work under a brutal system of labor exploitation. Under the convict-lease system, for a small fee state and county governments leased black convicts to plantation owners and industrialists, who in turn worked them on farms, in coal mines, in turpentine camps, and in railroad construction. Schools for Negroes were far inferior to those serving white children, primarily the result of discrimination in the appropriation and use of state school funds. As the end of the nineteenth century approached, Negro school funds were dwindling, while the average per capita expenditure for white children was rising slightly, increasing the divergence in per capita appropriations for the two races. In 1910 at least twice as much money per child was being spent for whites than for blacks in most southern states, the facts being reflected in the considerable variations in pupil attendance, length of school terms, quality of buildings, and teachers' qualifications and salaries. In no area of life were white and black southerners more separated than in the schoolroom.

As years passed and as more laws and customs were established, the two races came to be isolated from each other. Social contact, except when the Negro was clearly recognized to be in an inferior position, did not exist. If members of the two races mingled on the streets, each ignored the other. The Negro to a large extent became an "invisible man."

While the restrictions were enforced primarily to emphasize the difference in social status between whites and blacks, the white majority also was pledged to the Negroes' economic subordination. Whites living in the rural South did not look with favor upon an economically solvent freedman. Landless white tenants resented the black man's competition for annual tenant contracts, and small white farmers were no less resentful toward blacks who managed to acquire small farms. These lower-class, white, rural dwellers would have been happy if the black population in the South had suddenly disappeared. Large landowners opposed efforts to drive the Negro to the towns and cities, because they desired a large supply of labor to work in their fields, but the landed whites carried out deliberate practices to keep the Negro impoverished. Despite this formidable opposition, a few blacks prospered as landowners in the years following emancipation, but over 80 percent of the southern rural Negroes in 1920 labored as tenants, sharecroppers, or wage laborers, with little or no opportunity to improve their economic status.

In a region with a surplus of labor, particularly unskilled labor, lower-class whites also objected to the competition of black workers in southern factories and mills. Pressure from these whites brought others to support their objections, and employers often refused to hire Negroes if white laborers were available. The rapid growth of southern industry attracted both whites and blacks from the hills and farms of the rural South, but most of the jobs went to the whites. Some extremely undesirable tasks came to be designated as "nigger jobs," and whites tacitly and happily relegated the Negro to such positions, but the number of such jobs in the industrial plants were far short of the available supply of black labor. As years passed, even these assured jobs for blacks were jeopardized by white infringements. Small businesses often used Negroes for janitorial duties, and certain kinds of jobs such as garbage collecting were filled by blacks, but many men of the minority race were reduced to shining shoes, an occupation which depicted with moving irony the lowly position of the black race. When black men could not find employment, their wives became domestic servants for white families, often playing much the same role as household slaves during antebellum days. The matriarchal family that came to dominate black society in America was the direct result of these events. Black men experienced psychological emasculation, when they were continually denied employment and when their wives were compelled to support their families.

During the first three decades of the twentieth century, craft unions in the South barred—either openly or through subterfuge—virtually all Negroes from membership. Leaders of the southern unions assumed that blacks were incapable of becoming skilled laborers; therefore, union membership was unnecessary for them. This rationalization was accepted by the unions' national leaders, who were striving against many obstacles in their efforts to build membership in the developing industrial South. Unions had made little headway in the region in the early years of the century, and national leaders were willing to forego a drive for Negro membership which might prevent prejudiced southern white workers from joining the unions. The American Federation of Labor officially opposed discrimination, but like many pious declarations, this stand was not upheld. As late as 1944, twelve AFL craft unions specifically excluded Negroes constitutionally, seven regularly excluded them by tacit consent, and ten gave Negroes segregated auxiliary status, but with no policy powers.

Unlike the craft unions, which restricted their numbers to skilled laborers, the industrial unions desired to organize all the workers in an industry. In 1935 the Committee for Industrial Organization was formed, quickly making great strides throughout the nation. It set out to organize southern workers, regardless of race or color, but its efforts met resistance from such groups as the revived Ku Klux Klan. Planters and public officials expressed loud disapproval of efforts to organize black agricultural workers. The CIO experienced some success in the mining regions, however. In 1935 the United Mine Workers, a leading union in the new industrial organization, had about twelve thousand Negro members and a long record of interracial amity. The nature of coal mining compelled cooperation of workers in the mines, and this interracial cooperation also existed above ground. The UMW developed a standard pattern of mixed locals, even though at meetings blacks and whites usually were segregated. The CIO-affiliated Textile Workers' Union of America permitted separate locals in the South, but no other CIO locals had Jim Crow practices, and no CIO national excluded Negroes. But the total picture remained bleak for the Negro. In 1943 only 12 percent of the black labor force in southern industries was organized, in contrast to 20 percent of the southern whites and 44 percent of the black laborers in the North.

The general discriminatory conditions prevailing for the Negro employed in southern industries were reflected in the wages he received. Blacks often averaged less than one-fourth the wages paid to white workers. A study of Negro families in thirty-four towns and villages in four Deep South states in the mid-1930s revealed annual incomes of less than $330, compared with the average of $1,220 for white families in the same vicinities. Negro families with incomes of less than $250 comprised 17 percent of the total, and none of these was on relief in those depression days. Only 4 percent had incomes of $1,000 or more. Conditions were no better for the Negro living in the cities. At a time when the Works Progress Administration calculated that a family of four required a minimal annual income of $900, half the Negro families in Atlanta lived on less than $632, many subsisting on less than $332. A subsequent study in 1940 revealed that conditions had not improved. Some 30 percent of southern Negro urban and village families had annual incomes of less than $350. Jim Crow was more than a pickpocket; he was an insensitive robber who stole from paychecks before they were written. Thus, piece by piece the patterns of segregation, proscription, and racial subordination were firmly established in the society and economic life of the South during the early decades of the twentieth century.

Black Responses in the Age of Segregation

How did southern Negroes respond to the massive development of restrictive Jim Crow laws and customs? A large number meekly submitted to white domination, openly accommodating themselves in every way to the majority's demands and reinforcing southern white preconceptions that the Negro was lazy, infantile, and unambitious. The "Sambo" characteristics of many antebellum slaves prevailed, as Negroes refused to look a white man in the eyes, kept head bowed in the presence of whites, and manifested no imagination or intelligence. In the face of a hostile and determined white majority, many southern Negroes reasoned that this was the only way to survive; and for lower-class blacks this was often true.

Negroes with more intelligence and ambition also submitted to the Jim Crow atmosphere, and in the presence of whites they bowed and fawned as required, but within the Negro community, many of these Negroes came to profit from the existence of Jim Crow. As discrimination became more apparent, many Negroes realized that the black man must establish his own economic institutions for his people. When whites refused to serve blacks, they had no alternative but to establish their own stores, banks, funeral homes, realty associations, and insurance companies, as well as professional and other services for the black community. While these businessmen and professionals were denied a white clientele, they had almost a monopoly on the black population, and thus they were in a position to profit from segregation. One of the most important features of the changing nature of the Negro class structure in the early years of the twentieth century was the rise of this *petite bourgeoisie* of professionals and businessmen who gained their livelihood from serving the black masses. White-imposed traditions demanded that such steps be taken, and the surrender to demands for segregation in turn reinforced Jim Crow customs.

If some Negroes gained financially because of segregation, the great majority did not. Many of them responded to Jim Crow practices by leaving the South. Their social isolation and economic oppression was so great that they migrated to northern and western cities where racial antagonisms were less apparent and where economic opportunity appeared greater. The Negroes' flight out of the South during and immediately following World War I has been labeled the Great Migration, and August Meier has called it the "great watershed" in postemancipation American Negro history. While the Negro exodus was deeply rooted in a host of grievances, its immediate cause was World War I. War industries in the North needed more laborers, and when the war itself stemmed the tide of foreign immigration, northern industrialists looked to the region below the Ohio River to fill the labor vacuum. Before the United States became involved in the war, northern employers dispatched agents southward to entice domestic immigrants with promises of good paying jobs. Agricultural depression arising from floods and the onrushing boll weevil in 1915 and 1916 made the northern agents' jobs easier. Railroads made arrangements to transport trainloads of Negroes from the South, and several large corporations set up camps to care for the new immigrants until they were placed in jobs.

The migratory urge was strong throughout the South, and northern agents were not responsible for all of the Negro workers who went north. Most Negroes were influenced by friends and relatives who had preceded them and who wrote back about the money they were making. In many cases money was sent to help pay transportation costs for families or friends who indicated that they too were willing to leave the land of their birth for a modicum of economic opportunity in the North. Negro journals and newspapers supported the migratory movement, but there was no organization or leadership behind the Great Migration. Momentum increased, and a spontaneous mass movement developed as Negroes quietly moved out of the South, expressing mute protest to regional treatment accorded them.

The population movement which began during World War I and continued unabated in the postwar years was illustrated by the census returns. Until 1910 the center of the American Negro population had moved slightly south and west, reflecting the expansion of the southern frontier and southern economic development. In 1920 the center of the Negro population moved a few miles to the *northeast* (from Fort Payne, Alabama, to Rising Fawn, Georgia), permanently reversing a trend of more than a century. In the decade following 1910, 5 percent of the native Negro population of the Southeast in 1910 migrated from the region, and in the 1920s, 8 percent of the native Negro population in 1920 had joined the exodus. By 1930, 1,840,000 Negroes born in the Southeast no longer lived there. The trend all over the South was much the same, and it continued into World War II and in the postwar years.

The out-migrating Negro did not always move to the North. A few southern Negroes joined other black Americans and moved back to Africa. Playing upon the disillusionment and failing hope of black men in a dominant white society, a Jamaican citizen named Marcus Garvey in 1914 formed the Universal Negro Improvement Association to organize and transport Negroes to the home of their ancestors. Hoping to liberate both African and American Negroes from their oppressors, Garvey designated himself as provisional president of Africa, adopted a flag, and surrounded himself with a large group of subordinates who espoused his belief that Negroes should be proud of their blackness. Garvey desired to instill a sense of pride in black people, and he believed that all people of African descent ought to cooperate in their struggle for freedom—a kind of Pan-Africanism. He believed that white men would respect Negroes only after the latter successfully organized an all-black country. While proclaiming the merits of his proposals and making plans to establish a new country in Africa, Garvey aroused the interest and hope of literally millions of Negroes. These hopes were dashed, however, when their leader was prosecuted for illegal use of the mail in connection with the sale of stock in his steamship company, the Black Star Line. When Garvey was deported as an undesirable alien, the last great "back to Africa" movement expired, and Negroes unhappy with conditions in the United States turned to other forms of protest.

Besides submission or flight the Negro had at least one other alternative to react to Jim Crow restrictions. He could fight. And on occasion he did. As early as 1894 blacks boycotted Atlanta streetcars, successfully abrogating a newly instituted policy of segregation. In the decade following, when other southern cities provided Jim Crow trolley cars, Negroes resorted to the boycott, although they were usually unsuccessful. Negroes even organized their own transportation companies in Houston, Austin, Nashville, and Savannah, but their efforts were short-lived in an era when a white majority was determined to control blacks.

Protests often arose from a specific incident steeped in the frustrations of the Negro who felt the tightening screws of segregation laws and customs. On occasion this protest erupted into riots and violence. During World War I, when a disproportionate number of Negroes were drafted into the armed services, several ugly incidents occurred involving black troops stationed in southern army camps. In September 1917, resenting harassment by Houston police, Negro soldiers at Camp Logan resisted police suppression of their legitimate off-base activities, causing a full-fledged race riot which left seventeen whites dead. Thirteen soldiers were hanged and forty-one were sentenced to life imprisonment for their part in the riot. When tensions at Spartanburg, South Carolina, threatened to cause a riot, Negro soldiers were promptly shipped to France. Several clashes between blacks and whites occurred after the war was over, one of the worst being in Charleston, South Carolina, between black soldiers and white sailors.

The summer of 1919 ushered in one of the greatest periods of interracial strife in the nation's history, some twenty-five riots occurring before the end of the year. In July a group of angry whites entered the Negro section of Longview, Texas, looking for a black man who had purportedly damaged the reputation of a white woman. They burned Negro shops and homes, and they frightened many Negroes into fleeing from the area before state militia took control. One of the most publicized conflicts between whites and blacks occurred in Phillips County, Arkansas, in October 1919. Negro tenants in the area had formed a unionlike organization through which to express their grievances against landowners. Reports of plotting and insurrection began to circulate within the white community, and a shooting incident touched off interracial fighting. Five whites and at least twenty-five Negroes died. Newspapers in the nation carried great headlines about a black insurrection in Arkansas, and in the excitement a court sentenced twelve Negroes to death and fifty-four more to prison terms of from one to twenty years. After the hysteria died down, all of the twelve Negroes sentenced to die were freed, but not until some five years had passed.

Other racial disturbances interrupted the domestic peace in the years following the end of World War I. Two of the more important ones occurred in Oklahoma and Florida. In 1921 when an oil boom was underway in the Tulsa area, rumors of an impending lynching brought crowds of whites and blacks together in front of the city jail, where a riot broke out. Before the incident ended, whites had reduced forty-four blocks of Tulsa's Negro residential area to rubble. In Rosewood, Florida,

two years later, a white mob searching for an alleged Negro rapist entered the Negro section of town, burning six homes and a church and
killing six Negroes. Two whites were also killed in the melee. These incidents of racial disturbances should not leave the impression that the postwar pattern of rioting was solely a regional experience. Disorders were
also occurring in the North, undoubtedly because migrating black men
soon discovered that northern racial attitudes toward the Negro were little better than southern whites' attitudes.

If individual acts and mob rioting were illustrative of Negro
objections to discrimination, they also revealed the destructive side of
protest. Sober Negro leaders of the early twentieth century were happy
with neither the destructiveness of the rioters nor the submissiveness of
Booker T. Washington, whose gradualism and outward acceptance of
Negro inferiority advanced the position of the minority at a snail's pace,
if at all. These New Negroes, as they came to be called, who condoned
neither violence nor accommodation, were responsible for the formation of
a number of organizations which were to lead orderly opposition to Jim
Crow practices. Most of these New Negroes were northern intellectuals,
but their influence was great throughout the nation.

The most important leader of this group came to be W. E. B. Du
Bois, a Massachusetts Negro who studied at Fisk University and the University of Berlin and who received a Ph.D. from Harvard University. In
the 1890s when he was a professor at Atlanta University, Du Bois had
supported Booker T. Washington's program of gradualism, but when
segregation and discrimination increased at the very time Washington's
leadership was at its height, Du Bois came to believe that members of his
race could not advance themselves by voluntarily throwing away their
rights or continually belittling themselves. Rather Du Bois believed that
Negroes must constantly speak out against oppression and discrimination. He concluded that it was a mistake to assume that industrial training would raise up Negro leaders, arguing that a liberal arts education
would better help elevate blacks both culturally and economically. Du
Bois's ideas were widely read and publicized after 1903, the year in which
his volume of essays, *The Souls of Black Folk,* appeared. Besides being
highly critical of Washington's strategy, Du Bois in this volume also advanced the concept of the "Talented Tenth," that the cream of the Negro
population must assume the responsibility for uplifting the entire race.

In 1905 Du Bois led some of the "Talented Tenth" to inaugurate
the Niagara Movement, an organized program of public agitation for the
constitutional rights of Negroes. The Niagarans declared that the race
problem in America was due not to blacks but to whites. In crisp language Du Bois's group announced to whites that Negroes were dissatisfied with their progress toward freedom since slavery, and that they
would vigorously agitate for voting rights and "the abolition of all caste

distinctions based simply on race and color." Members of the Niagara
Movement actively opposed school segregation in Chicago and Philadelphia, and their legal redress committee won a lawsuit concerning railroad
segregation. The achievements of the Niagara Movement were limited
and it rapidly declined in influence, but its importance lay in its members' ability and willingness to articulate the Negroes' frustrations with
the social and economic system of the nation.

Liberal whites in the United States were also becoming increasingly alarmed over the rising tide of segregation, disfranchisement, and
racial violence, and in 1908, after a serious race riot in Springfield, Illinois, Oswald Garrison Villard, publisher of the New York *Evening Post,*
proposed that a "strong defense committee" be formed to protect and advance Negro interests. In the following year, in response to a call issued
by Villard, whites and blacks gathered in New York for a National
Negro Conference. This group issued statements demanding the ballot
for the Negro, denouncing mob violence, and calling for an end to segregation. Out of this conference grew the National Association for the Advancement of Colored People (NAACP). While the Niagara Movement
did not officially merge with the NAACP, many of its leaders, including
W. E. B. Du Bois, were active in establishing the new organization.

The NAACP quickly became an important agency for Negro advancement because of its interracial nature and because of the untiring
efforts of a small group of Negro leaders. Since it had the support and
prestige of many well-known white Progressives, such as Villard, Lillian
Wald, Jane Addams, and Clarence Darrow, the NAACP had greater financial support and a wider audience than it otherwise would have had.
Except for Du Bois, who became director of publicity and editor of the
Association's magazine, *Crisis,* all of the chief officers of the early organization were white. But the backbone of its support came from its
Negro members. By 1914 the Association had 6,000 members in some 50
local branches over the nation. The unsettling war years caused many
Negroes to turn to the NAACP as their major hope, and by the end of
1919 the Association claimed 300 branches, of which 155 were in the
South. Out of 88,448 members, 42,588 lived in the South. The New Negroes, the Niagarans, and the NAACP were committed to uplifting all
black Americans, and since the great majority of Negroes lived in the
South, the efforts of these individuals and organizations bore directly
upon that region. That few southern blacks were in places of leadership
and influence was irrelevant. The numerical strength of the NAACP in
the South was mute evidence of the southern Negroes' support of that nationwide organization.

Despite its rapid growth, the NAACP never strayed from its role
as an agency of legal protest. While it publicized lynchings and strove to
have lynchers prosecuted, it discouraged Negro mob reaction to this ille-

gal substitute for the nation's system of established justice. The Association's sustained efforts to have Congress pass an antilynching law were unsuccessful, but the publicity did reduce the incidents of the inexcusable practice. While the NAACP pointed to the small number of Negro voters, it encouraged Negroes not to lose hope in the American democratic system. It was to a large extent responsible for the Supreme Court's rejection of Oklahoma's grandfather clause in 1915, even though Oklahoma state election officials found ways to circumvent the decision. It was also behind the Court's action striking down municipal ordinances requiring residential segregation, but southern towns covertly practiced residential segregation despite the Court's ruling. The importance of the NAACP cannot be measured in terms of its specific successes or failure. It came to be recognized as the major organization in the nation devoted to helping the Negro. Its presence as a symbol was as important as its minor victories. Its existence in the Age of Segregation is a tribute to those blacks in both North and South who never lost hope that their race could be improved within the context of the laws of the nation.

Breakthrough in Education

Although the caste system was not firmly established in the South before the end of the nineteenth century, educational separation of the races was unfailingly present, sanctioned by the U. S. Supreme Court in the *Plessy* v. *Ferguson* decision. But for minor variations this basic ruling was applied to education for nearly sixty years.

Under the stimulus of the NAACP and other organizations, Negroes criticized the separate-but-equal doctrine throughout the Age of Segregation, although before 1930 this criticism was unorganized and lacked focus. In the 1930s they directed their attacks at the top levels of the southern biracial school system, facilities for Negroes being weakest here. Thus, they made efforts to desegregate professional and graduate schools of universities in the South, since the states had done practically nothing for the training of Negroes in the fields of law, engineering, dentistry, and medicine. When cases began to reach the courts dealing with the rights of Negroes to attend southern state universities, some states tried to equalize professional education by paying Negro students the difference between the cost of education in their home states and in northern universities which had no racial bars. The courts promptly outlawed such efforts. For example, in 1936 the Maryland Court of Appeals compelled the state's university law school to admit Donald Murray and other qualified Negroes, rather than pay their tuition to out-of-state schools, on the principle that out-of-state scholarships failed to meet the requirements of equal protection under the Constitution. The court said that instruction obtained elsewhere was not equal to in-state training for those who proposed to practice law in Maryland.

The same concept was accepted by the U. S. Supreme Court in 1938 in Lloyd L. Gaines's case against Missouri. This was the first time the Supreme Court reexamined the separate-but-equal doctrine laid down in 1896, and while the principle was not overthrown, the Gaines case became the first milestone to be passed by the Court in the ultimate destruction of that earlier ruling. The state of Missouri complied with the decision by setting up a separate law school for Negroes in St. Louis instead of allowing Gaines and other Negroes admission to the University of Missouri. Several other states followed this ploy by establishing separate law schools for Negroes. In Kentucky, Oklahoma, and Texas law schools were set up in the state capitols, and teachers from the state universities commuted to teach the students who enrolled in these makeshift schools. Few Negroes attended such schools, however, as their leaders continued their demands for integrated facilities.

When the Supreme Court in 1948 ordered the University of Oklahoma to provide truly equal facilities for a petitioning Negro named G. W. McLaurin, the president of the university declared that "you can't build a cyclotron for one student," and McLaurin was admitted to the university's graduate school. But when McLaurin attended classes he was set apart from white students, and in one class he was seated in an adjoining room where he could hear but not participate fully in the activities of the class. The Court ruled that this student must be afforded the same treatment as others, and in 1950 these strangely separated facilities were ended. After a long court struggle, Ada Lois Sipuel Fisher was admitted to the regular law school of the University of Oklahoma in 1949. In 1950 in the case of *Sweatt* v. *Painter* the Court ruled that Texas's separate law school for Negroes was inferior to the all-white law school at the University of Texas. In this case the Court came very close to the reasoning it was to use in the landmark decision of 1954, when it declared specifically that separate schools were inherently unequal. As a result of these and other decisions, a trickle of qualified Negroes began to be admitted to graduate and professional schools in the South. Also in the early 1950s, previously segregated private universities, colleges, and seminaries began opening their doors to Negroes, and shortly state institutions came to allow blacks into their undergraduate programs. By 1960 well over one-half of the 208 tax-supported colleges in the South were open to Negroes, and by 1970 nearly all of them had at least a sprinkling of black students.

The admission of Negroes to state university campuses did not come without some violence. In 1956, when Autherine Lucy was permitted to enroll in the University of Alabama, some students and townspeople encouraged mob action, and for several hours Miss Lucy's life was in danger. In the fall of 1963 the governor of Alabama stood at the front door of the University of Alabama in his attempt to prevent Negroes from enrolling in the school, but he yielded to the Court's orders and Negroes entered the school without violence. In 1962 James Meredith enrolled in the University of Mississippi, and his presence on the campus caused a riot in which two persons were killed. Despite the fact that the campus was in turmoil for several months, Meredith attended classes and was graduated from that institution. But Mississippi and Alabama were the headlined exceptions in a movement that was most successful. Generally few disturbances occurred when Negroes walked onto the southern campuses. In 1963 a black student enrolled in Clemson University in South Carolina without incident. Dozens upon dozens of campuses quietly enrolled Negroes, students and faculties usually adjusting quite rapidly to the presence of blacks on the campus. The most serious obstacle to the Negro on the campus was not white opposition; rather it was the inadequate preparation he received at home and in the preparatory schools. In the 1950s and 1960s a sprinkling of whites began attending formerly all-Negro schools in several states so that it became no longer a valid distinction to refer to "white" or "Negro" colleges. In 1966, however, 80 percent of the Negroes enrolled in college classes in the South were attending one of the 119 predominantly Negro institutions.

While the South was under the sway of the separate-but-equal doctrine, dozens of Negro colleges sprang up in the South. States and philanthropists had put some money into these schools so that able black students would not be completely denied an education. Some were fairly good institutions, but ordinarily these highly separate schools were hardly equal to those for whites. When whites began to open their doors to blacks, the Negro schools in turn lowered their racial barriers. In some cases states made extra efforts to raise standards at the Negro schools to encourage blacks to continue to seek schooling in them. As these formerly all-black schools became somewhat better, whites began to attend them. In the 1960s approximately 120 predominantly Negro universities and colleges existed in the South, over one-half of them enrolling at least a few white students. After serving the great majority of black students before 1954, these schools enrolled only 56.8 percent of all black undergraduates and only 25 percent of all black graduate students in college in September 1969, as many blacks took advantage of better opportunities in schools formerly closed to them. While most black professors who taught in the predominantly Negro schools had lifetime commitments to remain, some yielded to the temptation to move to better paying positions at prestigious northern and western universities, when these institutions accepted student demands for black studies programs headed by black professors. The shortage of qualified blacks compelled the larger nonsouthern schools to raid the faculties of the formerly all-black institutions.

Whether the latter could continue to retain their more able faculty members remained unanswered in 1970, but the competitive situation resulted in somewhat higher salaries and better working conditions for those who chose to stay. Even so, salaries lagged behind, teaching loads remained oppressive, library holdings were meager, and facilities were generally substandard at most of the predominantly black schools.

Around 1950 the NAACP sponsored a number of court cases challenging segregation in the nation's grade and high schools. Five of these cases from Kansas, Virginia, Delaware, and Washington, D. C. reached the Supreme Court, and in May 1954 the Court ruled on them collectively, specifically overturning the separate-but-equal concept by a unanimous decision. Flatly reversing the doctrine enunciated in *Plessy* v. *Ferguson* a half century earlier, this historic decision, called *Brown* v. *Board of Education (Topeka)* since the Kansas case was listed first, stated that separate schools were inherently unequal, even though physical facilities were on a par, and that segregated schools denied Negroes equal protection of the laws. The Court agreed with the plaintiff that separate schools created "psychological roadblocks" for members of the minority race. A year later the Court prescribed the manner in which racial segregation was to end by handing down an implementing decision providing that public schools were to be desegregated "with all deliberate speed." The Court recognized that many local school problems existed, and thus it set no specific time limit for the completion of the desegregation process. The Court's decision was to be implemented by local school authorities, and the federal courts were assigned the responsibility of deciding whether the pace and actions of school authorities constituted good faith as they proceeded along the line of desegregation. These decisions vested much power over the desegregation process in local school boards.

When the Supreme Court's decision was handed down, seventeen states, plus Washington, D. C., had segregated schools by law. Four other states (Kansas, Wyoming, New Mexico, and Arizona) allowed varieties of local option on segregation. The response from Washington and many states was to integrate as rapidly as possible, especially in the larger cities. President Dwight Eisenhower hoped to make the nation's capital a showplace for the integrating process, and Washington school officials began combined classes in the fall of 1954. Less than a month after the original Court decision, Baltimore, Maryland, announced a definite desegregation program. With 40 percent of its school population Negro, and no school district lines in the first place, that city simply continued its policy of allowing children to go to the schools of their choice, but now without any racial distinctions. Louisville, Kentucky, developed an elaborate program for integration, completely redistricting its school system in 1956 without regard to race. In December 1958 a Negro was elected to the city's Board of Education. St. Louis, Missouri, developed a plan which resulted in considerable mixing, especially in areas where Negro families were re-placing suburbanbound white families. In 1959 a Negro was elected to the St. Louis Board of Education. Other cities also complied with the Court's decision. In some areas where few Negroes lived, desegregation was effected but hardly any integration occurred. Thus, within two years after the Court's ruling, such states as Oklahoma, Missouri, and West Virginia were proudly proclaiming that they were 80 to 90 percent integrated. However, although school districts in which no black children lived were desegregated, because of residential patterns this official desegregation did not result in integration. De facto segregation continued in many areas despite the praise selected states received from those following desegregation's progress.

De facto segregation was not restricted to the South. Although the Court's decision was aimed directly at southern de jure segregation, it stimulated Negroes to strike back at segregated schools in the North and West. Legally segregation had not generally existed outside the South, but in actual fact numerous big city schools were as segregated as southern systems. That residential housing was primarily responsible for these situations did not deter black leaders, and they filed suits in California, Illinois, and other states against segregated school systems. The segregation-desegregation controversy became nationwide.

Not to be overlooked in the total picture was the fact that a few schools in the Deep South states were desegregated within a short time after the 1954 Court decision. While the percentages and numbers of Negro pupils in these situations were not large, that any integration occurred was worthy of note. Moreover, when school desegregation was implemented, violence seldom accompanied the action. News media made much of the violence of Little Rock, New Orleans, and Clinton, Tennessee, but these were the headlined exceptions. Although southerners indicated that the Court was interfering with their sacred traditions and constitutional prerogatives, and although they said that they would strongly resist school integration, when the moment of decision came, they generally did not carry out their threat. Despite their unhappiness, the great majority of southerners refused to engage in or condone violence.

By 1958 the desegregation process began to slow down considerably. The initial thrust in the large cities and in states with lower Negro percentages had ended, and each passing year saw fewer additional black pupils assigned to schools with whites. Before 1960 the desegregation movement was virtually at a standstill; the hard core of resistance to integration had been reached. In some cities, instances of resegregation occurred. When schools were desegregated, white families moved out of the districts, and they were often replaced by blacks. Formerly all-white schools went through a mixed stage when members of both races were in attendance, but within a few years those schools became virtually all-black. Thus, residential patterns affected the makeup of the school population. After 1963 the proportion of blacks enrolling in the same schools with whites in the southern states remained at about 1 to 10. If progress was made in one district, others were resegregating. While parts of the picture changed each year, the total scene remained fairly constant.

Although some Negro pupils were attending school with whites in every state in the South before the end of the 1960s, in some states the numbers were infinitesimally small as southerners were successfully resisting massive school integration. Six states had passed amendments or statutes providing for the closing of public schools in the event of forced segregation. Some had provided financial aid for students who wished to attend segregated, private, nonsectarian schools, if the public schools were either closed or mixed. Other states passed laws to deny state funds to school districts which integrated. Pupil placement laws to control or restrain desegregation were also passed. These laws empowered school officials to assign pupils to particular schools for various reasons, and while race was not mentioned, the purpose of the laws was obvious. Compulsory attendance laws were repealed in Mississippi and South Carolina, and teacher tenure laws were altered by some states so teachers could be dismissed in the event of desegregation. After federal troops were sent into Little Rock in 1957, some states passed laws providing for the closing of their schools if federal troops were used to enforce integration. Nearly five hundred laws dealing with the segregation-desegregation issue in the public schools were passed in the dozen years following the 1954 decision. The majority were designed to prevent or delay integration.

The Supreme Court's patience finally wore thin. In November 1969 the Court released a crisp, two-page statement in which it announced that segregation in fourteen Mississippi school districts—and by implication throughout the entire South—must cease "at once." This unanimous decision was a stinging rebuke to the go-slow desegregation tactics of the southern states. The Justices declared that such procrastination amounted to nothing less than "the denial of fundamental rights to many thousands of schoolchildren." In uncompromising language the Court swept away its own former criterion of "all deliberate speed" as "no longer constitutionally permissible." Also now gone was judicial toleration for often endless stages of negotiations before dual school systems were abolished. The order set forth the principle that in the future all pleas for exceptions to desegregation could be made only after integration was an established fact. With one stroke the Court sought finally to wipe out the dual systems still operating in much of the Deep South.

The delight expressed by civil rights activists was matched by an equal and opposite reaction from the South. South Carolina's Senator Strom Thurmond denounced the ruling as "pernicious," Mississippi's James Eastland predicted that it would result in "the destruction of the public-school system," and former Alabama Governor George Wallace warned that "in the not too distant future the people are going, by lawful means, to take back their children from the Supreme Court." In April 1970 Florida Governor Claude Kirk personally took charge of the Manatee County schools, after dismissing the system's school board when it prepared to implement a court-ordered desegregation plan which included the busing of children. Leaders of other southern states watched the legal skirmishing between the governor and a U. S. District Judge with care, since the results would have broad implications for the future of all school integration.

The urgency of the Court's 1969 decision threw many school administrators into confusion and panic, a reaction that could have been avoided had they been seriously working toward a gradual changeover to a unitary school system. Their deliberate delay forced the Court to act decisively, and they in turn damned the Court for disrupting their school programs in mid-year. Other reactions in the South were not unexpected. Most campaigns for school bond issues were halted immediately. The voters of Jackson, Mississippi, decisively defeated a $7,000,000 bond issue a few days after the "at once" ruling. During the spring and summer of 1970 additional private schools were founded—these were quickly called "segregation academies"—and in September approximately 400,000 pupils were enrolled in such schools in the eleven states of the old Confederacy. The private academies ranged from a physically inadequate, one-teacher school in Lamar County, Georgia, to the well-equipped, modern facility housed in a former Elks Club building in Montgomery, Alabama. Some prophets of doom predicted that the public school systems of the Deep South would soon disappear, but the likelihood was that the southern systems would survive the racial crisis despite the travail for many whites, especially parents.

During the Presidential campaign of 1968, Richard Nixon had given encouragement to many white southerners by implying that he approved of "freedom of choice" desegregation schemes, and after the Nixon administration had moved into the White House, it abandoned the tactic of halting federal funds to stubborn school districts. But after the "at once" decision of the Court, the administration promised to assist in the implementation of the Court ruling, much to the chagrin of Senator Thurmond who denounced what he called an "unjustified and arbitrary invasion" of southern states' rights. In the early summer of 1970 the Nixon administration instituted more than fifty lawsuits against recalcitrant southern school boards, directed the withdrawal of tax exemptions from segregated private schools, and made plans to send a team of federal lawyers and marshals to the South to keep tab on the progress of desegregation. In the face of this united front from the executive and judicial arms of the government some southerners remained adamant, but others were resigned to defeat. In Forest, Mississippi, a progressive, poultry-processing town east of Jackson, the school superintendent expressed the attitude of many: "We realize we can't operate a dual school system. When the federal government made up its mind and stopped toying around, that was it." Incidentally, in the two years prior to the "at once" decision, Mississippi had already moved from being the state with the least desegregation to the Deep South state with the most.

Efforts to ease the burdens were made in the feverish summer of 1970. Lawyers from the Department of Justice and the Department of Health, Education and Welfare met with school authorities in five states to make final mass efforts for federal-local agreements to implement school desegregation. The State Department of Education in North Carolina dispatched a three-man team (one black, two white) to consult with and aid troubled school districts. In Mobile, Alabama, the Center for Intercultural Education developed programs for pairing black and white teachers to work on new curricula; also, it offered films on common school problems, often racial, for discussion and consideration by school teachers. Despite predictions from the prophets of gloom, widespread violence did not occur in September when public schools across the South opened their doors.

By the fall of 1970 most southerners had come to accept school integration as inevitable, although they still hoped to delay it as long as possible in as many schools as possible. Despite Attorney General John N. Mitchell's boast that the South's school systems were 90 percent integrated in the fall of 1970, de facto segregation was commonplace. Residential housing patterns, calculated resegregation tactics, and movement by whites from one school district to another continued to affect the racial makeup of many schools. It appeared that years would pass before some schools in the region would actually be integrated.

Suggestions for Further Reading

The Woodward and Tindall volumes (previously mentioned) continue to have much relevant material in them. In addition, Woodward's volume entitled *The Strange Career of Jim Crow*,* 2nd rev. ed. (New York: Oxford, 1966) is an interpretive work in which the author argues that the origins of segregation were reasonably late. Some of Woodward's conclusions are based upon George B. Tindall, *South Carolina Negroes, 1877–1900* * (Columbia, S. C.: Univ. South Carolina, 1952). In sharp disagreement with Woodward and Tindall are: Charles E. Wynes, *Race Relations in Virginia, 1870–1902* (Charlottesville: Univ. Virginia, 1961); Joel Williamson, *After Slavery: The Negro in South Carolina During Reconstruction, 1861–1877* (Chapel Hill: Univ. North Carolina, 1965); Frenise A. Logan, *The Negro in North Carolina, 1870–1894* (Chapel Hill: Univ. North Carolina, 1964). Other volumes devoted primarily to the Negro since 1865 include: Vernon L. Wharton, *The Negro in Mississippi, 1865–1890* * (Chapel Hill: Univ. North Carolina, 1947); Alrutheus A. Taylor, *The Negro in Tennessee, 1865–1880* (Washington: Associated Publishers, 1944); Charles S. Mangum, Jr., *The Legal Status of the Negro* (Chapel Hill: Univ. North Carolina, 1940); Charles S. Johnson, *Patterns of Negro Segregation* (New York: Harper & Brothers, 1943); Pauli Murray, *States' Laws on Race and Color* (Cincinnati: Methodist Church Board of Missions, 1951); Hortense Powdermaker, *After Freedom: A Cultural Study in the Deep South* * (New York: Viking Press, 1939).

Booker T. Washington has been the subject of a number of volumes, beginning with that well-known Negro's autobiography *Up From Slavery* * (Toronto: J. L. Nichols, 1902). Also worthy of reading are S. R. Spencer, *Booker T. Washington and the Negro's Place in American Life* * (Boston: Little, Brown, 1955) and B. J. Mathews, *Booker T. Washington: Educator and Interracial Interpreter* (Cambridge, Mass.: Harvard Univ., 1948). W. E. B. Du Bois has been the subject of a surprisingly small amount of historical writing. Francis L. Broderick, *W. E. B. Du Bois: Negro Leader in a Time of Crisis* * (Stanford: Stanford Univ., 1959) and Elliott M. Rudwick, *W. E. B. Du Bois: A Study in Minority Group Leadership* * (Philadelphia: Univ. Pennsylvania, 1960) are recent biographical studies. For representative works by Du Bois himself, see: *The Souls of Black Folk* * (Chicago: A. C. McClurg, 1903); *Dusk of Dawn* * (New York: Harcourt, Brace, 1940); *Black Folks, Then and Now* (New York: H. Holt, 1939). Langston Hughes, *Fight for Freedom: The Story of the NAACP* (New York: Norton, 1962) and Warren D. St. James, *The National Association for the Advancement of Colored People* (New York: Exposition Press, 1958) are two volumes which enlighten their readers on the activities of the most important organization fighting for the Negro cause.

Gunnar Myrdal, *An American Dilemma: The Negro Problem and Modern Democracy,** 2 vols. (New York: Harper & Brothers, 1944) has become a monumental classic and remains valuable for an understanding of the Negro's presence in American society. *Black Moses* * (Madison: Univ. Wisconsin, 1955) by E. David Cronon is a biography of Marcus Garvey and the story of his movement. Margaret Just Butcher, *The Negro in American Culture* (New York: Knopf, 1956) is a well-balanced study. Two volumes which complement each other very well are August Meier, *Negro Thought in America, 1880–1915* * (Ann Arbor: Univ. Michigan, 1963) and I. A. Newby, *Jim Crow's Defense: Anti-Negro Thought in America, 1900–1930* * (Baton Rouge: Louisiana State Univ., 1965). Charles Wynes (ed.), *The Negro in the South Since 1865* (University, Ala.: Univ. Alabama, 1965) contains several relevant essays. An excellent general survey of the Negro in American life is John Hope Franklin, *From Slavery to Freedom: A History of American Negroes* * (New York: Knopf, 1947), while a brief but superb summary of recent scholarship may be found in August Meier and Elliott M. Rudwick, *From Plantation to Ghetto: An Interpretive History of American Negroes* * (New York: Hill & Wang, 1966). Rayford W. Logan, *The Negro in American Life and Thought: The Nadir, 1877–1901* * (New York: Dial Press, 1954) details the North's desertion of the Negro following Reconstruction. E. Franklin Frazier, *The Negro in the United States* (New York: Macmillan, 1949) is a sociologist's approach to the subject. Three volumes directed toward exposing the darker side of black-white relationships are Arthur F. Raper, *The Tragedy of Lynching* (Chapel Hill: Univ. North Carolina, 1933), Walter Francis White, *Rope and Faggot: A Biography of Judge Lynch* (New York: Knopf, 1929), and R. Ginzburg, *One Hundred Years of Lynchings* * (New York: Lancer Books, 1962).

The segregation-desegregation theme in regard to southern schools has attracted much attention. Don Shoemaker (ed.), *With All Deliberate Speed: Segregation-Desegregation in Southern Schools* (New York: Harper, 1957) is a study of the situation during the first few years following the Supreme Court decision of 1954, based upon statistics compiled by the Southern Educational Reporting Service. A. P. Blaustein and C. C. Ferguson, *Desegregation and the Law: The Meaning and Effect of the School Segregation Cases* * (New Brunswick: Rutgers Univ., 1957) is an early attempt to explain the legal implications of the 1954 Supreme Court decision. More interpretive is Benjamin Muse, *Ten Years of Prelude: The Story of Integration Since the Supreme Court's 1954 Decision* (New York: Viking Press, 1964). Muse also has a volume entitled *Virginia's Massive Resistance* (Bloomington: Indiana Univ., 1961). Bob Smith,

They Closed Their Schools * (Chapel Hill: Univ. North Carolina, 1965) is a thorough and detailed account of Prince Edward County, Virginia, which abolished its public school system because of the Court's order, while a more general work on Virginia is Robbins L. Gates, *The Making of Massive Resistance: Virginia's Politics of Public School Desegregation* (Chapel Hill: Univ. North Carolina, 1964). Robin M. Williams and Margaret W. Ryan (eds.), *Schools in Transition: Community Experiences in Desegregation* (Chapel Hill: Univ. North Carolina, 1954) describes the process of school desegregation in several upper South states prior to the Supreme Court decision of 1954. Omer Carmichael, *The Louisville Story* (New York: Simon & Schuster, 1957) is an excellent account of school desegregation of Kentucky's largest city. Dealing with two upper South states' experiences are essays by Monroe Billington: "Public School Integration in Oklahoma, 1954–1963," *The Historian,* vol. 26 (1964) and "Public School Integration in Missouri, 1954–1965," *Journal of Negro Education,* vol. 35 (1966). Truman M. Pierce and others, *White and Negro Schools in the South: An Analysis of Biracial Education* (Englewood Cliffs: Prentice-Hall, 1955) is a competent collection of essays which implies criticism of the South, while the southern position is expounded by James J. Kilpatrick, *The Southern Case for School Segregation* (New York: Crowell-Collier, 1962). Harry Ashmore, *The Negro and the Schools* * (Chapel Hill: Univ. North Carolina, 1954) contains the observations of an Arkansas newspaperman prior to the school desegregation crisis in Little Rock. Robert Penn Warren, *Segregation: The Inner Conflict of the South* * (New York: Random House, 1956) was written following the 1954 Supreme Court decision and its brevity is compensated by its depth of perception. Gary Orfield, *The Reconstruction of Southern Education: The Schools and the 1964 Civil Rights Act* (New York: Wiley-Interscience, 1969) is an excellent study focusing upon the activities of civil servants in the Department of Health, Education and Welfare who worked out policies to make effective the 1964 law, which authorized the withholding of funds from schools which refused to desegregate. Margaret Anderson, *The Children of the South* * (New York: Farrar, Straus & Giroux, 1966) is the moving story of the Negro children who desegregated the schools in Clinton, Tennessee; its emphasis is upon the human aspects of desegregation.

James Silver, *Mississippi: The Closed Society* * (New York: Harcourt, Brace & World, 1964) is the story of the desegregation of the University of Mississippi as told from the point of view of a white faculty member who favored lowering the color bars, while James H. Meredith, *Three Years in Mississippi* (Bloomington: Indiana Univ., 1966) is a recounting of his experiences by the Negro who successfully desegregated Ole Miss. For information on Negro colleges see Willard Range, *The*

Rise and Progress of Negro Colleges in Georgia, 1865–1949 (Athens, Ga.: Univ. Georgia, 1951) and Earl J. McGrath, *The Predominantly Negro Colleges and Universities in Transition* * (New York: Columbia Univ. Bureau of Publications, 1965).

* Available in paperback.

CHAPTER XVIII

THE CIVIL RIGHTS REVOLUTION

In 1940 Ralph Bunche, American Negro and later a high ranking official in the United Nations, wrote, "There are Negroes . . . who, fed up with frustration of their life here, see no hope and express an angry desire 'to shoot their way out of it.' I have on many occasions heard Negroes exclaim: 'Just give us machine guns and we'll blow the lid off the whole damn business.'" Even though only a very small minority of blacks actually desired to destroy American society, continued frustrations with the social and economic order and resentment of "whitey" greatly escalated black activities and demands in the four middle decades of the twentieth century. By the 1960s a civil rights revolution was in full swing, although no single individual or organization spoke for or led the blacks. The movement to elevate the Negro's position took many forms, the routes to the same goals were as different as were the travelers, and the goals of the various organizations were not always the same. If some observers saw the diversity which characterized the Negro movement as a weakening of the effect of Negro efforts in their own behalf, others saw it as strength, recognizing that many battles must be fought on many fronts by men and organizations whose temperaments, tactics, and strategies were necessarily multifarious. Since nearly one-half of the Negroes in the United States lived outside the South by 1960, the civil rights revolution

had become national in character. But the South was the seedbed for
much of the dissatisfaction, and many of the events and leaders in the
movement were in the South.

The Coalescent Years

The New Deal Era was in many ways a time of regression for the
status of the Negro, but at the same time it constituted a significant turning point in American race relations. This admixture of relapse and progress was evident in regard to the New Deal itself. Discrimination hovered around black men in almost every federal program, and these
programs provided little assistance for the Negro in the fields of agriculture, housing, jobs, or economic security during the dreary days of the
Great Depression. Under the National Recovery Administration, whites
took over Negro-held jobs when wages were raised, causing some blacks
to refer to the NRA as the "Negro Removal Administration." The NRA
codes established in various industries did not provide for wage differentials between the races, but in practice many loopholes existed. The Tennessee Valley Authority, conforming to southern separatist practices, excluded Negroes from model towns like Norris, Tennessee, and it placed
"white" and "colored" signs on toilet doors and above water fountains.
The TVA preferred whites for skilled jobs, and unskilled work crews
were segregated. Public Works Administration housing contracts in the
South called for the use of Negro workers, but blacks did not obtain a
specified percentage of the payrolls, as the law required. Public relief
monies made available to the states by the federal government were not
always distributed on an equitable basis, even though the South's Negro
population was the recipient of a large share of the total amount. Formu-
las were drawn up in some states and cities to prevent a disproportion of
the federal funds from gravitating to the lowly black man.

The Civilian Conservation Corps and the National Youth Administration often excluded Negroes from their programs, and only a few
were employed in the southern local offices of these agencies. State and
local officials told Negroes who inquired about work that the CCC was
for whites only, and when criticized for this policy, Georgia's director of
selection claimed young Negro men were needed "for chopping cotton
and for planting other produce." Before the CCC expired a small percentage of Negroes were enrolled in the total program, but they remained underrepresented in the Fourth Corps Area which covered most
of the South. The NYA had a Division of Negro Affairs under the direction of Mrs. Mary McLeod Bethune, a South Carolina native who had
become a national leader among her race. Under her leadership the NYA

avoided the controversies besetting the CCC, but relatively few southern blacks profited from the NYA programs.

Despite this overt discrimination in many federal agencies, particularly at the operational level in the South, many prominent New Dealers manifested interest in the welfare of American Negroes. Their concern was rooted in a broad humanitarian interest in all submerged classes of American society, but specifically it was related to the fact that Negro political power was rising. The migration of Negroes to the North had made that minority group one that could not be overlooked, and New Dealers and their supporters were wholly conscious of this. President Franklin D. Roosevelt had built a coalition of support which depended upon white southerners, and he hesitated to speak out for Negro rights for fear of alienating southern congressmen who could scuttle his entire economic program. However, in his first year in office, the President did appoint more qualified blacks to federal positions than the three Presidents preceding him had appointed in twelve years in office, and privately he communicated a sense of concern for the Negro's plight. To Mrs. Bethune, Roosevelt once said, "People like you and me are fighting . . . for the day when a man will be regarded as a man regardless of his race. That day will come, but we must pass through perilous times before we realize it." In a speech at all-Negro Howard University in Washington, D. C., he said that "there should be no forgotten men and no forgotten races" among American citizens. By overcoming a handicap of his own, Roosevelt became an inspiration for Negroes to rise above theirs.

If the blacks received more words than action from the President, they found that Mrs. Eleanor Roosevelt was willing to stand up for their cause, and she became the New Deal's symbol of support for the minority race. She appeared in public with Negro leaders, attended functions sponsored by Negro organizations, and had her photograph taken with Negroes, a practice prohibited by all her predecessors. At a Conference on Human Welfare in Birmingham, Alabama, Mrs. Roosevelt sat in the section set aside for Negroes. When police asked her to move to the white section, she put her chair in the aisle between the two groups rather than surrender completely. Manifesting a genuine humanitarian concern for race relations, the First Lady best illustrated her attitude in 1939, when she resigned from the Daughters of the American Revolution, after that group prohibited Marian Anderson from giving a recital in Constitution Hall in Washington. Miss Anderson, internationally famous as an operatic contralto, gave her concert from the steps of Lincoln Memorial, some seventy-five thousand people attending this Easter Sunday program. More than any other, the incident demonstrated the New Deal administration's concern for the status of the Negro.

Despite the discrimination common in the New Deal agencies,

many Negroes survived the depression because of the Rooseveltian relief programs. The significant fact about these programs was not that they saved the Negroes, but that blacks were included in them in the first place. The Public Works Administration built schools, hospitals, and homes for Negroes, federal education grants went to Negro colleges, and the National Labor Relations Board allowed blacks voting rights in labor disputes. The activities of the Works Progress Administration were no more than a stopgap program for the unemployed white laborer, but for the black man it was a significant step in his struggle for equality. For the first time in history, the American Negro received equal wages for the same amount of work done as the white man. A Georgia newspaper-woman, Lorena Hickok, wrote, "For these people to be getting $12 a week—at least twice as much as common labor has ever been paid down here before—is an awfully bitter pill for Savannah people to swallow. . . . The Federal Reemployment Director observed yesterday: 'Any nigger who gets over $8 a week is a spoiled nigger, that's all.'" A principle had been inaugurated, even though it was to take years to become well established. But Negroes had made a start toward being a part of the whole, and in 1936 they showed their appreciation by voting for Roosevelt in large numbers.

This expression of confidence in the Democratic party as their ray of hope did not mean that blacks believed they had won their battles. On the contrary, the 1930s witnessed increased activity by Negroes and Negro organizations in behalf of their race. Attacks upon biracial education in the 1930s led to partial successes in the postwar era. The practice of lynching also received the attention of various Negro groups, particularly the NAACP. The NAACP had long been an opponent of lynching, and perhaps because of the Association's activities, lynchings had declined in the 1920s. The depression reversed the trend and in 1930 lynch mobs killed twenty-one victims. Supported by the Commission on Interracial Cooperation, a Southern Commission on the Study of Lynchings carefully investigated the lynchings of 1930, making its report public in 1933. The Association of Southern Women for the Prevention of Lynching was founded under the auspices of the Commission. Several anti-lynching laws had been introduced into Congress earlier in the century, but when a southern filibuster killed the Dyer bill in 1922 and when lynchings declined, agitation for legislation had dwindled. These studies, the formation of new groups, and renewed demands by the NAACP for federal action focused attention once again on antilynching legislation.

An antilynching bill drafted by the NAACP was introduced in Congress in late 1933. Similar to the old Dyer bill, this act would provide for federal trials of mob members if states did not act, punish law officers who were derelict in their duties, and levy damage claims against counties in which lynching occurred. This bill and others like it were debated from time to time throughout the remainder of the decade, but filibusters or other parliamentary maneuvers always pushed them aside. In 1938 Texas's Tom Connally led a six-week filibuster. After two attempts to invoke cloture failed, the southerners successfully shelved an antilynching law. The nation was not ready to control the white supremacists, even though lynchings and the antilynching debates lowered the South in the eyes of the remainder of the nation. For a variety of reasons lynching declined in the late 1930s, and agitation for an antilynching law was overcome by other more pressing matters.

The stepped-up tempo for Negro equality in the 1930s was a precursor to the demands made during the crisis of World War II. Before the United States entered that great war, black leaders were already demanding full Negro participation in the defense effort. In September 1940 several leaders presented at the White House a program for total equality for Negroes in the armed services and the nation's defense industries. Here was an opportunity for advancing civil and economic rights never before available to the Negro. Despite the plea, the one million Negroes who served in the armed services both at home and abroad were generally segregated. Segregation existed not only in the field but also at camps, posts, and bases. The blacks were relegated to inadequate Jim Crow recreational facilities, quarters, and transportation accommodations. Even the blood banks were segregated. Life in the armed forces mirrored the society from which the Negro came, and racial incidents were fairly frequent. In the South white citizens often insulted Negro soldiers, and low morale was reported from the battlefronts because of prejudicial treatment of blacks by white Army officers. As a result of these events an order was issued in 1944 banning segregation in recreational and transportation facilities on Army bases, but Negroes were disappointed when the ban was not enforced.

At the beginning of the war, the Army raised Benjamin O. Davis to the rank of Brigadier General, and the Secretary of War and the Director of Selective Service named Negro assistants, but blacks considered these nothing more than token appointments. In 1940 the armed forces abolished segregation in all officer candidate schools of the Army, Navy, and Marines. The Air Force retained segregation of its training schools, one for Negro pilots being established at Tuskegee Institute. Some Negroes attended integrated officers' training programs, and the Navy began to accept Negroes for jobs other than messmen. During the Battle of the Bulge in early 1945, the Army distributed platoons of twenty-five hundred Negro volunteers from the Supply Service among eleven white divisions. These men fought throughout the succeeding drive across Germany, the only time during the war that ground combat forces were integrated.

When the nation's defense industries began to tool up for expanded production in 1940 and 1941, Negroes saw an opportunity for actual economic advancement. But unemployed whites filled most of these new jobs, and blacks remained without jobs or were used only for janitorial and other menial chores. The government theoretically opposed discrimination, and in August 1940 it urged employers with government contracts to hire on a nondiscriminatory basis. In October an appropriation act specifically prohibited discrimination in job training for defense industries, but the South circumvented this ruling by training Negroes only for jobs already open to them. When it was evident that discrimination remained in effect, Negro leaders protested vigorously and A. Philip Randolph, long-time activist on behalf of his race, conceived the idea of a mass march on Washington to dramatize job discrimination. After a highly publicized meeting in February 1941 at which organizational plans were laid, Negro leaders promised to mobilize 100,000 black workers for a July March on Washington. As the movement grew, government officials came to realize the import of the planned march and tried to head it off. The Office of Production Management once again encouraged defense contractors to hire black workers, and President Roosevelt called for "immediate steps to facilitate the full utilization of our manpower," but Negro leaders rejected these statements as meaningless. The administration then called a series of conferences between governmental officials and the Negroes out of which came a recommendation that the President proclaim an official statement against discrimination and establish a committee to hear grievances. In June 1941 President Roosevelt issued his famous Executive Order 8802 in which he forbade defense industries and training programs to discriminate, required defense contracts to contain nondiscriminatory clauses, and authorized the establishment of a Fair Employment Practices Committee (FEPC). The Negroes called off their march in view of this Presidential action.

The FEPC had no power to enforce its directives, and not once did it recommend that a defense contract be cancelled because a company practiced discrimination. The Committee spent much of its time publicizing the President's statement and seeking information, but little attempt was made to hear complaints about alleged discrimination. After the Committee was transferred from the jurisdiction of the War Production Board to that of the War Manpower Commission, hearings on complaints against southern railroads and unions were "indefinitely postponed." Three members of the Committee resigned because of this action, and a new Committee had to be organized. The new and enlarged FEPC was organized in May 1943, but it also lacked enforcement powers and was devoid of any real influence after impassioned critics, particularly southerners, attacked it. Despite the obstacles, the FEPC advanced Negro employment in war industries, and it successfully encouraged federal employment services in many communities to hire Negroes. Its greatest influence was on Negro morale. Even though discrimination was flagrant, Negroes had a federal agency—until June 1946 when it expired for lack of funds—which was specifically interested in their problems. Even though the FEPC was one of the least important of the various war agencies, it was a giant step toward economic advancement for black Americans in the postwar era.

World War II served as a coalescent period for the postwar civil rights revolution. The out-migration of Negroes from the South reached flood tide during the war—greater than the so-called Great Migration of the World War I era—as blacks searched for improved economic opportunities during a time of industrial expansion. Those who improved their status realized they remained behind the whites, and those who made no headway were more bitter than ever toward The Man and the system which held them down. The ideology of the war itself had a great impact upon Negro thinking. This was a war of democracies against dictatorships; it was a fight to defend the "Four Freedoms"—freedom from want, freedom from fear, freedom of speech, and freedom of religion. Negroes saw the inconsistencies of these ideals with actual practices at home and abroad. One Negro soldier said, "Just carve on my tombstone, 'Here lies a black man killed fighting a yellow man for the protection of a white man.'" Another soldier defiantly told his white tormentors during a confrontation, "If I've got to die for democracy, I might as well die for some of it right here and now." Soldiers returning from the war were particularly outraged at the paradoxes in American life. If fighting for the world's freedom was worth dying for, perhaps it was worth dying for the freedom of their race in the freest of the free nations. White Americans and southerners who had fretted at the restlessness of Negroes and their groups before and during World War II had yet to see Negro protest of great magnitude. It came in the postwar era.

The Catalytic Years

Negro aspirations during World War II brought on a not unexpected white reaction. Tensions among workers caused a series of racial disturbances, the most notable riot occurring in June 1943 in Detroit. If the South had fewer incidents of outright violence, the racial rumor mills worked overtime during the wartime emergency, and the efforts of many southern interracial agencies were needed to keep racial unrest at tolerable levels. Surprisingly, in contrast to the years immediately following World War I, no major postwar racial violence occurred when the demobilized soldiers returned home. But this was only the quiet before the storm broke. The relentless tide of events to make equality of race a fact in the United States had been set in motion, and there was no way for opponents to contain it.

Concurrent with and closely related to the postwar drive for Negro voting rights and school desegregation * were Negro demands for other concessions rightfully theirs: equal employment opportunities, non-discriminatory accommodations in private and public facilities, and fair housing conditions. The Negro's lot everywhere, but especially in the South, was still far below the status of the whites, and by 1955 Negro humility, patience, and forbearance had dried up. Black leaders recognized how much more needed to be done and that old methods were not effective. They determined to lead their people in campaigns of civil disobedience. The era of boycotts, freedom rides, sit-ins, and street demonstrations was about to begin. Why did the black man wait so long to espouse vigorously his own cause? Roy Wilkins, executive secretary of the NAACP, has given his opinion: ". . . this new push? It's cumulative. It's the emergence of Africa. It's being hungry. It's the G.I. Bill. It's major-league baseball with Negroes. It's the eight thousand to ten thousand Negroes graduating from college each year. It's kids being impatient. . . ."

A major catalytic agent in the forthcoming Negro revolution was the Montgomery, Alabama, bus boycott of 1955–56. Some observers call the boycott the opening battle of the revolution; most certainly it stirred the nation and was largely responsible for the Negro's move toward the use of direct action in the decades to follow. On December 1, 1955, Mrs. Rosa Parks took a seat on a Montgomery city bus in the section reserved for whites. When a white man boarded the filled vehicle, the bus driver ordered Mrs. Parks to relinquish her seat, but she refused and was arrested by the police. Negroes who had long repressed their exasperation at the Jim Crow system organized a protest boycott of the bus system for the day of Mrs. Parks's trial. Leaflets requesting support for the boycott were widely distributed, and Negro ministers implored their congregations to cooperate with the boycott. On December 5, the day of the trial, city buses traveled their routes with hardly any passengers. Blacks had constituted about three-fourths of the riders in the past, but the boycott was almost totally effective.

On that same day, leaders of Montgomery's Negro community formed the Montgomery Improvement Association. They resolved to continue the boycott until bus drivers accorded courteous treatment to Negro passengers, until black drivers were employed on predominantly Negro routes, and until the bus company agreed to change its policies in regard to seating arrangements on buses. The Negroes suggested that seating be done on a first-come, first-served basis, with blacks being seated at the rear of the bus, and progressing forward as the seats were

* See Chapters XVI and XVII.

filled. Whites would be seated at the front of the bus and progress toward the rear. The Association organized car pools in lieu of bus transportation. Over three hundred private automobiles traveled over the city transporting Negroes to and from jobs without charge. Private contributions paid for these costs, which ran about $5,000 per week. Whites expected the boycott to falter within a matter of days, but the blacks were determined to make their private transportation system an adequate substitute. The Montgomery Police Commissioner acknowledged that the Negroes' system moved with "military precision."

When white officials were unable to persuade Negroes to abandon the boycott, more stringent tactics were employed. Policemen gave tickets to Negroes for minor and concocted traffic violations. White hoodlums bombed the homes of black leaders, and later mass indictments based on a constitutionally questionable antilabor law were meted out. All Montgomery Improvement Association leaders were indicted, several being convicted and jailed. This action spurred the boycott to greater effectiveness. After the boycott had been in effect for several months, whites began to talk of economic retaliation against the Negroes. But the intertwining of the black and white economies was such that the threats were not carried out. Whites realized that if Negroes did not have jobs, they could not pay their rent to white landlords, meet their installment payments at the local stores, or make cash purchases at white-owned stores. White housewives were reluctant to fire their Negro cooks and maids, when they contemplated the prospect of doing their own cooking and household chores. Negroes recognized the advantage they held and determined to win the battle. The Montgomery Transit Company faced bankruptcy after operating the buses for months without passengers, and the white community grew weary of the impasse. The issue was settled in December 1956 when a federal court ordered the city bus company to operate desegregated vehicles.

The Negro victory can be attributed to determination and unity, and their leaders supplied much of both. The president of the Montgomery Improvement Association was the Rev. Martin Luther King, Jr., a twenty-seven-year-old native of Atlanta who had received his Ph.D. degree from Boston University before assuming his first pastorate in Montgomery a few months before the boycott began. King did not instigate the boycott, but his leadership became synonymous with it, and his oratory inspired the Negro masses during the crisis. King was a Christian pacifist, although his philosophy was deeply influenced by the life and writings of Mahatma Gandhi. In the tradition of Henry David Thoreau, King believed civil disobedience to be the most effective means to combat the tyranny of government and a closed society. As an act of nonviolent resistance, the bus boycott reflected King's philosophy. If this resistance resulted in jail terms or even death, King told his followers, the price for freeing the Negro race would be worth it. He thus placed the primary responsibility for race improvement upon the Negroes themselves. Day and night he preached passive resistance. The bus boycott skyrocketed King to national and international prominence. He traveled to India and Africa, where he was praised as a leader in the emerging people's fight for freedom. While the civil rights revolution had many leaders, King for a time came closest to being the spokesman for all Negro Americans. His charismatic leadership was recognized by whites and blacks alike.

Soon after the success of the Montgomery boycott, King and his followers organized the Southern Christian Leadership Conference (SCLC), designed to coordinate nonviolent, direct-action activities in southern cities. Bus boycotts in Tallahassee, Florida, and Birmingham, Alabama, were supported by the SCLC. Encouraged by King's successes, the Tuskegee Civic Association in June 1957 inaugurated a boycott of white merchants, after the state legislature had gerrymandered Tuskegee's boundaries in such a way that almost no Negroes lived within the city's voting district. Three years later the Supreme Court in *Gomillion* v. *Lightfoot* ruled the gerrymander illegal. This victory, sponsored by the NAACP Legal Defense Fund and coupled with the events in Montgomery, Tallahassee, and Birmingham, spurred actions among southern Negroes. They no longer feared white hoodlums, police night sticks, or jails. They determined to use their collective weight to crumble the towers of Jim Crowism, and the SCLC became a prime agent in that destruction.

In the spring of 1960 four students from North Carolina Agricultural and Technological College staged a sit-in at the lunch counter of a variety store in Greensboro. The store had welcomed the business of the Negroes, except that they were required to stand when served at the snack bar. The students sat on the stools at the counter and refused to move when ordered to do so. In the confrontation, the students requested support from the SCLC, and King's organization, now headquartered in Atlanta, rushed to their side. Before the spring ended, hundreds of black students engaged in dozens of similar sit-in demonstrations throughout the upper South, the Atlantic coastal states, and Texas. Following the SCLC's nonviolent direct-action approach and with moral and financial support from that organization, the college students' revolt was a decisive step in the civil rights revolution, as they successfully desegregated lunch counters in drug and variety stores. The campaign proved to be a failure in the Deep South, where arrests ran into the hundreds and where police brutality was evident in the breakup of the peaceful demonstrations, but the college students had captured the imagination of the nation's Negroes, and they were to remain in the forefront of the movement.

In April 1960 the Student Nonviolent Coordinating Committee (SNCC) was formed as a wing of SCLC, and as its name suggested, it was pledged to the philosophy of Martin Luther King. As the sit-in movement grew, the students concluded that King's organization was too cautious, and within a year after its formation SNCC had broken with SCLC. At this same time, the NAACP decided to make direct action a major part of its strategy. Having engaged in demonstrations only in a peripheral way in the past, the NAACP reactivated its college and youth chapters in the southern states with plans to take part in activism. Young people needed only the slightest nudge from their adult sponsors to become involved in the NAACP's direct-action strategy. With financial and legal backing from the national organization, the youth groups of the NAACP became eager leaders in the confrontations with Jim Crow. If some adults were reluctant to support the youths, they were swept along by the events which saw hundreds of Negro youths jailed for civil disobedience. A college student at the 1961 NAACP convention accurately remarked, "We don't need the adults, but they need us."

Closely related to the sit-in demonstrations were the freedom rides sponsored by the Congress of Racial Equality (CORE). Founded by pacifists and socialists during World War II and dominated by its white members for two decades, this biracial organization was dedicated to improving the lot of the Negro. It was virtually unknown to the general public until January 1961 when James Farmer became its national director. Farmer conceived the idea of headlining segregated transportation facilities by having groups of blacks ride interstate buses in the South, while refusing to abide by Jim Crow regulations. In the spring of 1961 hundreds of Negro youths began their freedom rides. Several students were injured when their buses were met at terminals by hostile whites, and one of the buses they were riding was burned in Alabama. Dozens upon dozens of the riders were arrested and jailed, and many of them spent a month or more in prison in Mississippi. But their efforts were not in vain. The Interstate Commerce Commission ordered the desegregation of all facilities used in interstate transportation, and although the South complied only partially, an important step was taken toward equality.

The final and signal victory of the first phase of direct-action strategy came after a series of events in Birmingham, Alabama. In the fall of 1962 Birmingham Negroes began an all-out boycott of white merchants in order to force desegregation of lunch counters and other facilities. Six months later, even though businesses were suffering, white merchants remained adamant, and Negro leaders agreed that a massive demonstration was needed. Police Commissioner Eugene (Bull) Connor refused to issue a permit for a march, but the Negroes defied him and marched anyway. When scores of blacks were jailed, the Birmingham Negro community was aroused and great mass demonstrations followed. City officials panicked and permitted fire hoses, electric cattle prods, and police dogs to be used to break up the demonstrations. On Monday morning following Easter Sunday, 1963, Negro children were encouraged to return to their churches to pray, sing, and dance. On the following Thursday, three thousand children skipped school to demonstrate in the streets. When these children were jailed too, more students demonstrated, and city officials could not cope with the tide of events. At the same time adults and older youths staged sit-ins, which resulted in further confrontations with the police when owners demanded that the "trespassers" be removed. Pictures of police dogs attacking Negro demonstrators damaged the South's and the nation's image around the world.

A civil rights aide from the Department of Justice was able to effect agreements between the businessmen and the Negroes, and by the end of the summer about two-thirds of the city's lunch counters and restaurants were desegregated. During the year following the riots in Birmingham, desegregation of privately owned public facilities was stepped up considerably throughout the region. Desegregated movie theatres in southern cities increased that year from 109 to 287, restaurants from 141 to 298, hotels and motels from 163 to 267, and lunch counters from 204 to 355. These figures indicated that the South was still a long way from full equality of private and public facilities, but the disturbances of the past two years had had their beneficial effects. Perhaps they most revealed to white merchants that the economies of the white and black communities were interdependent. When the merchants had to choose between continued segregation coupled with loss of profits or desegregation and money in the cash register, most of them chose the latter.

Racial unrest, demonstrations, and confrontations across the nation in the spring of 1963 stimulated important Negro leaders to plan another March on Washington in order to show the need for jobs and for federal action to advance Negro rights. After the Birmingham demonstration, plans for the march were stepped up, and emphasis was placed on passage of a civil rights bill then before the Congress. In August over 250,000 people, nearly one-fourth of whom were white, converged on Washington to hear addresses from the steps of the Lincoln Memorial by A. Philip Randolph, Roy Wilkins, and Martin Luther King, Jr. King caught the imagination of the nation as well as those present in his "I Have a Dream" speech in which he articulated the ever recurrent dream of Negroes that they might someday be fully included in the American society. While King said what blacks had been saying before, the situation and the times indicated that this mass March on Washington was a major step in the direction of freedom for Negroes. The march had the approval of President John F. Kennedy, and it undoubtedly aided in the passage of a civil rights bill the following year. More importantly, the march symbolized the new directions Negro activity would take in the future. While the march was orderly and peaceful, it stimulated a deeper concern for the problems of the Negro masses and it encouraged a new militancy among some blacks. The nation was about to witness The Violent Years of the civil rights revolution.

The Violent Years

The nationwide racial violence during and after 1963 did not bypass the South. Throughout the southern states, but especially in Mississippi and Alabama, the gulf between whites and blacks had become wider, communication was almost nonexistent, and the polarization of the two races was never greater. Racists cowed southern moderates into silence as they advocated white supremacy and vowed to defy the national government's racial policies. In June 1963 Medgar Evers, an NAACP official, was cut down with a rifle shot in front of his home in Jackson, Mississippi. After Evers's death, one Byron de la Beckwith was indicted for the murder, but two juries failed to convict the avowed segregationist even though the evidence against him was strong. In the middle of the summer of 1964 more violence came when white Mississippians resisted a voter registration drive in their state by some 200 volunteer college students from across the nation. Three of the students, one Negro and two whites, were killed and buried in a shallow grave at a dam construction site near Philadelphia, Mississippi. Four other students were injured by gunfire, 52 were beaten, and over 250 were arrested for various reasons. Thirty Negro churches were damaged or destroyed during the long, hot summer, as whites used any means possible to intimidate the blacks and their supporters.

Negroes had by this time become convinced that the road to their success lay in the voting booth. The voter registration drive in Mississippi was only one of many attempts to register Negroes to vote in the southern states. In January 1965 Martin Luther King led a group of followers in a registration drive in Selma, Alabama. When he was unsuccessful, King encouraged mass demonstrations in the streets and laid plans for a fifty-mile march from Selma to Montgomery, the state capital, to publicize the unavailability of basic political rights for Alabama Negroes. Using tear gas and clubs, mounted police aborted the attempt to march on Montgomery. This action spurred white citizens from other regions to rush to Selma to assist the Negro cause. Hoodlums savagely attacked four clergymen from the North; one of them, James J. Reeb, a white Unitarian minister from Boston, died two days after the brutal beatings. A few days later King resumed his march upon Montgomery, this time under the authority of a federal court order and protected by federal marshals, a nationalized Alabama militia, and dozens of FBI agents. Over twenty-five thousand marchers had gathered in Selma, although logistics de-

manded that only a few hundred be permitted to make the four-day trek
to the state capital. Governor George Wallace refused to meet King and
his followers at the end of the journey, but King used the occasion to assure the nation that Negroes would continue to press for their demands.
Within hours after King spoke, Mrs. Viola Liuzzo, who had come from
Detroit to support the march, was shot while driving demonstrators between Montgomery and Selma. The death of this white mother of five
children may have been as instrumental as the march itself in causing the
Congress to pass before midsummer an act to protect the rights of those
who desired to register and participate in the political process. But the
act as ultimately enacted promised more than it could deliver, and Negroes realized their battle was not won.

By 1965 many of the nation's Negroes were coming to believe that
legalism and direct-action strategy were not sufficient to attain the goals
they desired. Progress had been made through legal action in years past,
and Martin Luther King's nonviolent, direct-action approach had
brought additional results, but restless young blacks were not to be pac-
ified by what they considered only occasional crumbs from the white establishment. The tendency toward unity of strategy as symbolized by
King began to dissipate, and the movement for Negro rights became fragmented. In broad generalizations, most members of SNCC and many individuals in CORE constituted the militant left wing of the movement;
the conservative wing was made up of a large number of members of the
NAACP and Urban League officials, including Whitney M. Young, Jr.,
whose efforts were primarily directed toward obtaining jobs for Negroes;
Martin Luther King represented a middle or moderate position, which
included not only members of the SCLC but also many Negroes active in
CORE and the NAACP. The people in the militant left wing of the
movement began to criticize American society from a new perspective.
While Negro leaders in the past had almost always attempted to work
within the limitations of the law, young blacks began to talk more and
more in terms of "revolutionary" changes in the structure of American society. They became increasingly skeptical of "white liberals," whom they
began to consider not their friends. With much needing to be done over
the years, what had white liberals done to help them up to this point?
they asked. In fact, they began to suspect that the white liberals were representatives of the white establishment intent on infiltrating the Negro
movement ostensibly to show their friendship, when all the while their
main objective was to hold down black protest and violence. In the
same category with white liberals, these black militants placed Negroes
who cooperated with the white establishment. Many old leaders of the
NAACP had been appointed to high office, and despite their years of
protest, they were looked upon as "Uncle Toms" by the young militants.

Whitney M. Young, who had developed many contacts with high business and political figures, was referred to as "Whitey" M. Young.

After SNCC had broken with SCLC in 1961, it grew beyond the bounds of the campuses, when its staff of activists placed field workers in southern communities to bring about their desired goals. Howard Zinn has referred to the SNCC groups as "the new abolitionists." SNCC from the very beginning was an organization which directed its appeal to the working classes rather than to the bourgeoisie, and it retained its appeal to young Negroes. Unlike the NAACP, CORE, and other biracial organizations, SNCC was from the start a Negro-led and Negro-dominated organization. James Forman and John Lewis were early leaders of SNCC, but within a few years after it was formed, a group of extremists seized control of the organization under the leadership of Stokely Carmichael.

While Martin Luther King symbolized Negroes who were willing to press for their rights but hoped to avoid violence in the process, Carmichael was clearly preaching revolt, law-violation, violence, and revolution. He joined King as one of the two most charismatic leaders of the Negro movement, and his influence was every bit as great as King's. He had the ability to articulate the demands of the frustrated young black as no other leader had done. While the conservative and moderate organizations and leaders continued to aspire to be a part of the white man's world, Carmichael scoffed at such aspirations. Integration was as much a dirty word to Carmichael as segregation was to the old-line Negro leaders. Carmichael turned SNCC into what Ralph McGill called "a reverse Ku Klux Klan." Preaching hatred of whites, encouraging violence and property destruction, showing impatience with Negro moderates, Carmichael inspired young blacks as no other leader had done. He encouraged his followers "to think black" and he instilled racial pride in his brothers. "Black is beautiful" is a phrase associated with him, and he added to the American vocabulary the word "Honky," an opprobrious term referring to the white man. In 1966 while on a march in Mississippi, Carmichael in an angry mood impulsively shouted "black power," and thus gave emerging black militancy its most useful phrase.

The concept of Black Power has never been satisfactorily defined. To many Negroes it was a phrase expressing general discontent with the Negro's lot and embracing a vague notion that somehow the Negro might unite to help himself. To conservative and moderate Negroes it was a phrase used to characterize their efforts to bring about improvement in the Negro's status through economic and political channels. To militant blacks it expressed the growing attitude that Negroes must help themselves at the expense of whites. In any case, no other phrase excited American Negroes more. It removed despair and hopelessness from blacks, giving them something to live for. Militant Black Power advocates joined with moderate and conservative Negroes in singing "We Shall Overcome," and each group advanced toward that goal in its own way. If some Negroes remained alienated and in a state of despair, the concept of Black Power supported their acknowledged hopeless fight against the dominant society.

The logical extension of Black Power was a movement of separatism. If moderate Negro leaders continued to desire an integrated society, cynical young militants began to feel that this could never be attained, and even if it could, it was not a desirable goal. They came to believe that they could improve themselves only by remaining separate, by fighting their own battles, by developing pride of race, and by remaining united as a racial minority. They no longer accepted integration as the answer to their problems, and they scoffed at "black bourgeoisie" who aspired to higher socioeconomic status. But no modern Marcus Garvey arose to lead these separatists in a mass movement to Africa, and such a leader is not likely to appear in the future. The separatists probably would not follow such a person anyway. The concept of separatism in the 1960s was not one of physical separation, but rather one of realization that races were in fact separate despite their physical proximity. Separation was a fact of life for most Negroes, and the separatists were acknowledging a fait accompli. But they were doing more than that. They were in essence saying that since the white man had insisted upon separation in the past, they would now use that situation to their advantage. In throwing off the yoke of white paternalism, they manifested a new independence. By refusing to aspire to be black-skinned white men, they increased their racial pride. By referring to each other as "soul brothers," they were developing a unity never before experienced. In the past Negroes had passively accepted the white man's evaluation of black men, but they were now making their own evaluations, seeking their own identities, and learning not to be prejudiced against themselves.

A number of lesser organizations took up the cries of Black Power and separatism, the most important being the Black Muslims. Elijah Muhammad preached separation, and his rabid speeches chilled whites when they contemplated the possibility of violence in the wake of his orations. Actually the separatists, knowingly or unknowingly, functioned as a psychological safety valve for tense racial relations. By preaching separation, the Black Muslims were in effect accommodating themselves to the existing American social order, delaying direct confrontation between the whites and the blacks. If the separatists win the battle for the Negro's mind, violent racial warfare may occur sometime in the future, but as of 1970, despite rabid talk and occasional racial incidents, the separatists remained a minute minority of the American Negro population. Most Negroes saw the separatist movement for what it was: a futile and unrealistic attempt on the part of a minority group to destroy or dominate a democratic society. Some blacks flirted with Marxist doctrines, when their leaders encouraged them to fight back against vicious "slavemasters," but as in the past the majority of blacks rejected the clash of classes inherent in Marxian theory.

The final years of the 1960s were ones of racial turmoil for the entire nation. "Burn, baby, burn" became the cry of disillusioned blacks as riots in Harlem, Cleveland, Detroit, Chicago, and nearly every major city in the North (plus Los Angeles in the West) revealed how explosive and destructive race relations were in the country. Major southern cities were not entirely free from this wave of violence, although widespread property destruction and violence characteristic of the 1965 Watts riots in Los Angeles or the 1967 riots in Detroit did not occur in the South. But the South had no cause to bask in its good fortune. Mass communication media and high speed transportation systems overcame regional separateness in many ways, and this was particularly true in regard to race relations. National Negro organizations had local chapters all over the nation, including the South. Through television, national leaders appealing for Negro support entered the homes of southern Negroes as well as those in the North. Airplanes made it possible for Martin Luther King to speak in Atlanta and Chicago on the same day. Whatever else could be said about the Negro protest movement it was now national in scope. No longer was the "Negro problem" exclusively the South's concern, but neither did the nationalizing of race relations exclude the South from the time of troubles.

The Government's Response

President Franklin D. Roosevelt had been only mildly interested in the problems facing American Negroes, and his administration had given little overt attention to Negro requests. Financial relief for needy families during the depths of the depression and the President's executive order outlawing discriminatory employment practices in defense industries during World War II constituted the most important actions taken by the New Deal administration for Negro benefit. But the activities and words of President and Mrs. Roosevelt made it easier for President Harry Truman to go beyond his predecessor. Truman spoke out early for Negro rights, established a blue-ribbon committee to investigate and report on the status of civil rights in the nation, and made numerous recommendations to Congress for legislative action beneficial for minority groups.

Even though the Congress quashed Truman's legislative proposals for Negro equality, the President used his appointive and executive powers and his prestigious position for Negro advancement. In July 1948 he created the Committee on Equality of Treatment and Opportunity in the

Armed Forces. Called the Fahy Committee, after its chairman Charles H. Fahy, this group worked for a year and a half before the three main branches of the armed services agreed to treat all personnel equally. Years passed before all agreements were put into practice, but some policies were effected immediately, and the 1950s witnessed a significant breakthrough in regard to racial policies and practices in the armed services. In 1949 Truman appointed William Henry Hastie to the Third U. S. Circuit Court of Appeals, thus elevating a Negro to the highest judicial post ever held by a member of that race up to that time in American history. Perhaps Truman's greatest assistance to the Negroes resulted from his repeated public statements in which he thumped for equal rights. For the first time black men could look to the President of the United States for moral support, and they were not unaware of the implications of having the President take public stands in their behalf.

Although Truman has been criticized for coveting Negro votes by his actions, he was responding to the increasing demands of blacks and to the drift in public opinion toward a more liberal racial atmosphere. Truman's support in turn encouraged Negroes to step up their efforts for equality of the races. During the Eisenhower Presidential years, federal court decisions (not only the Brown decision of 1954 but also many lesser decisions ruling a variety of state and local segregation laws unconstitutional) gave Negroes cause for hope, despite the fact that Eisenhower himself was less responsive to Negro demands than was Truman. Numerous bills to advance Negro rights were submitted to the Congress, although opponents delayed congressional action. Finally, the increasing demands by Negroes and their supporters for legislative action resulted in the passage of the first civil rights legislation in the eight decades since the Reconstruction Era. Despite southern opposition and extended filibustering techniques, including a record 24-hour, 18-minute speech by Strom Thurmond of South Carolina, the Civil Rights Act of 1957 was passed.

This act was far from the sweeping proposal demanded by Negro leaders and supporters but in view of past failures at the hands of southerners, senators and congressmen supporting the legislation could rightly claim a victory. The act provided for the establishment of a civil rights division within the Department of Justice, and it empowered federal prosecutors to obtain court injunctions in the name of the United States government against actual or threatened interference with the right to vote. It also established a federal Civil Rights Commission with subpoena powers and the authority to investigate discriminatory conditions in the nation and to recommend corrective measures to the President. Until this act was passed, injunctive relief was not available to individuals who were unable to pay for long and complicated court litigation proceedings. Now the United States government would provide attorneys and pay the expenses of all lawsuits of cases involving the violation of Negro voting rights. The act gave federal district courts jurisdiction over such lawsuits, without the necessity of every state alternative being pursued first. For the first time in American history, the Department of Justice itself had the authority to sue in cases where voting rights were being denied, and the suit could reach the federal district courts months sooner than had formerly been possible.

For all these advancements, the Civil Rights Act of 1957 was less than effective when implemented. Individual lawsuits did not create widespread voting by Negroes, and since the powers of the new Civil Rights Commission were limited to fact finding, few tangible results were seen, even though the Commission set about doing its job with a flurry of publicity. Southern congressmen had been able to water down the bill before its final passage, and they were not surprised by its ineffectiveness. While the bill was being weakened before it passed the Senate, Richard Russell had said, "This bill is not going to work any hardship on the people of Georgia," and Herman Tallmadge had earlier criticized Thurmond's one-man filibuster, fearing that a strong stand against so weak a bill might bring stronger civil rights legislation in the future and an antifilibuster closure rule. The two senators were correct in the ineffectiveness of this bill's specific provisions, but they misread the future in regard to additional civil rights legislation.

The 1957 act was important not for the great specific advances it made for the Negro, but rather as a psychological lift for the black race. If Congress could finally push through a civil rights act despite southern opposition, Negroes correctly reasoned, with additional pressures more laws with teeth in them might soon be passed. Growing numbers of Negro voters in northern cities and the general mood of the nation toward the depressed minorities were influential in pressuring legislators to speak out for civil rights legislation. The states caught the spirit of the times too, and under pressure from the NAACP and similar organizations, northern and western states in the late 1950s began to outlaw discrimination in employment, housing, and public facilities. Coupled with federal court decisions requiring actions such as the desegregation of the city parks of New Orleans, the opening to Negroes of a public golf course of Greensboro, North Carolina, and the desegregation of buses within the state of Florida, these actions constituted a veritable revolution in the advancement of legal rights for Negroes.

Primarily as the result of the efforts of Democratic Majority Leader Lyndon Johnson, the Congress in 1960 passed a second piece of legislation dealing with civil rights. President Eisenhower hoped this act would deter "heinous acts of lawlessness," because it made federal crimes out of flight to avoid prosecution for any type of bombing offense and out of willful interference or obstruction to prevent the carrying out of federal court orders in regard to school desegregation. Under the provisions of the act, in areas where the court found a "pattern or practice" of discrimination federal judges were empowered to appoint referees to hear persons claiming that state elections officials had denied them the right to register and vote. Senator Thurmond said of the law while it was still being considered: "This proposal is extreme. It is punitive. It is flagrantly abusive. It is palpably and viciously anti-Southern. It would, in effect, treat the South as a conquered province to be ruled over, insofar as race relations are concerned, by a czar in the person of the Attorney General of the United States. . . ." Black leaders and liberals condemned the act as too mild, and in practice the law was hampered in enforcement because before the finding could be made and referee machinery started, the Justice Department had to bring forth specific cases to prove that qualified citizens had been denied the vote because of race or color.

Two days after taking office in January 1961, President John F. Kennedy wrote a memorandum to the officials of the Coast Guard Academy informing them that he had noticed that no Negroes were a part of the Coast Guard unit in the recent inaugural parade. Although Negro students had not been barred from the Academy, the Coast Guard took the hint and began a vigorous recruiting drive for black applicants. Near the end of his first year in office President Kennedy issued an executive order on "Equal Employment Opportunity," providing for "sanctions and penalties" for owners of businesses with government contracts who engaged in discriminatory employment practices. Administering the Kennedy directive, Vice President Lyndon Johnson called for meetings with government contractors, industrialists, and chamber of commerce executives. To each group Johnson said: "Some say Now; some say Never; let's all say Together." Favorable action was taken on 72 percent of the seventeen hundred complaints about discrimination by government contractors received during the first two years of the Kennedy administration. That administration secured the voluntary pledges of over one hundred major industrial employers and 117 labor unions to carry on an all-out attack on discrimination in employment. Also, the President ordered the Department of Labor to abolish discrimination in training programs under its general supervision, in referrals for employment, and in labor union operations.

In 1962 civil rights proponents introduced a bill to restrict arbitrary use of literacy tests to prevent voters from participating in federal elections. The bill stated that a sixth grade education should be considered sufficient evidence of literacy, but southerners waged a successful filibuster against the literacy test bill, and it was set aside after fourteen days of debate. The President and his brother, Attorney General Robert Kennedy, expressed disappointment with this action, and in June 1963 in a nationally televised speech, President Kennedy became the first Chief Executive since Abraham Lincoln to declare that the Negro's struggle for first-class citizenship was a moral issue involving every person living in the United States. The President also let it be known that by 1963 the Civil Rights Division of the Attorney General's office had twenty-four full-time lawyers, and that he was encouraging his brother to "keep pushing the cases" filed in behalf of Negroes desiring to vote. No President had so captured the imagination of the nation, including Negroes, and Kennedy's verve, style, and polished speeches aroused great hope in minority hearts. But Kennedy was President for only one thousand days before his assassination in November 1963, and few concrete results came from his efforts on behalf of the Negro cause during that brief period of time. He was notably unsuccessful in persuading Congress to enact meaningful civil rights legislation.

To a large extent the racial disturbances in 1963 and 1964 may have been a reaction to the go-slow policies of the national Congress. Negro vocal demands were loud, but the Congress's response was weak. This along with the rising tension related to the whole civil rights movement undoubtedly contributed to the disturbances. The riots and demonstrations, including the August 1963 March on Washington, combined with an aroused national conscience to pressure Congress into passing the Civil Rights Act of 1964, the most important national legislation yet passed on behalf of minority groups. Southern opposition did not readily capitulate. The bill was debated from time to time in both houses of Congress for over a year before its final passage. The longest filibuster in the United States Senate occurred in the spring of 1964 when southern senators, determined to block a final vote, talked against it for nearly eleven weeks. Mississippi's James Eastland and South Carolina's Strom Thurmond led the talk marathon. They received support from sixteen other southerners, but as the filibuster continued it became clear that some senators did not have their hearts in it. Ralph Yarborough of Texas and Lister Hill and John Sparkman of Alabama were considered liberal even by northern standards, but they would have committed political suicide if they had not joined in the opposition. William Fulbright (Arkansas), George Smathers (Florida), Russell Long (Louisiana), and Olin D. Johnston (South Carolina) were also less than enthusiastic about the filibuster even though they participated in it. Tennessee's senators, Estes Kefauver and Albert Gore, refused to support the filibuster, but neither would they join those who wished to limit debate through cloture.

The Civil Rights Act of 1964 was sponsored by President Lyndon Johnson's Democratic administration, but it would not have passed without Republican support. On June 10 when the Senate voted 71 to 29 to end the filibuster, all but six Republicans followed the lead of Everett M. Dirksen, Senate minority leader, and voted with the majority. As soon as the debate was ended, the Senate quickly passed the bill, 73 to 27, with 27 Republicans voting "yes." A bipartisan majority rushed it through the

House of Representatives on July 2, and President Johnson made the measure law a few hours later. Upon signing the bill the President attempted to heal sectional wounds with a conciliatory statement in which he expressed hope that the "springs of racial poison" would soon run dry. Ironically, within a few days after the President's statement, major race riots broke out in Harlem, Brooklyn, Chicago, Philadelphia, Rochester, and Jersey City. Five persons were killed, 750 injured, nearly 2,000 arrested, and millions of dollars of property damage occurred just as the nation began implementing the most sweeping civil rights bill yet passed.

The most important provisions of the Civil Rights Act of 1964 banned discrimination by businesses offering food, lodging, gasoline, or entertainment to the public; forbade discrimination by employers or labor unions when hiring, promoting, dismissing, or making job referrals; authorized government agencies to withhold federal money from any program permitting discrimination; authorized the Attorney General to file suit to force desegregation of schools, playgrounds, parks, libraries, and swimming pools; tightened provisions to prevent denial of Negro voting rights in federal elections by declaring that any person with a sixth grade education was presumed literate and that state literacy tests were not to be applied to him; established a federal agency to assist local communities in settling racial disputes; granted additional powers to the federal Civil Rights Commission and extended its life until 1966.

Alabama Governor George Wallace expressed the opinion of many white southerners toward the passage of the 1964 act when he declared, "This is a sad day for individual freedom and liberty." The white-man-on-the-southern-street was generally inclined to agree, but some white southerners were more willing to acknowledge reality. When the mayor of Nashville, Georgia, said, "Whatever the law is, we will abide," he was expressing an attitude not atypical of many small-town mayors and politicians in the Deep South. Southern Negroes were generally skeptical. Mississippian Charles Evers observed, "The passage of the bill is not the important thing. The most important thing is the implementation of it, that it is accepted by both races without too much hatred. . . ."

The public accommodations section of the 1964 law had drawn the most fire from congressional opponents, and it aroused the most opposition from the general public. In early test cases various courts held the section to be constitutional, and although occasional violations of the law were reported, businesses in the South's major cities generally accepted the fact that the matter had been permanently settled. Soon after the act was passed, the Mississippi Economic Council, a statewide business organization, issued a statement in which it said that "order and respect for the law must be maintained. Lawless activities in the state by individuals and organizations cannot be tolerated. . . . The Civil Rights Act of 1964 has been enacted by Congress as law. It cannot be ignored and should not be unlawfully defied." The voting section of this act promised more than it could deliver, and this weakness in the law stimulated Martin Luther King's demonstrations in Selma and Montgomery, Alabama. The march on Montgomery in turn was a large factor in the passage of an effective voting rights act.

The Voting Rights Act of 1965 provided for elaborate and effective federal machinery for registering voters and assuring the right to vote in areas where a literacy test was still required, and where less than 50 percent of the voting-age population voted or was registered to vote in November 1964. The wording of these provisions was so narrowly drawn that the bill's restrictions applied to only seven southern states where voter discriminations had been most blatant. Federal examiners were given the power within those states to decide whether Negroes were qualified to vote. To be registered, all an applicant had to do was fill out a simple form (with assistance from a registrar, if needed) giving his name, age, length of residence, and whether he had ever been convicted of a felony. If a person met these minimal qualifications, the registrar automatically added his name to a list of voters, and state and local election officials were required to accept the registrar's list. If they questioned the qualifications of a registrant, the challenge was to be heard before a federal judge and a decision made within two weeks. If an election was held during that period, the registrant was to be permitted to vote. Federal poll-watchers were instructed to observe the actual election process, both the casting and counting of ballots. Anyone who intimidated voters or tampered with ballots faced stiff criminal charges and penalties.

The need for this law was obvious. For example, in 1965 in Sunflower County, Mississippi, the home of Senator James Eastland, 80 percent of the county's 8783 white residents of voting age were registered, but only 1.1 percent of the county's 13,524 Negroes of voting age were on the rolls. So patently undemocratic was this situation that the United States Fifth Circuit Court of Appeals disallowed the 1965 election in Sunflower County. The Voting Rights Act of 1965 clearly closed many visible loopholes remaining from previous voting rights measures, and it was called the most effective civil rights legislation in the nation's history.

President Johnson continued executive action in the tradition of Presidents Truman and Kennedy. After the Department of Housing and Urban Development was raised to cabinet status in November 1965, Johnson appointed as its head Robert C. Weaver, the first Negro in the nation's history to serve as a secretary in the Cabinet. In 1967 the President appointed to the Supreme Court Thurgood Marshall, well-known Negro leader and long-time civil servant, then serving as Solicitor General. Marshall's appointment represented the highest governmental position any American Negro had ever attained in this nation's history.

In 1966 the House of Representatives passed another multipurposed civil rights bill by a comfortable margin. The bill was designed to prohibit discrimination in the selection of federal and state juries, to enable the Attorney General to initiate school desegregation suits, to forbid intimidation or physical harm of voters and civil rights workers, and to forbid discrimination in the sale or rental of housing by anyone selling or leasing more than three units in any one year. This bill would have been the first civil rights legislation to hit harder north of the Mason-Dixon Line than below it, and few senators were eager to go on record in support of it. Many Negro leaders, who hoped for a much stronger housing clause, maintained that the House-passed bill was so watered down that it was hardly worth a battle for its passage in the Senate. Since the bill's proponents were unenthusiastic, a languid filibuster in the Senate was successful, and the bill was soon abandoned. It automatically died when Congress adjourned late in the year.

In a special message in February 1967 President Johnson requested the Congress to pass legislation to implement the major provisions of the defunct 1966 bill. Following the President's suggestion and in view of widespread rioting in the summer of 1967, the House of Representatives passed a bill designed to make it a crime to harm or intimidate persons exercising federally protected civil rights or policemen and firemen trying to quell a riot, and to make it a crime to cross state lines or use interstate commerce facilities to incite violence. According to its sponsor, Representative William C. Cramer (Florida), this bill was directed toward black militants such as Stokely Carmichael and H. Rap Brown as much as it was toward white supremacists. A subcommittee of the Senate Judiciary Committee drastically altered the House-approved bill, but neither version reached the Senate floor. The President's suggestion for a fair housing bill likewise was not acted upon favorably by the Congress. While no major civil rights bills passed both houses of Congress in 1967, the life of the Civil Rights Commission was extended from January 31, 1968 to January 31, 1973, and a clarifying provision was added to the section of the 1964 Civil Rights Act dealing with nondiscrimination in federally assisted school programs.

Early in 1968 a comprehensive civil rights bill was at last passed by both houses of Congress and signed by President Johnson in April. Included in this new law were many of the features of the bills which had passed the House of Representatives in 1966 and 1967 but which had been stalled by the Senate. The most far-reaching provisions of the new act dealt with housing, lowering racial barriers by three stages for about fifty-three million housing units, some 80 percent of the nation's total. Effective immediately, the act barred discrimination in the sale or rental of federally owned housing and multi-unit dwellings whose mortgages were insured or underwritten by the Federal Housing Administration or the Veterans Administration. Beginning in December 1968 it banned discrimination in multi-unit housing, such as apartments and real estate developments. However, owner-occupied dwellings of four or fewer units, such as boarding houses, were excluded. Effective in January 1970 the act declared illegal discrimination in single family houses sold or rented through real estate brokers. Owners selling their homes without the aid of brokers could discriminate, but they were not allowed to use discriminatory signs or other such advertisements.

In other areas the 1968 act provided for stiff federal penalties for persons convicted of intimidating or injuring civil rights workers, made it a crime to use interstate facilities with the intent to incite a riot, and made it a criminal offense to manufacture, sell, or demonstrate the use of firearms or other explosive devices to be used in civil disorders. When President Johnson signed the act into law he said, "We all know that the roots of injustice run deep, but violence cannot redress a solitary wrong or remedy a single unfairness. . . . And we just must put our shoulders together and put a stop to both. The time is here. Action must be now." Perhaps it was significant that the bill was passed soon after the assassination and funeral of Dr. Martin Luther King, Jr.

In June 1970 President Richard Nixon signed a law extending the life of the Voting Rights Act of 1965 for another five years, and at the opening of the next decade the pattern of action for civil rights proposals had been pretty well established. If that tradition continued, civil rights leaders would not fail to press during each legislative session for bills dealing with various aspects of minority demands. A few of these laws would pass the House of Representatives, but most of them would be lost in Senate committees or be defeated by filibuster. Every other year or so, the nation could expect another major civil rights law, but none of them would solve all the problems, and pressures for additional legislation would continue. To white and black civil rights advocates, the process seemed excruciatingly slow. To many southern whites the progress was painfully rapid. To the neutral observer, the events represented important change in the nation's and the South's legal and extralegal traditions.

Suggestions for Further Reading

The current civil rights crisis has resulted in a spate of books being published on the subject. Since 1945 more than ten thousand periodical articles have appeared on the Negro, and books on the subject have been published at the rate of one a day for the past several years. Many are nothing more than quick production jobs to put profits into the hands of the authors and the publishers, but others are serious attempts to sort out the various factors in the revolution, order them, and give them meaning. Many of these volumes do not relate specifically to the South, but they usually include much material on the Negro revolution in the South.

One of the best volumes on the background of the contemporary Negro issue is Charles E. Silberman, *Crisis in Black and White* * (New York: Random House, 1964). The best general history of the crucial decade in race relations between the 1954 Supreme Court decision and the passage of the 1964 Civil Rights Act is Anthony Lewis (ed.), *Portrait of a Decade: The Second American Revolution* * (New York: Random House, 1964). Louis Lomax, *The Negro Revolt* * (New York: Harper, 1962) appeared early in the current crisis, and it has many valuable observations on the beginning of the movement. William Brink and Louis Harris, *The Negro Revolution in America* * (New York: Simon & Schuster, 1963) is based upon a nationwide survey by *Newsweek* magazine and has considerable relevance. Brink and Harris have also made a later study of racial attitudes in the United States, and their findings have been published in *Black and White: A Study of U. S. Racial Attitudes Today* * (New York: Simon & Schuster, 1967). A good general history of the development of civil rights is John P. Roche, *The Quest for the Dream: The Development of Civil Rights and Human Relations in Modern America* * (New York: Macmillan, 1963). Jack Greenberg, *Race Relations and American Law* (New York: Columbia Univ., 1959) studies the legal aspects of the desegregation process. Two general studies of the civil rights movement are Milton R. Konvitz and T. Leskes, *A Century of Civil Rights* * (New York: Columbia Univ., 1961) and Oscar Handlin, *Fire-Bell in the Night: The Crisis in Civil Rights* * (Boston: Little, Brown, 1964).

John W. Anderson has described the complex maneuverings necessary to pass the 1957 Civil Rights Act in *Eisenhower, Brownell, and the Congress: The Tangled Origins of the Civil Rights Bill of 1956–1957* (University, Ala.: Univ. Alabama, 1964). Richard M. Dalfiume, *Desegregation of the U. S. Armed Forces: Fighting on Two Fronts, 1939–1953* (Columbia, Mo.: Univ. Missouri, 1969) is a well-documented and scholarly account of the successful desegregation of the American military establishment. *Stride Toward Freedom: The Montgomery Story** (New York: Harper, 1958) by Martin Luther King, Jr. is more than the story of the Montgomery, Alabama boycott; it reveals King's philosophy as well. To be read along with King's volume is L. D. Reddick, *Crusader Without Violence: A Biography of Martin Luther King, Jr.* (New York: Harper, 1959). Also worthy of mention is Lerone Bennett, *What Manner of Man: A Biography of Martin Luther King, Jr.* (Chicago: Johnson, 1965), C. Eric Lincoln, *Martin Luther King, Jr.: A Profile** (New York: American-Century, 1969), and Don McKee, *Martin Luther King, Jr.* (New York: Putnam, 1969). *Mr. Kennedy and the Negroes** (New York: Fawcett World Library, 1964) by Harry Golden is broader than its title and summarizes recent race relations and legislation well.

An excellent introduction to the recent black protest movement may be found in a series of articles in the January 1965 issue of the *Annals of the American Academy of Political and Social Science,* vol. 357 (1965). Kenneth B. Clark (ed.), *The Negro Protest: James Baldwin, Malcolm X, Martin Luther King Talk with Kenneth B. Clark* (Boston: Beacon, 1963) is a collection of revealing interviews. James Baldwin's semiautobiographical novels *Nobody Knows My Name** (New York: Dial Press, 1961), *Go Tell It on the Mountain** (New York: Knopf, 1953), and *Tell Me How Long the Train's Been Gone** (New York: Dial Press, 1968) are basic readings for an understanding of the Negro mind. Francis L. Broderick and August Meier (eds.), *Negro Protest Thought in the Twentieth Century** (Indianapolis: Bobbs-Merrill, 1966) is a scholarly account of recent intellectual trends. Howard Zinn, *SNCC: The New Abolitionists** (Boston: Beacon, 1964) is a good, brief history of the beginnings of the student protest movement. *Diary of a Sit-In** (Chapel Hill: Univ. North Carolina, 1962) by Merrill Proudfoot is a participating white minister's vivid account of the desegregation of facilities in Knoxville, Tennessee. *The Free Men* (New York: Harper & Row, 1965) by John Ehle is a similar story of the successful integration of facilities in Chapel Hill, North Carolina. Dan Wakefield, *Revolt in the South* (New York: Grove Press, 1960) is an eyewitness account of recent events, particularly the era of the sit-in. Other volumes relating personal experiences include James Peck, *Freedom Ride* (New York: Simon & Schuster, 1962) and Nicholas Van Hoffman, *Mississippi Notebook* (New York: D. White, 1964). William Bradford Huie, *Three Lives for Mississippi* (New York: WCC Books, 1964) is an account of the brutal slaying of three young civil rights workers in 1964, while Walter Lord, *The Past That Would Not Die* (New York: Harper & Row, 1965) is a book about the South after James Meredith integrated the campus of Ole Miss.

Alan F. Westin (ed.), *Freedom Now! The Civil-Rights Struggle in America* (New York: Basic Books, 1964) is a collection of articles with conflicting viewpoints ranging from the integrationists to the Black Muslims. C. Eric Lincoln's *The Black Muslims in America* * (Boston: Beacon, 1961) is a scholarly description of a group which seeks complete geographic separation of the races in the United States, and Louis E. Lomax, *When the Word Is Given: A Report on Elijah Muhammad, Malcolm X, and the Black Muslim World* * (Cleveland: World Publishing Co., 1963) is a popular account of the same subject. To be read along with these volumes is the enlightening *Autobiography of Malcolm X* * (New York: Grove Press, 1965) by Malcolm Little.

* Available in paperback.

CHAPTER XIX

THE MODERN SOUTH

After being an eyewitness to the violence on the University of Mississippi campus in 1962 when the first Negro attempted to enroll in that school, Professor James Silver wrote *Mississippi: The Closed Society* (1964) in which he related his views and detailed his experiences in the events of that fateful week. In the course of his discussion, Professor Silver maintained that the Old South was far from dead and that the attitudes of southerners, at least those in Mississippi, were no different in the 1960s than they had been in the 1860s. Other recent writers, notably Francis B. Simkins, have also argued that the traditional South is still very much alive. By contrast, a number of writers have stressed the economic changes in the South to the extent that they have hailed the disappearance of the South as a distinct region. C. Vann Woodward has observed that "recent changes are of sufficient depth and impact as to define the end of an era of Southern history." Which is the true view?

Walter Hines Page once wrote that the three ghosts haunting the southern mind were the ghost of the Confederate dead, the ghost of religious orthodoxy, and the ghost of white supremacy. While these ghosts had become dim by the 1960s, evidence of their presence was still apparent. Additional vestiges of an earlier South remained, but they were mixed with changes apparent on every hand. The South appeared to be going through a transitional phase, and if it may someday disappear, it had not yet done so by the beginning of the 1970s. The historian of the twenty-first century may look upon the present century as the one in which the modern South truly emerged.

The Changing South

Rural isolation, long a characteristic of the South, rapidly diminished in the twentieth century. Many factors were responsible for this development, not the least of which was the construction of hard-surfaced roads. Throughout nine-tenths of its history, the South had lived with narrow, rutted roads, dusty in dry seasons and muddy quagmires after rains had fallen. Antebellum travelers seldom failed to mention the poor quality of roads in the South, Frederick Law Olmsted being a particularly harsh critic. This criticism of the South's inadequate roads was accurate until well into the twentieth century, although the South began to make some headway in alleviating the deplorably bad conditions early in the century. In the 1890s conventions had been held in Richmond, Atlanta, and Houston, when small groups of southern leaders realized the importance of adequate roads if the South was to overcome its economic backwardness. After the turn of the century, southern newspaper editors added their complaints about the region's poor roads, but their early columns went unheeded. The South had the labor supply necessary for road-building, but her financial resources were limited and counties and states were unwilling to levy additional taxes for road projects. As the campaign for good roads increased, politicians came to realize that rural voters were beginning to demand hard-surfaced, farm-to-market roads, and they could ill afford to ignore these voices entirely. By 1917 every southern state had created state highway commissions, and by 1924 all of them had designated a state highway system.

Construction, maintenance, supervision, and financing of highways and roads were assumed by both states and counties in the South, but the burden was great and southern congressmen in Washington began to demand federal aid. The Federal Highways Act of 1916, which made limited grants to rural post roads, spurred demands for greater appropriations. The Federal Highways Act of 1921 provided for federal money to be made available to the states for the building of a network of interstate roads throughout the nation. It resulted in the planning of an inter-southern highway system which ultimately brought the various sections of the South together and tied the South as a region to the nation as a whole. Passage of the early federal highway acts ended forever the debate over federal assistance for internal improvements, and in the four decades following 1921 the national government poured many millions of dollars into southern state coffers for road construction. The money was used for construction and maintenance of both primary interstate highways and secondary roads in the South. From 1921 to 1929 local, state, and federal expenditures for the building of southern highway systems increased by

157 percent. Concrete and asphalt began to seal in both dust and mud as surfaced roads in the South increased from 121,164 miles in 1921 to 209,-880 miles in 1930. Gradually it became possible for a southerner to travel for hundreds of miles on all-weather roads, unaware of when he moved from one political jurisdiction to another. Northerners who traveled southward hardly knew that they had moved from one region to another as they hurried across the countryside with the aid of solid footing. No longer did these outsiders complain about the poor land arteries as they had a century earlier.

By mid-century a web-work of improved roads covered the South, even the most remote southerner being able to travel on a hard-surfaced road which often passed not more than a few hundred yards from his home. In 1952 Louisiana made a comprehensive study of its highway needs, and two years later the state issued over $104,000,000 worth of bonds, to reach maturity by 1989. The interest payments on this enormous sum will be more than all the money Louisiana had spent on roads from the days of the French explorer LaSalle to World War I. This large sum of money has permitted the state to launch a massive highway building program which has in turn had a major effect upon the state's economy. North Carolina had long maintained one of the largest and best road systems in the South, and it made giant strides in the direction of even better roads after mid-century. In 1956 North Carolina took the bold step of issuing $200,000,000 in bonds to modernize and enlarge its road and highway network. If timid spirits shrank from such an enormous mortgage upon the state's resources, the action manifested its leaders' faith in the state's future. In 1917 South Carolina had a hopeless system of roads with hardly any funds being used to remedy the situation. Between 1917 and 1956, the state spent $395,000,000 for road improvement, this sum being supplemented by $98,000,000 from federal funds. The story was much the same in all other southern states, each moving forward on the road front.

In 1956 the Congress passed a measure providing for the construction of the National System of Interstate and Defense Highways, a carefully planned network of forty-one thousand miles of modern, limited access, four-lane highways to handle the nation's geometrically increasing numbers of automobiles and trucks. With the federal government providing 90 percent of the funds, the states willingly cooperated in the building of this new web of super highways which was over 98 percent completed or under construction by the fall of 1970. The South was an eager participant in this great project, the interstate system comprising a capstone to the South's Good Roads Movement of several decades. When the new system is completed by 1978, a traveler will be able to drive eastward on Interstate 10 from El Paso to Jacksonville, passing through Houston, New Orleans, and Mobile, without slowing down for a single traffic light.

He may begin on Interstate 20 in Dallas and travel uninterruptedly through Shreveport, Jackson, and Montgomery, or he may drive on Interstate 40 which passes through Oklahoma City, Little Rock, Memphis, Nashville, Asheville, and Greensboro. Running north and south Interstate 35 bisects the region in Oklahoma and Texas, Interstate 55 parallels the Mississippi River, Interstate 65 moves southward from Louisville through Nashville and Birmingham to Mobile, and Interstate 75 goes from Cincinnati to Tampa, via Lexington, Chattanooga, and Atlanta. While Interstate 85 traverses the Piedmont regions of Virginia and the Carolinas, moving on to Atlanta and Montgomery, Interstate 95 serves the coastal region from Baltimore to Florida. These and other spans of the interstate system have formed a cross-hatching pattern over the South so that no city with a population over fifty thousand is more than a few miles from one of these major arterial roads. Such an engineering and construction accomplishment is all the more striking when one is reminded that a few decades ago the traveler was bogged in mud or choked with dust as he attempted to traverse the South.

Good roads and highways would not have come had the age of the automobile not demanded them. Early automobile manufacturers successfully adapted the internal combustion engine to the four-wheel carriage, and by the 1920s Fords, Nashes, Reos, Oldsmobiles, and Studebakers were being mass produced. When the price of these autos placed the vehicles within the reach of the middle classes, production zoomed and auto owners in turn demanded hard-surfaced roads. Thereafter, the building of bigger and faster automobiles coincided with the pouring of money into highway construction, and long before mid-century the two enterprises were inextricably bound together. States partially financed costly highway construction projects by taxing both the automobile and the gasoline it burned. The presence of the good roads in turn encouraged more southerners to buy automobiles, the taxes upon them being used to finance additional ribbons of cement and asphalt. If the South lagged somewhat behind the nation as a whole in these developments, it nevertheless was a part of this nationwide movement, and automobiles and roads had much to do with the changing southern landscape. Besides providing construction jobs for laborers, road-building and the presence of the automobile had other economic consequences for the South. Automobile agencies, repair garages, service stations, roadside establishments for travelers who needed to sleep and eat, and trucking businesses mushroomed in the South and stimulated the southern economy. To discount the great economic influence of the automobile upon the South would be a gross error.

The social consequences of this Yankee contraption from the banks of the Great Lakes were just as great. In his new vehicle and on hard-surfaced roads, the southerner had a mobility never before experienced. Distance was no longer a barrier impossible to overcome. The bonds of the past could not retain a stifling grip upon the yeoman farmer, who came to view his automobile (he called it a machine) as his most prized possession. If installment buying of his car placed the southerner deeper in debt, the monthly payments forced him to consider occupations other than farming, with its uncertain year-end returns. The automobile freed the southerner to search more diligently for different jobs assuring him more economic security and an upgraded social status.

Where did the good roads in the South lead? Where did the southerner in his shiny new automobile search for better economic conditions? Towns and cities in the twentieth-century South came to play a role never before assigned to them in that most rural of rural regions. This is not to say that urban centers of sorts did not exist in the South prior to 1900. Charleston, New Orleans, Mobile, Memphis, and Richmond had long served as major centers of the South's urban population, but the overwhelmingly rural nature of the South's economy and culture relegated these urban centers to secondary positions. Automobiles and farm-to-market roads greatly assisted southern rural dwellers to make their way to the towns and cities, there to sell their produce, to partake of the benefits of urban offerings, and in many cases to be attracted like moths to the bright lights of city life and ways.

Although the South of the 1960s remained the most rural region of the nation, it boasted several major urban centers. Four of the ten largest cities in the nation in 1960 were southern: Baltimore (939,024), Houston (938,219), Washington (763,956), and St. Louis (750,026). Before 1969 Houston, the fastest growing large city in the country, had surpassed the 1,000,000 mark and had replaced Baltimore as the nation's sixth largest metropolis. In addition to these giant urban complexes the South in 1960 boasted of New Orleans (627,525), Memphis (497,524), Atlanta (487,455), Louisville (390,639), Oklahoma City (324,253), and Miami (291,688). The 1960 federal census revealed that in the South (sixteen states plus the District of Columbia) there were ninety-seven cities with more than 50,000 population, forty-four of these with more than 100,000.

Southerners not attracted to the metropolitan centers often found their way to small and medium-sized towns. The Federal Census Bureau's definition of an urban center as a population concentration of 2,500 persons or more meant that in 1960 the South had 1,657 such centers. Of the South's population figure of 54,973,113 in 1960, 32,160,250 southerners lived in these urban centers. Thus, 58.5 percent of all southerners were urban dwellers. While rural ways and attitudes dominated these smaller population centers, southerners were moving off the farms in large numbers and ultimately urbanization was to have a great effect upon the entire region. These figures reveal the flight of both the white and black man from the rural areas of the South. It was not uncommon in the

1960s for all the children of a tenant farmer to move from farm to town as soon as they were old enough to strive for economic independence, attracted by jobs, schools, proximity to the necessities of life, social activities, and a host of other advantages.

Many white and black southerners who left the farms scurried past or paused only briefly in the towns and cities of the South as they emigrated beyond the bounds of their native region. In the decade of the 1940s over 7,000,000 southerners left the South permanently. The Negro population in Ohio, Indiana, Illinois, Michigan, and Wisconsin was 930,450 in 1930 but had jumped to 1,803,698 by 1950, a not insignificant factor in these statistics being the increased migration of southern Negroes to the cities of the Old Northwest. During the same twenty-year period, the Negro population in five southern states (Louisiana, Arkansas, Alabama, Mississippi, and Georgia) remained almost static, rising from 4,280,466 in 1930 to 4,337,940 in 1950, as the birthrate barely kept ahead of the out-migration. The greatest period of emigration of southerners was during the four years of World War II, when more than 1,600,000 southerners moved north and west. Interestingly, Negroes comprised only about one-third of the migration between Pearl Harbor and V-J day. The postwar period witnessed further increases in migration from the South. Even though the birthrate there was the highest in the nation, the rate of the region's population growth was the lowest, reflecting the migration of both whites and blacks from the South. If the South did not particularly miss the masses of illiterates with limited skills who fled their native region, the loss of trained scientists, engineers, lawyers, doctors, teachers, and potential or actual business leaders verged on the disastrous. The South had everything to lose and nothing to gain by exporting its future leaders, who sometimes made significant contributions to the economy and society of other regions.

Indications were that the out-migration from the South was slowing down, although not reversed, by 1970. As the South's industrial economy expanded, need for more laborers was obvious, and the South's surplus laborers both white and black had greater opportunity to work at home, obviating the need to search for employment outside the region. As the civil rights revolution came into full swing, many southern blacks hesitated to migrate to the northern urban centers, fearing the uncertain life to be had in the North. Furthermore, their cousins who preceded them admitted that while they made more money, living conditions in the ghettos of the urban North were not pleasant, and these reports gave many southern blacks pause for contemplation, causing a significant number of them to abandon plans to flee the South. Then, too, since the race problem was now national, few southerners—black or white—were migrating from the South to avoid that pressing issue. Although the number of immigrants into the South was only minimal when compared to those who were emigrating, the industries and businesses of the South were actually attracting northerners in significant numbers, particularly in supervisory and managerial positions.

Southerners and the Environment

Perhaps nothing illustrated the changing South in 1970 better than southerners' concern for the environment. Americans had become impressed by the growing publicity generated by young people and other crusaders, who warned that the world's population was being endangered by water and air pollution, by the increasing complexities in the disposal of tons of refuse, and by assorted dangers to the balance of nature due to the use of pesticides, herbicides, mercury fungicides, lead, boron, nickel, arsenic, and hundreds of other toxic substances. Southerners joined with northerners to demand a halt to the wanton destruction of the nation's— and the world's—life-giving air and water.

The South had moved into the modern era with the coming of the automobile, but by 1970 idealistic young southerners looked upon horseless carriages, powered by air-polluting internal combustion engines, as unmixed material blessings. If many southerners praised the automobile for its rapid transit facility, others viewed with alarm the deadly carbon monoxide gas and smog ingredients such as nitrogen oxides and hydrocarbons pouring into the atmosphere from millions of exhaust pipes. Southerners had encouraged giant industrial plants to locate in their native region, but now many of them had second thoughts as they witnessed poisonous fumes emitting from the smokestacks of the industrial parks. Residents of Birmingham, Alabama, were subjected to low visibility and smarting eyes, when the unsightly clouds from the vast steel mill complex were not quickly blown away by friendly breezes. Despite the large economic benefits Atlanta, Georgia, derived from the numerous industrial concerns located on its outskirts, the city was too often shrouded in a haze of smoke and dust. The beautiful stretch along the Atlantic coast north of Charleston, South Carolina, had become dotted with stinking manufacturing plants, enticed to the region by the plentiful supply of water. The air of the Southeast had not become as foul as that of the Northeast, but when atmospheric temperature inversions did occur occasionally, causing sulfur dioxide, carbon monoxide, and other pollutants to hover near the ground for several days and resulting in coughing and watery eyes, east coast southerners were reminded that the clean air of their region was slowly but steadily disappearing.

In August 1970 officials of the National Pollution Control Administration released tentative rankings for the nation's cities in two major categories of air fouling: visible particulates, such as dirt, smoke, and soot; and sulphur oxides. Southern cities among the top ten in the nation in particular pollution were Charleston, West Virginia (no. 2), and Louisville, Kentucky (no. 8). High on the list of those cities in the nation with the worst composite sulphur oxide levels were Huntington, West Virginia (no. 3), St. Louis, Missouri (tied with Cleveland, Ohio, for no. 6), and Washington, D.C. (no. 8). Federal officials reported that more than thirty-three million tons of sulphur oxides fouled the atmosphere in 1970, three million tons more than in 1968. Southerners concerned about the quality of the atmosphere were not proud of their region's contribution to this national disgrace.

Numerous towns and cities had long dumped untreated sewage into almost every southern river and major tributary, and when industrial wastes were added in large quantities, the crystal clear waters became black with pollutants, and to this development came vociferous objections. Syndicated columnist Art Buchwald said the dead fish found floating on the lower reaches of the Mississippi River had not died from contaminated water; rather they had drowned because they did not know how to swim. Southerners smiled at this cute statement, but the truth about the disturbed marine ecology cycle prevented them from enjoying the joke too much.

Human life itself was endangered by rampant mercury pollution. A test made of the water of the Great Lakes in the spring of 1970 revealed that its mercury content was dangerously high; Secretary of the Interior Walter J. Hickel then ordered a survey of the mercury level of the nation's waters at all of its four thousand water quality stations. The survey revealed that river waters in every section of the country were in jeopardy, particularly in the South. Especially singled out for alarm were the Rio Grande from El Paso to Brownsville, Texas; the Mississippi River from one hundred miles north of New Orleans to its mouth; the Tombigbee River and the Mobile River and Bay in Alabama; the lower reaches of the Savannah River between South Carolina and Georgia; the Cape Fear River in North Carolina; and the Tennessee River from Lake Pickwick to its confluence with the Mississippi. Highly poisonous to living creatures, mercury had reached the South's streams and lakes from farmlands on which trees had been treated to prevent fungus, from chemical and plastic plants, and from paper mills which used the heavy metal to inhibit the growth of slime in their processing waters. Hickel urged the governors of seventeen states to bend every effort to eliminate discharges of quicksilver into the nation's rivers. In July 1970 Governor Albert Brewer of Alabama banned fishing in fifty-one thousand acres of lake and river water, including the Tennessee River, because of mercury pollution, and he requested that President Nixon declare portions of the state federal disaster areas. Alabamians were sternly warned against eating fish which had swum in mercury-polluted waters.

In August 1970 the Department of Justice filed suits against eight companies in seven states which had not moved as rapidly as others to end dumping of mercury into lakes and rivers. That same month congressional committees began holding hearings on the problem. As more Americans in both North and South were apprised of the situation through the mass media, greater pressures were placed upon the national government to act decisively in a potentially serious emergency.

Far too many cities and areas of the South suffered from both air and water pollution, including Birmingham, Atlanta, Louisville, and Memphis. In Texas the Houston-Beaumont area, wealthy beyond imagination because of the oil and gas refineries, suffered from both foul air and water. While the residents of Santa Barbara, California, led the national chorus of protest when a leaking offshore well spread messy oil along the beaches of the west coast, southerners near New Orleans identified with them when a similar situation developed in the nearby Gulf of Mexico. But the oil slick was only temporary; New Orleans residents often experienced prolonged breathing discomfort from the multimillion-dollar industrial installations located nearby on the banks of the great river.

Like most of the world's inhabitants, southerners and tourists in the South have assumed that the oceans are too immense to lose the battle of pollution. But overuse and misuse of southern coastlines was fast becoming a major problem. Summer vacationers began to find beautiful beaches covered with litter and debris. The blow-out of a few oil wells or the accidental sinking of an occasional tanker were highly publicized disasters, but as damaging as these catastrophes were, they were only part of a larger problem. As a Coast Guard law enforcement officer said, "It's the day-to-day stuff that's killing us—the chronic pollution that does not reach the headlines." An estimated forty-eight million tons of solid wastes were dumped off U. S. coasts in 1968. This is predicted to increase sevenfold within the next decade. Fin rot—a deadly bacterial disease linked to pollution—attacks a wide variety of valuable fish in the New York-New Jersey area; it seemed only a matter of time before marine life off the southern coast would also be in serious trouble.

While the South's coastal waters were being polluted by man's waste products and his tinkering with the environment, the Dade County (Miami) Port Authority aroused the ire of sensitive Floridians when it proposed to construct a major airport near the Everglades National Park. In the spring of 1969 attention was focused on that fascinating aquatic wilderness, "the last refuge of solitude along the eastern seaboard," when a single-strip training facility for commercial airline pilots began to be constructed in privately owned Big Cypress Swamp, forty miles west of Miami and six miles north of the park. Investigation revealed that plans called for the training strip to be only the first phase of a giant commer-

cial operation scheduled for completion by 1980. Planned as the largest
air terminal in the nation, the airport was to cover thirty-nine square
miles—larger than the city of Miami—and was to be designed to accommodate jumbo jets and supersonic planes. Planners estimated that the international jetport would service up to 40,000,000 passengers annually,
and they expected ultimately that a city of nearly 1,000,000 would spring
up around it.

Park officials, the National Audubon Society, the Tri-County Everglades Area Planning Council, Conservation 70s, Inc., and other interested groups raised serious questions about the advisability of construct-
ing such facilities in the chosen location. They pointed out that Big
Cypress Swamp supplied 38 percent of the water flowing into the park,
the very life stream of the park and its inhabitants; that water pollution,
air pollution, and the noise from overflights by jet planes would be inevitable when the project was fully developed; and that the combined impact
on the glades could be catastrophic. Conservationists warned that even
before the entire project materialized, pollution and the alteration of the
flow of the water into the park could upset the delicately balanced ecology of the park. Absolutely dependent on a cycle of summer flooding and
winter drought, the park would suffer from any change in the quantity,
quality, and rhythm of the flow of water. Biologists and ecologists added
their voices against the possible destruction of the nation's only subtropi-
cal forest, home to many rare species of plants, animals, and birds.

Port Authority directors disagreed and argued that the dangers to
the park were grossly exaggerated. One official dismissed the conservationists as "butterfly chasers" and referred to the rare and endangered
bird species in the park as "just a bunch of yellow bellied sapsuckers."
Another airport spokesman said, "The preservationists want everything
to remain the way it was; but it's not the way the great American [eco-
nomic?] system operates." Such statements spurred the critics forward, and
when the training strip began operations in the late summer of 1969,
with an average of five hundred training flights a day, they redoubled
their efforts. Their first victory came when they forced a two-year moratorium on any zoning changes on the 576-square-mile area surrounding the
proposed jetport. The area had been zoned A-1, or agricultural, and this
designation was not to be changed in order to provide a "cooling-off period" regarding the controversy.

The conservationists' protests resulted in a Department of the Interior study which stated flatly that the proposed jetport would "inexora-
bly destroy south Florida's ecosystem" and thus the park. It also said that
the existing pilot training airstrip on the jetport site near the park was
"intolerable" because it would lead to "urbanization and drainage" which
would destroy the ecosystem. With such firm support the conservationists
urged Secretary of Transportation John A. Volpe to order the relocation

of the proposed jetport. However, the National Academy of Sciences also made a study and reported that the training strip "would not appear to pose a severe problem to the region if various safeguards are instituted." Armed with this report, Secretary Volpe approved the continued use of the training strip, but with stringent precautions such as the banning of insecticides in the runway's vicinity, the preventing of interference with the Everglades water supply, and the limiting of residential and commercial development.

Shortly thereafter, in December 1969, a spokesman for the Department of the Interior announced: "The Secretary of the Interior is empowered to protect our national parks. The Everglades are vulnerable in this situation, and in view of the clear and present danger, we will protect the park." Both Secretary Volpe and Secretary of the Interior Walter Hickel withdrew their support of the plans for expansion of the facility, the result of enormous pressure applied on both state and federal officials by several conservation groups. By January 1970 the conservationists had successfully thwarted plans for the huge jet airport, and Dade County Port Authority officials began to search for other sites and other means to handle south Florida's increasing air transportation problems.

Approval for the operation of the training strip was for three years or until a new jetport site was found, and most conservationists were willing to accept this compromise, since their major fears were related to the expansion of the facility. Others believed that even this operation would be damaging, and in February 1970 two staunch conservationists filed suit to stop use of the training airstrip. The suit charged that the use of the strip would destroy the Everglades by altering the area's ecology, and it asked a permanent injunction forbidding use of the strip. Although the suit had not been settled by July 1970, the controversy over the airstrip and the jetport illustrated some southerners' concern for the ecological and conservation issues facing the entire nation at that time.

As the nation expressed its concern for pollution, ecology, and the preservation of resources, leading educational institutions quickly inaugurated courses, seminars, conferences, institutes, centers, and entire schools to study and discuss environmental problems. Southern colleges and universities joined the current fashion, and by the fall of 1970, glamour courses were being taught all over the region with titles such as Man and His Environment; Conservation of Resources; Water Resources and Environmental Radioactivity; Human Ecology; Aquatic Biology; Environmental Microbiology; Ecology and Management of Aquatic Areas; and Ecology in the Elementary School. Frostburg State College (Maryland) established a pilot program to investigate the effects of water pollution and mining practices in the Potomac River Basin, and the University of Florida designated one large structure as an Environmental Engineering Building in which conservation was the principal subject studied. Interest in environmental problems was not limited to the universities. In December 1969 the federal government sponsored a series of seminars for high school and college students in major cities around the country, including Kansas City, Missouri, and Atlanta, Georgia, in the hope of enlisting "the enthusiasm, vigor and fresh ideas of our country's high school and college youth in this battle to protect and preserve our precious and irreplaceable water resources."

Southerners joined with other Americans for a nationwide Earth Day observance on April 22, 1970, to protest the destruction of the environment. They expressed concern and engaged in antipollution drives from Annapolis, Maryland, on the dirty Chesapeake Bay to Laredo, Texas, on the sluggish Rio Grande; from Springfield, Missouri, in the debris-strewn Ozark Mountains to Coral Gables, Florida, where tourists did their part to spoil the Atlantic Ocean. Sponsored by the Episcopal Youth Churchmen of Christ Church, a group of students in Charlotte, North Carolina, piled old bedsteads, toilet seats, tires, charcoal grills, and other discarded junk on the lawn near the city hall, erected a flag, Iwo Jima style, and marched around it singing "America the Beautiful." After their demonstration, they dutifully cleaned up the mess. In Miami Beach, Florida, pollution protestors staged a Dead Orange Parade, the floats being loaded with toilets, bottled sewage, garbage, and individuals wearing gas masks. College students in Knoxville, Tennessee, pulled boatloads of junk out of a smelly river, and students held a contest on the campus of the University of the South to see if each contestant could gather up in one day the five pounds of debris that the average American supposedly discards each day. School children also did their part in the ecological drama. Grade schoolers in Jackson, Mississippi, formed KOP (Kick Out Pollution), and they spent a day picking up waste paper and other litter from vacant lots. Numerous universities and institutions in the South sponsored speakers and seminars. At Oak Ridge, Tennessee, where nuclear power plants befouled both streams and soil, a conference was held on the problem of the disposal of atomically generated hot water. The participants concluded that with proper treatment thermally polluted water could be beneficial to growing vegetables and to oyster beds.

Not all southerners were enthusiastic about Earth Day. Georgia State Comptroller James L. Bentley questioned the purposes and forces behind the occasion, pointing out that the observance fell suspiciously on Lenin's birthday. Other white southerners did not verbalize their fears about a possible plot, but in their everyday concern with inflation and higher taxes, many of them studiously ignored what was rapidly becoming one of the most pressing issues of the day. Black southern leaders were often unexcited about the whole ecological movement, viewing it as essentially a middle-class end run to divert attention and money from their race's needs. Julian Bond traveled from campus to campus in both

North and South preaching this theme. Whatever the reactions of various groups of southerners, the region, like the nation, was caught up in the excitement of the environmental crisis. Americans in both North and South pondered the implications of a statement Adlai E. Stevenson had once made: "We are all passengers on the Spaceship Earth with only limited amounts of food, water, and other resources available."

The Southern Mind

A detailed analysis of the southern mind in the twentieth century would encompass many facets, but perhaps the most prominent aspect of virtually every white southerner's mind has been his conscious or subconscious concern with race relations. Attitudes have often been translated into actions and organizations with the determination to subjugate the black man. The revived Ku Klux Klan of the twentieth century may have been overtly supported by relatively few whites, but the very existence of the Klan bespoke the sentiments of many other southerners. The second Klan was founded in October 1915 by Colonel William J. Simmons, when he and thirty-four other Georgians met on top of Stone Mountain near Atlanta to dedicate themselves to the maintenance of white supremacy. By linking the doctrine of white supremacy to nativism, patriotism, and Protestantism, the Klan had a mass appeal in the 1920s. Publicity agents capitalized on the confluence of the Klan's principles with those of the nation in the postwar period, and enrollments burgeoned rapidly. Simmons reported that in 1922 over thirty-five hundred persons joined the Klan every day. The Klan became a nationwide organization, and it actually became a powerful political organization in Indiana, Oregon, and Oklahoma. Despite all of its national publicity and influence, the Klan remained strongest in the South, an invariable development in view of the intensity of white southern attitudes toward blacks. The Klan's influence waned during the depression years of the 1930s, and for all practical purposes it ceased to exist by World War II.

During the postwar uneasiness, latent white southern attitudes were responsible for the establishment of a variety of Klans and Klan-like organizations. The White Knights of the Ku Klux Klan, Americans for the Preservation of the White Race, the Association for the Advancement of White People, the Original Ku Klux Klan, the United Klans of America, the Knights of the Ku Klux Klan, and a dozen other such names were adopted by local and southwide organizations pledged to white supremacy, God, country, home, and family. In a 1964 brochure, the Mississippi-based White Knights appealed for additional qualified members because the organization was Christian, fraternal, benevolent, democratic, dedicated, just, and right. Some of the Klans were more secret than others, some were more activist than others, and some made special appeals to families, but they all reacted to the growing civil rights movement and used the thinly veiled rhetoric of violence. One brochure read, "The issue is clearly one of personal, physical SELF-DEFENSE or DEATH for the American Anglo-Saxons."

As progress continued to be made on the civil rights front, Klansmen made more noise, but their memberships and influence were held in check by their own bad press, by the South's growing toleration of integration, and by stern measures of control. When Klansmen threatened to disrupt integrated Christmas parades in North Carolina in 1964, Governor Terry Sanford warned: "I would urge all members of the KKK to read the Christmas story and the message of goodwill to all men contained in the Bible. In the meantime, I am instructing the State Highway Patrol to provide all aid necessary. . . . If there are illegal acts on the part of the Ku Klux Klan, they will be prosecuted." No trouble arose.

Klansmanship in the post-World War II years was not strictly limited to the South's white lower classes, but all evidence pointed to its strength in that area of the social structure. By contrast, middle class southerners dominated the so-called White Citizens Council. The Council was established by fourteen men near Indianola, Mississippi, within a month after the Supreme Court had handed down its school desegregation decision in 1954. A leader of the original organization was Robert Patterson, a delta farmer and former football player at Mississippi State University. Patterson determined to establish local councils throughout the South, and he made public addresses, wrote letters, and printed brochures to that end. A leaflet describing the Citizens Council movement stated that it was "dedicated to the maintenance of peace, good order and domestic tranquility in our communities and in our state, to the preservation of state's rights." It declared that southern communities needed local councils as badly as they needed health and fire departments. If no immediate race problem existed, southern communities could soon expect to have one, since the "NAACP, aided by alien influences, bloc-vote-seeking politicians and left-wing do-gooders will see that you have a problem in the near future." The Citizens Council was to follow "the old paths of our founding fathers and to refuse to destroy ancient landmarks to appease anyone, even the internationalists. This integration scheme ties right in with the new, one world, one creed, one race philosophy fostered by ultra-idealists and international left-wingers."

The organizing campaign was successful, and local councils sprang up all over the South, the focal point for southerners dissatisfied with the prospect of school integration and the extension of other rights to Negroes. The groups disavowed secrecy and violence, appealed to the middle classes, and drew up grandiose plans for a nationwide organization to fight civil rights progress. If their plans did not materialize, the

councils were not without influence in the South. Fragmentary evidence
indicates that the councils placed economic and social pressures on both
blacks and whites to conform to their standards for a peaceful society.
Council members visited ministers in efforts to curb pulpit remarks not
in keeping with the council's objectives. The anonymous telephone call
was used to intimidate opponents. In 1956 local council members were
responsible for the purging of the voter rolls in a parish in Louisiana,
and as a result the names of 90 percent of the Negroes registered were removed because they had failed to fill out their registration cards properly. A check of the first one hundred white registrants' cards revealed
that only one met the exacting standards applied to the blacks, but no
white voters were disallowed. One of the councils' objectives was to
screen candidates for office to be sure they held the proper views, and
in some areas of the South a candidate could commit political suicide by
raising his voice against a council.

Many of the leading members of the Citizens Councils were respectable, small-town businessmen, causing the councils to be dubbed
"Main Street Klans." The appellation is not entirely accurate, but it is
too close to be dismissed as totally false. The councils operated openly
and omitted the ritual and symbolism of the Klan organizations, yet their
rhetoric was not far from the diatribes of the Klansmen. Speaking at a
council rally in Selma, Alabama, in 1955 Robert Patterson stated that the
"integration monster creates the most serious crisis in the South since the
Civil War. The people of the South have been complacent and apathetic
for many years. Every battle we have lost has been by default. Some great
philosopher once said, 'All that is necessary for the triumph of evil is for
good men to do nothing,' and that certainly applies to us. . . . If 50,-
000,000 of us can't keep our race white, then we aren't fit to be white,
and we won't be white very long. . . . Some people think we are the Ku
Klux Klan. We're not. We don't cover our faces and we aren't baiting any-
body. . . . In places like Chicago and Detroit they hate the Negro. Here
the Negro is our friend. But we in Mississippi will never stand for the integration monster."

Despite the efforts of the Klans and the Citizens Councils, integration was speeded up in the 1960s. At the very time the Negro was making
some considerable headway for first-class citizenship, his patience wore
thin and the disturbances of the early 1960s occurred. Violence, demonstrations, and property damage caused many white Americans to give second thought to the future of race relations in the nation. A "white backlash" developed in reaction to the militancy of some blacks. As periodic
public opinion polls showed, white Americans who were inclined to be
sympathetic to the Negro in the early 1960s developed serious reservations about the direction and speed the Negro movement was taking by
the end of the decade. Much of the violence of the last half of the decade

came as a result of this white backlash, and its consequences were tragic for the nation.

In April 1968 James Earl Ray assassinated Martin Luther King, while the moderate Negro leader was in Memphis preparing for a demonstration in behalf of the city's garbage collectors, most of whom were black. While few southerners would have willingly done so foul a deed, many felt that "he had it coming" and that "he had been asking for it." The nation mourned one of its most important leaders, but far too many in every section spoke incautiously about how other Negro leaders ought to be dealt with in like fashion. At the beginning of the 1960s Klansmen and Citizens Council members recognized that they were fighting a rearguard action in their opposition to Negro progress, and in their more honest moments they admitted that they were waging a losing battle, even though they wanted to prolong it as long as possible. By the end of the decade the tide of events gave them cause to believe that perhaps they had admitted ultimate defeat too early.

The revived Klans, the establishment of Citizens Councils, and the white backlash revealed that the South was in the midst of great change. Fear of the unknown, resistance to change, and a desire to retain old traditions were responsible for the growth of these organizations and this reaction. But not all southerners joined or approved of these organizations or their stated or implied beliefs, and not all southerners lashed back at militant blacks. As always, a small minority of southerners favored racial integration and a larger role for the national government in state affairs, and they did not see alien influences behind every action taken by the Supreme Court or the President. The presence of the "Segs" and the southern liberals justify references to the "divided mind of the South." But a greater justification for the use of that phrase devolves from the ambivalent mind of the "great silent majority" of southerners. Most southerners were inclined to want to keep the Negro in his place, yet the forces of change were so powerful that many secretly raised serious questions about some of their basic assumptions. While their long past tugged at them to revere old traditions and ways, economic and social forces of great magnitude compelled them to give second thought to their first impulses. While they wanted to stand on the solid rock of southern tradition, they realized that their own economic advancement could come only if they ventured into the choppy sea of changing social patterns.

This great majority of southerners in this quandary reflected the plight of the region itself. The future of the South lay in the hands of that great middle class of troubled southerners. How they ultimately responded to the voices of retreat or the forces of progress in the South in the last quarter of the twentieth century would in the final analysis determine the course of the South's future and history.

Suggestions for Further Reading

Georgia newspaperman Ralph McGill in *The South and the Southerner* * (Boston: Little, Brown, 1964) addresses himself to the changing mores of the South, while Mississippi newspaperman Hodding Carter reveals a deep knowledge of his native region in *Southern Legacy* * (Baton Rouge: Louisiana State Univ., 1950). W. D. Workman, Jr., *The Case for the South* (New York: Devin-Adair, 1960) is a plea for the South to return to the "good old days." A reasoned approach to the changing South is Brooks Hayes, *A Southern Moderate Speaks* (Chapel Hill: Univ. North Carolina, 1959), while Wilma Dykeman and James Stokely, *Neither Black Nor White* (New York: Rinehart, 1957) is a thought-provoking volume directed toward recent issues.

Volumes by southerners and others who have written about their personal experiences and reflections often illuminate the region: Jonathan Daniels, *A Southerner Discovers the South* (New York: Macmillan, 1938); Virginius Dabney, *Below the Potomac: A Book about the New South* (New York: Appleton-Century, 1942); Clarence Cason, *90° in the Shade* (Chapel Hill: Univ. North Carolina, 1935); William A. Percy, *Lanterns on the Levee* (New York: Knopf, 1941); Carl T. Rowan, *South of Freedom* (New York: Knopf, 1952); Ben Robertson, *Red Hills and Cotton: An Upcountry Memory* (New York: Knopf, 1942); Katharine Dupre Lumpkin, *The Making of a Southerner* (New York: Knopf, 1947); Charles Longstreet Weltner, *Southerner* (Philadelphia: Lippincott, 1966). William Peters, *The Southern Temper* (Garden City: Doubleday, 1959) and Henry Savage, Jr., *Seeds of Time: Background of Southern Thinking* (New York: Holt, 1959) delve into the mind of the modern southerner. Because he believes that the South has virtually disappeared, Harry Ashmore has written *An Epitaph for Dixie* (New York: Norton, 1958). By contrast Louis D. Rubin, Jr. and James Jackson Kilpatrick (eds.), *The Lasting South* (Chicago: H. Regnery, 1957) argue that the South will be present for years to come. *I'll Take My Stand* * (New York: Harper & Brothers, 1930), the famous agrarian manifesto by Twelve Southerners, continues to be relevant for readers concerned with the future of the modern South.

Clark's *The Emerging South* * (mentioned earlier) has a chapter on the modern South's Good Roads Movement. Charles C. Alexander, *The Ku Klux Klan in the Southwest* * (Lexington: Univ. Kentucky, 1965) is a study of the Klan in the 1920s in Texas, Oklahoma, Arkansas, and Louisiana, and is more valuable than J. M. Mecklin, *The Ku Klux Klan: A Study in the American Mind* (New York: Harcourt, Brace, 1924). Arnold S. Rice, *The Ku Klux Klan in American Politics* (Washington:

Public Affairs Press, 1962) examines the political activities of the Klan of the 1920s on both local and national levels. Approximately one-third of Kenneth T. Jackson's *The Ku Klux Klan in the City, 1915–1930* * (New York: Oxford, 1967) is devoted to the urban South. *The South Strikes Back* (Garden City: Doubleday, 1959) by Hodding Carter is a description of the growth and structure of the White Citizens Councils, and John B. Martin, *The Deep South Says "Never"* (New York: Ballantine Books, 1957) is a perceptive inquiry into the leadership and methods of resistance of the councils. A popular volume dealing with both the Klan and the councils is James G. Cook, *The Segregationists* (New York: Appleton-Century-Crofts, 1962).

Several volumes listed at the end of Chapter XII deal with population as well as economic changes in recent times. Information on migration from the South is fragmented, but the following are useful on the movement of blacks: Carter G. Woodson, *A Century of Negro Migration* (Washington: Association for the Study of Negro Life and History, 1918); Logan, "The Movement of Negroes from North Carolina, 1876–1894," *North Carolina Historical Review*, vol. 33 (1952); Henderson, "The Negro Migration of 1916–1918," *Journal of Negro History*, vol. 6 (1921). To be read along with these is Thomas Ford (ed.), *The Southern Appalachian Region: A Survey* * (Lexington: Univ. Kentucky, 1962), which reveals the drainage of human resources from this region of the South. Rupert B. Vance and Nicholas J. Demerath (eds.), *The Urban South* (Chapel Hill: Univ. North Carolina, 1954), Rupert B. Vance, *All These People: The Nation's Human Resources in the South* (Chapel Hill: Univ. North Carolina, 1954), and Howard W. Odum, *Southern Regions of the United States* (Chapel Hill: Univ. North Carolina, 1936) are basic for an understanding of the development of the urban South.

Racial problems and urbanization are dealt with in John Dollard, *Caste and Class in a Southern Town* * (New Haven: Yale Univ., 1937); Allison Davis and others, *Deep South: A Social Anthropological Study of Caste and Class* * (Chicago: Univ. Chicago, 1941); Hortense Powdermaker, *After Freedom: A Cultural Study in the Deep South* * (New York: Viking Press, 1939); M. Elaine Burgess, *Negro Leadership in a Southern City* * (Chapel Hill: Univ. North Carolina, 1962); Arnold M. Rose, *The Negro's Morale* (Minneapolis: Univ. Minnesota, 1949). A spritely account of life and change in a rural Alabama hamlet is presented in H. C. Nixon, *Possum Trot, Rural Community, South* (Norman, Okla.: Univ. Oklahoma, 1941).

* Available in paperback.

A BIBLIOGRAPHY OF SELECTED PAPERBACKS

At the end of each chapter is a brief list of readings particularly relevant to the material in the immediately preceding pages. These lists are intended to be suggestive rather than exhaustive, and those who desire to read further are directed to the bibliographies of the volumes indicated. A number of readily available scholarly articles have also been included in the chapter listings, particularly where secondary volumes are in short supply or when an article is especially suggestive.

Readers of southern history have been blessed by the publication of an exceedingly large number of excellent paperback volumes in recent years. Listed below are works appearing in paperback which were in print in 1970 * and which bear in whole or in part on the subject of the South's history. This list is not intended to be complete, its primary purpose being to indicate the availability of modestly priced books related to the South. The date in parentheses indicates the year the volume was originally published, whether in hardcover or paperback. Several of the works have been revised or reissued, but these dates have not been included, because they are ordinarily of less consequence than the original publication date. Each entry notes the paperback publisher as a convenience to the reader.

Anderson, Margaret. *The Children of the South* (1966). Dell.
Alexander, Charles C. *The Ku Klux Klan in the Southwest* (1965). University of Kentucky Press.
Allen, James S. *Reconstruction: The Battle for Democracy* (1937). International Publishers Company.
Aptheker, Herbert. *American Negro Slave Revolts* (1943). International Publishers Company.
———. *Essays in the History of the American Negro* (1945). International Publishers Company.
———. *Nat Turner's Slave Rebellion* (1966). Humanities Press.
Ashmore, Harry. *The Negro and the Schools* (1954). University of North Carolina Press.
Baker, Ray S. *Following the Color Line: American Negro Democracy in the Progressive Era* (1908). Harper & Row.
Baldwin, James. *Go Tell It on the Mountain* (1953). Dell.
———. *Nobody Knows My Name* (1961). Dell.
———. *Tell Me How Long the Train's Been Gone* (1968). Dell.

* See *Paperbound Books in Print* (New York: R. R. Bowker, March 1970).

Baldwin, Joseph. *The Flush Times of Alabama and Mississippi* (1853). Hill & Wang.

Barbour, Floyd (ed.). *Black Power Revolt* (1968). Macmillan.

Bardolph, Richard. *The Negro Vanguard* (1959). Random House.

Barker, Alan. *The Civil War in America* (1961). Doubleday.

Barnes, Gilbert H. *Antislavery Impulse: 1830–1844* (1933). Harcourt, Brace & World.

Beard, Charles. *An Economic Interpretation of the Constitution of the United States* (1913). Free Press.

Bennett, Lerone, Jr. *Before the Mayflower: A History of the Negro, 1619–1964* (1962). Penguin Books.

Billington, Monroe (ed.). *The South: A Central Theme?* (1969). Holt, Rinehart & Winston.

Blair, Lewis H. *Southern Prophecy* (1889). Little, Brown.

Blaustein, Albert and Zangrando, Robert (eds.). *Civil Rights and the American Negro: A Documentary History* (1968). Simon & Schuster.

—— and Ferguson, C. C. *Desegregation and the Law: The Meaning and Effect of the School Desegregation Cases* (1957). Random House.

Bond, Horace M. *Negro Education in Alabama: A Study in Cotton and Steel* (1939). Atheneum.

Boorstin, Daniel J. *The Americans: The Colonial Experience* (1958). Random House.

Bowers, Claude G. *Jefferson and Hamilton* (1925). Houghton Mifflin.

——. *Jefferson in Power* (1936). Houghton Mifflin.

——. *The Tragic Era* (1929). Houghton Mifflin.

Bradford, S. *Harriet Tubman, The Moses of Her People* (1961). Corinth Books.

Breitman, George. *The Last Year of Malcolm X: The Evolution of a Revolutionary* (1967). Merit.

Brink, William and Harris, Louis. *Black and White: A Study of U. S. Racial Attitudes Today* (1967). Simon & Schuster.

——. *The Negro Revolution in America* (1963). Simon & Schuster.

Brock, William R. *An American Crisis: Congress and Reconstruction* (1963). Harper & Row.

——. *The Civil War* (1969). Harper & Row.

Broderick, Francis L. *W. E. B. Du Bois: Negro Leader in a Time of Crisis* (1959). Stanford University Press.

—— and Meier, A. (eds.). *Negro Protest Thought in the Twentieth Century* (1966). Bobbs-Merrill.

Brooks, Cleanth. *William Faulkner: The Yoknapatawpha Country* (1963). Yale University Press.

Brown, Richard D. (ed.). *Slavery in American Society* (1969). D. C. Heath.

Bruce, Philip A. *Social Life in Old Virginia* (1910). Putnam.

Buck, Paul H. *Road to Reunion: 1865–1900* (1937). Vintage Books.

Buck, Solon J. *The Granger Movement: A Study of Agricultural Organization and Its Political, Economic, and Social Manifestations, 1870–1880* (1913). University of Nebraska Press.

Buckmaster, Henrietta. *Let My People Go: The Story of the Underground Railroad and the Growth of the Abolitionist Movement* (1941). Beacon Press.

Burgess, Margaret E. *Negro Leadership in a Southern City* (1962). College and University Press.

Carter, Hodding. *Southern Legacy* (1950). Louisiana State University Press.

Cash, W. J. *The Mind of the South* (1941). Random House.

Catton, Bruce. *The Coming Fury* (1961). Pocket Books.

———. *America Goes to War* (1961). Hill & Wang.

———. *Glory Road* (1952). Pocket Books.

———. *Mr. Lincoln's Army* (1951). Pocket Books.

———. *A Stillness at Appomattox* (1953). Pocket Books.

———. *Terrible Swift Sword* (1963). Pocket Books.

———. *This Hallowed Ground* (1956). Pocket Books.

Chalmers, David M. *Hooded Americanism: The History of the Ku Klux Klan* (1965). Quadrangle.

Clark, Thomas D. *The Emerging South* (1968). Oxford University Press.

Coit, Margaret. *John C. Calhoun* (1950). Houghton Mifflin.

Cornish, Dudley T. *Sable Arm: Negro Troops in the Union Army, 1861–1865* (1966). Norton.

Crane, Verner W. *The Southern Frontier, 1670–1732* (1929). University of Michigan Press.

Craven, Avery. *The Coming of the Civil War* (1942). University of Chicago Press.

———. *The Civil War in the Making, 1815–1860* (1959). Louisiana State University Press.

———. *Edmund Ruffin, Southerner: A Study in Secession* (1932). Louisiana State University Press.

———. *Reconstruction: The Ending of the Civil War* (1969). Holt, Rinehart & Winston.

Cronon, E. David. *Black Moses: The Story of Marcus Garvey and the Universal Negro Improvement Association* (1955). University of Wisconsin Press.

Cruden, Robert. *The Negro in Reconstruction* (1969). Prentice-Hall.

Cunliffe, Marcus. *The Nation Takes Shape: 1789–1837* (1959). University of Chicago Press.

Cunningham, Noble E., Jr. *Jeffersonian Republicans in Power: Party Operations, 1801–1809* (1963). University of North Carolina Press.

———. *The Jeffersonian Republicans: The Formation of a Party Organization, 1789–1801* (1957). University of North Carolina Press.

Current, Richard N. *John C. Calhoun* (1963). Washington Square Press.

Curtin, Philip (ed.). *Africa Remembered: Narratives by West Africans from the Era of the Slave Trade* (1967). University of Wisconsin Press.

Davis, Allison and others. *Deep South: A Social Anthropological Study of Caste and Class* (1941). University of Chicago Press.

Davis, Jefferson. *The Rise and Fall of the Confederate Government* (1881). Crowell.

Dethloff, Henry C. (ed.). *Huey P. Long* (1967). D. C. Heath.

Dick, Everett. *The Dixie Frontier* (1948). Putnam.

Dollard, John. *Caste and Class in a Southern Town* (1937). Doubleday.

Donald, David. *Lincoln Reconsidered: Essays on the Civil War Era* (1956). Random House.

Douglass, Frederick. *Narrative of the Life of Frederick Douglass* (1846). Doubleday.

Dowdey, Clifford. *Experiment in Rebellion* (1946). Doubleday.

———. *The Land They Fought For* (1955). Doubleday.

Duberman, Martin (ed.). *The Antislavery Vanguard: New Essays on the Abolitionists* (1965). Princeton University Press.

Du Bois, W. E. B. *Black Reconstruction in America* (1935). World Publishing Company.

———. *Dusk of Dawn* (1940). Schocken.

———. *Souls of Black Folk* (1903). Fawcett World.

Dumond, Dwight L. *Antislavery: The Crusade for Freedom in America* (1966). Norton.

———. *Antislavery Origins of the Civil War in the United States* (1939). University of Michigan Press.

Dunning, William A. *Essays on the Civil War and Reconstruction* (1898). Harper & Row.

———. *Reconstruction, Political and Economic: 1865–1877* (1907). Harper & Row.

Dupuy, Richard E. and Trevor N. *The Compact History of the Civil War* (1960). Macmillan.

Durden, Robert F. *The Climax of Populism: The Election of 1896* (1965). University of Kentucky Press.

Eaton, Clement. *The Freedom-of-Thought Struggle in the Old South* (1964). Harper & Row.

———. *The Growth of Southern Civilization, 1790–1860* (1961). Harper & Row.

———. *Henry Clay and the Art of American Politics* (1957). Little, Brown.

———. *A History of the Southern Confederacy* (1954). Free Press.

———. *The Mind of the Old South* (1964). Louisiana State University Press.

Elkins, Stanley. *Slavery* (1959). University of Chicago Press.

Essien-Udom, Essien U. *Black Nationalism: A Search for an Identity in America* (1962). Dell.

Filler, Louis. *The Crusade against Slavery, 1830–1860* (1960). Harper & Row.

Fishel, Leslie H., Jr. and Quarles, Benjamin. *The Negro American: A Documentary Story* (1967). Scott, Foresman.

Ford, Thomas (ed.). *The Southern Applachian Region: A Survey* (1962). University of Kentucky Press.

Franklin, John Hope. *From Slavery to Freedom: A History of Negro Americans* (1947). Random House.

———. *The Militant South* (1956). Beacon Press.

———. *Reconstruction: After the Civil War* (1961). University of Chicago Press.

——— and Starr, I. (eds.). *The Negro in Twentieth Century America* (1967). Random House.

Frazier, E. F. *The Negro Church in America* (1963). Schocken.

Freehling, William W. *Prelude to Civil War: The Nullification Controversy in South Carolina, 1816–1836* (1966). Harper & Row.

Freyre, Gilberto. *The Masters and the Slaves: A Study in the Development of Brazilian Civilization* (1946). Knopf.

Furnas, J. C. *Goodbye to Uncle Tom* (1956). Crowell.

Gara, Larry. *The Liberty Line: The Legend of the Underground Railroad* (1961). University of Kentucky Press.

Garfinkel, Herbert. *When Negroes March* (1959). Atheneum.

Garner, James W. *Reconstruction in Mississippi* (1901). Louisiana State University Press.

Garvey, Marcus. *Philosophy and Opinions of Marcus Garvey* (1923). Atheneum.

Genovese, Eugene D. *The Political Economy of Slavery* (1965). Random House.

Ginger, Ray. *Six Days or Forever? Tennessee v. John Thomas Scopes* (1958). New American Library.

Ginzberg, Eli and Eichner, Alfred E. *The Troublesome Presence: American Democracy and the Negro* (1964). New American Library.

Ginzburg, R. *One Hundred Years of Lynchings* (1962). Lancer Books.

Golden, Harry. *Mr. Kennedy and the Negroes* (1964). Fawcett World.

Goldwin, R. A. (ed.). *One Hundred Years of Emancipation* (1964). Rand McNally.

Grantham, Dewey W., Jr. *The Democratic South* (1963). Norton.

———. (ed.). *The South and the Sectional Image: The Sectional Theme Since Reconstruction* (1967). Harper & Row.

———. *Hoke Smith and the Politics of the New South* (1958). Louisiana State University Press.

Grebstein, Sheldon N. *Monkey Trial* (1960). Houghton Mifflin.

Green, Fletcher M. *Constitutional Development in the South Atlantic States, 1776–1860* (1930). Norton.

Guérin, Daniel. *Negroes on the March* (1956). Merit.

Hamilton, Holman. *Prologue to Conflict: The Crisis and Compromise of 1850* (1964). Norton.

Handlin, Oscar. *Fire-Bell in the Night: The Crisis in Civil Rights* (1964). Beacon Press.

Hansen, Harry. *The Civil War* (1961). Mentor Books.

Harlan, Louis R. *Separate and Unequal* (1958). Atheneum.

Harris, Marvin. *Patterns of Race in the Americas* (1964). Walker.

Hawkins, Hugh (ed.). *Booker T. Washington and His Critics* (1962). D. C. Heath.

Helper, Hinton R. *Impending Crisis of the South* (1857). Macmillan.

Henry, Robert S. *The Story of the Confederacy* (1931). Bobbs-Merrill.

Herndon, M. *Tobacco in Colonial Virginia* (1957). University Press of Virginia.

Hesseltine, William B. *Lincoln's Plan of Reconstruction* (1960). Quadrangle.

——— (ed.). *Tragic Conflict: The Civil War and Reconstruction* (1962). Braziller.

Hicks, John D. *Populist Revolt: A History of the Farmers' Alliance and the People's Party* (1931). University of Nebraska Press.

Higham, John (ed.). *The Reconstruction of American History* (1962). Harper & Row.

Hill, Samuel S., Jr. *Southern Churches in Crisis* (1967). Beacon Press.

——— and Torbet, Robert G. *Baptists: North and South* (1964). Judson Press.

Hofstadter, Richard. *The Age of Reform: From Bryan to F. D. R.* (1955). Random House.

Hoover, Dwight W. (ed.). *Understanding Negro History* (1969). Quadrangle.

Hopkins, V. C. *Dred Scott's Case* (1967). Atheneum.

Isaacs, Harold. *The New World of Negro Americans* (1963). Viking Press.

Jackson, Kenneth T. *The Ku Klux Klan in the City, 1915–1930* (1967). Oxford University Press.

Jackson, Luther P. *Free Negro Labor and Property in Ante-Bellum Virginia* (1942). Atheneum.

Jensen, Merrill. *The Articles of Confederation* (1948). University of Wisconsin Press.

———. *The New Nation: A History of the United States During the Confederation* (1950). Random House.

Jordan, Winthrop D. *White Over Black: The Development of American Attitudes Toward the Negro, 1550–1812* (1968). Penguin Books.

Kenyon, Cecelia M. *The Antifederalists* (1966). Bobbs-Merrill.

Key, V. O., Jr. *Southern Politics* (1949). Random House.

Killian, Lewis M. and Grigg, Charles. *Racial Crisis in America: Leadership in Conflict* (1964). Prentice-Hall.

King, Martin L., Jr. *Stride Toward Freedom: The Montgomery Story* (1958). Harper & Row.

Kirwan, A. D. (ed.). *The Confederacy* (1959). World Publishing Company.

———. *Revolt of the Rednecks: Mississippi Politics, 1876–1925* (1951). Harper & Row.

Koch, Adrienne. *Jefferson and Madison* (1950). Oxford University Press.

Konvitz, Milton R. and Leskes, T. *A Century of Civil Rights* (1961). Columbia University Press.

Kutler, S. I. *Dred Scott Decision: Law or Politics?* (1967). Houghton Mifflin.

Leiserson, Avery (ed.). *The American South in the 1960's* (1964). Praeger.

Leuchtenburg, William E. *Franklin D. Roosevelt and the New Deal* (1963). Harper & Row.

Lewis, Anthony (ed.). *Portrait of a Decade: The Second American Revolution* (1964). Bantam Books.

Lincoln, C. Eric. *The Black Muslims in America* (1961). Beacon Press.

———. *Martin Luther King, Jr.: A Profile* (1969). Hill & Wang.

Link, Arthur S. and Patrick, Rembert W. (eds.). *Writing Southern History: Essays in Historiography in Honor of Fletcher M. Green* (1965). Louisiana State University Press.

Little, Malcolm. *Autobiography of Malcolm X* (1965). Grove Press.

———. *Malcolm X on Afro-American History* (1967). Merit.

Litwack, Leon. *North of Slavery: The Negro in the Free States, 1790–1860* (1961). University of Chicago Press.

Logan, Rayford W. *Betrayal of the Negro: From Rutherford B. Hayes to Woodrow Wilson* (1954). Macmillan.

———. *The Negro in American Life and Thought: The Nadir, 1877–1901* (1954). Dial Press.

Lomax, Louis E. *The Negro Revolt* (1962). New American Library.

————. *When the Word Is Given* (1963). New American Library.

Long, Huey P. *Every Man a King: The Autobiography of Huey P. Long* (1933). Quadrangle.

Lubell, Samuel. *White and Black: Test of a Nation* (1964). Harper & Row.

Lynd, Staughton. *Reconstruction* (1967). Harper & Row.

Lyons, T. T. (ed.). *Reconstruction and the Race Problem* (1968). D. C. Heath.

McCarthy, A. and Reddick, L. *Worth Fighting For: A History of the Negro in the United States During the Civil War and Reconstruction* (1965). Parallax Publishing Company.

McDonald, Forrest. *We the People: The Economic Origins of the Constitution* (1958). University of Chicago Press.

McGill, Ralph. *The South and the Southerner* (1964). Little, Brown.

McGrath, Earl J. *The Predominantly Negro Colleges and Universities in Transition* (1965). Teachers College Press.

McKitrick, Eric L. *Andrew Johnson and Reconstruction* (1960). University of Chicago Press.

———— (ed.). *Slavery Defended: Views of the Old South* (1963). Prentice-Hall.

McPherson, James (ed.). *The Negro's Civil War: How American Negroes Felt and Acted* (1965). Random House.

————. *The Struggle for Equality: Abolitionists and the Negro in the Civil War and Reconstruction* (1964). Princeton University Press.

McWhiney, Grady (ed.). *Grant, Lee, Lincoln and the Radicals* (1964). Harper & Row.

————. *Reconstruction and the Freedman* (1963). Rand McNally.

Malone, Dumas. *Jefferson the Virginian* (1948). Little, Brown.

Mannix, Daniel P. and Cowley, Malcolm. *Black Cargoes: A History of the Atlantic Slave Trade* (1962). Viking Press.

Meier, August. *Negro Thought in America, 1880–1915* (1963). University of Michigan Press.

———— and Rudwick, Elliott M. *From Plantation to Ghetto: An Interpretive History of American Negroes* (1966). Hill & Wang.

Miers, Earl S. *The Great Rebellion* (1958). Macmillan.

————. *Robert E. Lee: A Great Life in Brief* (1956). Random House.

Miller, John. *The Federalist Era, 1789–1801* (1960). Harper & Row.

Miller, Loren. *The Petitioners: The Story of the Supreme Court of the United States and the Negro* (1966). World Publishers.

Mitchell, Broadus and Louise. *A Biography of the Constitution of the United States* (1964). Oxford University Press.

Mitchell, Joseph. *Decisive Battles of the Civil War* (1962). Fawcett World.

Moore, Glover. *The Missouri Controversy, 1819–1821* (1955). University of Kentucky Press.

Morgan, Edmund S. *Virginians at Home: Family Life in the Eighteenth Century* (1952). University Press of Virginia.

Murray, Paul. *The Whig Party in Georgia* (1948). University of North Carolina Press.

Myrdal, Gunnar. *An American Dilemma*, 2 vols. (1944). McGraw-Hill.

Nevins, Allan. *The Statesmanship of the Civil War* (1962). Macmillan.

Newby, I. A. *Jim Crow's Defense: Anti-Negro Thought in America, 1900–1930* (1965). Louisiana State University Press.

Nichols, Roy F. *The Disruption of American Democracy* (1948). Free Press.

Nolen, Claude H. *The Negro's Image in the South: The Anatomy of White Supremacy* (1967). University of Kentucky Press.

Norton, Clarence C. *The Democratic Party in Ante-Bellum North Carolina* (1930). University of North Carolina Press.

Nugent, Walter T. *The Money Question During Reconstruction* (1967). Norton.

Nye, Russel B. *William Lloyd Garrison and the Humanitarian Reformers* (1955). Little, Brown.

Olmsted, Frederick L. *The Slave States before the Civil War* (1860). Putnam.

Osterweis, Rollin G. *Romanticism and Nationalism in the Old South* (1949). Louisiana State University Press.

Owsley, Frank L. *Plain Folk of the Old South* (1950). Quadrangle.

Parrington, Vernon C. *The Romantic Revolution in America, 1800–1860* (1927). Harcourt, Brace & World.

Patrick, Rembert W. *Reconstruction of the Nation* (1967). Oxford University Press.

Perlo, Victor. *The Negro in Southern Agriculture* (1953). International Publishers.

Phillips, Ulrich B. *American Negro Slavery* (1918). Louisiana State University Press.

———. *The Course of the South to Secession: An Interpretation* (1939). Hill & Wang.

———. *Life and Labor in the Old South* (1929). Little, Brown.

———. *The Slave Economy of the Old South: Selected Essays in Economic and Social History* (1968). Louisiana State University Press.

Pollack, Norman. *The Populist Mind* (1967). Bobbs-Merrill.

———. *The Populist Response to Industrial America* (1962). Norton.

Pope, Liston. *Millhands and Preachers: A Study of Gastonia* (1942). Yale University Press.

Potter, David M. *Lincoln and His Party in the Secession Crisis* (1942). Yale University Press.

Powdermaker, Hortense. *After Freedom: A Cultural Study in the Deep South* (1939). Atheneum.

Pratt, Fletcher. *A Short History of the Civil War* [*Ordeal by Fire*] (1935). Pocket Books.

Pressly, Thomas J. *Americans Interpret Their Civil War* (1954). Macmillan.

Proudfoot, Merrill. *Diary of a Sit-In* (1962). College and University Press.

Puryear, E. L. *Democratic Party Dissension in North Carolina, 1928–1936* (1962). University of North Carolina Press.

Quarles, Benjamin. *Black Abolitionists* (1969). Oxford University Press.

———— (ed.). *Frederick Douglass* (1968). Prentice-Hall.

————. *The Negro in the Making of America* (1964). Macmillan.

————. *The Negro in the American Revolution* (1961). University of North Carolina Press.

Randall, James G. *Constitutional Problems under Lincoln* (1926). University of Illinois Press.

————. *Lincoln: The Liberal Statesman* (1947). Crowell.

Raper, Arthur F. *Preface to Peasantry: A Tale of Two Black Belt Counties* (1939). Atheneum.

Rawley, James A. *Turning Points of the Civil War* (1966). University of Nebraska Press.

Reid, Whitelaw. *After the War: A Tour of the Southern States, 1865–1866* (1866). Harper & Row.

Robert, Joseph C. *The Story of Tobacco in America* (1949). University of North Carolina Press.

Roche, John P. *The Quest for the Dream: The Development of Civil Rights and Human Relations in Modern America* (1963). Quadrangle.

Roland, Charles P. *The Confederacy* (1960). University of Chicago Press.

Rose, Willie L. *Rehearsal for Reconstruction* (1964). Random House.

Rubin, Louis. *Writers of the Modern South* (1963). University of Washington Press.

———— and Jacobs, Robert D. (eds.). *Southern Renascence: The Literature of the Modern World* (1953). Johns Hopkins University Press.

Rubin, Morton. *Plantation County* (1951). College and University Press.

Ruchames, Louis (ed.). *The Abolitionists: A Collection of Their Writings* (1963). Putnam.

Rudwick, Elliott. *W. E. B. Du Bois: Propagandist of the Negro Protest* (1960). Atheneum.

Rutland, Robert A. *The Birth of the Bill of Rights, 1776–1791* (1962). Macmillan.

Saloutos, Theodore. *Farmer Movements in the South, 1865–1933* (1960). University of Nebraska Press.

Sandburg, Carl. *Abraham Lincoln: The Prairie Years and the War Years,* 3 vols. (1926–39). Dell.

Saunders, D. E. (ed.). *The Kennedy Years and the Negro* (1964). Johnson Publishing Company.

Scheiner, Seth M. (ed.). *Reconstruction: A Tragic Era?* (1968). Holt, Rinehart & Winston.

Sellers, Charles G., Jr. (ed.). *The Southerner as American* (1960). Dutton.

Sellers, James B. *The Prohibition Movement in Alabama* (1943). University of North Carolina Press.

Shannon, Fred A. *The Farmer's Last Frontier: Agriculture, 1860–1897* (1945). Harper & Row.

Sharkey, Robert P. *Money, Class and Party: An Economic Study of Civil War and Reconstruction* (1959). Johns Hopkins University Press.

Shenton, James P. *The Reconstruction: A Documentary History of the South after the War, 1865–1877* (1963). Putnam.

Silberman, Charles E. *Crisis in Black and White* (1964). Random House.

Silver, James. *Mississippi: The Closed Society* (1964). Harcourt, Brace & World.

Simkins, Francis B. *Pitchfork Ben Tillman: South Carolinian* (1944). Louisiana State University Press.

Sindler, Alan P. *Huey Long's Louisiana: State Politics, 1920–1952* (1956). Johns Hopkins University Press.

Sitterson, J. C. (ed.). *Studies in Southern History* (1957). University of North Carolina Press.

Smith, Bob. *They Closed Their Schools: Prince Edward County, Virginia, 1951–1964* (1965). University of North Carolina Press.

Smith, Timothy L. *Revivalism and Social Reform: American Protestantism on the Eve of the Civil War* (1957). Harper & Row.

Spencer, Samuel R., Jr. *Booker T. Washington and the Negro's Place in American Life* (1955). Little, Brown.

Spero, S. D. and Harris, A. L. *The Black Worker: The Negro and the Labor Movement* (1931). Atheneum.

Stampp, Kenneth M. *And the War Came: The North and the Secession Crisis, 1860–1861* (1951). University of Chicago Press.

———. (ed.). *The Causes of the Civil War* (1959). Prentice-Hall.

———. *The Era of Reconstruction, 1865–1877* (1965). Random House.

———. *The Peculiar Institution: Slavery in the Ante-Bellum South* (1956). Random House.

——— and Litwack, Leon F. (eds.). *Reconstruction: An Anthology of Revisionist Writings* (1969). Louisiana State University Press.

Stanton, William R. *The Leopard's Spots: Scientific Attitudes toward Race in America, 1815–1859* (1960). University of Chicago Press.

Staudenraus, P. J. *The Secession Crisis* (1963). Rand McNally.

Sydnor, Charles S. *Slavery in Mississippi* (1933). Louisiana State University Press.

Tannenbaum, Frank. *Slave and Citizen: The Negro in the Americas* (1947). Random House.

Taper, Bernard. *Gomillion versus Lightfoot: Apartheid in Alabama* (1962). McGraw-Hill.

Tate, Thaddeus W., Jr. *The Negro in Eighteenth-Century Williamsburg* (1965). University Press of Virginia.

Taylor, William R. *Cavalier and Yankee: The Old South and American National Character* (1961). Doubleday.

Thomas, John L. (ed.). *Slavery Attacked: The Abolitionist Crusade* (1965). Prentice-Hall.

Tindall, George B. *South Carolina Negroes* (1952). Louisiana State University Press.

Turnbull, Andrew. *Thomas Wolfe* (1968). Pocket Books.

Turner, Arlin. *George W. Cable* (1956). Louisiana State University Press.

Twelve Southerners. *I'll Take My Stand: The South and the Agrarian Tradition* (1930). Harper & Row.

Unger, Irving. *Populism: Nostalgia or Progressive?* (1964). Rand McNally.

Van Deusen, G. G. *The Life of Henry Clay* (1937). Little, Brown.

Van Doren, Carl. *The Great Rehearsal: The Story of the Making and Ratifying of the Constitution of the United States* (1948). Viking.

Wade, Richard C. *The Negro in American Life* (1965). Houghton Mifflin.

———. *Slavery in the Cities: The South, 1820–1860* (1964). Oxford University Press.

Waggoner, Hyatt H. *William Faulkner: From Jefferson to the World* (1959). University of Kentucky Press.

Warren, Robert P. *The Legacy of the Civil War* (1961). Random House.

———. *Segregation: The Inner Conflict in the South* (1956). Random House.

Washington, Booker T. *Up from Slavery* (1902). Bantam Books.

Weinstein, Allen and Gatell, Frank O. (eds.). *American Negro Slavery: A Modern Reader* (1968). Oxford University Press.

——— (eds.). *The Segregation Era, 1863–1954* (1970). Oxford University Press.

Wharton, Vernon L. *The Negro in Mississippi, 1865–1890* (1947). Harper & Row.

White, Leonard D. *The Jeffersonians* (1951). Macmillan.

———. *The Republican Era* (1958). Macmillan.

White, Theodore H. *The Making of the President, 1960* (1961). New American Library.

———. *The Making of the President, 1964* (1965). New American Library.

———. *The Making of the President, 1968* (1969). New American Library.

Wiley, Bell I. *Plain People of the Confederacy* (1963). Quadrangle.

A BIBLIOGRAPHY OF SELECTED PAPERBACKS 451

————. *Southern Negroes, 1861–1865* (1938). Yale University Press.
Williams, T. Harry. *Americans at War* (1960). Crowell.
————. *Beauregard* (1955). Macmillan.
————. *Lincoln and His Generals* (1957). Random House.
————. *Lincoln and the Radicals* (1941). University of Wisconsin Press.
————. *Romance and Realism in Southern Politics* (1961). Louisiana State University Press.
Williamson, Joel. *After Slavery: The Negro in South Carolina During Reconstruction, 1861–1877* (1965). University of North Carolina Press.
———— (ed.). *The Origins of Segregation* (1968). D. C. Heath.
Wish, Harvey (ed.). *Ante-Bellum: Three Classic Writings on Slavery in the Old South* (1960). Putnam.
———— (ed.). *The Negro Since Emancipation* (1964). Prentice-Hall.
———— (ed.). *Slavery in the South* (1964). Farrar, Straus & Giroux.
Wolfe, John H. *Jeffersonian Democracy in South Carolina* (1940). University of North Carolina Press.
Woodman, Harold D. (ed.). *Slavery and the Southern Economy: Sources and Readings* (1966). Harcourt, Brace & World.
Woodward, C. Vann. *The Burden of Southern History* (1960). Louisiana State University Press.
————. *Origins of the New South* (1951). Louisiana State University Press.
————. *Reunion and Reaction: The Compromise of 1877 and the End of Reconstruction* (1951). Little, Brown.
————. *The Strange Career of Jim Crow* (1966). Oxford University Press.
————. *Tom Watson: Agrarian Rebel* (1938). Oxford University Press.
Wright, Nathan, Jr. *Black Power and Urban Unrest: The Creative Possibilities* (1967). Hawthorn.
Ziegler, B. M. (ed.). *Desegregation and the Supreme Court* (1958). D. C. Heath.
Zinn, Howard. *SNCC: The New Abolitionists* (1964). Beacon Press.

Index